SCHOOLCRAFT COLLEGE LIBRARY
W9-ANB-674

The Pentecostals

The Pentecostals

The Charismatic Movement in the Churches

W. J. Hollenweger

Augsburg Publishing House
Minneapolis, Minnesota

Translated by R. A. Wilson from the German
Enthusiastisches Christentum: die Pfingstbewegung in Geschichte und Gegenwart
Theologischer Verlag Rolf Brockhaus Wuppertal
Zwingli Verlag Zürich 1969
with revisions by the author

THE PENTECOSTALS
First United States Edition 1972

Library of Congress Catalog Card No. 70–176103
International Standard Book No. 0–8066–1210–x

Printed in Great Britain

CONTENTS

PART TWO · BELIEF AND PRACTICE

ABBREVIATIONS

AdD	Assemblées de Dieu; Assemblee di Dio; Assembléias de Deus; Asambleas de Dios
AoG	Assemblies of God
ASTE	Associaçâo de Seminários Teológicos Evangélicos
AUCECB	All-Union Council of Evangelical Christians-Baptists
Bloch-Hoell I	Nils Bloch-Hoell, *Pinsebevegelsen. En undersøkelse av Pinsebevegelsens tilblivelse, utvikling og saerpreg med saerlig henblikk på bevegelsens utformning i Norge.* Oslo: Universitetsforlaget, 1956
Bloch-Hoell II	Nils Bloch-Hoell, *The Pentecostal Movement. Its Origin, Development, and Distinctive Character*, London; Allen & Unwin, 1964
ChoG	Church of God
ChoGE	*Church of God Evangel*
CWME	Commission on World Mission and Evangelism
ET	English translation
FGBMFI	Full Gospel Business Men's Fellowship International
Fleisch I	Paul Fleisch. *Die moderne Gemeinschaftsbewegung in Deutschland.* Vol. I: Geschichte der deutschen Gemeinschaftsbewegung bis zum Auftreten des Zungenredens, 1875–1903. Leipzig, 3rd ed. 1914
Fleisch II/1	Paul Fleisch, *Die moderne Gemeinschaftsbewegung in Deutschland.* Vol. II, Part 1: Die Zungenbewegung in Deutschland. Leipzig, 3rd ed. 1914
Fleisch II/2	Paul Fleisch. *Die moderne Gemeinschaftsbewegung in Deutschland.* Vol. II, Part 2: Die Pfingstbewegung in Deutschland, Hanover: Heinr. Feesche Verlag, 1957
FO	Faith and Order series, Geneva: WCC (duplicated typescript)
GPH	Gospel Publishing House
ICh4G	International Church of the Foursquare Gospel
IRM	*International Review of Mission*
Krust I	Christian Krust, *50 Jahre deutsche Pfingstbewegung Mülheimer Richtung*, Altdorf bei Nürnberg: Missionsbuchhandlung und Verlag, 1958
Krust II	Christian Krust, *Was wir glauben, lehren und bekennen.* Altdorf bei Nürnberg; Missionsbuchhandlung und Verlag, 1963
MD	*Materialdienst, Längsschnitt durch die geistigen Strömungen und Fragen der Gegenwart*, Stuttgart
Moore	Everett LeRoy Moore, *Handbook of Pentecostal Denominations*

	in the United States, M.A. thesis, Graduate Studies in Religion, Pasadena College, 1954 (unpublished)
P	Pentecostal, Pentecôte, Pfingsten, etc.
P	*Pentecost* (the journal)
PE	*Pentecostal Evangel*
PAoW	Pentecostal Assemblies of the World
PGG	Walter J. Hollenweger, *Enthusiastisches Christentum. Die Pfingstbewegung in Geschichte und Gegenwart.* Wuppertal: Theol. Verlag R. Brockhaus, Zürich: Zwingli-Verlag, 1969
PHCh	Pentecostal Holiness Church
RGG	*Die Religion in Geschichte und Gegenwart*, Tübingen: Mohr, 2nd ed. 1927–1932; 3rd ed. 1957–1965
SE	Studies on Evangelism, Geneva: WCC (duplicated typescript)
SPM	Schweizerische Pfingstmission (Swiss Pentecostal Mission)
Sundkler	Bengt G. M. Sundkler, *Bantu Prophets in South Africa.* London: Oxford UP, *1948, 2nd ed. 1961
TDNT	G. Kittel (ed.), *Theological Dictionary of the New Testament* (ET of *TWNT*), Grand Rapids, Mich.: Eerdmans, 1964ff.
TWNT	G. Kittel (ed.), *Theologisches Wörterbuch zum Neuen Testament.* Stuttgart: Kohlhammer, 1932ff.
US 1936 Census	*Religious Bodies 1936, I-II.* United States Department of Commerce Bureau of the Census, Washington 1941
VdV	*Verheissung des Vaters* (Zürich 1909–1968)
WCC	World Council of Churches
WChH	H. Wakelin Coxill and Sir Kenneth Grubb (edd.), *World Christian Handbook*, London: Lutterworth, 1962, 1968
Y	Youth Department studies, Geneva: WCC (duplicated typescript)

Numbers (e.g. 02a.02.115) point to my *Handbuch der Pfingstbewegung* (Geneva, 1965/67, dupl., 10 vol.). This handbook consists of three parts. The *first part* (1 vol.: 'Sektierer oder Enthusiasten?') is a 'Résumé of the piety, the history and the doctrine of the Pentecostal Movement'. The *second part* (6 vols.) deals with all the Pentecostal denominations in all countries. The *third part* (3 vols.) contains a research review, a sociological analysis of 400 Pentecostal pastors and an annotated bibliography. The numbers in the first position mean:

00	Résumé	06	Introduction to the third part
01	Africa	07/08	Pentecostal literature written by Pentecostals
02a	North America		
02b	Latin America		
03	Asia	09	Literature written by non-Pentecostals
04	Australia	10	Literature on the Holiness movement
05	Europe	11	Other literature

To my friends and teachers in the Pentecostal Movement
who taught me to love the Bible

and to my teachers and friends in the Presbyterian Church
who taught me to understand it.

PREFACE

THE origins of the Pentecostal movement go back to a revival amongst the negroes of North America at the beginning of the present century. The enthusiasm of these revival groups, however, quickly became institutionalized, which often leads in the theoretical writings of the Pentecostal movement to the use of conservative and rationalizing expressions and concepts. This fixing of enthusiasm in systematic forms, and especially the view that the baptism of the Spirit is to be recognized by the 'initial sign' of speaking in tongues, became a constituent element in the *formal structure* of the Pentecostal movement, especially in North America. Much more important, however, for the *growth* of the Pentecostal movement was its ability to make use of the North American negro's faculties of understanding and communicating by way of enthusiastic spiritual manifestations to build up a community and fellowship. These means of communication (hymns, speaking in tongues, dreams, spontaneous forms of worship) are of decisive importance in the Third World. Information and impulses are exchanged by means of a kind of 'atmospheric communication'. Jacques Rossel, the President of the Basle Mission, has described this language, in a different context, as follows: For the African and Asiatic truth or untruth lies at a more profound level than for the white man. 'It is not the correspondence of the words which concerns him, but the interior correspondence of sentiments.' Similarly, Emil G. Léonard, in his study of Brazilian Protestantism, affirms that for many Brazilian Protestants the age of the book is followed by the age of the Spirit, an expression which denotes the same as Rossel's phrase 'correspondence of sentiments'. The Baptist theologian Harvey Cox follows McLuhan in believing that the post-literary age has begun for the West as well. The age of books and the newspaper as the most important means of communication is past. But what does this signify for Protestantism, the religion of the book *par excellence*? According to Harvey Cox it means the reduction of Protestantism to the ever decreasing minority of readers, unless it makes room within itself for other means of communication.

The continuous spread of the Pentecostal movement in many countries must be interpreted as the discovery of new means of communication in a specific social field, which can be clearly defined for each Pentecostal group. Thus when in Chile, Brazil and other countries it has more adherents than all other Protestants, when in France and Russia, Nigeria and South Africa it is far and away the most rapidly growing religious group, and when even the intellectuals of Europe and America rediscover with its aid long buried levels of human existence, it is not surprising that Roman Catholic theologians and sociologists and even atheist anthropologists and experts in African studies are beginning to take an interest in the phenomenon. European theologians, however, have been the last – what else could one expect? – to enter the dialogue. They differ in their judgment on the Pentecostal movement, Some see in it a return to the charismatic church of primitive Christianity. Others believe it displays demonic imitations of the true life of the Spirit. Most regard it as mental overactivity, or as an illusion essential to the lives of some people, which should not be resisted but ignored. Most observers stand somewhere between these three positions. Those who are *familiar* with the movement are more reserved in their evaluation, because sweeping judgments on a movement which constantly changes and displays wide differences between one country and another, and one group and another, can hardly be just.

For some time the World Council of Churches has also joined in the discussion. The majority of the churches of the Third World do not belong to the WCC, and many of the non-member churches are of the Pentecostal type. On the other hand the WCC has recognized that the absence of the churches of the Third World makes it illusory to describe itself as a *world* council. Thus there were profound inherent reasons why at the Assembly at Uppsala in 1968 a representative of the Pentecostal movement, as well as the observer from the Roman Catholic church, should speak at a plenary session. On this occasion the Pentecostal speaker pointed out that it was necessary for the Pentecostal movement and ecumenical movement to get to know each other better.

This is the purpose of the present book. But to make the Ecumenical movement and the Pentecostal movement better known to each other is not a simple matter. How can one present in a book – the means of communication of Protestantism – a movement whose main characteristic is not verbal agreement but correspondence of sentiments? This difference in levels of communication has given rise on both sides to many misleading pictures of the other. Much patience and endurance are necessary (from the reader too!) to be able to distinguish accurately, across differences of language, both factual differences and factual agreements. Both movements have much in common. Both are *movements*. Both wish to renew the church from within. Both consist of numerous denominations with differences that are sometimes considerable.

This study does not gloss over the differences between different Pentecostal groups. Some friends from the Pentecostal movement will not fail to comment that the choice is one-sided and inappropriate, although the whole work has been written in constant dialogue with the Pentecostal movement. When baptismal rites or washings of feet are described – and these play an important role in some Pentecostal groups – they will say in dismay: we have never seen anything like that. They will rub their eyes in amazement at many of the statements they see and say: I have never heard anything like that in our church and I have been thirty years in the Pentecostal church. But it is not possible to draw the conclusion: What I, as a member or pastor of the Pentecostal movement, do not know, does not exist. One of the tasks of this ecumenical book is to discover with

Pentecostals the rich variety of the Pentecostal movement. Thus no specific expression of Prentecostal faith can be put forward as *the* interpretation of the Bible.

Finally, with regard to the mention of more extreme and more recent Pentecostal revivals, these may not be neglected, even if they are often quite small groups. In many countries the Pentecostal movement has been and is being ignored by opponents on account of its relatively small size. At the beginning of its development it was dismissed with a reference to extreme utterances and the small numbers of its adherents. No one can tell whether the Latter Rain movement or the apostolic type of Pentecostal belief may not yet develop into a great revival movement. Other Pentecostals should not cold shoulder these groups, on the grounds that they do not – as is said in an incomprehensible misunderstanding of the situation – belong to the 'official' Pentecostal movement, because anyone who has to describe himself as 'official' – and there is no supreme international body in the Pentecostal movement – cannot protest if another Pentecostal group regards itself as more genuinely Pentecostal, as a more official Pentecostal movement.

The differences between individual groups are by no means unimportant. A Canadian Pentecostal, H. H. Barber, says himself:

> In the city of Winnipeg are people who claim to be Pentecostal who are hyper-Calvinists [i.e. they hold a strict doctrine of predestination], some who are strong Arminians [i.e. they hold that man has free will]; some who look upon the doctrine of the Trinity as a pagan superstition [the so-called 'Jesus Only' groups], others who are staunchly Trinitarian; some who believe in baptismal regeneration, others who deny any regenerative virtue of baptism. Some cherish a rabid type of independence, others are loyal to the requirement of ordered denominational affiliation.

The differences must be interpreted not only theologically, but also in terms of social psychology. But what is the common factor? Most Pentecostals would say that the distinguishing feature is the experience of the baptism of the Spirit with the 'initial sign of speaking in tongues'. Thus this book includes as Pentecostals all the groups who profess at least two religious crisis experiences (1. baptism or rebirth; 2. the baptism of the Spirit), the second being subsequent to and different from the first one, and the second usually, but not always, being associated with speaking in tongues.

But in their own account of themselves, Pentecostals have a tendency to deny that groups which represent a type of Pentecostal belief and worship different from their own belong to the Pentecostal movement at all. Depending upon what kind of Pentecostal is criticizing this book, the Church of God (Cleveland), the Latter Rain movement or the independent South African churches will be regarded as wrongly included in an account of the Pentecostal movement. By an objective account of the Pentecostal movement most Pentecostals mean an account written from the point of view of the *present day* – not necessarily the original – belief and practice predominating in *their own group*. These writers have a perfect right to make a value judgment in their own writings, and to describe particular Pentecostals as marginal groups and others as main-stream groups. But they need to be aware that they are using as a standard the practice and doctrine of their own group (an awareness which is equally to be desired in the studies of other denominations produced in most of the so-called historic churches).

In choosing quotations I have been guided by the following principles. In Part I: History, confessions of faith are quoted as fully as space permitted. In Part II: Belief and Practice, I have first described the average opinion of the majority. But for the sake of ecumenical responsibility the views of minorities who hold a different position have not been overlooked. For reasons of space, however, I have had to limit myself to an account of a few characteristic views. I have not made improvements on the language of Pentecostals, not only because of their unintentional humour, but out of respect for the spontaneity of Pentecostal statements.

To assist interested scholars (and also Pentecostals who may complain the quotations have been taken out of context) to check the academic material, the quotations in their original language, the original *Sitz im Leben* and the context of individual quotations, I give the references to my *Handbuch der Pfingstbewegung*, in which the material can be found under the appropriate heading.

A note on the translation: this English translation is based on the German text. But this has been revised, and the account brought up to date. Similarly quotations from Swiss or German sources have sometimes been replaced by the equivalent English or American document. Two chapters on Switzerland and one chapter on Germany have been replaced by three chapters on the British Pentecostal movement. Similarly the French translation will include an account of the French and Congolese Pentecostal movements (including the important Kimbanguist church).

Where the footnotes give a source in a foreign language, the translation has been made either from the original or a German version made or quoted by the author. References to English sources are either to the English original or to the translation named.

Finally, it is a pleasure to record my thanks to the following: my teacher, Professor Fritz Blanke, who gave valuable encouragement and advice in the early stages of this book, and whose early death is a great loss; the many Pentecostals who have so readily supplied me with written and verbal information; the colleagues mentioned by name in the preface to my handbook; the translator, Mr R. A. Wilson, for his sensitive translation; my publishers for their willingness to take on so large a work; and last but not least my wife, who not only wrote and filed innumerable letters, but also put up with numerous conversations at home on the subject of the Pentecostal movement.

Geneva and Birmingham
1968/1971

PART ONE

History

THE UNITED STATES OF AMERICA

I

Pentecost Outside 'Pentecost': Speaking with Tongues in the Traditional Churches of America

RABBI Jacob Rabinowitz belonged to an old rabbinic family. For seventeen generations his ancestors had been rabbis. When Rabinowitz began to discover the truth of the New Testament, he felt like a traitor. He was afraid to become a 'converted Jew' – terrible word! The proud history of a rabbinic tradition reaching back over the centuries came into conflict with the words of the rabbi Jesus of Nazareth. Rabinowitz had become a disciple of this rabbi, but a secret disciple with a guilty conscience. In the summer of 1960 a friend invited him to a service of the Assemblies of God (see ch. 3) in Pasadena, Texas. He accepted the invitation reluctantly. It was a typical Pentecostalist service: easy hymns and choruses, in harmony and sung with enthusiasm, accompanied by a Hammond organ and a pianist who improvised jazz-like rhythms and arpeggios during pauses in the tunes. The congregation clapped their hands in time with the tunes and ventilated their joy in spontaneous testimony. After a short address, the evangelist invited anyone present who had a personal problem to kneel on the red carpet in front of the altar step to receive the blessing of the congregation.

Jacob Rabinowitz longed to be able to lay down the burden of his demanding double life. He knelt down with others in front of the altar. When the preacher asked him what his particular problem was he could not reply. 'That's all right,' replied the preacher, 'God knows what your needs are better than you know yourself.' And he invited the congregation to pray for Rabinowitz 'in the spirit'. Several men left their seats, came up to Rabinowitz and laid their hands on his head and shoulders. Others stood round the kneeling men and inclined their heads in prayer. Then they all began to pray together, some in English, others in tongues.

Suddenly Rabinowitz stood up and asked with tears in his eyes, 'Which one of you is Jewish?' No one answered. 'Which one of you knows me? You'll forgive me: I don't recognize you.' Still no answer.

Now the whole church became silent. 'It came from right here, behind me,' the rabbi pointed out. 'Just exactly where you're standing,' he said to one of the men. 'Are you Jewish?'

'Me?' The man smiled. 'My name's John Gruver. I'm Irish.' 'That's the voice,' said Rabinowitz, 'but tell me where you learned to speak Hebrew so well.'

'I don't know a word of it,' replied Gruver. 'That's where you're wrong,' retorted Rabinowitz, 'because you were speaking Hebrew just now.' And how did you know my name and the name of my father? You said in perfect Hebrew, "I have dreamed a dream that you will go into the big populated places and there you will preach. The ones who have not heard will understand you because you, Jacob, son of Rabbi Ezekiel, come in the fullness of the blessing of the Gospel of Jesus Christ." '

This incident, described by the well-known American journalist John L. Sherrill,[1] raises a number of different questions: What is the explanation of speaking with tongues and what is its theological significance? Do we have here a revival of the phenomenon of which Paul says, 'Thus, tongues are a sign not for believers but for unbelievers. . . .' (I Cor. 14.22)? We shall have to return to these questions later.[2]

First, however, we must put the incident described above and similar events, which have led to a rediscovery of the gift of speaking with tongues in the traditional churches of America, into their historical context.

1. *The Origin of the Pentecostal Movement within the American Churches*[3]

A variety of impulses led to the recovery of the experience of baptism in the Spirit with speaking in tongues[4] in the traditional churches of America. It is very difficult to discover the extent of the revival and its sources, as many clergy and members of congregations who speak with tongues keep quiet about it, partly through natural restraint and partly because they are afraid of sanctions from the church authorities.[5] Among such unknown sources of revival would be, for example, the Latvian Lutherans who emigrated to America on the basis of a prophecy, and the Catholic Apostolic Christians[6] who are scattered among a number of churches in America.[7]

The known sources of revival at the beginning of the nineteen-sixties are:

(*a*) *The van Nuys revival*

A young Anglican couple had received the baptism of the Spirit with speaking in tongues at an alliance meeting. From then on they surprised the vicar of their Anglican church by regular tithing – i.e. giving ten per cent of income to the church – and vigorous participation. His one fear was that they were in danger of becoming fanatics. To sober them down, he introduced them to another couple. Thereupon these, too, experienced the baptism of the Spirit. The astonished vicar told his superior, Father Bennett, about the affair. But now he, too, began to pray for the baptism of the Spirit. Seven hundred members of his congregation, among them a Ph.D. and a brain surgeon, thereupon sought and found the experience of Spirit baptism.[8] Among them was Mrs Jean Stone, wife of a director of Lockheed. Though she assiduously prayed in the way that is required in the Anglican church, went to all the services and gave a good deal of money to the church, she 'felt a void in my life, which nothing but more of him could fill'.[9] Because she was a woman she could not be ordained in the Anglican church, because she was a mother she could not become an Anglican nun and because her husband had no vocation to the mission field, she could not become a missionary. So she saw no possibility of active work in the church. But when she was filled with the Holy Spirit, she saw that it was not her destiny to waste her life with aimless conversations at parties with the 'high society' of California. Her home became a meeting place for clergy and laity from the upper levels of society[10] who sought the baptism of the Spirit. She herself gave lectures to Pentecostals and non-Pentecostals about Spirit baptism; Pentecostals who had long sought the baptism of the Spirit in Pentecostal prayer times received it when this Anglican laid her hands on them, though they had been told that the Pentecostal experience was very hard to have outside the Pentecostal movement. Some of these Pentecostals later came to the Anglican eucharist, the quiet congregational devotion of which caused them to come over to the Anglican church.[11]

Jean Stone summed up the result of the baptism of the Spirit in the following way: it brought a deeper understanding of the love of God, a desire to read the Bible; experience of the baptism of the Spirit made anyone who had not previously believed in the infallibility of Scripture into an 'Anglican fundamentalist'; it brought a deeper recognition of sin, power to testify and power to pray with the sick.[12]

The speaking with tongues brought about tensions in the community which caused the vicar, Dennis J. Bennett, to retire.[13] But the revival could not be halted, and spread all over America and indeed to Europe.[14] A United Protestant pastor, A. Bittlinger, and a number of other observers[15] describe charismatic services within the church whose solemn beauty was deeply impressive. Contrary to their expectations, they heard no hand-clapping, no sighing and no interspersed exclamations. The advocates of this revival are agreed that it is

> a spiritual movement that is defrosting a frigid church; . . . that is converting cocktail Christians into tithers; that is relaxing stiff-necked Pharisees confirmed in the faith but firmed in a past experience long dead; that is rocking the chairs of worldly bishops who make investigations in order to control the Holy Spirit; that metamorphoses social butterflies into spiritual dynamos.[16]

Occasionally children, too, were invited to receive the baptism of the Spirit.

Dr John Alexander Mackay, at one time President of the famous Theological Seminary at Princeton, said: 'If it is a choice between the uncouth life of the Pentecostals and the aesthetic death of the older churches, I for one choose uncouth life.'[17] The outbreak of speaking with tongues in Anglican and high-church Lutheran and Reformed churches does, however, make such an alternative superfluous.

(*b*) '*Full Gospel Business Men*'[18]

Many ministers of traditional churches were made aware of the Pentecostals and their message by the television broadcasts of Oral Roberts, the healing campaigns of T. L. Osborn, W. Branham and others, by the rapid growth of the Pentecostal communities, by the evangelization of drug addicts[19] and by intermediary organizations like the Full Gospel Business Men's Fellowship International (FGBMFI). Despite vigorous criticism, the mass meetings made many ministers wonder why the churches were unsuccessful in interesting the 'little people', the blue- and white-collar workers, in their services. At the banquets of the 'Full Gospel Business Men' they were brought together with Pentecostals in a context that fitted their place in society. In seeking thus to move sociologically beyond the stage of the sect, the Pentecostals made conversion very much easier, and as a result many ministers took over Pentecostal ideology and experience uncritically.

The FGBMFI mentioned in the preceding paragraph is a lay organization. It includes business men – the leading managers are very rich industrialists – who have set as their goal the evangelization of the world and the spreading of the message of the baptism of the Spirit and the healing of the sick, as this is understood by Pentecostal healing evangelists, in non-Pentecostal circles. It was founded by the Armenian American Demos Shakarian; he himself did not want to become a preacher, but appointed evangelists who seemed to him to be promising, paid their expenses and remunerated them generously. He regarded this as a contribution towards the building of the kingdom of God befitting a great industrialist. Evidently the resolution of the Assemblies of God not to accept those who were not full-time pastors into their regional leadership[20] contributed considerably to the expansion of this lay organization. This also explains the polemic which appears every now and then against the clericalism developing in the Assemblies of God. Only *men* can become members of the FGBMFI; no preachers can be elected to the leading circles, although they appear regularly at the conferences and banquets of the FGBMFI.

The 'Full Gospel Business Men' can claim credit for having gained a hearing for the healing evangelists[21] in the non-Pentecostal churches and in the Anglican Order of Saint Luke.[22] It played a decisive part in financing the newly-founded Pentecostal Oral Roberts university in Tulsa, Oklahoma – one of the most modern in the world.[23] Its conferences have been addressed by Oral Roberts, Reformed and Lutheran pastors, Roman Catholic priests, William Branham and Billy Graham, Adventists, Methodists and Baptists. The fellowship has formed groups all over the world. However, the European director, Adolf Guggenbühl, together with the European branch, has broken off from the international Centre in Los Angeles.[24]

The organization has made a decisive contribution towards the spreading of Pentecostal ideas all over the world.[25] At the same time it is critical of the Pentecostal denominations for their (sociologically conditioned) narrow-mindedness and the clericalism of their preachers. The preachers of the Pentecostal movement, on the other hand, accuse the organization of being moulded in its structure and methods of propaganda by worldly business efficiency and not by the guidance of the Spirit.[26] In fact the overwhelming optimism of these business men, not only reminiscent of the Old Testament but also typically American, is quite incomprehensible to the European reader, as for example when it is said that the person who is full of the Holy Spirit will prove more successful in business, make better tractors and automobiles than his competitors, live in a finer house and, if he is a footballer, score more goals than the person who is not converted or is not baptized with the Spirit.[27]

(*c*) *The influence of David J. Du Plessis*

By his witness, David J. Du Plessis, a South African descendant of exiled Hugenots and a leading functionary in the South African Apostolic Faith Mission,[28] for a long time General Secretary of the World Pentecostal Conferences, co-worker with the healing evangelists and advocate of ecumenical contacts between the Pentecostal movement, the World Council of Churches and traditional churches, has communicated the experience and the doctrine of the baptism of the Spirit to many non-Pentecostals. He has talked with participants at a number of ecumenical conferences[29] and with senior Catholic dignitaries at the Vatican Council. Although he has never had an academic theological education, he has lectured at many American universities and seminaries.[30] All this has corrected the picture held by many theologians and parish clergy of the narrow-minded sectarian that they had thought a Pentecostal preacher to be. He reports a steadily increasing interest in the baptism of the Spirit, not within fundamentalist churches and communities, but in the liberal churches and the member churches of the World Council.[31]

The Swedish Pentecostal leader Lewi Pethrus[32] and the leadership of the Assemblies of God[33] have repudiated Du Plessis' attempts at ecumenical communication. It seems that the Assemblies of God were chagrined because the Holy Spirit had used this false channel and not extended the baptism of the Spirit to the traditional churches by means of the official committees of the Assemblies of God. In 1962 Du Plessis was disfellowshipped from the Assemblies of God because of his contacts with the World Council of Churches. Donald Gee, however, supported him.[34]

(*d*) *Roman Catholic Pentecostalism*

Since 1962, individual Catholics, laity and priests, had taken part in meetings of the 'Full Gospel Fellowship' and in so doing had also experienced and taken over Pentecostal spirituality.[35] The breakthrough did not come, however, until 1966/67:

> Several Catholic laymen, all members of the faculty of Duquesne University in Pittsburg, were drawn together in a period of deep prayer and discussion about the vitality of their faith life ... Not satisfied with a life of ivory tower scholarship, they concerned themselves with the problems of renewal in the Church ... In recent years they had been involved in the liturgical and ecumenical movements, with civil rights, and with the concerns of world peace.[36]

The most prominent people in this group of Catholic intellectuals were the Ranaghans, a married couple with academic theological training. At the end of 1966 they read the story of the Pentecostal evangelist David Wilkerson, who had proved prayer and the gifts of the Spirit to be the most effective means of fighting against the teenage drug problem.[37] John Sherrill's account of the charismatic revival[38] within the Protestant churches made them curious to make its acquaintance at first hand. Through William Lewis, an Anglican rector, they came into contact with an ecumenical charismatic prayer group. Soon they received the gift of speaking with tongues. The revival spread from Duquesne via Notre Dame University all over America. The movement is said already to include 10,000 Catholics.[39] St John's Abbey, Collegeville (Minnesota) commissioned the Benedictine Kilian McDonnell to investigate the revival and its roots, and this has led to a series of noteworthy publications both about the Pentecostal denominations and about the Roman Catholic Pentecostals.[40]

The prayer meetings of the Catholic Pentecostals 'shattered the "economic-deprivation" theory that had routinely been set forth as an "explanation" of the older, classical Pentecostalism'.[41] It was not the uneducated but the intellectuals, not the uncritical but the critical exegetes, not frustrated Puritans but quite normal Christians who took part in these meetings. There is not only speaking in tongues but critical discussion of theological and social problems; not only the singing of hymns but the composition of new hymns, not only praying, but eating, drinking and smoking.

The Catholics concede that this revival movement has its roots outside the Catholic church. Although Edward O'Connor tolerates no doubt about the sound Catholic theology behind it, he asks the question,

> Is it conceivable that the Holy Spirit should be more operative in certain other Churches (viz. the Pentecostal) than in that Church which alone is held to be fully authentic, and that the latter could receive from the former a new influx of the gifts of the Spirit?

His answer is:

> This may be God's way of demonstrating to members of the Church that he alone is sovereign Lord, and that all institutions and hierarchs on earth, even in the Church, are nothing but instruments and ministers . . . We need to have it demonstrated for us that God's action transcends the action of the Church as well as all human calculation.[42]

Although the *Pentecostal Evangel* of the Assemblies of God is of the opinion that the Vatican Council 'produced so little worthy of note',[43] it must be realized that a charismatic movement like that described above could hardly have laid claim to so much freedom as it enjoys at present without the decrees of the Council. As the Decree on the apostolate of the laity lays stress on the necessity of charismata for the whole people of God,[44] the movement has so far aroused no fundamental criticism even among the American bishops. In the 'Report of the Committee on Doctrine of the National Conference of Catholic Bishops' on 'The Pentecostal Movement in the Catholic Church in the U.S.A.' they merely asserted:

1. The movement appeared to be theologically sound;
2. There were dangers involved in it;
3. They wished that more priests would get involved in it.[45]

The theology of this movement, which is only just beginning to develop, is substantially different from that of the Pentecostal denominations, as it is from that of the charismatic movement within the Protestant church. It is closest to the theology of the charismatic movement within the German churches[46] and the free church Mülheim Association of Christian Fellowships.[47] The Pentecostals who hitherto have seen the Catholic church simply as a prefigurement of the 'great whore'[48] are puzzled by the combination of spirituality and freedom (smoking and drinking), prayer and critical exegesis, which is so uncharacteristic of their own denominations. It is no coincidence that apart from some notes[49] there had been no mention of the Pentecostal revival in the Catholic church in the *Pentecostal Evangel* up to the end of 1969.

2. *A Summary of the Doctrine of the Pentecostal Movement within the Churches*

(*a*) *Baptism of the Spirit*

In contrast to the Catholic Pentecostals, the greater part of the Pentecostal movement within the Protestant churches seems to have taken over the Pentecostal doctrine of the two sorts of Christians, those who have been baptized in the Spirit and those who have not.[50] The former are qualified by speaking with tongues. A difference is also made between speaking with tongues as a sign of the baptism of the Spirit (which is received by all those who are baptized with the Spirit) and speaking with tongues as a gift of the Spirit which is acquired only by certain persons.[51] Jean Stone wrote to a clergyman:

> You stated, 'I have learned that not everyone has the same initial experience.' If you mean by that that they do not all need to speak with other tongues to be filled with the Holy Spirit, I must confess that I do not agree with you. I am well aware that God is omnipotent and can do anything. But I feel that He normally operates in an orderly, fathomable and practicable fashion.[52]

A similar view is put forward in the Blessed Trinity Society's pamphlet *Why Tongues, Why Divisions?*:

> If we only wish to perform the barest minimum essential for life everlasting, then once we have repented of our sins and accepted Jesus Christ as our personal Saviour, we may live and obtain life eternal. But how much more there is for the serious Christian! How much more rewarding is the life of commitment and service a dedicated Child of God may participate in . . .[53] For surely the unknown tongue is the initial, audible evidence of the infilling of the Holy Spirit.[54]

The Anglican rector mentioned earlier, Dennis J. Bennett, wrote:

> Thus in many places the New Testament explicitly and implicitly makes it clear that there is a 'baptism in the Holy Spirit' that is to be distinguished from the 'baptism of repentance'.[55]

In the New Testament, the expectation was that a person should be converted and baptized and thereupon experience the baptism of the Spirit. Today in churches which practise confirmation, he is expected to be converted (in theory, if not in practice), be baptized and receive the laying on of hands,

> but not to have any recognizable experience of the Holy Spirit, nor manifestation of the same. The New Testament rule has become the exception: the New Testament exception has become the rule. Is it any wonder that there is confusion with regard to confirmation? And confusion will remain until enough people experience the Holy Spirit with recognizable power to make the theologians take notice.[56]

We can pass over the journalistic polemics in the American press. Even the pastoral letter by the Anglican bishop of California, James A. Pike,[57] does not seem to me to be very helpful. Certainly we must agree with Pike when he tries to understand speaking with tongues as a natural phenomenon and when he points to the difficult problems which are presented by the dogmatics which are borrowed from the classical Pentecostals. But what does Pike have to say about the right use of speaking with tongues? Nothing! One can see all too clearly the anxiety of the church leader at a phenomenon which he does not understand.

On the other hand, the Lutheran pastor Larry Christenson asserts, 'The cure for abuse is not disuse, but proper use'.[58] Christenson stresses strongly the significance of speaking with tongues for personal prayer life and has found in it a source of spiritual refreshment alongside his strenuous intellectual daily work. He refuses to accept that speaking with tongues is the only sign of the baptism of the Spirit, but because he believes that it is essential for the prayer life of every Christian, he gives suggestions as to how it might be achieved.

> In order to speak in tongues, you must quit speaking in any other language which you know, for you cannot speak two languages at once. After you have come to the Lord with prayers and petitions in your native tongue, lapse into silence and resolve to speak not a syllable of any language you have learned. Focus your thoughts on Christ. *Then simply lift up your voice and speak out confidently*, in the faith that the Lord will take the sound which you give Him, and shape it into a language.[59]

Because of his social background he discourages

> the copying of any set traditions, customs or mannerisms (of the Pentecostals) in our prayer groups. We have nothing against these traditions from other Christian groups, but we don't feel they are essential to the manifestation of the gifts of the Spirit. It is unnatural for our people to pray in loud voices, or frequently to intersperse another person's prayer with 'Amen', 'Hallelujah' 'Praise the Lord'.[60]

Following the final conclusions of the report of the American Lutheran Church on speaking with tongues,[61] he enjoins:

> When a person feels that this experience is not for him, that the Holy Spirit is working in his life in other ways, that is his decision, and there should be no implication that he is 'less of a Christian' than someone who speaks in tongues. The person who speaks in tongues is 'not better than someone else, but better than he himself was before'.[62] As in the last resort it is not a question concerned with the way of salvation, we believe as a community that we ought to take still more time to acquire wisdom and maturity before we talk about it to our children (in instruction).[63]

An Anglican assistant priest who was also a physicist in the research division of a chemical undertaking attempted to make as it were a scientific psychological investigation of his own speaking with tongues and came to the conclusion: 'Speaking in tongues is prayer.'[64] Another Anglican points to the long underestimated significance of the emotional element for the spiritual and religious health of men:

> I do believe that the Church must cease to deprecate the emotional element in religion, for the matter is truly important, and simple will power is not sufficient to meet it. Since becoming aware of psychological factors in life some ten years ago, I have had occasion to observe how often those who trust primarily in institutional theories of religion break down emotionally. And many of those who do not break live lives of intense and tortured emotional repression. In fact, the very objection to 'emotionalism' we hear so often is a symptom in many cases of severe emotional repression and strain. We must conclude that trust in and adherence to an ecclesiastical system cannot, of itself, bring that salvation of which St Paul spoke, and which Jesus offered.[65]

It is difficult to say how far the writings of Mrs J. E. Stiles are representative of the Pentecostal movement within the American church. They give similar counsel to Christenson's aids towards receiving the Holy Spirit, but contrast these with the usual practice of the Assemblies of God, a fact which indicates thorough acquaintance with the Pentecostal tarrying meetings. Mrs Stiles attacks the Pentecostal preachers who are not in a position to impart to members of their communities the baptism of the Spirit and speaking with tongues.

> The Full Gospel movement has today in its ranks literally thousands of such people over the world. You meet them everywhere you go, if you make any inquiry along this line. They will no longer seek the Holy Spirit because they have been disappointed so many times . . .[66]

She asserts that what is taught in the Pentecostal movement, especially in groups with a three-stage way of salvation,[67] simply is not true – that the baptism of the Spirit is only given to the believer when he is ready for it. Receiving the baptism of the Spirit and speaking with tongues are an act of will on the part of the believer, so that he no longer wants to speak in his mother tongue. The fruit of the Spirit and the gift of the Spirit can grow almost independently of one another and are not constantly to be associated with each other.[68]

She pertinently describes the normal testimony of a Pentecostal at one of the annual camp meetings:

> I came to camp meeting last year feeling very much down in spirits, but the third night I was here the power of God came down in a wonderful way, and I got gloriously re-filled. I spoke with other tongues for an hour and a half, and it was such a wonderful refreshing. I really lived in another world for a solid week. It seemed as if I hardly touched the ground, I was so lost in God and heavenly things. About that time we had to go home, and I began the daily round of duties that kept me busy from morning till night. Well, it just seemed that I was so busy with cooking, and washing and sewing, and added to that, the tying up of cut fingers, and kissing of bumped heads, that I didn't have much time to read my Bible, or pray as I should. Little by little the joy seemed to slip away, and it wasn't long before I felt as if I was in a spiritual desert. I was so dried up and so hungry. How I have been looking forward for months to this year's camp meeting so that I could be filled again. Well, last night it came, and Oh! how the glory poured down on me. I surely feel like a new person today. I spoke in other tongues for hours, and words can't express how wonderful it was. Heaven really came down, and flooded my heart to overflowing. Praise the Lord for His wonderful goodness to me.[69]

Mrs Stiles remarks that this same person will experience the same regression again in a few weeks, and that after a few repetitions of the cycle of heavenly joy and barren desolation will perhaps lose all interest in these camp meetings, in prayer and in the Bible. This she sees as a principal problem of Pentecostal pastoral care.

Her suggestion for a solution to the problem is unusual. Instead of saying, like Luther, 'Baptizatus sum', instead of relying, like the Catholics, on the sacrament or trusting, like the Reformed, on the word of preaching, the Pentecostal is to say: 'There, in that baptism of the Spirit and speaking with tongues, God's Spirit has come to me objectively. Quite independently of what I know feel or experience: this one fact remains unshakable.' This position might be called a kind of sacramentalism of speaking with tongues.

Mrs Stiles rightly describes the tragedies that arise from the Pentecostal doctrine that the Holy Spirit can only come into purified hearts:

1. The most upright Christians never receive the baptism of the Spirit, because they know themselves well enough to be aware that they can never regard themselves as purified.
2. Those who receive the baptism of the Spirit automatically rise to a higher class of Christians, whereas
3. those who have not received the baptism of the Spirit seem to be Christians of an inferior quality.
4. This often results in the arrogance of those who have received the baptism of the Spirit.
5. Therefore it must now be said of the Pentecostal preachers that those baptized with the Spirit who later have an excessive opinion of themselves have not really been baptized by the Spirit of God, even if they have already spoken in tongues: they have only been anointed by the Spirit, and this will be followed later by a true filling with the Holy Spirit.
6. A recognition of this will discourage the best Pentecostal preachers from ever preaching about the baptism of the Spirit.
7. Baptism of the Spirit wrongly becomes a goal, instead of a means.

In contrast to the Protestant charismatic movement within the church, the parallel Catholic movement rejects the 'methodology of fundamentalism'. To quote Ranaghan again:

> Too often in the past Christians experiencing baptism in the Holy Spirit have adopted not only the cultural environment of denominational Pentecostalism but also the thought categories of the fundamentalist milieu.

The denominational Pentecostals are not of course to be criticized for their fundamentalism. Presumably it is part of their social milieu.[70] Nevertheless, it seems necessary to Ranaghan that, in so far as Pentecost is really an experience of the whole church and not the doctrine of a particular group within the church, the charismatic element should be approached in theological discussion from different standpoints, including that of critical exegesis.[71]

It follows from this that the charismata must not be regarded as something supernatural. As in the charismatic movement within the German church,[72] community casework, journalism[73] and run-of-the-mill administration[74] can therefore also be regarded as charismata.

It is only logical that the concept of 'baptism in the Holy Spirit' should be used with restraint. This concept has been borrowed from fundamentalist Pentecostals 'who don't have the sacramental theology needed to relate it to the whole context of water baptism'.[75] Catholic charismatic theology must therefore speak of a renewal of the receiving of the Spirit rather than of an initiation into the life of the Spirit.[76]

(*b*) *Spirit and sacrament*

One of the brightest aspects of this charismatic revival is the recognition that a *liturgy* rooted in the past of the church, an Anglican, Lutheran or Roman Catholic understanding of the sacraments, need not necessary conflict with a charismatic understanding of the Spirit. On the contrary, in a hierarchically, liturgically and sacramentally 'protected' church far more room can be accorded to the charismata than in Pentecostal communities with no tradition or in unliturgical fellowship groups. Lutheran, Anglican and Roman Catholic clergy testify unanimously that the ministry of the altar and liturgy have become a need and an experience after their baptism with the Spirit:

> When it seems that one can know God's nearness and love to such depth following the baptism of the Holy Spirit, why these forms . . . ? Why have moments of quiet, when one's heart is bursting to praise the Living God? These are legitimate questions. The answer is that we cannot exclude either the fixed form of the liturgy and the sacraments or the charismatic breath of the Spirit. Both belong to worship.[77]

Catholic Pentecostals can also recognize this form of the baptism in the Holy Spirit as 'sacramental in the broad sense of the term, that is, as all physical realities speak to us of the grace of God'.[78]

(*c*) *Ethics*

The *Protestant* wing of the charismatic revival has so far made no contribution to the theme of ethical rigorism in *Pentecostal* circles, to the opening up of the all too narrow personalistic horizon of the Pentecostal movement. This is disappointing.[79] We shall wait expectantly for R. R. Rice's book *Charismatic Revival*, which is to contain a chapter on the relationship between charisma and ethics. Meanwhile one can only be amazed that e.g. in the writings of the wife of the great industrialist Mr Stone, the ethical consequences of this revival, 'turning the world upside down', are restricted to abstention from cocktails and smoking.[80] I have not been able to find any contribution to the race question in any of the publications of the Trinity Group. It is astounding that in a revival brought about by the Spirit of God, God seems completely to have forgotten the most important problems with which the churches of America are struggling at present. The Anglican Wilbur O. Fogg writes with disconcerting superficiality:

I do not believe that it is a question of 'speaking the language of the twentieth century' (though that certainly has its value), but of returning ourselves to a simple and solid experience of the spiritual facts that empowered the Apostles and early Christians to turn the world upside down. So far as I can tell, they did not try to 'meet the world where it was', but as a matter of fact, they challenged the position of the world. They called upon the world to 'move out' from where it was, and affirmed very strongly that they would stand on the Rock of Jesus Christ whether the world came with them or not. They could do this, not because they had learned to 'communicate in contemporary terms' but because they had experienced the grace and power and presence of the Risen Christ.[81]

3. *Assessment and Conclusions*

It will become harder and harder to make a clear-cut distinction between American Pentecostals and American non-Pentecostals in the future, now that the experience and message of the baptism of the Spirit have found a way into all the American denominations. Russell Chandler reckons that over a thousand Presbyterian pastors have experienced the baptism of the Spirit and speaking with tongues. Retreat houses, in which 'charismatic services' are arranged, extend the experience. Du Plessis reckons that ten thousand Catholics have experienced the baptism of the Spirit and speaking with tongues. Bishop Chandler W. Sterling estimates the number of Anglican clergy in the USA who speak with tongues at ten per cent of the total (about 700).[82] Some well-known journalists in the United States make the message of the baptism of the Spirit known to a wider public. In Germany and Switzerland people like to make a fundamental distinction between Billy Graham and the Pentecostals,[83] but that is no longer possible now that Billy Graham, who in any case had been influenced before his conversion by a friend from the Pentecostal movement,[84] has accepted invitations to the 'Full Gospel Fellowship' and has made most approving statements about the Pentecostals on a number of occasions.[85] Donald Gee had encouraged the theologians of the Protestant charismatic revival within traditional churches not to despise their theological education and not to stake everything on the one card of spiritual experience.[86] Unfortunately, however, it must be said by way of summary that by and large the Pentecostal movement within the American church has thrown this admonition to the winds. With the exception of Christenson, who attempts to dissociate himself from the Pentecostal theory of the baptism of the Spirit, the Pentecostal theories are taken over without criticism. Frank Farrel[87] and Arnold Bittlinger therefore hope that soon theologians will appear who will take a decisive stand against a doctrine of the 'baptism of the Spirit'.[88]

This wish now seems to be being granted in an unexpected way as a result of the charismatic revival in the Catholic church. In this the Catholics are supported by an investigation of the Anglican Morton T. Kelsey.[89] Taking further the historical and psychological analysis of speaking with tongues made by George Barton Cutten, Kelsey, a clergyman who does not himself speak with tongues but who has a group in his parish which does, sets out to understand the phenomenon of speaking with tongues against a background of Jungian psychology. Kelsey stresses the connection between the Pentecostal movement and the new charismatic revival more strongly than does, e.g. Bittlinger, but this is only an incidental feature of his account. More important, for him, is speaking with tongues as an expression of the collective psyche. According to Kelsey, for certain people – not just primitive or uneducated people – it has the same healing function as dreams and is by no means to be dismissed as a phenomenon of sickness. On the other hand, forced speaking with tongues does damage to the character and the psyche both of the person who forces it and of the recipient. This shows up the doctrine of the baptism of the Spirit taught in the Trinity Group as also being wrong from a psychological point of view (a point which seems to have escaped Donald Gee in his positive review of the book).[90] The author, who has a thorough knowledge of all the relevant psychiatric literature, regards speaking with tongues as an extremely effective medicine, but one that can be dangerous if applied to inappropriate patients.

By way of summary it must be said:

1. Anglican and Lutheran Pentecostals seem to have succeeded in directing emotional outbursts into channels where the churches have some control over their theological, ecclesiastical and social consequences. In this way they take up a legitimate need of even academically educated Christians for non-intellectual forms of worship.

In most instances the experience of the baptism of the Spirit is described in the thought categories of Pentecostal doctrine and is therefore in danger of being exposed to all the misunderstandings of Pentecostal doctrine. This danger is all the greater when the philosophical (the division of the phenomena of the world into natural and supernatural) and exegetical (the acceptance of Acts as a normative protocol of the first normative Christianity) presuppositions remain unclarified.

2. The consequences of an emotional outburst for social and ethical problems, which ought not to be neglected by these more highly placed strata precisely because of their social prestige and their intellectual competence, have so far not been considered. What is the meaning of 'turning the world upside down', 'having experienced the presence of the Risen Christ' in a world which is at its wits' end over the problems of racial division, war, individual and social ethics and needs more than ever the ministry of Christian thought?

3. We must follow with great interest further developments in the Roman Catholic church. Perhaps the composure with which the Catholic theologians approach these problems reveals the gifts of the Pentecostal movement (inside and outside the traditional churches) for the whole Christian world. It is, however, very hard to say how a Pentecostal revival within the Roman Catholic

church will influence the relationship between denominational Pentecostalism and Catholicism or between those two groups and the ecumenical movement. The silence on this theme in the Pentecostal periodicals at any rate shows that this revival cannot be interpreted in the usual categories.

NOTES

1. J. L. Sherrill, *They Speak*, pp. 89f.; cf. also J. Robins, *Full Gospel Men's Voice* 8/6–7, July–Aug. 1960, pp. 9f.
2. Cf. ch. 24.5, pp. 342ff.
3. Evidence, documents, literature: 02a.02.206–16. Main periodicals: *Trinity*, *Testimony*, *Voice in the Wilderness*, *Faith Conquest*, *Acts*, *Charisma Digest*. Cf. also the series by J. Jensen (bibliography) and the books published by Logos, Plainfield, New Jersey (e.g. D. G. Lillie, *Tongues*; D. J. Bennett, *Nine o'Clock*).
4. For this concept cf. ch. 24.4, pp. 330ff.
5. *Living Church* 164, 10.7.1960, p. 5.
6. A revival group within the church from the last century. Cf. F. S. Mead, *Handbook*, p. 62.
7. A. Bittlinger, letter to W.H., 18.11.1963.
8. *Trinity* 1/2, 1962, pp. 5, 48; *Time* 78, 15.8.1960, p. 55; 81, 29.3.1963, p. 52; *Nationalzeitung*, Basel, 30/31.5.1964; many articles in American newspapers and periodicals. Cf. also J. T. Nichol, *Pentecostalism*, pp. 240-4. For the latest development see R. Chandler, *Christianity Today* 12/4, 24.11.1967, pp. 39f.
9. *Trinity* 1/2, 1962, p. 30. J. Stone, *Trinity* 1/2, 1962, pp. 8–11; *Christian Life*, Nov. 1961, pp. 38–41.
10. Instances: J. E. Hadley, *Trinity* 1/4, 1962, pp. 24f.; N. G. Scovell, *Trinity* 1/3, 1962, pp. 2–4.
11. J. Weddle, *Trinity* 1/2, 1962, pp. 19f.
12. J. Stone, *Trinity* 1/2, 1962, pp. 10f.
13. D. J. Bennett, *Trinity* 1/2, 1962, pp. 6f. (farewell speech).
14. Cf. the writings of A. Bittlinger, M. Harper and R. F. Edel.
15. Instances: E. B. Stube, P. E. Hughes, J. H. Hanson.
16. E. Newman, *Trinity* 1/2, 1961, pp. 18, 20.
17. Quoted in J. L. Sherrill, *They Speak*, p. 140.
18. Evidence, documents, literature: 02a.02.205.
19. D. R. Wilkerson, *Cross*.
20. On this cf. ch. 3.2(*a*), p. 34.
21. On this cf. ch. 25, pp. 353ff.
22. The International Order of Saint Luke, San Diego, California, is a fellowship of doctors and ministers who want to bring new life to prayer for the sick in churches. The order is closely related to Pentecostal healing evangelists and occasionally takes over their theses, cf. 02a.02.209. Journal: *Sharing*.
23. In detail, 02a.02.177; cf. ch. 25.2(*b*), pp. 363ff.
24. Internationale Vereinigung Christlicher Geschäftsleute (IVCG), located in Zurich; there is co-operation from Hans Bruns, various European pastors, intellectuals and businessmen. Periodicals: *Actes – Geschäftsmann und Christ*.
25. A banquet is described in detail by J. L. Sherrill, *They Speak*, pp. 117–23.
26. D. Gee, *MD* 21, 1958, p. 131.
27. E. Braselton, *Full Gospel Men's Voice* 6/2, March 1968, p. 15.

28. Cf. ch. 9.3(*a*), pp. 120ff.

29. Cf. 02a.02.208.

30. H. Bredesen, *Trinity* 2/2, 1963, pp. 3–5, gives an account of baptisms of the Spirit at Yale university.

31. D. J. Du Plessis, *Pentecost outside 'Pentecost'* and *The Spirit Bade Me Go*.

32. L. Pethrus, *Dagen*, 2.3.1963; but cf. more recently *Dagen* 24/131, 9.7.1968; 24/135, 13.7.1968 – *Dagens Nyheter*, 13.7.1968.

33. Cf. ch. 3.4, pp. 42f.

34. D. Gee, *P* 21, 1952, p. 12; *P* 24, 1953, p. 17.

35. F. J. Schulgen, *Testimony* 4/1, First Quarter of 1965, pp. 1–7; L. O'Docharty, *ibid.*, p. 8.

36. K. and D. Ranaghan, *Catholic P*, p. 6; J. Connelly in Ranaghan, *Spirit*, pp. 211–232.

37. D. Wilkerson, *Cross.*

38. J. Sherrill, *They Speak*, cf. pp. 3f.

39. The most important account and most balanced assessment is given by K. McDonnell, *Dialog* (Winter 1970), pp. 35–54. Further literature (cf. also the following footnotes and the literature on ch. 30.3, pp. 437ff.): T. Barbarie, *Triumph* 4 (April 1969), pp. 20–2; J. Cavnar, *Prayer Meetings* (typescript); *id.*, *Acts* 1/5, 1968, pp. 14/19; *id.*, *Scholastic* 109, 21.4.1967, p. 14; St B. Clark, *Confirmation and 'The Baptism of the Spirit'* (typescript); *Baptized in the Spirit*; *Spiritual Gifts*; P. Damboriena, *Tongues*, pp. 63f.; J. M. Ford, *Jubilee* 16/2, June 1968, pp. 13–17; D. Francis, *Twin Circle* 2/29, 21.7.1968, p. 6; B. Ghezzi, Acts 1/2, Sept.–Oct. 1967, p. 34; M. Killian, *The Priest* 25 (Nov. 1969), pp. 611–16; A. Molina, *Voice* 17 (Oct. 1969), pp. 30–3; D. Murray, *Scholastic* 109, 14.4.1967, pp. 18–20; E. O'Connor, *Ave Maria* 105, 3.6.1967, pp. 7–10; 106, 19.8.1967, pp. 11–14; *id.*, *The Ecumenist* 6/5, July–August 1968, pp. 161–4 (all three reprinted in revised form in: O'Connor, *Pentecost in the Catholic Church*); *American Ecclesiastical Review*, Sept. 1969, pp. 145–59; Synan, *P Movement*; M. Papa, *National Catholic Reporter* 3/29, 17.5.1967; 4 (5.6.1967), pp. 1, 2; K. Peters, *Ave Maria* 108 (17.8.1968), pp. 8–12; J. F. Powers, *America* 119/2, 20.7.1968, pp. 43f.; K. Ranaghan, *National Catholic Reporter* 3 (26.4.1967), p. 4; *Charisma Digest* 2, 1969, pp. 14–18, 22–4; *Religious News Service*, 25.10.1969, 'Report on The Leader's Workshop', Lansing, Mich. (12.3.1968); M. Sandoval, *National Catholic Reporter*, 12.6.1968; *St Mary's Chapel* (Ann Arbor, Mich.), 4.2.1968, pp. 1–3; P. A. Thibodeau, A Study of the Catholic Pentecostal Movement in Ann Arbor, Michigan (unpublished sociological report); *Time*, 14.6.1968, p. 64; K. Wullenweber, *St Anthony Messenger* 76, Jan. 1969, pp. 18–27; *Acts* 1/2, Sept.–Oct. 1967, pp. 25–30.

40. K. McDonnell, *Worship* 40/10, December 1966, pp. 608–29; *id.*, *America* 118/13, 30.3.1968; *id.*, *Journal of Ecumenical Studies* 1967/8, pp. 105–26; *id.*, *Continuum*, Winter 1967/68, pp. 673–85; *id.*, *Sisters Today* 40 (May 1969), pp. 497–506; *id.*, *Commonweal* 89, 8.11.1968, pp. 198–204; H. J. M. Nouwen, *Scholastic* 109, 21.4.1967, pp. 15–17, 32; *id.*, *Ave Maria* 105, 3.6.1967, pp. 11–13, 30; N. L. Gerrard, *Transaction*, May 1968, pp. 22–30.

41. *Religious News Service*, 25.10.1969.

42. E. O'Connor, *Ecumenist* 6/5, July/August 1968, pp. 161–4; cf. also Ranaghan, *Catholic P*, p. 153.

43. C. A. Bolten, *PE* 2703, 27.2.1966, pp. 6f.

44. Quoted in Ranaghan, *op. cit.*, p. 184.

45. Cf. C. Rigby, *Ecumenist* 7/5, July/August 1969, pp. 73–6; the report was presented by Bishop A. Zaleski of Lansing, Mich., to the Bishops in their meeting in Washington, D.C., 14 Nov. 1969. Compare the battle the charismatics had to fight in the United Presbyterian Church of the USA (*Acts* 1/5, 1968, pp. 13f.).

46. Cf. ch. 18, pp. 244ff.
47. Cf. ch. 17, pp. 231ff.
48. Cf. ch. 30.3, pp. 436ff.
49. *PE* 2860, 2.3.1969, p. 10. *PE* 2785, 24.9.1967, pp. 6–7, 13; but cf. Ranaghan, *Spirit*, pp. 114f., 141.
50. Cf. ch. 24.4, pp. 330ff.
51. *Trinity* 1/1, 1961, p. 51; cf. ch. 24.5, pp. 342ff.
52. J. Stone, *Trinity* 1/3, 1962, p. 22; similarly, T. W. Ewald, *Trinity* 1/4, 1962, pp. 6f. and E. B. Stube, *Trinity* 1/3, 1962, pp. 39–46.
53. Blessed Trinity Society, *Why Tongues?*, p. 1.
54. *Ibid.*, p. 2. This is word for word the teaching of the Assemblies of God (cf. ch. 3.1(*c*), pp. 32f.) and other American Pentecostal circles. It is disputed by British, Chilean, Swiss and German *classical* Pentecostal denominations (cf. ch. 14.2, p. 200) and by A. Bittlinger and recently by Catholic Pentecostals (cf. p. 14).
55. D. J. Bennett, *Pentecostal Testimony*, special ed. (Pentecostalism in the Church Today).
56. *Trinity* 1/4, 1962, pp. 2–4.
57. J. A. Pike, Pastoral Letter 1963.
58. L. Christenson, *Speaking in Tongues: A Gift*, pp. 11, 27.
59. L. Christenson, *Speaking in Tongues and its Significance*, p. 130.
60. L. Christenson, *Speaking in Tongues: A Gift*, p. 30.
61. 'Christians who believe that they have experienced the phenomenon of speaking with tongues or other ecstatic utterances should not be forbidden to practise these gifts. But they should be reminded in Christian love to observe the admonition of the apostle Paul in I Cor. 14.' Quoted by A. Bittlinger, *Deutsches Pfarrerblatt* 1963, pp. 333f.
62. L. Christenson, *Speaking in Tongues: A Gift*, p. 36.
63. L. Christenson, *Gabe des Zungenredens*, p. 28 (only in the German edition).
64. W. O. Swann, *Trinity* 1/3, 1962, p. 16.
65. W. O. Fogg, *Trinity* 1/4, 1962, p. 41.
66. J. E. Stiles, *Gift*, pp. 97, 129.
67. For terminology see ch. 2.4, pp. 24f.
68. J. E. Stiles, *op. cit.*, p. 143.
69. *Ibid.*, pp. 24f.
70. Ranaghan, *Catholic P*, p. 261; K. McDonnell, *Dialog*, Winter 1970, p. 41.
71. Ranaghan, *op. cit.*, p. 260; D. L. Gelpi, *Pentecostalism.*
72. Cf. ch. 18, pp. 344ff.
73. Ranaghan, *op. cit.*, p. 159.
74. *Ibid.*, p. 249.
75. C. Rigby, *Ecumenist* 7/5, July/August 1969, pp. 73–6.
76. St B. Clark, Confirmation and 'The Baptism of the Holy Spirit' (typescript).
77. R. M. Harvey, *Trinity* 1/3, 1962, pp. 6–7, 10.
78. Ranaghan, *op. cit.*, p. 150; *Spirit*, p. 8.
79. All that can be said for the moment about the ethics of the Catholic wing is that (*a*) they are not rigorist and (*b*) the ecumenical contacts of the Catholic charismatics have the political aspects of a Christian spirituality.
80. J. Stone, *Trinity* 1/2, 1962, p. 10.
81. W. O. Fogg, *Trinity* 1/4, 1962, p. 38.
82. R. Chandler, *Christianity Today* 12/4, 24.11.1967, pp. 39–40.
83. E.g. A. Müller, who asserts that Graham has a negative relationship to the Pentecostal movement (*Das missionarische Wort* 13/5, May 1959, pp. 135–47).
84. C. Brumback, *Suddenly*, pp. 311f.
85. See the writings by Graham in the bibliography.

86. D. Gee, *P* 58, 1962, p. 17.
87. F. Farrel, *Christianity Today* 7/24, 13.9.1962, pp. 3–7.
88. A. Bittlinger, letter to W.H., 18.11.1963.
89. M. T. Kelsey, *Tongue Speaking*.
90. D. Gee, *P* 70, 1965, p. 3.

2

'In the Upper Room':[1] The Rise of the American Pentecostal Movement

1. *The Holiness Movement*

WE HAVE seen that apart from some exceptions, the Pentecostal movement within the churches in America took over uncritically from the Pentecostal movement proper its strengths and weaknesses, the experience of the baptism of the Spirit and the fundamentalist interpretation placed on it.

We go on to give a brief summary of the rise of the American Pentecostal movement.

John Wesley, the founder of the Methodist Church, had already made a distinction between the sanctified, or those who had been baptized in the Spirit, and ordinary Christians.[2] This view was adopted and simplified by the evangelists and theologians of the American Holiness movement. Some of these theologians of the Holiness movement, such as Asa Mahan and C. G. Finney, were also involved in the struggle for the Negroes, for women's university education, and for the workers. On the basis of his experience of the baptism of the Spirit, T. C. Upham proposed the foundation of a League of Nations. But of the writings of these Holiness preachers, the only ones to influence the Pentecostal and revivalist movements were those which were concerned with the theory and practice of the baptism of the Spirit. To Asa Mahan, however, it was clear that he needed the 'power of the Holy Spirit' not 'to get to Heaven', nor 'to save souls', but in order to tackle concrete problems of politics and social morality. How ill-acquainted European and American revivalist Christians are with their American masters![3]

The philosophical, political and social endeavours of the Holiness evangelists were forgotten. Their theory of the two distinct turning points in Christian experience (conversion and sactification) remained. The only difficulty was to find the criteria for the second crisis experience. This uncertainty was removed by the early Pentecostal movement.

2. *The Topeka Revival*[4]

In a Bible school in Topeka, Kansas, run by Charles Parham, speaking in tongues was recognized as a distinguishing characteristic of the baptism of the Spirit. In many towns Parham held large meetings in which, as can be seen from press reports,[5] the participants were converted, sanctified, baptized with the Spirit and healed of sickness. One group of Parham's followers later organized the Apostolic Faith Churches, Baxter Springs, Kansas,[6] which at the present day are led by his son, Robert L. Parham, and which like Parham himself are also adherents of the British Israel theory. This is the theory that the Anglo-Saxons are the descendants of the ten tribes of Israel that disappeared in the Assyrian captivity.[7] Charles Parham was no more fortunate than most of the charismatic pioneers of the Pentecostal movement. The following generation of Pentecostal preachers ignored him, never mentioned him, and secretly regarded him as a sectarian, even though the Pentecostal movement as it is at the present day would never have come into being without the 'sectarianism' of its leaders.

3. *The Los Angeles Revival*[8]

One of Parham's pupils, the Negro preacher W. J. Seymour, was invited to Los Angeles by the woman pastor of a Negro Holiness church,[9] Neelly Terry. Joseph Smale[10] and Frank Bartleman, Baptist preachers who had been influenced by the revival in Wales,[11] had already worked there. Seymour arrived in Los Angeles, accompanied by his two women assistants J. A. Warren and Lucy F. Farrow,[12] and preached on Acts 2.4: 'Anyone who does not speak in tongues is not baptized with the Holy Spirit', although Seymour himself had not received the baptism of the Spirit with speaking in tongues. 'The older members (of the Holiness Church) had claimed the "baptism of the Holy Spirit" for years, and here was a stranger telling them they were only "sanctified" and that there was yet another spiritual "experience". This was more than they could accept. . . .'[13] Neelly Terry put Seymour out, whereupon he held meetings in the homes of members of the congregation. On 9 April 1906 'the fire came down' at a prayer meeting in Bonnie Brae Street.[14] It appears that the first to receive the baptism of the Spirit was an eight-year-old Negro boy.[15] Many, mostly members of the Church of the Nazarene[16] and other Holiness denominations,[17] experienced the baptism of the Spirit. Seymour hired an old Methodist church at 312 Azusa Street; this Azusa Street Mission is regarded by Pentecostal publicists as the place of origin of the world-wide Pentecostal movement. For three years without interruption prayer meetings took place here with speaking in tongues, singing in tongues and prophecy. Stories of the Azusa Street revival, in a distinctly legendary form, are retold amongst Pentecostals; for example:

> They shouted three days and three nights. It was the Easter season. The people came from everywhere. By the next morning there was no way of getting near the house. As the people came in they would fall under God's Power; and the whole city was stirred. They shouted there until the foundation of the house gave way, but no one was hurt.[18]

The ecstatic outbursts in the original church, where the floor was covered with sawdust and the pews made of planks laid on empty packing cases, sometimes knew no limits. Alma White's secretary[19] could tell of men and women kissing each other.[20]

The early stages of the revival met bitter opposition from the Holiness churches, and other churches also; they were a laughing stock to the press. The *New York American* of 3 December 1906 reported:

> Faith Gives Quaint Sect New Languages to Convert Africa. Votaries of Odd Religion Nightly see 'Miracles' in West Side Room. Led by Negro Elder. The leaders of this strange movement are for the most part Negroes.

The first edition of *Apostolic Faith* identifies the press with the devil.[21] In general, however, the press campaign provided free publicity.

Originally Parham was the leader of the Azusa Street revival,[22] but from November 1907 on his name no longer appears on the official letterhead.[23] In 1908 the whites withdrew.[24]

The confession of faith of the Apostolic Faith Movement of Los Angeles is given in the appendix.[25] In interpreting this confession of faith, it is important to notice not only what it contains, but also what it omits (e.g. no baptism of believers!). The uncertain English and orthography is also to be noted.

According to this declaration the Azusa Street Mission belongs quite clearly to the Pentecostals who profess the three-stage way of salvation,[26] in contrast to the majority of the groups that arose from this revival and which soon reduced the three-stage pattern to a two-stage one. To this extent Arthur G. Allen[27] and Georgia Bond[28] are correct in reproaching the rest of the Pentecostal movement for having betrayed its original teaching. This is admitted, moreover, by the Assemblies of God.[29] The British Israel theory,[30] the conviction that sanctification precedes the baptism of the Spirit, and fellowship with the American Negroes – the three outstanding characteristics of the early Pentecostal movement in America – have all been abandoned at the present day by the greater part of the American Pentecostal movement.[31]

By the end of 1906 there were already nine Pentecostal assemblies in Los Angeles,[32] some of which were not on good terms with each other. Besides the Azusa Street Mission, which lasted until 1923, we also know of the 'Upper Room Mission', 327 South Spring St., the Eighth Street and Maple Street Missions (Bartleman and Pendleton).

The 'Pentecostal experience of Los Angeles' was neither the leading astray of the Church by demons (as the German Evangelical movement claimed), nor the eschatological pouring out of the Holy Spirit (as the Pentecostal movement itself claims) but an outburst of enthusiastic religion of a kind well-known and frequent in the history of Negro churches in America which derived its specifically Pentecostal features from Parham's theory that speaking with tongues is a necessary concomitant of the baptism of the Spirit.

I do not wish to assert here that the Holy Spirit was not at work in the Los Angeles revival. I agree with the pioneer British Pentecostal Alexander A. Boddy who wrote:

> It was something very extraordinary, that white pastors from the South were eagerly prepared to go to Los Angeles to the Negroes, to have fellowship with them and to receive through their prayers and intercessions the blessings of the Spirit. And it was still more wonderful that these white pastors went back to the South and reported to the members of their congregations that they had been together with Negroes, that they had prayed in one Spirit and received the same blessings as they.[33]

4. *W. H. Durham: Chicago*

Until about 1908 the whole Pentecostal movement in America taught the doctrine of a three-stage way of salvation. Like the *Church of the Nazarene* and other non-Pentecostal Holiness churches it was held that sanctification was a sudden and distinct second work of God's grace, which *followed* conversion and could be distinguished from it. To these two stages (conversion and sanctification) they added the baptism of the Spirit, which was characterized by speaking in tongues. W. H. Durham, a respected and successful evangelist in Los Angeles and Chicago, who had received the baptism of the Spirit in 1907 in Los Angeles, reduced this three-stage pattern to a two-stage one. Under the influence of the Baptists he regarded conversion and sanctification as simultaneous, and sanctification as 'a self-abandonment to God's promise':

> I began to write against the doctrine that it takes two works of grace to save and cleanse a man. I denied and still deny that God does not deal with the nature of sin at conversion. I deny that a man who is converted or born again is outwardly washed and cleansed but that his heart is left unclean with enmity against God in it . . . This would not be salvation. Salvation is an inward work. It means a change of heart. It means a change of nature. It means that old things pass away and that all things become new. It means that all condemnation and guilt is removed. It means that all the old man, or old nature, which was sinful and depraved and which was the very thing in us that was condemned is crucified with Christ.[34]

Durham was expelled by Seymour from the Apostolic Faith Church although Seymour had earlier prophesied that 'wherever this man preaches, the Holy Spirit will come down on the people'.[35]

Since the difference between Seymour and Durham came in the years that followed to be the substance of the disagreement between the Pentecostals who teach a three-stage way of salvation and those who teach a two-stage way, we set it out here in tabular form:

	Stage 1	*Stage 2*	*Stage 3*
Holiness Churches	*Conversion*, also called regeneration	*Sanctification*, distinct in time and content from conversion; also called 'baptism of the Spirit' or 'second blessing'. Known as the 'Wesleyan understanding' of sanctification. Sanctification at a definite fixed time.	
Parham/Seymour; three-stage Pentecostals (ch.2.2–3)	*Conversion*, also called regeneration	*Sanctification*, distinct in time and content from conversion, and also called 'second blessing'. Sanctification at a definite fixed time. The pastoral theme behind this understanding of sanctification is that the Holy Spirit can only enter purified hearts.	*Baptism of the Spirit*, with speaking in tongues.
Durham; two-stage Pentecostals (ch.2.4):	*Conversion*, also called regeneration.	*Baptism of the Spirit*, with speaking in tongues. (Here sanctification is understood as a process continuing throughout life; known as the 'Baptist understanding of sanctification'.)	

There was much opposition to Durham in his time, although he has remained up to the present day the one original theologian of the American Pentecostal movement. Indeed, the first Pentecostals believed that the Devil had led Durham to his theory. A certain Sister Rubley had a vision: The demons were discussing what to do, now that the Holy Spirit had come to the world again. But when at last a 'very distorted demon said, "I have it, give them a Baptism on an unsanctified life", all the demons clapped and roared in approval'.[36] To this day the disagreement between the Pentecostals who teach a two-stage way of salvation and those who teach a three-stage way has not been resolved. Together with the unsolved questions of the doctrine of the Trinity, it represents the most difficult theological problem facing the American Pentecostal movement.

5. *Sociological and Geographical Summary*

Bloch-Hoell has published a table[37] showing the percentage of Pentecostals in the different states of the USA. This shows that in 1936 Pentecostals were principally to be found in the southern states. In 1936 the number of women in Pentecostal churches was greater than the number of men, and the proportion of Negroes greater than in the population as a whole.[38] The average income of members of Pentecostal churches was lower than that of members of American churches as a whole,[39] and less even than that for members of Negro churches.[40] These figures give a clear picture of the sociological structure of the Pentecostal movement before the second world war, but they are now largely out of date. Except for individual denominations, no reliable figures are available, for the 1936 census in the USA was not repeated.

NOTES

1.
The pow'r that fell at Pentecost
When *in the upper room*,
Upon the watching, waiting ones,
The Holy Ghost had come.

C. H. Morris, *Redemption Hymnal*, 1958, 219.

The Upper Room is the place where the first disciples received their Pentecost (Acts 1.13). The Pentecost of Acts 2 was repeated in the pouring out of the Spirit in Los Angeles (ch. 2.3) and is repeated in the personal experience of every Pentecostal. Cf. the brilliant interpretation of this experience of the Spirit by Mahalia Jackson, *In the Upper Room with Jesus* (Metronome, Decca, MEP 1099, NCB).

2. Wesley himself was strongly influenced by Catholic (Lorenzo Scupoli, Juan de Castañiza, Gregor Lopez, Jean Baptiste de Renty) and Anglican (Henry Scougal, Jeremy Taylor, William Law) devotional literature. Full discussion of sources: 05.28.004 and M. Schmidt, *John Wesley*, I, pp. 13f., 48ff.

3. Full account of the sources, doctrine and biographies of the Holiness evangelists: C. G. Finney (02a.02.002), A. Mahan (02a.02.003), D. L. Moody (02a.02.004), R. P. Smith (02a.02.005), R. A. Torrey (02a.02.006), T. C. Upham (02a.02.007).

4. Documents and discussion of sources for the origin of the Pentecostal movement in America: 02a.02.060.

5. 02a.02.061c; 08.088.001.

6. Details: 02a.02.061.

7. C. Parham, *Kol kare bomidbar*.

8. Most detailed and accurate account: Bloch-Hoell, II, pp. 30–52. See also H. V. Synan's excellent Ph.D. dissertation (*The Pentecostal Movement in the US*). He treats the Azusa Street Revival under the significant title 'The American Jerusalem' (pp. 113ff.).

9. (Black) Church of the Nazarene, Santa Fe Street (02a.02.020). S. H. Frodsham, *With Signs*, 3rd ed., 1946, p. 31; R. Crayne, *20th Century P*, p. 10; C. Brumback, *Suddenly*, p. 35; K. Kendrick, *Promise*, p. 64; H. V. Synan, *P Movement*, p. 128; *PE* 6.4.1946, p. 6.

10. Smale came from Wales in July 1905. He later founded the New Testament Congregation (*Evangelii Härold*, 1916, pp. 118, 170); F. Bartleman, *Azusa St*, pp. 12–13; Bloch-Hoell, II, p. 33.

11. Details: 05.13.001.

12. The latter went later as a missionary to Liberia. E. Linderholm, *Pfingströrelsen* I, 1924, p. 243; G. E. Söderholm, *Svenska pingstväckelsens historia* I, 1929, p. 169; R. C. Dalton, *Tongues*, p. 39; *Evangelii Härold*, 1916, p. 173; Bloch-Hoell II, p. 37.

13. K. Kendrick, *Promise*, p. 65.

14. G. Bond, *Life*, p. 158: 'Bonnie Bray [*sic*] Street among colored saints (sanctified people)'.

15. Discussion of the confused state of the sources in Bloch-Hoell II, pp. 38, 196 n. 99. Other sources: *Apostolic Faith*, Sept., Oct., Nov., 1906; C. F. Parham, *Life*, pp. 148ff., 155, 164; *PE* 1607, 24.2.1945, pp. 2f. (with extracts from the earlier Pentecostal journal *The Upper Room*); W. E. Pickthorn, *PE* 1610, 17.3.1945, pp. 2f.; *PE* 1787, 7.8.1945, pp. 2, 6f.; 1786, 31.7.1948, pp. 3, 6f.; 2696, 9.1.1966, pp. 10f.; 2697, 16.1.1966, pp. 8f., 26; E. S. Williams, *PE* 2711, 24.4.1966, p. 7; R. Carter, *PE* 2726, 7.8.1966, p. 9 (Int. ed.); A. A. Boddy, *Pfingstgrüsse* 5/8, 24.11.1912, p. 63; 5/18, 2.2.1913, pp. 141f.

16. 02a.02.020.

17. E.g. William Pendleton. Those baptized with the Spirit also included the President of the 'Holiness League in Southern California'. (F. Bartleman, *Azusa St*, p. 53; *Apostolic Faith*, Oct. 1906; Bloch-Hoell II, pp. 32f.).

18. *PE* 6.4.1946, p. 6.

19. *Pillar of Fire* (02a.02.040).

20. E. Linderholm, *Pingströrelsen* I, 1924, p. 266; Bloch-Hoell II, p. 200, n. 172. Alma White's accounts should be used with caution.

21. *Apostolic Faith*, Sept. 1906.

22. Bloch-Hoell quotes the letterheads of the Azusa Street revival, which he found in T. Barratt's papers: 'The Apostolic Faith Movement. Chas. F. Parham, Projector: W. J. Seymour, Pastor' (Oct. 1906). Bloch-Hoell II, p. 48.

23. 'The Pacific Apostolic Faith Movement. W. J. Seymour, Pastor and Manager; Clara Lunn, Secretary; Headquarters: 312 Azusa Street; Hiram Smith, Deacon; Jenny Moore, City Missionary [later Seymour's wife, cf. A. Boddy's account]; Phoebe Sargent, City Missionary; G. Cook, Ass't State Manager; Florence Crawford, State Director; G. W. Evans, Field Director' (Nov. 1907). Bloch-Hoell II, p. 48.

24. Bloch-Hoell II, p. 54, on the basis of a letter from Frodsham, March 1949.

25. Cf. Appendix: 1, p. 513.

26. Cf. p. 25.

27. A. G. Allen, 'The Apostolic Faith', Portland, Oregon, letter to W.H., 10.5.1963 (02a.02.063).

28. 'No one was ever taught to seek for the baptism of the Holy Ghost, except they had first sought for and received a definite experience in sanctification.' G. Bond, *Life*, p. 158.

29. S. M. Horton, *PE* 2526, 7.10.1962, p. 9, cf. H. V. Synan, *P Movement*, p. 191.

30. For this theory see above p. 22.

31. There are exceptions; cf. ch. 4, pp. 47ff.; for the concept of 'sanctification' cf. ch. 24.3, pp. 325ff.

32. *PE* 1787, 7.8.1948, p. 2; *Apostolic Faith*, Oct. 1906; Bloch-Hoell II, pp. 53, 204, n. 6.

33. A. A. Boddy, *Pfingstgrüsse* 5/8, 24.11.1912, p. 63. (The article appeared first in the British paper *Confidence*. I am basing the above statement on the German translation.) A similar declaration was made by F. Bartleman. For him 'the "color line" was washed away in the blood' at the Azusa Street revival (F. Bartleman, *Azusa St*, p. 29). For a contemporary discussion of the race problem in American Pentecostalism see H. V. Synan, *P Movement* (*passim*) and W. J. Hollenweger, *Black Pentecostal Concept*, and below, ch. 31.2, pp. 469f.

34. W. H. Durham, *P Testimony*, June 1911; quoted in Brumback, *Suddenly*, p. 99; cf. also *Faithful Standard*, Nov. 1922; quoted in Brumback, *op. cit.*, p. 98.

35. *Ibid.*

36. Crayne, *20th Century P*, p. 53. Crayne adds: 'This information was received from Sister Agnes Shirlaw of Atascadero, California, whose mother was told the vision by Sister Rubley.'

37. Bloch-Hoell II, p. 57.

38. Average figure for whole of USA, 78·5 men per 100 women; 9·7% of the population were black.

Figure for the Pentecostals: 52·04 men per 100 women, 14·54% Negroes. (US Dept. of Commerce, Bureau of Census, 1936, I, pp. 87, 74, 695ff., 840ff., quoted in Bloch-Hoell II, p. 60.)

39. Average for USA: $2749. For Pentecostals: $735. (US Dept. of Commerce, 1936, I, pp. 27, 85; quoted in Bloch-Hoell II, p. 61.)

40. $749.

Additional Note Only after the completion of this book was L. P. Gerlach and V. H. Hine, *People*, *Power*, *Change*, available to me. This fascinating comparison between Black Power and Pentecostalism will be dealt with in a later publication.

3

A Church in spite of itself: The Organization of the Assemblies of God into a Church

I HAVE counted about two hundred Pentecostal denominations in the USA. In this book I shall describe in greater detail two of them: the Assemblies of God, the largest white Pentecostal organization in the United States, which preaches the two-stage way of salvation,[1] and the Church of God (Cleveland), which puts forward the three-stage way of salvation.[2]

1. *The Beginnings of the Assemblies of God*

(*a*) *Origin*

For the earliest Pentecostals it was more important to pray than to organize. For example, Arch P. Collins used to pray in the night for each individual member of his congregation, before the doors of their houses.[3] The first Pentecostals rejected every kind of organization. In the assemblies, 'if more than one minister were present, the leader would say "Now we will look to the Lord, and the person to whom the Lord gives the word, he is going to be the speaker." '[4] As Kendrick observes, this practice often brought the less capable, but consequently more self-confident persons into the foreground. Some minimal organization was therefore necessary if total anarchy and confusion was not to result, for 'each person regarded himself as the final authority between heaven and earth',[5] an authority which each based on ever more profound knowledge and ever more glorious experiences of salvation. Similarly an organization was necessary in order to provide 'credentials' (i.e. to prove that the bearer is a minister of religion), particularly so that pastors could use the cheap rail tickets available for ministers in the USA. Various attempts were made to set up a loose brotherhood. Just as in the more recent Pentecostal bodies set up since 1950,[6] the founding fathers of the Assemblies of God did not wish to set up a Pentecostal denomination, but tried to establish a fraternal fellowship which

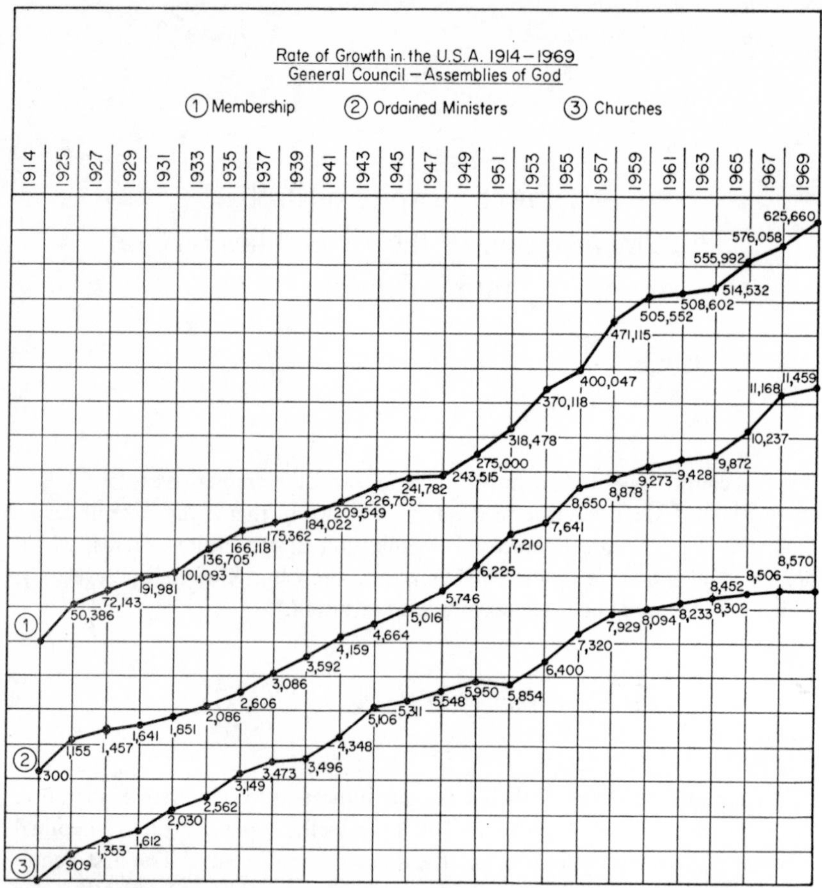

would serve the whole church.[7] The names given to the brotherhood were temporary and unofficial. Two titles occur frequently:

> *Church of God*;[8] for a short time there was co-operation with the *Church of God in Christ*,[9] a Negro body. In general, the influence of the Negroes on the Pentecostal movement must not be underestimated.[10]
>
> *Apostolic Faith Movements*;[11] the name originated in a Los Angeles revival. Many journals were called *Apostolic Faith*. Naturally, the bodies still known by that name believe that they have remained most faithful to the original vision.[12]

When representatives of these two loose fellowships were invited to establish a more structured organization J. Roswell Flower said, 'This goes to show that the Pentecostals are tired of individualism'.[13] E. N. Bell drew attention to the necessity of founding a Bible school.[14] The minutes of the first conference observe that 'all kinds of chaotic conditions have been manifested', every man being a law unto himself.[15]

Mario G. Hoover, a grandson of W. C. Hoover, the founder of the Chilean Pentecostal movement, is the author of a history of the constitution of the Assemblies of God.[16] He has made a careful study of the minutes, and describes the struggles that were necessary before agreement was reached on a common declaration of faith, a common journal, a central administration and Bible schools for the training of future preachers. The first attempt at a constitution, which consisted simply of the gathering together of the motions passed at earlier conferences of pastors of the Assemblies of God, was rejected by a large majority, and those who had initiated this attempt at a constitution were 'fired'.[17] In spite of this, a similar constitution was accepted two years later, leading J. R. Flower to the melancholy observation:

> We declared we were not a sect and not an organization, and then we turned right round and organized. Whether we admit it or not we are in a measure a sect. But that does not mean that we are going to have a sectarian spirit.[18]

Hoover concludes his study with the statement:

> Churches and districts were originally much stronger than they are to-day. With growth, delegated responsibility and organizational development, power has accrued to the central agency at the expense of the local church and the district. Imperceptibly, innocently, and often for the sake of expediency and efficient operation, there has been a shift of power toward the centre.[19]

(*b*) *The 'Jesus Only' dispute*

> A preacher who did not dig up some new slant on a Scripture, or get some new revelation to his own heart ever so often; a preacher who did not propagate it, defend it, and if necessary be prepared to lay down his life for it, was considered slow, stupid, unspiritual . . . Calling a man 'a compromiser' killed his ministry far and wide. Because of this, no doubt, many new revelations began to cause confusion.[20]

This was the origin of the 'Jesus Only' movement. John G. Scheppe, a participant in a Pentecostal camp meeting in Arroyo Seco, California, so rejoiced at the name of Jesus, which had worked miracles in that meeting, that he leapt up for joy and cried out to those at the camp, how great a discovery the glory of the name of Jesus had been to him in that night of prayer: The slogan was adopted by Glenn A. Cook, Frank Ewart and others. They sought to find the significance of the name of Jesus in Scripture, and discovered that in the Acts of the Apostles baptism was always 'in the name of Jesus', and that this was therefore the correct way to carry out the command to baptize in Matthew 28. This showed that preachers baptized with the trinitarian formula had less authority, for they were foolish enough to try and give a better interpretation of the formula of baptism than the apostles themselves. New baptism services were brought in, in which baptism was 'in the name of Jesus'. Almost all the baptized had already been baptized once as adults with the trinitarian formula, and most of them as infants as well. A large number of the leaders of the Pentecostal movement of the time[21] were baptized a second time 'in the name of Jesus'. It was now realized that the recently formed Assemblies of God would have to take action against the innovators, as vigorously as the Methodists, Baptists and Holiness denominations had acted against themselves ten years previously. In 1915 the following doctrines and practices were rejected as false: the use of wine in the Lord's Supper, the identification of regeneration and baptism in the Spirit, and the identification of Father, Son and Holy Spirit.[22] The last point was directed against the modalist doctrine of the Trinity held by the 'Jesus Only' group. They taught that Jesus was the name for God the Father, God the Son and God the Holy Spirit.

Thus the 'Jesus Only' doctrine was rejected. Over 150 preachers left the Assemblies of God, to found their own organization.[23]

(*c*) *The dispute about speaking in tongues*

Only a few years later another controversy arose. F. F. Bosworth, A. G. Canada and others did not regard speaking with tongues as the sole sign of baptism in the Spirit. They also wanted to recognize other gifts of the Spirit as signs of baptism in the Spirit.[24] Bosworth demanded a discussion of the question at the Pastors' Conference of 1918, but the vote went against him. From now on, it was no longer possible to be a pastor of the Assemblies of God and at the same time deny the distinctive doctrine of the Assemblies of God that speaking with tongues had necessarily to accompany baptism in the Spirit.[25]

In theory the Assemblies of God regard speaking with tongues 'initial evidence'.[26] A distinction was made between conversion and baptism in the spirit.

> Isn't it [the baptism in the Spirit] always received at conversion? No. Paul visiting the Ephesian Christians asked them this pointed question: 'Have you received the Holy Ghost *since ye believed*?' (Acts 19.5). Obviously they had not received *when* they had believed. It is, of course, true that conversion is the work of the Holy Spirit, but there is a vast difference between having the Holy Spirit with you and being filled by him. What is the sign of receiving the baptism of the Holy Spirit? The sign of the infilling of the Spirit is speaking with other tongues.[27]

The question of the relationship between conversion and baptism in the Spirit cannot be answered either from the Gospels (for the Spirit is only promised there) or from the New Testament epistles (which deal only with practical, not fundamental, questions concerning the reception of the Spirit). The only source that must be allowed in answer to this problem is the narrative account of the normative baptisms in the Spirit, the Acts of the Apostles:

> Where the results are described there is always an immediate supernatural outward expression convincing not only the receiver but the people listening to him, that a divine power is controlling the person; and in every case there is an ecstatic speaking in a language that the person has never learned.[28]

The literature of the Assemblies of God is full of testimonies concerning baptism in the Spirit. J. Roswell Flower, originally a lawyer, and later a leading figure in the Assemblies of God, confirms in his description of his own baptism in the Spirit that at first the Assemblies of God also taught the three-stage way to salvation.[29] When he received the baptism of the Spirit,

> It seemed as though my very flesh was laughing within me. I was almost beside myself, but too timid to let it out, so I decided to slip out of the church and go home as fast as I could.[30]

Billie Davies, who was of gypsy origin, and is active in the Sunday school work of the Assemblies of God, records:

> Suddenly I seemed to relax. The hollow, empty frustration melted away and I was filled with love for the Lord, so that I raised my hands spontaneously toward heaven and praised him with complete abandon. Where before I had always been a little uncertain of God's love for me, I now began to realize that He was indeed a loving Father, and He was right there with me. . . .[31]

It is well known that there are today many members of the Assemblies of God who have *not* experienced the baptism of the Spirit. These members are under a constant mental pressure. A possible alternative exists for them in those traditional churches which are open to charismatic revival.[32] A change in the dogmatic position of the Assemblies of God can hardly be expected, as they have invested too much energy, zeal and prestige in their Pentecostal theory.

2. *The Path to Organization as Churches*

(*a*) *The decline of enthusiasm*

In 1944 S. Braden[33] pointed out once more that the traditional churches had lost two million members, 8 per cent of their membership, between 1926 and 1936, whereas the Pentecostals had shown a phenomenal growth in the same period (in the case of the Assemblies of God, an increase of 208.7 per cent). According to more recent statistics the outward growth of the Assemblies of God has slowed down. Other groups, characterized by the Assemblies of God as extreme or fanatical, seem to be taking over their inheritance. Thus Muelder tells of a schism in an Assembly of God in California, which came about because the more simple church members no longer felt at home in the newly built chapels of the Assemblies of God. For now they could no longer cry 'Amen' in a loud voice.[34] Walter Goldschmidt had already noted twenty years earlier that pastors of the Assemblies of God were losing contact with the lower social groups. They played golf with people of social standing and no longer preached against make-up and cinema-going, 'letting too much of the world creep in'.[35]

It is clear why new revivals, such as the healing evangelists and the Latter Rain movement,[36] have a great attraction for those whose longing for 'revival' is not yet dead.[37]

> One cannot help but observe that the fervor of the Holiness and Pentecostal movements cooled as the social and economic status of the participants improved.[38]

On the other hand Hutten reports that in 18 months, out of 45,826 Puerto-Rican immigrants to New York, 32,159 were accepted into Spanish-speaking Pentecostal congregations (but not solely Assemblies of God) and only 13,667 into other Protestant congregations.[39]

The first pastors of the Assemblies of God had little regard for formal education. According to Kendrick, they appealed to John 16.13: 'When the Spirit of truth comes, he will guide you into all the truth.' The second coming of Jesus was expected in the immediate future. They regarded evangelization as more important than education. Many pastors came from levels of society in which it had been impossible for them to go further than elementary school.[40] Many of them had another job, apart from their ministry. Since then the Assemblies of God had set up Bible schools, which provided pastors for their constantly growing congregations. But those who were not pastors had also risen on the social scale – some of them had become efficient and prosperous businessmen, who were required to make great financial sacrifices for the growing financial needs of the movement,[41] but who had become very discontented since about the 1950's; for although they were represented at the pastors' conference, they could not be represented in the highest decision-making body of the church. Brumback, who is himself a pastor, deals very curtly with this legitimate desire when he writes:

> One must look in vain in the New Testament to find a layman in final places of authority, either over one congregation or a group of congregations.[42]

This was the degree to which the Assemblies of God had, in forty years, adopted the formal organization of a church. The abrupt rejection of non-pastors in the highest decision-making body has led, amongst other things, to the setting up of a lay organization, in which ministers are not allowed to hold any directing office.[43]

The building up of a church organization can also be seen in the increasing value placed on legal forms. In the minutes of the General Assembly for 1961 explicitly parliamentary rules for sessions and regulations are laid down.[44]

A precisely defined terminology is laid down for the procedure whereby a minister is struck off the list. If he withdraws of his own volition, he must appear in the minutes as 'withdrawn'. If he appears in the minutes as 'removed' he has been struck off for a less serious offence (authoritarian behaviour, incapacity or unwillingness to preach the Pentecostal gospel). If he is noted as 'dropped', he has been struck off for a grave moral offence.[45]

The development of written liturgies,[46] the printed programme issued for each Sunday service in the style of other American churches, the gowns for the members of the choir, all point in the same direction. It is clear why some are asking: 'Are we becoming too formal?'[47]

(*b*) *The break with the healing evangelists*

The attacks of most of the healing evangelists on the local Pentecostal ministry, whose 'feeble efforts' they readily denounced, was according to Brumback the reason why the *Pentecostal Evangel* refused any longer to publish the reports of the healing evangelists. Brumback gives further reasons for the rejection of the healing evangelists: their moral lapses, their 'supreme egotism', their arrogant attitude, their over-emphasis on bodily healing and their doctrine that prosperity is an undeniable sign of piety. The healing evangelists therefore operated outside the Assemblies of God, and founded their own periodical. When Brumback suggests that the healing evangelists have lost their following,[48] he is deceiving himself. For how could they pay for their radio programmes, their huge missionary activity in Europe and Africa, their tons of printed material? Moreover, it must not be forgotten that the healing evangelists do not represent any more extreme a view than what was known until a short time ago in the Assemblies of God as 'the full gospel', e.g., in the writings of the Assemblies of God evangelist Dr Lilian B. Yeomans. Lilian Yeomans (a medical doctor) was cured of severe morphine addiction by John Alexander Dowie. She gives the exact doses and the kind of morphine that she took, and describes her unsuccessful medical treatment by several specialists.[49] She puts forward the teaching of the healing evangelists, which is today rejected by Brumback:

> Many of us have been taught to pray, 'if it be Thy will, heal me'. That wasn't the way David prayed . . . (Ps. 6.2–9). There were no ifs, no buts in that prayer . . . And we, God's people of this day, should be as free from doubt regarding our Father's will for our bodies as they were, for it is as clearly revealed in the Word as His will concerning the salvation of our souls.[50]

Up to 1960 at least the Assemblies of God held the view:

> The Bible teaches us that it is God's will to heal our bodies if we will bring our lives into conformity with His Word and ask in faith.[51]

(*c*) *The relaxation of ethical rigorism*

As a Holiness church, the Assemblies of God began by making rigorist demands upon its members. Make-up, the theatre, the cinema, and even secondary schools (high schools) and universities lay outside the social horizons of its founders and religious taboo was therefore placed on them. This changed in time. The men earned more money, and consequently the women wanted to be better dressed and the children wanted to take their education further. In this respect the leaders of the Assemblies of God are constantly on the retreat, because they will not risk losing their influence on future generations. J. O. Savell remarks bitterly:

> Our 'negative preaching' in the past resulted in positive living; today our 'positive preaching' results too often in negative living.[52]

Moreover the basic emotional and fundamental impulse of the Assemblies of God seems, in spite of all assertions to the contrary by its headquarters, to be flagging in many places. Sometimes one has to ask oneself whether one is in a Pentecostal Assembly or not – so Brumback observes in reference to the 'worldly' dress of those present.[53]

> [He] might also have made reference to the alarming decline in attendance at the Sunday evening services across the land; or to the brevity of the after-meeting at the altar; or to the crowded condition of the church calendar which will not permit some assemblies to engage in revival campaigns; or the ever-increasing emphasis upon the recreational aspect of the camp meetings; or to the expression 'our denomination' which in these days is often on the lips of members of the Assemblies of God.[54]

Not only outsiders like Braden and Goldschmidt[55] draw attention to the relaxations of ethical rigorism in the Assemblies of God. In 1940 Lester F. Sumrall could still write a thunderous attack on the 'Worshippers of the Silver Screen'.[56] In the preface, Edith Mae Pennington, formerly a film actress and now a preacher in the Assemblies of God, tells how she became Beauty Queen of America, was invited into the most sophisticated clubs, and got into the theatre and films. But she goes on, 'I grew restless and tired of dances, luncheons, flowers, cars and ceremony. . . . I was deeply horrified by the apparent immorality on every side.' But today the Assemblies of God publish religious romantic novels.[57] The *Pentecostal Evangel* admits that many Pentecostal women and pastors' wives use make-up,[58] while members of the youth groups, in spite of their ministers' protests, visit the cinema and are rock-and-roll fans.[59]

The older leaders, such as Williams and Riggs, maintain for the moment their rejection of worldliness. It is true that Williams leaves open the question of whether military service can be reconciled with the Christian conscience. Everyone must decide this according to his own conscience. But that one should not play volley-ball on a Sunday afternoon is quite clear to him; it is a compromise with the world:

> How then are we an example of reverence for God, for his worship, and for his day as set apart for worship?[60]

At a period when many American Christians – and many Swedish Pentecostals[61] – have seen the questionable nature of the Vietnam War and published declarations to this effect, there is no sign of such ideas in the *Pentecostal Evangel.* On the contrary, the title page frequently carries pictures of Pentecostal army chaplains in Vietnam. The accompanying articles tell of their fruitful evangelization and services amongst soldiers and civilians. While German Pentecostals are increasingly rejecting military service in favour of a substitute civilian form of service,[62] a different tendency can be observed in the Assemblies of God.[63] Biblical arguments are used in favour of the retention of capital punishment,[64] and America is regarded as the best country on earth:

> We thank God for America because it has provided the greatest liberty in the world; freedom of speech, press, assembly and worship. America has given opportunities for preaching the gospel unknown in other lands. It has permitted foreign missionary work. It has been given prosperity envied by all other peoples the world around. Here the poor have, and still can, become great.[65]

(*d*) *The struggle over the schools*

The Sunday school The Sunday school is the real backbone of the Assemblies of God and can be regarded as a preliminary stage for all the rest of the school system. Every age group, from the three-year-old to the adults, has its own Sunday school magazine; the teachers at each level are likewise provided with their own magazines. Often the same material (adapted to each age group) is used simultaneously in every class. Imagine the effect of the Sunday school on a family in which, according to the normal practice of the Assemblies of God, father, mother and children, either as teachers or pupils, study the same theme in small Sunday school classes of fifteen persons at most, before going in to the preaching service! Here a thorough grounding is given in tithing, the understanding of the Bible, the baptism of the Spirit, and missionary responsibility. Besides this, the Bible, albeit limited by a fundamentalist interpretation, becomes the book which will be their companion throughout their lives.

The works of Myer Pearlman, Frank M. Boyd, and Ralph M. Riggs, listed in the bibliography, are obligatory teaching material for the Sunday schools.[66] In order to assess the quality of a Sunday school, and for each class to compete with the others, an elaborate grading system has been worked out:

1. Attendance – 20 points. (A gain of at least 20% in average attendance each year)
2. Sunday school equal to church in size – 10 points. (Having a Sunday school enrolment at least equal to church membership)
3. Attendance of pastor – 5 points. (Pastor required to attend at least 95% of regular sessions as well as staff meetings)
4. Attendance of superintendent – 5 points. (Superintendent required to attend at least 95% of regular sessions as well as staff meetings)

5. Attendance of teacher – 20 points. (Teachers required to attend at least 90% of regular sessions as well as staff meetings)
6. Teacher training – 5 points. (One subject completed each year; at least 12 classes of 45 minutes each)
7. Church attendance – 9 points. (90% of pupils remain for morning worship service)
8. Evangelism – 6 points. (3% of enrolled pupils make decisions for Christ)
9. Increase in regular offerings – 5 points. (20% increase over previous year)
10. Increase in missionary offering – 5 points. (20% of increase over previous year.
11. Cradle roll – 5 points. (Cradle roll to equal 5% of Sunday school enrolment)
12. Home department – 5 points. (Home department to equal 5% of Sunday school enrolment)

In 1961 the Assemblies of God had 992,366 Sunday school pupils, against 514,317 members. But Kendrick points out that when he wrote more attention was being paid to quantity than to ethical and educational aims and that the participants were enticed into the Sunday school by all kinds of gifts rather than any good teaching.[67]

Teen Challenge Center David Wilkerson undertook an impressive project amongst the deprived youth of Brooklyn, Los Angeles and Chicago. Wilkerson, a pastor of the Assemblies of God, saw in *Life* magazine in 1959 a picture of a seventeen-year-old youth sentenced to death for murder. This led him to start something for these young people. In the three cities mentioned he founded 'Teen Challenge Centers', to which he added a 'rehabilitation farm' near Rehrersburg, Pennsylvania. Through Wilkerson's enterprise, the project attracted the attention of non-Pentecostals.[68]

Junior High Schools and Evangel College To an increasing extent the Assemblies of God have concerned themselves with the setting up of Pentecostal junior high schools, in order to provide young Pentecostals with a secondary education uncontaminated by modern scientific errors such as the theory of evolution or by worldly behaviour on the part of pupils and teachers.[69]

Evangel College is a central liberal arts college and teacher training college. The following subjects are taught:

> Accounting, business education, management, secretarial education, psychology, elementary or secondary education, modern languages, art, music, speech, English, religion and philosophy, biology, chemistry, mathematics, history, pre-law, pre-social work, sociology.[70]

The leaving certificate is recognized by the University of Missouri. The building (originally the hospital of Springfield) was given to the Assemblies of God by the Springfield Town Council (a cheap way for the town to get a liberal arts college). Scholarships are also given to non-members of the Assemblies of God.[71] Within the Assemblies of God there seems to be a considerable resistance to the setting up of liberal arts colleges, especially as Evangel College (together with the other high schools) costs the Assemblies of God $100,000 a year. The plan to extend Evangel College to include a high school was accepted in 1961 by the General Assembly of the Assemblies of God only after a vote of 565 for and 378 against.[72]

Central Bible Institute The Central Bible Institute, for which land was also donated by the town of Springfield, offers two courses:

- a three-year program for future pastors and other officials of the Assemblies of God;
- a four-year program (undergraduate collegiate course in religion). This includes a 'general course' with religion and 'theology'. If the course is completed successfully, a 'baccalaureate degree' is awarded. The subjects are: Bible, 'theology', religious education, missions, English and speech, languages, social science, and music.

Applicants to the college must be at least 19 years old. A high school or academy education was most desirable up to 1930. But applicants of more advanced years were admitted, if they proved themselves able in other ways. From 1931 all those who had not been to high school had to take an entrance examination. From 1948, only those who had secondary education were accepted. Further conditions are: Approved Christian character, willingness to do hard work and to submit cheerfully to the discipline of the school. A clear vocation to be a pastor is very desirable, but those who have no calling are also accepted, if they fulfil the other conditions. The students are under strict control with regard to their way of life, especially dress, attitude to the opposite sex, absence from the campus, abstinence from tobacco and alcohol, and leisure time activities.

The educational aims of the Central Bible Institute and the other Bible schools have from the very beginning of their history been that of a fortress of fundamentalism.

> This school will stand for the Bible as the inspired word of God, against all destructive criticism of the blessed old Book; for the atoning blood of the Lamb as the only way of salvation; for a never-changing and wonder-working God; for a Divine Saviour with all power in heaven and in earth; for a path to look for the same wonders, signs and gifts of the Holy Ghost as promised in the New Testament.[73]

These aims were reiterated thirty years later. The motto is still 'Our School – Our Bulwark':[74] The schools must cling firmly to fundamentalist teaching. Their education claims not to be naturalistic and man-centred, like that of other, non-fundamentalist, schools, but supernaturalist and God-centred. Thus even today attacks are still made on prehistoric archaeology and the theory of evolution, in favour of the biblical creation stories, on the grounds that these are more plausible and more satisfying than the theory of a natural evolution.[75]

The Situation as a Whole All schools of the Assemblies of God are members of the 'Accrediting Association for Bible Institutes and Colleges'. Up to 1960 they have graduated in all 13,332 students.

From 1914 to 1949 the schools provided 36% of all pastors and 74% of all missionaries. From 1949 to 1953 this proportion increased to 60% of pastors and 93% of missionaries;[76] that is: almost all missionaries and a majority of pastors were trained at schools belonging to the Assemblies of God.

At the same time, a remarkable shift towards secular subjects took place. In 1956 86.1%of the students were Bible students or theology students and 13.9% were 'liberal arts students'. But by 1960 only 60% were Bible students and theology students. Since then the proportion of 'liberal arts students' has increased even more.

A further tendency is that more and more students belonging to the Assemblies of God are studying at liberal arts and other colleges which do not belong to the Assemblies of God. There were 950 by 1962, but as many as 2,350 in 1963.

These three tendencies together mean that most pastors and missionaries of the Assembly of God are trained in their own Bible schools. Although the students are specializing more and more in courses that do not lead to the profession of pastor, an increasing number of students from the Assemblies of God are attending non-Pentecostal colleges. There is no doubt that this is one of the observations that led Oral Roberts to found his university.[77]

3. *Present-day Teaching: 'Back to the Bible!'*

The Assemblies of God profess a clear-cut fundamentalism. 'The infallible rule for the life and practice of Christians' is the Bible, not an ecclesiastical hierarchy.[78] European theology is completely rejected as modernism. Its principal exponents, known only superficially, are dealt with under the heading 'sects': Schleiermacher, 'This gentleman with the long German name (pronounced Schly-er-mock-er, first syllable rhymes with "sly"),' Sigmund Freud 'pronounced Froid to rhyme with annoyed', and Karl Marx.[79] Karl Barth, as a representative of neo-orthodoxy, is also included amongst the sectarians, but was judged somewhat more leniently. He is said to be a German(!) pastor who during the first world war found great difficulty in preaching the goodness of man to German widows. In this way he discovered the corruption of man, and so achieved a new attitude to the Epistle to the Romans.[80]

The defence of fundamentalist standpoints in the letter columns of the *Pentecostal Evangel* suggests that they are being strongly criticized by younger members of the Assemblies of God. However, the enquirer who wants to know when man was created gets no answer.[81] According to Williams[82] innocent children will probably be present at the rapture.[83] He avoids giving an answer to the question whether Christ is *seated* at the right of God (Heb. 10.12), or *standing* (Acts. 7.55).[84] He interprets the difficult passage II Sam. 24.1–2, which tells how God made David take a census, for which David was then punished, by reference to I Chron. 21.1,[85] where this is glossed over. He says that the promise of Matt. 16.21, that some of the disciples before their death will see the Son of Man coming to his kingdom, was fulfilled on the mountain of the Transfiguration (Matt. 17).[86]

The help of other fundamentalists is welcomed. Thus 'a Californian doctor' writes that he prefers the Pentecostal movement to the absolutely corrupt groups of so-called believers.

> Take the Baptists for instance – and I was saved among the Baptists – look at their colleges . . . Every one of them is honeycombed with bastard Modernism.[87]

The author of the above tract then tells the story of a Baptist girl student, who burned her Bible because she could no longer trust a book of lies. The weaker the arguments for a fundamentalist understanding of the Bible, the stronger the attack on the unbelieving ministers of the 'modernist' churches. Thus Bishop James A. Pike's rejection of a narrow Christianity based on conversion[88] is attacked:

> It is indeed a pity that men with such doubts choose to remain in the ministry. The Lord Jesus said that religious leaders who lack the light of truth are blind leaders of the blind. The trouble is that if the blind lead the blind, both shall fall into the ditch (Matt. 15.14). If a man wishes to take to the ditch, why does he not jump alone without dragging others with him?[89]

Flower expresses his belief in fundamentalism as follows:

> We can say like Paul, 'I am a fundamentalist, of the strictest sect of the fundamentalists am I one.' But that is not enough. Paul was more than a Pharisee. The Pharisees believed in the resurrection; they believed in angels; they believed in the supernatural – but it was all in the past. Paul believed in it – the past and in the present also. We are fundamentalists, but we are more than that.[90]

That is, like present-day fundamentalists (the Pharisees), the Pentecostals believe in all the miracles of the Bible. But like Paul they also expect miracles at the present day: the healing of the sick through prayer, prophecy, conversions, speaking with tongues. This 'supernatural world view' is summed up in the declaration of truth of the Assemblies of God (in force from 1916 on).[91] It was taken over with minor changes from the Christian and Missionary Alliance[92] and underlies the declarations of faith of many Pentecostal bodies outside America.

4. *Relationships with Other Churches*

The Assemblies of God have succeeded in establishing co-operation with other fundamentalist churches. The National Association of Evangelicals (NAE) has even chosen the President of the Assemblies of God, Thomas Zimmermann, as their president.

For the time being, the Assemblies of God are prevented by their fundamentalist understanding of the Bible from joining the World Council of Churches. Kendrick quotes from *United Evangelical Action* ten points, setting out why the Pentecostals reject the Ecumenical Movement. The main reasons are: The World Council of Churches does not profess belief in a fundamentalist view of the Bible; it has taken many free-thinkers into its ranks; it has set up an ecclesiastical oligarchy; it gives support to social revolution and neglects the missionary task of the church.[93] In 1962 the General Assembly of the Assemblies of God unanimously adopted a resolution in which every pastor of the Assemblies of God was urged not to have dealings with representatives of the World Council of Churches,[94] although in 1940 there had been ungrudging co-operation with the WCC (then in formation) with regard to the distribution of the Bible to prisoners of war.[95]

> We vigorously disagree that the joining of any [Chilean] Pentecostal group with the WCC constitutes in any degree an answer to Christ's prayer. Rather, we would observe that this constitutes a real menace to such groups, and this trend, if continued, will bring true believers into a snare.[96]

Frank M. Boyd agrees with the *Moody Monthly* in affirming that the integration of the International Missionary Council with the World Council of Churches at New Delhi (1961) 'will cripple the witness of true evangelicals'.[97] Boyd is concerned because the 'harlot church (and her daughters) of Revelation 17 is being formed rapidly'.[98] The National Council of Christian Churches (USA) and the World Council of Churches are, according to Boyd, the crystallization of this apostasy:

> They do not believe in the inspiration of the Scriptures nor are they true to the Person of Christ. They feel that the Church's mission in the world is to make a total impact upon the social, political, legislative and spiritual areas of humanity. They are not committed to the Great Commission as a missionary body entrusted with a ministry of the gospel for individual, personal acceptance. The leaders of these apostate bodies use evangelical terms constantly in their pronouncements, but with quite different connotations. In the final analysis these groups are universalist . . .[99]

Citing Clyde W. Taylor and an American Air Force Manual, the *Pentecostal Evangel* asserts that the WCC is not merely liberal but also Communist. 'Liberal theology is what draws some clergymen into "pro-Communist fronts, projects and publications" '.[100] Even the attempt to produce an ecumenical text of the

Bible is criticized and condemned.[101] It is clear that in the eyes of the Assemblies of God the World Council of Churches is a hindrance to evangelization in the Pentecostal sense. Its main aim is not the salvation of souls. The vision of men to be saved from hell, men rushing into the 'bottomless abyss full of wailing and gnashing of teeth', is alien to it.[102]

NOTES

1. Documents, records and full details of literature: 02a.02.115. Statistics: 625,660 members, 11,459 ordained ministers, 8,570 churches (*PE* 2829, 28.9.1969, p. 9). Main journal: *Pentecostal Evangel* (*PE*).

2. Cf. ch. 4.2, pp. 50ff.

3. R. Alford, *PE* 9.7.1921.

4. K. Kendrick, *Promise*, p. 71.

5. *Ibid.*

6. E.g. FGBMFI, ch. 1.1(*b*); *Full Gospel Fellowship of Churches and Ministers International* (02a.02.169).

7. C. Brumback, *Suddenly*, p. 151.

8. 1907: H. G. Rodgers, Alabama; J. W. Ledbetter. The name 'Church of God' was later dropped, when it was discovered that it was already being used by the Church of God (Cleveland).

9. 02a.02.075.

10. Leading figures in the early Pentecostal movement were negroes: W. J. Seymour, G. T. Haywood, the composer of many well-known hymns used in the Pentecostal movement. According to H. V. Synan (*P Movement*, pp. 172, 215), 'many of the men who founded the white AoG church in 1914 were thus ordained in the (black) ChoG in Christ by Bishop Mason.' At the present day the AoG are drawing away from the negroes (L. Steiner, *VdV* 40/12, Dec. 1947, pp. 16–18). A list of American negro Pentecostal denominations: 02a.02.051, n. 246, and W. J. Hollenweger, *Black Pentecostal Concept*.

11. E. N. Bell, C. Parham, Arch P. Collins, H. A. Goss, W. F. Carother.

12. 02a.02.061; 02a.02.062; 02a.02.063.

13. AoG, *Early History*, p. 11.

14. E. N. Bell, *Word and Witness* 9, 20.12.1913, p. 1.

15. AoG, *Minutes, 2–12 April, 15–29 Nov. 1914*, p. 2; quoted in K. Kendrick, *Promise*, p. 83.

16. M. G. Hoover, *Origin*.

17. *PE* 10.10.1925, pp. 8–9; quoted in Hoover, *op. cit.*, pp. 68f.

18. J. R. Flower, *PE* 8.10.1927, pp. 5–9; quoted in Hoover, *op. cit.*, p. 74.

19. Hoover, *op. cit.*, p. 188.

20. E. E. Goss, *Winds*, p. 155; quoted in C. Brumback, *Suddenly*, p. 191.

21. A. H. Argue, F. Bartleman, E. N. Bell (his testimony in *The Weekly Evangel*, Aug. 1915), W. E. Booth-Clibborn, G. A. Cook, A. G. Carr, H. A. Goss, L. C. Hall, G. T. Haywood, B. F. Lawrence, H. v. Loon, the whole McAlister family and almost all Canadian pastors (02a.01.013a, bb), A. S. McPherson, D. C. O. Opperman, H. G. Rodgers (E. F. Smith, Los Angeles, letter to Moore, 19.12.1954; Moore, p. 240; F. J. Ewart, *Phenomenon*, pp. 98f.).

22. Quoted from the minutes by C. Brumback, *Suddenly*, p. 202.

23. The most important is the United Pentecostal Church (02a.02.140). Full list 02a.02.131–02a.02.140.

24. '... I do not believe, nor can I ever teach, that all will speak in tongues when baptized in the Spirit.' F. F. Bosworth, letter to J. W. Welch, 24.7.1918; quoted in C. Brumback, *Suddenly*, p. 216.

25. Quoted from the minutes by C. Brumback, *Suddenly*, p. 223. This has been confirmed by J. R. Evans, the General Secretary of the AoG (E. Clark, *Small Sects*, p. 107).

26. 'In addition and subsequent to conversion a believer may experience an enduement of power whose initial oncoming is signalized by a miraculous utterance in a language never learned by the speaker.' M. Pearlman. *Knowing the Bible*, p. 310.

27. AoG, *You Have Accepted Christ*, p. 5 (italics in original; the quotation is from a text of the Australian AoG).

28. M. Pearlman, *Heavenly Gift*, p. 56.

29. J. R. Flower, *VdV* 26/4, April 1933, pp. 1–5; 26/5, May 1933, pp. 12–16.

30. J. R. Flower, quoted by I. Winehouse, *AoG*, p. 71.

31. B. Davies, *PE* 2054, 20.9.1953, pp. 11f.

32. Cf. the writings of Mrs Stiles, ch. 1.2(*a*), pp. 12f.

33. S. Braden, *Christian Century*, 61/4, 26.1.1944, p. 108.

34. W. G. Muelder, *Christendom* 10, 1954, p. 454.

35. W. R. Goldschmidt, *Social Structure*, p. 445.

36. For a South African Latter Rain Assembly, cf. ch. 11, pp. 140ff.

37. J. R. Flower, *PE* 1640, 13.10.1945, pp. 2–3, 5–8.

38. K. Kendrick, *Promise*, p. 45.

39. *MD* 24, 1961, p. 103.

40. K. Kendrick, *Promise*, p. 117.

41. 'Commercialism was the farthest thing from primitive Pentecost ... There were no high pressure drives for money in the early days.' (E. S. Williams, *PE* 1946, 26.8.1951, p. 4.)

42. C. Brumback, *Suddenly*, p. 326.

43. Cf. ch. 1.1(*b*), pp. 6f.

44. AoG, *Minutes 1961*, p. 100.

45. AoG, *Minutes 1961*, pp. 66f.

46. E.g. AoG, *Service Book* (contains liturgies for congregational and special services, e.g. two different forms for the burial of a converted person and an unconverted person).

47. D. A. Womack, *PE* 2430, 4.12.1960, pp. 3, 31f.

48. C. Brumback, *Suddenly*, p. 334.

49. L. B. Yeomans, *Leaves of Healing* 4, 1897, p. 350.

50. L. B. Yeomans, *Healing*, pp. 22f.

51. *PE* 1301, 15.4.1939; R. Vinyard, in D. Gee (ed.), *Fifth Conference*, pp. 71f.; R. C. Cunningham, *PE* 2415, 21.8.1960, p. 2 (quotation).

52. Quoted by C. Brumback, *Suddenly*, p. 336.

53. C. Brumback, *Suddenly*, p. 350.

54. *Ibid.*

55. Cf. nn. 33 and 35.

56. L. F. Sumrall, *Worshippers*.

57. M. E. Frey, *The Minister*; A. Pryor, *Tangled Paths* (for a note on their content, see bibliography).

58. E. S. Williams, *PE* 2449, 16.4.1961, p. 13.

59. E. S. Williams, *PE* 2448, 9.4.1961, p. 15.

60. E. S. Williams, *PE* 2440, 12.2.1961, p. 11.

61. B. Wirmark, 'Politik in der schwedischen Pfingstbewegung' in W. J. Hollenweger (ed.), *Pfingstkirchen*, pp. 256–64.

62. L. Eisenlöffel, *Ein Feuer*, p. 116; W. Sardaczuk, *Ich hatt' einen Kameraden.*

63. D. Gee, *PE* 1356, 4.5.1940, p. 4; E. S. Williams, *PE* 1362, 15.6.1940, pp. 4f.; *PE* 1368, 27.7.1940, p. 5; J. R. Flower, *PE* 1518, 12.6.1943, pp. 6f.; *PE* 1521, 3.7.1943, pp. 2f.; *PE* 2708, 3.4.1966 (Int. Ed.), p. 11.

64. *PE* 2385, 24.1.1960, p. 4.

65. L. E. Krogstad, *PE* 1444, 10.1.1942, pp. 6f.; R. M. Riggs, *PE* 1621, 2.6.1945, p. 1.

66. K. Kendrick, *Promise*, p. 121.

67. *Ibid.*, p. 126.

68. D. Wilkerson, *Cross; Bridegroom's Messenger* 51, Nov. 1962, p. 5; G. Fannin, *PE* 2733, 25.9.1966 (Int. Ed.), p. 19; K. McDonnell, *America* 118/13, 30.3.1968, pp. 402–6; E. Wakin, *Sign* 48/3, Oct. 1968, pp. 27–32.

69. AoG, *Minutes 1929*, p. 83; quoted in K. Kendrick, *Promise*, p. 136.

70. K. Kendrick, *Promise*, p. 137.

71. J. R. Ashcroft, *Advance* 5/1, 1963, p. 8.

72. AoG, *Minutes 1961*, pp. 38f., 51

73. *PE* 27.11.1920, p. 11.

74. C. W. R. Scott, *PE* 2472, 24.9.1961, pp. 12f.; cf. T. E. Cannon, *PE* 2888, 14.9.1969, pp. 6f.; F. J. Highfill (*PE* 2825, 30.6.1968, p. 23) says of his non-Pentecostal teachers: 'They were spreading socialism, communism, modernism and infidelity to many, many young minds . . . Leftwingers, socialists, liberalists and agnostics have no kinship with the fine people who taught me patriotism and faith in God.'

75. B. Williams, *PE* 2471, 17.9.1961, pp. 4f.; C. E. Robinson, *Blacky.*

76. AoG, *Reports 1953*, p. 34; quoted in Kendrick, *Promise*, p. 136. Kendrick gives further literature on the Bible schools.

77. Cf. ch. 25.2(*b*), pp. 363ff.

78. AoG, *Assemblies of God*, p. 4.

79. R. W. Harris, *Cults*, pp. 85f.

80. R. W. Harris, *ibid.*

81. E. S. Williams, *PE* 2444, 12.3.1961, p. 13.

82. E. S. Williams, *PE* 2443, 5.3.1961, p. 11.

83. For this term see ch. 29.2, pp. 415f.

84. E. S. Williams, *PE* 2482, 3.12.1961, p. 12.

85. E. S. Williams, *PE* 2488, 14.1.1962, p. 11. This passage is discussed further in ch. 21.4, pp. 302ff.

86. E. S. Williams, *PE* 2502, 22.4.1962, p. 11.

87. GPH, *A Defence.*

88. 'I no longer regard grace, or the work of the Holy Spirit, as limited explicitly to the Christian revelation . . . The kind of god I first believed in, who would limit salvation to a select group of people who happen to have heard the news and heard it well . . . is an impossible god. As to this god, I am now an atheist' (J. A. Pike, *Christian Century* 77/51, 21.12.1960, p. 1496). The Pentecostals' criticism of Pike has recently grown less, because he described the baptism of the Spirit as a valuable experience (R. Chandler, *Christianity Today* 12/4, 24.11.1967, pp. 39f.).

89. *PE* 2444, 12.3.1961, p. 2.

90. J. R. Flower, *PE* 2187, 8.4.1956, pp. 23f.

91. See Appendix, pp. 514ff.

92. C. Brumback, *Suddenly*, p. 94 (02a.02.013).

93. *United Evangelical Action*, 13 and 15.1.1955, p. 10; quoted with approval by Kendrick, *Promise*, pp. 204f. The whole document is given in the Appendix: 3. For

the rejection of these charges cf. ch. 30.4(*d*), pp. 444ff. For Th. Zimmermann's criticism of the Russian Orthodox Church cf. *ChoGE* 52/6, 9.4.1962, p. 15.

94. R. C. Cunningham, *PE* 2526, 7.10.1962, p. 3.
95. S. H. Frodsham, *PE* 1386, 30.11.1940, pp. 4f.
96. F. M. Boyd, *PE* 2526, 7.10.1962, p. 4.
97. *Moody Monthly*, March 1962, quoted by F. M. Boyd, *loc. cit.*
98. *Ibid.*
99. *Ibid.*; cf. also G. Duty, *PE* 2846, 24.11.1968, pp. 10f.
100. *PE* 2392, 20.3.1960, p. 2; F. Smolchuck, *PE* 2700, 13.2.1966, p. 3.
101. R. C. Cunningham, *PE* 2751, 29.1.1967, p. 4.
102. A vision of the evangelist Mary Woodworth-Etter, *VdV* 6/1, 1.1.1914, pp. 1–5.

Additional Note This chapter was unfortunately completed before the publication of W. W. Menzies, *Appointed to Serve*. Menzies is Chairman of the Department of Biblical Studies and Philosophy in the Evangel College, Springfield, Mo. He presents the history and development of the Assemblies of God from the point of view of an AoG official, using valuable and otherwise almost inaccessible source material, particularly from AoG archives.

4

'If I Gained the World . . .': Holiness in the Church of God (Cleveland)

1. *Origin and History*

The largest part of the American Pentecostal movement consists of Pentecostals professing the two-stage way of salvation. A significant group of organizations teaches the original, three-stage way of salvation.[1] The principal groups are the Churches of God – I counted thirty different Churches of God in the USA, amongst them very large and important black denominations – and the Pentecostal Holiness Church.[2]

In this chapter we shall deal solely with the Church of God (Cleveland).[3] According to Conn, the accurate and talented historian of this church, the mountain people of the border between North Carolina and Tennessee had at the end of the nineteenth century become deprived both in religion and in material matters. On week days they wore clothes of home-woven material. A school education was a luxury quite out of their reach. The only books that were available were Bunyan's *Pilgrim's Progress* and Webster's Dictionary. Those who were illiterate depended on others reading aloud.[4] Their monotonous daily work was interrupted only by the Sunday church services. These were the event of the week, their education and their entertainment.

One of the Baptist pastors working there was Richard B. Spurling. He was devout, but convinced that both the Baptists and also the Holiness preachers of his time, not to speak of the reformers of the sixteenth century, had failed in their task. He accused the latter especially – and this is typical of the knowledge of the history of the European Reformation amongst the pioneers of American Pentecostalism – of having once again submitted to the yoke of doctrinal creeds: 'They adopted the law of faith when they should have adopted the law of love', and 'failed to reserve a right way for the leadership of the Holy Ghost', although it was true that 'they were awakened to the fact that God's Church existed only where His law and government was observed by His children'.[5] Because of the failure of the churches of the time, Spurling, together with eight others who shared his views, founded a better church, which was the forerunner of the Church of God (Cleveland) and a number of other churches that later separated from it.[6] They were called at that time the 'Christian Union', in order to express the idea that it was not a new denomination, but a body which would extend across, enrich and revive the churches. Anyone who wanted to join this union for revival had to be 'free from all man-made creeds and traditions'.[7]

'For ten years this servant of God, Spurling, prayed, wept and continued his ministry against much opposition and under peculiar difficulties, before seeing real fruits of his labours'.[8] At last, after many years, a revival broke out in Camp Creek, Cherokee County. Many experienced the baptism of the Spirit with speaking in tongues. The little group rapidly increased in numbers, but at the same time a persecution began. At that time, it must have been like the Wild West in those hills. The houses of those who belonged to the revival were reduced to ashes, their chapels were several times burnt down or blown up, sometimes with the help of the sheriff and other officials. In some cases, believers were shot, and even the Ku-Klux-Klan paid them a visit. At the height of the persecution the County of Cherokee intervened and brought the persecutors before the court, but at the request of the persecuted revivalist congregation let them go without punishment.[9] But now the revival turned into a wild fanaticism. Irrational regulations about food and dress were counted as a sign of particular spirituality. The baptism of the Spirit with speaking in tongues was no longer sufficient. People wanted baptism of 'holy dynamite', 'holy lyddite', 'holy oxidite' and other explosives. These scenes almost led to the collapse of the little group.

Twenty people from this tumultuous revival reorganized themselves and took the name 'Holiness Church' at Camp Creek.

In 1902 A. J. Tomlinson, a colporteur of the American Bible Society, joined the group, and a year later was made its pastor. The movement grew, and under Tomlinson's leadership tried to organize itself more formally. But the minutes of its first Assembly include the following preamble composed by Tomlinson:

> We hope and trust that no person or body of people will ever use these minutes, or any part of them, as articles of faith from which to establish a sect or denomination. The subjects were discussed merely to obtain light and understanding. Our articles of faith are inspired and given us by the Holy Apostles and written in the New Testament which is our only rule of faith and practice.[10]

The minutes accurately reproduce the feeling of the founders when they note:

> After considering the ripened fields and open doors for evangelism this year, strong men wept and said they were not only willing but anxious to go.[11]

In 1907 the headquarters of the Church was moved to Cleveland, Tennessee, and the name altered to Church of God. Amongst the themes dealt with in the early annual assemblies, the debates on smoking and divorce should be emphasized. Smoking was declared incompatible with membership of the Church of God, while up to the present day the Church of God has not taken an unambiguous position against divorce.[12] Divorce 'only because of fornication' (Matt. 5.31–32)[13] and remarriage of the innocent party are allowed.[14]

In 1909 a revival took place in Cleveland. A circus setting up its tent near the mission tent of the Church of God would have been envious of the masses that moved past its own tent to that of the Church of God.[15] Under A. J. Tomlinson's leadership, the church continued to increase. The minutes of the Assembly of 1915 contain a passage in which in solemn legal language the title 'Holy Roller' is repudiated.[16]

In 1920 there was another crisis, when the Assembly accepted the proposal of A. J. Tomlinson, who had been elected General Overseer for life, to pay all tithes in the future direct to him; he would then pay them back to each pastor. This practice almost led to the financial and religious ruin of the organization. Whether the cause was Tomlinson's inability to administer large sums, or improper motives on his part, is difficult for an outsider to judge. What is certain is that from the first Tomlinson greatly overestimated himself. His self-adulation took on increasingly blatant forms. He was simultaneously General Overseer, manager of the publishing department, editor-in-chief of the monthly journal and head of the orphanage and the Bible school, and he automatically controlled all salaries (between $70,000 and $80,000 a year). The pastors of the Church of God tried to limit the completely unrestricted power of their General Overseer by various organizational changes, but Tomlinson declared these steps unbiblical. The struggles lasted for years, and towards the end even came before the public courts, but they concluded with the expulsion of Tomlinson, who thereupon formed with his own supporters a new Church of God, known as the Church of God of Prophecy.[17]

Under the new General Overseer, F. J. Lee, the church recovered relatively quickly, increased in numbers, began missionary work in new areas, and restricted the powers of its leading officials through organizational safeguards.

In 1951 it amalgamated – through the mediation of David J. Du Plessis – with the Full Gospel Church, South Africa, which from then on became known as the Full Gospel Church of God.

Since dozens of churches in the USA are called 'Church of God' it has become usual to add a distinguishing name in brackets. There are Churches of God which belong to the Holiness movement.[18] The churches listed in the note below[19] have presumably separated themselves from the Church of God (Cleveland). But the table which follows shows only those Churches of God which can actually be shown to have come into being by separating from the Church of God (Cleveland). There are a large number of other Churches of God which originated independently of the Church of God (Cleveland).[20]

Churches of God which can be shown to go back to the Church of God (Cleveland) (02a.02.067).

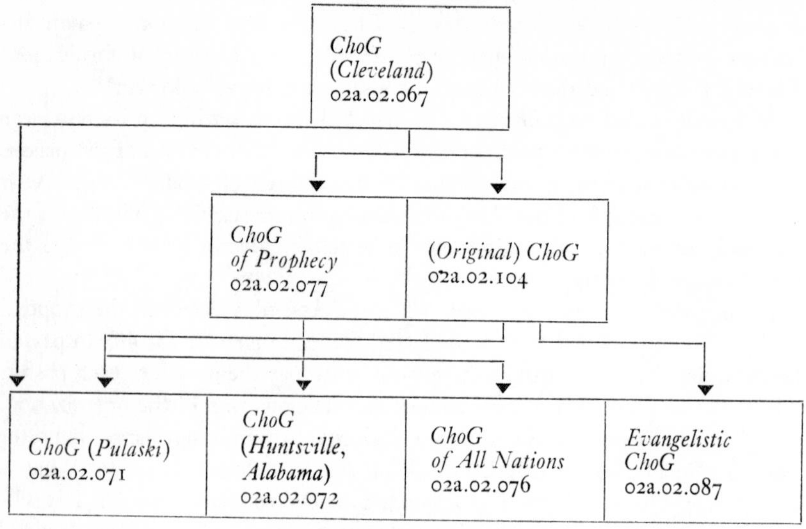

2. *Doctrine and Worship*

The confession of faith of the Church of God (Cleveland) is given in the appendix. It contains the usual articles of Pentecostal doctrine. The Church believes 'in speaking with other tongues as the Spirit gives utterance, and that it is the initial evidence of the baptism of the Holy Ghost'. But by contrast with the Assemblies of God, it also teaches sanctification, as a particular and decisive experience, distinct from the baptism of the Spirit and from conversion. Latterly, however, doubt seems to have been cast upon the description of it as the 'Second Work of Grace'.[21] This experience of sanctification is described as a justification within the soul, a certainty of the joy of salvation, a quietist absorption of oneself into Jesus, and a condition for the baptism of the Spirit which comes later.[22] The Church also practises the washing of feet.[23]

(*a*) *Ethical rigorism*

The ethical rigorism[24] of the Church of God (the prohibition of mixed bathing, of permanently waved hair, of going to the cinema or the theatre[25] and of make-up) seems according to some observers no longer to be exercised very strictly, especially with regard to women's fashions. The young people's magazine of the Church of God features Patricia Lockhart, a fashion artist who belongs to the Church of God. Some of the very modern designs produced by her are illustrated.[26] One of the reasons for the relaxation of ethical rigorism is probably the development of the schools run by the Church of God (Cleveland). At Lee College there are 804 students at the present time. The more talented amongst them can gain a BA in 'biblical education', 'church music', 'Christian education' and 'combined areas of Bible and music'. The school is a member of the Association of Bible Colleges and the Evangelical Teacher-Training Association. It goes to great trouble to expand its library (10,000 new purchases a year), has begun a building programme that will cost $700,000, and has set up a language laboratory for its future missionaries.[27] On the other hand, smoking is still considered to justify expulsion.[28] At first military service was also rejected. From 1917 to 1921 the minutes of the General Assembly of the Church of God carried condemnation of members of the Church who carried out military service. From 1928 to 1945 this condemnation was limited to members who served in combatant units. Today every member decides for himself whether or not he will do military service.

(b) The attitude to fundamentalism

The Church of God is a radically *fundamentalist Pentecostal group*. In his first-class history of the Church of God, Conn charges the traditional churches with having allowed the ideas of Kant, Emerson, Newman, Voltaire, Schleiermacher, Carlyle, 'and a confusion of theologians, philosophers, and poets' to have a greater influence on many pulpits than the Word of God.

> The most famous of these writers was Renan, who stated in his biography of Christ that he was a mere man, and that both the New Testament and the Old Testament contained numerous myths and legends. Both modernism and Socialism resulted in much scepticism among the masses.[29]

In its 'Answers to Correspondents' the *Church of God Evangel* replied to a question about the difference between Luke 7.36–50 and Matt. 26.6 in a fundamentalist sense, saying that Simon the Pharisee and Simon the leper were two different persons. The woman in Luke 7.37 and those in Matt. 26.7, Mark 14.3 and John 12.3 are likewise different, and none of them is identical with Mary Magdalene.[30]

Jack J. Chinn, a missionary of the Church of God, criticizes the Theological Seminary of Berkeley, California, because it did not support the evangelization campaign of Billy Graham.

> Intellectuals have had their opportunity in the last century to prove what *men* can do; now there is a theology emerging [in the Church of God] proving what *God* can do.[31]

Earl P. Paulk, a prominent young pastor of the Church of God, the son of a Pentecostal preacher, makes in his account of Pentecostal teaching a remarkable attempt to reconcile academic scholarship and fundamentalism. The book is written in clear English, intelligible to those with no theological background. Paulk nevertheless attempts to proceed in a scholarly manner. In the opening chapter he defines Pentecostals as those 'who receive the same experience as those "on the day of Pentecost" (Acts 2.1, 4)'.[32]

He rejects the church and experience as the final authority for faith. God is the final authority:

> The fact that man has power to reason points to a Higher Mind. That man has a sense of good and evil indicates that there is an Almighty Judge . . . The Pentecostal position is that any form of revelation of God is valuable and is to be taken into account. However, the highest and most perfect revelation of God is Jesus Christ.[33]
>
> It is well to note, however, the Bible is not authoritative to the Pentecostal because of its historical value. It is so because God moved the hearts of men to receive the events of his saving grace through Jesus Christ.[34]

After the doctrine of God, dealt with in the traditional way, the passage on the divinity of Christ defends the virgin birth at length. The only available accounts tell of a virgin birth. The Christian tradition of a virgin birth is unbroken. Matthew and Luke bear independent witness to it, but agree. John does not dispute it. The oldest creed, the Apostles' Creed, teaches it. Anyone who denies the virgin birth must explain the origin of the birth narratives. Although the Old Testament has no high regard for virginity, both Luke and Matthew, both markedly Hebraic in their thinking, tell of the virgin birth. There is no evidence that the early church ever taught the incarnation of Jesus apart from the virgin birth. Since Paul and John regard Christ as a supernatural person, it must be concluded that they too taught the virgin birth. The unique life and work of Jesus seem to postulate a supernatural birth. There is no indication that Mary, who knew the facts, disputed the accounts of Matthew and Luke.[35]

This is not the place to discuss the above assertions. Paulk shares with all American fundamentalists an ignorance of the debate about the exegetical background of the narrative of the virgin birth.

The doctrine of the Spirit is on the same lines as elsewhere in the Pentecostal movement. The chapter on 'Man' rejects the theory of evolution – 'the Pentecostal thinker cannot accept the theory of evolution'.[36] The doctrine of predestination is misunderstood as determinism and rejected, because man is 'a free moral agent'.[37] Sin is regarded as a 'wilful transgression of the law'. This means that one's motive is to do wrong.[38] The chapter on the sacraments refers not only to baptism and the Lord's Supper, but also to the 'commandment' of 'washing the saints' feet'.[39] The chapter on ethics condemns in a very restrained way 'worldly dress' in women, and waved hair,[40] and recommends restraint in the use of 'unnecessary jewels', a phrase that sounds a great deal less dogmatic than the corresponding passages in the Church's confession of faith.[41] In the chapter on the family a passage on means of contraception refuses to condemn them.[42] The chapter on 'social responsibility' brings the usual superficial American condemnation of communism[43] as the 'mystery of iniquity'.[44] Soviet Russia, 'with her atheistic Communist Party' is contrasted with the

United States of America, 'a democracy of God-loving and believing people'.[45] But 'the world ignores . . . misunderstands and misjudges the acts of mercy and generous gifts which they have received' from the United States. 'Instead of reaping love and gratefulness from the world, America has received distrust, hatred and jealousy. So it has been from the beginning of the world until now'.[46]

There is considerable disagreement with other fundamentalists. The fundamentalist American Council of Christian Churches,[47] which is accused of despising the Pentecostals, had tried to cut the Pentecostals off from the non-Pentecostals in the National Association of Evangelicals, by rejecting an amalgamation of the National Association of Evangelicals with the American Council of Christian Churches, and inviting the members of the National Association of Evangelicals to apply *individually* to be members of the American Council of Christian Churches; the applications of the Pentecostals would then have been turned down. 'The founders of the National Association of Evangelicals refused to forsake their [Pentecostal] friends and brethren'.[48] The writings of H. R. Gause reveal the tendency to enter into dialogue at least with the more conservative of the traditional churches.[49] At any rate, the identification of the Church of God (Cleveland) with the Church of God in the absolute sense is rejected.[50] On the other hand, when John F. Kennedy was campaigning for election there was opposition on the part of the Church of God (Cleveland), as also among the Assemblies of God,[51] to a Catholic president of the United States,[52] while the World Council of Churches is rejected out of hand.[53]

(*c*) *Pentecostal religious practice as an expression and overcoming of deprivation*

In 1942, Liston Pope gave the following description of a service in the Church of God (Cleveland):

> One traverses a grassless, rutted yard, climbs precarious 2 x 6 steps into a long, bare room filled with crude pews, and takes a seat in the Church of God. It is Sunday night, and the building is filled to overflowing, with about a thousand people present. Many stand in the doors or in the front yard of the church, including a large group of young men watching the girls go in and out. An ice cream vendor has placed his portable refrigerator near the church door, and is doing a thriving business. About 65% of those present are women between the ages of fourteen and fifty-five, many of whom have sleeping babies in their laps. The atmosphere is expectant and informal; members of the congregation move about at will, and talk in any tone of voice that suits their fancy.
>
> A crude pulpit, a piano, and a section of pews for the choir are placed at the far end of the oblong building. Back of the pulpit to the left is a homemade board on which to register weekly attendance; beneath the board, in sprawling letters, the question:
>
> HOW WILL YOUR
> REPORT IN HEAVEN BE

To the right of the pulpit is another sign:

GOD IS ABLE

A band, including three stringed instruments and a saxophone, plays occasional music.

The service begins at eight o'clock or thereabouts. Rather, the actions of the congregation become more intense and concerted in character; there is almost nothing by way of formal announcement. The choir, in co-operation with the pastor, breaks into a rhythmic hymn, and the congregation follows suit. The hymn has an interminable number of stanzas, and a refrain, reminiscent of mountain ballads both in music and in narrative form. The hymn looks toward a narrative climax, and the excitement of the congregation increases as the singing proceeds. The stanzas are punctuated with loud shouts of 'Hallelujah', 'Thank you, Jesus', 'Glory', and the rhythmic clapping of hands and tapping of feet. Almost immediately, various members of the congregation begin to 'get the Holy Ghost' (as a teen-age boy awesomely remarks). One young woman leaves the front row of the choir and jerks about the pulpit, with motions so disconnected as to seem involuntary, weird. A man's head trembles violently from side to side. Another man, tieless and red-face, laughs boomingly at odd moments, in a laugh resembling that of intoxication.

Half a dozen songs follow in succession. Then comes a prayer, with everybody kneeling on the floor and praying aloud at the same time, each in his own way. Some mutter with occasional shouts; others chant, with frequent bendings backward and forward; the volume of sound rises and falls, without unified pattern or group concentration. The pastor's voice booms out occasionally above all the others. Then, as if by a prearranged but unobservable signal, the prayer abruptly ends; the onlooker is amazed to see emerging from the confusion a concerted return to a sitting position. The cacophony of prayer is ended as suddenly as it began.

Then the pastor reads 'the Scripture', after confessing that he 'ain't had no time to study today', and after attempting to induce a layman in the congregation to 'say something' – without avail, because the layman confesses that he 'ain't had no time to study neither' and insists, 'You go right ahead, brother'. Reluctantly the pastor begins to read, explaining each verse with amazing exegesis and equally amazing insight. Each verse becomes the subject for a homily, and the reader works up to a climax in its exposition – a climax reflected in increase of rhythmic motions and hortatory shouts from members of the congregation. Having finished the Scripture lesson, the preacher takes up a collection, counts it, announces that he has to have 'a little more', and runs around in the congregation to garner proffered contributions, acknowledging each with a receipt 'God bless you, brother', and finally emptying the collection plate into his pocket.

Then the service moves toward a climax; the taking of the collection has been an emotional interlude. The preacher begins a sermon; more precisely, he enunciates verbal symbols that arouse immediate response from the congregation. Such motifs play through his shoutings as 'sanctification', 'the

Second Coming', 'the world despises and misunderstands and lies about the Church of God', 'Jesus can heal your body and soul', 'believe the Word', 'follow the knee-route'. The Church of God is depicted as a remnant of those who have escaped from the 'coldness' of the Methodist and Baptist churches. Lay preaching is urged, and personal evangelistic work. Attention is called to a number of prayer meetings to be held at various houses during the subsequent week, and to persons for whom prayer is desired – especially the family of a four-year-old girl who has just died, because 'they can't hardly get over it'.

Then there is a testimony meeting in which a large number of the more faithful testify to their personal experience and joy in religion, some mutteringly, some loudly, fervidly. One woman defends her right to wear long-sleeved, high-necked dresses in the summer time, because 'the Spirit told me to'. Nearly all say that they are proud to speak for Christ, and not ashamed to speak out for their Master in church. The man who has been indulging the intoxicated laugh defends his right to laugh in church, saying that his religion makes him feel good all over and is not like the stiff coldness of the Methodist church. Recurring phrases appear in the testimonies: 'I'm glad I got over bein' too proud to be a Holiness and get all there was of the Holy Ghost'; 'I'm a better wife and I've got a better husband because I joined the Church of God'; 'the Baptists are all right, but I wanted more of the Lord than they had.' Several testify to marvelous cures of physical illness during the past week, through prayer and the 'laying on of hands'.

All the while waves of ecstatic rhythm have been sweeping over the congregation, with the actions of the preacher setting the pace. There are patterns to the rhythmic actions: running around the pulpit, holding trembling hands to the sky, very fast clogging of the feet, swinging the arms in sharp, staccato motions. One girl leaps from her seat as though struck by an electric shock, races four times around the aisles of the church, screaming 'O God . . . O Jesus . . . O God . . . Glory, glory, glory . . . give me more . . . more . . . glory, glory, glory'; falling over backward with hands outstretched, her whole body quivering and rhythmically jerking, she collapses at last in a dull heap on the floor, and stays there in comatose condition for several minutes. Others rise and shout at the top of their lungs for five minutes, or bang on something in staccato rhythm. The same persons respond again and again, with perhaps seventy-five individuals represented. Each responds with an individual pattern of motions, but all motions revolve around a few general types. The motions appear to have been culturally conditioned, whether immediately conditioned by the agent or not. One wonders if some form of mass hypnotism is at work.

About ten o'clock the pastor calls for sinners to come to the front and kneel around the altar (constructed of a bench quickly placed before the pulpit). About ten come, including one five-year-old boy. A hundred members of the congregation gather about, and a tremendous tumult ensues as they attempt to 'pray and shout the sinners through', interspersed with wild demonstrations of joy as one is 'saved'.

It is nearly 11 p.m., but one stays and wonders. They cry out, and cry; they are drunken, but not with wine; they stagger, but not with strong drink . . .[54]

In the famous work from which this passage is taken, *Millhands and Preachers*, Liston Pope was studying the role of the churches in one of the most severe social struggles America has known, the strike of textile workers in Gastonia, N. Carolina. His findings are based on years of investigations, personal interviews, study of the Church and political press in Gaston County, all minutes of meetings of most of the churches and sects. What was the contribution of the churches to the calming down of the precarious situation in a town where there was a very bitter strike? The ministerial association of Gastonia, during the years 1932–1939 dealt amongst other things with the following:

Held a program on the dangers of unemployment (May 2, 1932)

Pledged support to the United Dry Forces of North Carolina (September 4, 1933)

Commended city officials for banishing slot machines (December 2, 1935).

Held two joint meetings with colored ministers of the city at one of which a Negro minister spoke 'with deep humility' (January 3, 1937, January 3, 1938).

Protested against the flying of airplanes at low altitudes over the city on the Sabbath (May 2, 1938).[55]

The following recommendation is given as a proposed solution to the employment situation: 'When we all (not just a few) properly adjust our relations to our God and to our fellow-man, all other problems, small or great, will adjust themselves around them'.[56] 'Religion is the medicine for industry.'[57] Liston Pope's judgment on the ignorance of the ministers about problems of national economics is sweeping:

Despite the years spent in professional preparation, almost none of the mill pastors in Gaston County have had any special training for work in an industrial parish. Under ordinary circumstances they follow conventional, standardized programs in their churches, aping the policies of uptown churches of their denomination and the sermons of the uptown preachers who speak at their denominational gatherings. In most instances their knowledge of economic processes, labor relations, management problems, trade union tactics, and culture analysis is no more extensive or competent than that of their village parishioners, and they are easily convinced by the only persons who presumably do know about such matters – the mill owners and managers. When conflict occurs between the social classes, the mill pastors almost invariably adopt the analyses presented by the 'most intelligent' and 'best informed' citizens in the vicinity, who always are members of the uptown class. Uptown pastors, though their economic insight is frequently even less acute than that of their colleagues in the mill parishes, give the cues by which all their ministerial brethren are guided, citing mill owners and other persons 'in the know' as their source of authority. Lacking economic and socio-

> logical perspectives wider than those of their own communities, ministers of all types of churches fail to appraise the opinions of community leaders as being in themselves highly relative; instead, they incline to accept them at face value or to modify them in minor details only. Though they are acknowledged experts in the field of religion and continually profess to be troubled by the gap between ethical ideals and social practice, they do not possess criteria for judging social possibilities, and thus in effect become instruments of social inertia.[58]

Social distress and the extremely deficient solidarity with the textile workers shown by the traditional churches provide the background, at least for the time and place which Pope is investigating, for the growth of 'new sects' (in which Pope includes the Pentecostal movement). Pope discusses the *reasons for this growth* in connection with the description of worship in the Church of God. It had at first been supposed that there was a relation between the *mobility of a family* and its membership of the 'new sects'.[59]

> A close study of the entire membership of one sect group in Gastonia revealed that 98 per cent of its members had been living in the community for more than five years.[60]

Others have seen the reason as the *ignorance and lack of education* of potential converts to the Pentecostal movement. 'But this judgment is based on an external standard and contributes little to understanding.'[61]

Others again make the *failure of the traditional churches* responsible for the growth of the Pentecostals. According to Pope, this last hypothesis is justified. 'At least 80 per cent of the numbers of such groups had previously belonged to established' mainly Baptist, churches.[62] And for this reason there is very frequent mention in Pentecostal services in this region of the dullness of Baptist and Methodist services.

It has also been pointed out that the Pentecostals principally attract the *economically weak sections of the population*, whom they help to bear their misery by promising a better world to come. Pope regards this explanation as true, but inadequate.[63]

He attempts to give a fuller diagnosis of the phenomenon of the growth of Pentecostalism with the aid of *psychological categories.*

> Frenetic religious services represent release from psychological repression, it is said, fulfilling a need for self-expression and for identification of one's self with a greater power. Life in a mill village is monotonous and dull, production processes in the mills are largely mechanical in character, and the worker has little opportunity for choice as to any of the basic factors that control his daily life.

But the Church of God is a lay movement,

> The entire membership participates in most of the services ... The unusually high percentage of women who belong and who appear to be most active

participants in semi-hysterical religious practices is also significant; of the members of one Church of God in Gaston County, 57 per cent were women, almost all of whom were between the ages of seventeen and fifty-four. A psychologist observing the religious ceremonies of the Church of God might conclude that the sex factor is crucial in explanation. Certainly members of these groups are widely accused of being immoral, and a considerable degree of sexual laxity is undoubtedly a concomitant of their services. An uptown boy explained, standing outside a Church of God while a service was in progress: 'It'll get hot in there pretty soon. A lot of women come over here, which is why all the boys are hanging around. I got started out late tonight and all the dates are taken, so I have to take what I can get. Mill girls are the best-looking girls nowadays anyhow.' Rhythmic music, supported by stringed instruments and saxophones, tendencies towards exhibitionism, and injunctions to 'let yourself go' for 'possession by the Spirit' are surcharged with sex stimulation.[64]

3. *Assessment*

The pastors of the Church of God ascribe the growth of their church to the zeal of their adherents. Inspired by their fiery preaching, all members become missionaries and sacrifice unimaginable sums from their small incomes. 'People are gettin' disgusted with professional religion and demandin' to get results in their religion.' The typical pastor of the Church of God explains in part the rapid growth of the Church of God, but not why it came into being. In Gastonia, it is notable that the textile workers' pastors were factory workers themselves and preached part-time, or had been factory workers and were called by a congregation to be its pastor. They had had little education, often no more than a few years in primary school (fourth grade in the public schools) with a few weeks at the Bible School, and were content with the low salary of a factory worker.

One must not underestimate the enormous increase in self-esteem which a working man gains by being accepted into the Church of God. He sees a spiritual career in front of him which leads not only far beyond what is possible for a working man, but also gives him the chance to do better than members of the Methodist Church, who in other respects are richer than he to a degree he cannot hope to attain. As a member of the Church of God he is certain of being truly and finally saved. But in addition he can also be sanctified and receive the baptism of the Spirit, and perhaps even become a pastor. What does it matter that a Methodist has more money, but is only saved at best, and certainly not sanctified or baptized in the Spirit?

If I gained the world but lost the Savior,
Were my life worth living for a day?
Could my yearning heart find rest and comfort
In the things that soon must pass away?[65]

Christians who belong to the traditional churches may let their wives use jewelry and make-up. But this is not necessary for a member of the Church of God, for his wife is adorned with spiritual gifts. All the deprivations he has to suffer he can turn into witness and spiritual gifts. And finally, he rejoices in heaven, where nobody can push him about any more:

> Had I wealth and love in fullest measure,
> And a name revered both far and near,
> Yet no hope beyond, no harbour waiting,
> Where my stormtossed vessel I could steer.[66]

Thus he pities other Christians, who are still in the forecourt of the sanctuary. 'By the thousands and scores of thousands, the lower economic classes abandoned Protestantism which had first abandoned them.'[67]

The introduction of emotional outbursts and erotic undertones into worship need not be absolutely condemned by a psychological observer. With a strict liturgical guidance it could be seen as a substitute for the lack of moral direction to which the members of the Church of God were exposed, according to their own testimony, before their conversion. The services would then have a sublimatory function and would be a help in integrating the emotional into the whole personality. It would be desirable for an expert psychologist at some time to examine this phenomenon from his own point of view.

The picture of the Church of God given by Pope and Curran was true up to the second world war. Since then, a steady rise on the social scale has altered the sociological position of the Church of God. Other Pentecostal groups, particularly of Negro Pentecostals, have taken over its functions. Liberation from psychological stress situations is still, however one of the most important functions of the Church of God, but it is now the stress situations of the middle class, of supervisors and managers.

The Church of God has rapidly developed into a middle-class church. Its rigorist understanding of salvation has been modified,[68] and it has adopted the patriotic values of the American middle class.[69] The more the churches of the Reformation and the Catholic church reject the values of the American middle class, the more they protest *for* the Negroes and *against* the war in Vietnam, the greater is the potential membership of the Church of God and other similar Pentecostal groups. A remarkable change of side has taken place. The church of the poor, which protested against the way in which the New Testament was overlaid by the values of church and bourgeosie, is in the process itself of becoming a conservative middle-class force, while former traditional churches suddenly appear revolutionary.

NOTES

1. Cf. above, ch. 2.4, pp. 24ff.

2. 02a.02.110.

3. Records, documents, literature: 02a.02.067. Statistics: 253,434 members, 4,388 congregations (letter of Ray H. Hughes, Assistant General Overseer ChoG [Cleveland] to W.H., 4.2.1970). Main periodical *Church of God Evangel* (*ChoGE*).

4. C. Conn, *Army*, p. 3.

5. L. H. Juillerat, *Brief History*, quoted in C. Conn, *op. cit.*, pp. 6f.

6. See n. 20 below.

7. L. H. Juillerat, *op. cit.*, quoted in C. Conn, *Army*, p. 14.

8. *Ibid.*

9. At least this is how Conn describes the affair in his very careful and accurately documented history of the ChoG.

10. ChoG, *Minutes* (*First Assembly, 1906*), 1; quoted Conn, *Army*, p. 65. The claim that the Church of God was organized as the 'Christian Union' in 1886 is contested by H. V. Synan. According to him, the 'Christian Union' 'completely disbanded before 1892 and there is no evidence of direct connection with the revival of 1896. The first continuous organization of the present ChoG (Cleveland) was the "Holiness Church at Camp Creek" which was organized in 1902. The claim that the ChoG (Cleveland) is "America's oldest Pentecostal church" is not based on contemporary documentary evidence and seems to be a much later interpolation' (*P Movement*, p. 98).

11. ChoG, *Minutes* (First Assembly, 1906), p. 16: quoted Conn, *op. cit.*, p. 68.

12. V. D. Hargreave, letter to W.H., 19.12.1963; E. P. Paulk, *Neighbour*, pp. 202–4.

13. *ChoGE* 50/50, 15.2.1960, p. 13.

14. *ChoGE* 53/5, 1.4.1963, p. 14.

15. *The Journal and the Banner*, 17.9.1908; quoted Conn, *Army*, p. 87.

16. 'Be it known to all men everywhere and unto all nations that we, the Church of God . . . do hereby and hereafter disclaim and repudiate the title "Holy Rollers" in reference to the Church of God.' ChoG, *Minutes* (Eleventh Assembly, 1915), p. 200; quoted C. Conn, *Army*, p. 131.

17. 02a.02.077.

18. Church of God (Anderson) (02a.02.017); Church of God (Apostolic) (02a.02.018); Church of God (Holiness) (02a.02.018A).

19. Church of God (Bishop Poteat) (?) (02a.02.070): Church of God, Inc. (Pulaski) (02a.02.071); Church of God (formerly Queen's Village, now Huntsville, Alabama) (02a.02.072) (this and other information on Churches of God from A. C. Piepkorn); Church of God of All Nations (02a.02.076); Church of God of Prophecy (02a.02.077); Church of God of the Mountain Assembly (?) (02a.02.068); Evangelistic Church of God (02a.02.087); (Original) Church of God (02a.02.104).

20. Church of God (East Harlem) (02a.02.068); Church of God (Holiness) (Negroes) (02a.02.068A); Church of God (Holiness) USA (Negroes) (02a.02.068B); Church of God (Mother Horn) (Negroes) (02a.02.069); Church of God (Mother Robinson) (Negroes) (02a.02.073): Church of God in Christ (Negroes) (02a.02.075); Church of God of the Bible (USA) (02a.02.079); Church of the Living God (Christian Workers for Fellowship) (Negroes) (02a.02.082); Church of the Living God, The Pillar and Ground of Truth (Negroes) (02a.02.083); Churches of God (Holiness) (Negroes) (02a.02.084); Free Church of God in Christ (02a.02.090); Glorified Church of God (02a.02.092); Holiness Church of God, Inc. (Negroes) (02a.02.093); Interracial Church of God (Negroes and Whites) (02a.02.100); Justified Church of God (02a.02.101); Non-

Digressive Church of God (USA) (02a.02.103); Pentecostal Church of God of America (02a.02.127). Some of the churches listed in n. 20 probably belong to n. 19. Those marked (?) in n. 19 cannot be said with absolute certainty to derive from the ChoG (Cleveland) (02a.02.067).

21. T. O. Dennis, *ChoGE* 53/41, 7.10.1963, pp. 8f.; P. H. Walker, *ChoGE* 52/24, 21.8.1961; F. W. Lemons, *ChoGE* 52/25, 28.8.1961, p. 5.

22. Cf. ch. 23.3, pp. 265ff., where experiences of sanctification are described.

23. P. H. Walker, *ChoGE* 52/19, 9.7.1962, pp. 4f.

24. W. H. Horton, *et al.*, *ChoGE* 51/3, 7.3.1960, pp. 28f.

25. L. Ward attacks a 'sex-laden Ingmar Bergman production' and deplores the fact that *King of Kings* did not get an Oscar (*ChoGE* 51/42, 1.1.1962, pp. 4f.).

26. P. Lockhart, *Lighted Pathway* 33/12, Dec. 1962, p. 18.

27. *P* 70, 1964, p. 10.

28. ChoG, *Minutes* (Third Assembly, 1908); Conn, *Army*, p. 82.

29. C. Conn, *Army*, p. xx (quoted from A. Hyma, *World History*, p. 335).

30. *ChoGE* 52/4, 14.1.1963.

31. J. J. Chinn, *Christianity Today* 5, 1961, p. 880.

32. E. P. Paulk, *Neighbour*, p. 20.

33. *Ibid.*, p. 24.

34. *Ibid.*, p. 25.

35. *Ibid.*, pp. 42f.

36. *Ibid.*, p. 71.

37. 'Zwingli, and perhaps Calvin, supported the idea that God chose some to be saved and some to be damned even before the creation or fall of Adam' (*ibid.*, p. 77).

38. *Ibid.*, p. 89.

39. Washing the Saints' Feet 'is a commandment of the Word of God and it is to be done even as the Lord's Supper' (*ibid.*, p. 166).

40. *Ibid.*, p. 194.

41. *Ibid.*, p. 195.

42. *Ibid.*, pp. 210ff.

43. *Ibid.*, pp. 222ff.

44. *ChoGE* 52/24, 20.8.1962, p. 14.

45. C. C. Cox, *ChoGE* 51/24, 22.8.1960, pp. 8f.

46. M. Gaines, *ChoGE* 53/8, 22.4.1963, p. 19.

47. 15 Park Row, New York 38. Listed in B. Y. Landis, *Yearbook 1963*, p. 8, with the remark: 'Information declined'.

48. H. Lindsell, *Park Street Prophet*, pp. 118–20; quoted in Conn, *Army*, p. 259.

49. H. R. Gause, *ChoGE* 51/33, 23.10.1961, pp. 8–10; 52/34, 29.10.1962, pp. 3f.

50. J. D. Bright, *ChoGE* 51/25, 28.8.1961, pp. 6f.

51. G. L. Ford, *PE* 2408, 3.7.1960, pp. 4f., 21–3; *ChoGE* 51/23, 15.8.1960, pp. 3–5, 10f.; M. Gaston, *PE* 2421, 2.10.1960, pp. 6f., 28f.; *PE* 2422, 9.10.1960, p. 10.

52. *ChoGE* 51/11, 16.5.1960, pp. 3–5, 11; 51/24, 22.8.1960, p. 5; G. L. Britt, *ChoGE* 51/12, 23.5.1960, pp. 7, 10; C. W. Fisher, *ChoGE* 51/32, 17.10.1960, pp. 5f.

53. *ChoGE* 51/48, 12.2.1962, p. 15; 51/50, 26.2.1962, p. 15; 51/2, 5.3.1962, p. 14; 52/39, 3.12.1962, p. 12.

54. L. Pope, *Millhands*, pp. 130f.

55. *Minutes of the Gaston Ministers Association*, 1932–1939, ms., quoted by Pope, *Millhands*, pp. 166f.

56. *Gastonia Gazette*, 4.6.1938, quoted in L. Pope, *op. cit.*, p. 172.

57. *Ibid.*, p. 170.

58. *Ibid.*, p. 115.

59. E. R. Hartz, *Social Problems*, pp. 132, 136.

60. L. Pope, *Millhands*, p. 133.
61. *Ibid.*
62. Information given by Pope on the basis of interviews with three pastors of the ChoG in Gastonia, 27.7.1939; L. Pope, *op. cit.*, p. 134.
63. A. T. Boisen, *Social Action*, 15.3.1939.
64. L. Pope, *op. cit.*, pp. 134f.
65. A. Ölander, in N. J. Clayton, *Melodies of Life*, 9.1.
66. *Ibid.*, 9.2.
67. F. X. Curran, *Major Traits*; quoted in J. Campbell, *PHCh*, p. 93.
68. J. A. Cross, *ChoGE* 51/28, 19.9.1960, pp. 13–15.
69. R. E. Day, *ChoGE*, 51/26, 5.9.1960, pp. 4–5, 13; *ChoGE* 53/24, 19.8.1963, p. 23. Cf. above, pp. 52f. and nn. 43–6.

5

'Unto the end of the World': The Spread of Pentecostalism

THE Pentecostal movement spread like wildfire over the whole world. I believe that the statistics are mostly too low, not because they accord to individual denominations too few members – there are a few cases of exaggeration – but because there are large Pentecostal bodies which are unknown to the Pentecostals themselves, and about the size of which they have no information.

1. *Europe*

During a fund-raising journey in America, T. B. Barratt, a Norwegian Methodist minister, a talented pupil of Grieg, and of Celtic British origin, was attracted by the Los Angeles revival.[1] He wrote enthusiastic letters from America back to Norway, and after his return to Oslo held great Pentecostal meetings. 'Many were filled with the Spirit, and many souls sought God'.[2] Barratt himself declared that he had spoken in eight different tongues[3] including French and Italian. He was so beside himself with joy that he began to dance in the Spirit.[4] The press began to notice what was happening and printed headlines about the 'idiot factory',[5] thus involuntarily providing publicity for the revival.

From Oslo the Pentecostal movement spread into the other Scandinavian countries – in Finland and Norway it is the largest Free Church, and in Sweden the second largest – and also into Germany,[6] Switzerland[7] and Great Britain.[8]

In the established churches of the Swiss cantons and German provinces, a massive criticism of the theological work of the universities had been accompanied by a longing for revival that had reached boiling point. 'We need the March storms to make way for the latter rain.'[9]

At provincial church assemblies, there were sermons about the Pentecostal fullness, the fullness of the Holy Spirit, the baptism of the Spirit, which the believing church can experience if only she earnestly desires it.[10] In 1905 the German pastor Modersohn was baptized with 'power from above'. 'The children of God prayed fervently for the onrush of power, and it came.'[11] Prayer in concert, that is, prayer in which the whole congregation utters prayers together and in spontaneous confusion, was designated as a 'divine ordinance'.[12] Criticism of the suggestive method of evangelization was firmly rejected.

The Reformation teaching that as long as we are alive there is no complete deliverance from sin was dismissed as 'blasphemy'.[13] Scholarly theological study was condemned as 'the work of Satan'. The 'cry of rage of the Jews in the liberal journals' – a contemptuous reference to specialist theological journals – was seen as being a compliment to the revival rather than a condemnation of it.[14] Anyone who would not define a miracle as an intervention which upset the normal course of nature was 'no longer a Christian theologian', according to the journal *Reichgottesarbeiter* ('Worker for the kingdom of God').[15] Thus there was rejoicing at the rise of the Pentecostal movement on the part of other evangelical Christians. This made it all the more difficult for Conservative Evangelicals in Germany and Switzerland to understand why the leaders of the Evangelical movement should suddenly turn against the Pentecostal movement. In the 'Berlin Declaration' of 1909, the bill of divorcement of the Evangelical movement', the leaders of the Conservative Evangelical movement condemned as the work of the devil the revival that they had first praised.[16] The Berlin Declaration has kept the Evangelical movement and the Pentecostal movement apart to this day, and was of great importance not merely in Germany but also in Switzerland and in Slavonic countries.[17]

In Italy the Pentecostal movement had more adherents than all the other Protestant groups together, and exercises a social influence which is respected by communists, liberals and sympathetic Catholics after suffering for many years severe persecutions by the Fascists and the Catholic Church.[18] In France, it is the second largest Protestant Church, the Reformed Church being the largest. Most of its members came from Catholicism, as the Catholic scholar H. C. Chéry has established.[19]

2. *Latin America*

In many countries in Latin America the Pentecostal movement is the largest Protestant Church. In Chile 14% of the population belong to it, while only 1% belong to other Protestant churches. There is no doubt that there is a connection between the influence of Pentecostal pastors on the workers and peons of Chile, and the fact that politics are no longer wrongly seen to present a simple choice between communism and feudalism. In its turn the relatively calm political climate in Chile has favoured the growth of the Pentecostal movement.[20] In Mexico the Pentecostal movement has not very many members, but has had to brave severe persecutions, in the course of which one of Obregón's police chiefs, who was directing the operation, was converted – the Pentecostals always seem to be involved in such dramatic stories. In the Bahamas, to choose one example from the islands of the West Indies, 10% of the population and 20% of the Protestants are Pentecostals, half being members of the Iglesia de Dios (Cleveland).[21] In Haiti the Pentecostals demythologize the heathen Voodoo cult and have set up many schools. They were persecuted in most South American countries, but most violently in Colombia, where one of their pastors was posted to the members of his congregation in pieces; 'Here is a part of your pastor, whom you loved.'[22] Pentecostalism in Brazil is the most numerous Protestant body in any country having a Latin language. There are approximately four million Pentecostals in Brazil (about 70% of all Protestants in Brazil) and by contrast with the Catholic Church and many Protestant churches, they have succeeded in becoming a 'Brazilian' Church, that is, one which integrates the latent Brazilian illuminism into Christian worship.[23] The Brazilian Assembléias de Deus (with almost two million members) is recognized by the Brazilian government, and indeed highly placed government officials insist on being present in person at the consecration of Pentecostal churches. Similarly, at the World Pentecostal Conference in Helsinki in 1964, an official reception was given for the Brazilian ambassador in Finland.[24]

3. *Africa*

The Pentecostal movement also established a foothold in Africa. It has tried to make the mission churches as quickly as possible independent practically, organizationally and spiritually, of the mother church conducting the mission. Some of these African mission churches, however, have become independent too quickly. I believe I have shown that the Zionist wing of the South African independent churches (almost 400 groups) goes back to missionaries led by John Alexander Dowie. Dowie's Black followers were taken over by the Apostolic Faith Mission[25] and ordained as evangelists, before they could read or write; far less had they received even the slightest theological training. If the Black South Africans had received the 'power from on high', this was sufficient grounds for the Pentecostal missionaries to institute them as preachers and missionaries. All the important Zionist leaders of the first generation go back to this missionary activity by the Pentecostal movement. Today the Pentecostal movement rejects the Zionists as extremists. There is no question that some have combined paganism with Christianity, but many of them have simply remained faithful to the enthusiastic practices of the first Pentecostal missionaries. It is easy, particularly in the present situation in South Africa, to understand the psychological reasons why the Pentecostal missionaries reject these disciples of Pentecostalism, most of whom were baptized *before* the present missionaries came to Africa. And if a Pentecostal preacher has not himself experienced something within the Pentecostal movement he cannot be persuaded that it is an historical fact. How can a church historian in Switzerland, it might be said, understand the history of the Pentecostal movement in South Africa better than a

Pentecostal missionary who has worked there for thirty years? But one cannot dispute the historical fact that the Zionists of South Africa, who have a million followers, came into being from an impulse given by the Pentecostal mission.[26] Besides these independent churches there are large missionary churches in South Africa. One of their main leaders is Nicholas Bhengu, originally a Lutheran, but for whom *simul justus – simul peccator* is incomprehensible, as for the European Pentecostals. On the contrary, anyone who has been baptized no longer sins; he is not an *udlalani*, no longer a Don Juan. Bhengu's sermons must be overwhelming.

> Do not always ask the white people to do anything and everything. For you are not even satisfied today for them to build you free houses, but also expect them to furnish them for you (loud laughter from all the congregation, who know he has touched them on a weak point). It is a scandal that you saddle others with everything. You yourselves have willpower and human reason....[27]
>
> God, who created these young people, this athletic young man and this shapely girl, plump and fat, intended thereby to show his glory and thought of you instead of himself. But the Tempter, the Evil One, took this model of God's creation and spoiled it by sin and disease. This marvellous vessel became the devil's horse, which he rode on, whose beauty he spoiled and whose strength he undermined. He filled it with filthy sins, with crime and disease....[28]
>
> You, you strong young men, must become politicians with a constructive policy.[29]

The Pentecostal movement has also provided the starting point for the growth of large independent African churches in Nigeria and Ghana, but not in the Congo.[30] Some of these churches were represented at the World Pentecostal Conference in Helsinki in 1964.[31]

4. *Asia and Australia*

Malcolm Calley, an Australian anthropologist, who describes himself as a non-Christian, lived for six months amongst Australian aboriginal Pentecostals, learnt their language, studied the relationship between Pentecostal and heathen Australian religion, and came to the important conclusion that for these Australians Pentecostal religion is a transitional stage in their gradual assimilation to the newcomers from the West. By contrast to the missionaries of the *International Church of the Foursquare Gospel* he is not surprised at the ability of the Australians to experience the baptism of the Spirit, for they were acquainted with similar experiences from their Australian religion.[32]

It is scarcely realized that the Pentecostal movement plays an important role in the Communist part of the world. In China – as in Russia – the Pentecostals set up co-operative settlements *before* the Communists, and these were at first highly praised by the communist government, but later dissolved, since a religious *kolchoz* which functioned better that the state ones could not be permitted. But the Pentecostal movement is still spreading in China. But the theological poverty of the Pentecostal movement brings little profit in the encounter with Communism. The older Protestant churches must either adopt a religious practice like that of the Pentecostals, including speaking in tongues, or else admit their inability to survive in this stress situation and disappear.[33]

Elsewhere in Asia, there is particular interest in the large Pentecostal movement in Indonesia, in the sizeable movement in India, autonomous and independent of missionary churches, and in the situation in Japan. 'In few countries in the world are there so many Pentecostal missionaries at work as in Japan',[34] but so far they have been practically without success. During the war the mission churches of the Assemblies of God, the Iesu-no Mitama Kyokai, separated from their American mother church and now exist *alongside* the renewed missionary activity of the Americans, the Nihon Assemburizu Kyodan.[35] The Iesu-no Mitama Kyokai has in its turn begun to send missionaries to the United States.[36] The indigenous Japanese Pentecostal churches far outnumber the Pentecostal missionary churches. Perhaps the Japanese 'Non-Church Movement' can be included amongst the former.[37]

5. *The World Conferences*

In order to draw together the international Pentecostal Movement, international conferences have been held since 1939.

The first Pentecostal Conference, for all Europe, took place in 1939 in Stockholm. The very instructive minutes are a mine of information about the controversial questions within Pentecostalism, and about Pentecostal churches in socialist countries. The most important questions discussed (put by Leonhard Steiner) were:

> Is it right to base our conception of the baptism of the Spirit on the Acts of the Apostles, and the experience of the twelve Apostles? Can this experience be deduced from the Epistles written by them?[38]

In spite of the criticism implied in the way the question was put, the leadership of the Pentecostal movement proclaimed the usual Pentecostal view, with the exception of George Jeffreys, who wished to see a less strict connection made between speaking in tongues and the baptism of the Spirit.[39] The rest of the discussion turned on such questions as: Can we formulate our view in a declaration of faith? Would this be of help to us? Can we organize ourselves as a world-wide denomination? In spite of the urgent pleas of the Slav and Baltic representatives for dogmatic and organizational unification, no agreement was reached on these matters.

At the World Conference in Zurich (1947) the first attempt to found a World Pentecostal Fellowship was a failure.[40] A second attempt at the World Conference in Paris (1949), where a full-blown plan was presented for a World

Pentecostal Fellowship with statutes and declaration of faith, was so decisively wrecked by the Scandinavian Pentecostals[41] that since then no further attempts have been made, even though in London in 1952 David J. Du Plessis affirmed

> . . . a great need for better co-ordination in the missionary services across the world. Fortunes are being spent fruitlessly in foreign lands because we do not take the trouble to sit down with our brethren from overseas and develop plans in co-operation with them.[42]

The report of the World Pentecostal Conference in Stockholm in 1955[43] contains a number of representative speeches, including a historical survey by J. Roswell Flower, two addresses on the Baptism of the Spirit by Paul Rabe and G. R. Wessels, an address on speaking in tongues and prophecy by Donald Gee and an important contribution on the healing of the sick by prayer by the Norwegian doctor and Pentecostal, Oswald Orlien.

The only real debate – the last up to the present day – took place at the fifth World Pentecostal Conference in Toronto in 1958.[44] Leonhard Steiner's address is of particular interest, for it is as it were his farewell to the World Conferences. But the most important points made by Steiner concerning 'Divine Healing in God's Redemption'[45] were, like Jeffrey's views in Stockholm,[46] not recorded in the minutes of the Conference, for although they received lively support they also aroused violent dissent. In particular, Steiner suggested that the healing evangelists[47] wanted as it were to make God their servant, and in their prayers for healing had ignored the limitation that man must always make: 'Thy will be done.' Consequently God had not confirmed their preaching in the last ten years. It had to be stated with sadness that after the rush of enthusiasm those who remained healed were only a very small percentage.

> The apostles practised divine healing without making a special point of preaching it, whereas we preach it, but fail to practise it.[48]

The second keynote address to the Conference was that of J. A. Synan,[49] Bishop of the Pentecostal Holiness Church, and is characteristic of the growing fundamentalist tendency in Pentecostal circles. He sees the principal task of the Pentecostal movement as a battle against those Christians who no longer believe in the 'supernatural'. 'Higher criticism' comes under heavy fire, for it turns the miracles of Christ into 'the inventions of overzealous disciples', and the doctrine of heaven into 'a beautiful dream that will never come true'.

> But we Pentecostals believe the Bible to be the inerrant and infallible, the divinely-inspired Word of God. We accept all of it: we believe that, till heaven and earth pass away, one jot or one tittle of the Word shall in no wise fall, till all be fulfilled.

Thus Synan calls for a battle for 'a dogmatic declaration of great Bible truths, regardless of how they may be received'; that is, he demands the strict following of the American fundamentalists, and the rejection of all dialogue with the ecumenical and sceptical scholarship.

The third keynote address was given by Donald Gee[50] and has been printed in many Pentecostal journals.[51] He vigorously defends the Pentecostal dogma that 'only he who speaks in tongues has received the baptism of the Spirit'.

> With all due respect we refuse to be satisfied that so-called 'Pentecostal' experiences without a physical manifestation are valid according to the scriptural pattern or even common logic.

As is described below[52] Gee combined this strict Pentecostal view with a broad-minded ecumenical outlook, even with regard to non-fundamentalists.

The report of the sixth World Pentecostal Conference in Jerusalem (1961)[53] is interesting because of the considerable degree to which the Israeli state participated in the conference – for example, Ben Gurion spoke to the Pentecostal delegates.

It seems that the subsequent conferences (Helsinki, 1964; Rio de Janeiro, 1967) no longer produced any disagreements or statements of the Pentecostal position, but rather served the purpose of public demonstrations. In Rio de Janeiro, according to usually well-informed circles, the American Assemblies of God sought to bring under their control not only the World Conference, but also the important Brazilian Assembléias de Deus, and to make them theologically and economically dependent on America. This attempt, however, met with bitter and successful resistance from the Brazilians. In the judgment of a Chilean Pentecostal pastor the Pentecostal World Conference in Dallas, Texas (1970) had pushed the great indigenous Pentecostal denominations of the Third World into the background. He observed, that the missionary success of the Assemblies of God and of the Church of God (Cleveland) gives them 'the complex of superiority and power in the Pentecostal World Conference'.[54]

6. *An Attempt to Classify the Theology of the Different Pentecostal Organizations*

To the outsider, the Pentecostal movement seems to consist of an unlimited profusion of greater and lesser organizations. The impression is often given that each is in conflict with the others. On the other hand, the great Conferences give a profound impression of the unanimity of members of different organizations who are taking part. Both impressions are deceptive. As far as the latter is concerned, it is impossible for a Pentecostal conference to hold worship otherwise than with one mind, even though there are profound theological and human differences in the background.

The Pentecostal movement is not an unstructured chaos. One obviously well-ordered area is to be found in the hundreds of Pentecostal Journals. The Pentecostals originally could not find publishers for their literature, partly for stylistic reasons, but largely on doctrinal grounds. Moreover, the publishers failed to recognize the market there was. For today Pentecostal literature is a huge business. Pentecostals buy books for themselves, their relations and their acquaintances. One may note the huge output of the Gospel Publishing House of the Assemblies of God. In 1963 the printing works of this firm printed ten tons of literature a day. In 1958–59 it was already selling \$5½m. worth of books and magazines; in 1969 it was selling 5,000,000 tracts and about 40,000 books, employed 600 people and had an annual wage bill of \$3m. The Brazilian Pentecostal publisher, O. S. Boyer, sells 2,000,000 books and tracts a year in Brazil and is reckoned to be the most widely read living author in Portuguese.[55]

Since the Pentecostals were forced to set up their own publishing system, their books are found neither in official bibliographies, nor in libraries, nor in book-sellers' catalogues. Nevertheless, large editions of Pentecostal journals are printed and read, not only by Pentecostals. Any minister can see this for himself. For example, there are few towns in the world where the *Herald of His Coming* is not read in some translation by members of traditional churches. There must be few villages and hardly any minister's house in Holland where *Kracht van Omhoog* ('Power From On High') cannot be found. There are few congregations in Switzerland and Germany where there are not some members at least who read *Sieg des Kreuzes* ('The Victory of the Cross'). And there must be few hospitals in Europe and America where there are not some patients or nurses reading or distributing the literature of the healing evangelists. Thus it is not surprising that each denomination has set up one or more publishing enterprises.

Some of these journals have very large circulations. In 1961 the total circulation of all the journals of the Assemblies of God was more than two million. Certain numbers of *Mehr Licht* ('More Light') had a circulation of more than 100,000. But this is exceptional. Normally each denomination produces a number of journals for different groups of readers. The differences in presentation and quality are considerable. Thus there was the illustrated new magazine *Pentecost* (which unfortunately ceased publication after the death of Donald Gee), the two British Pentecostal journals *Elim Evangel* and *Redemption Tidings*; journals in Brazil (*Mensageiro da Paz*), Mexico (*Mensajero Pentecostes*), Italy (*Risveglio Pentecostale*) and France (*Viens et Vois*), the *Pentecostal Evangel*, very pretentious in its layout and typography – circulation 230,000; the Swedish daily paper *Dagen*; the cheap paperback propaganda writings of the healing evangelists; the conservative German *Heilszeugnisse*; the modest *Verheissung des Vaters*, which has existed since 1909, and the *Pentecostal Testimony*, which also discusses political matters. There are specialist journals for preachers, Sunday School teachers, Sunday school superintendents, for children, teen-agers, students, the blind, the deaf and dumb, for soldiers, for Pentecostal army chaplains, for musicians and choirmasters, etc. Almost every country and every language has its Pentecostal literature.

Most (but not all) of these journals are published by an organization. But they are read not only by the members of the organization that publishes them, but also by Pentecostals who belong to other organizations and by members of majority churches and established churches. This overlapping of published material (and of the equally important radio broadcasts and record publishing enterprises) must be taken into account in considering the relationship between the different organizations.

An important aspect of Pentecostal journals is their international character. It is common to find in a Pentecostal magazine articles on the Pentecostal movement in countries behind the Iron Curtain or even in China. Most of these articles are retranslated from Swedish or English translations. The international co-operation of Pentecostal journals can perhaps best be compared with that of the banks. Sometimes the name of a branch in Hamburg or New York will correspond to that of the parent company. But it is sometimes impossible to tell from the name of a journal that it largely consists of news and articles from a particular Swedish or American Pentecostal denomination, particularly as Pentecostal articles rarely give exact details such as places, names of organizations, etc. News and articles are passed along an invisible network, which can nevertheless be disentangled by a practised observer.

It is not possible here to set out the exact degrees of relationship between the different Pentecostal organizations. We shall do no more than attempt to list the main types, looked at from the point of view of the doctrines and ideas they hold.

(*a*) *Pentecostals who teach a two-stage way of salvation*

This is far and away the largest group of organizations. Representatives of this group are the American and British Assemblies of God (chs. 3 and 15), Assembléias de Deus (ch. 6), Assemblee di Dio (ch. 19), Nicholas Bhengu (ch. 10), Elim Pentecostal Church (ch. 14), Congregação Cristã do Brasil (ch. 7), and the Protestant wing of the Pentecostal movement within the existing churches in America (ch. 1).

(*b*) *Pentecostals who teach a three-stage way of salvation*

This group is represented by the Church of God (Cleveland) (ch. 4) and its missionary churches, the Pentecostal Holiness Church[56] and others.

(*c*) *The 'Jesus Only' groups*

These accept only the baptismal formula 'in the name of Jesus'.[57] The most important representatives of this group are the United Pentecostal Church[58] and almost the entire Indonesian Pentecostal Movement.[59]

(*d*) *Pentecostals with a Quaker, Reformed, Lutheran or Roman Catholic doctrine*

With the exception of the Roman Catholic Pentecostals and the charismatic movement within the established churches in Germany (ch. 17), this type is not, as might be supposed, to be found principally in the Pentecostal movement within the existing churches. On the contrary, the bulk of the Protestant wing of the Pentecostal movement within existing churches in the USA belongs to type (*a*). On the other hand almost the entire Chilean Pentecostal movement (Methodist), the German Mülheim Association of Christian Fellowships (Lutheran and Reformed, ch. 15), part of the Swiss Pentecostal movement,[60] and the Quaker Pentecostals of the USA[61] belong to this group.

(*e*) *Independent African Pentecostal churches*

The most important groups are in South and West Africa. Examples are given in ch. 12.

(*f*) *The Latter Rain movement*

The Latter Rain movement occurs throughout the world as an enthusiastic wing of existing Pentecostal organizations. In various places it has become independent and is now in competition with existing, more traditional Pentecostal denominations. Examples are found in the Latter Rain churches in Germany[62] and in South Africa (ch. 11).

(*g*) *Pentecostal denominations of the Apostolic type*

These groups have institutionalized the offices of apostle and prophet. In the early stages of the denomination prophecy played a major role, and the church was guided by it. The theory has not altered, although the practice seems less spontaneous at the present day. This type is represented by the Apostolic Church[63] (ch. 13.4).

NOTES

1. Cf. ch. 2.3, pp. 22ff.
2. *Byposten*, 12.1.1902, p. 2; quoted in Bloch-Hoell I, p. 141.
3. *Verdens Gang*, 4.1.1967, pp. 1f.; quoted in Bloch-Hoell I, p. 142.
4. *Byposten*, 12.1.1907, p. 2; quoted in Bloch-Hoell I, p. 142.
5. *Social-Demokraten*, 4.1.1907, p. 1; quoted in Bloch-Hoell I, p. 145.
6. Cf. chs. 16–18, pp. 218ff.
7. Cf. *PGG*, pp. 252ff.
8. Cf. the biography of A. A. Boddy (07.150.001) and chs. 13–15, pp. 176ff.
9. J. Lohmann, *Sabbathklänge*, 21.7.1906, p. 46; quoted in A. Goetz, *Mehr Licht*, 28/19–20, 1954, p. 7.
10. *Allianzblatt* 1903/4, n. 18; quoted in Fleisch, I, p. 447.
11. *Auf der Warte* 2/33, 13.8.1905, pp. 7f.
12. *Reichgottesarbeiter* 3, 1906, p. 138.
13. Regehly, *Auf der Warte* 3/31, 29.7.1906, pp. 4f.
14. Busch, *Licht und Leben*; quoted by Jansen, *Zeitschrift für Religionspsychologie* 1, 1907, p. 329.
15. *Reichgottesarbeiter* 2, 1905, p. 189: answers to correspondents.

16. For the legend of the diabolic origin of the Pentecostal movement cf. ch. 16, pp. 218ff.
17. E.g. A. B. (A. Adolf?), *Nové hnutí*.
18. Cf. ch. 19.2, pp. 254ff.
19. H.-Ch. Chéry, *Offensive*, p. 329.
20. 02b.28.
21. A missionary church of the ChoG (Cleveland), cf. ch. 4, pp. 47ff.
22. Sources for this event: 02b.20.001.
23. Cf. chs. 6–8, pp. 75ff.
24. C. Lemke, *Leuchter* 15/8, Aug. 1964, pp. 3–6.
25. The evidence for this dependence is given in full in 01.36.038, and in shorter form in chs. 9 and 12.
26. Cf. ch. 12, pp. 149ff.
27. K. Schlosser, *Eingeborenenkirchen*, p. 29.
28. *Ibid.*, p. 30.
29. August Kast, a missionary of the Swiss Pentecostal Mission, who has corrected this section, deleted the last sentence. But it was printed by Bhengu in *Back to God*, July 1955 (Schlosser, *op. cit.*, p. 34). For a full account see ch. 10, pp. 126ff.
30. For the Congo cf. 01.18 and the French edition of this book.
31. D. Gee, *P* 68, 1964, p. 2; 67, 1964, p. 16.
32. M. Calley, *Aboriginal Pentecostalism.*
33. W. J. Hollenweger, *Monthly Letter on Evangelism*, Nov.–Dec. 1965.
34. D. J. Du Plessis, *History*.
35. 03.12.032.
36. 02a.02.137B.
37. 03.12.B II.
38. Formulation and justification of the question in Förlaget Filadelfia, *Europeiska*, 1939, pp. 50–7.
39. This passage does not appear in the official Swedish report of the conference, but in Steiner's own account (L. Steiner, *VdV* 33/2, Feb. 1940, p. 11). Cf. below n. 46.
40. L. F. Sumrall, *PE* 1725, 31.5.1947, pp. 6, 10–12; 1726, 7.6.1947, pp. 6f.; L. Steiner, *PE* 1728, 21.6.1947, p. 7.
41. *PE* 1833, 25.6.1949, pp. 8–11. Duplicated statutes for a World Pentecostal Fellowship in the possession of the author.
42. D. Gee, *Wind and Flame*, p. 247; *P* 21, 1952, pp. 1, 3–5; *PE* 1995, 3.8.1952, pp. 11f. The souvenir brochure (H. W. Greenway, D. Gee, I. Macpherson, eds., *World Conference 1952*) was published *before* the conference and does not contain any reports of discussion.
43. Förlaget Filadelfia, *Världpingstkonferensen, 1955*.
44. D. Gee (ed.), *Fifth Conference, 1958*.
45. L. Steiner in D. Gee (ed.), *Fifth Conference, 1958*, pp. 139–48. This speech by Steiner follows in its essentials his earlier statements, e.g. L. Steiner, *VdV* 50/4, April 1957, pp. 7–8, 10f.; 50/5, May 1957, pp. 2–7.
46. Letter from L. Steiner to W.H., 14.4.1960. The suppression of displeasing or controversial statements in what purports to be an official record gives an odd impression.
47. Cf. ch. 3.2(*b*), p. 35, and ch. 25, pp. 353ff.
48. Letter from L. Steiner to W.H., 14.4.1960.
49. J. A. Synan, 'Purpose', in D. Gee (ed.), *Fifth Conference, 1958*, pp. 27–36.
50. D. Gee, 'The Pentecostal Experience', *ibid.*, pp. 43–52.
51. Cf. bibliography.
52. Cf. ch. 15.2(*b*), pp. 208ff.

53. D. Gee (ed.), *Sixth Conference, 1961*.
54. G. E. Valdivia, letter to W.H., 10.12.1970.
55. *Revista Bibliográphica*, quoted in *P* 55, 1961, p. 3.
56. 02a.01.110.
57. Cf. ch. 3.1(*b*), pp. 31ff.
58. 02a.02.140.
59. W. J. Hollenweger, in *Nieuwe creative vormen van christen-zijn* (in preparation).
60. *PGG*, pp. 252–75.
61. 02a.02.D.V.
62. 05.07.034, 05.07.035, 05.07.036, 05.07.037.
63. 05.13.022.

BRAZIL

6

A Worker Founds the Largest Protestant Church in Latin America: Daniel Berg and the Assembléias de Deus in Brazil[1]

1. *Origin*

THE ORIGIN of the Assembléias de Deus in Brazil is indissolubly bound up with the life of the simple Swedish workers Daniel Berg and Gunnar Vingren.

Berg was born in Southern Sweden in 1885 or 1884, baptized in a Swedish Baptist community in 1899, and emigrated to the USA in 1902. In 1909 he was on a visit to Sweden where a friend, who meanwhile had become a preacher, told him about the baptism of the Spirit which he experienced in the same year. On his return to the United States he joined W. H. Durham's congregation in Chicago.[2] His friend Vingren was shown in a dream that the two of them were to go as missionaries to Pará.[3] They did not know where Pará was, but they discovered from the City Library in Chicago that it was a state in Brazil. They saved $90 for their fare, but had to give it to a Pentecostal newspaper as the result of a revelation. Shortly afterwards, however, they again got enough money for their fares.

They came to Belém in 1910. Berg earned his living as a foundryman in a steel works and while doing so learned Portuguese. Originally they had little success with their missionary work within the Baptist congregation of Belém. They held prayer meetings in the cellar of the Baptist chapel and waited for a revival in Brazil. When some of the Baptists began to speak in tongues, experienced the baptism of the Spirit and soon carried out missionary work with fiery zeal in their neighbourhood, the Baptist preacher of Belém found himself compelled to intervene.

In what follows I shall compare Berg's account with that of the Baptist preacher of Belém:

One evening the local preacher appeared in our simple premises. When he opened the door, a wave of song and prayers struck him. We got up and invited him to take part in our improvised service. He refused and declared that it was now time to make a decision. He said that a short time before he had discovered that people had dared to engage in a discussion of doctrine,[4] something that had never happened before. He accused us of sowing doubt and unrest and of being separatists.

Gunnar Vingren got up and declared that we did not desire any division. On the contrary, we wanted unity among everyone. If only everyone had the experience of the baptism of the Spirit, we would never be divided. On the contrary, we would then be more than brothers, like a family.

The local preacher spoke again. The discussion was open. He said that the Bible did indeed speak about the baptism of the Spirit and also said that Jesus healed the sick. But that was in *those* days. He said that it would be absurd if educated people of our time believed that such things could happen today. We had to be realistic – he continued – and not waste time with dreams[5] and false prophecies. Nowadays we had knowledge to know what to do with it. 'If you do not mend your ways and recognize your error, it is my duty to inform all the Baptist congregations and to warn them about your false doctrine.'

Vingren listened to these words very quietly and then replied: 'Brothers, we should not allow themes as important as those we have discussed to be lost in a personal dispute. We are both servants of God and so we both want to stand in the truth, for he to whom we pray is the truth. In my view we are colleagues and not competitors.[6] *Who* brings souls to God is a matter of secondary importance. What is important is the fact that more and more souls are saved. I would not want to say that the brother does not stand in the truth but that he has not found the whole truth. [He does not have] the truth of the baptism of the Spirit and the healing of the sick by Jesus, as we can experience them today.'

When Vingren had finished, the preacher looked round at all those present in the hope that someone would support him. But no one did so. Then he looked pointedly at a deacon and waited for his judgment on the question. This deacon, one of the oldest pillars in the church, stood up after he had been looked at in this way and remarked in the name of all those present: 'I can understand your feelings very well, pastor. You say that you have come into a group of traitors who have departed from your teaching. You think that we are not following the way you have shown us. But that is not true. We have never been so certain our of cause as we are now. We have never had as much faith as we have now. We have found even more: faith and power of the Holy Spirit.

'We do not hold it against you that you did not say these things to us, for you did not know them yourself and so you could not teach them. But we very much want you also to receive these blessings from God. Then we shall understand each other better and feel the same unity with the brothers who have come to us from abroad.

'All the members of this church, pastor, are now on "higher ground" and nearer to heaven. You yourself said that you wanted to be a realist. Very good, I will give you some instances of realities of the healing power of Jesus in our days: these sisters, who have belonged to our congregation for years, used to have to walk on crutches (perhaps you never even noticed). Now they no longer need them. The crutches hang on the wall of their house, visible to everyone, so that all can see the wonderful way in which Jesus has healed them. And Jesus has healed not only them, but also a tumour on the throat.

'Dear preacher', the deacon continued, 'we cannot and will not accuse you. You have worked to win souls for Jesus. You have asked Jesus for strength to stand fast in sickness. But you have not prayed for healing from sickness, because you did not believe in that. Now you have seen with your own eyes the instances which I have mentioned.'

Hoping for an expression in his support, the preacher let his eyes sweep round the room. In vain. He turned to me and brother Vingren and said, 'I have come to a decision. From now on you may not meet here any longer. Look for another place. After what has happened here we no longer want you.' Then he turned to the small group of people and asked, 'How many of you are in agreement with the false teaching?' Eighteen people resolutely raised their hands.[7] They knew that that meant their expulsion from the church.

We thanked the preacher for the common life (that lay behind us) and hoped that he would soon receive the blessing of the baptism of the Spirit. He did not reply, but turned his back on us and walked out . . .

(The account then goes on to tell of the move into the house of one of the group, where 'the first Pentecostal service in Brazil was officially celebrated'.)[8]

The Baptist author de Mesquita reports the matter as follows:

In April 1911, two Swedish missionaries, Gunnar Vingren and Daniel Berg, landed in Belém. They called themselves Baptists . . . They immediately went to Nelson,[9] their fellow-countryman, to find shelter with him. They were offered the cellar of the church; they put up there and learnt the language in order to be able to *help*[10] Nelson in the work of evangelization. The good missionary [Nelson] then made one of his numerous journeys into the state of Piaui and left these two behind in the church, in the sweet hope that even though they could not speak [Portuguese], they would be able to continue the work.[11] After a short while, however, these (so-called) Baptists began to quiver and shriek in a meeting. Soon Brazilians imitated them. What had happened? What kind of a new religion was this, people asked. They replied that it was the baptism of the Spirit. The speaking with tongues and the cackling made the services frightful. Nelson was away, and the work of the congregation was under the supervision of a young man without any experience. . . . The whole church was infected, because so many people were already talking in this so-called speaking with tongues, with the exception of the deacons, whom this development did not escape. The evangelist called a meeting of the congregation with the help of the organist, declared the Pentecostals, who were already in the majority, to be outside the order and with the help (of the minority who had remained Baptists) excommunicated those who had falsified sound doctrine. The latter attempted to assert their rights as the majority, but they were excluded. In this way the congregation was decimated ... That was the beginning of the Pentecostal movement in Brazil.[12]

Growth of the Assembléias de Deus (M=Member C=Congregation)

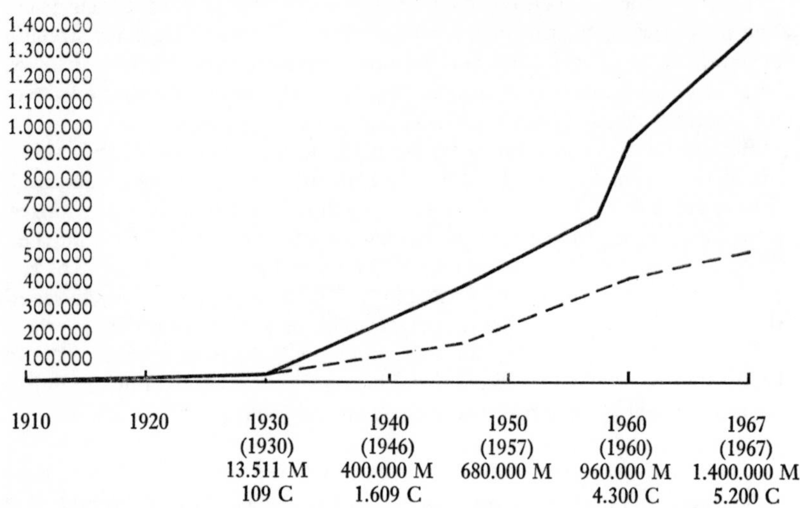

From Belém, the Pentecostals did missionary work in the Amazon region; in the twenties they pressed south into the industrial and coffee growing areas and founded large communities in the cities of Rio de Janeiro, São Paulo, Pôrto Alegre etc. In 1930, a number of preachers from the Igreja de Cristo (Mata Grande, Alagoas), an American evangelical church, joined forces with the Assembléias de Deus. From that year they moved also into the interior. At a very early stage (from 1913), missionaries were sent to Portugal,[13] and later also to Madagascar and France.[14]

Many of their churches have several thousand members, the largest in Recife comprising about 7,000. In Rio they have 6,500 communicants, hold 180 services a week, run 15 Sunday schools, 3 grammar schools, a Bible class and a trade school.[15] In São Paulo they baptized 10,000 converts in a year.

Workers have gone where the people are. Churches have been established first in the metropolitan areas; then branches have been established later in the interior. As a result about 80% of the Assembléias de Deus membership is concentrated in strategic centres where 93% of Brazil's population lives.[16]

Today the Assembléias de Deus are by far the largest evangelical church in Brazil. Along with the Catholics they are the only ones to be represented in all the states of Brazil. As William R. Read rightly remarks, 'Singer sewing machines, Coca-Cola, Lucky Strike and the Assemblies are there.'[17] And they have done all this through their own resources, unlike the other evangelical churches, which are generously supported with money and personnel from USA.

Quite apart from the difficult problems of obtaining accurate statistics,[18] which will not be discussed here, the growth of the Assembléias de Deus is unparalleled in recent church history and its significance for theology and the ecumenical movement is not to be underestimated.

Although Emilio Conde believes that only faith can rightly record the history of the Assembléias de Deus,[19] his *História das Assembléias de Deus* is a remarkably dry enumeration of names, places and dates, like a chronicle or even an annal. The book is based on reliable reports, personal interviews, letters, newspaper articles (but all without documentation), and can be regarded as a good source. But it is difficult to read. One cannot yet expect a historical treatment from the Brazilian Pentecostal movement.

The conversion of Jose Gomes Moreno, later a preacher and broadcaster, may be typical of their kind of evangelistic work. Moreno was originally a player in the 'Corinth' football team in São Paulo. One day he kicked the ball into the crowd instead of the goal, and a woman was so badly hurt that she had to be taken to hospital. Tormented by conscience, he visited her. She heaped insults on him: 'You useless man! Watch out that you do not become a murderer. Some "*crentes*", members of the Assembléias de Deus, who visited me here, told me that Jesus is the same yesterday, today and to all eternity, and that useless people like you can again be set on the right way.' The sick woman, Dona Amelia, regarded herself as a good Catholic, and did not need the help of these '*crentes*'.

Moreno obediently went to the meeting, as he was bidden, and thought to himself, 'I have seen Jesus in the circus, the theatre and the cinema, but never in a church. I wonder what he looks like?' He thought Jesus was a famous actor.

The preacher made hell hot for Moreno, by describing the latter's dissolute life. 'You'll end up killing your own father,' he shouted. At the end of the sermon he pointed to him and said, 'This young man is to come forward and give his heart to Jesus.' Moreno came forward and was converted. After three days he returned and asked to be prayed for. He thought that he was not normal any more, because for three days he had not been able to smoke, but he was told that non-smoking was normal for a Christian. After several months he visited Dona Amelia again and prayed for her health. She was immediately cured and converted.[20]

2. *Social Work*

The Assembléias de Deus recruit their members from the great mass of the Brazilian people, i.e. from the lower strata, including those of mixed race and

Indians.[21] They have a very high opinion of Martin Luther King.[22] Political and social engagement goes hand in hand with evangelization.

> Christ attached an extraordinary value to man. So much so, that he died on the cross. That is sufficient reason for the Christian leader to attach considerable importance to human problems. In one sense Jesus was a humanist *par excellence*.[23]

Communism does not arise – as is so often said – by alien infiltration, but in the 'trough of misery'. It 'is nourished by poverty and injustice'. 'Communism denies God, but *laissez faire* (*comodismo*) denies one's neighbour. Both are equally unjust.'[24] However one cannot deny that in recent years members of the middle class have joined them.[25] They carry on an aggressive programme of education among their members, teach those who are still illiterate, print and distribute an incredible amount of literature,[26] build community libraries, day nurseries[27] and carry on Portuguese courses. They have established a provident fund for expectant mothers, the sick and the orphaned, which is supported by public means because, as Conde proudly remarks, 'it does valuable service to the public'.[28]

Church organization is a remarkable mixture of free congregationalism and the takeover of certain functions by the central authorities. Thus the 'ministerio' (as the united community is called) of Ipirange (São Paulo) was originally independent; in 1942 it became part of the 'ministerio' of Belenzinho; in 1952 it again gained its independence. In São Paulo and surroundings it has six preachers, nine elders, an evangelist and thirty communities with a total of three thousand members. It runs a tile factory. In its community centre there is a polyclinic and a dental clinic (with reduced prices), schools for Portuguese, typewriting, sawing, music and a primary school. The secretary of the 'ministerio' remarked to Key Yuasa: 'God cares for our souls, so we have to care for bodies.' A hospital, an old people's home, a secondary school and a Bible school are in process of construction. The different 'ministerios' overlap geographically. But they have the same newspapers, the same radio programme, and the same regional and general conferences. One can often hear the expression: 'Many "ministerios" but one "assembly of God".' This, then is a type of church which for the first time realizes community on a large scale in non-parochial structures.[29]

So far, no hostility to education can be detected. On the contrary, the journal *A Seara* reports:

> We are delighted to note a further victory for our church. Thanks to state grants, Alcidio Donato, a young member of the church born in humble circumstances, has been able to complete his medical studies.[30]

When high officers of the General Staff, the Governor, members of Congress or even the Vice-President of Brazil take part in the consecration of a new church, the fact is noted with satisfaction.[31] Perhaps there have been some changes here in the last twenty years, since Emilio Conde wrote in 1944 that the call for educated preachers would be a return to Egypt.[32]

3. *Relationships with Other Churches*

(*a*) *With the Roman Catholic church*

Occasional persecutions have been carried on by the lower Catholic clergy. But according to the sources at my disposal, the Protestants are protected by the secular authorities, as e.g. the Varjão family in Picos (Piauí). The incitement of the priest of Picos to boycott the Pentecostal family in the shops even led to the expulsion of the 'wicked priest' and caused the bishop of Oeiras to declare on a visit to Picos that the people of the city were committing a crime if they persecuted the evangelicals. He added, 'All should bow their heads, be ashamed of themselves and ask God for forgiveness for this sin.'[33] Nevertheless there are still occasional polemical articles in the *Mensageiro da Paz*, asserting that Rome has not really changed, it merely uses different tactics.[34]

(*b*) *With the Ecumenical movement*

At local level, the Assembléias de Deus are prepared to practise intercommunion with other Pentecostal groups and with Baptist churches.[35] Nor is their relationship with the other Brazilian Protestants a bad one. But the influence of the fundamentalists in the Protestant churches of Brazil and the general mistrust of the Ecumenical movement by the evangelical church of Brazil has led the Assembléias de Deus to speak out against the ecumenical movement.

The General Assembly of Preachers of the Assembléias de Deus declared in 1963: 'Ecumenism', represented by the World Council of Churches and the Vatican Council in Rome, has a tendency towards apostasy. Fellowship with churches which manifestly practise 'idolatry' and which believe in justification by good works (the Roman Catholic church) and on the other hand with churches which deny the divinity of Jesus or his virgin birth, the necessity of rebirth, the resurrection of Christ and his second coming (World Council of Churches), is impossible for a Pentecostal. The Protestants in the World Council of Churches have betrayed those who died as martyrs for the sake of the faith.[36] Nevertheless, two 'delegate observers' of the Assembléias de Deus[37] took part in the Full Assembly of the World Council in Uppsala (1968). Conde could not refrain from uttering polemics against pagan modernism in the Protestant churches,[38] which are guilty of being the 'church without brilliance'.[39] The churches have not imitated the bees, who for centuries have kept collecting the same flowers and the same honey and live off that, but have thought that they had to change the honey of the gospel for their own sugared water.

(*c*) *With the North American Assemblies of God*

In the mission statistics of the North American Assemblies of God, the Assembléias de Deus figure as their mission church. In contrast, the Brazilian Pentecostals regard themselves as an independent church. Certainly, there are some North American 'fraternal workers' among the several thousand Brazilian Pentecostal preachers who are principally involved in directing Bible schools and radio programmes.[40] They are regarded by the Brazilians as technical specialists, but not acknowledged as superiors, unless the recent visit of the Assemblies of God Chaplain John A. Lindvall (who as chaplain of the American paratroopers in the Dominican Republic in 1965 met Brazilian troops)[41] had political connotations.

4. *Doctrine*

The Assembléias de Deus have published a summary of their doctrine for brothers from other denominations:

> We, the believers of the Assembléias de Deus, believe, like you, that Jesus is the unique and sole sufficient Saviour, that salvation is entirely by grace, by means of faith in Jesus Christ. We believe in all the doctrines taught by Jesus and by the apostles, and we also believe that 'Jesus Christ is the same yesterday, today and eternally'. For that reason, and for that reason alone, we believe that he still baptizes with the Holy Spirit, since he is still the same. 'For indeed, John baptized with water, but you will be baptized with the Holy Spirit.'
>
> The baptism of the Holy Spirit is not received at the hour of salvation nor at the hour of baptism with water. The believers of Samaria were saved and baptized in water, but they had not yet received the baptism of the Holy Spirit (Acts 8.15f). Those who believed at the house of Cornelius were saved and received the baptism of the Holy Spirit before receiving baptism with water (Acts 10.44).
>
> The sign of the baptism of the Holy Spirit is speaking in foreign tongues. That is what happened on the day of Pentecost (Acts 2.4); in the house of Cornelius (10.46); at Ephesus (19.6). At Samaria, the same sign occurred after Simon had offered money to the apostles: at that time a sign came on those who were baptized with the Holy Spirit (7.19).
>
> . . . The baptism of the Holy Spirit is not salvation. Salvation comes by faith; but the baptism of the Spirit is a blessing that derives from salvation. To accept the salvation that God offers and to reject or neglect the baptism of the Spirit that he has equally offered cannot but be a grave sin against the honour of the heavenly Father. Brothers of the denominations, all you who are saved, rediscover the baptism of the Holy Spirit.[42]

For their domestic use they took over the confession of the North American Assemblies of God.[43]

NOTES

1. Evidence, documents, literature: 02b.05.012. Statistics: 1,700,000 members, 5,000 communities, 5,500 preachers (1968). Main journal, *Mensageiro da Paz.*

2. Cf. ch. 2.4, pp. 24ff.

3. According to Du Plessis, *History*, the word 'pará' kept cropping up in the speaking with tongues.

4. D. Berg, *Enviado*, p. 37.

5. A clear dig at Berg's dream.

6. Vingren, who came straight from the Baptist Bible School in Chicago, was thus indicating indirectly that while he had saved more souls than the local preacher, he was ready to recognize him as a colleague, though not as a superior.

7. Conde enumerates the names of 17 people (E. Conde, *História*, pp. 25f.).

8. D. Berg, *Enviado*, pp. 37–41. Cf. too I. Vingren, *Pionjärens dagbok.*

9. A Swedish Baptist missionary.

10. De Mesquita stresses the word ironically.

11. 'Trabalho' is the designation for community life used by the activist Protestant churches of Brazil.

12. A. N. de Mesquita, *História* II, pp. 136f.

13. E. Conde, *História*, 36; *Mensageiro da Paz* 39/19, 15.10.1969, p. 6.

14. Edison da Costa Navarro, *Mensageiro da Paz* 39/21f., 30.11.1969, pp. 8, 6. O. and M. Lagerstrom, *Mensageiro da Paz* 38/11, 1.6.1968, pp. 1, 5.

15. E. Conde, *P* 57, 1961, p. 1. Read gives much higher statistics: Rio de Janeiro, 40,000; Pôrto Alegre, 25,000; Belém, 30,000; Recife, 22,000; São Paulo, 30,000 (W. R. Read *et al.*, *Latin American Church Growth*, p. 68).

16. *PE* 2712, 1.5.1966, pp. 8f.

17. W. R. Read, *New Patterns*, p. 131.

18. Special statistical questions are discussed by W. R. Read, *New Patterns*, and H. Meyer, 'Die Evangelische Diaspora', *Jahrbuch des Gustav-Adolf-Vereins* 39, 1968, pp. 9–50.

19. E. Conde, *História*, p. 9.

20. N. L. Olson, *PE* 2472, 24.9.1961, pp. 6f.

21. Cf. the critical report on the Hearing of the Fundação Nacional do Indios on the massacre of Indians in Brazil, *Mensageiro da Paz* 39/19, 15.10.1969, p. 8.

22. Joanyr de Oliveira, *Martin Luther King e a Igreja hodierne*, 1968; *Mensageiro da Paz* 38/11, 1.6.1968, p. 5.

23. Joanyr de Oliveira, *Mensageiro da Paz* 38/11, 1.6.1968, pp. 4f. (interview with Lewi Pethrus).

24. Joanyr de Oliveira, 'Nem Comunismo, nem comodismo', *Mensageiro da Paz* 39/19, 15.10.1969, p. 2.

25. Thus e.g. the police sergeant Paulino F. Rodrigues, who later became prefect of Pindaré-Mirim (E. Conde, *História*, p. 95).

26. Cf. ch. 5.6, pp. 69ff.

27. R. Alencar, *A Seara* 2/6, Nov.–Dec. 1957, p. 51.

28. E. Conde, *História*, p. 154.

29. I am grateful to Key Yuasa for this information.

30. *A Seara* 2/6, Nov.–Dec. 1957, p. 50.

31. E. Conde, *P* 57, 1961, p. 1; O. S. Boyer, *P* 25, 1951, p. 1.

32. E. Conde, *Etapas*, p. 109.

33. E. Conde, *História*, p. 112.

34. *A Seara* 2/6, Nov.–Dec. 1957, pp. 40, 42; Antonieto Grageiro Sobrinho, *Mensageiro da Paz* 39/17, 15.9.1969, p. 2; *Mensageiro da Paz*, 31.10.1969, pp. 4, 7.

35. E. Conde, *Testemunho*, p. 181.

36. A. P. dos Santos, *Mensageiro da Paz*, 33/3, Feb. 1963, p. 8; reprinted: 38/4, 16.7.1968, pp. 1, 6.

37. Ezequias Ribeiro Brizola, Antonio de Oliviera Rocha.

38. E. Conde, *Pentecoste*, p. 23.

39. E. Conde, *Igreja sem brilho*, p. 30.

40. S. Nyström, *PE* 1586, 30.9.1944, pp. 6f.; C. Carmichael, *PE* 2771, 18.6.1967, pp. 21f.; T. R. Hoover, *PE* 2858, 16.2.1969, pp. 18f.

41. J. A. Lindvall, *Mensageiro da Paz* 39/17, 15.9.1969, pp. 8, 7.

42. *Mensageiro da Paz*, 15.2.1950; quoted by E. G. Léonard, *L'illuminisme*, pp. 65f.

43. AoG, cf. ch. 3: the confession of the AoG is in Appendix: 2 (pp. 514ff.); there are too the characteristic alterations made by the AdD.

7

A Religion by Word of Mouth: The Waldensian Luigi Francescon and the 'Congregaçâo Cristã do Brasil'[1]

1. *Origin and religious character*

IN 1910, Luigi Francescon, an Italian American, came to Brazil and brought to South America the Pentecostal message which he, like Berg and Vingren, had come to know in Chicago. In the Jardin da Luz, São Paulo, he met an Italian who was converted and served as a stepping stone to other Italians in Brazil. The first two communities were founded in Santa Antonio da Platina, from former Catholics, and in São Paulo, from former Protestants. Since then the church has experienced a steady growth which is all the more astonishing in that the members of the Congregação Cristã, unlike other Pentecostals, do not hold open air meetings and do not publicize themselves either by printed matter or by radio programmes;[2] they rely entirely on the personal testimony of their members. The community does not employ any pastors in the traditional sense. The elders and deacons carry on the preaching; often the same elder performs different functions in different communities (see diagram 2). During the service anyone can give testimony or prophecy, but the community passes judgment on everything (I Cor. 14.29). The only full-time functionary is the book-keeper. The whole proclamation is oral (geared to illiterates).

The following table shows the astounding growth of the Congregação Cristã:

	Growth rate members	Number of Communities	Number of Buildings	Resources (*cruzeiros*)
1936	2,100	244	32	857,521.—
1946	7,377	513	107	5,130,296.—
1956	16,246	1,095	477	96,910,909.50
1957	17,383	1,176	499	122,015,254.90
1958	17,224	1,278	552	152,977,047.80
1967		2,500		

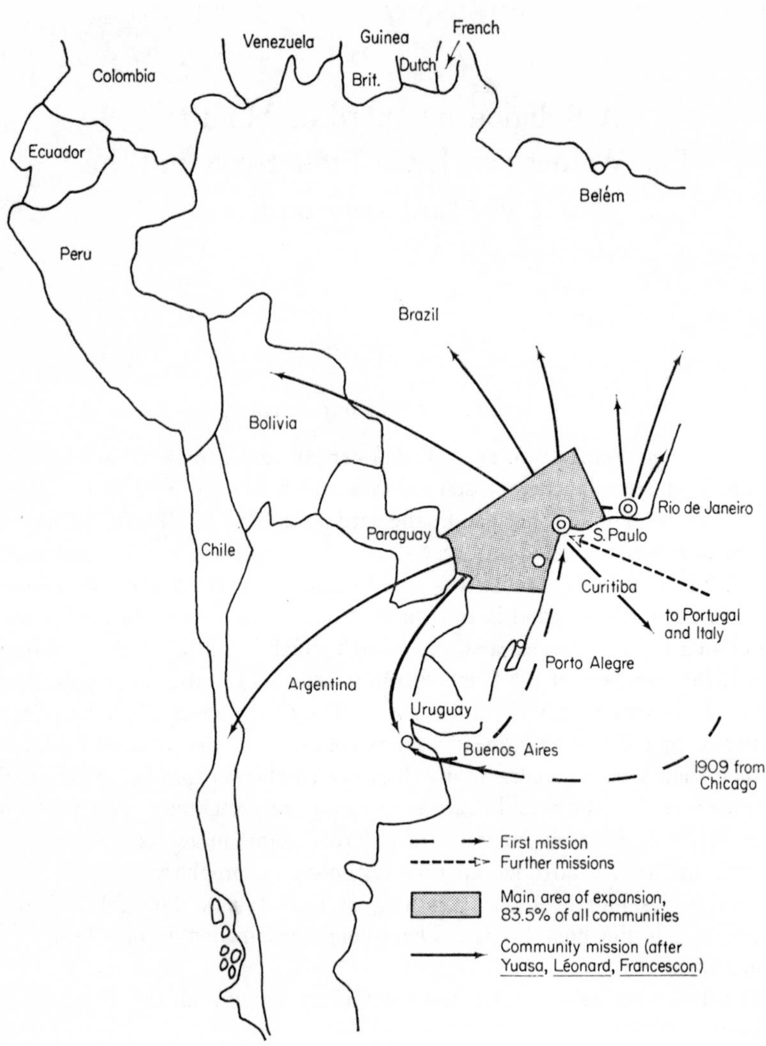

Expansion of the Congregação Cristã do Brasil

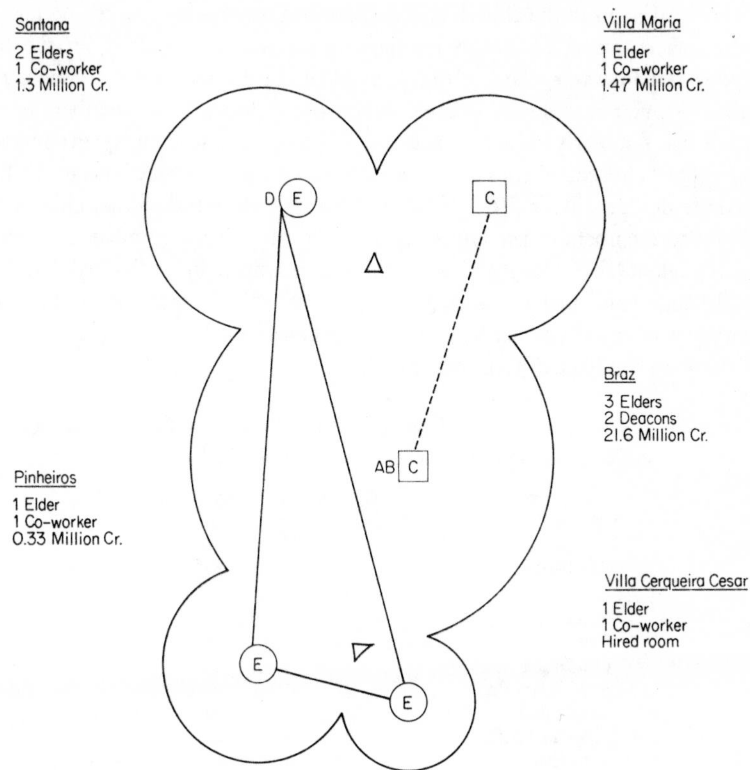

(All details follow the *Relatorio e Balanco* for 1958, ed. 1959, after notes by Yuasa; in each case the lowest line gives the value of the church building in millions of cruzeiros.)

Schematic plan

Functions of the elders in different communities

Income for 1958 was 36,559,753·50 cr., of which 5,768,850 cr. (i.e. a sixth) was set aside for the 'obra de piedade' (see p. 90 below).

The focal point of the church is in and around São Paulo. The reason for this is the concentration of Italian immigrants in this city. Indeed, in the first decades Italian was spoken in the services of the Congregação. It was a real 'Italian popular movement' (Read). When the 'Glorias' – as members of the church are familiarly called – meet on Wednesday and Sunday evenings at their central church, which holds 7,000, there are regular traffic jams in the Rua Visconde de Parnaiba in Brás. While for example the Presbyterian church has only 8,000 members in the city of São Paulo, the Glorias number 110,000 in this city alone!.[3] A classification of the communities by individual states in Brazil,[4] and baptismal statistics from the year 1962,[5] clearly show the predominance of the church in São Paulo. The Congregação can even stand comparison with the Roman Catholic church:

Number of Catholic communities and communities of the Congregação in some dioceses in the neighbourhood of São Paulo (1948)

Diocese	Catholic communities	Congregação Cristã
São Paulo	129	82[6]
Santos	25	5
Sorocaba	32	71(!)
Assis	28	16
Cafelandia	44	55(!)
S. José Rio Preto	41	41
Jaboticabal	24	9
Ribeirão Preto	51	28
S. Carlos	42	26
Campinas	42	17[7]

Obviously a community of the Congregação Cristã does not have the social weight and the size of a Roman Catholic parish. But if, on the other hand, only the numbers of members are compared, an equally false picture arises, because the Roman Catholic church counts all nominal Christians, including infants and those who rarely come to church, if at all, whereas the Congregação Cristã, like all free churches, counts only adult members. The significance of the small but vigorous communities is greater than might be expected from their numerical strength. The fact that the communities have their focal point in the industrial centre of Sorocaba shows immediately the influence of this worker-church. This does not prevent the church from also finding a way to farmworkers and peasants in the interior of the country. Among them are a number of members of the professions, but 'it has not yet pleased the Lord to make them elders'.[8]

The women dress carefully for worship, and wear imitation jewellery and bright hair bands. Make-up and nail varnish are not forbidden, but they are not used. The community passionately rejects any kind of legalistic ethic, explicitly dissociates itself from the Anglo-Saxon observance of Sunday (a position which is regarded as heretical by the other evangelical churches) and even rejects the regulation tithe which is practised so widely among the Pentecostals.[9]

The time of persecution was endured with silent suffering, without retaliation by informing the police. The young community regarded the persecution not primarily as a question of 'religious freedom', but as 'testing sent by God', who had told them: 'If this flock remains true to my word, I will increase it by those who are called to be saved.'[10] The church regards its own history as a fulfilment of the promises given to Luigi Francescon.[11]

Léonard, too, has discerned that hymns and choruses are the liturgical elements in their services by the aid of which the leader of the assembly pilots the community safely through the strongest storms of feeling. Many hymns have a definite function. Every member knows, for example, that general intercessions rather than personal prayers and testimonies are made after the chorus 'Praise, Honour and Glory', that the notices come after 'Under the Blood . . .', etc. This happens in most Pentecostal communities, but the different choruses do not always have the same function in the different communities. Davis and Read have given vivid descriptions of the prayers repeated by the whole community in shouts and whispered words and of the enthusiastic singing, often accompanied by great orchestras.[12]

Léonard gives many instances of conversions. For instance, there is the Negro elder of Piracicaba, Bento. A 'Gloria' gave a testimony on the basis of the Bible to Bento who at that time had not yet been converted. Bento got his Bible so as to be able to contradict the 'Gloria'. But – alas – he was forced to make the discovery that his Bible was a history of the saints. Now he began to compare the sermons of his favourite priest with the Bible, which he read night-long, and in 1937 this led to his conversion.[13]

Another instance: Lucas A. and his wife had become alcoholics. Lucas was a bully. He always carried a weapon. He took part passionately in the 'cururu', a singing competition in which each competitor had to continue the theme or the story of the previous singer as skilfully and dramatically as possible. The themes of the 'cururu' singers were often taken from the Bible, so Lucas A. also owned a Bible and read it. When he contracted tuberculosis, he sought relief among the fetishists and the Macumbas. A 'Gloria' visited him and wanted to teach him about the Bible. At that point, however, the 'cururu' singer proudly showed off his knowledge of the Bible. The 'Gloria' built on this foundation and showed him the way to conversion and to liberation from his alcoholism.[14]

A girl student, Celisah Ulhôa Tenória, gives the following description of a meeting of the 'Glorias':

They kneel down. They all pray individually in louder or softer voices. Beside me, someone is praying: 'O Jesus, your name is holy! Glory be to your holy name!' Another prays: 'The Lord have mercy on our souls! May he have mercy on our sins!' Another says, 'Have pity on those who do not know you, glorious Father! Holy one, your name is holy!'

The sounds of praise increase; the murmur of voices grows louder. Some women pray in foreign languages . . . In the midst of this tumult the Holy Spirit gives the word to one of the faithful who begins to speak, uttering loud cries. The murmuring of the brothers increases and all pay attention. He asks for help for young children, that they may not learn what is bad; for widows and widowers: some women weep. Waves of prayer come and go; there are sounds of approval for the words of the one who is thus inspired. These waves of fervour now increase, now diminish in intensity; sometimes they reach a real paroxysm of religious exaltation. The man speaks louder and louder. He appeals to God for the work and the power of the Lord to continue. In the midst of this exaltation many people weep. All the men simultaneously make a backwards and forwards movement. The man continues, 'Send your word, Lord, so that we may go from here filled with your wisdom. Come, Lord of glory, bless us all.' During all this time he speaks in good, fluent Portuguese. The contrast between the man's uncultivated exterior and what he says is remarkable.[15]

2. *The Social Function*

Despite its indifference to education, the church exercises an educative effect on the lowest classes, because it helps them towards an ordered, responsible life. The Waldensian heritage (Francescon) leads to the demand for a high degree of responsibility towards fellow men, going beyond the individualistic understanding of the average Protestant, as evidence of faith in the Holy Spirit. Its preaching is protected against fragmentation into individual testimony and authenticated by what is called 'works of devotion' (obra de piedade). The 'obra de piedade' in São Paulo were described to me by Key Yuasa as follows: Every Tuesday, about 390 people gather together for a prayer meeting. After the meeting, about 100 women (mostly illiterates) remain behind to be given 'works of devotion' (probably following the early Christian office of widow). A committee of eight, six women and two men (the only men who have access to the 'works of piety') take their places at a table in front of the meeting. If one of the women knows of any need in her neighbourhood, she can come forward and report the matter to the committee. Then the whole meeting prays silently for the guidance of the Holy Spirit. After that a definite form of help is proposed, either money or direct aid. The proposal of a single individual is not enough; it has to be confirmed by a second person, otherwise the request is not accepted. If the request is supported by a second woman, the money, if monetary help is required, is paid out immediately. The person who has made the request has the task of making clear to the recipient that this help does not come from an individual, but from the church, in God's name. The recipient is not to feel humiliated because of the money; at the same time, however, it is to be used rightly, because it is God's money. This is a very tangible way of teaching responsibility for possessions and towards one's fellow men. Help is not restricted to the members of the Congregação Cristã. In addition the church has developed even greater industrial undertakings in order to deal with unemployment. In these industrial undertakings it preaches the gospel by ruling that on grounds of principle only a small proportion of those involved (about 6%) are to belong to its community.

This is an attempt to take up the Waldensian tradition of co-operative help and at the same time to avoid a complicated institutional apparatus involving both church and state. Whether this will also be possible in the future, e.g. by stronger engagement in industrial mass-production, is a vital question.

The income of the church from the collections of its members is significant, although the tithe is not obligatory. Thus in 1945, 190,000 cruzeiros were sent to Italy; in 1958 the income of the 'obra de piedade' amounted to 5,768,850.80 crs.[16]

3. *Doctrine*

Doctrine is basically that of the Pentecostal movement as a whole, but it has some typically Brazilian features and shows some signs of Waldensian influence.[17] The criteria for distinguishing between true prophecy and false are practical and effective: 'Anyone who in prayer or witness shows any antipathy towards a brother has not been guided by the Lord, but by his feelings.' Rules about travelling church members and elders have been established which recall parallel ordinances in one of the earliest community rules in the history of the church, the Didache: on journeys for their ministry they are given hospitality by members of the community, but on private journeys they are to spend the night in a hotel. The repudiation of all marriage and funeral ceremonies is a protest against the luxuriant festivities of Brazilian catholicism. In the section on 'sin' a distinction is made between sins committed before conversion and those committed afterwards. The former 'will be forgiven, however great they may be, if the sinner believes in him (Jesus)'. 'Sins which are committed after receiving the Lord will be judged by the church.' The refusal of gifts of real property which cannot be used directly by the church is realistic, and should be understood as a protest against the property politics of the Catholic church in Brazil.

Léonard sees in this 'oral form of Christianity' the danger of a neglect of the written word. Knowledge of the Bible in this church seems modest in contrast to the rest of the Pentecostal movement. No Sunday school work is carried on. The judgment of an investigator, 'The Holy Spirit teaches them; any ass can become one of their preachers; it is a religion against study and against progress',[18] is probably too harsh. Nevertheless, in the eyes of the Congregação Cristã, any study is useless for the spiritual life. Léonard asks:

> Have we in fact reached an age which is . . . no longer that of the book? Is the Congregação Cristã a Protestant church which reaches those proletarians who accept their fate without wanting to break out of it?[19]

This criticism by Léonard must be compared with Harding Meyer's judgment. He claims that the authority of holy Scripture can hardly be stressed more strongly than in the statutes of the church and in the 'articles of faith'.[20]

> Of course, it is another question how far *de facto* they have surrendered Scripture as a binding force. Here Léonard's criticism may to some degree be justified. Thus, for example, sermons are as a rule intended to be expositions of Scripture in that they begin from biblical texts. But as the Spirit only 'calls' the preacher during the service and no one knows beforehand who will have to preach, the degree to which such a sermon is really bound by and based on Scripture, as it is when preceded by exegesis and meditation, is surely highly questionable.[21]

Here, as often in the Pentecostal movement, practice raises afresh a theological question which had been thought to be settled. The question that we must ask must therefore be: does control by the community guarantee that a sermon is based on Scripture? Or does the absence of preceding exegesis and meditation put in question this relationship to Scripture? If we take into account the preaching of the early church and the Reformers, we may have to modify the question in the following way: In what conditions can the spontaneous (and indeed the prepared) sermon be scriptural?

NOTES

1. Evidence, documents, literature: 02b.05.017. No journal! Statistics: 700,000 members, 2,500 communities (1968).

2. Congregação Cristã, *Resumo Convençã*, 1936, 1948, p. 24; E. G. Leonard, *Revista de História* 5, 1952 (no. 12), p. 438; *id.*, *L'illuminisme*, p. 71.

3. W. R. Read, *New Patterns*, p. 23.

4. São Paulo, 758; Federal district, 2; Alagoas, 1; Paraná, 330; Rio de Janeiro, 15; Sergipe, 3; Minas Gerais, 90; Santa Catarina, 3; Ceará, 3; Bahia, 24; Rio Grande do Sul, 2; Mato Grosso, 27; Espiríto Santo, 2; Goiás, 17; Pernambuco, 1. Total 1,278 (Yuasa).

5. W. R. Read, *New Patterns*, p. 30.

6. In the capital there were 43 in 1948, 70 in 1958 and at least 119 in 1967.

7. According to E. G. Léonard, *L'illuminisme*, p. 71.

8. Elder's MS. to Key Yuasa.

9. E. G. Léonard, *L'illuminisme*, p. 98.

10. K. Yuasa, notes.

11. The prophecy is quoted in L. Francescon, *Resumo*, 3rd ed., 1958, pp. 15f., as 'Eu, o Senhor, permaneci no meio de vós e se Me obedecerdes e fordes humildes Eu mandarei convosco todos os que devem ser salvos' (I, the Lord, will remain in the midst of you, and if you obey me and are humble, I will entrust to you all who are to be saved).

12. J. M. Davis, *How the Church Grows in Brazil*, pp. 82f.; W. R. Read, *New Patterns*,

pp. 20–2; E. G. Léonard, *L'illuminisme*, p. 88, quotes the orchestral forces of one community. It had six violins, one flute, five (!) clarinets, six cornets, a trombone and a Hammond organ.

13. E. G. Léonard, *L'illuminisme*, p. 91.

14. *Ibid.*, p. 94.

15. *Ibid.*, p. 86.

16. According to Yuasa, notes.

17. Congregação Cristã, *Estatutos*. (H. Meyer, 'Pfingstbewegung', pp. 27–9, quotes the whole confession from my *Handbuch*.)

18. E. G. Léonard, *L'illuminisme*, p. 99.

19. *Ibid.*, p. 100.

20. Reproduced: 02.05.017c.

21. From H. Meyer, *op. cit.*, p. 27. He gives an excellent account of the Brazilian Pentecostal movement.

8

Brazilian Illuminism: An Attempt at an Assessment of the Brazilian Pentecostal Movement

1. *Brazilian Illuminism before the Emergence of the Pentecostal Movement*

EVEN before the emergence of the Pentecostal movement there was an autochthonous Brazilian illuminism; two of its representatives may be mentioned briefly here.

According to Léonard, *José Manuel da Conceição*,[1] a well educated Catholic priest, was one of the greatest evangelists, and most profound mystics in the history of the church. By reading the Bible and by preaching in the Reformation tradition, he became an evangelical and on 23 October 1863, accepted baptism from the Protestant missionary Blackford. He now worked with the Protestant missionaries, although he did not understand their theory of conversion. For him conversion was a long and toilsome way from to uncertainty to faith, for the Anglo-Saxon missionaries it was the recollection of a few blessed moments. Mocked as 'padre louco', a crazy priest, he went on foot from village to village and comforted and encouraged the poorest people of Brazil.

His friends from the Presbyterian mission had taught him that conversion brings peace into a man's heart. How, then, was it that his temptations did not cease:

> I had my tears as my food, the darkness of the night as my companion and my soul sank into a sea of sorrow. Men's glances made me tremble. I had to hide myself from everyone as a vagabond and a fugitive.[2]

His friends from the Presbyterian mission could not understand his struggles in prayer and described them as 'moral or intellectual aberrations'.[3] Yet da Conceição had opened up the way for the Protestant mission in many places.

Another Brazilian illuminist was *Miguel Vieira Ferreira*,[4] who sought out the worship of the Presbyterian church of his own accord. After a sermon he discovered that he was incapable of moving from his place.

> His body was not rigid, but he remained in the position in which he was or in which anyone put him. He stayed this way for almost half an hour, and during this time he only opened his eyes once, and then only for a moment. However, when he came to himself, he knew perfectly well what had been done or said around him. Among his first words were, 'Now I accept the Bible as the word of God, true and inspired, and Christ as a divine saviour, and I wish to profess the faith in this Presbyterian church.'[5]

Ferreira became an elder and lay preacher in the Presbyterian church. The church was proud of its convert, as he was a skilled engineer and mathematician, and had access to the leading levels of Brazilian society. He was so attracted by the gospel that he refused a professorship at the Polytechnic so that it would not hinder him in his unpaid lay preaching. While the Presbyterians had accepted his conversion with joy, they repudiated the effect of his testimony, because they feared that as a result of his conversion experience there would be similar illuminist experiences among their churchgoers. As he did not want to keep silent about his conversion experience, which for him had been the way to the gospel, he was deprived of his office as elder. Ferreira attempted to stay in the church that he loved with all his strength. But in vain; he had to write a farewell letter:

> I have spoken with God face to face. If God had spoken with you, you would know that I am speaking the truth. But you say that God has never spoken to you, and that is true, and that you do not believe that he ever speaks to you as he has spoken to me! Truly, I tell you, you will judge me, but you can never be my judges.[6]

On 11 September 1879, he founded the Igreja Evangélica Brasileira with 27 members. The further development of this church and the restraining mysticism of its founder, his love for the Brazilian people and the sharp rejection of his spiritualism by the traditional church have been described with sympathy and profound knowledge by Léonard.

So far it has not been possible to demonstrate any historical connection between da Conceição, Ferreira and the Pentecostals. This is improbable, simply because both come from a milieu inaccessible to the Pentecostals. They do show, however, how a Protestantism in Brazil must develop if it is to be a Brazilian Protestantism for the Brazilians; it will have to take seriously the latent illuminism of Brazil and develop it theologically. There are signs that the Pentecostal movement is succeeding here, not on a rational plane, but more intuitively. The time will come when it will have to follow up intellectually what it is doing in practice. Will the other churches be able to help it here and be ready to do so? Will it be ready to accept help?

2. *The Function of the Brazilian Pentecostal Movement in relation to Psychology and Social Psychology*

In his fundamental study *O Protestantismo brasileiro*, Léonard speaks of the Christianity of the sacrament, the Christianity of the book and the Christianity of the Spirit.[7] He asks in all seriousness whether – in South America, at any rate, – the age of the book is not past. He tells the story of a minister who asked a woman who had recently learnt to read, whether she now read the Bible with increasing enthusiasm. He received the answer: 'Your Bible? Oh! no. I've finished the Bible course now. I just read political newpapers and sports magazines.'[8] In the age of the radio, the television and the telephone, book readers are dying out.

> The 'modern' Christians 'of today', as e.g. members of Moral Rearmament, speak to God directly on the telephone and receive a direct answer. This makes the Bible unnecessary. The radio replaces the book as a direct means of communicating human ideas; is it not natural that the Spirit replaces the Bible in the communication of divine ideas? . . . The Bible requires the meditation of the solitary thinker. A hedonistic, degenerate and mechanized civilization does not favour meditation, whether individually or communally.

But here the Spirit helps.

> Illuminism is Brazil's real problem – not liberalism, ecumenism or fundamentalism – for the latter are imported goods, whereas illuminism has grown up on Brazilian soil.[9]

How far are the Christian churches of Brazil Brazilian, and how far have they taken seriously the 'real problem of Brazil'? Catholicism has not yet succeeded in becoming a Brazilian church. Not only does it suffer from a chronic shortage of priests, so that it is hardly able to look after its nominal church membership – a priest has to care for 10,000 to 12,000 souls,[10] but many are responsible for 30,000 souls and *Brasil Católico* in 1947 assigned 150,000 souls to the cure of Itambacuri (Minas Gerais) – but even more significant, the majority of priests are foreigners:[11] in one diocese, Upper Parana, all the priests except the bishop are foreigners, whereas in the same diocese all the evangelical ministers are Brazilians.

As a result, the conversion of 1,000 people a day to Protestantism, which in Brazil means almost exclusively to the Pentecostal movement, is not surprising.[12] Furthermore, the fear of a 'churchman in high circles' that Brazil will no longer be Catholic in 20 years if the present development continues, is well founded.[13]

Brazilian Protestantism, which numerically is the most important Latin-language Protestantism in the world, has so far been involved in a strong defensive reaction against the 'real problem of Brazil'. Exorcisms, healing of the sick, voices and visions are either rejected as 'diabolical' or mocked as superstitious. So far it has not had the patience to take seriously enough the second part of Ferreira's confession (God can always speak directly to men, but he no longer reveals anything [new]), because it has had to gird itself up immediately to refute the first part of the confession.

Key Yuasa, a Japanese Brazilian who does not belong to the Pentecostal movement but knows it thoroughly, and to whom I owe many of the observations and notes in this chapter, describes the attitude of the Brazilian Pentecostal movement as follows:

> Whereas the Protestants reject this superstition on more or less rationalistic or dogmatic grounds, the Pentecostals, because of their belief in the existence of demons, etc., seem to be right in the heart of the controversy with the world of magic and belief in spirits. But they fight the spirits with the Spirit. I saw the best example in the Igreja Apostolica, where an important part of the service consisted in prayer for the sick, exorcisms (with direct address to the demon causing the sickness); it claims to be the only church that is effectively fighting against 'Macumba, magic, bewitchments and other evil deeds'. If we reflect on this practice long enough, we shall possibly discover that the involvement of the Pentecostal with the spirits leads to a kind of demythologizing of their power, a power which is feared by the people because it is uncontrollable, but which also arouses in them the longing for liberation and peace.[14]

The French sociologist Bastide also comes to the same conclusion: at the moment when 'the member of the Congregação Cristã seems to be most African, is seized with trembling, speaks in tongues, is dominated by the Holy Spirit, he is in fact furthest removed from that, and is on the way towards being Westernized'.[15]

The German-American sociologist Emilio Willems, who knows the churches of Brazil and Chile[16] at first hand, describes the social and psychological function of the Brazilian Pentecostal movement in a different way from Léonard, Bastide and Yuasa, but he does not disagree with them. In particular, he points to a tendency that is already present in Catholicism towards indigenization which cannot be realized in a society which is becoming increasingly more mobile because of the structure of the church, imported from Europe and largely superimposed on local conditions. If a Brazilian Catholic has to move his home several hundred kilometres in search of work – and migrations of this kind happen often in the interior of Brazil – he cannot take his priest or his local saints with him, as both are tied to a particular location. By contrast, the Pentecostal movement can be found everywhere, as the religious character of the Pentecostal congregation is not dependent on either a particular preacher or a particular local community.

Willems emphasizes the inestimable help offered by the Pentecostal community towards the 'coming of age' of illiterate Brazilians. In the Pentecostal congregation a man learns to form an opinion and to express it. Furthermore, the community exercises moral control over its members, which is a considerable restraint on the double sexual morality which is common elsewhere in Brazil. Whereas pre-marital and extra-marital intercourse is regular in the case of the Brazilian man, a married Brazilian woman cannot in any circumstances give rise to even the slightest suspicion that she is infringing the unqualified right of her husband to her faithfulness. In the Pentecostal community, on the other hand, as in all the Protestant churches in Brazil, the same moral demands are laid on man and woman alike. Among the lower classes reached by the Pentecostal movement, this leads to a great improvement in the status of the woman. One step towards conversation between husband and wife as equals is the introduction of grace and family singing at meals, both practices which are impossible in male-dominated Brazilian society. With the introduction of grace – at any rate, in Willems' view – the family meal becomes an encounter between husband and wife. In contrast to other Brazilians of the same social stratum, the Pentecostal does not sit down at the table without a word, eat his food as quickly as possible, and then disappear again.[17]

A parallel development to this revaluation of the family which is controlled by the 'family of the community' is the improvement in the reputation of the Pentecostal for work. Like other Protestants, he enjoys the reputation of being a reliable worker. Personnel managers of the large firms therefore employ Pentecostals by preference, and in individual cases, conversion to the Pentecostal movement represents an impressive commendation in any search for work.

The Brazilian sociologist C. Procópio F. de Camargo comes to a similar conclusion. He too describes the Pentecostal community as a 'large family' which overcomes the climate of impersonality in the great cities with its personal and direct contacts and interprets the neglected everyday life of the Brazilian within a pattern of religious values which incorporate the small decisions of daily life into a context of salvation history.[18] Beatriz Muñiz de Souza, a young Presbyterian sociologist from São Paulo, in her investigation of the Pentecostal movement in São Paulo, concludes that 'despite the process of secularization in the society of São Paulo, Pentecostalism offers its adherents a possibility of understanding and overcoming reality'.[19] Furthermore, Miss de Souza deals not only with the great Pentecostal denominations, but also with the medium- to small-sized organization – of which the majority are nevertheless larger than the Protestant denominations – which are usually neglected. In a large number of tables, she shows where and why the Pentecostals are increasing. She puts special emphasis on the Pentecostal radio programme (more than twenty-six hours a week).[20]

According to Léonard, Bastide, Yuasa, Willems, de Camargo and de Souza, then, six witnesses beyond suspicion, the Pentecostal movement is making relevant progress over 'Brazil's real problem'. But how far has illuminism penetrated on the intellectual side?

Until recently, theological work was not the strong point of Brazilian Protestantism, either inside or outside the Pentecostal movement. The reason for this was that most pastors and Pentecostal preachers had to spend their time in other work. Léonard cites an extract from the diary of one such pastor. Every six months the poor man had to spend 106 days travelling,[21] baptize 13 infants, give 118 sermons and hold 18 eucharists, take part in 18 administrative meetings, receive 3 'professions of faith', make 102 visits and read 125 chapters, 1,011 verses, in the Bible. If in addition to that he has to carry on his profession as advocate, merchant or teacher, he is left little time or inclination for study and meditation. It is hardly beside the point that church life in Brazilian Pentecostalism is called 'O Trabalho', work. Léonard, however, calls for deeper study, for without *theological control*, illuminism comes dangerously near to Brazilian spiritism:

> There are two possibilities. Either Protestantism will not be willing or able to cope with these dissidents, in which case there will be the risk that they will turn to extravagance and then to religious indifference, as happened when Luther's rejection drove the Anabaptists to the excesses of Münster ... Or, it will keep contact with those who have 'gone over'[22] and work on them with friendly conversations, so as to bring them to understand the importance of the Bible. Their message, bound up with the gifts of the Spirit, will then finally reach that class (of workers) which was too often repudiated by the Reformation all too soon after it had attracted them.[23]

There are more levels to the problem than Léonard supposes. At this point the pressing question arises: how can a conversation in partnership be carried on which transcends the limitations imposed by culture, education and society? Pentecostals who had studied theology in the theological faculty at Buenos Aires have so far been used only to a very limited degree as interpreters between the cultures, because they have tended to be ashamed of the old language and as yet in inadequate control of the new. Furthermore, traditional theological education in Brazil – and perhaps not only there – seems to have become dysfunctional, as has recently been shown by the Armenian theologian Aharon Sapsezian, General Secretary of the Associação de Seminários Teológicos Evangélicos (ASTE).[24] A conversation in partnership between Protestants and Pentecostals would require a form of theological education in which there was equal acceptance of critical exegesis, practical theology and testimony in the market-place, sociological analysis and spontaneous improvisation. This is usually rejected as impossible. But has anyone ever tried it?

3. *A New Ecumenical Development*

(*a*) *Free Pentecostal communities*

The conversations desiderated by Léonard in the fifties now seem to be beginning. Before that could happen, however, a third family of Pentecostal denominations needed to arise. H. Meyer calls them the 'free Pentecostal communities', a title he uses to designate twenty to thirty Pentecostal denominations which arose in the fifties. The boundaries between these groups and the historical churches – especially between them and the Assembléias de Deus – are fluid. New demarcations and agreements with outher groups take place regularly. H. Meyer emphasizes their readiness for interdenominational collaboration[25] and their stress on *cura divina*, healing by prayer.

The most important organization is the Igreja Evangélica Pentecostal 'Brasil para Cristo', under the direction of the famous evangelist Manoel de Melo.[26] The Lutheran Meyer calls it 'without doubt one of the most remarkable phenomena in the church life of Brazil'.

> From Pernambuco, where he was active as pastor of the Assembléias de Deus, his course took him to São Paulo. A few years later, he broke away from the Assembléias there and put his extraordinary gifts as an evangelist, his famous oratorical talent and his inexhaustible capacity for work at the service of the Cruzada Nacional de Evangelização.[27] There were gigantic attendances at his evangelization meetings in tents, in open places and in parks, which often resulted in astonishing cures of the sick. All he needed for such meetings was an easily transportable loudspeaker system and a couple of musicians, whose songs first attracted the attention of the people. It is said that meetings with an audience of 100,000 were by no means rare and he himself estimated the audience for his morning radio programme at five million.

Mayer relates:

> I was there when one Thursday he had to bring forward the regular service in his provisional main church in São Paulo, a former market hall, from its appointed time on Saturday to Friday evening. Despite this, the church was packed with more than five thousand believers so that there was not even standing room; people were left outside the doors and even on the streets. The two-hour service had all the marks of Brazilian Pentecostal services with their lively, joyful, even hilarious mood: there was vigorous and extremely rhythmical singing emphasized by hand-claps and accompanied by an *ad hoc* 'orchestra' of violins, flutes, clarinets, horns, etc.; all five thousand joined in loud spontaneous prayer which went on for minutes and swelled to a crescendo, suddenly dying away at a sign from the preacher. (Individuals who seemed to have lapsed into speaking with tongues were silenced with an imploring yet sharp 'silêncio!'.) The sermon – about the parable of the five foolish and five wise virgins – was very emotional and had a strongly admonitory tone, but it was an extraordinarily clear, concrete and attractive exposition of the biblical text. The attention of the congregation did not slip for a moment, and their intensive preoccupation could be seen and heard in movements, laughter, loud interjections and – above all after certain key expressions – cries of 'Glória a Deus', 'Alleluia' or 'Louvada seja o nome do Senhor!'
>
> Without question this temperamental, dark Pernambucan with his squat

figure and harsh voice is one of the most popular figures in Brazil and surely the best-known evangelist in the country, admired by some, attacked and criticized by others. When he founded his own movement, a large number of his adherents from the Cruzada Nacional de Evangelização followed him. His own estimate of the annual rate of growth is about 80,000. Of course, it is impossible to confirm that for the moment. Nevertheless, his church may be the fastest growing in Brazil. His own verdict goes even further: 'This work grows faster than any other in the whole world.'[28]

(*b*) *An ecumenical symposium*

In the autumn of 1965 about fifty theological leaders and pastors from Brazil met with Pentecostal leaders from several groups for a symposium on 'The Holy Spirit and the Pentecostal Movement'. The symposium was attended by Adventists, Baptists, Methodists, Presbyterians, Roman Catholics, Holiness people, Lutherans, Anglicans and others on the one hand, and Pentecostals on the other. It produced a highly significant report, but because it was written in Portuguese, it has so far remained virtually unknown outside Brazil.[29]

The convener of the consultation was Aharon Sapsezian. In his introduction, he observed that the Pentecostals' vision of

> a world full of supernatural and invisible powers, where miracles and divine healing are not only happening, but are made to happen, seems to contradict Bonhoeffer's 'world come of age' and Cox's 'exorcism in the technopolis'.

And all of this is interpreted in the framework of the Pentecostal understanding of the baptism in the Spirit. But Sapsezian went on to ask:

> Could the well-known proximity of the Pentecostals to the disinherited strata of society give us the right to expect from them a deeper and more realistic understanding of their problems and a genuine comprehension of the saving and liberating power of the gospel for the oppressed?[30]

Or, on the contrary, do their aspiration for social status and ecclesiastical recognition, their building[31] and educational programmes lead them to a situation similar to that of our own churches?

The question was well expressed. What did the Pentecostals answer? Pentecostal evangelism – according to them – is characterized by three qualities:

1. It maintains solidarity with the poor.
2. It does not confine itself to soul-saving.
3. It can only be effective in an ecumenical context.

1. There is a messianic note in Manoel de Melo's declaration:

> Rome has brought to the world idolatry, Russia the terrors of communism, the USA the demon of capitalism; we Brazilians, nation of the poor, shall bring to the world the gospel.[32]

Lawrence Olsen described this in practical terms by saying that Pentecostals adopt the missionary pattern of the early Christians, not only in concentrating strategically on the cities, but also in working with the poor. If Paul's target has been exclusively the middle and upper classes, as often happens with churches today, Christianity would perhaps have been short-lived. This means that the Pentecostal pastor belongs to the same sociological stratum as those whom he wants to win for Christ. Otherwise he will not be able to make himself comprehensible to his audience. The communication is spontaneous, and is sometimes wrongly termed 'emotionalism' by some outsiders. But the joyful noise of the Pentecostals is surely no less normal than the deafening roar of a football match. K. Yuasa, who is well acquainted with the Brazilian Pentecostal movement, characterized this means of communication based solely upon the receptivity of the congregation as a 'pneumatocentric missiology', in that it takes seriously Bonhoeffer's concept of the 'church for others'.[33] The Pentecostals, of course, would never describe their evangelism in terms of Bonhoeffer's theology. They use fundamentalist language, for this is their only *rational* means of communication with non-Pentecostals. But their fundamentalist description of evangelism and the way they evangelize are two different things.

2. Levy Tavares sees the practice of the healing of the sick through prayer in direct relation to the Brazilian context:

> It is the reality of Brazil itself that draws people to Pentecostal meetings, for in a country that has a great lack of hospitals, in which medicine is too costly for the majority, one logically expects that the promise of divine healing, which happens through faith in God alone, attracts the masses not so much because of their desire to attend worship as because of their need to be freed from suffering and sickness.[34]

Thus the prayer of the Pentecostal preacher is the first step in accepting the bodily reality of the poor in Brazil. But prayer for the sick does not exclude medical care.[35]

Political evangelization was stressed by Levy Tavares, Geraldino dos Santos[36] and Manoel de Melo. For these Pentecostals, active engagement in politics is the logical consequence of their understanding of evangelization.[37]

The Roman Catholic speaker at the symposium, Francisco Lepargneur, Professor at the Dominican Theological Seminary in São Paulo, began his paper by stating that he did not want to give 'an apologetic refutation of the Pentecostal movement'. On the contrary, the Pentecostals had adopted into their churches a number of Catholic truths which had sometimes been forgotten by the Catholics themselves.[38] He gave a good account of the practice of glossolalic prayer in the writings of the Church Fathers, and stressed the fact that the distinction between two kinds of believers, 'semi-believers' and charismatically equipped born-again believers, is well known in patristic literature.[39] In contrast, however, he stressed that according to Paul the supernatural quality is not the criterion which distinguishes the charismatic from the psychical or natural, as Paul includes a list of ordinary and natural gifts among the gifts of the Spirit.[40] According to Lepargneur, a characteristic of pagan religions is to identify the extraordinary or the supernatural with a divine gift. Therefore the characteristic of spiritual gifts should be their 'service to the whole community'.[41]

This paper was received with a mixture of joy and scepticism by the Pentecostals. Although Lepargneur had backed his statements with massive quotations from the Church Fathers and the Second Vatican Council, Manoel de Melo asked whether Lepargneur's progressive opinion was just his own, or whether it could be taken as the expression of a change in the attitude of the Roman Catholic church to the 'sectarians'.

3. Lepargneur's characterization of the gifts of the Spirit as an expression of 'service for the whole community', and the Pentecostals' second point[42] lead directly to the statement of Geraldino dos Santos: 'in the era of ecumenism, we are sure that the unity of Christians is imperative for the salvation of the world.'[43] The astonishing thing about this statement is not only the reference to the 'era of ecumenism' but the direction of Christian unity towards service in and to the world, i.e., for dos Santos, in and to Brazilian society.

One aspect of this Pentecostal ecumenism is the hope of 'Pentecostalizing' the whole church, i.e. passing on their specific gifts to all the existing denominations. Theoretically, the traditional churches agree with this. Could any church refuse to be Pentecostal in the widest sense? But as soon as some of their pastors and congregations begin to exercise the charismatic gifts which are common in Pentecostal churches (above all, glossolalia and divine healing), tensions arise which often, though not always, lead to splits within churches.[44]

In evaluating the consultation of October 1965, the Pentecostals agreed with the traditional churches that they need help in establishing their Pentecostal seminaries.[45] The traditional churches, on the other hand, believe that they could do with a bit more Pentecostal zeal. Harding Meyer,[46] who was present at the consultation, does not agree with such an interpretation. He thinks that the very practice of Pentecostal evangelism is a theological contribution and, although the Pentecostals may not be able to describe their method in theological terms, their evangelism in Brazil should be reflected upon at a theological level. By beginning where the people are, with their sickness (healing of the sick through prayer), with their irrational articulation of joy and fear (glossolalia), with their emphasis on archetypal means of communication (music and singing), they exemplify the phrase of a WCC study, 'The world provides the agenda'.[47] The Brazilian situation determines the themes and means of communication of the Pentecostal worship. That does not, of course, mean that the Pentecostals merely repeat what Brazilians are thinking and saying, but that they set out to bring the gospel to the points of tension in Brazilian society.[48]

This is a hermeneutical approach which is well-known to traditional churches as a principle for New Testament exegesis. They know that the New Testament documents have to be understood in their social and literary context. Traditional churches have also learned that communication today involves first of all an enquiry about the actual context of their times. But the traditional churches have so far developed no instrument by which they could perceive the hermeneutical context in a largely non-bourgeois, inarticulate stratum of society, where there is a need for 'atmospheric' means of communication which is not afraid of emotional and intuitive channels. Furthermore, recent observations have shown that these channels of communication seem to be relevant even for those who do not belong to the usual Pentecostal constituency. They would, in fact, apply to Paul himself, who thanked God that he spoke in tongues more than the Corinthians (I Cor. 14.18). We find here a parallel to the Negro spirituals and the jazz which emerged in the rationally inarticulate milieu of the American Negro communities, but which overflowed their original social context.

A dramatic turn in the relationship between the Ecumenical movement and the Pentecostal movement came about when Manuel de Melo, in an interview given to the Methodist newspaper *Expositor Cristão*,[49] announced that his church would join the World Council of Churches. This intention was realized at the meeting of the Central Committee in Canterbury in 1969.[50] He had not been impressed by the services which he had attended as an observer in Uppsala. He felt like 'Ezekiel in the valley of the dry bones'. In his view, as far as worship was concerned the World Council was pedalling a bicycle in the age of jet aeroplanes. But, de Melo continued, it is not enough to arrange nice services, to sing and to pray, important though that may be. 'While we convert a million, the devil de-converts ten millions through hunger, misery, militarism, dictatorship.' De Melo mentioned the Roman Catholic bishop Helder Câmara as the model of a true evangelist. The church in Brazil had to have the help of the World Council to be able to fulfil its function as a prophet and a reviver of social and political conscience. De Melo also made practical suggestions as to how this might come about.

> Why not transform the hundreds of church buildings into schools during week days, and even into trade unions and associations in order to train the people?

In this way, the Igreja Evangélica Pentecostal 'Brasil para Cristo' became the largest member church of the World Council in Latin America. Manoel de Melo has resolved to break down prejudice against the World Council in Latin America by a series of 'ecumenical revival meetings'. In this way, he hopes to obtain the help of traditional member churches of the World Council in Brazil. It is to be hoped that they will not leave him in the lurch.

The world-wide Pentecostal movement has received the entry of de Melo into the World Council with mixed feelings, where it has not passed over the matter in silence. To begin with, an attempt was made to say that his church did not really belong to the Pentecostal movement. Where this was not possible, 'serious anxiety' was expressed. While it was conceded that the Pentecostal movement had no solution to offer for the social and political problems of Latin America, it was 'surely a very serious question whether social concerns, desperate though they might be, permitted entry into the ecumenical movement.'[51]

(*c*) *The importance of the Pentecostal movement for the Catholic church*

Since the Second Vatican Council, feelings towards the Pentecostals in the Catholic church of Brazil have changed radically. Abdalazis de Moura from Recife, Regional (secretary) of the National Conference of Brazilian Bishops, stresses the importance of the Pentecostal movement for the Catholic church in an excellent analysis.[52] He begins by asking, 'What are the possibilities and difficulties with which an ecumenical dialogue with the Pentecostals must come to grips?' He defines the Pentecostal movement as a 'conscious or unconscious protest against existing political, social, economic or religious forms'. Despite its supreme theological importance, so far no theological works have appeared – de Moura does not count polemic as theological works.[53]

As the theologians have so far ignored the Pentecostals, the Pentecostals are not interested, understandably enough, in theology. In any case, Pentecostal theology is not carried on in rational categories, but in categories of intuition and experience. The theologians, and not the Pentecostals, are to blame for this segregation, because they have developed a false understanding of what academic theology is. Furthermore, a false interpretation of the maxim 'No salvation outside the church' on the Catholic side has made dialogue almost impossible. 'Salvation which is exclusively bound up with the confessional formulation of one church hinders the recognition of the sovereignty of Christ.'[54] Even the various Catholic and Protestant attempts at social revolution do not reach those for whom they are intended. 'They are the monopoly of a privileged élite which has access to a particular jargon.'[55] As a result, among the mass of Brazilian people the symptoms of poverty are taken as its cause. It is not surprising that the Pentecostals are not informed any better or any worse than the other churches here, as the historic churches have not given any reasonable teaching for centuries. For the Pentecostals, however, the tragedy is that there is no 'popular organization' worth mentioning outside the Pentecostal denominations in Chile and Brazil.[56]

Granted, the Catholic church is attempting to bring worship nearer to ordinary people by liturgical reform. But this is quite inadequate patchwork. What has so far been lacking in all the historical churches is a 'criativadade no culto liturgico', the possibility of a liturgy in which the people play a spontaneous part, as demonstrated by the Pentecostals. As long as the Catholic church means to keep the alterations under strict control, no spontaneous new creations will arise.[57] Even the prayer groups and Bible groups which have arisen in slum areas are quite inadequate. The bourgeois who go to the poor and instruct them allow themselves to be 'wondered at and reverenced by the poor', so that the presence of social superiors is a psychological hindrance to the poor in the development of their specific gifts.[58] The Pentecostals have overcome this difficulty by having as teachers neither priests nor intellectuals nor the middle class, but poor workers like themselves.

In his criticism of the Pentecostal movement, de Moura points to its obvious limitations: biblicist fundamentalism, devaluation of history ('A faith which is lived outside history will not find any significance in the actual situation')[59] and an individualism which as a result of its disengagement from politics acts as an upholder of the *status quo*.

De Moura sees the greatest danger for the future in the possible alienation of the poor, once these no longer accept the comfort of their preachers, as when a worker is consoled over the death of his child with the words, 'One more angel in heaven'. On the other hand, according to de Moura an accommodation with classical academic theology would be 'the death of the Pentecostal movement' and 'a betrayal of its own important insights'.[60] Unfortunately, however, this development is precisely the one that the historic churches want to force on the Pentecostal movement.

What other possibilities does de Moura see? Like H. Meyer,[61] he calls for a theology that does not begin with theory but with Pentecostal practice. The Pentecostals have brought about this practice without an ecclesiology to correspond with it. How did it come about that the Pentecostals 'developed a practice which matches the thought of the best of our theologians without their profound considerations?'[62] Without our theoretical insights into group processes they have recognized the natural leaders of the poor community as key figures in their net of communication.[63] That means that we who have developed these good theories but have not put them into practice have a great deal to learn from their method of theology, which begins with experiment.[64]

Consequently, dialogue with them must begin with the 'bases populares', with 'experiência e do fato concreto'. Arguments will never convince a Pentecostal that he must take political or industrial action. But if among those engaged in politics and industrial work he meets Christians with an authentic Christian witness instead of atheists and agnostics. he will be made to think. Arguments will never convince a Pentecostal that the return of Christ has something to do with the building of a better world. But if he comes across a missionary and warm-hearted community of Christians whose concern is the building of a better society, that will carry conviction. Arguments will never convince a Pentecostal that he must build up solid exegetical insights. But if he meets popular evangelists who can communicate with the people and who at the same time have a positive attitude towards critical exegesis, they will lead him to re-examine his own fundamentalist position.[65]

As a result, dialogue with Pentecostals does not depend so much on our arguments as on our style of religious practice and communication. The question is whether the Pentecostal can recognize them as authentic and therefore as appropriate to their subject-matter.

4. *Political Influence*

Among the participants in the symposium mentioned above were two active Pentecostal politicians.[66] After initial resistance against political careers for 'preachers baptized with the Spirit'[67] and some disappointments in co-operation with existing political parties, Manoel de Melo decided to intervene actively in politics. In the present suspension of Parliament in Brazil his hope of having an evangelical Vice-President for Brazil is, however, more than questionable. This development, which is still hard to assess, must be seen in connection with the rise of a political Pentecostal party in Sweden[68] and the active intervention of Pentecostals in the politics of Chile,[69] Russia[70] and Switzerland.[71] Clumsy though individual attempts may seem, it is at least clear to these Pentecostal preachers that the gospel and politics are not two realities that can be separated from each other. We can understand their dismay at the dominant regime when they read in the newspaper that two thousand and forty children die of hunger in Brazil every day, while tremendous Brazilian resources are hoarded in Swiss banks.[72] On the lines of James 5.4, the alternative to Communism that is required is voluntary renunciation of excess income. This fine theory, which however lacks political persuasiveness, will soon put the Pentecostal movement either on the wing of the conservative forces which defend the *status quo* or compel them to develop a social and economic programme that can actually be put into practice. Here the Brazilian Protestants need to look for the help of the best Western traditions. The first beginnings of such a development can be seen in the contributions from Latin America made at the World Council of Churches Conference on Church and Society at Geneva in 1966.

To sum up, it may be said that because of its extent – it has more than four million adherents, i.e. seventy per cent of Brazilian Protestantism – its growth and its access to hitherto neglected but increasingly important strata of the population, the Brazilian Pentecostal movement occupies a key position not only in Latin American Protestantism but also in Brazilian politics. We cannot be indifferent to the question of the kind of theological and philosophical knowledge (or ignorance) with which it approaches this task. One of the most urgent tasks of 'inter-church aid' is therefore an intensive contact with these Pentecostal churches.

This view was shared by the Latin American Pentecostal 'observers' at the Fourth Assembly of the World Council of Churches in Uppsala (1968). They told me: The people here seem to be like the wise men from the East. They have seen the star and are on the way to the manger with their treasures. But they have not yet knelt down. They are under-developed religiously and in this respect can learn something from us. But we must learn from their insight into the social and political situation.[73]

NOTES

1. E. G. Léonard, *L'illuminisme*, pp. 14–19; *id.*, *Rev. de l'Ev.* 7/38, July–August 1952, pp. 214–17.

2. B. Ribeiro, *Padre Protestante*, p. 120 (quotation from da Conceicão's unpublished 'Confession of evangelical faith').

3. *Ibid.*, p. 146.

4. Léonard, *L'illuminisme*, pp. 19–58; *id.*, *Rev. de l'Ev.* 7/38, July–August 1952, p. 217; *id.*, *Revista de História* 3, 1952, no. 12, pp. 428–32.

5. Léonard, *L'illuminisme*, p. 22 (report by Blackford, a missionary, to his American committee, 24.4.1874). The source question is complicated. The best and most literal sources are in Léonard, *L'illuminisme*, and in his church history of Brazil, which appeared in *Revista de História*. But the new impression of these articles published in 1963 suppresses the quotations that are most interesting to us in this context.

6. Parting words of Ferreira in the church register of the Presbyterian church, quoted by E. G. Léonard, *L'illuminisme*, p. 25. The words contain the most important and effective motto of the churches: 'Deus pode sempre falar diretamente aos homens, mas Êle nada mais revela' (God can always speak directly to men, but he does not reveal anything [new]). Following Léonard, *Revista de História* 3, 1952, no. 12, p. 430.

7. Léonard, *Protestantismo brasileiro*, p. 33.

8. *Ibid.*, p. 338.

9. *Ibid.*

10. Léonard, *Rev. de l'Ev.* 7/38, July–August 1952, p. 222.

11. 2,000 out of 3,419.

12. According to *La Razón*, S. Paulo, ca. 20.6.1962: Hay mas Protestantes.

13. H.K., *Orientierung* 19/1, 15.1.1955, pp. 9–11.

14. K. Yuasa, notes.

15. R. Bastide, *Les religions*, p. 515.

16. E. Willems, *Kölner Zeitschrift fur Soziologie und Sozialpsychologie* 12, 1960, pp. 652–71.

17. E. Willems, *Followers*, pp. 169–73.

18. C. Procópio F. de Camargo, in: J. V. Freitas Marcondes, Osmar Pimentel, *São Paulo*, p. 377.

19. Beatriz Mũniz de Souza, *Experiência*, p. 163: German summary in W. J. Hollenweger (ed.), *Die Pfingstkirchen*, pp. 294–300.

20. Beatriz Mũniz de Souza, *op. cit.*, p. 127.

21. 2,340 kilometres by railway, 1,102 by bus, 53 on horseback, 24 by lorry, 19 on foot, 18 by car, 13 by ox-cart.

22. 'transfugés'; Léonard means those who have gone over from the traditional churches to the Pentecostal movement. No complaints should be made about this 'falling away'. 'Those who have fallen away' have an important function in the Pentecostal movement.

23. Léonard; *Rev. de l'Ev.* 7/38, July–August 1952, p. 235; cf. also *L'illumnismie*, p. 113.

24. A. Sapsezian, *Monthly Letter on Evangelism*, Oct.–Dec. 1968.

25. A characteristic of each new Pentecostal denomination, cf. ch. 12.2, p. 153.

26. 02b.05.037. Estimated membership between 110,000 (W. R. Read, *New Patterns*, p. 154) and 900,000 (M. de Melo, quoted in H. Meyer, 'Pfingstbewegung').

27. A new group in Brazil (02b.05.028) originally dependent on the International Church of the Foursquare Gospel (02a.02.124).

28. H. Meyer, 'Pfingstbewegung', pp. 43f.

29. ASTE, *O Espirito Santo.*

30. A. Sapsezian, in ASTE, *op. cit.*, p. 4.

31. One example is the new Manoel de Melo church. It is said to be the biggest church in the world: 25,000 square metres, 25,000 seats and room for 15,000 standing, 46 different halls and rooms, a great library, a bookshop, a restaurant, a hairdresser's, a tower 300 m. high at the top of which 300 people can stand, seven illuminated fountains, an artificial lake, etc. Total cost was one million dollars (W. R. Read, *New Patterns*, pp. 152f.; de Souza, *Experiência*, pp. 43f.).

32. H. Meyer, *Pfingstbewegung*, p. 50.

33. K. Yuasa in ASTE, *op. cit.*, pp. 68–70. Yuasa is a pastor in the Igreja Evangélica Holiness (02b.05.004).

34. L. Tavares in ASTE, *op. cit.*, p. 36. Tavares was originally a Methodist preacher. Today he belongs to Melo's church. He is a deputy in the federal parliament. See his speeches there on 'Wasting money on armaments', 'Humanizing the money market', 'Suppression of religious freedom in *South* Vietnam', 'Nobel prize for a Negro preacher' (L. Tavares, *Minha patria*).

35. Cf. ch. 6.2, p. 80.

36. G. dos Santos, originally a Methodist preacher, today co-operating with Melo and a deputy in the Parliament of the state of São Paulo.

37. See p. 104.

38. This is not an isolated remark by Lepargneur, cf. ch. 8.3(*c*) p. 104, A. Gaëte, SJ, 'Un cas d'adaption', and the literature in ch. 30.3, pp. 437ff.

39. For the connection between Catholic and Pentecostal piety cf. 05.28.004a: *PGG*, pp. 256f. Also H. V. Synan (*P Movement*, p. 266) stresses the Roman Catholic elements within Pentecostalism: 'As a product of Methodism, the Pentecostal-holiness movement traces its lineage through the Wesleys to Anglicanism and from thence to Roman Catholicism. This theological heritage places the Pentecostals outside the Calvinistic, reformed tradition which culminated in the Baptist and Presbyterian movements in the United States.' Similarly E. O'Connor, *P Movement*, p. 23.

40. On this see ch. 25.4, p. 372.

41. F. Lepargneur in ASTE, *op. cit.*, p. 55.

42. Evangelism refers to the total reality of man, physical, social, political and psychological, see above, p. 101ff.

43. G. dos Santos, ASTE, *op. cit.*, p. 32.

44. Cf. e.g. the battle waged by E. Tognini, leader of the Pentecostal-like Baptist Movimento de Renovação Espíritual (ASTE, *op. cit.*, pp. 76–82: E. Tognini, 'Batismo'). There are similar groups among German and French Baptists (05.09.001) and in all the traditional churches of the USA (ch. 1, pp. 3f.), Great Britain (ch. 13.2, pp. 184ff.) and Germany (ch. 18, pp. 234ff.).

45. A. Sapsezian, in ASTE, *op. cit.*, p. 6.

46. Dr Harding Meyer, Research Secretary of the Lutheran World Federation, in an interview with the author.

47. See the WCC report, *The Church for Others*, Geneva 1967.

48. See section II of the 'Drafts for Sections', p. 31, for the Fourth Assembly of the World Council of Churches, Uppsala (Geneva 1968).

49. M. de Melo, *Monthly Letter on Evangelism*, Feb.–March 1969.
50. *Ecumenical Press Service* 36/30, 21.8.1969, pp. 3–5; O. Brekke, *Voort Land* 25/232, 7.10.1969, p. 6.
51. J. Zopfi, *Wort und Geist* 1/7, July 1969, p. 8.
52. A. de Moura, *A importância das Igrejas Pentecostais para a Igreja Católica.*
53. De Moura, *op. cit.*, p. 3.
54. *Ibid.*, p. 20.
55. *Ibid.*, p. 24.
56. *Ibid.*, p. 35.
57. *Ibid.*, p. 25.
58. *Ibid.*, p. 27.
59. *Ibid.*, p. 31 (quotation from A. Dumas, *Ideologia e fe*, pp. 15f.).
60. *Ibid.*, p. 34.
61. Cf. p. 103.
62. *Ibid.*, p. 26.
63. *Ibid.*, p. 28.
64. *Ibid.*, p. 38.
65. *Ibid.*, p. 37; cf. also de Moura, *Revista Eclesiástica Brasileira* 31/121, March 1971, pp. 78ff.
66. See notes 34 and 36 above. Similarly *Luz do Mundo* 6/49, Oct. 1966, p. 5; on the Movimento de Redenção Nacional, cf. 02b.05.039.
67. S. O. E. Martins, *Luz do Mundo* 2/10, Nov.–Dec. 1962, p. 6.
68. Cf. B. Wirmark, 'Politik in der schwedischen Pfingstbewegung', in: W. J. Hollenweger (ed.), *Pfingstkirchen*, pp. 256–64.
69. 02.08.001.
70. Ch. 20.3(*c*), pp. 279ff.
71. *PGG*, p. 283.
72. *Diario da Noite*, 18.8.1963; quoted in S. O. E. Martins, *Luz do Mundo* 2/15, Aug.–Sept. 1963, pp. 1f.; at length in 02b.05.025.
73. The Swedish press reported on the conversations between Pentecostals, Protestants and Catholics in Uppsala: *Dagens Nyheter*, 13.7.1968, p. 7; E. S., *Dagen* 24/138, 18.7.1968, pp. 1, 8; *Uppsala* 68/7, 19.7.1968, p. 20; *Dagen* 24/131, 9.7.1968; 24/135, 13.7.1968, pp. 1, 8.

SOUTH AFRICA

9

'The Full Blessing of Pentecost': Andrew Murray, John Alexander Dowie and the Early Days of the Pentecostal Movement in South Africa

1. *Andrew Murray*

(*a*) *His life*

MURRAY (1828–1917) was descended from a family of Scottish sheep farmers in Aberdeenshire. Murray's father, Andrew Murray (died 1866) was minister of the Dutch Reformed Church in Graf Reinet, South Africa, and has almost a thousand descendants of the same name in South Africa. The African explorers Livingstone and Moffat were regular visitors to his house. His sons sometimes heard him in his study 'praying aloud and fervently for the outpouring of the Holy Spirit'.[1]

Andrew Murray was sent in 1838 with his brother John to continue his studies in Aberdeen, where they lived with their uncle, John Andrew. 'It is said that the boys never gave their hosts any cause for reproach or punishment, which can be ascribed to the constant prayer offered for them back at home.'[2] In 1845 they both passed their M.A. examinations, and were sent to Utrecht to study theology and learn Dutch, with which they were still so unfamiliar that prayers, discussions and the exposition of Scripture had to be carried on in Latin on their account. They kept away from social life, from tobacco and from alcohol. 'Resist both these abominable habits', their father wrote. As a result they became known as the 'Cocoa Club' or the 'Prayer Club'.[3] In 1845 Andrew wrote home to tell of his rebirth: 'Your son has been born anew.'[4] From Holland, the brothers travelled on foot to visit Pastor Johannes Christoph Blumhardt. In 1848 they were ordained as ministers of the Dutch Church in the Hague.

Andrew was thereafter a minister in Bloemfontein, Worcester, Wellington and Cape Town. The people respected him, even though the Boers regarded clergy paid by the British crown with hostility.

In Worcester in 1860 there was a revival:

> On a certain Sunday evening there were gathered in a little hall some sixty young people. I was leader of the meeting, which commenced with a hymn and a lesson from God's Word, after which I engaged in prayer. After three or four others had (as was customary) given out a verse of a hymn and offered prayer, a coloured girl of about fifteen years of age, in service with a farmer from Hex River, rose at the back of the room and asked if she too might propose a hymn. At first I hesitated, not knowing what the meeting would think, but better thoughts prevailed, and I replied, 'Yes'. She gave out her hymn-verse and prayed in moving tones. While she was praying, we heard as it were a sound in the distance, which came nearer and nearer, until the hall seemed to be shaken, and with one or two exceptions, the whole meeting began to pray, the majority in audible voice, but some in whispers. Nevertheless, the noise made by the concourse was deafening. . . . [Mr Murray] had preached that evening in the English language. When service was over an elder passed the door of the hall, heard the noise, peeped in, and then hastened to call Mr Murray, returning presently with him. Mr Murray came forward to the table where I knelt, touched me, and made me understand that he wanted me to rise. He then asked me what had happened. I related everything to him. He then walked down the hall for some distance, and called out, as loudly as he could, 'People, silence'. But the praying continued. In the meantime I too kneeled down again. It seemed to me that if the Lord was coming to bless us, I should not be upon my feet but on my knees. Mr Murray then called again aloud, 'People, I am your minister, sent from God, silence!' But there was no stopping the noise. No one heard him, but all continued praying and calling on God for mercy and pardon. Mr Murray then returned to me and told me to start the hymn-verse ['Aid the soul that helpless cries']. I did so, but . . . the meeting went on praying. . . .[5]

Now prayer meetings took place every day, led by Murray. He tried without success to lead them along a more peaceful path; but his father was enthusiastic and said to him: 'Andrew, my son, for how many years have I longed like these people.'[6] His wife also supported the revival, in the course of which there was not only much excitement, with people sometimes fainting, but also fifty young men offered themselves for the ministry. Professor Hofmeyr, an eyewitness, made the following comment:

> We cannot conceal our fear that not a few mistake the natural, sympathetic influence of one mind upon another for the immediate action of the Spirit of God. . . . We are greatly grieved at the self-deceit to which emotional people such as these are subject; but in the present condition of human nature we can expect no revival which does not stand to this danger. However this may be we thank the Lord that we have good reason to affirm that since the revival began many have been added to the Lord's flock. Some of them lived in open sin. . . .[7]

In order to provide a guide for the many converts from the revival movement, Murray wrote his book *Abide in Christ.*

In his last ministry, in Wellington, he had a similar experience. One of his daughters describes it:

> The first Whit Sunday after father's return from England [from the great Holiness Conference of 1871] brought him a great harvest of souls in Wellington. The elders asked him to preach about hell. During his sermon many men and women began to shudder, but soon found peace under the tender breathing of God's love in Jesus Christ.[8]

In 1862 Murray was made Moderator of the Reformed Church in South Africa. During the Boer War he took the side of the Boers and fought for the removal of the concentration camps set up for the Boer prisoners. He opposed slavery and advocated total abstinence. In his doctrine of holiness and in his practical Christianity he was decisively influenced by Moody, Boardman, Smith, Stockmayer and Miss A. von Wattenwyl; he knew most of them personally. He testified to his own baptism of the Spirit in Keswick in 1895:

> I remember in my little room in Bloemfontein how I used to sit and think 'What is the matter? Here I am knowing that God has justified me in the blood of Christ, but I have no power for service.' . . . Perhaps if I were to talk of consecration I might tell you of an evening there in my own study in Cape Town. Yet I cannot say that that was my deliverance, for I was still struggling. I would say that what we need is complete obedience. . . . Later on my mind was much exercised about the baptism of the Holy Spirit and I gave myself to God as perfectly as I could, to receive this baptism of the Spirit. Yet there was failure . . . I can help you more, perhaps, by speaking not of any marked experience, but by telling very simply what I think God has given me now. . . .[9]

This remarkably colourless account may be due to the revision that the writings of the ancestors of the Pentecostal movement have undergone since the Pentecostal movement proper started. This process can be observed in the case of Stockmayer, Markus Hauser and the American Holiness evangelists But it may be due to Murray's own reticence. If the latter is true it would distinguish him from most of the Holiness preachers of his time.

He remained in constant contact with the Holiness movement. 'I constantly followed what was happening in Oxford and Brighton, and they all helped me. . . .'[10] For twenty years he was president of the Holiness movement in South Africa.

His biographer, Alfred Stucki, describes Murray as one of those 'from whom, as the Scriptures say, streams of living water flow'.[11] His sincerity, devotion, coupled with humour, intelligence, good taste and culture cannot in my view be doubted. Because of his inadequate theological training (he was ten years old when he went to Scotland, and a minister by the time he was twenty), he also introduced the two-stage way of salvation and the doctrine of the baptism of the Spirit to South Africa, as well as a doctrine concerning the healing of the sick by prayer which was in many respects one-sided.

(*b*) *Murray's doctrine of the baptism of the Spirit*

In his doctrine of the baptism of the Spirit Murray makes a clear distinction between 'rebirth' and the 'indwelling of the Spirit' or 'baptism with the Holy Spirit'.

> The former is that work of the Holy Spirit, by which He convinces us of sin, leads to repentance and faith in Christ, and imparts a new nature. Through the Spirit God thus fulfils the promise: 'I will put a new spirit within you.' The believer is now a child of God, a temple ready for the Spirit to dwell in. Where faith claims it, the second half of the promise is fulfilled as surely as the first. . . . How are these two parts of the Divine promise fulfilled? – simultaneously or successively? . . . From God's side the twofold gift is simultaneous. The Spirit is not divided . . . and yet we have indications in Scripture that there may be circumstances, dependent either on the enduement of the preacher or the faith of the hearers, in which the two halves of the promise are not so closely linked. . . . [Here follows a discussion on the relevant passages in Acts.] When the standard of spiritual life in a Church is sickly and low, . . . we must not wonder that, even where God gives His Spirit, He will be known and experienced only as the Spirit of regeneration.[12]

In common with the whole Pentecostal movement he describes the baptism of the Spirit as an 'enduement with power'.[13] It is not what makes possible the life of prayer, but is the crown awarded to perseverance in prayer.[14] Obedience and prayer (and here too Murray is a ready pupil of Lucan theology)[15] must precede the baptism of the Spirit.

> They err who want the fulness of the Spirit before they obey, no less than those who think that obedience is already a sign that the fulness of the Spirit is there. . . . It has been thought that only those who had the fulness of the Spirit could be obedient. It was not seen that obedience was the lower platform – that the baptism of the Spirit, the full revelation of the glorified Lord . . . was something higher, the Presence that the obedient should inherit. . . . *The obedient must and may look for the fulness of the Spirit.*[16]

This doctrine is set out even more clearly in his book *The Full Blessing of Pentecost*, which is sold nowadays only by the Pentecostals:

> In these chapters it is my desire to bring to the children of God the message that there is a twofold Christian life. The one is that in which we experience something of the operations of the Holy Spirit, just as many did under the old covenant, but do not yet receive him as the Pentecostal Spirit, as the personal indwelling Guest, concerning whom we know that He has come to abide permanently in the heart. On the other hand, there is a more abundant life in which the indwelling just referred to is known and the full joy and power of redemption are facts of personal experience. It will be only when

Christians come to understand fully the distinction betwixt these two conditions, and discern that the second of these is in very deed the will of God concerning them, and therefore a possible experience of each believer; when with shame and confusion of face they shall confess the sinful and inconsistent elements that still mark their life; that we shall dare to hope that the Christian community will once more be restored to its Pentecostal power.[17]

In these words Murray formulates the principle of the Holiness movement, which he makes clear in the passage that follows:

For a healthful Christian life, it is indispensable that we should be fully conscious that we have received the Holy Spirit to dwell in us.

This baptism of the Spirit, which is 'something higher' and 'different' from conversion[18] is imparted 'through laying on of hands and prayer'.

The minister of the Spirit whom God is to use for communicating the blessing as well as the believer who is to receive it, must meet with God in an immediate and close intercourse.[19]

Nevertheless this gift 'does not always come, as on the day of Pentecost, with external observation'.[20] In spite of this, 'Back to Pentecost; without this the work cannot be done!'[21]

The Church of Pentecost was not merely an example and pledge of what God could do, leaving us to choose if we would enjoy the same blessing. Nay, it is much more – a revelation of God's will as to what His Church ought to be, and of what is absolutely indispensable if there is to be any real hope of securing obedience to the command to bring the gospel to every creature.[22]

(*c*) *Murray's doctrine of healing through prayer*

In his doctrine of healing through prayer, if not in his practice of prayer with the sick, Murray came dangerously close to the theories of the American healing evangelists. Thus it is not surprising that one of the first propagandists of Dowie's church, the Christian Catholic Church,[23] was a disciple of Murray's (Le Roux, later leader of the Pentecostal Apostolic Faith Mission). He came from a Huguenot family which had settled in Wellington, where Murray worked for forty-five years.[24] Influenced by Stockmayer, Murray wrote:

Sick Christian, open thy Bible, study it and see in its pages that sickness is a warning to renounce sin, but that whoever acknowledges and forsakes his sins finds in Jesus pardon and healing. Such is God's promise in His Word. If the Lord had in view some other dispensation for such of His children whom He was about to call home to Him, He would make known to them His will, giving them by the Holy Spirit a desire to depart; in other special cases, He would awaken some special conviction; but as a general rule, the Word of God promises us healing in answer to the prayer of faith. . . . 'This is the will of God, even your sanctification' (I Thess. 4.3), and it is by healing that God confirms the reality of this. When Jesus comes to take possession of our body, and cures it miraculously, when it follows that the health received must be maintained from day to day by an uninterrupted communion with Him, the experience which we thus make of the Saviour's power and of His love is a result very superior to any which sickness has to offer.[25]

2. *John Alexander Dowie*

(*a*) *Outline of his life*

Dowie was born in Edinburgh in 1847. His mother was illiterate, while his father was a tailor, and a part-time preacher. When he was six years old he tried smoking; it made him ill, and this is clearly the explanation of his later aversion to tobacco.[26] In 1860 the young Dowie emigrated to his uncle in Australia, who set him to work as a shoe salesman. In an open air meeting he was converted by Henry Wright. Through poverty and sickness he was able to attend school only irregularly; in 1868 he received private tuition in Australia, in order to prepare himself to become a minister. From 1869 to 1872 he was a student in Edinburgh, and became a kind of honorary chaplain in an Edinburgh hospital. There he had the opportunity to overhear the conversation of the surgeons as they operated, which may explain his later antipathy towards doctors. The further information we have about his studies is contradictory.[27]

In 1872 he became a Congregationalist minister in Australia, and in 1878 an independent evangelist. In 1882 he opened his own tabernacle, but had to face bitter opposition from the clergy of Sydney. He tried without success to become a member of the Australian parliament, opened a church in Melbourne, fought a bitter struggle against the liquor companies, and was imprisoned for holding open air meetings without permission. All this only brought more publicity for his work, something for which he hungered throughout his life. The liquor manufacturers had a bomb set off in his church. But Dowie was warned beforehand by visions and voices, so that he escaped the attempt on his life.

During an epidemic of plague, he was seized with anger at the impotence of the medical profession. He refused to explain the death of those who had the plague as 'the will of God' and began to heal the sick through prayer.

In financial affairs he always seems to have been unfortunate. At any rate his wife wrote to him in 1877, at her father's instigation, to ask him to leave the administration of their finances to her, since she could not regard the financial risks he was taking as justified by his religious attitudes[28] and since he was neglecting his duty to maintain his wife and children.

He received an invitation to an international conference on divine healing and sanctification, which was taking place in 1885 under the leadership of the Methodist preacher Boardman in London.[29] Since Dowie could not attend himself, he sent a letter, which was later published. In it he proclaimed to the world that within three years he would set out on a 'world-wide mission'.[30]

In 1888 he arrived in America, in order to preach the 'full gospel'[31] there,[32]

In 1893 the Zion Tabernacle, which had been built in the meantime in Chicago, was full to overflowing. 'The miraculous healing of a cousin of the martyred President of the United States, Abraham Lincoln, who was brought in a dying state from Clinton, Ky., and the restoration of hundreds of sick people of every kind'[33] made him increasingly well-known. But he also met mockery and opposition. He himself boasted that he had been taken to court a hundred times, but had always won his case.[34] Although according to Dowie the city of Chicago was at that time physically and morally intoxicated, between 3,000 and 7,000 people came to his services to seek salvation and healing. After rejecting him at first, the theologians began to modify their theology.[35]

Dowie did not despise academic theology,[36] but put it to his own use. Thus in Zion College, Zion, Illinois, Hebrew, systematic theology, canon law and church history were taught, while in the preparatory school (a kind of grammar school) Latin, history, Greek, mathematics, natural science, English, etc., were taught. The teachers had had an (American) academic education. 'Careful attention will also be given to the study of Greek and Hebrew.'[37]

In 1896 Dowie proclaimed: 'The Church must have a business fellowship, a fellowship in getting money, in saving money, and in spending money for Christ.' He had a vision of building an industrial city without any institutional links with sin, disease and poverty. In Zion, Ill., there should be neither liquor stores, theatres, pork abattoirs, doctors nor hospitals; the latter were in any case unnecessary in the holy city. Instead a vast temple for 25,000 people was built, together with an industrial area, particularly for lace making on a co-operative basis.[38] In addition the members of Zion were to subscribe to shares in Zion at the Bank of Zion,[39] which even had a branch in Zürich.[40] On New Year's Eve 1900, on the stroke of midnight, Dowie unveiled in his temple a painting which showed the future city of Zion to his astonished congregation.

From 1901 on Dowie's highly individual personality seems to have taken on delusions of grandeur. He first of all tried to reintroduce into his church, the Christian Catholic Church, the rank of apostle.[41] From 1902 he asserted that churches which did not join his Zion were without further hope.[42] In 1903, with his 'Restoration Host', he organized large meetings in Madison Square Gardens. The eight special trains required to transport the members of Zion cost $250,000. He appeared dressed all in black, with a bodyguard of 1,000 men and a choir of hundreds of girls, all dressed in white. But this demonstration in New York was a mistake from the point of view both of finance and propaganda. The *New York World* had published unpleasant letters from Dowie to his father, in which Dowie questioned his relationship with his father,[43] and this led Dowie to misuse the meeting in New York to defend his own position. His self-adulation now knew no limits. 'John the Baptist was – I say in all humility – like me, not proud'.[44] In spite of his biblicism, he dared to say: 'Paul would have done better to keep quiet about some things.'[45] He wildly exaggerated his healings, when he stated that in one of his witness meetings more healings were reported than in the whole Bible.[46] 'We[47] were sent to destroy sin, to prepare the people of God and to restore the kingdom of the Lord.'[48] From now on he no longer used the name Dowie of himself: 'If we are not Elijah the Restorer, who is?'[49] He put on a high priestly garment and in 1904 undertook a world tour. In course of this he visited Zürich, which he chose to be the centre of his European branches. In response to the provocations of the reporters, he called down rain on them like Elijah.

In 1905 he was half-paralysed by a stroke. As a result of unwise financial policies the Zion manufactures and the Zion banks could no longer meet their obligations and the enterprises failed.[50] There was a famine in Zion, and Dowie was deposed. His successor was Willson Glen Voliva. Dowie died, an abandoned, broken and sick man, in his villa in Zion. Before his death he expressed the hope that he would return during the millennium. His son Gladstone became an Anglican clergyman and died in 1945. This was the end of a beautiful dream of the possibility of overcoming sin, if only men would at last begin to listen to God. But this has not prevented Holiness and Pentecostal evangelists of all lands from continuing to preach this dream up to the present day. But they have lacked Dowie's strength and courage to put the dream to the test in real life.

Of all the Pentecostal healing evangelists, it is Dowie who brought back the healing of the sick into the foreground. Many of his followers in Switzerland, Holland, South Africa and the USA[51] were leading Pentecostal preachers. The Anglican Dr K. Mackenzie called him a 'giant of faith'.[52] But the Lutheran pastor W. Lotze judges differently:

> In our eyes the man is a skilled performer, with a rare talent, a gripping orator, a marvellous organizer, a financial genius of the first rank, who had a masterly understanding of how to bind weak souls to himself and to hold his faithful together.[53]

The final word has not yet been said about Dowie. It would be particularly worthwhile to study the connection between his zeal for evangelism and his Utopian political and economic programme.[54]

Charles Kessler, the associate editor of *Leaves of Healing*, which is still published by the Christian Catholic Church, Zion, has given a critical summary of the driving force behind Dowie in the following words:

> The 'secret' of Dr Dowie was not his concept of spreading Zion cities over the world. It was not the spirit of controversy with which he attacked various denominations, individuals and the press. . . . I am convinced that Dr Dowie's zeal for justice, his hatred for racial discrimination, his plea for pacifism, his interest in equal universal education, his belief in universal redemption *together with* his passion for Divine Healing, and his hatred of these things that destroy the individual *all stem from his intense inner*, *spiritual commitment to the compassion and love of God.*[55]

(b) Worship and doctrine

Dowie set out his doctrine of the healing of the sick in eight points:

God's way of healing is a person, not a thing.
The Lord Jesus Christ is still the healer.
Divine Healing rests on Christ's atonement.
Disease can never be God's will.
The gifts of healing are permanent.
Divine Healing is opposed by diabolical counterfeits (Christian Science, Mind Healing etc.)
Multitudes have been healed through faith in Jesus.
Belief cometh of hearing, and hearing by the word of God.[56]

Dowie must have been a compelling preacher, understanding how to carry his audience with humour and irony, a quick wit and apparent logic:

> Where is the science of medicine? *Scientia* means accurate knowledge, does it not? It means sure and certain knowledge about a thing. Where is the sure and certain knowledge about medicine? See, here is a man steps up. 'I am an Allopath.'
>
> 'An allopath. Well how do you cure people?'
>
> 'Well, if they have got a disease in them, a poison, I look along the list of my medicines, all that pharmacy has taught me (You sorcerer!) and I find another poison stronger than the poison that is in the man, and I say, "Now open your mouth, and shut your eyes, and see what I have sent you," (laughter) and in it goes.'
>
> 'Well, what do you do?'
>
> 'I have knocked out that first poison.'
>
> 'Well, now Mr Allopath, after this stronger fellow has got in, what is he going to do?'
>
> 'Oh, well, after a while he may give us some trouble.'
>
> 'What are you going to do then?'
>
> 'I look along the line of my pharmacy, and I pick out another fellow, and I say, "Shut your eyes, and open your mouth," and I put him in and knock that one out.'
>
> 'That is very good. Now, what is the next thing? Supposing that strong poison you have put in gives the man trouble with the kidneys or liver, or his stomach, or something?'
>
> 'Well then I look along the line of my pharmacy, and I say, "Shut your eyes, and open your mouth," and I put in another and knock him out.' (laughter)
>
> 'Well, Mr Allopath, when does this stop?'
>
> 'Oh, it never stops until we knock the man out.' (laughter)[57]

There are similar passages on homoeopathy. He rejected the idea that sickness was a 'chastisement' or 'pedagogy from God'. Who would ask the teacher, in the interests of a child's education, to put out his eye in the first term, to break his leg in the second term, and in the third term to give him a suitable dose of diphtheria?[58]

In the Republic of South Africa Dowie's teaching and example has become typical of the important independent African churches. 'And that was the kind of Church which was to attempt to save the Africans lingering in utter darkness.'[59]

(c) *Dowie's 'Christian Catholic Church in Zion' in South Africa*

On 8 May 1904 the first missionary of Dowie's Christian Catholic Church, the overseer Daniel Bryant, arrived in Johannesburg and baptized twenty-seven Africans by threefold immersion.[60] The greater part of this church later developed into the Pentecostal Apostolic Faith Mission.[61] The healing practice of the Christian Catholic Church provided the example that has been followed by the South African Pentecostal movement and the independent churches[62] that have broken away from it. To this day the threefold immersion at baptism remains a mark of distinction between the Apostolic Faith Mission, influenced by Dowie's doctrine of baptism, and the other South African Pentecostal churches.

3. *The Beginnings of the Pentecostal Movement in South Africa*

(a) *The Apostolic Faith Mission*[63]

In 1908 a group of Pentecostal missionaries came to the South African Christian Catholic Church.[64] 'They brought the Pentecostal light to South Africa.'[65] They discovered that 'Zion taught immersion and divine healing, but *not* Pentecost'.[66] 'Meetings were first conducted in conjunction with the Apostolic Faith Church in Zion' – as the Christian Catholic Church was known in South Africa at that time.

In 1910 the Apostolic Faith Mission of South Africa was founded with Thomas Hezmalhalch as its first President.[67] Other prominent pastors were J. H. Greef, John G. Lake, who had formerly been an elder in Dowie's Christian Catholic Church in Zion, and P. L. le Roux, originally a missionary of the Dutch Reformed Church and a disciple of Andrew Murray,[68] later a pastor in the Christian Catholic Church in Zion, and finally, for 29 years, President of the Apostolic Faith Mission. Le Roux had already experienced his 'Pentecost' or 'baptism in the Holy Spirit' in 1907.[69]

From about 1915 onwards the African pastors of the Apostolic Faith Mission were either left to themselves or made themselves independent. This is something which at the present day is very embarrassing to the leaders of the Apostolic Faith Mission and which they deny, although it is perfectly obvious from their own records.[70] The derivation of hundreds of independent Bantu churches from the Christian Catholic Church in Zion, or from the Apostolic Faith

Mission, can be seen not only from the historical development which we set out in full below, but also from the following characteristics:

1. The names of the churches include the words 'Zion', 'Apostolic' or 'Pentecost'.
2. Like Dowie and the Apostolic Faith Mission, they almost all practise baptism with threefold immersion.
3. The food taboos are almost without exception the same as Dowie's.[71]
4. The theocratic leaders of these churches have the same titles (overseer, Elijah, King, etc.) as Dowie in the Christian Catholic Church and are honoured by the same liturgical terminology.
5. Medicine is rejected and there is absolute reliance on the healing of the sick through prayer.
6. The parallels between the Pentecostal concept of the Spirit and the concept of *uMoya* (the Spirit) in the Bantu churches, the function of women and prophets, the phenomena of possession and speaking in tongues in both groups are described in detail below[72]
7. The Christian Catholic Church and the independent Bantu churches both delight in uniforms, theatrical processions, and a complicated hierarchy. Many of the African churches surround their leader with a bodyguard, such as accompanied Dowie.

The important similarities between the independent African churches, the Pentecostal movement and the Christian Catholic Church are not surprising. The African churches constantly receive fresh stimulus from the Pentecostal movement, and back numbers of Dowie's *Leaves of Healing* are still read and revered.[73]

The first meetings of the Apostolic Faith Mission were held in Doornfontein (Johannesburg). The Pentecostal missionaries gained entry not only into the Christian Catholic Church, but also into the Reformed Churches of South Africa. Non-Christians, including the son of a rabbi, were also converted. The Apostolic Faith Mission spread principally amongst the Afrikaans-speaking Boers. This fact, together with their Reformed background (*geen gelijkstelling* – 'no equality') has made it easy for the Apostolic Faith Mission to support the apartheid policy of the South African Government.[74] For this reason F. P. Möller has severely criticized my account of the South African Pentecostal movement.

> The Republic of South Africa and Southern Rhodesia are the only countries on the continent of Africa where you still have religious liberty.[75]

The members of the Apostolic Faith Mission seem to be well integrated in the white ruling class of South Africa. A cabinet minister, B. Schoeman, was the brother of a high official of the Apostolic Faith Mission (Abilenes J. Schoeman). Another leading member of the church, G. Wessels, was a member of the Senate in 1964.[76]

It is also interesting that a member of the Apostolic Faith Mission, E. M.

van Vivier, wrote the first psychological study of speaking in tongues by a Pentecostal.[77] There is not space here for a full account of the doctrine and history of the Apostolic Faith Mission, which is of interest and of some importance in South African society. We shall mention only what is necessary to understand the Pentecostal African churches (or Zionists).[78]

(*b*) *Assemblies of God*[79]

In 1914 the newly founded Assemblies of God in the USA[80] accepted as part of their organization the missionary churches that had been founded by R. M. Turney and others in South Africa. In 1925 the Assemblies of God in South Africa became an independent district and in 1932 were separated from the parent organization in the USA. They originally formed a non-segregated missionary church with the emphasis on the African element. The growth of white participation in this church and the political polarization of South Africa forced the Assemblies of God to separate the organization of the African and the white sectors of their work. The Assemblies of God were able to unite a hundred Swiss, English, North American, Scandinavian and South African missionaries in an association. But whether the Joint Executive Council, which consisted of five whites (European and American) and five black South Africans, is still functioning, is unknown. 'However, the fellowship is simply on a spiritual basis, and separate dining rooms and quarters are provided for whites and Africans.'[81] Fred Burke set up a notable Bible School for the leaders of the 'independent Churches'.[82] Five hundred African evangelists, including the well-known evangelists Nicholas H. B. Bhengu[83] and Philip Molefe, still work with the foreign missionaries. Their doctrine is similar to that of the American Assemblies of God.[84]

Blacks still considerably outnumber whites in the Assemblies of God. As the influence of Bhengu constantly increased, the American missionaries accused him of dictatorship, and the Assemblies of God split into the Assemblies of God of Southern Africa (with Bhengu, the Canadian, South African and other missionaries and the black evangelists) and the International Assemblies of God (which in spite of its name consists entirely of American missionaries). The latter body is not recognized by the government.[85]

NOTES

1. A. Stucki, *Andrew Murray*, p. 10.
2. *Ibid*., p. 12.
3. J. Du Plessis, *Andrew Murray*, p. 59; Stucki, *op. cit*., p. 16.
4. Du Plessis, *op. cit*., p. 64; Stucki, *op. cit*., p. 17.
5. Du Plessis, *op. cit*., pp. 194f., quoting the Rev. J. C. de Vries; cf. Stucki, *op. cit*., pp. 27f.; D. G. Molenaar, *De doop*, pp. 236–8.
6. Stucki, *op. cit*., p. 29.

7. Du Plessis, *op. cit.*, p. 197; Stucki, *op. cit.*, pp. 30f.
8. Stucki, *op. cit.*, p. 38.
9. Douglas, *Andrew Murray*, pp. 166, 168; Stucki, *op. cit.*, pp. 56–8; D. G. Molenaar, *De doop*, pp. 233–5.
10. Stucki, *op. cit.*, p. 58.
11. *Ibid.*, p. 5.
12. A. Murray, *Spirit of Christ*, pp. 14–16.
13. *Ibid.*, p. 22.
14. Murray, *School of Prayer*; in his doctrine of prayer Murray prefers texts from St Luke, e.g. Luke 18.1–8 (cf. *Ministry of Intercession*, pp. 43–54; *Key to the Missionary Problem*, pp. 127ff.).
15. Cf. ch. 24.4, pp. 336ff.
16. Murray, *Spirit of Christ*, pp. 51f.
17. A. Murray, *Full Blessing*, p. 12.
18. *Ibid.*, pp. 12, 14.
19. *Ibid.*, pp. 16f.
20. *Ibid.*, p. 115.
21. Murray, *Key*, p. 132.
22. *Ibid.*, p. 119.
23. Cf. p. 120.
24. Cf. p. 120.
25. A. Murray, *Divine Healing*, pp. 70f.; full bibliography on Murray, 01.36.003.
26. G. Lindsay, *Life of Dowie*, pp. 12f.
27. It is not known where he received his doctorate (cf. G. P. Gardiner, *Bread of Life*, March 1957, pp. 3ff.).
28. The whole correspondence is given in G. Lindsay, *op. cit.*
29. *Semaine Religieuse de Genève*, 30.1.1886, p. 19. According to *Guérison et Sanctification par la Foi*, 1886, pp. 112 ff. (Conference report) the following spoke at this conference: Mr and Mrs Boardman, Elias Schrenk, A. B. Simpson (founder of the Christian and Missionary Alliance, 02a.02.013).
30. J. A. Dowie, *Leaves of Healing*, 15.1.1900, pp. 512–16; H. Besson, *Mouvement de Sanctification*, 1914, p. 79; *Le Dieu qui te guérit*, Feb. 1887, p. 7.
31. An expression which later became a standard concept in the Pentecostal movement.
32. J. A. Dowie, *Leaves of Healing*, 15.12.1899, pp. 1–6; cf. *Democrat*, Clinton, 8.3.1894.
33. J. A. Dowie, *Leaves of Healing*, 15.12.1899, p. 2.
34. E. S. Bates, art. 'J. A. Dowie', *Dictionary of American Biography*, 1930, p. 413.
35. J. A. Dowie, *Leaves of Healing*, 15.12.1899, pp. 1–6.
36. This naturally did not prevent him from making violent attacks on the theologians, especially German theologians (J. A. Dowie, *Leaves of Healing*, 19.7.1902, pp. 424 f.).
37. *Leaves of Healing*, 15.1.1900, pp. 917f.
38. J. A. Dowie, *Leaves of Healing*, 15.6.1900, p. 298.
39. W. S. Peckham, *Leaves of Healing*, 15.11.1909, p. 1.
40. Verbal communication from former members of the *Zionsgemeinde* ('Church of Zion'), Zürich. The reason for subscription to Zion shares was often the hope of emigrating.
41. Minutes of the conferences quoted in G. Lindsay, *op. cit.*, pp. 152–6.
42. G. Lindsay, *op. cit.*, p. 203; J. A. Dowie, *Leaves of Healing*, 1902, p. 419.
43. Perhaps Dowie was born out of wedlock or from an adulterous union. His mother's name was in fact Ann McFarlane-McHardie (Lindsay).

44. *Blätter der Heilung*, 1904, p. 236; W. Lotze, 'Dowie', in E. Kalb, *Kirchen und Sekten*, 1905, p. 491.

45. *Blätter der Heilung*, 1902, p. 136; W. Lotze, *loc. cit.*

46. J. A. Dowie, *Leaves of Healing*, 1900, p. 760.

47. He is now referring to himself with the royal 'we'.

48. *Blätter der Heilung*, 1902, p. 177; W. Lotze, *op. cit.*, p. 487.

49. J. A. Dowie, *Leaves of Healing*, 23.8.1902, p. 591.

50. A.W.N., *Leaves of Healing*, 7.4.1906, pp. 437–9.

51. Full list, 02a.02.047, n. 203.

52. G. P. Gardiner, *Bread of Life*, March 1957, pp. 3ff.

53. W. Lotze, *op. cit.*, p. 492.

54. Sources, documents, literature, 02a.02.047.

55. C. Kessler, *Leaves of Healing*, 55/2, March–April 1969, pp. 11–19.

56. *Leaves of Healing*, 23.2.1902, p. 593.

57. J. A. Dowie, *Leaves of Healing* 3/40, 41.7.1897, p. 636.

58. *Blätter der Heilung*, 15.7.1900, p. 185.

59. Sundkler, p. 48.

60. Sundkler, p. 48; first missionaries: Mordred Powell, F. M. Royall.

61. Documents, sources, literature: 01.36.011. Statistics: 250 congregations, 10,000 members (WChH 1962; WChH 1968: no entry).

62. Cf. ch. 12.4(*e*), pp. 159ff.

63. Documents, sources, literature: 01.36.017. The account above has had to be considerably abbreviated. Statistics: 535 congregations, 100,000 members. Journal: *Trooster/Comforter*.

64. The names of the Pentecostal missionaries of this early period, which can be ascertained, are: W. J. Kerr, originally of the South African Interior Mission; J. O. Lehman; John G. Lake, originally of the Christian Catholic Church; Verna G. Barnard; Louis Schneiderman (*Trooster*, Aug./Sept. 1940; Sundkler, p. 224; F. P. Möller, letter of 20.3.1962 to Atter, quoted in G. F. Atter, *Third Force*, pp. 201f.; J. R. Flower, *PE* 2177, 29.1.1956, p. 30).

65. F. P. Möller, *loc. cit.*

66. Sundkler, p. 48.

67. F. P. Möller, *loc. cit.*

68. D. J. Du Plessis, *PE* 1264, 30.7.1938, pp. 2–4.

69. Sundkler, p. 48; P. L. le Roux, 'Pentecostal Signs', *PE* 1674, 8.6.1946, pp. 3, 8.

70. Cf. ch. 12.2, pp. 150ff.

71. A Zionist local church leader told Sundkler that he had left the Anglican Church 'because they mix Christianity and heathenism by allowing tobacco, beer, and pork.' One of the European leaders of the Christian Catholic Church told Sundkler: 'Zion said, Zion does not allow beer, medicine, tobacco and pork. Dowie was against pork. We felt sick if we ate it. And as you know it is forbidden in the Bible' (Sundkler, pp. 216f.).

72. Cf. ch. 12.4(*c*), p. 157.

73. Sundkler, p. 243.

74. This is the slogan of the Dutch Reformed Churches of South Africa. The English-speaking Anglicans and the Roman Catholics are in principle (unfortunately not in practice) opposed to the Apartheid policy of the South African government. (M.-L. Martin, Notes, p. 4.)

75. F. P. Möller, letter to W.H., 4.6.1964.

76. A. Kast, letter to W.H. 16.4.1964; D. Gee, *Wind and Flame*, p. 269.

77. L. M. Vivier-van Eetveldt, *Glossolalia*; *id.*, 'Glossolalic', in T. Spörri, *Ekstase*, pp. 153–75.

78. Full details: 01.36.017. Doctrine: F. P. Möller, *De Apostoliese Leer.*

79. Sources, documents, literature: 01.36.019. Statistics: 21,676 members, 225 congregations. Journal: *Fellowship.*

80. Cf. ch. 3, pp. 29ff.

81. E. G. Wilson, *Making Many Rich*, p. 216.

82. E. F. Burke, *Fellowship*, 4/4–5, April/May 1963, pp. 11, 15; E. F. Burke, *PE* 2711, 24.4.1966, p. 10; E. F. Burke, *Monthly Letter on Evangelism*, Dec. 1966/Jan. 1967, Geneva: WCC (!).

83. Cf. ch. 10, pp. 126ff.

84. Cf. Appendix: 2, pp. 514ff.

85. Verbal communication from D. J. Du Plessis, 4.8.1968. C. Carmichael (*PE* 2386, 15.9.1968, pp. 19–26) describes the matter somewhat differently.

10

Nicholas B. H. Bhengu: A Charismatic African Prophet

1. *His Significance and his Life*

NICHOLAS BHENGU was born in 1909 in Entumeni in Zululand, and was the son of a Lutheran pastor.[1] Known as the 'black Billy Graham', he is of particular importance because of his intermediary position between the independent African churches[2] and the Pentecostal mission churches.[3] He might serve as a model for the study called for by Dorothy Emmet of the relation between the 'hypnotic' and 'charismatic' types of leader. The latter 'is concerned to build up his followers in what we may call a vocational group, in which their responsibility is developed'.[4] Emmet sets out to show that the requirement of a consciousness of responsibility can only be made by a prophet who has a prophetic consciousness that derives from a *vocation* experience which lifts him out of his society without isolating him from it. Bhengu and the church founded by him (Assemblies of God, East London) present a model in which one can observe the situation that comes about between a 'charismatic' leader and the community which is dependent upon him, but which is also indispensable to him.

Bhengu was originally a teacher and speaks perfect and vigorous English and elegant Zulu. In Cape Province he speaks in Xhosa and in Swaziland in Seswati. He also speaks Shangaan, Sotho and Afrikaans.

He attended the Lutheran missionary school in Entumeni, and from 1925 the Roman Catholic missionary schools in Inkamana and Marianhill.[5] In the intervals of his studies he earned the money for his keep as a clerk in a solicitor's office. He was attracted to the trade union movement and was employed in the office of the Durban leader, Mr Champion. He became suspicious of the extreme course the union was following. He 'ran away' to Kimberley, 'where there will be neither my people nor my companions who influence me to sin and lethargy'.[6] But in Kimberley he came into contact with even more radical circles. He joined the Communist Party, and by his own account became 'one of the leading noise-makers and demagogues'.[7] He also joined the International Bible Students

Association and the Seventh Day Adventists, though without losing touch with the Schreuder Mission. The upheaval that led to his subsequent career was his conversion in the course of a mission by two young Americans belonging to the Full Gospel Church.[8] He broke off his connections with the Communists, the Bible Students and the Seventh Day Adventists. Two things in particular had attracted him in the revival preaching; the American pronunciation and intonation of English, and the simplicity of the interpretation of Isaiah 53. Verse for verse, line for line, the two evangelists built up their preaching on their personal experience. Thirdly, the joy and sincerity with which they proclaimed their message aroused in him the desire to be one of their followers. But he asked himself whether people of his race could equal the two young white men.

Bhengu gives a vivid description of the inner restraints he had to overcome before he could manage to speak to the preachers. He would willingly have gone forward when sinners were called to the penitents' bench. But he was afraid to lose prestige in the eyes of his girl friend. At least he did not want to be the first to come forward, and no one else led the way. But the conviction that if he were not converted that night he would never be saved and would die a sinner drove him to ask to speak to the preachers. Bhengu's account clearly indicates that it was fear of eternal damnation which drove him to this step. From his own experience Bhengu now hammers home to his audience the lesson: 'Do not delay the decision! Tomorrow may be too late! Do not wait for another to take the step first!'

Bhengu had to overcome other psychological difficulties before he could come to the knowledge that he was saved. After talking and praying with one of the preachers, he was asked whether he now felt he was saved. Bhengu said 'I do not feel anything yet.' The preacher then asked whether Bhengu had any money on him and could feel that. Just as he had no need to feel the money to be sure that he had it with him, so he could take his salvation for certain. 'From that time faith came into my heart; I did not wait for feelings of any kind but took the word of God and thanked him in prayer.'[9] But he first felt the effect of his conversion the next morning, when he found himself incapable of smoking and drinking as usual. The mere smell of tobacco and gin made him feel sick.[10] He asked,

> What is gone wrong with me? A thought came – maybe this is the result of salvation. I knelt down to pray for the first time from the heart and I said, 'Thank you God for Jesus your Son who died my death and now I am saved and have eternal life. My name is in the Book of Life.'[11]

When he testified in his Lutheran church at home that God had set him free from his sins, he was astonished to find himself condemned for teaching error, on the grounds that this is something no one can know on this side of the grave. He then tried to join the Salvation Army, after hearing their testimonies in street meetings. But he had approached a group of whites, and was refused membership on grounds of racial separation. He thereupon set up his own free assemblies in Kimberley. He gathered people together for common Bible study and to testify in the streets. Following a vision in which Jesus showed him how he could help black people from the most diverse language groups in Africa, who were drowning in a great sea and calling for help, he intensified his Bible study. From 1934–36 he attended the South Africa General Mission Bible School in Dumia. In 1937 he returned to his earlier place of work as a court interpreter.[12] In 1938 he was ordained as an evangelist of the Assemblies of God. Many missionaries regard Bhengu as having no denominational allegiance, which is wrong. He certainly accepts invitations from all churches (Plymouth Brethren, Lutherans, Church of the Nazarene,[13] Free Methodists,[14] etc.). But the church he founded on 1 January 1945 belongs to the Assemblies of God. The consecration of the church, which had cost $28,000, took place within the framework of the Annual Conference of the Assemblies of God; 3,000 Africans took part in the consecration, which was concluded by a feast for which ten oxen were slaughtered.

From 1945 on he undertook long journeys: to Portuguese East Africa, several to Europe and America,[15] to Kenya, to the World Pentecostal Conference in London (1952), to Japan. He was a member of the Advisory Committee for the Fifth World Pentecostal Conference in Toronto (1958). His great revival campaigns in South Africa, and especially his fight against crime, gained him the favour and support of the South African government. He cannot understand why his Lutheran mother church did not accept his testimony. He quotes as the examples he has followed Huldrych Zwingli, John Calvin, John Knox, John Wesley, Evan Roberts,[16] David Livingstone, Robert Moffat, Henry M. Stanley, Charles G. Finney, Dwight L. Moody and Reuben A. Torrey.[17]

2. *His Teaching*

Bhengu's declaration of belief is given in the Appendix.[18] Although Bhengu's churches form 'part of a Pentecostal church of (White) American origin'[19] and Bhengu teaches Pentecostal doctrine in his sermons, it is notable that the declaration of belief does not mention the typical Pentecostal doctrine of the baptism of the Spirit. There are no doubt reasons why it is not included in the declaration. His forms of worship, his pastoral practice and his views on the baptism of the Spirit, believers' baptism and the healing of the sick through prayer, are all in the best tradition of the Pentecostal movement, even though this is not expressed in his declaration of belief and although, because of his above average intelligence, he avoids the kind of statement made by white missionaries in South Africa.

Katesa Schlosser, who has made a lengthy study of Bhengu in her outstanding work *Eingeborenenkirchen in Süd- und Südwestafrika* ('Indigenous Churches in South and South-West Africa'), sums up his teaching under three headings: (*a*) the proof of God through the healing of the sick, (*b*) the preaching of Jesus as redeemer, (*c*) the struggle against ancestor worship. To these three points one may add a fourth, the doctrine of baptism; while his doctrine of the Spirit will be dealt with in the section on worship and devotion.

(*a*) *The proof of God through the healing of the sick*

'I will prove that there is a God and that he is stronger than the Devil!' He does this by faith healings, 'for without them my church would be as empty as the other Protestant missions'. 'If I was not convinced that the missionary command had to be carried out in all its parts, both teaching *and* healing, I would not have begun to preach.'[20] Katesa Schlosser reports:

> Bhengu regards hostility to medicine as a regrettable mistake on the part of many Pentecostal churches . . . I have never heard testimonies about healings of organic diseases. This seems once again to be in contrast to the white American Pentecostal churches. [Bhengu] affirmed on 8 April and 2 November 1953 that in East London he cooperated with two doctors, to whom he sent everyone suffering from an organic disease.[21]

According to Katesa Schlosser, this does not stop Bhengu proclaiming the healing of the organically sick.[22] In the vernacular his church is known as the 'Healer's Church' (*icawe kamphilisi*).[23]

> God desires a healthy mind in a healthy body. The body is the temple of God It is our duty to keep this temple pure and to avoid everything that can harm it. And therefore I do not need to forbid my followers to smoke and drink. I only draw their attention to the ruin of their health – and their finances! And the result? None of my people smokes or drinks.[24]

(*b*) *The preaching of Jesus as redeemer*

Bhengu adopts the latent perfectionism of the Holiness and Pentecostal movements and teaches that Jesus' redemption is final. The *simul justus, simul peccator* of Lutheranism is completely incomprehensible to him, the son of a Lutheran (admittedly African Lutheran) pastor – as it is to every Pentecostal preacher. A summary of his view is:

> The White Protestant missionaries definitely give a false interpretation of the Bible 'when they always drag the burden of sin around with them'. This is a doctrine of which as Africans they can make nothing. For the White missionaries easily conclude that from that the Blacks have to bend their backs to carry the burden of sin laid upon them.[25]

This idea is also expressed in the testimonies made at conversion:

> Today I believe in the existence of God Almighty and I fear him, for I have learnt that the fear of the Lord is the beginning of wisdom. I am no longer what I used to be, *udlalani*, an aimless lover of women.[26]

(*c*) *The struggle against ancestor worship*

Bhengu allows a general veneration of ancestors, but forbids praying to them as gods.[27] God Almighty rules over the ancestors of the 'red people'.[28] 'The spirits of the ancestors may indeed be watching our steps though they are subject to God.'[29] 'A third of Bhengu's followers come from paganism,[30] a high proportion in comparison to other sects who prefer "to steal the sheep of other shepherds".'[31] August Kast notes that 'many witch doctors have been converted'.[32] In spite of this 'he cannot be said to have succeeded notably in the main strongholds of paganism.'[33]

(*d*) *Baptism*

The *Daily Dispatch* of 15 April 1952 reports a mass baptism in East London, in the course of which 1,300 converts were baptized under the direction of Nicholas Bhengu and in the presence of white representatives of the Assemblies of God. In his baptismal address Bhengu said:

> For those who are baptized today, it does not mean that they are free to sin again. They all know that. There is only one baptism.[34] And if they were to sin again afterwards, they would know that they would then become sinners for ever.[35]

Thus Bhengu follows Heb. 6.4–6 in recognizing only *one* repentance and forgiveness, preceding baptism. After baptism there is in principle no more sin.[36]

3. *Worship and Devotion*

Bhengu realizes the great effectiveness of hymns.

> The hymns sung in East London by a thousand or more people in six to eight parts must have done a very great deal to overcome the feeling of abandonment on the part of the detribalized and to maintain the fortifying consciousness of belonging to a larger community.[37]

Naturally he uses American and African rhythms.

Katesa Schlosser describes two of Bhengu's services. She is surprised at the difference between them. One, during which a hailstorm came down on the corrugated iron roof of the cinema in which the service was taking place, turned into an apparently unrestrained, ecstatic confusion (though anyone who is acquainted with Pentecostal services knows that even in the most extreme frenzy certain liturgical laws prevail, which the leader has to follow). In the second service, the excitement of the same congregation was not even as great as that before the ecstasy in the first service.[38]

The following sermon, which Bhengu gave at the Fifth World Pentecostal Conference in London, supplements Katesa Schlosser's description, and is typical of Bhengu's rhetorical style, devotion and concept of the Spirit. I still recall the powerful impression that this forceful, lucid preacher made on the Conference.

There is a tribe in South Africa . . . the Masutos. When a woman has a baby she stays indoors for three months. She doesn't go out. This woman I am talking about now, had a baby almost three months old. She was indoors, and the tornado took place. She couldn't leave her baby and run away. She decided to kneel and cover the baby with her body. The bricks passed over her. The roofing iron scraped her body. You know what a tornado does. Her back was ripped open. You could see lungs inside. Still she covered the baby, and she died . . .

I drove 700 miles to go see the baby whose mother had done such a noble act. Came to the hospital – I wanted to see the baby. I knelt and prayed and thanked God. And this thought came to me – this is what Jesus has done for us . . . Jesus died on the Cross that we should not die. Those who believe in Jesus have passed from death unto life. I just preach this message. Some people say that this is an old message. But this is the message that is saving souls in Africa today. Jesus! We glorify Jesus! His death! . . .

And while we preach we get a cripple over there – he jumps up. He makes a noise; he throws his crutches away; he walks; he runs about; he creates an uproar. We didn't pray for him. Jesus healed him; and he shouts; and the people know Jesus heals . . .

Now when the Lord started to baptize in East London it was on an Easter Monday. We were outside in the open. There were over 7,000 people. There were missionaries there from all denominations who had come to East London on holiday. Everyone who came to East London wanted to see this revival. Lutheran missionaries, Dutch Reformed missionaries – they all had their umbrellas. And I said to God, 'I hope nothing will happen today.'

And while we were singing the chorus, 'There is power in the Blood of the Lamb', He came down upon the whole crowd half past ten in the morning until it was dark. The people didn't know where they were. Small boys twelve years old talked in tongues and prophesied. We had a wonderful day. And from that day on God was filling people with the Holy Spirit. It was impossible to preach. The rain came down upon the people. And people came from all over to see what this noise was – and they got converted – and the numbers increased, and the Lord baptized.

Some of the things you may think we are exaggerating. We had to send for buses – people couldn't walk – they were like dead . . . The bus drivers and conductors picked the people up, put them in the buses. The same conductors were under the power of the Holy Spirit when they touched these men! . . . They said, 'As soon as we touch them this comes into us.'

In East London God saved all[39] the bus conductors, and all the bus drivers . . . In East London we closed down a theatre hall – a very big theatre hall, very popular. We closed it down. No man could go there. It was empty. Until the men came to us and begged us to rent it from them. We took it over, and there were no shows in that city. We showed Christ. That is what God has done for us . . .[40]

Jesus! That is what the apostles preached. You know why Missions have failed? They preach Jesus from the head – not filled with the Holy Ghost. And you know why we fail? We preach the Holy Ghost and leave Jesus – and then we both fail. The purpose of the Holy Ghost is to bring Jesus to us . . .[41]

4. *Is Bhengu a Pentecostal?*

Katesa Schlosser doubts whether Bhengu is capable of ecstasy. Moreover he denied to her – after ascertaining that she was a Lutheran – that he had had any ecstatic experiences, such as are frequent elsewhere in Pentecostal churches. He explicitly denied dreams and visions, and any direct command from God. But in his book *Revival Fire* and in his sermons he appeals not only to a direct divine command, but also to visions. Katesa Schlosser considers that the question cannot be resolved: did he make concessions to the Lutheran European or to the Africans, of whose fondness for supernatural things he is only too well aware?

In addition Bhengu emphasizes that he is by no means invited to preach only by Pentecostal churches, and that those whom he has converted could even join the Anglican Church. He said several times to Katesa Schlosser: 'I am not a simple Pentecostal man. I belong rather to the Plymouth Brethren and to the Baptists.'[42]

On the other hand the following points must be noted:

(i) In all respects Bhengu's services are in the best tradition of the Pentecostal movement.

(ii) Bhengu received his decisive conversion experience in a Pentecostal congregation.

(iii) Bhengu's organizational link with the Assemblies of God of South Africa, by which he was ordained in 1938 and whose certificate of baptism he uses in his baptismal services, has remained unbroken for 25 years. It is also expressed in his international links with the Pentecostal movement and in his acceptance of the Presidency of the African section of the Assemblies of God of Southern Africa.

(iv) His work with the sick, his view of baptism of the Spirit, his position between Pentecostal missionary churches and independent African Pentecostal churches are possible only within the framework of the religious outlook and organization of the Assemblies of God. For in spite of the theological guidance they lay down, they give wide scope in matters of worship and devotion; and while a headquarters gives organizational support the local congregation is guaranteed as much freedom and autonomy as possible. In what other organization in South Africa could Bhengu give expression to as many aspects of his ministry as in the Assemblies of God?

That he should maintain his links with other evangelical bodies likewise belongs to the best traditions of the Pentecostal movement, which sets out to serve the whole church.[43] On the other hand Bhengu's declaration of faith,[44] which omits the definition of the baptism of the Spirit, so important to Pentecostals, suggests he has certain reservations about the Pentecostal doctrine of the baptism of the Spirit.

Bhengu's attitude to the World Council of Churches is unknown. But it is possible that if he was approached the Ecumenical movement would find in him a skilled and powerful, albeit independent spokesman for its cause. He does not call himself a simple Pentecostal, and this expresses his criticism of the sectarian narrow-mindedness of many Pentecostals, and of their indifference towards the social and political questions which are of importance for him. It is also a mark of his objection to the undiscriminating rejection of all medical assistance by some Pentecostal groups. As far as the matter of ecstasy is concerned, no Pentecostal would ever describe his spiritual experiences by the term ecstasy, which is drawn from comparative religion. He rejects this word for describing his religion, for the emotional outbursts experienced in Pentecostalism do not normally lead to the elimination of the personality. If this nevertheless happens, Pentecostals fear a demonic influence, for they say that the Holy Spirit does not overpower us, he ennobles us. But paganism lives by and in ecstasy. His denial of the revelatory function of dreams and visions comes from the same attitude. It is quite clear as a matter of fact that Bhengu has had dreams and visions. But even if they have been the experiences which have led him to decisions, they could not have any theological standing as ultimate revelation. This is excluded by the fundamentalist theology of the great majority of Pentecostals, whose final authority is the Bible interpreted in a fundamentalist sense. In the *theological system* of the Pentecostals dreams and visions have the function of interpretations of the Bible which are subordinate to it. This may well be *in contradiction to their reality as experiences*. In his testimony in *Revival Fire* Bhengu argues on the level of experience, but to the European Lutheran he argues on the theological level. Pentecostal theologians often do not keep the two separate.

5. *Bhengu's Concern for Social Ethics*

Bhengu has a clearly thought out, modest yet well-balanced and realistic social programme. When one considers the prevailing uncertainty and naivety in these matters amongst fundamentalist bodies, this is a great achievement. On the basis of Katesa Schlosser's studies and the reports made by Philip Mayer[45] and A. A. Dubb,[46] one can sum it up as follows: (*a*) Brotherhood between 'red people' and 'school people'.[47] (*b*) A struggle against crime amongst Africans in the locations by preaching against bad films,[48] alcohol, smoking, and sexual licence, and an emphasis on the blessing of work and the necessity of observing the ten commandments even in relations with white people. (*c*) The strengthening of the self-confidence of the Africans towards the whites. (*d*) The struggle against the independent African Pentecostal Churches.[49] (*e*) A more remote aim – communal village settlements for his followers.[50]

(*a*) *Brotherhood between 'red people' and 'school people'*

In the traditional European churches of South Africa there are mostly only 'school people', while the independent African churches and 'low class churches' consist only of 'red people'. In Bhengu's church both classes live together. Former pagans, who are still not masters of the European way of life, can come together with 'school people', Africans who live in a European style; because of their mutual rejection this is extremely rare elsewhere. In Bhengu's church a friendly greeting is given to former pagans, and the 'school people' do not show them any condescension. The fellowship between them and the rejection of those who are outside this 'new tribe' is greater than the natural aversion of the 'school people' for the 'red people'. The distinguishing marks of the 'tribe' are the rigorist requirements of the Pentecostal movement: dancing and the cinema are forbidden.[51] On the other hand, purity, cleanliness, education,[52] industriousness, prayer, Bible study and the 'spreading of the gospel'[53] are tribal virtues:

> In heaven the streets are shining gold and the dresses shining white. Let us, as good Christians, be as clean and shining in our appearance as we can, even here. . . . It is difficult for people to break away from their old customs. Africans in the country like to relieve themselves in the bush, but here we have lavatories. Use them. I shall not be pleased to hear that dirty paper is lying about in them. I see that you are even too lazy to flush the lavatories. That is being very dirty. This church, too, is cleaned every day, but look at it just now, with all these papers lying around. It is this kind of thing that makes the location streets unecessarily dirty too.[54]

The quotation shows not only the difficulty of the task that Bhengu has taken on, but also that the necessary alternative to the apartheid policy of South African government is not as simple as is imagined in Europe.

Dubb questioned the 767 persons present at a Sunday service about their social origin. Twenty-nine per cent were of 'red' origin. Of these a third were men, a high percentage for an African church in East London. The 'red people' were half former 'farm people', who had been employed on a daily basis, and half peasants from the reserves.[55] But farm people and widows (Bhengu's church has many widows) are amongst the deprived groups of 'red' village society. So far Bhengu has not exercised any great influence on the 'red' immigrants who still have firm roots in their village. The 'red' people whom one meets in Bhengu's church tend to be those who have received *more* education than most of the 'red people' who come to the town.[56] Thus Bhengu has won over to Christianity many pagans who have become unsure of their paganism through their acquaintance with European civilization and decreasing contact with the place where their traditional religion was practised. We should not underestimate the value of this work of reintegration for a class pressing violently for improvement. 'Here, it seemed, the demons of the town were being tamed by a higher power.'[57] There are also middle-class white people amongst Bhengu's congregations.

(b) The fight against crime amongst the Africans

In the locations, the black quarters of South African towns, families break up, and children lead a disorganized life,

> because everyone has to go to work and only comes home late at night. The whole country is faced with the problem of the rising generation. The whites are afraid of the increasing crime wave, anarchy and law-breaking amongst the Africans. African parents are also appalled and dismayed, and go in fear of their own sons, who rob, plunder, murder and wound whoever they come across. The police are powerless and social workers have no answer. One asks the other what can be done. My solution has always been [says Bhengu]: Jesus is the answer.[58]

While the battle for and against apartheid was raging in Africa, Bhengu said to Katesa Schlosser that he preached apartheid before Malan's government:

> Only through apartheid can we Bantu gradually achieve so much that the Europeans will finally . . . themselves have to grant us social recognition.[59]

This attitude of Bhengu's is reflected in the sermons mentioned above. 'You, you strong young men, must become politicians with a constructive policy'.[60]

(c) The struggle against the independent African Pentecostal churches

He attacks and mocks them:

> They beat drums, blow horns and dance throughout the night. This is certainly not God's will. God has ordained the night for sleeping, so that we can work during the day. The Zionist services are held for money. It is money that divides us. These services are not meant for the worship of God, but for the income and pleasure of the preacher, for 'they like to eat meat'.[61]

(d) Strengthening the self-confidence of the Africans towards the Whites

Bhengu exorts his followers to obey the government and to behave honestly towards the whites, but does not reproach only the Africans for their sins in his sermons. 'Many Europeans are far greater heathen than can be found amongst the Bantu.' 'Most Bantu find nothing wrong in stealing little things up to the size of a camera – though bank robberies are carried out by Europeans.' (Loud applause.)[62]

(e) Communal village settlements

The ideal Bhengu has in mind is a kind of Soviet *kolchoz*, which is familiar to him from Marxist literature.

> Instead of the scattered settlement usual here I would if necessary enforce settlement in compact villages. The centre point of the village must be a

cultural centre. Every family should have its own house and garden. There must be enough employment for men to remain with their families and not have to migrate temporarily. All work must be done in common. But women must completely withdraw from earning money and devote themselves solely to their families.[63]

6. *Bhengu in the Crossfire of Politics*

Katesa Schlosser writes:

> Bhengu pleads for peace with the whites – a phenomenon amongst 'educated natives' in the Union of South Africa – and is consequently branded and threatened as a 'traitor' by the nationalist natives who belong to the African National Congress.[64]

In fact in South Africa it is no longer so easy even for a Pentecostal pastor to remain outside politics, something which is incomprehensible to most of his colleagues in other countries. Albert Luthuli, who died in 1967 while under house arrest, was a lay preacher of the American Congregational Church and President of the African National Congress, and in his youth was a teacher in a village near Bhengu's home. Katesa Schlosser reports:

> He told me that he respected Bhengu as a sincere and honest man. Bhengu, who is conscious of the danger that threatens him from the extremists of the African National Congress, has in his turn a great human respect of Luthuli; 'He is one of the best Christians we have. But I do not understand why he has declared his support for the passive resistance movement.'[65]

On the other hand Manilal Ghandi, the son of Mahatma Ghandi and President of the Natal Indian Congress,

> spoke in completely derogatory terms about Bhengu, and indeed branded him as a traitor to the cause of non-Europeans in South Africa: 'Bhengu has been bought by the government and inculcates the natives with their doctrine, that is, that the natives are exploited by Indian merchants.'[66]

But Katesa Schlosser says: 'Bhengu is far from being a blind admirer of the whites, but he is too reasonable to be a fanatical black nationalist.'[67]

It is regrettable that both the South African and the World Pentecostal movements have left Nicholas Bhengu to deal with these difficult problems completely on his own. Compare the deletions made by August Kast listed in the notes in the above chapter. Kast is a missionary of the Swiss Pentecostal Mission in Lesotho, and clearly hopes to resolve these difficult and unanswered questions by suppression. But why does the spirit of prophecy in these Pentecostals express itself on the subject only of food taboos, women's dress, the difference between the baptism of the Spirit and rebirth, and not about the great riddles of human existence, with which Bhengu is faced?[68]

NOTES

1. American Lutheran Mission, Schreuder Mission.

2. Cf. ch. 12, pp. 149ff.

3. Of the many Pentecostal mission churches only the Apostolic Faith Mission (ch. 9.3[*a*]) and the Assemblies of God (ch. 9.3[*b*]) are discussed above.

4. D. Emmet, *Journal of the Royal Anthropological Institute* 86, 1956, p. 21.

5. It is noteworthy that Bhengu does not mention the Catholic school in his autobiography, *Revival Fire in South Africa.*

6. N. Bhengu, *Revival Fire*, pp. 1–2.

7. N. Bhengu, *ibid.*, p. 2. August Kast, a missionary of the Swiss Pentecostal Mission in Basutoland (01.05.033) has kindly corrected and commented on the sections on South Africa. The mention of Bhengu's Communist past was clearly embarrassing to Kast, and he put the following interpretations on it: 'When he came to East London, he spent whole nights reading about Communism, since so many of the blacks believed in it, and he wanted to help them to leave Communism. He said to me that in East London 30% of his large congregation of 4,000 members were former Communists.' (A. Kast, letter to W.H., 16.4.1964, p. 2.) K. Schlosser makes what in my view is the right comment: 'The Communists gave him [Bhengu] simply the chance to "let off steam". At any rate the Communist influence on him was certainly not greater than that of the Catholic mission schools, the Bible students, etc.' (K. Schlosser, letter to W.H., 3.3.1964.)

8. 01.36.013. At the present day the church is called the 'Full Gospel Church of God' and has been amalgamated with the Church of God (Cleveland) (ch. 4).

9. N. Bhengu, *Revival Fire*, p. 5.

10. Cf. the conversion of Jose Gomes Moreno (above, ch. 6.7, p. 79).

11. N. Bhengu, *Revival Fire*, p. 5. The account is given in full in K. Schlosser, *Eingeborenenkirchen*, pp. 22–4.

12. Cf. ch. 9.3(*b*), p. 122.

13. 01.36.004.

14. 01.36.005.

15. He studied for nine months at the Methodist Taylor University in Indiana.

16. A leading evangelist of the revival in Wales.

17. The last three are nineteenth-century American Holiness evangelists, cf. ch. 2.1, pp. 21f.

18. Cf. Appendix: 5.

19. P. Mayer, *Townsmen*, p. 193.

20. K. Schlosser, *Eingeborenenkirchen*, p. 25. Katesa Schlosser's quotations are taken either from sermons, from conversations with Bhengu, or from newspapers which are not accessible to me.

21. K. Schlosser, *op. cit.*, p. 26.

22. K. Schlosser, letter to W.H., 3.3.1964. She adds: 'When those who have organic diseases come to him, it must be easy for Bhengu to convince them that one or another doctor – who has the psychological understanding to make a proper approach to Pentecostals – is a tool in God's hand, which a sick person should use.' Bhengu regards all scientific progress as God's grace (K. Schlosser, *op. cit.*, p. 26). I cannot see here any fundamental difference from the Pentecostals; cf. Oral Roberts (ch. 26.2(*b*), pp. 363ff.) and the Pentecostal psychologist L. M. Vivier-van Eetveldt mentioned above (p. 122).

23. P. Mayer, *op. cit.*, p. 195.

24. K. Schlosser, *op. cit.*, p. 26.

25. *Ibid.*, p. 40.
26. P. Mayer, *op. cit.*, p. 199.
27. K. Schlosser, *op. cit.*, p. 28.
28. 'Red people' here are not Communists but heathen, and similarly 'ex-red' are former heathen, so-called because among the Xhosa it is still customary to wear red blankets. (K. Schlosser, letter to W.H., 3.3.1964.) 'School people' are Africans who have adopted a European way of life.
29. P. Mayer, *op. cit.*, p. 199.
30. Principally from the detribalized.
31. O. F. Raum, 'Von Stammespropheten', in E. Benz (ed.) *Messianische Kirchen*, p. 66.
32. Communication by August Kast.
33. P. Mayer, *op. cit.*, p. 194.
34. This is an attack on the repeated purification rites of the independent African churches (Zionists, ch. 12), and also against the repetition of baptism by those Pentecostal groups which do not recognize the baptism of another Pentecostal group.
35. K. Schlosser, *op. cit.*, p. 45.
36. This passage was deleted by August Kast, But it is confirmed by Mayer's researches, which are independent of those of Katesa Schlosser. Mayer quotes a member of Bhengu's church, a former 'red' man: 'What I like very much about Bhengu's church is that once your sins are forgiven you can no longer sin. You are holy, you have been washed in the blood of the Lord Jesus, you have conquered the devil. . . . Other churches preach that no man is perfect, that we sin and must pray for forgiveness all our lives, but Bhengu's church says this is not true.' (P. Mayer, *op. cit.*, p. 196.)
37. K. Schlosser, *op. cit.*, p. 38.
38. *Ibid.*, p. 52 (August Kast deletes the whole section).
39. August Kast corrects this to 'many'.
40. Bhengu rented the theatre for seven years for daily meetings. (Communication from August Kast.)
41. N. Bhengu, 'Christ', in D. Gee (ed.), *Fifth Conference, 1958*, pp. 92–5.
42. K. Schlosser, *Eingeborenenkirchen*, p. 47. August Kast deletes both sentences and comments: 'Bhengu would strongly deny this!'. Mayer states: 'Ever since joining the Assemblies of God some twenty years ago he has indicated that he belongs as much to the Plymouth Brethren and the Baptists as to the Pentecostals proper' (*Townsmen*, p. 193).
43. Cf. ch. 32.4, pp. 504ff.
44. Cf. Appendix: 5.
45. P. Mayer, *Townsmen*, pp. 192–205.
46. A. A. Dubb, *Role.*
47. Cf. n. 28.
48. He even approached a film renting company with the (vain) request to be allowed to censor films. (August Kast deletes this sentence.)
49. Cf. ch. 12, pp. 129ff.
50. This passage is deleted by August Kast.
51. P. Mayer, *Townsmen*, p. 200.
52. *Ibid.*, pp. 197, 200.
53. *Ibid.*, p. 204. Bhengu himself claimed that every member of his church was a preacher ('Christ', in D. Gee (ed.), *Fifth Conference, 1958*, p. 90).
54. Bhengu at a Convention of the Assemblies, quoted by Mayer, *op. cit.*, p. 200.
55. *Ibid.*, p. 194.
56. About half the men and a third of the women stated that they had attended school.

57. P. Mayer, *op. cit.*, p. 195.
58. K. Schlosser, *Eingeborenenkirchen*, p. 28.
59. *Ibid.*, p. 29.
60. Deleted by August Kast. The whole sermon is given in K. Schlosser, *op. cit.*, pp. 30–4, and in N. Bhengu's periodical *Back to God* (July 1955); cf. above ch. 5.3, p. 66.
61. K. Schlosser, *op. cit.*, p. 34.
62. *Ibid.*, p. 35. August Kast contradicts Bhengu: 'All bank robberies in South Africa are done by blacks.' (Communication from August Kast.)
63. K. Schlosser, *op. cit.*, p. 35. August Kast deletes the whole section. M. L. Martin observes: 'I wonder if Bhengu is thinking of a kind of "Soviet *kolchoz*". It is a typical phenomenon of the "sects" in South Africa that they form "church colonies", in order to replace the former centre of the tribe, the "home", that has been lost. The stress on this is even greater in the Republic of South Africa, where the land question is so important . . .' (M. L. Martin, Notes, p. 2).
64. K. Schlosser, *op. cit.*, p. 12. Cf. *VdV* 49/12, Dec. 1956, pp. 13f.: attack on the evangelists Bhengu and Molefe. Tsotsi attempt to assassinate native evangelists.
65. K. Schlosser, *op. cit.*, p. 56.
66. *Ibid.*
67. *Ibid.*, p. 57.
68. Cf. ch. 24.6, pp. 345ff.

II

Back to Pentecost: The Latter Rain Assemblies as a Protest Movement against the decline of enthusiasm in the Older Pentecostal Churches

In several countries a new protest movement in the Pentecostal movement itself has arisen against the decline of enthusiasm and the various tendencies towards formal church organization. A typical example is the Latter Rain Assemblies of South Africa (*Spade Reën Gemeentes van Suid-Afrika*)[1] – although they are relatively few in South Africa.

1. *Origin and Faith Homes*

Typical characteristics of the Latter Rain Assemblies are:

1. The repeated confession of sin in the presence of a trustworthy witness,
2. The dominant position of the prophetic ministry.[2]

It is therefore not surprising that the Latter Rain Assemblies began with a nine-month period of confession of sin. According to Maria Fraser, the founder of the Latter Rain Assemblies in South Africa, the Pentecostal Churches,[3] to which she originally belonged, had at first still been spiritual.

> But gradually sin began to creep in more and more. It was then that the Lord, through tongues and interpretation of tongues and discernment of spirits, began revealing to us what was taking place.[4]

Confessions of sin were the only way 'to climb to the most exalted and most holy platform of santification'.[5]

Maria Fraser accused the Apostolic Faith Mission not only of stifling the Spirit of God, but also of individual moral failings on the part of its lesser officials. Although according to her own account the prophecies were always justified, she met with increasing opposition from the leaders of the Apostolic Faith Mission. In 1927 the Lord revealed to her that he 'would establish a work where all the gifts of the Holy Spirit would operate freely, a work after the Lord's heart, where sin would not be able to persist.'[6] When sinning Pentecostals or visitors came to her daily hours of prayer at 10 a.m. or to the regular weekly services, their inmost thoughts were revealed. Wizards had to hand over their potions, defrauders of the insurance companies and murderers were unmasked, adulterers uncovered and sent back to their wives;[7] a cancerous tumour formed on the face of an elderly Pentecostal pastor, and vanished only when he confessed the sins he had committed during the Boer War. The Holy Spirit passed a terrible judgment on those who had mocked Maria Fraser and her friends or even denied their spiritual authority. They could be grateful if they escaped with their lives.

During the nine-month period of preparation[8] the new Latter Rain Assembly experienced periods of heavenly ecstasy, singing in tongues in harmony, holy dances,[9] laughing in the Spirit and visions of angels. Towards the end of 1927 the Holy Spirit spoke and told to the tiny congregation

> that at that moment a man-child had been born, i.e. this Holy Spirit Movement – a movement after the heart of God, in which the Holy Spirit would bring into full operation all the nine gifts of the Spirit; where sin would be revealed and exterminated; a movement where Christ as the Head would lead and direct His people.[10]

Similarly the Lord showed Maria Fraser in a vision

> the 'blue dress', telling me that He wished us to wear that, as the Lord wanted us to be isolated from the world and honourably clad. Together with the blue dress with its long sleeves, its high neck with a collar, we should wear black shoes and stockings, but nothing was to be made of silk.[11] The blue dress was laid down for the six weekdays and the same in white for Sundays.[12]

The leaders of the Apostolic Faith Church now intervened and sent the Benoni circle an ultimatum (the giving up of the 'uniform', the 'Spirit of judgment', and the 'uncovering of sins'; the handing over of the key to the room; and the ceasing of publication of the *Spade Reëns Boodskapper*). When Maria Fraser and her faithful followers would not agree, they were excommunicated; with the help of the police they were ejected from the chapels which for the most part they had built with their own money, and these were sold by public auction, but with the reservation that on no account were they to be sold to members of the new Latter Rain movement.

The Latter Rain congregation was by no means discouraged; it soon went on to set up its first 'faith home' in Benoni. A faith home is a kind of monastery in which married and unmarried people live together and share their goods. At four in the morning the brothers hold the first prayer meeting; at six, ten and in the evening general prayer meetings are held. In addition there is an uninterrupted chain of prayer throughout the day and night. The prayer room must never be empty.

Thrice daily one or two inmates go through all the buildings and rooms, and over the premises to plead the blood of Jesus against all spiritual evil in the air, praying that everything be cleansed and that peace may reign.[13]

Silence has to be maintained; no one is allowed to speak loudly or shout on the premises, or run; no idle talk and jesting is allowed whereby the holiness and peace of the Holy Spirit can be disturbed. When there are special needs for the house, the inmates sometimes pray day and night for this (this does not include the usual chain-prayer which in any case goes on), or they may praise the Lord round the buildings, just as the Lord may lead.[14]

Collections are not taken either in the meetings or for the faith home. The various publications in French, German, Afrikaans, English and various African languages are not sold, but given away. Each can give what he thinks proper. In everything trust is placed in the help of God.

At the conferences, which hundreds attend, all who take part are fed.

Those who can afford to do so bring foodstuff, and those who cannot afford anything do not bring a thing. . . . Nothing which is not in the Bible is allowed, and nothing is done contrary to the Scriptures.[15] Youngsters who are still at school are also sent here by the parents with the consent of the Holy Spirit. When they are here, they are out of the world and are able to serve the Lord.[16]

2. *Doctrine*

(*a*) '*Praying through*' *and* '*full confession*.[17]

The confession of all sins is obligatory.[18] But since no person can remember all his sins, he must from time to time be 'prayed through'. This is the name given to the action in which

the Holy Spirit reveals the sins of the person who is being 'prayed through'. He kneels in an empty room, while the prophet stands or lies behind him. First there are all sorts of noise and whispering, and then come tongues and prophecy. Through the prophecies sins going right back to youth are uncovered.[19]

The result of the 'full confession' is a kind of state of perfection.[20]

(*b*) *Baptism*

Since the Apostolic Faith Mission in South Africa is violently opposed to the 'Jesus Only' groups,[21] it uses not only the trinitarian formula but also requires a threefold immersion of the candidate.[22] As a result, there has been tension for many years in South Africa between the Apostolic Faith Churches and other Pentecostals. Maria Fraser believes that she has helped to resolve this controversy, since in her movement either type of baptism is possible according to the wish of the candidate. But she believes that the church will recognize threefold immersion as biblical.[23]

(c) The 'blood of Jesus'

The threefold 'sprinkling' with the blood of Jesus has been mentioned above.[24] The members of the Latter Rain Assembly

> must continually imbibe through faith this Blood, this Life. This we can do by focusing our attention on the quickening and strengthening power of the Blood, the Life, and especially when we partake of communion.[25]

The Latter Rain Assemblies distinguish between 'unpurified Christianity', that is, conventional Christians in name only; a narrower circle of Christians who have allowed themselves to be washed by the water of baptism; and the 'priests', who daily bring the blood of Jesus over themselves, their churches, their houses and their employment. Even car tyres are protected from punctures by the blood of Jesus.[26] And 'we quietly encircle' unpleasant neighbours 'with the blood of Jesus and bind and banish the Spirit of malice and argumentativeness.'[27]

(d) Absolute claims

> [Since] the birth of the Latter Rain Assembly in South Africa, in 1927 . . . there is once again a church on earth which is in truth ruled and guided exclusively by the Holy Spirit. In this church, which he has founded himself, he can once again as in the beginning reveal all sins (Acts 5.1–11) and protect it from its otherwise inevitable ruin. The unceasing growth of the Latter Rain Assemblies, brought about by the Spirit, is therefore equivalent to the final and ultimate unmasking of the devil, who consequently persecutes it and seeks to destroy it with deathly hatred.[28]

Anyone who blasphemes against the Spirit of God, that is, calls the gifts of the Spirit found in the Latter Rain Assembly diabolical, becomes possessed by 'the Spirit of eternal Death': that is, he can 'no longer anoint unto life, but only unto death', when he prays with the sick and anoints them with oil in accordance with James 5.14. A smell of death comes from him.[29] Thus the Latter Rain Assemblies take care that their members do not come into contact with other churches:

> The Lord does not wish us to insinuate ourselves casually and occasionally into other congregations and sects to enjoy spiritual food there, or to read books which the Holy Spirit has not approved. For it is so that any preacher, or writer, however skilful, who has not thoroughly purified the contents of his vessel, that is, his heart, through the proper and full confession of his sins, is actually giving his hearers or readers water to drink out of a dirty well.[30]

Of course the World Council of Churches is rejected as a sign of Antichrist.[31] We are in the last days, and therefore all compromises have to be avoided. On the basis of prophecy

> we must expect Scotland shortly to be separated [from Great Britain]. All that is now necessary is for the Western Balkans to unite in one kingdom, and then the ten toes [the original Roman Empire] – or the ten kingdoms –

will have been made ready to be struck by the stone [from the Book of Daniel].[32]

(*e*) *Ethical rigorism*

The Latter Rain Assemblies accuse the rest of the Pentecostal movement of worldliness.

Why is it that so many sisters paint themselves and curl their hair? Whom are they awaiting? With hair all made up there are far too many Jezebels looking through windows today . . .[33]

In God's House are found far too many vain peacocks who cannot possibly kneel down when they pray, for the God of fashion has seen to it that their dresses are far too short to allow them to kneel.[34]

Pentecostals are to be found in all places of worldly pleasure. If their pastors were really spiritual men, they would never listen to the radio, this 'source of evil'.[35] In all these matters the Latter Rain Assemblies take a firm stand against the world. In addition, their members avoid pig's flesh: 'Anyone who eats pig's flesh is a pig.'[36] A prophet can give an order to lick the dust as a sign of humility; against the forces of lechery a sackcloth girdle is worn, and ashes are strewed on the head as a sign of penitence.

(*f*) *Demonology – illustrated from prayers*[37]

Father, I bring myself wholly beneath the dear blood of Jesus, I sprinkle my head with it . . . etc. I pray, purify me from all evils that cling to me.

Father, I pray, purify also the place in which I pray . . . the whole room . . . from all the powers at work here . . . bring a double protecting wall of blood and faith over me.

Bind all powers that whisper temptation and eavesdrop, and the calling voices[38] of magical powers . . . the spiritist powers . . . and the key powers[39] of the spiritist powers. Make them helpless and cast them into outer darkness . . .

Father, I pray, send a mighty angel with a two-edged sword to hack away all undermining threads of thought[40] and nets, so that my prayer can rise up to the throne of grace . . .

Lord, in thy name I cut away all threads of thought . . . from and behind springs and channels of unrighteousness. I close these channels with the blood of Jesus, bind this evil this side and the far side of the channels, and also the powers that come close and cast them into outer darkness (Isa. 5.18). I set up a wall of blood before the well of blasphemy.[41]

Father, burn away from me, I pray, with the fire of thy Holy Spirit all veils of false peace . . . reject all prayers from persons who are surrounded and infected by false peace and other princes of unrighteousness . . .

Father, cut off all contrary prayers of churches, sects, brotherhoods and sectaries. . . . I pray, set up a wall of blood against the undermining that comes upon your children through prayers against them.

Father, join together all threads of blessing that have been cut off . . . bind

> all evil spirits who have cut off the blessings . . . make them powerless . . . close the wells of the underminings of hatred, wrath, jealousy, the spirit of Antichrist, magic powers and the devil of marriage.

3. *Criticism of the Latter Rain Movement by the Rest of the Pentecostal Movement*

All the rest of the Pentecostal Movement rejects the 'Children of the Latter Rain'. The Apostolic Faith Movement disputes the 'blood theory' of the Latter Rain Assemblies.[42] The German Pentecostal Ludwig Eisenlöffel of the Working Fellowship of Christian Churches in Germany[43] makes the curt remark: 'There is no doubt that the Latter Rain movement is a sect.' He finds the constant appeal to the Holy Spirit 'repugnant'.[44] In addition, he states, the movement in South Africa is fizzling out and has split into three separate groups. Thus Eisenlöffel is arguing in exactly the same way as the Conservative Evangelicals argued in the early days of the Pentecostal movement. Unfortunately he gives no details, names or figures; and the missionary activity of the Latter Rain movement shows that it has not fizzled out yet. He is right to criticize the 'spiritual strip-tease':

> I have been at public meetings of this movement where married men and women publicly confess sins in their sexual life in the presence of many young girls and boys, and I felt as if a bucket of filth was being emptied out over these young people, to stain perhaps pure consciences.[45]

4. *The Characteristic Features of the Latter Rain Movement*

The Latter Rain Movement is numerically insignificant, but we have given a detailed account of it for the following reasons:

1. It clearly demonstrates the similarities in worship and religious experience between Dowie's Christian Catholic Church and a Pentecostal church in the early stages of its development.
2. The Latter Rain Assemblies provide a good picture of the essential features of a Pentecostal church in its early stages, when it is still led by prophets and spontaneous inspirations.
3. It provides a striking parallel to the independent African churches (the importance of prophecy, the magical conception of the blood of Jesus, food taboos, demonology, full confession, etc.).

F. P. Möller and August Kast take objection to the section on the Latter Rain Movement.

> Its leader was admittedly once a Pentecostal, but has fallen into error, and all Pentecostals in this country will warn you against the 'Latter Rain Assemblies'. They have nothing to do with the Pentecostal movement, but were

> expelled from it. So write about the Pentecostal movement from the point of view of a true Christian and to the edification of the Church of Christ.[46]

Möller observes:

> The 'Spade-Reën' movement is so small and insignificant in this country that it is more or less an unknown quantity in the religious life. To give an elaborate and detailed description of this group, even devoting more attention to it than to the major Pentecostal bodies, gives a wrong and distorted picture of Pentecost in South Africa.[47]

Kast's view is based on an assumption which is otherwise rejected by Pentecostals, that there is an official Pentecostal organization. Do not the Pentecostals constantly repeat that Pentecost is not a denomination, but an experience? Do they not continuously campaign against organizations that might serve to distinguish Christians and sectarians? Can one destroy ecclesiastical organizations, as the Pentecostals have done in Africa and elsewhere, and then claim an inherent authority for one's own organization to decide who belongs to the Pentecostal movement and who does not? Möller also bases his argument on a principle the Pentecostals otherwise reject. Fifty years ago in South Africa, as in many countries at the present day, the Pentecostal movement was still 'so small and insignificant' that it was ignored by most commentators on Christian denominations. Who knows whether the Latter Rain Assemblies will not undergo a process of sobering down and growth similar to that of the other Pentecostal denominations?

NOTES

1. Documents, Sources, Literature: 01.36.034. Journal: *Latter Rain Evangel/Spade Reën Boodskapper*. Missionaries in Germany, Holland and Switzerland!

2. Letter from the German Latter Rain Mission (05.07.034) to W.H., 17.5.1963.

3. Probably the Apostolic Faith Mission (ch. 9.3[*a*]). Cf. Maria Fraser's attitude to baptism by threefold immersion (p. 42). The original Pentecostal mission she belonged to is therefore given throughout as the Apostolic Faith Mission, although she herself never gives the name of her original church in her writings.

4. Maria Fraser, *Faith Life*, p. 12; Afrikaans: *Getuienis*, 2nd ed. 1962, p. 14.

5. M. Fraser, *Faith Life*, p. 14. Afrikaans: 'op 'n hoogheilige plat van heiligmaking' (*Getuienis*, 2nd ed., 1962, p. 14).

6. M. Fraser, *Faith Life*, p. 13; *Getuienis*, 2nd ed., p. 13.

7. 'Adam, Adam, you are busy biting an apple which will cause much pain. You are in love with your brother's wife,' was the prophecy (M. Fraser, *Faith Life*, p. 16; *Getuienis*, 2nd ed., p. 16).

8. The nine months are meant to be an explicit parallel to pregnancy, with respect to the 'man child' who was to come into the world. Cf. the Afrikaans chapter heading '6. *Lydensworstelings tot Geboorte van Spade Reën*', a nuance of travail or birthpangs which the English version, '6: The Birth of the Latter Rain Assemblies' does not contain.

9. See the commentary of M. Fraser: *Deplorable State* (no pagination): 'Scripture tells us the reason why the dancing in the Spirit has stopped, "Woe to us, for we have sinned" (Lam. 5.15–18).'

10. M. Fraser, *Faith Life*, pp. 21–2; *Getuienis*, 2nd ed., p. 23.

11. *Ibid.*, p. 23 (pp. 24f.).

12. The last sentence is missing from the English and Afrikaans text, but contained in the German translation (M. Fraser, *Persönliche Erfahrungen*, no date, p. 24).

13. M. Fraser, *Faith Life*, p. 38; *Getuienis*, 2nd ed., p. 40.

14. *Ibid.*, p. 38 (41).

15. *Ibid.*, p. 39 (pp. 41f.).

16. *Ibid.*, p. 40 (43).

17. The Afrikaans technical term for 'praying through' is *deurbid.*

18. 'Although the Lord himself in the times of ignorance [i.e. before the birth of the Latter Rain movement. W.H.] imparted to thousands of souls a glorious measure of redemption and conviction, the reality now testifies through the Word and the Spirit that the liberating effect is not complete as long as the soul has not admitted all its sins by name before witnesses . . .' (A. V. Krige, *Rundbriefe der Deutschen Spätregenmission* 3/7, Sept. 1961, p. 12).

19. *MD* 24, 1961, pp. 184–92, 'Die Spätregenbewegung' (cited from offprint, p. 9). (All kinds of ridiculous gesticulations are described.)

20. 'The mystery of the new covenant is: these laws are now written in our hearts . . . We now no longer swear or steal and also no longer kill, not because the law forbids it, but because grace has given us a life that *cannot* steal or swear or kill.' (A. V. Krige, *Rundbriefe* . . . 3/6, Aug. 1961, p. 3; italics original).

21. Cf. ch. 3.1(*b*), pp. 31f.

22. Taken over from Dowie's Christian Catholic Church, cf. ch. 9.2(*c*), p. 120.

23. A. V. Krige, *Rundbriefe* . . . 3/10, Dec. 1961, p. 15.

24. Cf. p. 142.

25. Latter Rain Assemblies of S.A., *The Blood of Jesus.*

26. 'The Lord also taught us and warned us not to get into a motor-vehicle with hearts that have not been cleansed by confession. In addition we must be careful to plead the Blood of Jesus around and over and through the vehicle before we depart . . . The fact is, moreover, that all types of evil spirits wherever they find opportunity creep in and tuck away or adhere to whatever they can to await their chance to overcome the unwary. By now pleading the Blood of Jesus as instructed, such are then driven out of their hiding-places. Where this has been done then the journey will prove pleasant and successful, because we are thereby protected against dangers and accidents, and even against punctures and other adversities.' *Ibid.*

27. *Ibid.*

28. K. Born, *Wahrheit*, p. 4.

29. M. Fraser, *Faith Life*, p. 69; *Getuienis*, 2nd ed., p. 70.

30. *MD* 24, 1961, pp. 184–92, 'Die Spätregenbewegung' (offprint, p. 9); (*Rundbriefe* 1/7, Sept. 1960).

31. P. C. de Jager, *Signposts*, pp. 40f.

32. P. C. de Jager, *Zeichen* (German version of *Signposts*; the passage is lacking in the English and Afrikaans versions).

33. Cf. II Kings 9.30.

34. M. Fraser, *Deplorable State.*

35. This is the same kind of argument as was advanced by the traditional Pentecostal movement against the other churches fifty years ago.

36. *MD* 24, 1961, pp. 184–92, 'Die Spätregenbewegung' (offprint, p. 10). Cf. also Dowie's Christian Catholic Church, ch. 9.2(*c*), p. 120.

37. The following most instructive prayers are taken from L. Eisenlöffel's duplicated work, *Spätregenbewegung*, pp. 25–6.

38. Calling voices are powers which constantly call upon other powers to help, because the former powers have already been bound.

39. Key powers are used by spiritist powers as keys with which to open the minds of the saints in order to know their plans, and so to organize resistance to them in the realm of darkness.

40. Hostile persons spin undermining threads of thought over the saints, in both directions, until eventually a complete network is formed over them, and their prayers can scarcely reach the throne of grace.

41. Many powers work through a person who has blasphemed the Holy Spirit. They form a well or source of blasphemy and defile all who are associated with them.

42. *Trooster*, 34/8, Aug. 1962, pp. 14–15.

43. 05.07.015. (German title: Arbeitsgemeinschaft der Christengemeinden in Deutschland.)

44. L. Eisenlöffel, *Spätregenbewegung*, pp. 1, 5.

45. Quoted from a letter from South Africa by L. Eisenlöffel, *op. cit.*, p. 8.

46. A. Kast, letter to W.H., 16.4.1964, p. 3.

47. F. P. Möller, letter to W.H., 4.6.1964.

12

uMoya – the Spirit in the Independent African Churches [1]

1. *Investigation into Typology*

MOST authorities follow Sundkler in dividing the independent African churches into three groups: (*a*) Ethiopian, (*b*) Zionist, and (*c*) Messianic. Minor variations in this scheme can be ignored here.

(*a*) *The Ethiopian churches*

These separated from the historical missionary churches at the beginning of the century because of racial discrimination. They mostly teach a traditional form of Christian doctrine and had originally nothing to do with the Pentecostal movement. Consequently they are not discussed in this chapter.

(*b*) *The Zionist churches*

> Sundkler calls them 'Zionist', because most of them originally sprang from the missionaries of the Holy Catholic Apostolic Church in Zion, Illinois,[2] and employ the name Zion.[3]

Since these missionaries are largely identical with the pioneers of the Pentecostal movement in South Africa I refer to this group both as 'independent African Pentecostal churches' and also as 'Zionist'. They exercise an increasing influence on the Ethiopian churches. Marie-Louise Martin calls these groups 'prophetic movements'. They have a 'Jordan', a 'Bethesda', for baptisms and washings. 'The Holy Spirit manifests himself in speaking with tongues (like the spirit of the ancestors among the heathen . . .)'.[4]

Sundkler gives the following definition of the Zionists. They are syncretistic groups, who stress the healing of the sick and speaking in tongues. Each group has its typical taboos and purification rites, and makes an effort to have a taboo or purification rite peculiar to itself. In spite of this there is between them an astonishing similarity in basic features, 'caused no doubt by certain fundamental needs and aspirations in the broad masses of these Churches, which needs and aspirations find their satisfaction in the behaviour patterns of the movement.'[5]

(*c*) *The Messianic sects*

These arose from Zionist churches when one of their prophets was proclaimed Messiah. By contrast with the Congo, the Messiahs were at first relatively few in number in South Africa. In this chapter Messianic sects are not discussed, because I agree with the conclusions of the analysis of independent African churches made by the World Council of Churches,[6] which states that a group which replaces the functions of the historic Jesus as revealed by an African Christ has excluded itself from the circle of Christian churches.

2. *Origins*

The historical dependence of the Zionist churches upon Dowie's missionaries and the early Pentecostal movement can no longer be disputed. The Zionists of South Africa say, 'We do just as in Zion City, Illinois.'[7]

As early as 1909 the Pentecostal missionaries accepted the consequences of their doctrine that the most important qualification for the office of pastor is the baptism of the Spirit – a qualification acquired with extraordinary speed by the black converts[8] – and gave certificates to preach to the Africans:

> This is to certify that we recognize Brother E.M.L. of Pretoria has been called by the Holy Ghost as an evangelist in connexion with the (Apostolic Faith) Mission of Johannesburg for the year 1909 and as long thereafter as he shall maintain the unity of the Spirit with us, to preach the Gospel of Jesus Christ. To lay hands on the sick, To perform Native marriages. To baptize disciples by triune immersion, To administer the Lord's Supper, To concrete [should read 'to consecrate'] children.[9]

Sundkler finds the assertion that the Pentecostals were the first to bring the glorious fire of the Holy Spirit to South Africa[10] tragi-comic: 'One nowadays wades through the ashes resulting from such fires.'[11]

Since then the development of the Zionists has in part led them far from their original Pentecostal fathers; although this development was already contained in the missionary policy of the Pentecostals, when they said that the baptism of the Spirit was more important for the Negro evangelists than theological training. Today this fact is embarrassing to the Pentecostal missionaries. They prefer to deny the connection between the Pentecostal movement and the Zionists.[12]

A different solution is sought by Fred Burke, a missionary of the Assemblies of God in South Africa. He feels a responsibility for these independent churches and has set up a Bible correspondence school for their 'bishops'. He claims to have thousands of participants. In spite of its fundamentalist theology this Bible School can be regarded as an important bridge between traditional Christianity (in this case in the form of the Assemblies of God) and the independent churches.[13] B. A. Pauw, who has made a study of the independent churches in a limited area in which the Pentecostals also have congregations, has come to the conclusion that of all the missionary churches the Pentecostals still at the present day have the greatest influence on the independent churches.[14] Thirty-seven per cent (756 out of 2,070) of all the independent churches belong to Pentecostal or Seventh Day Adventist types.[15]

But what is the deep reason for the rise of these many[16] independent African Pentecostal churches? In South Africa and in other countries with black populations the Pentecostal movement was in fact no more than the safety valve which released a pressure that existed already. According to Sundkler, racial discrimination is the reason for the coming into being of these churches; and in the situation in South Africa he no longer asks why there are so many independent churches, but 'How is it that this or that African minister still continues in the mission?'[17]

Other reasons are the numerous ecclesiastical divisions in South Africa, the tensions between different African tribes (Zulu – Sotho; Zulu – Swazi) and the bid for power which individual prophets make everywhere in the world.

The most recent and most probable theory – which applies to the whole of Africa – is that put forward by David B. Barrett. He gives a list of eighteen measurable and quantifiable conditions,[18] and specifies how many of these conditions must be fulfilled before an independent church is formed. Since most of these conditions will occur to an increasing degree in the future, one must anticipate an accelerated growth of independent groups of all kinds (and not only Pentecostal and Zionist groups). Barrett discusses at length the limits and margin of error of his schema.[19]

The names of the first black colleagues of the Apostolic Faith Mission are known,[20] as are the names of the churches they founded (see diagram). After the African Pentecostals separated from the Apostolic Faith Mission between 1914 and 1917 (or were allowed to drift away), most of the churches subdivided at an increasing rate. Because all the emphasis was laid on the prophetic quality of the leader, each personal struggle for power led to the foundation of new churches. Besides this, the development of a tribal church is a natural one for Africans. Each clan develops its own particular form of tribal religion, a 'cultic unity with its own ancestors', but the high god, if there is one, remains the same, and the way in which he is worshipped is the same.[21] The divisions are seen as similar to the kraal divisions (*ukukhipa ikhanda*) of the Zulu, that is, to the custom that when a son reaches adult years, he leaves his father's kraal and founds his own.[22] Some of the constitutions of the African churches formally anticipate a division in the future and make legislative provision for it.[23]

Since the African Pentecostal churches see the history of the Reformation through the eyes of their Pentecostal teachers, it is not surprising that they sometimes appeal to Luther: 'We do as Luther did on 31 October 1517.'[24]

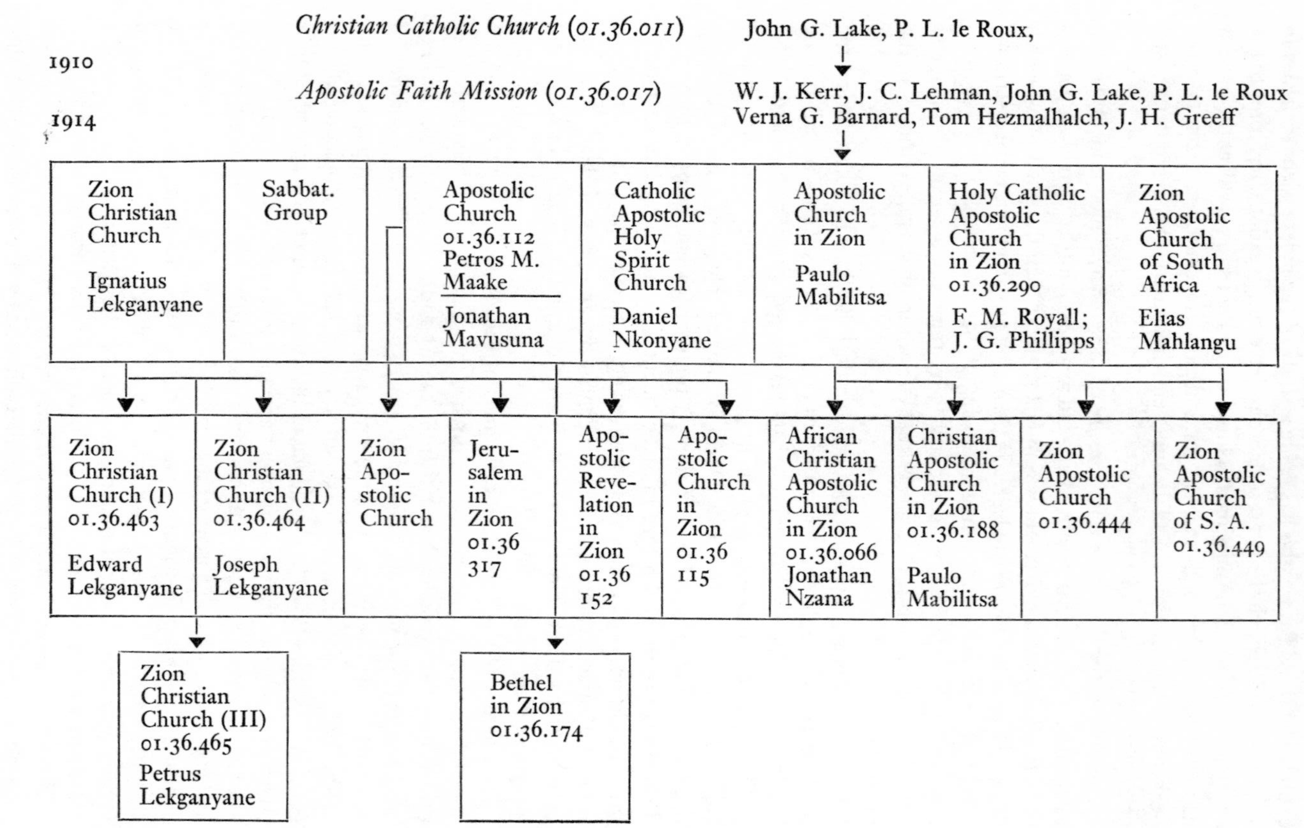
1910
Christian Catholic Church (01.36.011)
John G. Lake, P. L. le Roux,
1914
Apostolic Faith Mission (01.36.017)
W. J. Kerr, J. C. Lehman, John G. Lake, P. L. le Roux
Verna G. Barnard, Tom Hezmalhalch, J. H. Greeff
Zion Christian Church Ignatius Lekganyane
Sabbat. Group
Apostolic Church 01.36.112 Petros M. Maake
Jonathan Mavusuna
Catholic Apostolic Holy Spirit Church Daniel Nkonyane
Apostolic Church in Zion Paulo Mabilitsa
Holy Catholic Apostolic Church in Zion 01.36.290 F. M. Royall; J. G. Phillipps
Zion Apostolic Church of South Africa Elias Mahlangu
Zion Christian Church (I) 01.36.463 Edward Lekganyane
Zion Christian Church (II) 01.36.464 Joseph Lekganyane
Zion Apo-stolic Church
Jeru-salem in Zion 01.36 317
Apo-stolic Reve-lation in Zion 01.36 152
Apo-stolic Church in Zion 01.36 115
African Christian Apostolic Church in Zion 01.36.066 Jonathan Nzama
Christian Apostolic Church in Zion 01.36.188 Paulo Mabilitsa
Zion Apostolic Church 01.36.444
Zion Apostolic Church of S. A. 01.36.449
Zion Christian Church (III) 01.36.465 Petrus Lekganyane
Bethel in Zion 01.36.174

On the other hand there are also movements towards reunion. Not all the leaders of independent African churches define the church in the way that some are caricatured as doing by Sundkler: 'I belong to that universal and invisible church, of which I actually am the only member.'[25] 'It is not unfair to say that any Zulu leader who breaks away from his parent Church is immediately ready to become a champiou of Church union.'[26] Many such attempts at reunion have failed.[27] Since 1965 the Ethiopian [28] and Zionist[29] churches seem to have formed themselves into two main groupings.[30]

3. *Relationship to the State*

(*a*) *Net Vir Blankes* – '*Whites only*'

Land for Whites only

> 'The Native question *is* the land question.'[31] The increase in the number of Bantu independent churches could be shown on a diagram as a parallel to the tightening squeeze of the Natives through land legislation.[32]

This legislation (Natives Land Act 1913) prohibited the natives, simply because they were natives, from buying or renting land, except in precisely defined areas. This meant, for example, that in Natal 132,000 Europeans had at their disposal a stock of 25,000 square miles of land, while a million Zulu were restricted to 4,000 square miles (1921). In the whole of South Africa, a million Whites had more land than five million Africans. It was natural for the natives to say in bitter confusion; 'At first we had the land, and you had the Bible. Now we have the Bible, and you have the land.' '*Siyanghaphi?* Where were we to go?'[33] Katesa Schlosser gives an objective account of this problem and tries to give a fair hearing to the South African government in the face of international attacks. While 87% of the land is in white hands, large parts of present day South Africa have never belonged to the Bantu, but to the Hottentots and Bushmen, against whom the Bantu fought fiercely when they advanced into the country. 47% of the natives live in reserves, which comprise 13% of the land; but because the rainfall there is higher than average they represent a higher value than the percentage suggests. Nevertheless the reserves are not enough to support the natives, and therefore the men have to go into the towns. The reserves are at present being enlarged.[34]

Marie-Louise Martin, who as a foreign missionary in South Africa had to be careful about what she published, made special mention of the Natives Land Act of 1913 as a reason for the springing up of the independent African churches.

> [The Act] prevented the Africans from acquiring by purchase the land reserved for Whites, . . . restricted them to relatively small territories, the 'reserves', and made them squatters on the farms of the Europeans or proletarians in the towns.[35]

Well-paid professional work for Whites only

The same rule, 'Whites only', also applies to well-paid professional work. African trade unions were permitted, but were not recognized as negotiating bodies. They were also forbidden to strike. 'Whites only' applied to the right to strike. 'Hat in hand, the African is supposed to say "Yes, Sir" to anything that a White man, simply because he is White, tells him to do.'[36]

And just as in North America a century ago, the Whites in South Africa today will tell you, 'Look at the African in the street, how happy he is. He doesn't want any more.'

Reformed Churches for Whites only

The rule of the Calvinists is *geen gelijkstelling* – no equal rights for Black and White in church or state. Many of the leaders of independent Black churches have been refused entry to White churches. A striking example of this is Nicholas Bhengu,[37] who adopts a sympathetic mediatory position, and who in spite of the humiliations to which he has been subjected is reasonable enough to plead for co-operation with the Whites. 'Separatism has been the result, to a very large extent, of the presence of the colour bar within the Christian Church.'[38]

(*b*) *The struggle for recognition by the Government*

Recognition by the Government is important for the African churches, not only for psychological reasons, which must not be underestimated, but also for the following reasons:

It allows them to build churches and schools in the native reserves.[39]
Their pastors can carry out native marriages.
It entitles pastors to reduced rail fares.
It permits them to buy wine for the Lord's Supper.[40]

Originally certain definite criteria were laid down for the recognition of an independent church.[41] Today, however, recognition or non-recognition is wholly at the discretion of the government.[42] Thus in 1960 recognition had been accorded to only ten out of all the independent African churches (Ethiopians, Zionist and Messianic). None of these was Zionist (Pentecostal). In 1965 there were 75, 'when the government decided not to proceed further with registrations since too much land was being set aside'.[43]

The Africans consider the non-recognition tactics of the government to be

> deliberate humiliation and stigmatization under the White rule that professes and confesses Christianity . . . This sort of thing is absolutely incompatible with the fundamental principle of God found in the Holy Scriptures, and is also incompatible with the principle of all democratic powers of the world.[44]

The above account of what Sundkler calls 'the most repressive clause' in the South African government's policy has been severely criticized by South African

Pentecostal missionaries who have read this book in manuscript. One of the leaders of the Apostolic Faith Mission, F. P. Möller, writes:

> The reference you quote as should there be no complete religious liberty in South Africa is not true. I know of no country in the world where there is more religious liberty. We have no state Church, or a church favoured by the state. While there is religious liberty it is on the other hand impossible to have each of the ca. 2500 Bantu sects registered Church bodies. That will mean endless headaches for the registrar of companies and would amount to an administrative chaos.[45]

The Swiss Professor of Missiology in Lesotho, Marie-Louise Martin, has criticized the expression 'most repressive clause' which I have borrowed from Sundkler.[46]

> Can you call it the 'most repressive clause' where an attempt is made to set a limit to the number of sects? At any rate, many Africans would *not* agree with you.[47]

Since I have not been to South Africa myself, it is impossible for me to give a final decision on this very complicated situation.

4. *Belief and Worship*

(*a*) *Fundamentalism*

The translation of the Bible into the vernacular is an important condition for the coming into being of the independent churches.[48] Even for the independent African Pentecostal preachers, who cannot read, the Bible plays an important role as an object of veneration and bearer of *mana*. Churches which have pastors who can read often abuse it in 'Bible ping-pong', that is, in disputes with the aid of Bible quotations (*ukushayana ngamavesi*). 'The Bible is bought, but rarely read continuously for personal edification . . . Its place is in the services, that is, in the cult.'[49] This is the background against which we must understand the statement of a Zionist who said, 'I left (the mission church) because of the Book.'[50] And one church constitution reads: Our leader 'explains the Bible from the following chapters Amen: Jer. 1.4–5, Proverbs 8.22–26. Amen.'[51] Another church offers the following hermeneutic key: We believe in the Old and New Testaments 'by the interpretation of the river'.[52] A third believes in the Old and New Testaments and the doctrines of John Dawi (*sic!* i.e. Dowie).[53]

The missionary churches of the revival movement were slow to recognize that careful theological training cannot be neglected with impunity. Their African pastors are nowadays waking up to the realization that the Bible is not only 'dangerous' but actually a 'forest'.[54] Theo Schneider, a Swiss missionary, strikes the nail on the head when he writes:

> Certainly the Bible is in the hands of all the Ethiopian bishops and all the

Zionist prophets . . . But it is not enough to possess the Bible, one must also know how to read it . . . One must be able to interpret it in accordance with its centre, Jesus Christ. What becomes of the Word when this centre is whittled away?[55]

(*b*) *Baptism, purification rites, the Lord's Supper*

Baptism

Many independent African churches practise baptism by threefold immersion.[56] As in the early Pentecostal movement and the present day Latter Rain Assemblies[57] baptism is preceded by a rite of the uncovering of sins and a full confession.[58]

The Lutherans are mocked for being afraid of immersion.[59] Infant baptism is the sign of the beast, for in Rev. 13.1 we read that the beast, just like the white churches with their infant baptism, comes out of the sea.[60] Baptism usually takes place in the kraal in the reserves which serves as the headquarters. Here each Zionist group has its 'Zion', its 'Bethesda'.[61] Here in baptism there takes place the 'crossing of Jordan' (*ukuwela i Jordan*).[62] Baptism washes away *imikhokha*, that is, 'a train of ugly, unpleasant consequences which a person brings along with him, e.g. from committal of some crime or contagious disease'.[63]

Pauw and Sundkler describe the prayer over the water which precedes baptism (*umkhuleko wamanzi*, water prayer), which drives out the water monster or water snake with the aid of the staff (*izikhali*, weapon) and the water angel (John 5.4).[64]

In a country like South Africa, where water is recognized as source of life much more than here, water takes on enormous power in worship and even in magical uses. It is medicine, 'vital force', which for the African is often identical with the presence of God. It is not for nothing that the Zulu journal of the Assemblies of God is called *Amanzi Okuphila* (Water of Life).

Purification rites

Many Zionist groups do not restrict themselves to a single baptism. Baptism is repeated and becomes a purification rite as in African religions. It also has to fulfil the function of the eucharist, since the Africans cannot get wine for the celebration of the Lord's Supper. The devaluation of the one baptism through the abuse of numerous rebaptisms, the disputes about baptism amongst the white South African Pentecostals, and the non-recognition of baptism administered by Lutherans, Reformed Churches, and even other Pentecostal groups, has made it much easier for the one baptism to be changed into a repeatable rite of purification. The purification rite is necessary to wash away the impurity caused by a burial, childbirth, drunkenness or sickness.[65]

In spite of the phenomenological parallels between heathen and Christian purification rites, the independent African Pentecostal churches make a conscious distinction in principle between them. This distinction is expressed in the terminology. Christians do not call their purification rites *ukophothula*, like the pagan Zulu, but *ukuhlambulula*[66] or *ukusefa*, an Afrikaans loan word.[67]

(*c*) *The Holy Spirit* (uMoya)

Like the rest of the Pentecostal movement the independent African Pentecostal churches distinguish between

> *uMoya* as the agent of sanctification (the fruit of the Spirit), and
> *uMoya* as the giver of supernatural gifts.

In certain circumstances the gifts of the Spirit can act in relative independence of the fruits of the Spirit; this is also the teaching of North American Pentecostals.

They agree with their white teachers in regarding being endowed with the Holy Spirit as the most important condition for the office of pastor and prophet. As a result they have many pastors who have had no schooling, and bishops who have only attended school for five years. Elias Nduli wrote to a Zulu newspaper:

> I see that many ministers have been instructed in colleges and go overseas to learn the ministers' work. I have never heard of any place where Christ is supposed to have been taught. I challenge whomsoever it may be of the ministers in European churches to tell me the Bible verse where it is said that Christ was instructed in the Gospel.[68]

The Zionists fight against demons with the weapon of the Spirit and are therefore in line with the whole Pentecostal movement.

Sundkler gives a number of testimonies of Spirit baptism: 'I felt that I was full (*ngisuthile*). 'I almost burst, yes, I was made ready to burst.' 'He is made sick by the *uMoya* (*uyaguliswa uMoya*).'[69] 'It was like being burnt, or as "the lighting of a match" within me.' When the attention of independent Pentecostals was brought to the phenomenological parallel between possession by the spirits of ancestors and the baptism of the Spirit, they replied to Sundkler that someone possessed by the spirit of an ancestor danced differently from someone possessed by the Holy Spirit. (*uMoya oyingcwele akasini. Amandiki namandawe ayasina.*)[70] This information is meaningful, if the speaker means that those possessed by the Holy Spirit remain in command of their senses, while those possessed by the spirit of an ancestor lose their personality for a time.

(*d*) *The function of the prophet*

The Zionist prophet as heir of the Zulu kingship

In Zulu history the king played a very large part. He was the 'essence of the vital force of the tribe and therefore of prosperity, of well-being'.[71] He carried out the most important religious actions. He healed the sick, and when he could not heal someone, that person was as it were incurable. He was the richest man in the tribe. Gathered round him in his military barracks were his 'regiments' (*amaбutho*), the periodically changed military units whose duties included singing and dancing.

The Zulu have not forgotten the magnificent past of their kings. On the contrary, it still lives in the prophets and priests of the independent Pentecostal churches. Their president, bishop or superintendent is really a king, an *inkosi*, and his church is his tribe. Thus the Zionist pastors even declare that they are of royal descent,[72] and in the case of some Pentecostal pastors this is true.[73] The 'king' has a great interest in owning land, for he will give his people back the land that was taken from the Africans in the Land Act of 1913.[74] In the Bethesdas of the Zionist leaders the 'regiments of the king' dance and sing like the soldiers of the great Zulu king Shaka.

But the parallels with white Pentecostal pastors and with Dowie should not be underestimated. Dowie also bought land for his people, in order to build the town of Zion, Illinois. He also called himself a king. And just like independent African Pentecostal pastors, white pastors are doctor, judge and priest in one.

The Zionist prophet as heir of the Zulu medicine man (isangoma)

Not only the tradition of the king but also that of the medicine man (*isangoma*) is carried on by the independent African Pentecostal pastor. He is ultimately a prophet. And adherents of such a prophet believe that he has eyes in his feet, which stay awake when he sleeps.[75] He prophesies, and like his fellow prophets of the Old Testament has experienced a call in a vision. By taking over this double function from Zulu tradition, the Zionist prophet, travelling through the country, has an advantage, in spite of his limited schooling, over the head of an Ethiopian church, who sits in Johannesburg and types letters.

The first appearance of visions and dreams was not in Pentecostalism. Sundkler asked the Christians of the Lutheran Ceza Mission Station in 1940–42 and 1958, why the first Zulu left their tribal religion and became Christians.

> The answer was often that this had happened in some crisis of illness. The powerful White Christ had cured them through his messengers and they had therefore transferred their allegiance to the white group. But the transition was very often made by way of response to a direct revelation of God by a dream. They saw a figure of dazzling brightness, which they identified as the White Christ preached by the missionaries; or they thought they saw themselves dressed in the white baptismal robe. There could be no more discussion: they had to break with all opposition and cross the boundary dividing traditional society from the Christian Church, and be received in baptism into the new tribe of the White Christ.[76]

But a conflict soon arose, for the Lutherans had black gowns and black clothes for the evangelists, and black blouses and skirts for the deaconesses or women catechists (*abasizikazi*). And since conversion to the Lutherans based on a vision was never questioned by the missionaries, it is easy to see that later visions of persons clad in white were bound to lead people to the Pentecostal baptismal services, where white is worn. Thousands of independent Pentecostals, when asked why they left the mission church, answer: 'I had a dream.'

(*e*) *Healing through prayer*

The Zulu and the Sotho distinguish between mild diseases brought about by natural causes, and severe diseases caused by bewitchment. Different words are used to refer to the two kinds of illness.[77] In the African view, the cause of *severe* illness is African and also European medicine. Because they reject both the African and the European medicine man (= doctor) and because if they have a disease 'cast' on them by magic or worked in them by magic medicine they cannot be cured by herbs or ordinary medicine, they are dependent for a cure on contrary magic, which in this case means healing by prayer.[78]

One of the most important ailments dealt with is the infertility of women; snakes sent by the bewitcher penetrate into the woman's womb and kill the foetus.[79] Thus the healing of these women requires the exorcism of this snake demon.

Sundkler gives a remarkable example of a Lutheran women, Melika, afflicted with innumerable ailments:

> Her case history in the hospital was as follows: Age 32. Examined September 18, 1939. Had been ill for many months with abdominal troubles, and ulcer on the right hip. Diagnosis: Syphilis and gonorrhoea. In hospital September 19 to November 8 1939. Was treated for syphilis. Developed pneumonia and pleurisy, and the treatment for syphilis had to be postponed for a while, but was later resumed. Further diagnosis showed also bilharzia, but not treated for this, as it was felt that she should rest between treatments. Next stay in hospital February 15 to March 11, 1940. She was then pregnant, sixth to seventh month. Treated for threatening abortion, gonorrhoea and bilharzia. Delivery May 1, 1940, normal. Some time after birth the child came out in a rash, Melika brought him regularly to the hospital for injections. He recovered, but when some eight months old was brought to the hospital with a big abscess on the arm. He had been cut by his father when trying to cure the infant of some ailment. The mother now refused to stay at the hospital, and the child was treated as an outpatient. The abcesss healed, but a few days later the child got conjunctivitis. Treated at the hospital service, with marked results. One day the father reported that they could not bring the child, as it had got diarrhoea. He asked for medicine and was instructed to bring the child to the hospital. It was too late, however, for it died the same day. February 19–25, 1941, Melika was treated after abortion. After that she disappeared from the hospital for a long time.
>
> We discovered that while visiting the mission hospital Melika had also sought the following treatments:
>
> (1) She visited another European doctor living some twenty miles away, who

was believed to possess specially effective medicines; she procured a bottle from him for 5*s*. 6*d*.

(2) She was treated by an *inyanga* for three weeks, and paid one beast and one goat for this.

(3) She stayed two months at prophet Ntshangase's Bethesda, where she went through an intense vomiting-cure, to get rid of demons and internal snakes.

(4) She was being prayed for daily during that whole period by the Sangweni Zionists, the method used being chiefly pummelling with holy sticks.[80] And all this over a period of seventeen months![81]

The last word has not been said about the relationship between European and indigenous medicine. The African view of the relationship between soul and body is a naive one, but seems to retain important elements of an integral understanding of man which medicine is at the present time taking seriously.[82]

(*f*) *Worship*

Although the prophets do not use any written liturgies, like the white Pentecostals they form in their churches oral 'liturgies' which are typical of each particular group. A congregation may pray 'Thou Eagle of Judah', or 'Thou God of Meshach, Shadrach and Abednego', or 'Thou with the wounded side'. The hymns used extend from Bach to Sankey. Sometimes hymns of their own are written. Thus the *Aбantu бaka Moya* (People of the Spirit) sing on the mountains:

Jesu, woza noyihlo	Jesus, come with Thy Father,
Aбantu бayafa	People are dying,
lapha emhlaбeni	Here on earth.[83]

(*g*) *Ethical rigorism: taboos*

The Anglican Church is accused of syncretism, for it mixes Christianity and paganism by allowing the use of tobacco, beer and pork.[84] The rejection of pig's flesh[85] is another reason why the Zionists cannot unite with the Ethiopians. The immediate reason for the prohibition of pork lies in the example of Dowie, who stormed against pig's flesh in fiery sermons. Besides, pork was introduced by the whites and was used by the Zulu medicine men (*izangoma*) as a magic material. And did not Jesus drive out the demons into pigs (Mark 5)? But this taboo can be relaxed, as is seen from the Zionist who prayed the following grace over pork: 'I bless you. Now you are no longer pig's flesh.'[86]

The numerous varieties of other taboos (the cutting of the hair, Sunday and Sabbath, uniforms, the washing of the prayer staff following ancient Zulu tradition, taking off shoes in church) serve the purpose of uniting and identifying the congregation.[87]

5. *Assessment*

(*a*) *Theological criticism*

Peter Beyerhaus follows Augustine in distinguishing between schismatics (who have cut the bond of love) and heretics (who have cut the bond of faith). He counts the Ethiopian churches as schismatics and the Zionists as heretics.

> [The latter] can by no way be a partner for reunification, but only an object of mission. We see that this is not clear to all ministers of our church unfortunately. We observe sometimes that some of us show an irresponsible attitude to toleration and even ecumenicity towards Zionists, as if they were only partly erring but anyway brethren and valid ministers of the Word and the Sacraments. Here we have to think of II John 9-11 . . .[88]

Beyerhaus wrote the article from which this quotation is taken in 1961, and even then he felt bound to admit that 'the religious concepts of Christians inside our Churches are often hardly different from those already won by the sects'. Beyerhaus admits that the independent Pentecostals were able to give to Africans plagued by demons an answer which was more comprehensible and of more help than that given by the Lutheran Missionary Church.

> And because of our lack of an answer to these problems which to him are the only important ones, he silently turns his back on us and consults the witch-doctor, or leaves us completely and joins a syncretistic sect which gradually brings him back to Heathenism.[89] . . . These sects are South Africa's attempt to escape the Cross.[90]

He consequently regards it as important in all contacts with these groups, for example when one of their prophets is invited to give fraternal greetings in a Lutheran congregation, 'that it be clear to the members of one's own church that this is not an ecumenical but a missionary activity'.[91] Even if their 'Bishops' seek further theological training, while this should not be refused, the instruction 'will have something of the character of baptismal instruction, even if this cannot be made clear for tactical reasons.'[92] Nor is Beyerhaus convinced by H. W. Turner's study of a number of sermons from independent Nigerian Pentecostal churches (known as *aladura*),[93] in which he demonstrates a more or less orthodox content in the prayers, hymns and sermons. For Beyerhaus argues that just as important as what the preachers say is what their congregations understand. This observation is true, but it applies just as much to European as to African churches.[94]

At the conclusion of the article just quoted, Beyerhaus mentions a criticism which seems to me very important. The church is not merely a society, but also has the task of saving human society outside the church. Part of this task is preparation for 'responsible citizenship' and a 'conscious acceptance of the secularisation of many religious concepts of the past'.[95]

This theological criticism does not prevent Beyerhaus from seeing the positive sides of the Zionists' methods and practices, their joyful worship, and the integration in their worship of African means of expression.

I also feel that in his inaugural lecture in Tübingen he put his criticism in less categorical terms and more in the form of questions, and in part admitted to sharing the theological dilemma of the Zionists.

> Behind the questions we have posed lie problems which have not yet been solved by the sending churches of the West and their theology, partly because our churches and their doctrinal structure are from an ecumenical point of view only fragments, and partly because all theological knowledge is always fragmentary.[96]

In his theological criticism Beyerhaus is supported by Gründler, though the latter makes hardly any distinction between Zionist and Ethiopian churches and clearly has little information about the spread of the Zionists. His comment, that 'they mostly lead a miserable existence'[97] is true of many individual groups, but not of some of the larger groups or of the Zionists as a whole.

Hans Häselbarth,[98] Marie-Louise Martin,[99] B. A. Pauw and Jacqueline Eberhardt all hold a similar view of the Zionists. In her article 'The Church Facing Prophetic and Messianic Movements'[100] Marie-Louise Martin gives a general survey of the history and subdivisions of the independent churches, and of the reasons why they came into being. Apart from the sociological and political factors, to which she gives full weight (the destruction of the ancient tribal structures, the South African government's land policy and racial policy, the decline of the chief's authority), she pays particular attention to the theological reasons for the rise of independent churches and comes to the following conclusion: The Whites removed the non-historical, cyclical understanding of history which the African peoples had held. From then on it was possible for them to think in historical terms.

Eschatology became possible and replaced a cyclical picture of history. But African congregations turned this eschatology into a future expectation of their unfulfilled longings and desires.[101] This did not only take place in the sphere of eschatology.

> We missionaries or African ministers are speaking about the Saviour; non-Christian Africans understand the word 'saviour' in their own way. We speak about the kingdom of God – they interpret it against the background of their own hopes. We speak about sin – they mean the old taboos. We speak about the Spirit – they think of 'power' or ancestor-possession. We speak about God – they coupled it with the conception of their own 'god'.[102]

The vocabulary in which the gospel is preached is taken over from paganism and brings its associations with it. Revelation is understood in the context of dreams and visions. They want a Messiah adapted to their desires and consequently avoid the crisis of all real faith in the cross. But this is the very reason why dialogue with them must be sought and sustained.

> We have no illusions about converting them and their members to the Church of Christ. They may resist not only our attempts, but the truth of the Gospel itself. We are aware of the post-Christian character of these movements and their 'anti-messianism',[103] we realise that in the final analysis they try to escape the *skandalon* of the cross.[104]

The same state of affairs is attested by Pauw. In an independent Pentecostal congregation he had listened to a sermon on the law, and used the invitation to speak

> to point out that faith in Jesus Christ and forgiveness in his Name is the essence of our salvation. The leader's wife, who was the next speaker, thereupon explained that 'forgiveness is when we behave well' (*tšhwarêlô ke ha re itšhwara sentlê*).[105] The expression 'faith is work', which I heard in several churches, is perhaps the most explicit expression of this tendency.[106]
>
> The sociologist Jacqueline Eberhardt makes the same observation:
>
> The resurrection is a well known and familiar theme to the Bantu. The critical distinction between our idea of Christ and that of the Zionist Prophet is the theme of the 'death [of Christ] for our salvation'. The believer is healed by the Prophet; he knows Jehovah thanks to the Prophet; the Prophet provides an assurance of his fertility and that of the crops; he offers him a refuge in the 'high places', leading him on to the 'gate of heaven'. But does he save him as an act of grace alone? In fact we have never encountered this notion. . . .'[107]

The question is simply whether Africans in general are in a position to understand the Reformation interpretation of the New Testament.

> Man certainly has an immediate intuitive understanding of legalism, and orthodox Protestant doctrine, according to which the redemption of the individual is not dependent on any legalism, and is therefore uncertain in every case, is something which for many men is simply too much to ask of their mental capacity. Thus the movement away from strict Protestant churches towards legalist churches represents a return to a more primitive form of church, which is more comprehensible to non-intellectuals in its demand than the strictly Protestant form. Besides this, a legalist religion probably provides its adherents with a greater power of resistance to the injustice of everyday life, because it is 'more certain'.[108]

Marie-Louise Martin makes a careful analysis of the *avoidable* weaknesses of the missionary churches, but affirms that the *theologia crucis* will always remain a stumbling block for the African, as for the European. In so far as these independent churches try to avoid the cross, they must be regarded as a danger and a threat to the gospel. But Marie-Louise Martin is not of the opinion that there is no place in a church in the Reformation tradition for prophecy which is under the control of the Bible and the Church, for the healing of the sick which avoids hard selling publicity, and for worship which brings into play the African soul within liturgical limits.

The African tradition should be assimilated by theology, but not adopted uncritically. This demand was made by Diedrich Westermann as early as 1926:

> Schools have been started, and mission work has been carried on without any consideration for the state of mind of those who were to be educated or evangelized. The Africans have been treated by us as having no religion, no language, no traditions no institutions, no racial character of their own, as empty vessels to be filled with European or American goods. Even more: People who are responsible for African education have considered the intentional destruction of Native forms of life and of thought a condition of success.[109]

The Africans' mother tongue was forbidden, their traditions ridiculed and set aside as sinful. In 1926 this approach was still practised, but was no longer dominant. But Westermann is clear that many elements of African tradition cannot be taken over at all (e.g. slavery), while others are only acceptable in a fragmented form.

H. von Sicard has a similar view:

> The view of the missionary as a 'new medicine man' is one of the most serious restrictions on the full acceptance of the biblical message of redemption. For the 'righteousness which is acceptable to God' finds no place in the gospel as it is interpreted in the legalist African sense, where it is a vital force not qualified by the considerations of Christian ethics. For the Africans 'good' is what aids fertility; 'bad' is what hinders it or works against it. The repentance which Christ called for is most difficult to understand. The belief is that vital force can be gained without sanctification. Direct personal guilt before the holy God is one of the parts of the Christian message which is hardest to understand.[110]

(*b*) *A sociological assessment*

Katesa Schlosser tries to assess the Zionists from the sociological point of view. Since they fulfil a necessary and important function which used to be that of the tribes and for which no substitute yet exists, her view of the groups is the more favourable, the better they fulfil this task. In this assessment Bhengu and Shembe, who does not belong to the Zionist groups, but to the Messianic, come out best.

Theo Schneider, who is familiar with the independent groups from his own observation, calls above all for the necessary adaptations in missionary policy:

> It is easy to reject the racial and nationalist aspect of the dissident Bantu congregations. But what have we done to help the blacks to resolve their basic economic problem, that of land? Here our mission farms could play a vital role . . . It is easy to be offended by ecstatic forms of worship, the use of drums in the church, and wild processions. But what have we done to

respond in accordance with the truth to the emotional nature of the blacks? . . . Error must be opposed by truth and not by a vacuum.[111]

(*c*) *An ecumenical study*

In the first edition of his book *Bantu Prophets in South Africa* (1948), Sundkler still treated the independent African churches as a bridge to paganism, over which the Christians from the missionary churches were returning to paganism. In the second edition of his book (1961) he considers this view to be too western in its outlook.

> To the African masses . . . their Churches appeared as definitely Christian organizations, adapted to their own real needs, and as bridges to a new and richer experience of life. In the city, with its rapidly industrialized civilization, they functioned as 'adaptive structures'. In Zululand and Swaziland they were, relatively speaking, reaching the difficult transition period from traditional religion to new structures and a new ideology.[112]

They can now accept apartheid as a new expression of the Bantu caste.[113] For this reason the government has recently been giving a certain degree of support to independent churches. 'The mine is always interested to have church services in order to tame the boys.'[114] But one should not be deceived by this. With some exceptions, Africans who are politically aware are hardly to be found in the Zionist Pentecostal groups.

On the other hand, in South Africa, as in North and South America, it seems that a powerful movement for social improvement is taking place amongst the members of the independent Pentecostal groups (Zionist). This is shown by the following table:

Number of Pupils from Different Denominations

	Elementary School	*Technical School*	*Secondary School*
Methodists	5572	3567	808
Lutherans	4319	2925	609
Anglicans	4149	2472	528
Roman Catholics	3298	1951	301
Ethiopian Churches	5596	3020	525
Zionist (Pentecostal) Churches	6898	1962	208[115]

Emotional worship seems everywhere in the world to be able to bring about a desire to change the outward conditions of life. The Zionists have gone on to concern themselves with agricultural reform; they have tried out new methods of cultivation; in a township in the Rand an independent church filled the governing body of the Anglican parish school with its own people.[116]

They also seem to be looking for a compromise over the rejection of medical help. Pentecostals from independent churches are now treated in hospitals.

When they are discharged they have to be decontaminated from the harmful influences of European medicine by their pastors, through prayers and purification rites. The student nurses include a number of daughters of Zionist Pentecostal pastors, and these told told Sundkler with a smile that 'doctors and nurses have the spirit of Christ'.[117]

> Bantu independent Churches are an outcome of the political, social and denominational situation in South Africa. Without deep-going changes in these fields we must expect that the strong inherent leadership qualities of the Bantu will express themselves in terms of Utopian movements such as those described here. But when we Europeans lament the appalling strife and friction among leaders and followers in the Bantu's own church, we should be careful to take our share of responsibility for the situation.[118]

This judgment seems to take insufficient account of the theological factors which led to the rise of the independent churches. Perhaps it is not possible to to make sense of the phenomena of the Zionists with the aid of theological categories. At any rate the theological and sociological assessment of the churches does not yet seem to have made sufficient progress. In my view further clarification can only be reached by examining the question *in co-operation* with them. Care is taken to leave the question open in a comment made by the editors of the *Evangelisches Missionsmagazin* on the article by Beyerhaus quoted above:[119]

> It is not immediately obvious that one must follow Marie-Louise Martin in seeing these groups as a 'new African syncretistic religion'. But is it any more obvious that the diminished emphasis placed on the crucified Messiah should be seen as a 'revolt against the way of revelation given by God in Christ'? It may well be that we European Christians, with our thorough theological grounding, try to make a general theological judgment, on the basis of the second article of faith, about groups upon whom the third article of faith has taken a particular hold, without their having succeeded so far in making the proper connection between the Holy Spirit and the historical Jesus Christ. We should pay attention to the statement of Bijlefeld:[120] 'The starting point of our "ecumenical" thinking is our own Church, and from this centre we decide whom we can still accept as fellow Christians.'[121]

To overcome this caricature of 'ecumenical' thought the World Council of Churches has for some time been carrying out a dialogue with the African mission churches in the presence of representatives of the independent churches, and is attempting to lay down guide lines which will make possible a proper judgment of the Zionists and other native churches. Account has been taken of the different phenomena within the independent groups. In the report of the consultation of Kitwe Mindolo (6–13 September 1962) there is emphasis on the link between salvation and sanctification, and a study of exorcism in the Bible is called for. There is also a call for a new understanding of the function of dreams, visions and prophecy, and for a more human attitude to polygamists who were already polygamists when they were converted. It is also suggested that means should be sought to provide women with more active forms of co-operation.

In order to make possible a unified approach in this matter, the following guide lines are laid down for the acceptance of independent churches into National Councils of Churches:

1. Acceptance of the basis (the basic formula of faith) of the World Council of Churches.
2. Acceptance of the Bible as the Word of God, wherein is found the full Way of Salvation.
3. Sufficient evidence of stability in life and organization, an established programme of Christian nurture and evangelism, affirmation of the principles of stable Christian home life, and arrangements for adequate training of the ministry.
4. Acceptance of the aims, objects, and constitution of the Council, together with the declaration of desire to co-operate in Christian fellowship with all other constituent member bodies of the Council.
5. Recommendation for membership by two churches which are member bodies of the Council.[122]

This ecumenical spirit and willingness to make contact are not to be understood as an easy-going relativism. This is made clear in an unambiguous rejection of the Messianic sects:

> The term *Messianic* is used to describe groups which, centred around a dominant personality, claim for him special powers involving a form of identification with Christ. It should be noted that when this identification becomes substitution, the group has in our opinion moved outside the sphere of the Christian church.[123]

This means that the Messianic groups which Viktor Maag discusses, which 'can as little be called churches as Islam',[124] are not considered to be possible members of the National Councils of Churches and the World Council of Churches.

Since 1962 discussions have gone further. A number of small independent groups have been accepted into the National Councils of Churches and into the All Africa Conference of Churches.[125] In 1969 the largest independent church, the *Église de Jésus-Christ sur la terre par le prophète Simon Kimbangu* from the Congo (Kimbanguists)[126] was accepted as a member of the World Council of Churches.

A new approach has been made by David B. Barratt in his analysyis of six thousand contemporary movements in Africa. He places the South African Zionists in their context in the whole of Africa, and on the basis of a list of eighteen measurable and quantifiable conditions, he mades unambiguous forecasts about where, when, and under what conditions one may expect new groups

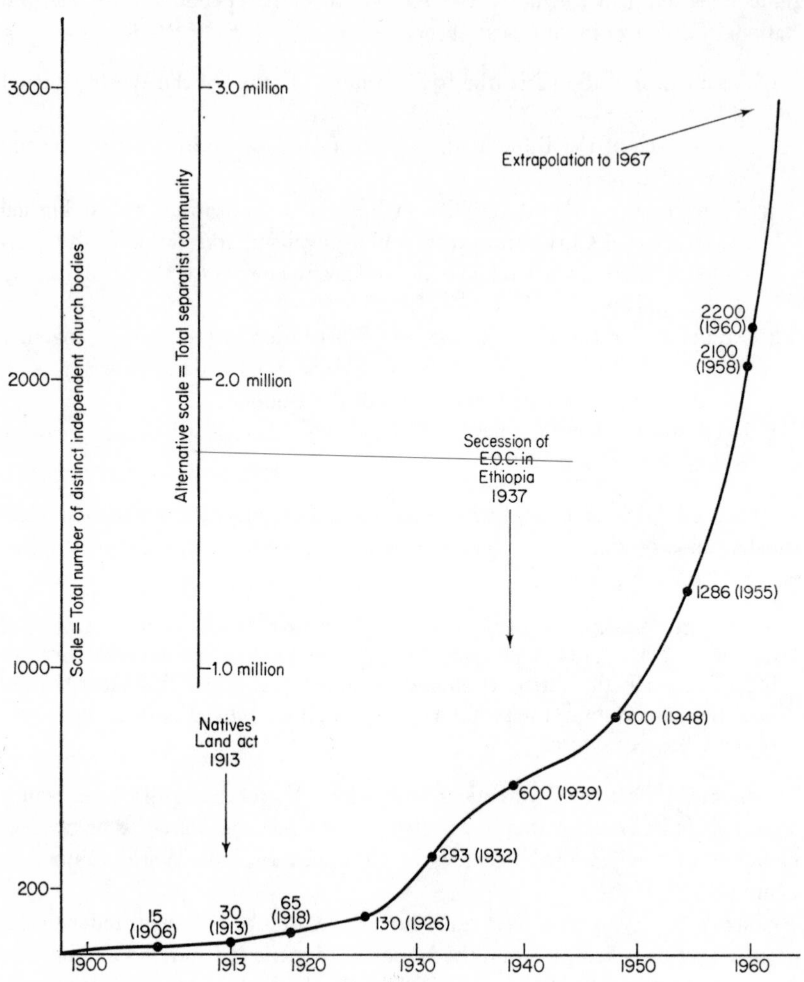

Growth of Independent Churches in South Africa, 1872–1967
(*Source: government censuses, reports and archives, and estimates by missions and social scientists; the numbers are of bodies, with related date in brackets*)[127]

to arise. Since these conditions will occur to an increasing extent, it is likely that independent churches will come into being at a growing rate.

Barrett describes these churches from a theological point of view as resembling 'both the remnant communities of Israel in the Old Testament and also the large number of small autonomous local churches in the New'.[128] They are the natural evangelists of Africa. While the achievements of traditional missionary work must not be minimized it becomes increasingly clear that the urgency of the task of evangelizing the 'two billions', the direct evangelistic task, can be carried forward more efficiently by these groups than by European missionaries and evangelists, which does not mean that the latter no longer have a contribution to make in Africa, but rather that their task will no longer be direct evangelization, particularly as these churches – at least in Barrett's judgment – have grasped Bonhoeffer's profound insight of 'a church for others'[129] to a very remarkable extent.[130]

In his discussion of the future of these movements Barrett expects that this type of Christian body will play an increasingly important role in Latin America and Africa. In fact he even predicts that the number of Christians in these two continents will exceed those in the rest of the world in year 2000.[131] He detects a large dormant sector of independency within the traditional African churches (see diagram),[132] which in the future will emerge to the surface as the preconditions are met.

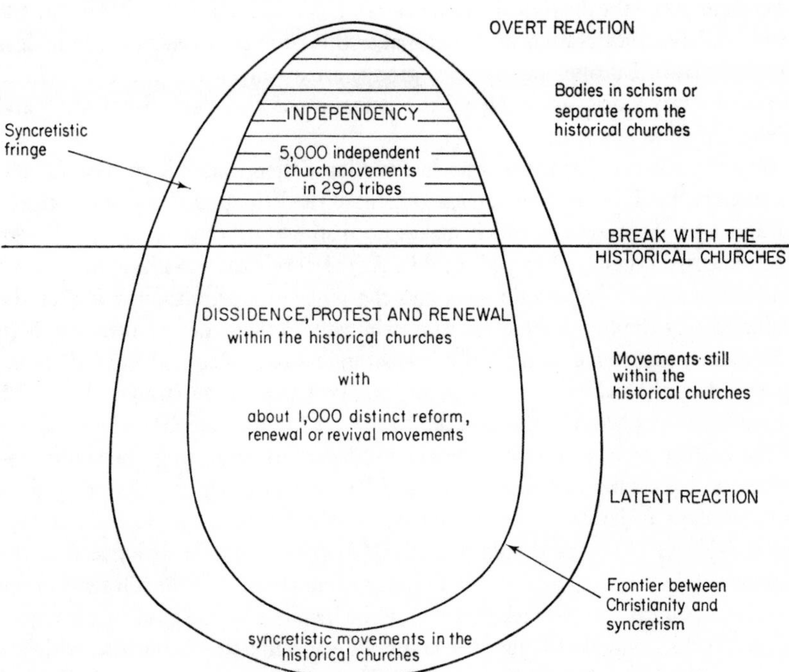

In a very interesting subsection Barrett discusses the 'perils of prediction':[133] The *first* possibility is that his prediction will prove to be a false or unfulfilled prophecy; this would be due either to the analysis having assessed the situation falsely, or to the emergence of some new and unexpected factor. The *second* possibility is that the predicition will be approximately fulfilled. The *third* possibility, and probably the most disastrous of the four, is that the prediction might become a self-fulfilling prophecy; that is, an initially fallacious prediction based on a false definition of the situation which evokes a new behaviour that makes the originally false conception come true. The *fourth* possibility and doubtless the most satisfactory of all, is that his prediction might prove to be a self-destroying prophecy: that is, an initially accurate prediction based on a correct definition of the situation which evokes a new behaviour that prevents fulfilment of what would otherwise come to pass. Historical churches might realize the gravity of the situation and attempt a full *rapprochement* once and for all.

One might consider that the different attempts at ecumenical fellowship on the part of these independent churches are a step in the direction of a self-destroying prophecy. It is true that many of these churches have tried to be accepted in National Councils and the All Africa Conference of Churches as well as in the WCC. Most of them have up to now been refused, and this forces these groups to set up their own ecumenical groupings, a fact which might well divide the ecumenical movement in the future into what I could call literary Christianity (in the historical churches) and non-literary Christianity (in the newer independent churches). What makes this problem even more difficult is the fact that in Europe and America groups are arising which must be defined as post-literary Christianity. Hence the attraction of Neo-Pentecostalism[134] and of the hippie movement.

One thing is certain; there is no justification either academic or pastoral and missionary, for a description and assessment of the Ethiopian, Zionist-Pentecostal and Messianic groups which makes no distinction between them. All who have discussed them are agreed on this. At the very least a distinction must be made between the Messianic sects and the other groups, although it must be admitted that the limits are often indeterminate. Perhaps the Zionists will help Christianity to survive its time of hibernation in Africa. A possible parallel may be found in the categories of thought, many of them very strange, by which Christianity was brought through the European Middle Ages.[135] The existence of the Zionist groups in which there is no longer any preaching, 'but only confession and speaking in tongues', is based 'on needs for which psychotherapists are nowadays available in Western civilizations'.[136] It seems to be essential that the missionary churches should not miss the opportunity for dialogue with the Zionists, if they wish to become the Ecumenical movement in the full sense of the word ecumenical. In this task they should be inspired by the guiding principles of the World Council of Churches, taking into account the theological criticism set out in the first part of this chapter.[137] The problems presented by individual phenomena (dreams, healing through prayer, prophecy, speaking in tongues) are the same as are presented in white Pentecostal churches, and do not need to be discussed separately here.

An independent Zulu pastor summed up his Christian witness as follows: *Umuntu ungumuntu ngomuntu*[138] (Man becomes man through Him who became man.) This is a theologically and linguistically mature expression of the Christian heritage. A church which is capable of this cannot be ignored by the missionary churches.

NOTES

1. Sources, Documents, Literature: 01.36.037–01.36.488.
2. Cf. above ch. 9.2(*c*), p. 120.
3. M.-L. Martin, *Ministry*, Lesotho, 3/2, Jan. 1963, pp. 53, 55.
4. M.-L. Martin, *op. cit.*, p. 53.
5. Sundkler, p. 55.
6. V. E. W. Hayward (ed.), *African Movements*, pp. 70–82; cf. pp. 166ff.
7. Sundkler, p. 180.
8. Cf. the account in *The Upper Room* of 7.6.1909 (quoted in *PE* 1607, 24.2.1945, pp. 2–3), which describes these baptisms of the Spirit, which took place in a baptism service taken by Le Roux. Similarly M. Harper, *As At the Beginning*, p. 94.
9. Sundkler, p. 116.
10. *Trooster*, Aug.–Sept. 1940, quoted in Sundkler, p. 243; J. Lake, *Die sichere Grundlage*.
11. Sundkler, p. 243.
12. F. P. Möller of the Apostolic Faith Mission (see ch. 9.3[*a*], pp. 130ff.), in a letter to W.H., 4.6.1964: 'All the Bantu groups as mentioned in your ms. are *not* Pentecostal. It is also a gross mistake to classify all ecstatic African groups under Pentecost. Their ecstasy can be better explained in the light of their heathen background. The only groups in Southern Africa which can be classified under the heading Pentecost are those linked with white Churches, like the AFM [Apostolic Faith Mission], Full Gospel Church of God [01.36.013], Assemblies of God [ch. 9.3(*b*), p. 122], Pentecostal Holiness Church [01.36.015].' August Kast writes: 'I repeat in all seriousness that the more than 400 "independent Pentecostal Churches" which you refer to have nothing to do with the Pentecostal movement and also do not count themselves a part of it, nor do they derive from it . . . There are a number of fairly large groups of Zionists based on Evaton (Transvaal), which possess notable gifts of healing, but deal with the spirits of the ancestors, which they naturally often call "Holy Spirit" . . . Consequently I must reject with all seriousness the referring to these Zionists as "Pentecostal Churches", and I confidently hope that that you will delete the whole section on independent Pentecostals from your book. Some of these Zionist leaders claim to go back to men like Le Roux, the first leader of the Apostolic Faith Mission, or Alexander Dowie. In recent years individual Zionists here and there have attached themselves to the Apostolic Faith Mission, but give it a lot of trouble and usually return to the Zionists.' (Letter to W.H., 16.4.1964.) On the other hand D. J. Du Plessis agrees with my account. Du Plessis has for many years held a leading position in the South African Apostolic Faith Mission. According to Du Plessis (who refers to statements of the previous secretary of the Apostolic Faith Mission, I. D. W. Bosman), in 1932 112 out of 400 Zionist groups

could be shown to be offshoots of the Apostolic Faith Mission (communication from Du Plessis, 4.8.1968).

13. F. Burke, *Monthly Letter on Evangelism*, Dec. 1966/Jan. 1967, WCC, Geneva.

14. B. A. Pauw, *Religion*, p. 236.

15. *Ibid.*, p. 227.

16. Sundkler knows of a list which contains the names of over 2,000 groups. Not all these groups still exist. Some have disappeared, others have amalgamated; but new groups constantly appear. M.-L. Martin gives a figure of 3,000 groups with 1,593,909 adherents (M.-L. Martin, *Biblical Concept*, p. 123). The rate of growth is sensational: 1918, 78; 1926, 120–40; 1938, 320; 1948, 800; 1960, 2,100; 1963, 3,000. In 1967 a quarter of all Bantu Christians (more than three millions) belonged to these groups (Sundkler, *RGG*, 3rd ed., vol. V, col. 1665; C. Loram, *IRM* 15/59, July 1926, pp. 476-482; D. B. Barrett, *Schism*, p. 78).

17. Sundkler, *Frontier* 3/1, 1960, p. 19.

18. D. B. Barrett, *Schism*, p. 109.

19. Barrett, *op. cit.*, p. 252.

20. Elias Mahlangu, Ignatius Lekganyane, Fred Luthuli, Petros Mabunya Maake, Jonathan Mavunsuna, Paulo Mabilitsa, Daniel Nkonyane, J. G. Phillipps.

21. M.-L. Martin, Notes.

22. Sundkler, p. 168.

23. E.g. National Swaziland Apostolic Church of Africa: 01.39.011.

24. Sundkler, p. 170.

25. *Ibid.*, p. 296.

26. *Ibid.*, p. 50.

27. The Bantu Independent Churches Union of South Africa (01.36.167); United Churches of Christ (01.36.427); Transvaal African National Congress (01.36.417); African Pentecostal Church (01.36.081); United National Church of Africa (01.36.431).

28. African Independent Churches' Association.

29. Assembly of Zionist and Apostolic Churches.

30. D. B. Barrett, *Schism*, p. 23.

31. Sundkler, p. 33 (quoting W. H. Macmillan).

32. Sundkler, *ibid.*

33. Sundkler, pp. 33f.

34. K. Schlosser, *Eingeborenenkirchen*, pp. 327f.

35. M.-L. Martin, *Ministry* 3/2, Jan. 1963, p. 55.

36. Sundkler, p. 35.

37. Cf. ch. 10, pp. 126ff.

38. E. H. Brookes, *A Century of Missions*, p. 32; quoted in Sundkler, p. 37; so also M.-L. Martin, *Ministry* 3/2, Jan. 1963, p. 55.

39. In spite of an explicit prohibition, however, churches and schools are built by 'unrecognized' churches.

40. Apart from this wine is not sold to natives (Liquor Act no. 30, 1928; Sundkler, p. 79) – though this has since been changed (K. Schlosser).

41. Age, size, stability, etc. (C. Loram, *IRM* 15/59, July 1926, pp. 476–82; Sundkler, p. 74).

42. Letter of the Native Affairs Dept. to Sundkler, 15.10.1941; quoted in Sundkler, p. 76.

43. Sundkler, p. 78.

44. Examples given of attempts to be recognized: African Baptized Apostle Church (01.36.055); Holy Cross Catholic Apostolic Christian Church in Zion (01.36.297); New Faith Gospel Apostolic Church of Jesus Christ (01.36.365); Pilgrims Apostolic Sabbath Church of Jesus Christ in Zion (01.36.393).

45. F. P. Möller, letter to W.H., 4.6.1964.
46. Sundkler, p. 70.
47. M.-L. Martin, Notes.
48. D. B. Barrett, *Schism*, p. 189 *et passim*.
49. H. v. Sicard, *RGG*, 3rd ed., vol. I, col. 151.
50. Sundkler, p. 275.
51. Sundkler, p. 276.
52. National Church of God of South Africa (01.36.342); Sundkler, p. 208.
53. Congregational Catholic Apostolic Church of Zion in South Africa (01.36.228); Sundkler, p. 55.
54. Sundkler, p. 276.
55. Th. Schneider, *Verbum Caro* 6, 1952, p. 125.
56. Sundkler (p. 208) is not correct when he states that churches which derive from Pentecostal or Baptist groups practise baptism by single immersion, while those which derive from the Catholic Christian Church in Zion, Ill., practise threefold immersion. Threefold immersion at baptism was, however, introduced into Africa by the Catholic Christian Church, and passed on to the Africans by way of the Apostolic Faith Mission.
57. Cf. ch. 11., pp. 140ff.
58. Sundkler, p. 211.
59. *Ibid.*, p. 164.
60. *Ibid.*, p. 207.
61. E.g. Jerusalem Sabbath Church (01.36.320); Zion Christian Church (01.36.463).
62. Sundkler, p. 208.
63. A. T. Bryant, *Zulu–English Dictionary*, Pine Town, Natal: 1905, p. 310, quoted in Sundkler, p. 202.
64. E.g. Sabbath Holy Apostolic Zion Church of South Africa (01.36.401); Sundkler, p. 207; B. A. Pauw, *Religion*, pp. 191–7: Examples for baptism: Christian Apostolic Faith Assembly in Zion of South Africa (01.36.189); Jerusalem Sabbath Church (01.36.320); Holy Catholic Apostolic Church in Zion (the blessing of children: 01.36.290).
65. B. A. Pauw, *Religion*, pp. 191f.
66. Derived from *ukuhlamba* (wash). Meaning: to make thin, free, unrestricted. In heathen Zulu the term is used for purification rites in connection with initiations (Bryant, *Zulu–English Dictionary*, p. 239, quoted in Sundkler, p. 210).
67. From *te sif*, to sift, winnow, riddle. For a comparison between a heathen and a Christian purification rite cf. ch. 27.2, pp. 393ff., and Sabbath Zionist Church (01.36.402), St Paul Apostolic Faith Morning Star (01.36.412), Zion Apostolic Church of South Africa (01.36.449).
68. E. Nduli, 'Amabandla azimeleyo' in *Llanga lase Natal*, 9.6.1945, quoted in Sundkler, p. 125.
69. This expression is also used in Zulu for possession by the spirit of an ancestor.
70. Sundkler, p. 247.
71. M.-L. Martin, Notes, p. 3.
72. E.g. United National Church of Christ (01.36.432); Holy Catholic Apostolic Church in Zion (01.36.290), Swaziland (01.39.008).
73. E.g. Paulo Mabilitsa (07.883.001).
74. Bhengu's plan for collective settlements must be seen in this context (cf. ch. 10.5 [*e*], pp. 135f.
75. Sundkler, p. 165.
76. Sundkler, *Frontier* 3/1, 1960, pp. 17f.
77. Mild diseases, colds: *umkhuhlane-nje* (Zulu); *bolwetsi bja mmele* (Sotho). Death, severe disease: *ukafa* or *ukafa kwa6antu* (Zulu).

78. Sundkler, p. 225; P. Beyerhaus, *Ministry* 1/4, July 1961, p. 8.
79. E.g. Christian Zion Sabbath Apostolic Church (01.36.214).
80. Sundkler, pp. 222f.
81. Further examples: African Castor-Oil Dead Church (01.36.060), Foundation Apostolic Church in Jerusalem (01.36.260), Holy Catholic Apostolic Church in Zion (01.36.290).
82. Cf. ch. 25.1(*e*), pp. 360ff.
83. Sundkler, p. 279.
84. *Ibid.*, p. 216.
85. The Latter Rain Assemblies also reject pork; cf. ch. 11.2(*e*), p. 144.
86. K. Schlosser, *Eingeborenenkirchen*, p. 340.
87. Further examples: Congregational Catholic Apostolic Church of Zion in South Africa (01.36.228), Ethiopian Catholic Church in Zion (01.36.241), Ethiopian Holy Baptist Church in Zion (01.36.244).
88. P. Beyerhaus, *Ministry* 1/4, July 1961, p. 5.
89. *Ibid.*, p. 12.
90. *Ibid.*, p. 9.
91. P. Beyerhaus, *Ev. Missionsmagazin* 11/2, 1967, p. 80.
92. *Ibid.*
93. H. W. Turner, *Profile.*
94. P. Beyerhaus in P. Beyerhaus (ed.), *Weltmission heute*, 33/34, p. 65.
95. P. Beyerhaus, *op. cit.*, p. 69.
96. P. Beyerhaus, *Zeitschrift für Theologie und Kirche* 64/4, Nov. 1967, p. 517.
97. J. Gründler, *Lexicon*, No. 0348.
98. H. Häselbarth, in P. Beyerhaus (ed.), *Weltmission heute* 33/34, pp. 11–25.
99. See the works cited below (notes 100 and 104); also in P. Beyerhaus, *Weltmission heute* 33/34, pp. 40–56.
100. M.-L. Martin, *Ministry* 3/2, Jan. 1963, pp. 49–61.
101. Cf. V. Maag, *Saeculum* 12, p. 125.
102. M.-L. Martin, *Ministry* 3/2, Jan. 1963, p. 56.
103. In this context 'anti-messianism' means opposition to *biblical* messianism.
104. M.-L. Martin, *Biblical Concept*, p. 210.
105. Perhaps because the words for 'behave well' and 'forgiveness' are derived from the same stem (*go tšhwara*, to take hold of). B. A. Pauw, *Religion*, p. 142 n. 1.
106. *Ibid.*, p. 142.
107. J. Eberhardt, *Archives de Sociologie des Religions* 2/4, July–Dec. 1957, p. 54.
108. K. Schlosser, letter to W.H., 3.3.1964, pp. 7–8.
109. D. Westermann, *IRM* 15/59, July 1926, pp. 426f.
110. H. v. Sicard, *RGG*, 3rd ed., vol. I, cols. 151–2.
111. T. Schneider, *Verbum Caro* 6, 1952, p. 126.
112. Sundkler, p. 302.
113. Cf. Bhengu, ch. 10.5(*b*), p. 135.
114. Sundkler, p. 305.
115. These figures were obtained in 1958 and covered 186 schools in Zululand and Natal, with altogether 60,585 children from 116 denominations (Sundkler, pp. 308f.).
116. Sundkler, p. 86.
117. *Ibid.*, p. 310.
118. *Ibid.*, p. 179.
119. P. Beyerhaus, *Ev. Missionsmagazin* 11/1, 1967, pp. 12–27; 11/2, 78–87.
120. W. A. Bijlefeld, *IRM* 55/220, Oct. 1966, p. 440.
121. *Ev. Missionsmagazin* 11/1, 1967, pp. 14f.
122. V. E. W. Hayward (ed.), *African Movements*, pp. 70–82.

123. *Ibid.*

124. V. Maag, *Volkshochschule* 32, 1963, p. 76.

125. All Africa Council of Churches. *Engagement*, pp. 122f.

126. Ecumenical Review 19/1, Jan. 1967, pp. 29–36; WCC, *Minutes, Central Committee, Canterbury 1969*, pp. 11, 64. For the Kimbanguists see the French edition of this book.

127. D. B. Barrett, *Schism*, p. 69.

128. D. B. Barrett, *op. cit.*, p. 171.

129. D. Bonhoeffer, *Letters and Papers from Prison*, p. 211; cf. WCC, *The Church for Others*, 1967.

130. D. B. Barrett, *Schism*, p. 173.

131. D. B. Barrett, *IRM* 59/233, Jan. 1970, pp. 39–54.

132. D. B. Barrett, *Schism*, p. 6.

133. *Ibid.*, pp. 251ff.

134. Cf. ch. 1, pp. 3ff.; ch. 13.2, pp. 184ff.; ch. 18, pp. 244ff.

135. J. W. C. Dougall, *IRM* 45/179, July 1956, p. 263.

136. K. Schlosser, letter to W.H., 3.3.1964, p. 8.

137. Cf. pp. 161ff.

138. Sundkler, p. 337.

13

A Blending of Aristocratic Anglicanism and Welsh Revivalism: The Origin of Pentecostalism in Great Britain

THE following three chapters deal with parts of the history of the British Pentecostal movement. Chapter 13 describes the origins of the British Pentecostal movement in the revival in Wales. It took the form of a charismatic movement within the existing churches. The rise of West Indian Pentecostal churches is also discussed in this chapter. Then the three largest of the twenty or so Pentecostal organizations in Great Britain are described in rather greater detail: the Apostolic Church as an example of a Pentecostal group of the apostolic type (ch. 13.4); the Elim Pentecostal Churches as an example of conflict between a charismatic founder and the institution that came into being as a result of his work (ch. 14); and the Assemblies of God as an example of a body originally meant to be a revivalist association within the existing churches, but which developed under the influence of the greatest teacher of the Pentecostal movement, Donald Gee, into an independent church organization (ch. 15). It should be stressed that there has been no room to provide an exhaustive account of these three examples.

1. *The Revival in Wales*

(*a*) *Origin*

The Celtic population of Wales is distinguished by a deeply emotional enthusiasm for singing, the Welsh language, and its resistance to the established Anglican Church. From time to time there have been religious revivals in Wales, which have been remarkable for their links with Welsh patriotism and longing for independence, and with the ancient musical culture of Wales.

The revival of 1904, which played such an important part in the origins of

Pentecostalism, began in Joseph Jenkins' church in New Quay on Cardigan Bay. After a sermon, Miss Florrie Evans went to Jenkins. She told him that she could not acknowledge Jesus as her Lord, because she could not know in advance what he would demand of her. The conversations that followed were without success. But at a testimony meeting in Jenkins' church she said 'If no one else will, I must say that I do love my Lord Jesus Christ with all my heart.' These words had an indelible, electric effect on the congregation. Instantly the Holy Spirit came down upon the meeting. They were all seized with indescribable excitement. A flood of tears burst forth. One after another all stood up and placed their lives under the rule of God. The revival had begun. Now at last there was proof of the presence of God, for he was in the midst of them.[1]

Those converted included Evan Roberts, his brother Dan Roberts, the Davies sisters – the 'Singing Sisters' who later accompanied him – Mrs Mary Jones, Evan Lloyd Jones and Sydney Evans.

(*b*) *Characteristics of the revival*

The characteristics of the services of the Welsh revival were the hour-long singing of Welsh hymns in harmony, the decline of the sermon, prayer in concert by the congregation, interruptions from the congregation, an emphasis on the experience of the baptism of the Spirit and the guidance of the Spirit, and *hwyl*, which Martin Schmidt inadequately describes as 'a liturgical intonation on the part of the preacher at the end of the sermon'.[2]

Prayer Henri Bois quotes several prayers which he heard and which are remarkable for their brevity and naive simplicity. A young woman asked for the conversion of her menfolk 'if only for the sake of the little children you have given them'. Someone else prayed: 'Before we had to wait so long for your answer when we prayed. But now you answer by return of post.'[3] Boys and girls took part in the prayers. The congregation commented on the prayer with sighs, Amens, and sometimes even with loud laughter. Often all prayed together in spontaneous confusion.

Interruptions Like the prayers, the short addresses were also commented upon by interruptions. But it is possible for these interruptions to lose their spontaneous freshness and be introduced as a matter of form at points where they are quite out of place. Thus for example when someone was reading 'They neither marry nor are given in marriage' (Matt. 22.30), someone uttered a heartfelt 'Amen'. The preacher looked at the interrupter and said, 'I understand, you have had enough of it!'[4]

Hwyl is a typically Welsh phenomenon which also occurs in secular context.[5] Bois, following Stead, describes it as follows. It is a half spoken, half sung scale in a chromatic or minor key, which ends in a hymn, or in a cry of thanks or repentance. The scale is not always that of our tonal system. In Bois' view it is a throw-back to one of the most primitive forms of human expression, and two conditions are necessary for it to take place. There must be a people whose means of expression is hampered (the suppression of the Welsh language), but which at the same time is above average in its musical ability. If these two conditions are satisfied, this people is thrown back upon a form of expression which goes back to a more primitive period of human history. This explanation by Bois is based on the belief that singing preceded speech in human evolution.

(*c*) *Opponents and supporters*

Many German critics of the revival in Wales have contended that preaching is overshadowed by singing and prayer.[6] They did not know about the Sunday schools which have existed for many years in Wales, where not only children, but adults too, are instructed in the reading and writing of Welsh and introduced to Welsh literature (including secular literature) and music. For adults the Sunday school also functioned as a popular theological college. They could study the theological works of Welsh theologians, and books by English theologians translated into Welsh. Like the American churches, the churches of Wales had built up an educational institution, the Sunday school, which enabled them to some extent to separate the task of preaching and teaching from the actual services and to lay more emphasis on worship.

The journals of the Evangelical movement in Germany provide a continuous account of the revival in Wales. In Germany, these accounts helped to raise the expectation of a revival 'almost to boiling point'.[7] The 'powerful evangelistic talent' of Seth Joshua[8] was stressed. 'It is evident that Evan Roberts is conscious that he has received a gift of prophecy through his baptism of the Spirit.' E. Lohmann defended the revival against all criticisms with the argument: 'What do they mean? They mean nothing other than: we will not repent.'[9] Johannes Seitz tells of a meeting in Hirwaun:

> The moment Evan Roberts opened the Bible he suddenly fell down, his face distorted with sorrow, and lay for ten minutes sobbing on the floor. When he arose, a deep majestic peace spread over his face, and he told his audience, who listened with bated breath, that he had just gone through one of the most terrible inward struggles that can be imagined, but that in this hour of Gethsemane Jesus had come very close to him.[10]

> In a prayer meeting the prayer uttered by a fourteen-year-old boy through the Spirit brought the whole congregation to their knees, so that a highly respected minister called this the finest hour of his life. Where the Spirit is at work, there is no need for us to make divisions. With us, men often want to separate the wheat from the tares, even if we don't exactly burn the tares, as the Catholic Church used to. In Wales the winnowing is done by the Holy Spirit . . . How sad the situation in Germany looks when seen in this light.[11]

R. Mummsen[12] tried to present the revival movement as a variation on the Evangelical movement in Germany, while L. Parker shared with many others the conviction that 'a new Pentecost, a new outpouring of the Holy Spirit' had come.[13] These judgments were mostly made by writers who a short time later condemned the Pentecostal movement as of diabolical origin.

(*d*) *Bois' description of the evangelist Evan Roberts*

Here I propose to look more closely at the account of Evan Roberts given by Henri Bois, because his description is an example of how it is possible to describe an irrational revival in a way which is both discriminating in its judgment and rational in both human and theological terms. Evan Roberts was born in 1888 in Loughor in Glamorgan, near Swansea. He had six brothers and three sisters. His father was a devout miner, and Evan himself was an exemplary schoolboy. When he was twelve he had to go down the mine with his father. Nevertheless, he read everything on which he set eyes. He was converted by the preaching of the Methodist minister Seth Joshua, founded a Sunday school for the children of miners, and made it his aim to become a preacher. Every free moment he possessed, even in the mine, he read the Bible. He had a poetic vein, and published poems in the *Cardiff Times* under the pseudonym of Bwlchydd. For three months he made a regular two-hour journey to a friend to learn shorthand.[14] In addition he taught himself to be a blacksmith. He describes his baptism of the Spirit as follows:

> For thirteen years I prayed that I might receive the Spirit. I had been led to pray by a remark of William Davies, one of the deacons: 'Be faithful! Supposing the Spirit were to come down and you were not there. Remember Thomas, and how much he lost from not being present on the evening of the Resurrection.'
>
> So I said to myself: 'I want to receive the Spirit at any price.' And I continually went to meetings despite all difficulties. Often, as I saw the other boys putting out to sea in their boats, I was tempted to turn round and join them. But no. I said to myself, 'Remember your resolution to be faithful', and I would go to the meeting. Prayer meeting on Monday evening at the [Methodist] chapel, prayer meeting for the Sunday school on Tuesday evening at 'Pisgah', meeting at the church [Church of Wales?] on Wednesday evening, Band of Hope meeting on Thursday evening. I supported all these faithfully for years. For ten or eleven years I prayed for revival. I spent whole nights reading accounts of revivals or talking about them. It was the Spirit who in this way was driving me to think about revival.
>
> One Friday evening that spring (1904), as I was praying at my bedside before going to bed, I was taken up into a great expanse – without time or space. It was communion with God. Up to that time I had only had a God who was far off. That evening I was afraid, but that fear has never come back. I trembled so violently that the bed shook, and my brother was awakened and took hold of me, thinking I was ill.
>
> After this experience I woke each night about one o'clock in the morning. It was the more strange, as usually I slept like a log and no noise in my room was enough to wake me. From one o'clock I was taken up into communion

with God for about four hours. What it was I cannot tell you, except that it was of God. About five o'clock I was again allowed to sleep until about nine o'clock. I was then taken up again and carried away in the same experience as in the early hours of the morning, until about midday or one o'clock.

At home they questioned me, and asked why I got up so late . . . But these things are too holy to speak of. This experience went on for about three months . . .

Bois comments: 'During that time Roberts was working for the entrance examination for the school at Newcastle-Emlyn.'[15] He speaks of an *idée fixe* which Roberts had of receiving the baptism of the Spirit at any price. This *idée fixe* was accompanied by the hope of a revival.

> Evan Roberts's subconscious was continually and increasingly charged up until the discharges took place: that is, the extraordinary experiences which are reported at Loughor, Newcastle Emlyn, and Blaenannerch.[16]

Bois interprets these experiences as a 'taking up', a feeling of expanse, and the loss of the sensation of space and time.

The experiences were repeated at the school, although there, probably for external reasons, they were reduced to half an hour. During a period of illness they once more grew longer. 'In the last four nights I was bathed in sweat (the result of the cold and of communion with God).'[17] Stead reports a conversation with Roberts:

> 'For the space of four hours I was privileged to speak face to face with Him as a man speaks face to face with a friend. At five o'clock it seemed to me as if I again returned to earth. 'Were you not dreaming! I asked. 'No, I was wide awake.' . . . May I ask,' I said, 'If He of whom you speak appeared to you as Jesus Christ?' 'No,' said Mr Roberts, 'not so, it was the personal God, not as Jesus.' 'As God the Father Almighty?' I said. 'Yes,' said Mr Roberts, 'and the Holy Spirit.'[18]

Stead, who gave the most important report of the experiences, refers in his account to similar phenomena in the history of the church (St Teresa, Jakob Boehme, George Fox, Ignatius Loyola), and interprets these phenomena with the aid of William James' *Varieties of Religious Experience*. But the psychological digressions were omitted by the French translator Rochat, presumably because he was afraid they would interfere with the edification of his readers. Bois says of Stead, that this psychological excursus shows that 'it is perfectly possible to be carried away by the revival, and yet to possess and retain in one's own mind a proper concern with religious psychology'.[19]

Roberts himself called the experience described above the baptism of the Spirit, and distinguished it sharply from conversion.[20]. Using detailed source material, Bois describes Roberts's further visions and overwhelming experiences, and also those of the young women who accompanied him and assisted him as evangelists and especially in prayer.[21]

Immediately after this, Roberts preached for six months without a break. The *Western Mail* sent a reporter, Awstin, to follow him, and published every month a tract with reports and sermons. The main Welsh papers gave regular reports on him, as did the whole church press of Europe. There were mass conversions in the mining communities of Wales.

He made all his journeys dependent upon the 'guidance of the Spirit', which could lead him to call off obligations to speak which he had undertaken, with an appeal to the Spirit, and to go to another meeting instead. One day he withdrew without motive into silence. Only Annie Davies was allowed to look after him and to communicate with him in writing. He kept an exact journal of the 'seven days of silence'. The greater part of his notes have been published (in the *Western Mail*) and are of great psychological value. He gives an exact date and time for every entry. He writes:

> I am pleased, because I have been moved by the eternal Spirit to write it. I do not know what the notebook you bought for me cost, but I know today that it is priceless. It has become very dear to me because of the precious things it contains. It contains a large amount of our experience while we were passing through that strange period.[22]

It almost seems, writes Henri Bois, that Evan Roberts is intending to set this notebook beside the writings of the New Testament, when he sends it to a certain Mr Jones with the words:

> Dear Mr Jones, You can have this prayer. It will be a blessing to thousands, for it is the fruit of the Holy Spirit. I want thousands of copies to be printed without altering a word or a comma or a verse, and particularly want the parts I have underlined to be preserved, for they give it life. The Holy Spirit 'puts soul into it' and makes it a living prayer.[23]

Roberts was a prophetic type, hypersensitive, nervous, and not a particularly good speaker. But he had an unusually acute sense of what was happening in the audience he faced, its tensions, resistances, cares, fears and questions. There is a connection between these perceptions and his visions and telepathic abilities. They 'are not the cause but the effect' of his inner life,[24] and are compared by Bois with those of Pascal, Paul, Socrates, Descartes and the prophets of the Old Testament. There is no reason to be suspicious either of the prophets of old or of Roberts because of their visions. 'Nothing would be more wrong than to regard them as unhinged.'[25] According to Henri Bois, Roberts had the gift of seeing what he thought, and could convey this in a dramatic form to his audience. For example, he once made all the men between thirty-three and thirty-four years of age stand up. He then burst into tears and for some time could not speak for weeping. 'What if these young men whom you see were crucified and had to suffer the terrible pains of Christ?' At this the meeting broke into the passion hymn *Dyma gariad fel y moroedd* (Streams of Love and Grace).[26]
In Liverpool he cried out:

> There are five people here who are stopping the revival. They must leave the meeting. Three of them are preachers of the gospel, and are envious in their hearts because of the many conversions. *Pluga nhw, Dhuw!* (humble them, O God).'[27]

Another time he closed the meeting shortly after it had been opened and refused to preach because of resistance on the part of certain of the congregation.[28]

There was once a rumour that he wanted to get engaged to Annie Davies. This was denied by Annie Davies in the following words: 'People really don't know how close Roberts is to God. If they knew, they wouldn't say such things.' The *Revival Number* of the *Western Mail* observed:

> It is reassuring to think that Evan Roberts and Miss Davies have decided not to let themselves be disturbed by these stupid rumours. The best way to put an end to this sort of story is to press on with one's work as if nothing had happened.[29]

The rest of Roberts' life is obscure. It is said that from 1910 until his death in 1947 he lived a retired life. He abandoned his rigorist ethics, went to football matches and smoked a pipe.

There are very different opinions about him. Many Welsh people see in Evan Roberts a true prophet who was the instrument of a miraculous revival. Dr Walford Bodie, who was himself a hypnotist, regarded Roberts as a highly talented hypnotist.[30] Others saw in him an honest but misguided preacher of the gospel. Every journal of the German Evangelical movement spoke of him in terms of the highest enthusiasm. Peter Price spoke of a genuine and a false revival in Wales. The latter, he claims, took place under the influence of Evan Roberts. He accuses him in particular of an exaggerated opinion of himself, and says that according to Roberts there was a fourth person of the Trinity, Roberts himself. 'He does not conduct himself like one who is led by the Spirit, but as one who leads the Spirit.'[31] Price also disparages him on account of the depressions, the frequent dark moods into which he lapsed when anything went wrong, his habit of breaking obligations he had made by an appeal to the Spirit, and his other habit of turning up during the course of a service and not at the beginning of it. The *Western Mail* published the lengthy controversy between Price and Roberts' followers in a pamphlet ('The Rev. Peter Price and Evan Roberts'). Roberts himself did not intervene in the dispute.

The considered judgment given by Bois is not only important for an assessment of Roberts; it also forms a valuable guide for an assessment of the revival in Wales and the Pentecostal movement. Bois observes:

> Everything that comes from his subconscious is regarded by Roberts as the guidance of the Spirit, while everything that comes from reason or from the good advice of his friends is human counsel.

This is an attitude which Pentecostalism and the revival in Wales took over from extreme right-wing Protestantism. In time Roberts seems to have become so unhinged and overstrained by his numerous meetings, mental upheavals and telepathic experiences that he had to withdraw to recover. This explains his later rejection of all 'super-spiritual things' and his polemic against the Pentecostal movement.[32] Bois cannot understand why the use of telepathic abilities should be a sin, a view which led some to reject Henri Bois' judgment, and led others to reject Evan Roberts. Bois acknowledged Roberts' devotion and love, but criticized the unfortunate *application* of his telepathic abilities, which he used to lay people bare in an impudent fashion in large meetings. Roberts' identification of the spontaneous and the outpourings of the subconscious with the Holy Spirit, and his suspicion of the rational, is highly questionable.

Donald Gee, who was brought to the Pentecostal movement by the revival in Wales, compares Evan Roberts with the healing evangelists of Pentecostalism. In his view, the revival in Wales

> touched only a small thickly populated mining district in South Wales. It never reached England and maintained its full intensity for only about a year. At its highest point it carried everything before it like a spiritual torrent. Many glorious and permanent results remain in the form of individual conversions, and it is still possible to point to them at the present day . . . However, the acknowledged leader of the movement, Evan Roberts, remained an enigma right up to the time of his death a few years ago. By his own decision he withdrew into silence and carried out no further public work for the gospel. The revival disappeared, and has made those valleys in Wales almost inaccessible to any further divine visitation. The faithful of Wales have a nostalgia for the past, but unfortunately nothing else.

He regrets their national pride and their cult of leading personalities.[33]

(*e*) *A considered criticism*

To give a 'natural explanation' of the revival in Wales is not to condemn it.[34] One 'natural explanation' which can be given is its context in the peculiar history and characteristics of Wales.[35] This approach would not condemn the revival in Wales for theological statements which from a Reformation point of view are questionable. It would agree with Henri Bois and Stead[36] that the way to loosen the grip of the vices of drunkenness, which destroyed whole villages, and gambling and prostitution, all of which have an emotional basis, is not better instruction but better, purified, decent emotional feeling. The chapel replaces the public house. Stead rightly remarks that you do not send a sluggard a tract on astronomy to give him a better explanation of the sunrise; you shake him thoroughly.[37] Every observer agrees that the upheaval caused by the revival overcame the craze for gambling, drunkenness, idleness and prostitution over wide areas for at least half a generation. When this aspect is considered, one must revise one's judgment, although one may still regret the neglect of theological study and the naive identification of mental upheaval with the Holy Spirit in the revival in Wales and in the Pentecostal movement which arose from it. The first step towards an intellectual attack on the problems which rose from the revival can be seen in the libraries and reading rooms which came into existence everywhere.[38] There is also much in Stead's remark that the revival in Wales helped to overcome the unchristian superiority of men over women.[39]

One cannot accept Holthey's attempt to remove criticism of the movement in Wales from the battlefield of rational psychological and theological criticism with the remark: 'Spiritual things must be judged spiritually. And these are spiritual things . . .'[40] Criticism is not shown to be spiritual by the fact that one ignores certain areas of reality.

(*f*) *The origin of the Pentecostal movement in the revival in Wales*

Amongst the 'children of the revival' (*Plant y Diwygiad*) from Wales speaking in tongues became very prominent in the early days of the Pentecostal movement. The Jeffreys brothers were products of the Welsh revival movement (Maesteg).[41] Donald Gee[42] was converted by the preaching of the Welsh Methodist Seth Joshua. The father of the British Pentecostal movement, the Anglican priest A. A. Boddy,[43] took part in the revival movement in Wales and worked with Evan Roberts. He was convinced that the Pentecostal movement was a direct continuation of the revival.

2. '*Preferring Dead Saints to Living Revolutionaries*': *Speaking in Tongues in the Church of England*[44]

(*a*) '*The wind bloweth*':[45] *Alexander A. Boddy and Cecil Polhill*

The Anglican parish priest Alexander A. Boddy was drawn into the Pentecostal movement in 1907 in Oslo by T. B. Barratt,[46] and through his efforts the parish hall of All Saints', Sunderland, where he was vicar, became a centre for those in Britain who sought the experience of the baptism of the Spirit. Many experienced there the baptism of the Spirit with speaking in tongues, including G. R. Polman, Holland and Smith Wigglesworth, all of whom worked in Britain, Stanley H. Frodsham, who worked in Britain and later in the USA, and others.

> A silent witness of those unforgettable days of blessing was erected at the entrace of the parish hall in the form of a memorial tablet with the eloquent inscription: 'September 1907. When the fire of the Lord fell it burned up the debt.' For in fact, as a result of the revival, a considerable debt on the building was paid off in a short time.[47]

> There amongst others was the pianist from the cinema; he too was converted and went from house to house and told people what Jesus had done for his soul. A dancing teacher had also been converted, as well as the notorious prostitute of Cwmtwrch, and so had one who had been an ordinand, but had now sunk to the level of a tramp.[48]

To the day of his death Boddy remained a priest of the Anglican church, although for many years he was a leading personality in the international Pentecostal movement. He regarded it as a revival within the church, and for this reason associated himself in 1909 with the work of the Pentecostal Missionary Union, which was meant as a body within the church.

Another leader of the Pentecostal Missionary Union was Cecil Polhill, the squire of Howbury Hall, who had been at Eton and as one of the 'Cambridge Seven' (a group which also included C. T. Studd) had formerly been a missionary in Tibet. He had received the baptism of the Spirit in Los Angeles.[49] It made a great impression on the Pentecostals that he, a wealthy upper-class landed proprietor, should preach in their meetings and should share his hymn book at street meetings with a servant girl.

When the Pentecostal Missionary Union was dissolved and replaced in 1924 by the Assemblies of God, organized as a free church[50] – the Elim Pentecostal Churches[51] and the Apostolic Church[52] had already come into organized existence previously – the influence of Boddy and Polhill in the British Pentecostal movement declined more and more.

(*b*) *The wind drops; the revival is ignored*

M. Harper has already pointed out that the British Holiness movement, one of the sources of which was the Keswick Conventions, either rejected the Pentecostal movement out of hand or ignored it,[53] although much in Pentecostal teaching is a legacy from Anglicanism, through the mediation of Wesley.[54] However, this one-sided condemnation was corrected after the second world war. As Horton Davies emphatically stresses,

> Pentecostalism is not a heretical group within Protestantism. Its articles of belief are indistinguishable from those of any conservative Protestant group.[55]

> They are orthodox Biblically conservative Protestant Christians, and not heretics. Their intense and fervid faith, the warmth and generosity of their fellowship, their missionary zeal and support of their charitable institutions, as well as their specialized ministries to prisoners and lepers, are wholly admirable and authentically Christian. Moreover, many second-generation Pentecostalists have become excellent members of the historic Christian Churches, adding to their unabated zeal a concern for the relationship of Christianity to culture and for the Gospel's transformation of the socio-economic life of the world.[56]

He suggests, however, that

> this, in itself, is an indication of the narrowness of the first-generation Pentecostalism with its ethics of flight rather than fight, and its uncharitable insistence that the Churches have utterly betrayed Christ. This 'holier-than-thou' attitude reflects pride rather than Christian humility.[57] Ethically they are world-condemning pietists . . . What is perhaps more disturbing . . . is

that Pentecostalists do not appear to be interested in such problems of Christian social ethics as social justice or the removal of the colour bar.[58]

We shall discuss below how far this latter judgment by Davies is accurate.[59]

(*c*) *'The second wind'*:[60] – *'Pentecost' in the Anglican church at the present day*

Following contacts with the Pentecostal movement within the historic churches in America, there have been similar phenomena within the Anglican church in Britain. The Anglican priest Philip L. C. Smith describes three services taken by a Pentecostal preacher (Richard Bolt) in his church, which included speaking in tongues, exposition of Scripture, prayer for the sick and a call to conversion.[61] Through contacts with the Pentecostals or with American Neo-Pentecostals, the baptism of the Spirit has also been experienced in other churches.[62] Prayer for healing of the sick, given a liturgical setting in public services, has existed for some time.[63]

The literature published by the Fountain Trust (London) shows that these churches have taken over not only the experience, but also the theological interpretation placed upon it by Pentecostals, that is, the two-stage way of salvation and speaking in tongues as a necessary sign of the baptism of the Spirit.[64]

This has led to criticism. In spite of all his admiration for Pentecostal worship 'in the thrill of which it is extraordinarily easy to get caught up unless one is being very deliberately detached and coldly critical',[65] D. Webster draws attention to the familiar weaknesses of Pentecostal belief and practice. He points to the almost complete absence of theological thinking; the ignorance of church history, resulting in the idea that between the Acts of the Apostles and the Azusa Street revival in Los Angeles nothing of importance took place in the history of the church apart from sporadic revivals; the pietistic failing of not seeing the world as God's world; the absence of any preaching which gives due place to the prophetic Christian concern for social ethics; the readiness to form schismatic groups. In Webster's view none of these failures are peculiar to Pentecostals; they share them with most fundamentalists and certain groups within the Anglican church.

His comment on speaking in tongues in the Anglican church is as follows: It should not be permitted in public worship, nor encouraged in private prayer meetings, but not forbidden in personal prayer. The history of the mystics shows that in the course of church history the gift of speaking in tongues has been 'interiorized'. 'There is nothing wrong in ecstasy, provided it comes as a gift from God and not as a self-induced state.'[66] But Webster gives no indication that an emotional outpouring, of which speaking in tongues may form part, can easily have an important social and political function.

Lindsay Dewar has made an interesting contribution to this dialogue. In his profound study of the Holy Spirit in the Bible and in church history the Reformers, and in particular Luther, are sharply criticized. He ignores works of exegesis and church history produced outside Britain, which is a serious weakness in the historical part of his book. But his psychological assessment is of great value:

> To the pscyhologist *qua* psychologist, the ravings of a maniac patient and the utterings of a saint alike may come through the same mechanism – if the phrase may be allowed. But to separate the precious from the vile is the work, not of science, but of philosophy and religion. It may indeed be true that there are certain types of individual in whom these lines of communication are broader than is the case with the average person's. This is suggested by the well-known saying that genius and madness are closely allied. But this does not alter the fact that the Holy Spirit may, according to His own purposes, make special use of persons with this kind of make-up. Indeed what else should we expect Him to do?[67]

Here he avoids the temptation of passing from the observation of phenomena to a value judgment. According to Dewar this critical function is properly that of the church – but not as an organization, nor as a commission of theological experts or as the guardian of tradition, but as a group (in a sense in which the word is used in psychology) which is ready and willing to bear and endure to the very end the tensions that are present.

3. *Crossing the Race Barrier: West Indian Pentecostals*[68]

Michael Harper,[69] Alexander A. Boddy[70] and Frank Bartleman[71] have all pointed out that the beliefs and practices of Pentecostalism offer the opportunity of breaking down racial barriers. This is true in so far as they have gained increasing acceptance in the racial sub-cultures of the world. In Great Britain, too, the Pentecostal movement is growing amongst West Indians. In spite of this, C. S. Hill regards the practices of Pentecostalism as an 'apartheid religion'.[72] Although this view of Hill's has been disputed, we shall begin our account with Hill's view of the beliefs and practices of West Indian Pentecostalism.

(*a*) *The West Indian immigrants' drift away from the churches*

From 1951 (the date of a catastrophic hurricane in Jamaica) to 1962 (Commonwealth Immigrants Act, 30.6.1962) a mass immigration of West Indians to Great Britain took place. From 1955 to 1962 there were 260,000 West Indian immigrants. No figures are available for the years 1952–55. Sixty-nine per cent of these immigrants regularly attended church in the West Indies, a proportion which grew rapidly smaller on their arrival in Great Britain. Hill explains this drift away from the churches by the shock and confusion of the West Indians at the discovery that England is not the Mecca of Christianity. 'It is like discovering that one's mother is a liar and a hypocrite.' It made no difference, according to Hill, that the British churches went to considerable trouble to make the West Indians welcome. Hill regrets that the churches, which might have been destined to become a place of integration for the West Indian immigrants, are failing in spite of their good-will to take any effective measures against racial prejudice. A minister could take it for granted that he would be well received by the West Indians, for they bring with them from their home country a love for the church and the clergy. But ministers should beware that they are dealing with poor but proud people, who are ashamed of their difficulties. In particular, he must have an understanding of their different marriage customs, and bear in mind that until 150 years ago West Indian slaves were forbidden to marry. 'It is a great mistake to try to deal with West Indian family problems according to accepted English standards and practices.'[73] It is not unusual for a West Indian couple to marry *after* the birth of the children. They live together and do not marry until they have saved the money to pay for the extravagant wedding celebrations. Similarly, ministers ought to recognize and make allowances for the unpunctuality of West Indians, for example at funerals.

(b) The coming into being of West Indian Pentecostal churches

Originally West Indian immigrants who were Pentecostals joined the English Pentecostal churches. But soon they founded their own churches with West Indian pastors and elders.[74] Only a very small number of British Pentecostal churches have West Indian members. The reason which Du Plessis gives for this development is as follows:

> In some instances the American brethren were compelled to open works in England because many of their members from other parts of the world immigrated to the British Isles and began to form separate churches.[75]

Their growth is astonishing. In 1964 Malcolm Calley found 23 congregations belonging to the 'New Testament Church of God', while two years later C. S. Hill counted 61 congregations with 10,500 members.[76]

Malcolm J. C. Calley, an anthropologist who had already made studies of the independent Pentecostal churches in Australia, lived for months amongst West Indian Pentecostals, in order to get to know their history, the nature of their belief and practice, and the social function of their worship.

According to Calley the following factors can be excluded as reasons for the rise of West Indian Pentecostal churches:

> Differences in doctrine and liturgy.[77]
> The site of the chapel.[78]
> Links with a mother church in the West Indies.

The reason Calley gives for the mushrooming of West Indian Pentecostal churches – every year half a dozen churches come into being in London – is as follows:

> West Indians join sects led by West Indians; the clergy of the three sects with the largest following are predominantly West Indian; in two they are all West Indian. The most successful sects were established by immigrant West

Indian preachers; those established by Englishmen before the great influx of West Indians are much less successful. West Indians have imported their preachers and their sects ready-made; they have not joined sects they found already operating in England.[79]

(*c*) *Assessment*

Hill has a very low view of West Indian Pentecostal churches, because of their exclusiveness and schismatic tendencies.

> The very beliefs and teachings of the Pentecostals must lead to a 'separatist' movement. Their mode of worship is far more likely to appeal to West Indians than to English people. This in turn tends to a voluntary segregation and to the formation of all-coloured churches.[80]

Where Anglicans or other churches let their church buildings to Pentecostal churches, their churches simply become identified in the eyes of other West Indians with the Pentecostals. West Indian Pentecostals have sufficient opportunities of joining British Pentecostal churches; separate West Indian churches emphasize racial barriers. Consequently – still according to Hill – the coming into being of West Indian Pentecostal churches is not in the interest of the West Indians.

Calley's view is different:

> As West Indians have come to England mainly as isolated individuals it was perhaps inevitable that they should import with them the social group that transplants most easily, the religious sect. At this stage it is difficult to say whether, in the long run, their presence will inhibit or facilitate assimilation. It is likely that, as time passes, the larger ones at least will change as native English Pentecostal sects have changed, and come to terms with society, becoming progressively less like the churches founded by the Apostles, embattled against society, and more like other religious denominations that exist in harmony with it. Most of the smaller groups must diasppear.[81]

In his fine work *God's People* Calley has given a summary of his analysis. He again points out that the Pentecostal does not approach religion and life intellectually, but rather ritually. If the West Indian Pentecostal does not understand something, he does not look it up in a commentary or an encyclopedia; he rather prays for enlightenment. Religion is not something to be understood, but rather to be experienced, whence the importance of the taboos and also of the religious rites. Calley's interpretation of speaking in tongues is that it allows the intellectually weaker member to contribute on an equal basis with others to the worship service, a point which has already been underlined by Bryan R. Wilson.[82] A successful leader 'is one who can stimulate his congregation to respond as a group, who can make members lose their own individuality in an impassioned, sometimes hysterical identification with the church'.[83]

Calley then goes on to ask: Why do nearly all West Indian immigrants join their own Pentecostal churches rather than native English Pentecostal churches? One might be tempted to make the British Christian's race prejudices responsible. But this is not usually the case. West Indian Pentecostal churches have depended upon the goodwill of English clergy. They have allowed them the use of Anglican and Baptist churches. Anglican ministers have performed their marriage rites. A Unitarian minister gave them the use of a Unitarian meeting hall for services.

> The Unitarian minister used to attend some of the services and was prepared to accept their manner of worship as a valid form of Christianity, even if very different from his own.[84]

West Indian Pentecostal churches have sprung up because some West Indians belonged to Pentecostal or Pentecostal-like Baptist churches in the West Indies, and in cold, foggy England there is little opportunity to meet and chat with one's neighbour on the street. The West Indian, therefore, wrongly thinks that he meets a racial barrier when he is really discovering that human relations in England, and Christian England itself, are very different from what he expected them to be. The most radical separation from this world, the best protection from these cold surroundings, is a warm West Indian Pentecostal service.

> [West Indians] who lack characteristics (occupation, education, possessions) carrying prestige in society at large, are persuaded that such things are unimportant; were not Christ and his disciples equally lacking in the things of the world? The 'world' has not treated sect recruits with conspicuous generosity, and in its terms they are lacking in status, poor and powerless, but these characteristics are precisely those which are pleasing to God. In their devotion to him, members make a virtue out of a necessity, rejecting the values of the world which anyway they could not hope to achieve.[85] . . . Perhaps in this frustration can be discerned the feeling of guilt and original sin that is a doctrinal cornerstone of all Pentecostal sects.[86] . . . Native English Pentecostal sects [who have advanced sociologically] remain as a memorial to such conditions in the past, but there have been no revivals for more than a generation.[87]

Calley concludes with the comment:

> The thoroughgoing, obsessive, ritual withdrawal of the saint from the world appears to be out of all proportion to the actual difficulty of the situation he is withdrawing from. I think this can only be understood historically. . . . There is in the West Indies a long tradition of seeking magico-religious, rather than practical solutions to problems.[88]

Calley thinks this attitude will soon prove to be inadequate in England. In the meantime West Indian Pentecostal sects are 'a buffer between the immigrant group and society'; they make life easier 'by greasing the wheels of social change in the long run'.[89]

4. *Apostles and Prophets – the Apostolic Church*[90]

(*a*) *Origins*

In the early years of the Pentecostal movement in Wales a dispute arose about the understanding of prophecy.

> By some the gift of prophecy was acknowledged, but the prophet with his words of guidance was not accepted as scriptural. They believed that the prophetic utterance was for exhortation, edification and comfort (I Cor. 14.3), but they did not believe that the prophetic office was for guidance and for leading the church.[91]

The Pentecostal congregation of Penygroes (Apostolic Church) believed that the latter view was the right one and called a miner, W. J. Williams, to the newly discovered office of prophet, while his brother D. P. Williams was called to the office of apostle. In 1918 Andrew Turnbull's Burning Bush Assembly in Glasgow joined the new movement. Others followed.

While at the present day the Apostolic Church has more congregations in Scotland (45 meeting places) than the Assemblies of God or the Elim Pentecostal churches,[92] in Great Britain as a whole it forms one of the smaller groups. But in Nigeria it has succeeded in becoming one of the largest Protestant churches.[93] It also carries out missionary work amongst the Australian aborigines[94] and on the continent of Europe, in both cases with considerable success. It is remarkable that in Switzerland it has succeeded in winning the allegiance of a number of theologians with university training.[95]

The sacrifices made for its missionary work are astonishing. It has built the largest assembly hall in Wales, the Apostolic Convention Hall, which can seat 3,000.

(*b*) *Organization*

Every variety of church constitution can be found within the Pentecostal movement, ranging from the purely congregationalist,[96] through a centralized presbyterianism,[97] to episcopal organization.[98] These varieties of organization derive from the nationality and denominational origin of the founders of each particular group. In the case of the Apostolic Church organization and doctrine are very closely linked. On the one hand, the church possesses a ministry organized as a strict hierarchy (apostles, prophets, shepherds, teachers, evangelists, elders, deacons, deaconesses). Originally, the members of this hierarchy were without exception chosen by the word of prophecy; and it culminates in the college of apostles. On the other hand, it gives greater play to the gifts of the Spirit than Pentecostal groups which are congregationalist in their organization. In contrast to most other Pentecostal groups, it allows prophetic utterances on concrete subjects of ethics, personal matters, and world and church politics. This it can do because the church is protected by the authority of the 'ministries' from utterances which go too far. Other Pentecostals do not reject 'ministries' in the church, when they are understood in a functional way, but prefer to institutionalize only those of shepherd (i.e. pastor) and evangelist.[99] In particular, there is controversy about the offices of apostle and prophet.

Apostles The Apostolic Church distinguishes between the 'apostles of the Lamb' (Rev. 21.14), who consist only of the twelve apostles, including Matthias who replaced Judas Iscariot (but not including Paul), and those others who are also called apostles in the New Testament.[100] There can no longer be 'apostles of the Lamb' at the present day, for it is a condition of this apostolic office to have been an eye-witness of the life, death and resurrection of Jesus. But the church at the present day *must* have other apostles. The Apostolic Church possesses such apostles. Their apostolate includes the laying on of hands to impart the Holy Spirit, the ordination of elders and the government of the church in other respects. They are distinguished by patience, humility and divine wisdom.[101]

The constitution, a strictly juridical church order with a casuistic element, explicitly accords ultimate authority to the apostles, whose office is for life.[102] William Henry Lewis describes the ministry of the apostles as follows. Apostles have 'authority to loose, authority to bind, authority to excommunicate, authority to re-admit, authority to establish churches'. They are 'elective in their calling, immutable in their setting, distinctive in their call, comprehensive in their ministry, exemplary in their character'.[103]

Prophets In the Apostolic Church the office of prophet is more and more subject to regulation. 'Present day prophets are not infallible.'[104] They can call others to some ministry, 'but the acceptance of these calls is still the responsibility of the Apostleship'.[105] Members who are undergoing church discipline are not allowed to prophesy, and in general the exercise of the 'gift of prophecy' is dependent upon the 'sanction of the presbytery'.[106]

(*c*) *Doctrine and ethical teaching*

The doctrine set out in the confession of faith of the Apostolic Church[107] is similar to that of the rest of the Pentecostal movement where the three-stage way of salvation is taught,[108] apart from the special position accorded to apostles and prophets.

Its casuistic ethic is laid down in its constitution. I give as an example the provisions concerning marriage:

> No believer and unbeliever should be joined together in marriage . . . but whenever there is a request for a marriage between a believer and an unbeliever, the parties must be seen by the Pastor and the Scriptural position fully pointed out to them with the consequences that are bound to ensue. If after being seen they are still insistent that the ceremony must take place, the Pastor has liberty of conscience to perform it or otherwise.[109]

Similarly a wedding can take place in the Apostolic Church even between 'unbelievers' or between 'members guilty of fornication and desiring marriage', but the Pastor cannot be obliged to perform it.[110] Precise and detailed regulations are given for divorces.[111] Unnecessary journeys on Sunday should be avoided.[112] Members may be absent from service on at most three successive Sundays. The Apostolic Church 'is definitely and absolutely against war' and gives those of its members who do not wish to carry out military service the usual support before the courts, but does not oppose those of its members who carry out military service.[113]

(*d*) *Relationships with other Pentecostals*

Although the Apostolic church at the present day is a member of the British Pentecostal Fellowship,[114] for many years there was tension between it and other Pentecostals, both in Great Britain and also in Denmark, Switzerland and Germany. After many years of observation and numerous close contacts with representatives of the Apostolic Church, Donald Gee maintained his earlier view:

> To bestow New Testament titles of offices upon men and women and then consider that by doing so we are creating apostolic assemblies parallel to those of the Primitive Church is very much like children playing at churches.[115]

Arnold Hitzer, a Lutheran theologian and now a German Pentecostal pastor, affirms flatly:

> The system of ministries in the Apostolic Church hinders the true power of ministries truly instituted by God, and its false badges of office are an obstacle to them.[116]

NOTES

1. Henri Bois, *Le Reveil dans le pays de Galles*, p. 62; W. T. Stead, *The Revival in Wales*, pp. 36f. This chapter is based on Bois' extensive work (613 pages), which in its turn is based on his own observations and his knowledge of the literary evidence, much of which is no longer extant. Bois was sympathetic to the revival, but as a professor of theology and psychological analyser of religious phenomena, he had the necessary equipment for a proper judgment. Cf. also J. Jenkins, *South Wales Daily News*, 16.11.1903. Full bibliography 05.13.001g.

2. M. Schmidt, Art. 'Wales', *RGG* 3rd ed., vol. VI, col. 1537.

3. Bois, *op. cit.*, p. 312; Paxton Hood, *Christmas Evans*, p. 235.

4. Bois, *op. cit.*, p. 304.

5. E. V. Hall, *Annales des sciences psychologiques*, May 1905, p. 300; quoted by Bois, *op. cit.*, p. 278.

6. P. Glage, *Wittenberg oder Wales?* ('Wittenberg *or* Wales?') For the opposite view, A. von Bernstoff, *Auf der Warte* 3/2, 7.1.1906, pp. 3f.

7. Fleisch I, p. 447.

8. E. Lohmann, *Auf der Warte* 2/44, 29.10.1905, pp. 7f.
9. E. Lohmann, *Auf der Warte* 2/48, 26.11.1905, pp. 3f.
10. J. Seitz, *Auf der Warte* 2/9, 25.2.1905, p.7.
11. J. Seitz, *Auf der Warte* 2/11, 12.3.1905, pp. 6f.
12. R. Mummsen, *Wittenberg und Wales!* ('Wittenberg *and* Wales').
13. L. Parker, *L'Evangéliste* 53/2, 13.1.1905, p. 6.
14. H. Bois, *op. cit.*, pp. 66ff.
15. Retranslated from Bois, *op. cit.*, pp. 70ff., as W. T. Stead, *The Revival in Wales*, was not available; but cf. Stead, *The Revival in the West*, p. 43.
16. Bois, *op. cit.*, p. 73.
17. *Ibid.*, pp. 73f. The last phrase, 'the result of the cold and of communion with God', was omitted by Mme Saillens in her French translation.
18. W. T. Stead, *The Revival in the West*, p. 43.
19. Bois, *op. cit.*, p. 76.
20. *Ibid.*, p. 78.
21. Cf. the biographies of Annie Davies (10.202.001), Marie Jones (10.413.001), Joseph Jenkins (10.406.001), Evan Lloyd Jones (10.412.001), and Sidney Evans (10.245.001).
22. Bois, *op. cit.*, p. 460.
23. *Ibid.*, p. 461.
24. *Ibid.*, p. 408.
25. *Ibid.*, p. 409.
26. *Ibid.*, p. 413.
27. *Ibid.*, p. 475.
28. *Ibid.*, p. 501.
29. *Ibid.*, p. 549.
30. *Ibid.*, p. 484.
31. P. Price, *Western Mail* 31.1.1905.
32. *Zeitschrift für Religiönspsychologie* 1, 1907, p. 471; cf. E. Roberts and Mrs Penn-Lewis, *War on the Saints*, 1912.
33. D. Gee, *VdV* 48/12, Dec. 1955, p. 5.
34. E. Ponsoye, review of Bois, *op. cit.*, in *Christianisme au XXe siècle*, 4.10.1906, p. 303.
35. E. Durand, *Journal de Bruxelles; Chrétien Belge* 55, 1905, p. 109.
36. W. T. Stead, a brilliant journalist, editor of the *Review of Reviews*, advocate of the poor, opponent of the Boer War; see M. Lelièvre, *L'Evangéliste* 53/4, 27.1.1905, p. 13; 53/5, 3.2.1905, p. 17; 53/12, 24.3.1905, pp. 45f.; F. W. Whyte, art. 'William Thomas Stead', *Dictionary of National Biography, 1912–1921*, pp. 507f.
37. Stead, *The Revival in Wales*, p. 26.
38. *Ibid.*, pp. 35ff.
39. *Ibid.*, p. 32.
40. Holthey, preface to German edition of Stead, *op. cit.* (*Die Erweckung in Wales*), p. 3.
41. The legendary ideas in Wales which identify the Celts with Israel, and the powerful emphasis on Old Testament social laws in opposition to the English central government, reappear in Jeffreys's teaching in the form of the British Israel theory (05.13.037). The struggle between the spontaneous revivalist preacher Jeffreys and the efficient secretary Phillips in the Elim Pentecostal Church (ch. 14.1[*b*], pp. 198f. below) can be seen as a repetition of the conflict between the emotional Celtic Welsh and the calculating English.
42. Cf. below, ch. 15.2(*a*), p. 208.
43. Cf. ch. 13.2(*a*), pp. 185f.

44. The title is taken from M. Harper, *As at the Beginning*, p. 23.
45. The title is taken from M. Harper, *op. cit.*, pp. 15ff.
46. A. A. Boddy describes his baptism of the Spirit as follows: 'Taking a nap in the afternoon I awoke feeling my jaws working on their own account. My jaws and tongue began to work, but there was no voice.' About midnight 'it seemed to me as if an iron hand were laid over my jaws. Both jaws and tongue worked incessantly, speaking and praying with very little intermission until four o'clock in the morning.' (Fleisch, II/2, p. 76.)
47. L. Steiner, *Mit folgenden Zeichen*, p. 41; M. Harper, *op. cit.*, p. 41.
48. *Pfingstgrüsse* 5/25, 23.2.1913, pp. 107f.
49. Cf. above, ch. 2.3, pp. 22ff.
50. Cf. below, ch. 15, pp. 206ff.
51. Cf. below, ch. 14, pp. 197ff.
52. Cf. ch. 13. 13.4, pp. 191ff.
53. Sir R. Anderson, *Spirit Manifestations*, 3rd ed., 1909; *Tongues of Fire*, April 1907, p. 6; July 1907, p. 6; Sept. 1907, p. 9; Oct. 1907, p. 11; Jan. 1908, p. 7; quoted in Bloch-Hoell II, pp. 81ff.; Cf. also M. Harper, *As at the Beginning*, pp. 23, 93; *Third Force*, p. 28.
54. Jeremy Taylor, William Law. (Details: 05.28.004a.)
55. Horton Davies, *Christian Deviations*, pp. 83f.
56. *Ibid.*, p. 96.
57. *Ibid.*
58. *Ibid.*, p. 95.
59. Cf. ch. 31.2, pp. 467ff.
60. The title is taken from M. Harper, *As at the Beginning*, pp. 51ff.
61. P. L. C. Smith, *P* 71, 1965, p. 7; cf. also W. H. Urch, *Spiritual Gifts*, pp. 6f.
62. D. Webster, *Pentecostalism*, p. 36; cf. the writings of M. Harper published by the Fountain Trust.
63. Iona Community, *Divine Healing*; I. Cowie, *Healing Christ*; G. F. Macleod, *Place of Healing*.
64. 'As our prayer is answered and we are filled with the Holy Spirit, so we should begin to speak in tongues as the Spirit gives us utterance.' M. Harper, *Power*, p. 41; I. Cockburn, *Renewal* 23, Oct.–Nov. 1969, pp. 23ff.; 24, Dec. 1969–Jan. 1970, pp. 21ff.
65. Webster, *op. cit.*, pp. 13f.
66. *Ibid.*, p. 39.
67. L. Dewar, *Holy Spirit*, p. 191.
68. Documents, statistics, literature: 05.13.021. In addition to a number of independent single congregations there are the New Testament Church of God (61 churches, 10,500 members, journal *New Testament Church of God News Bulletin*, 05.13.029); Church of God in Christ (11 churches, 1,000 members, 05.13.030); Church of God of Prophecy (16 churches, 1,000 members, 05.13.131); International Evangelistic Fellowship (journal, *International Evangelistic Fellowship News*, 05.13.032); Kingston City Mission (05.13.033); Victorious Church of God (05.13.035); Church of the Living God, the Pillar and Ground of the Truth (journal, *News and Gospel Messenger*; a 'Jesus only' church; 05.13.043). (This list is probably out of date by now.)
69. M. Harper, *As at the Beginning*, p. 17.
70. A. A. Boddy, *Pfingstgrüsse* 5/8, 24.11.1912, p. 63; cf. above, ch. 2.3, pp. 22ff.
71. F. Bartleman, *Azusa Street*, p. 29.
72. C. S. Hill, *Race and Religion*, p. 9.
73. Hill, *West Indian Migrants*, pp. 1, 5f., 61.
74. E.g. New Testament Church of God (05.12.029).
75. Du Plessis, *History*.

76. Hill, *Race and Religion*, p. 8.
77. 'Sect members are distinguished from non-members not by their beliefs, but by whether or not they attend Pentecostal meetings and perform Pentecostal rituals. Membership must be defined in terms of ritual practice, not in terms of belief. West Indian Pentecostals never ask: "Do you believe such and such?", but always, "Do you do such and such?" ' (M. Calley, *New Society*, Aug. 1964, p. 17).
78. Calley, *Race* 3/2, May 1962, p. 57.
79. *Ibid.*, p. 58.
80. Hill, *West Indian Migrants*, pp. 73f.
81. Calley, *New Society*, 6.8.1964, p. 18.
82. B. R. Wilson, *Sects and Society*. Cf. ch. 14.3, p. 203; ch. 24.5, pp. 342ff.
83. M. J. Calley, *God's People*, p. 74.
84. *Ibid.*, p. 125.
85. *Ibid.*, p. 134.
86. *Ibid.*, p. 135.
87. *Ibid.*, p. 136.
88. *Ibid.*, p. 145.
89. *Ibid.*
90. Records, documents, literature; 05.13.022. Statistics: 230 churches, 300 pastors, 10,000 members, 60 missionaries. Journals, *Apostolic Herald*, *Riches of Grace*.
91. T. N. Turnbull, *What God Hath Wrought*, p. 16.
92. J. Highet, *Scottish Churches*, p. 41.
93. 01.28.009. H. W. Turner, 'Nigerien', in W. J. Hollenweger (ed.), *Die Pfingstkirchen*, pp. 115–24; Turner, *History of an African Independent Church*.
94. 04.01.006; 04.08.003; 04.09.001; 04.11.003.
95. *PGG*, pp. 276ff.
96. E.g. Sweden (05.07.006).
97. E.g. Assemblies of God (ch. 15, pp. 206ff.)
98. E.g. PHCh (02a.02.110).
99. For the discussion between the Apostolic Church and the European Pentecostal churches: 05.05.002, 05.07.011, 05.09.009, 05.28.024.
100. Apostolic Church, *Fundamentals*, p. 25.
101. W. H. Lewis, *And He Gave Some Apostles*.
102. Apostolic Church, *Its Principles and Practices*, pp. 41ff.
103. Lewis, *op. cit.*
104. *Ibid.*
105. Apostolic Church, *Its Principles*, p. 95.
106. *Ibid.*, p. 124.
107. Cf. Appendix: 6, p. 518.
108. Apostolic Church, *Fundamentals*, p. 16f.
109. Apostolic Church, *Its Principles*, pp. 145f.
110. *Ibid.*
111. *Ibid.*, p. 160.
112. *Ibid.*, p. 147.
113. J. Highet, *Scottish Churches*, p. 61.
114. 05.13.045.
115. D. Gee, *Wind and Flame*, p. 74.
116. A. Hitzer, *Die (sogenannte) Apostolische Kirche*, p. 7.

14

Charisma and Institutional Organization: The Elim Pentecostal Churches[1]

1. *History*

(*a*) *The Jeffreys family*

THE Elim Pentecostal churches were brought into being by George and Stephen Jeffreys. The two brothers came from a very simple home in Wales. Their father was a miner. At the age of twelve, Stephen had to go with his father down the mine and earn his own living. Like his brother George he was drawn into the revival in Wales, and besides his ordinary job worked as an evangelist. He soon became famous for his sermons, which were packed with meaning, straight to the point and spiced with humour, as well as for the astonishing healings he accomplished. Sympathetic accounts of the latter were given in numerous articles in the British press. He politely declined the offer of a doctorate of theology (*honoris causa*). He was later to leave the Elim movement and become an evangelist of the Assemblies of God.

His brother George was originally a salesman in the Maesteg Co-operative Society. In 1914 he went to Bible school, became a Congregational minister, and by the time he was twenty-seven was so famous that in the largest and most expensive halls in Britain he commanded audiences of thousands. He captured his audience by his musical voice, but also by the logical clarity of his always brief but powerful sermons.

In 1915 George Jeffreys founded the 'Elim Evangelistic Band', an evangelization team which assisted him in carrying out his gigantic missions – first of all in Wales, and later in Ireland and England. In 1926 the Elim Four Square Gospel Alliance of the British Isles was founded, with the intention that it should become an umbrella organization for all Pentecostals in Great Britain. The plan failed; only Elim members joined. The logical step of changing the name from 'Alliance' to Elim Pentecostal Churches was taken a few years ago.

In his early years George Jeffreys had displayed an ecumenical attitude within the fundamentalist churches.

> Thank God, we are living in days, when, as far as spiritual people are concerned, denominational walls are falling flat before the trumpet call to stand uncompromisingly for the whole Bible and nothing but the Bible.[2]

B. R. Wilson's comment on this is that 'in fact exactly the reverse process was occurring', so that in 1939 P. S. Brewster could write:

> No matter how much you love a certain denomination or particular church, it is dangerous to your soul and future welfare if its teaching is not the full gospel.[3]

However, in the meantime the Elim Missionary Society had joined the Evangelical Missionary Alliance and become an observer member of the Conference of British Missionary Societies. The Elim Pentecostal Churches are also a member of the British Pentecostal Fellowship and the Evangelical Alliance. But they still reject the World Council of Churches.

(*b*) *The breach between George Jeffreys and his church*

From the middle of the 1930s there was tension between George Jeffreys and the other leaders of the church.

> Publicly he remained the figurehead, privately his power was curtailed by the new organisational structure, where the instruments of power were legal documents and constitutional technicalities which the charismatic leader could not manipulate, nor even, perhaps, fully understand.[4]

Jeffreys's comment on this is:

> Pastor E. J. Phillipps [the Secretary] came determined to fight with legal weapons for a continuation of the system, whereas I could do no other than return to fight with the Word of God against the system.[5]

The system which Jeffreys is opposing here was a centralized church organization. The keynote was set no longer by the Holy Spirit, but by an oligarchy of officials. At the European Pentecostal Conference in Stockholm (1939) George Jeffreys had declared both a congregationalist and a centralized church organization to be equally legitimate.[6] But by the end of 1939 there had been a breach between him and the Secretary of the Elim Pentecostal Churches, so that George Jeffreys was obliged to resign, and founded the Bible Pattern Church Fellowship.[7] In his statement 'Why I Resigned from the Elim Movement' he gives four reasons for this unusual step:

1. Because the Ministerial conference had made lay representation so remote a prospect.
2. Because local churches had no title or trust deeds giving them control over

church property which they had paid for and no control over procedure in church or over church finance.

3. Because the Irish churches had been granted elders by the Conference (since in Ireland elders already existed in many churches) in addition to deacons, while the churches in England, Scotland and Wales had been restricted to deacons.
4. Because he himself could not be bound by the resolution which prohibited him from writing or printing in protest against the control of the governing body of the Elim Alliance.[8]

The comments of the Elim Four Square Alliance were at first evasive. They wished to avoid an open controversy. They stated that Jeffreys had been released from his administrative tasks in order to give more time for his spiritual work, etc. But in spite of attempts at reconcilation, the break became final. In spite of the great respect which he enjoyed in many circles both within and outside the Pentecostal movement, Jeffreys henceforth became an outsider.

Bryan W. Wilson, a sociologist at the University of Oxford, has written an illuminating sociological study of the Elim movement.[9] His view is that the breach with George Jeffreys became unavoidable the moment the Elim Pentecostal Churches changed from a 'tribal community' drawn together by a single leader into a denomination with a complete organizational structure, in which the charismatic leader no longer felt at ease and had to give way to the master of organizational routine, the Secretary of the movement. Wilson does not regard Jeffreys's struggle simply as a struggle for power. In his view Jeffreys was profoundly disturbed by the institutionalization that was taking place, once he became aware of it.[10] On the other hand, it was necessary for the movement, if it was to survive in the struggle for existence between the denominations, to introduce the impersonal machinery of routine administration. Wilson's account has been welcomed by the present-day leaders of the Bible Pattern Church Fellowship,[11] but rejected by the leaders of the Elim Pentecostal Churches. The latter assert that Wilson's sources[12] are unreliable, and that Wilson sought his information solely amongst the adherents of Jeffreys.[13]

The Elim Pentecostal Churches see the main reason for the breach in the growing emphasis laid by Jeffreys on the British Israel theory.[14]

One of Stephen Jeffreys's sons, Edward Jeffreys, who was also a great evangelist and a talented singer, founded another organization, the Bethel Evangelistic Association,[15] which no longer taught the baptism of the Spirit in the Pentecostal sense (the second generation!),[16] although Edward Jeffreys had received this experience as a boy. The Jeffreys brothers possessed extraordinary natural talents, such as the Pentecostal movement, in Europe at least, has scarcely ever produced since. These talents did not consist of 'American gimmickry'. By simple, powerful and logically structured addresses they captured the minds and hearts of audiences thousands strong.

(*c*) *The transformation into an organized church*

In the successive issues of the *Elim Evangel* one can observe two parallel processes: the improvement of the social standing of Elim members and the decreasing emphasis on the characteristic doctrines of Pentecostalism:

> God does not bless us just because we have creeds and 'fundamentals'. We are often in danger of being more concerned with verbal assent to a set of fixed doctrines as the criterion of rightness than a heart experience of Jesus Christ. I feel that God meets a man not on how much he knows about 'truth' but upon his reaching out after Himself. Cornelius is an example. The Holy Spirit came on him *and* his family before they made any verbal 'confession of faith'. It is rather shattering to read David Du Plessis saying that there is a great outpouring of Pentecost today among the 'liberal' and 'ecclesiastical' sections of Christendom, but none at all among the 'Fundamentalists'. Why? Is it because the latter are more taken up with the 'letter that killeth' than the 'Spirit which giveth life'?[17]

The confession of faith made by young Elim members does not include the specific doctrines of Pentecostalism.[18] Young Elim members are no longer characterized by their refusal to use cosmetics.[19] To this extent Wilson's sociological study is already out of date.

2. *Points of Doctrine*

The confession of faith of the Elim Pentecostal churches[20] shows that it is a moderate Pentecostal group, but contains a number of notable contrasts with American Pentecostals. It teaches the inspiration of the Bible,[21] but not a 'mechanical inspiration, in which it is implied that the human writer was no more than the passive amanuensis'.[22] But the doctrine that speaking in tongues is the 'initial sign of the Baptism' is rejected as 'not valid'.[23] The gifts of the Spirit are important, but they should be restricted in accordance with precisely defined criteria.[24] With regard to the healing of the sick through prayer, Elim maintains the rational principles set forth by Jeffreys: 'There is no authority in Scripture for the view that every saint who is suffering from sickness and disease is out of line with the will of God.'[25] However, the newspaper *Mercury* investigated a number of cases of healing performed by Jeffreys and 'found no relapse in cases of healing of curvature of the spine and blindness'.[26]

There was originally great emphasis on the expectation of the imminent second coming of Jesus. In 1931 it was proclaimed that 'Bible students' had recognized that the year 1932 would be a year of crisis,[27] and it was announced that the second coming of Christ would be 'the next great world event'. Although apocalyptic theories were an important theme in evangelization at the beginning of the Elim movement, to the extent that in their light even pacifism was rejected and actually singled out as unbiblical,[28] such theories no longer seem to have any hold upon the members. In a commentary on a Pentecostal hymn which expresses a longing for a world to come, the *Elim Evangel* can make the statement that no one believes in it. We are all worldly, even those who do not go to the cinema, for in its place we have built up an entertainment industry of our own (choirs, film shows).[29] In fact the Welsh origin of the Elim movement has meant that music has always played a prominent part in it. The Elim Crusader Choir, led by a talented musician, Douglas Gray, often sings on the radio and in prisons. In a well-informed article Gray puts the case for the recognition by the church of the value in its congregational services of musicians who have had a proper musical training. He asks that organists, trumpeters, clarinettists and singers, many of whom have had a first-class musical training, should not suddenly have to abandon in the Elim meetings everything which at their schools of music they have been taught to take for granted. This problem is becoming an urgent one for a considerable number of professional musicians who belong to the Elim movement.[30] Perhaps in this observation Gray has in mind his colleague J. H. Davies, who condemns jazz as an immature form of music.[31]

In the encounter with the natural sciences most members of the Elim Churches in fact accept that there is a long interval of time between Gen. 1.1 and Gen. 1.2.[32] Similarly, the Elim movement allows the expression of different views about the time taken for the creation of the world. The six days of creation can be understood in a symbolic sense. But no concessions are made beyond this. During the 1930s there were attacks on the theory of evolution in almost every number of the *Elim Evangel*. For believers it was only a 'fairy tale'. The same view was repeated in 1953, with the regretful comment:

> The sad part about it is that this kind of nonsense is . . . taught from textbooks of the tax-supported schools . . . broadcast over the wireless, and headlined across the great dailies and the best magazines . . . Evolution is the greatest farce ever foisted on an unsuspecting public.[33]

Recently Russel Evans[34] attempted with the aid of the theory of relativity, the introduction of the concept of the 'realms of non-physical reality', in which the laws of causality are supposed not to hold, and by means of a new understanding of the *creatio continua*, to establish a better relationship between natural science and faith.

There is cause to believe that the ethical rigorism described by Wilson is no longer in force at the present day. Originally there was a firm insistence on the traditional English Sunday,[35] the ten commandments,[36] the prohibition of illustrated magazines,[37] the radio,[38] and the cinema.[39] But at the present day these ordinances seemed to have lost their hold.

3. *The Elim Pastor and his Congregation*

Wilson devoted a special study to the Elim pastor, entitled 'Role Conflicts and Status Contradictions of the Pentecostalist Minister'. On the one hand the pastor has to be loyal to the ethical, dogmatic and administrative provisions of the central administration, while on the other hand he has not to resist the moving of the Spirit in the congregation. It is the pastor's task to bring into harmony order and spontaneity, fundamentalism and enthusiasm. To this end, he has no better organizational structures at his disposal than those possessed by other churches. On the contrary, Pentecostal organizational forms are according to Wilson mostly antiquated. The result, he believes, is that in the Elim movement, even more than in the Reformation churches, everything depends upon the pastor.

> Thus in the matter of doctrinal conformity, the minister is specifically committed to headquarters, and his pulpit preaching is firmly circumscribed by formal rules; but no such attempt is made to ensure correct doctrine in laity, who need know little more than that they are born-again believers, eligible for Spirit baptism. The minister stands to bridge the gap between these two social systems of which he forms a part; he mediates the demands of headquarters to his own congregation, informs them of decisions, and builds up their confidence in 'our movement' and 'our God-blessed leaders'.[40]

Since the pastor's relationship to his congregation is based upon a shared emotional experience (and not upon a common confession of faith, a common concrete task, membership of the same social class,[41] or a common pattern of life),[42] the suitability of a pastor depends entirely upon his success in building up and maintaining this relationship in spite of the authoritarian functions which he has to exercise on behalf of the central administration and the Bible understood in a fundamentalist sense.

Finally, Wilson describes the contradiction between the status which the pastor enjoys within the Elim congregation and that which he holds outside it. As a *pastor* he has a very high status within the congregation, but as a *Pentecostal* he has a very low status in society. Consequently, he lives in a permanent condition of contradiction with regard to his status, which is made even more severe by the fact that other ministers and pastors are inclined to deny the Pentecostal pastor the status of a minister of religion; in their eyes he is an upstart 'with only an elementary education and ungrammatical speech with a marked regional accent'.[43] Consequently he is rarely invited to the local 'inter-denominational council'.

To sum up, one can say of the Elim pastor that he is the vital link between the rigid organization at the top of the Elim Pentecostal Church and the loose organization at its grass roots; and he has to come to terms psychologically with the tensions that result from this, which can lead to a conflict between his roles as agent of the central administration and as shepherd of the local congregation. Again, he experiences a tension resulting from the contradiction between his status as pastor in his congregation and as a Pentecostal pastor amongst the ministers of other churches. These tensions cannot be resolved in argument, for he cannot express them in dialogue with his colleagues (for example in a pastors' meeting), nor even make them known. This means that there is an ecumenical task for other ministers, to find a way of removing the blockage which prevents this dialogue.

The Elim pastor's *congregation* was originally composed of people from the depressed areas of society. Although women have no official part to play in the organization, many have found themselves at home in the meetings with 'tears, heavy breathing, groans, utterances of joy and rapture'.[44] But the traditional churches give people a bad conscience if they actually enjoy the services:

> The churches have done their jobs so well that the average man now believes that anything but Gothic, with music to match, would be wicked, and that religion in modern dress would be sacrilege. He assumes it is not 'proper' religion unless it is garbed in the fashion of the Middle Ages. The masses like Pentecostal services, but their breeding makes them suspicious of a service they can actually enjoy and appreciate.[45]

Today the Elim church itself has to struggle against 'chills' in its services – otherwise it would not have to make appeals for greater warmth of feeling towards newcomers.[46]

According to Wilson, the poverty of Elim members should not be overemphasized. It is true that the Elim movement grew great at a time of economic depression, but the reasons why a distinctive religious group came into being are not always the same as the reasons why it continues in existence.[47] Wilson describes the Elim church as a place in which individual neurosis can be drawn up into the worship and utilized in this common liturgical activity. Admittedly, it has developed its own methods for this, but there is much to be said for the analogy of group therapy under the guidance of a minister of religion. The frequent and emotionally intense services with their spontaneous testimonies create a situation similar to that of the therapeutic dramatic encounters experienced in group therapy. The Elim member, afraid to express himself in public, experiences a feeling of dramatic tension which is resolved when the psychological blockage is overcome in speaking in tongues – which is analogous to the practice of free association in the group-dynamic process. The Elim congregation is carrying out an unconscious psycho-therapeutic function, helps to overcome loneliness, anxiety and fear, releases emotional blockages in cathartic sessions and makes it possible for the individual to integrate himself into a community by passing through and leaving behind him a shared experience of guilt for the past (loneliness, misfortune, remorse, and everything else associated with sin).

It is interesting that the Elim pastor H. W. Greenway gives a similar interpretation of Elim services. He draws attention to the ways in which emotional tension can be released in art and sport, and to the lack of these in the church. But emotional stress situations, he points out, cannot be overcome by argument.

> It is foolish in these cases to say: 'Pull yourself together.' That is exactly what these folk are unable to do; the torment of unsatisfied desire is too strong for that, and all attempts to repress natural urges only seem to complicate the nervous tension. Nor does a pose of horror help. People with nervous breakdowns resulting from sexual causes, are usually overwhelmed with shame at having to confess defeat on this particular level. Virtue is their objective, but impurity their experience; or at least, that is how they feel about it. The thing must be faced for what it is; sexual difficulties are not resolved by ignoring them.

Greenway explicitly draws attention to the possibility of sublimation and describes the Elim church as a place in which there is 'ample scope for this re-channelling of the emotions into profitable social and spiritual services'.[48]

NOTES

1. Sources, Documents, Literature: 05.13.024. Statistics: 308 churches, 270 pastors, approx. 40,000 members and adherents. Journal: *Elim Evangel.*
2. G. Jeffreys, *Miraculous Foursquare Gospel* II, 1929, p. 2; quoted in B. R. Wilson, *Sects*, p. 47.
3. P. S. Brewster, *Convert's Handbook*, 1939, quoted with comments, Wilson, *op.cit.*, p. 41.
4. Wilson, *op. cit.*, p. 47.
5. N. Brooks, *Fight*, pp. 56f., quoted by Wilson, *op. cit.*, p. 48.
6. G. Jeffreys, 'Answer to Question no. 4', Forlaget, Filadelfia, *Europeiska Pingstkonferensen 1939*, pp. 192ff.
7. 05.13.036.
8. G. Jeffreys, *Why I Resigned*, quoted in B. R. Wilson, *Sects*, p. 53.
9. B. R. Wilson, *Sects and Society*. This work is a summary of a sociological thesis for the University of London (*Social Aspects of Religious Sects*, 1955, 2 vols., dupl.). Since Wilson lived for months amongst the Pentecostals and studied their religious belief and practice from within, his account is very valuable, and compares favourably with many theological polemics against the Pentecostals, even though Wilson declares himself to be a non-Christian.
10. Wilson, *op. cit.*, p. 49.
11. D. H. Macmillan, *Pattern* 22/10, Oct. 1961.
12. Especially the journal *Pattern* and N. Brooks, *Fight for Faith and Freedom.*
13. Wilson states, however, that he tried unsuccessfully to meet the leaders of the Elim Pentecostal Churches to discuss the matter.
14. D. Gee, *Wind and Flame*, pp. 181ff.
15. 05.13.002.
16. D. Gee, *Wind and Flame*, p. 153.

17. Squintus, *Elim Evangel* 43/51–52, 25.12.1962, p. 824.
18. Quoted in H. W. Greenway, *Labourers*, p. 41.
19. P. J. Brewster, *Elim Evangel* 43, 1962, p. 586.
20. Cf. Appendix: 7, p. 519.
21. G. Jeffreys in D. Gee (ed.), *Phenomena*, pp. 48f.
22. H. W. Greenway, *Labourers*, p. 12.
23. G. Jeffreys, *Pentecostal Rays*, p. 34.
24. W. H. Urch, *Spiritual Gifts*.
25. G. Jeffreys, *Healing Rays*, p. 81.
26. *Mercury*, 15.8.1927, quoted in Wilson, *Social Aspects* I, p. 131.
27. *Elim Evangel* 12, 1931, p. 266; quoted in Wilson *op. cit.*, I, p. 91.
28. J. McWhirter, *The Bible and War*.
29. Squintus, *Elim Evangel* 43, 1962, p. 581.
30. Douglas Gray, *Youth Challenge* 2, 1963, pp. 24ff.
31. J. H. Davies and H. W. Greenway, *Youth Challenge* 1, 1962, p. 25.
32. *Elim Evangel* 1933, quoted in Wilson, *Sects*, p. 85.
33. *Elim Evangel* 11, 1930, pp. 129f.; quoted in Wilson, *Sects*, p. 86. The same view is held by the Assemblies of God (A. J. R. Sharp, 'Evolution or Creation?', *Redemption Tidings* 43/5, 3.2.1967, pp. 12f.; Paul Newberry, 'Man or Monkey', *Redemption Tidings* 45/50, 11.12.1969, pp. 8f.).
34. R. Evans, *Youth Challenge* 2, 1963, pp. 6f.
35. *Elim Evangel* 14, 1933, p. 11; quoted in Wilson, *Sects*, p. 91.
36. *Elim Evangel* 6, 1925, p. 192; quoted in Wilson, *Sects*, p. 91.
37. *Elim Evangel* 29, 1948, p. 63; quoted in Wilson, *Sects*, p. 85.
38. *Elim Evangel* 31, 1950, p. 5; quoted in Wilson, *Sects*, p. 83.
39. *Elim Evangel* 28, 1947, p. 25; quoted in Wilson, *Sects*, p. 82.
40. Wilson, *American Journal of Sociology* 64, 1959, pp. 500f.
41. As a pastor, he no longer belongs to the same class as his congregation, even if he originated in it (cf. D. Gee, below, ch. 15.2(*c*), p. 211). In the 1930s this was shown by the fact that he alone possessed a car.
42. His pattern of life is markedly different from that of the members of his congregation. Until a short time ago he would be the only self-employed person, with a relatively large responsibility.
43. Wilson, *op. cit.*, p. 504.
44. Wilson, *Sects*, p. 107.
45. G. Canty, 'Twentieth Century Miracle', in H. W. Greenway (ed.), *Power Age*, p. 13.
46. L. E. Lambert, *Youth Challenge* 1, 1962, p. 27.
47. Wilson, *Sects*, p. 321.
48. H. W. Greenway, *This Emotionalism*, p. 144.

15

From a Revival Fellowship within the Existing Churches to an Independent Church: Donald Gee and the Assemblies of God[1]

1. *Origins*

IN THE course of the years, the conferences organized in Kingsway Hall, London, by Cecil Polhill[2] took on more and more the character of an interdenominational evangelical conference and lost their specifically Pentecostal note. Although prophecy and speaking in tongues were not suppressed, they were no longer encouraged, 'more through fear of inability to deal with resultant situations'[3] than for any reason of principle. Donald Gee recounts an example which seems to him typical:

> A lady soloist was announced for a sacred song of the professional type. Just as the accompanist was going to strike up the opening chords on the piano, a Pentecostal Missionary Union[4] missionary in the congregation, home on furlough, began to speak in tongues. The Lord graciously gave the accompanist[5] the interpretation, but the soloist had to stand waiting until it was completed before she could proceed with the music. In a more truly Pentecostal atmosphere such an informal interruption would have been charming; but in this case the lady probably was considerably embarrassed. However, we went through with the piece.[6]

Once the Apostolic Church[7] and the Elim Pentecostal Churches[8] had adopted the formal characteristics of distinct organizations, many small congregations came into existence throughout the country, which gave general support to the Pentecostal Missionary Union and its missionaries through its Missionary Committee, but otherwise had no organizational link. Many Pentecostals still belonged to other churches, especially since up to the 1920s the counsel of the Anglican clergyman A. A. Boddy was generally accepted: 'Receive the Baptism in the Holy Spirit, but remain in your church, whatever the denomination may be.'[9] As the Pentecostal influence in Polhill's Kingsway Hall conferences declined, the tendency towards an evangelical interdenominational structure for the Pentecostal Missionary Union grew less. In spite of this there was resistance to the formation of the Assemblies of God, for many of its founders had experienced in their own persons the disadvantages of an organized church. But there was no longer any way to avoid organization. In the founding assembly of 1 February 1924 it was resolved:

1. That we do not intend identifying ourselves as, or establishing ourselves into, a sect, that is a human organization, with centralized legislative power.
2. We do, however, recognize the need and recommend the adoption of scriptural methods and order for worship, unity, fellowship, work and business for God, disapproving of all unscriptural methods.[10]

By contrast with the centrally organized Elim congregations, most of which had been founded by George Jeffreys, the Assemblies of God consisted of local congregations which had come into being independently of each other, which did not wish to abandon their congregational autonomy, and which could therefore only join a federal organization of the congregationalist kind. In spite of this, the step to organization as a separate and distinct church had been taken under the pressure of circumstances. In 1925 the Pentecostal Missionary Union was dissolved and the Assemblies of God took over its missionaries. As a result the Anglicans Boddy and Polhill lost their influence in the British Pentecostal movement.

Now followed a period of large evangelization and healing campaigns with Stephen Jeffreys, Smith Wigglesworth,[11] John Carter and others. The story is told of Stephen Jeffreys, 'a miracle in the hands of God', that in Sunderland people were queueing outside the assembly hall as early as ten o'clock the night before, to obtain admission the following afternoon: for often several thousand people could not obtain admittance to his evangelization meetings.

In his assessment of the healing campaigns Donald Gee does not overlook their questionable features: mechanical and auto-suggestive methods of healing, the relatively small numbers healed, the considerable difference between those who 'professed conversion in the campaigns' and those who later joined the Assemblies. On the other hand the campaigns brought the concern of the Pentecostal movement for evangelization to the public notice and into the press. Nor should the fact be overlooked that the sound human understanding of the British evangelists restrained them from too great extravagances.

In spite of these large evangelization campaigns the British Pentecostal movement has remained a relatively small group (altogether just under 100,000). Donald Gee has examined the reasons for this development, so different from that in the Scandinavian, Italian and French Pentecostal movements. He comes to the following conclusion. The leaders in the early years understood the Pentecostal movement as a revival movement within the existing churches, and therefore did not encourage the setting up of distinct Pentecostal congregations.

The first Pentecostal pastors were often men of good-will, but 'crude and ungifted'. 'The baptism in the Spirit was construed as making its recipients not only "witnesses", but competent preachers and leaders in the Assemblies.'[12] In addition there were sometimes also 'crudities of behaviour', neglect of external factors, and a disproportionate emphasis on foreign missions. In my view the reason for the phenomenon seems to be one which Gee does not mention. As long as the Pentecostal movement remained within the existing churches, there was little room for the activity of capable non-theologians in the service of the congregation. At that time there had not even been a theoretical discovery of the laity in ecumenical discussions! Thus many of their pastors preached part-time; the best people were – with a few exceptions – sent into the mission field and to the continent. This is also a reason for the decisive importance of the British Pentecostal movement for many European Pentecostal bodies. We now go on to give a fuller account of the most important of its teachers.

2. '*A Pentecostal Gentleman*': *Donald Gee* (*1891–1966*)

(*a*) *His life*

Originally a Congregationalist, he was converted in 1905, during the revival in Wales, by the Methodist preacher Seth Joshua.[13] He came into contact with the Pentecostal movement in 1912, by way of Baptist groups. He describes his baptism in the Spirit as follows:

> Increasing glory now flooded my soul in the meetings as well, until I began to speak in new tongues publicly. Also I would sing very much in the Spirit in new tongues, when the little Assembly would be moved in this way by the Holy Spirit during our times of prayer and worship.[14]

For a long period he was the pastor of the Assembly of God in Edinburgh,[15] while from 1934–44 he was vice-chairman of the British Assemblies of God, and from 1948 on chairman. He undertook long journeys throughout the world as a Bible teacher (not as an evangelist). The World Pentecostal Conference at Zürich (1947) entrusted him with the editorship of *Pentecost*, an important Pentecostal news magazine, which, however, closed after Gee's death. From 1947 on he was the sole ex-officio member of the committee of the World Pentecostal Conferences. Up to 1964 he was in charge of the Bible School of the Assemblies of God in London.

(*b*) *Donald Gee as Pentecostal and ecumenist*

Donald Gee was a determined champion of the doctrine that the baptism of the Spirit is obligatorily accompanied by speaking in tongues (the 'initial sign') and also of intensive co-operation with non-Pentecostal churches. His literary influence is powerful. One of his works (*Concerning Spiritual Gifts*) has been published in French, German, Portuguese, Dutch, Chinese and Swedish. If one looks through a year's issues of almost any Pentecostal journal, it is virtually impossible not to come across an article by him. Even the critics of the Pentecostal movement have had to take his works into account. However, they have dealt with only a fragment of his whole output. Because his writings on co-operation with the World Council of Churches and about the 'initial sign' of the baptism of the Spirit are of fundamental importance, they will be discussed in detail below. As early as 1925 Donald Gee was putting forward this typical Pentecostal view, which he thereafter defended regularly in numerous articles and books:[16]

> The doctrine that speaking with other tongues is the initial evidence of the baptism in the Holy Spirit rests upon the accumulated evidence of the recorded cases in the books of Acts where this experience is received. Any doctrine on this point must necessarily be confined within these limits for its basis, for the New Testament contains no plain, categorical statement anywhere as to what must be regarded as *the* sign.[17]

In *Pentecost* 1958[18] and at the Fifth World Pentecostal Conference in 1958 he put forward the same view:

> To teach a presumed Pentecostal experience without emotional manifestation is to emaciate the doctrine beyond all recognition as being according to the Scriptures. . . . There must be *some* outlet of deep feeling. Why not accept the form of outlet that God, in His wisdom, has ordained? Why oppose speaking with tongues? . . . The physical manifestations accompanying the baptism in the Holy Spirit . . . provide the only immediate evidence to the onlooker that the Comforter has come indeed in all His glory and power. To see the shining faces of those first praising their Lord in new tongues is to taste something of the very gate of heaven.
>
> . . . . *that speaking with tongues is the scriptural initial evidence* of the baptism in the Holy Spirit I hold . . . to be right. . . . The soul becomes intoxicated with such a divine ecstasy that it is beyond all ordinary forms of speech. . . . With all due respect we refuse to be satisfied that so-called 'Pentecostal' experiences without a physical manifestation are valid according to the scriptural pattern or even common logic.[19]

He had not changed his opinion in 1962.[20] But it was always accompanied by his untiring struggle for an understanding of the non-fundamentalist churches, although he himself was a fundamentalist.[21] He found this struggle very hard, since he was opposed not only in Britain,[22] but above all by the American Assemblies of God.[23] He made skilful use of the positive response which Pentecostals had received in various circles within the existing churches,[24] and could point to the experiences of the baptism of the Spirit in American Protestant churches.[25] But this did not prevent him from giving a friendly warning to the Protestant and Anglican theologians who had experienced the baptism of the Spirit:

> Many of you are trained theologians with a good academic background. Do not, now you have tasted spiritual gifts, become fanatical in your repudiation of consecrated scholarship. Let the Spirit of truth set it all on fire and use it for the glory of God. Some of us in our early folly set a premium upon ignorance.[26]

From the time of the Full Assembly of the World Council of Churches in Amsterdam he kept up a friendly commentary on the efforts of the World Council. Gee's view of these efforts towards the unity of Christians, 'that they all may be one', was

> that it would be churlish, to say the least, not to welcome its progress. . . . It is all very well to talk about the unity of the Spirit as transcending our denominational and ideological differences, but that fact does not absolve us from efforts at manifesting an outward fellowship also.[27]

He tried to give encouragement to his friend David J. Du Plessis, who because of his open-minded attitude to the World Council of Churches had been expelled ('disfellowshipped') from the American Assemblies of God.[28] Under pressure from the same fundamentalist majority within the Pentecostal movement which made life bitter for Du Plessis and claimed that the World Council of Churches was 'miles apart from the Pentecostals', he had to turn down an invitation to the Full Assembly of the World Council of Churches in New Delhi.[29]

Instead he presented his disputatious friends with a fiery article entitled 'Are We Fundamental Enough?' In answer to the charge that at the present day we are not living at a time in which we can compromise, he replied:

> True . . ., but they are days for deep searchings of heart, and perhaps for reassessment of some things we have cherished in easier days, when we could afford the luxury of denominational strife and division. We are making ourselves liable to become companions of John and excommunicate those who have not signed on our dotted lines. We want all men to be 'with us' rather than 'for' the Son of God. Heresy-hunting is often a mark, for the discerning, of a receding fullness of the Spirit. We persecute, and we are persecuted, for things that are only relatively important. Yet we pride ourselves, we are fighting the battle of the Lord.[30]

His expression of approval of ancient liturgical forms in his dialogue with the Pentecostal movement within the existing churches is a fine example of his lack of prejudice:

> There may be a deep wisdom in this new charismatic revival that is touching so many in the older denominations if they can maintain their liturgies and forms of public worship under a new touch of the Spirit. There is no fundamental reason why time-honoured orders of worship cannot be touched with

Pentecostal fire, unless they embody some unscriptural error. . . . The need is for re-vitalizing, not destruction by an explosion of fanaticism. The last error may be worse than the first. We believe that there is a beauty of holiness that is not human but divine. . . . The 'open' type of meeting . . . can degenerate into something more wearisome and stereotyped than any devoutly used liturgy. . . . Much needless anxiety would be spared the sincere disciple if it was recognized that the normal is the will of God. It leads to a hopeless contradiction of ideas if Revivalism insists upon making the abnormal the regular pattern. The Christian life is walking with God . . ., not a system of jerks along the upward way.[31]

(*c*) *Self-criticism and a sense of humour*

His self-criticism of the Pentecostal movement, flavoured with his delicate sense of humour, is one of the most refreshing things to be found in Pentecostal literature. If we believe in the inspiration of the whole scripture, he wrote in 1936, we must not despise the sound wisdom of Proverbs.[32] Let us not eat too much honey (Prov. 25.16).

The kiss with which the Father greeted the returning prodigal must have been like sweetest balm upon his poor weary wounded spirit; yet no one would suggest that the Father kept on kissing him all the time. . . . Some Christians tend towards the superlative, and we have to confess to a feeling approaching nausea at their sugary language.

This is particularly true of hymns.[33] He likewise criticizes Pentecostal biographies, which he describes as the 'worst examples of unctuous flattery'.

The type of cheap 'Heroes' series beloved amongst the Assemblies for Sunday School prizes is responsible for a lot of false ideals and ideas about famous preachers and missionaries and missionary work.[34]

There could be better biographies about the same people if they were not written by the wrong authors and put out by the wrong publishers.[35] On the other hand, he wrote a favourable review of C. W. Conn's missionary history of the Church of God (Cleveland),[36] because Conn also mentions the failures of the missionaries, something unusual in Pentecostal missionary histories. He severely criticizes the young Pentecostals who crowd into the very full Bible schools in order, if at all possible, to become pastors of a tiny congregation. When their training is finished they renounce the language of the social milieu from which they come,[37] and are therefore as worthless to the Pentecostal movement as the missionaries in the Congo who could not speak Kilubu properly. Let them follow the example of the worker priests! Gee attacks the slogan 'Bible schools are unnecessary',[38] although he himself was wholly self-taught. He censured the pastors at the World Conferences in Paris and London because their sermons were too feeble. Pentecostals had to learn to prepare their sermons in writing and to deliver a sermon properly, following a manuscript. This is also something that needs practice and is anything but contrary to the expectation that a sermon should be inspired by the Holy Spirit. He gives as an example of this the Pentecostal sermons on the radio.[39]

This brings us to the numerous works by Gee which deal with misunderstandings and extravagances within the Pentecostal movement. He tried to refute the Pentecostal Unitarians of the 'Jesus Only' groups,[40] called the extremist Latter Rain Movement[41] to reason,[42] made an exhortation to unity,[43] and mocked the pilgrims who imagined that at the World Pentecostal Conference which took place at Whitsuntide 1961 in Jerusalem (Pentecostals at Pentecost at the place of the first Pentecost) they could expect a special Pentecostal blessing.[44] In important disputes with healing evangelists he pointed out that in the New Testament, as in Pentecostal Assemblies at the present day, not all who believe are healed.[45]

He took a very close look at the Pentecostal healing evangelists and the Full Gospel Business Men. The kind of publicity their evangelization received 'smelt more of high pressure salesmanship than of the guidance and power of the Spirit of God.' 'It is a bad day when leadership in the churches is usurped by rich men as such, just because they are rich.' To confuse prosperity with blessing 'would be to sound the knell of all Pentecostal grace and blessing'.[46]

> There comes to the editor's desk a flood of Pentecostal papers from all over the world with the name of leaders made prominent who but a few years ago were unknown. Admittedly they are a mixed bag – as their fathers were! A lot of it is sheer personal propaganda. With some there is obvious personal ambition and thrusting for the limelight. In some cases we greatly fear there is making merchandise of gullible souls, but even Peter knew that (II Peter 2.3).[47]

(*d*) *Dogmatic and ethical writings*

Gee's various dogmatic writings are studied in greater detail in the second part of this book. They contain an average fundamentalist Pentecostal theology.

His ethical writings are more interesting. By contrast with many Pentecostals and pietists, he was not unaware of the social-ethical aspect of Christianity.

> It is not enough to give men an assurance that their souls are securely labelled for heaven because of a decision in some mass meeting . . . better citizenship should be a direct result of all sound Pentecostal evangelism.[48]

He therefore asked for understanding and respect for Pentecostals who take an active part in politics.[49]

He made himself very unpopular with an article on 'the end of Acts 2'.

> We may find excellent reasons for rejecting the idea of communism, but those professing to be filled with the Spirit of Christ have the responsibility of showing a realistic alternative.[50]

He made an urgent call to the representatives of the charismatic revival within the historic churches: do not depend wholly on personal experience! We hope for more than the repetition of pietistic Pentecostal individualism in a rather higher stratum of society.[51]

His works on individual ethics deal with the basic principles of ethics.[52] He studied the question why many new converts lapse,[53] but in his journal for pastors also dealt with questions of sexual ethics and family planning in a progressive way.[54] He tried to bring about understanding for the proper psychiatric treatment of the depressed within the Pentecostal movement[55] and produced a kind of Pentecostal 'handbook of etiquette'.[56]

(*e*) *Historical writings. Conclusion*

His historical writings contain much valuable source material and numerous acute observations, although they do not make or possess any claims to scholarship. The autobiographical sketch *Bonnington Toll* contains striking impressionistic pictures of a Pentecostal Assembly in the early period, written by a man whose love for the Pentecostals does not prevent him from observing their weaknesses accurately and critically. He wrote two histories of the Assemblies of God in Great Britain,[57] and several accounts of the international Pentecostal movement,[58] which he collected together in his well known book *Wind and Flame*.

I have known Donald Gee for years, first as an occasional guest preacher in the Pentecostal mission in Zürich, then as a teacher at the International Bible Training Institute, Leamington Spa. I later translated regularly for him and worked with him at three World Pentecostal Conferences. Shortly before his death, in the spring of 1966, I once again discussed in full with him the basic features of the Pentecostal movement. On the occasion of this visit, I became aware that the range of his theological reading was astonishing for one of his advanced years. At the suggestion of one of his sons, who had studied theology, he was studying Tillich, and was reading Tillich's *Systematic Theology*. Perhaps I can best conclude this brief protrait of a 'Pentecostal gentleman' with the words with which he bade me farewell. 'Never give up hope of winning the Pentecostals over to an ecumenical outlook! It will be a long time, for the Pentecostals are afraid. And fear is hard to overcome.'

3. *The Doctrine and Religious Practice of the Assemblies of God*

The confession of faith of the Assemblies of God exists both in a full form[59] and a shorter form.[60] They set out the usual Pentecostal doctrines, including that mentioned above, the doctrine of the baptism of the Spirit with speaking in tongues as the 'initial sign'.[61] On the other hand, the present teaching seems to have superseded the assertions of Harold Horton:

> You will never hear modernists or ritualists speak with tongues . . . you will never see the modernist and the ritualist heal the sick, for they either ignore the ordinance altogether, or travesty God's appointed anointing, corrupting

> it into the rubbishy ritual of 'extreme unction' for the dead . . . What is there left for God's blood-bought heritage, His spiritual Israel, his precious flock? Nothing inside the organized Churches. Revival is *outside* the churches today and will be till Jesus comes.[62]

But man proposes and God disposes, and A. F. Missen, the General Secretary of the Assemblies of God, affirms that Pentecostal experience and practice has burst 'into circles where we would least have expected it', although he goes on to criticize the new charismatic movement for its efforts to keep its distance from the separate Pentecostal churches ('in the main holding aloof from the recognized Pentecostal bodies').[63] A. F. Missen also modifies Horton's basic assumption that 'spiritual gifts are unmistakable evidence of fundamental belief in God'.[64] He says: 'Any philosophy that experience matters more than doctrine is fraught with danger.'[65] This means nothing less than that the original standpoint, that experience takes precedence over doctrine, is being reviewed. There are also signs of the decline of enthusiasm in the sphere of liturgy, and in the position of the pastor and the missionary. Thus the Overseas Missions Secretary compares the earlier situation with that of the present day:

> Whereas in earlier times of pioneering our men came home from the fields covered with glory, showered with respect and gifts, and continually upheld by ardent prayer, our present-day missionary can meet with a completely changed attitude and response to his testimony. When we gave a lion story or two, and an account of souls being saved, assemblies would weep with joy, and take inspiration to pray and give. Nowadays, they come home weakened with toiling under the new conditions, having left behind dozens of nationals whom they have trained in the art of soul-winning and flock-feeding, who have the natural assets as masters of the language and local conditions, to help them in their work. When they get home, I have met them sometimes when there has been nobody else to welcome them back.[66]

The same is true of the pastor. Under the title 'Could this happen to us?', F. J. B. Sumner describes the tragic suicide of a Presbyterian minister. In objective, sympathetic and accurate terms – in part by quoting Talmadge – Sumner describes the senselessness of expecting all the work and all the inspiration to come from the pastor, something which clearly also seems to be becoming usual in the Assemblies of God. Who would not agree with his complaint:

> It is not hard study that makes the minister look pale. It is the infinity of interruptions and botherations to which they are subjected. If I die before my time, it will be at the hand of committees that want an address or a lecture.[67]

Sumner makes the sober observation:

> It is sad to realise that many of our ministers have suffered nervous break-

downs – some more than one. Often distress over financial matters has been a major contributing factor.[68]

An observant reader points out that pastors share the blame for this situation. The first Christian congregations

> were a body of men functioning as a body, and had it been left to the same man each time, week after week, month after month, year in year out, he would soon have felt the strain, and isn't this the position of many of our pastors today, how many we hear of having to rest with nervous trouble.

But he wonders if the first Christians

> sat in rows listening to one man all the evening. . . . We do not need to be fed on the Word, we need to *feed* on the Word: a big difference. If I was still feeding my children in their teens with a spoon, then something would be drastically wrong. At this age they feed themselves . . .[69]

Thus it is not surprising that in Great Britain there is a decline in membership not only in the traditional churches, but also amongst Pentecostals,[70] and that there are Pentecostals who prefer to meet in small ecumenical house groups, rather than in their chapels. How to plan regular services both informally and at the same time according to a pattern which is both rational *and* spontaneous is one of the problems which Pentecostals and supporters of the ecumenical movement must face as a *common* task.[71]

In the sphere of demonology the Assemblies of God have published a work which is of a higher standard than the usual Pentecostal publications on this subject. This is Raphael Gasson's study of Spiritualism.[72] The author was originally Jewish, and then, as a result of his musical interests, became organist in a Christian church, and came into contact with one of the numerous Christian spiritualist circles in London. He himself became a successful spiritualist medium, but turned away from spiritualism and discovered that mediums who were professed atheists obtained the same, if not better, results. In the meantime he came into contact with a Pentecostal congregation. He was astounded at the ignorance of its pastors and members, but convinced by the profundity and sincerity of their religious experience. In his book he describes many extraordinary spiritualist phenomena (levitations, clairvoyance and other parapsychological phenomena), but he endeavours to give an objective account and also describes those who have not been successful. As one converted from spiritualism he now completely rejects spiritualist practices, for one exceptional experience in the Bible (the witch of Endor) ought not in his view to be made the basis of a doctrine. He regards the phenomena of spiritualism as a deceit of the devil and is firmly convinced that there is a fundamental difference in doctrine and experience between spiritualism and the Pentecostal movement. But he considers it of great importance not only to reject the phenomena of spiritualism, but also to contrast with them the genuine miracles of the Bible. This book should be read by everyone who condemns the Pentecostal movement as tainted by spiritualism, for it is written by one who can compare them both. He proposes a 'demythologizing' of ghosts not by denying the existence of demons, but on the pattern of the Epistle to the Colossians, where they are subordinated to Christ. His account of the different schools of spiritualism and their history is also of value.

NOTES

1. Sources, Documents, Literature: 05.13.023. Statistics: 534 churches, 540 pastors, 65,000 members and adherents. Journal: *Redemption Tidings*.

2. Cf. above, ch. 13.2(*a*), pp. 184f.

3. D. Gee, *Wind and Flame*, p. 111.

4. Cf. above, ch. 13.2(*a*), pp. 184f.

5. This must refer to Donald Gee himself, who was often the pianist at meetings. Cf. the 'we' in the last sentence.

6. D. Gee, *Wind and Flame*, p. 112.

7. Cf. above, ch. 13.4, pp. 191ff.

8. Cf. above, ch. 14, pp. 197ff.

9. D. Gee. *Wind and Flame*, p. 88.

10. *Ibid*., p. 127.

11. Cf. ch. 31.4, p. 478.

12. D. Gee, *Wind and Flame*, p. 89.

13. *Ibid*., p. 34.

14. D. Gee, *Pentecost* (hereafter cited as *P*), 1932, p. 9.

15. D. Gee, *Bonnington*, 1943.

16. A selection: D. Gee, *Redemption Tidings* 1, Dec. 1925 (article reprinted 1959); 1932, pp. 26f.; *VdV* 20/5, May 1932, pp. 1ff.; *Phenomena*, 1931, p. 10; *P* 17, 1951, p. 17; *P* 25, 1953, p. 17; *P* 34, 1955, pp. 10f.

17. D. Gee, 'Initial Evidence', *Redemption Tidings* 1, Dec. 1925 (reprinted separately 1959); *PE* 2357, 12.7.1959, p. 3.

18. D. Gee, *P* 45, 1958, p. 17.

19. D. Gee, 'Pentecostal Experience', in D. Gee (ed.), *Fifth Conference, 1958*, pp. 43ff.

20. D. Gee, *Der Leuchter* 13/8, Sept. 1962, p. 4; *VdV* 55/7, July 1962, pp. 4ff.; *Die Wahrheit* 15/10, Oct. 1962, pp. 1f.; *MD* 25, 1962, pp. 166f.; *PE* 2387, 7.2.1960, pp. 6f.

21. D. Gee, *Concerning Spiritual Gifts*, 2nd ed., 1937, p. vi.

22. 'Ecumenism is bedevilled with two evils: the evil of Romanism and the evil of liberal theology' (A. F. Missen, *Redemption Tidings* 42/30, 22.7.66, p. 12). The entry of de Melo (ch. 8.3[*b*], p. 104) into the World Council of Churches was viewed by G. Jeffreys Williamson 'with great alarm' (*Redemption Tidings* 45/49, 4.12.1969, p. 5). Cf. also B. Barrett, *Redemption Tidings* 38/34, 24.8.1962, pp. 10ff., and William H. Hannah, *Redemption Tidings* 45/31, 31.7.1969, pp. 8f. For a less categorical view H. P. Benney, *Redemption Tidings* 45/23, 5.6.1969, p. 11.

23. Cf. below, ch. 3.4, pp. 42f.

24. D. Gee, *P* 22, 1952, p. 17; *P* 54, 1961, p. 2.

25. D. Gee, *P* 58 and 59, cf. ch. 1, pp. 3ff.

26. D. Gee, *P* 58, 1962, p. 17.

27. D. Gee, *P* 6, 1948, p. 17; cf. also *P* 30, 1954, p. 17; *P* 59, 1961, p. 17.

28. D. Gee, *P* 21, 1952, p. 12; 24, 1953, p. 17.

29. D. Gee, *P* 57, 1961, p. 16.
30. D. Gee, *P* 57, 1961, p. 17.
31. D. Gee, *P* 63, 1963, p. 17; cf. also D. Gee, *Study Hour* 5/2, 15.2.1946, pp. 27ff.
32. D. Gee, *Proverbs*, Introduction.
33. *Ibid.*, pp. 9f.
34. Circumspectus (pseudonym for Gee), *Study Hour* 9, 1950, p. 54.
35. *Ibid.*, p. 55.
36. C. W. Conn, *Where the Saints have Trod.*
37. Circumspectus, *Study Hour* 9, 1950, pp. 36f.
38. D. Gee, *P Testimony* 38/8, Aug. 1957, p. 8.
39. D. Gee, *P* 46, 1958, p. 17.
40. J. N. Gartner, D. Gee, H. Pickering, *Water Baptism.*
41. Cf. above ch. 11, pp. 140ff.
42. D. Gee, *P* 20, 1952, p. 17.
43. D. Gee, *All with One Accord*, 1961.
44. D. Gee, *P* 55, 1961, p. 17.
45. D. Gee, *Trophimus*; *P* 36, 1956, p. 17; *PE* 2426, 6.10.1960, pp. 3, 35.
46. D. Gee, *VdV* 50/12, Dec. 1957, p. 6; *MD* 21, 1958, p. 131; cf. above, ch. 1.1(*b*), p. 6f.
47. D. Gee, *P* 71, 1965 (cover).
48. D. Gee, *P Testimony* 41/2, Feb. 1960, p. 8.
49. D. Gee, *P Testimony* 40/4, April 1959, pp. 2, 30; *P* 47, 1957, p. 17. Cf. also below, ch. 31.2, pp. 467ff.
50. D. Gee, *P* 14, 1950, p. 17; Circumspectus, *Study Hour* 9, 1950, p. 167.
51. D. Gee, *P* 68, 1964, p. 17.
52. D. Gee, *Fruit of the Spirit: Fruitful or Barren.*
53. D. Gee, *Keeping in Touch.*
54. D. Gee, *This is the Will of God; Herald of His Coming* 20/9 (no. 237), Sept. 1961, p. 5; *Study Hour* 9, 1950, pp. 154 ff.
55. *Study Hour* 9, 1950, pp. 7ff., 33ff.
56. D. Gee, *Proverbs.*
57. D. Gee, *Glory of the AoG; Story of a Great Revival.*
58. D. Gee, 'Histoire', *L'Ami* 1932, pp. 203ff.; *To the Uttermost Part; Upon All Flesh.*
59. 'Statement of Fundamental Truths approved by the General Council' published in: AoG in Great Britain and Ireland, *Year Book 1962/1963*, pp. 6ff.
60. Cf. Appendix.
61. H. Horton, *Gifts*, pp. 135ff.; *Baptism*, pp. 13f.; J. E. Hindmarsh, *Redemption Tidings* 43/6, 10.2.1967, pp. 5ff.
62. H. Horton, *Gifts*, p. 206.
63. A. F. Missen, *Redemption Tidings* 42/30, 22.6.1966, p. 15.
64. H. Horton, *Gifts*, p. 206.
65. A. F. Missen, *Redemption Tidings* 42/30, 22.6.1966, p. 13.
66. W. B. Hawkins, *Redemption Tidings* 45/11, 13.3.1969, p. 9.
67. F. J. B. Sumner, *Redemption Tidings* 45/30, 24.7.1969, pp. 3f.
68. *Ibid.*
69. K. E. M. Clark in a letter in *Redemption Tidings* 45/43, 23.10.1969, p. 11.
70. *Redemption Tidings* 44/26, 27.6.1968, pp. 8ff.
71. K. Munday, *Rdeemption Tidings* 44/45, 7.11.1968, pp. 3f.
72. R. Gasson, *Challenging Counterfeit.*

16

The 'Legend of the Diabolical Origin' of Pentecostalism Demythologized: The Origin of the Pentecostal Movement in Germany

1. *The 'Pentecostal Atmosphere' in German Established and Free Churches before the Beginning of the Pentecostal Movement*

(*a*) *The attack on academic theology*[1]

THE German Conservative Evangelicals attempted, by passionate attacks on academic theology, to salvage the authority of fundamentalism. E. Lohmann was not ashamed to attack such a conservative theologian, profoundly rooted in the Bible, as Adolf Schlatter, because in his *Introduction to the Bible* Schlatter expressed his approval of 'Wellhausen's source hypothesis, that the five books of Moses are a later compilation of different accounts which actually often contradict each other . . .'.[2] He attacked Bousset, Gunkel, Jülicher and Weiss without restraint. 'This is the modern battle against the Bible.'[3] The fact of variations between different manuscripts of the biblical text was dismissed with the statement that we 'can trust the Lord to guide the hearts even of scholars'.[4] Taking one thing with another, 'our "moderate theologians" make too many concessions to biblical criticism'.[5]

There was a demand for 'humble submission to the entire word of God'.[6] In practice this led to a very high-handed dismissal of natural scientists[7] and the confusion of conversion with unquestioning assent to orthodox teaching.

> That doubts on this matter can come from *conscience* is one that you [evangelical Christians] will never entertain. You virtually never make sincere attempts to come to terms with modern thought. Rather, you always approach it with brutal rejection.[8]

For those who think in this way, the same writer continued, are trying at all costs to avoid being amongst those 'who prise one jewel after another out of our Saviour's crown and cut page after page out of the Book of Books until only the cover is left'.[9]

The doctrine of literal inspiration became the crucial issue in the attack by

Conservative Evangelical leaders against the Eisenach theologians, and Lepsius in particular, who were trying to co-operate with the Evangelicals. Lepsius' own standpoint was wholly that of positive theology and the Evangelical movement. He had made an 'attempt to restore the original text of Genesis 1–11'. His intention was 'to demolish piece by piece' the theory of Wellhausen. He declared that

> The Conservative Evangelical movement itself, now that it has passed the climax of its period of enthusiasm, needs a powerful biblical theology, if it is not to collapse as a result of an unhealthy theological dilettantism and the practical consequences thereof.[10]

There followed the most violent attacks upon Lepsius. Characteristically, these were not aimed at the fairly obvious academic weaknesses of his hypothesis, but condemned him out of hand because he did not endorse the doctrine of literal inspiration. The comment of the journal *Auf der Warte* ('On Guard') was 'The sacrifice of Abel reduced to a love story!'[11] Lepsius defended himself in vain against a declaration from the Conservative Evangelicals in which his hypothesis was disposed of by reference to II Peter 1.21, John 10.35 and Matt. 11.35. He wrote:

> One must be aware of the objections which are made against the truth and reliability of the historical tradition of Scripture, and refute them. Anyone who has any ability to do this . . . will find me at his side.[12]

This only strengthened the hostility of the Evangelical leaders towards Lepsius. At the eighteenth conference of the movement, 24–28 August 1903, he was put on trial. All his friends except Jellinghaus and Jonathan Paul, the later leader of the Pentecostal movement, abandoned him. Stockmayer compared him to Uzzah and Achan. Rubanowitsch cried: 'It is a real matter of conscience for every child of God to point out his brother's sin and utter it.'[13] But Jonathan Paul observed:

> Dear brethren, it is really worth remarking . . ., that if Martin Luther, with his views about Scripture, reappeared today among Evangelicals, we would pass the same judgment upon him as upon brother Lepsius.[14]

'The gentlemen present had clearly no reply to this observation.' But this did not prevent Vetter, 'without the slightest knowledge of the theological issues', from writing in *Die Bibel, das Schwert des Geistes* ('The Bible, the Sword of the Spirit'):

> Biblical criticism has introduced a new religion which is no more Christianity than the moon is the sun . . . Biblical criticism began in the Garden of Eden. The first biblical critic was the devil himself. Biblical critics are 'servants of the devil' and 'disciples of Satan'.[15]

A critical listener to revivalist sermons would long ago have noticed that this view was accompanied by an unconsidered but nevertheless effective principle of selection which silences large parts of the Bible.

> [The Old and New Testaments] are uncritically and unscrupulously shuffled together as though the scholarly exposition of Scripture did not exist. The things that are read into the Old Testament are beyond description. And it is no better with the New Testament. The treatment of individual texts naturally suffers in the same way. Not only are texts chosen from a one-sided point of view, but are all stamped in the same mould by the interpretation given them. The specific message of each is glossed over: the text is forced to say what it was never intended to. Authority is recognized more in principle than in practice. The devotional pattern [of revivalist preaching] . . . is what governs the content, not faithfulness to the Bible.[16]

Schian, the author of the above criticism, also reproached the preaching of the established Lutheran Church for often failing to be 'anything except a religious discourse, sometimes witty, sometimes not'. He considers it necessary that Protestant preaching should learn from the Evangelical movement 'to try to be effective again':[17] but it should avoid the unsuitable images, foolish tales and nonsense which the revivalist preachers use to rivet the attention, without putting over a single coherent idea. According to Schian the revival preaching of the Evangelical movement is like

> a person with a middle-aged way of life and outlook who dresses up to the latest fashions. In its message this preaching is not in touch with the modern age . . . Its modernity is merely an outward veneer; the method by which it obtains a revival is a one-sided adaptation to false piety and emotionalism. As a form of modern Protestant preaching it is always interesting, worthy of respect in many ways, but on the whole not to be imitated.[18]

Schian particularly objects to the use of examples from modern life merely as a useful peg on which to hang clever comparisons and illustrative references.

> Those who do so are very far from really getting down to modern life and casting any profound light on the situations it presents . . . [For example, a preacher asks:] 'At a national election three hundred miners cast not a single vote for the Socialists. Why is this? Each has his own house on his own patch of land.' [He then takes two – exactly two – sentences to draw the social consequences of the situation he describes. But then he abandons this subject and follows the biblical pattern in giving it a religious application:] 'In religion too one can have a patch of one's own land!' This is what the sermon is about . . . This is characteristic. The situation to which he alludes is taken from present-day life; but it provides him only with a starting point, a spring-board. He does not make full use of it, he does not examine it, he uses it only as a simile and gives it a spiritual interpretation.[19]

From the point of view of the Evangelicals this was justified. As they saw it, the call of the moment, in an age which was shaken by social struggle, was not for a profound examination of the situation, but for conversion:

> Is this conversion of the godless not the greatest success that can be achieved in the social field? For the converted, are not most so-called social problems in fact resolved without the expert intervention of the professional social politician? Just ask a worker who has bid farewell to the vice of drunkeness and carries out his daily work in the name of God as an act of worship.[20] No one can save a man by filling his belly. Bring him into contact with Jesus and he will soon be able to buy his own dinner.[21]
>
> Men who have fallen far . . . even Socialists . . . can be converted.[22]

In spite of Blumhardt they did not hesitate to conduct a polemic against the Social Democrats, who were spreading 'fanatical hatred against authority', 'jealousy and envy towards others', and were 'pulling down the fences of moral dignity'.[23] The difficulties of Christian Socialist pastors in Switzerland were remarked upon with satisfaction.[24] The same journal, however, recommends plays for the celebration of the Kaiser's birthday within the Evangelical fellowships; these included C. Offermann's *I am a Prussian* and Karl Lorenz's *In Enemy Country*. And in general, during the first world war, Evangelical Christians showed an enthusiasm for the war which seems extremely questionable to a present-day reader.

After weary years spent reading the literature of the Evangelical movement around the turn of the century, I have become convinced that by its polemic against academic theology, its blindness to questions of social policy and its exaggerated apocalyptic views, the Evangelical movement did not merely prepare the way for the Pentecostal movement, but by neglecting scholarly exegesis deprived itself of the only means of putting to rational use the fruitful impulses that came from the Pentecostal movement, without becoming completely at their mercy, and rendered itself incapable of making a pertinent criticism of the Pentecostal movement without accusing it of being of diabolical origin.

(*b*) *The propagation in the German Evangelical movement of the baptism of the Spirit, later condemned as 'diabolical'*

In Germany in 1904 the expectation of a revival, under the influence of events in Wales, 'had risen almost to boiling point'.[25]

> There was preaching about the fullness of Pentecost, the fullness of the Holy Spirit, the baptism of the Spirit, which the believing congregation can experience if only it earnestly longs for it.[26]

Various American Holiness evangelists came to Germany and Switzerland, including Torrey, who was celebrated in Germany as the new Moody.[27] Edel wrote in the *Allianzblatt* about his meetings at the Blankenburg conference in 1905:

> After Dr Torrey . . . had set out the conditions laid down in the Bible for baptism with the Holy Spirit . . . he made stand up all those who were ready

> to give everything, even what was dearest and best, in order to receive everything from God. Several hundred of the children of God stood up in the hall. Torrey now prayed that the Holy Spirit might come down upon all who desired him . . . I can only say of myself that a marvellous gentle stream of fire came down over me from above, and it seemed to me that if I had opened my eyes, which I had covered, I would have seen a flame of fire throughout the whole hall.[28]

When a certain P. Friedrich published a criticism of these events in the journal *Die Wacht* there was a great feeling of indignation, and people were inclined to count him amongst the 'mockers' who said on the day of Pentecost: 'They are filled with new wine'.[29]

In Blankenburg, according to Dallmayer, 'not only was the baptism of the Spirit preached, but there was already sufficient feeling there for it to be received'.[30] Modersohn described the conference as the 'hoofbeat of the white horse'. 'There the rider on the white horse had come and had shot his arrows into their hearts.'[31] Every Evangelical journal published enthusiastic reports of the beginnings of the Pentecostal Movement in Wales and India. Critical articles in the press were dismissed with the argument: 'What does it signify? All it signifies is, "We will not repent".'[32]

An account of the Pentecostal doctrine of the baptism of the Spirit, which was later bitterly contested, was reproduced in the Evangelical journal *Auf der Warte*. The author of the article was a Pentecostal lady missionary in India.[33]

Fleisch, a careful and well informed student of the German Evangelical movement, Kurt Reuber[34] and others have demonstrated from an overwhelming quantity of source material that the doctrines of the Pentecostal movement, which to this very day are condemned as 'diabolical', were not invented by Pentecostalism, but arose in the Evangelical movement, and particularly in those parts of it which were *within the established Churches*:[35] 'We are using the March storms, which prepare the way for the latter rain.'[36] According to the *Reichgottesarbeiter* ('Worker for the kingdom of God') anyone who would not define a miracle as a violation of the order of nature was 'no longer a Christian theologian'.[37] According to the same journal, in 1906 the German Evangelical movement was still too sober.[38] Likewise prayer in concert, that is, prayer in which the whole congregation utters prayers together and in spontaneous confusion, was designated as a 'divine ordinance'.[39] Objections based on the Bible and systematic theology were insolently rejected:

> We do not need to investigate whether it is biblical to speak of a baptism of the Spirit and a new experience of Pentecost, for we can see all around us men and women, and not only individuals, who can testify from their own blessed experience that there is such a thing. For it is spiritually that it must be judged.[40]

Pastor Busch was of the opinion that the 'cry of rage of the Jews in the liberal [theological] journals' was to be seen as a compliment to the Pentecostal movement rather than a condemnation of it.[41]

> The cloud of blessing under which we stand comes lower and lower, and in many and various places one can see how the streams of grace are pouring down and bringing forth new life in the wilderness.[42]

2. *The Pentecostal Movement 'Not from Above but from Below'*[43]

A reversal in the assessment of the baptism of the Spirit and the Pentecostal movement took place after the meetings held by two Norwegian lady missionaries in the Blue Cross House[44] in Kassel, under the direction of Heinrich Dallmeyer. Detailed accounts were given in the religious and political press. There were scenes of great tumult.[45] The leaders of the Evangelical movement, including Elias Schrenk, were not sure what to make of it. Dallmeyer was not in a position to guide the emotionally charged congregation in a more acceptable direction. At first he defended the emotional outburst, but at the end of 1907 he declared that the meetings at Kassel were diabolically inspired. He has given an incontrovertible account of the unhealthy currents within the Evangelical movement up to the time that speaking in tongues appeared: the separation of justification and sanctification,[46] the subjectivism,[47] the undervaluing of infant baptism,[48] the doctrine of the removal of man's sinful nature and that of the baptism of the Spirit.[49] His intention was to show that at decisive moments in the course of his ministry he had been falsely advised by the theologians and leaders of the Evangelical movement. This perception on the part of Dallmeyer can scarcely be ignored. Dallmeyer could only explain to himself the way he fell under the spell of the Pentecostal movement by supposing that he was led astray by the spirit of a powerful angel of Satan.[50] Rubanowitsch,[51] Ernst Lohmann,[52] Johannes Seitz,[53] and Bernhard Kühn,[54] also saw the devil at work in the Pentecostal movement. This view of the situation was summed up in what is known as the 'Berlin Declaration', which was signed by the main leaders of the Evangelical movement.

By contrast to this summary condemnation there were doctors and psychologists at the time whose judgment gave due weight to both sides of the matter.[55] And there were theologians who, without condemning the Pentecostal movement as diabolical, put their finger on its weak points, the theory of stages of salvation, the doctrine that some people will be taken up selectively before the general rapture, the exaggerated doctrine of perfection, and the contempt for scholarly exegesis. To this day these theologians have remained virtually unheard, in the Evangelical movement as well as in the Pentecostal movement, to the disadvantage of both the quarrelling brothers. If the Evangelical movement and the Pentecostal movement had listened to Fleisch, Bruckner, Sippel, Simon, and others, not only would they have avoided an unnecessary and nowadays almost ludicrous battle, they might even have been a blessing to the church. Thus in 1908 Friedrich Simon could already write:

> The established churches in the twentieth century can only reject 'speaking in tongues' as 'enthusiasm' as long as they are prepared to admit what the study of comparative religion shows to be the case: that in the New Testament, alongside the pinnacles of divine revelation in Jesus Christ, certain sub-Christian elements are also present. Enthusiasm is such an essential element in the life of the New Testament church that it is impossible to deal with a similar aberration within the Evangelical movement by a call to return to 'biblical sobriety'. The church is now suffering the consequences of its failure, in spite of all the critical editions of the New Testament text, to make generally known throughout its congregations the apocryphal character of Mark 16.9ff., and of v. 17 in particular.[56]

And in 1909 Bruckner made a statement which is still true today. In his view the main fault of the Pentecostal movement was

> the unhealthy religious feeling present in many Evangelical circles, which seems to have its main roots in a false, mechanical view of Scripture.
>
> This in fact has led numerous Evangelical theologians to a completely unbiblical fragmentation of the doctrine of the process of salvation. All the expressions of the New Testament writers which are used to illustrate what the individual experiences in his redemption, expressions such as justification, sanctification, the forgiveness of sins, rebirth, and so forth, are taken by them and interpreted as a series of particular and distinct acts of conversion. This leads them to the weird and completely unbiblical idea that these individual acts of conversion take place one after the other and at different times, so that the separate parts of the spiritual life are successively imparted to the Christian.

And, he continues, even though the converted Christian

> believes that he has obtained one part after the other, a final part of his whole spiritual armament is always lacking, so that he can never completely rejoice in his salvation. He therefore has a morbid longing for every new gift amongst those which are offered to him, because he believes that this alone can give him the full stature of a man in Christ.
>
> But in this way the Christianity of many members of the Evangelical movement sinks back to the level of Roman Catholic piety, which also believes that the grace of God can only be achieved in separate portions by one's own exertions.
>
> *It is at this point that the theology which the radical Evangelicals abhor as 'satanic' can be of the greatest value to it, by bringing it back in this and in other respects ... to a wholesome and truly evangelical view of the Scripture.*[57]

Wilhelm Nitsch regarded the condemnation of the Pentecostals because of their enthusiasm or their alleged diabolical origin as without scholarly justification. If there had been newspapers at the time of St Francis, they would also have had headlines about the 'enthusiastic movement at Assisi'. They would have called on Francis and his brethren 'to stick to their work in quiet simplicity'. And when George Fox was at work there were also those who sent for the police.

> But we now understand and respect this reckless, powerful energy of faith and witness, which expressed itself in these strange forms. The contemporaries of Fox and Penn regarded their way of life with extreme repulsion; their response to it was a terrible hatred, and years of bloody persecution . . .
>
> It is wild and unbridled enthusiasm, said the people of that time, who found it so disquieting; but nowadays we regard it as a mighty movement of the Spirit, albeit mixed up with many strange features.[58]

Sippel and Fleisch both agree that the Evangelicals had to declare the Pentecostal movement to be diabolical, because its views were too close to their own, and they did not want to be confused with it.[59]

Theodor Jellinghaus, the respected and honoured Evangelical theologian,

> now sees with deep sorrow, the 'doctrine of the Keswick Conventions' which he has taught for many years, as the source of all evil, and feels himself personally responsible for the rise of the Pentecostal movement . . . With his own hand he is destroying his life's work and is himself taking the blame for the wrong turning which the German Evangelical movement has taken.[60]

A systematic treatment of the problem of fundamentalism and the theory of stages of salvation is given in the second part of this book.[61]

3. *A Mentally Ill Girl Fools the Leaders of the German Evangelical Movement*

The 'Berlin Declaration', which even today is still regarded as fully in force by the Gnadauer Gemeinschaftsverband (Gnadau Evangelical Union) states that an infernal spirit is at work in the Pentecostal movement. What are the reasons for such a severe judgment? The Declaration alleges human failures within the Pentecostal movement, dogmatic errors, arrogance, pride, Pharisaism, the confusion of worthless utterances with the inspiration of the Holy Spirit, and the whole catalogue of vices with which the opponents of Christianity have always reproached the whole Christian church, even the church of primitive Christianity – sometimes rightly, as in I Corinthians! But it was left to the Gnadau Union to go on from these weaknesses in the Pentecostal movement, which individually were not to be taken lightly, to call the whole movement 'satanic'. If they were logical, they would also have to apply the term to the church in Corinth.

An important part in confirming the judgment that the Pentecostal movement was of satanic origin was played by the statements of a mentally ill girl which were published in 1911 by Johannes Seitz and Ernst F. Ströter. The name of the girl was not given, and they were presented as 'the "Pentecostal spirits" unmasking themselves'. They were reprinted in 1962 (!) by a certain Pastor Richard Eising. This 'self-unmasking' claims to be a verbatim report of utterances made by the girl, which were supposed to be made by a demon which had taken possession of her in Pentecostal meetings. In statements in a dramatic style, but of enormous naïveté, the demon 'unmasks' its purpose of putting the Christian church to confusion by means of the false teaching of Pentecostalism. 'Now the abomination, the swindle of Pentecostalism, has come into the open, and I cannot stop it,'[62] whines the demon, who in the face of the concentrated power of prayer of Seitz and his helpers has been forced to give up his secret. Jonathan Paul[63] pointed out that the so-called Pentecostal demon had made serious errors about the times events were supposed to have taken place, which made it impossible for his statements to be those of a demon endowed with supernatural knowledge, and showed them to be the product of the girl's diseased imagination. Then the psychiatrist Alfred Lechler felt obliged to refute from the psychiatric point of view the false assertions which were constantly being made in connection with the 'self-unmasking'.[64]

He begins by pointing out that in its condemnation, the Evangelicals had relied upon Seitz. But it was recognized that Seitz had falsely diagnosed many cases of psychiatric illness as demonic possession.[65]

'It is impossible for a psychiatrist to regard the phenomena which have taken place within the Pentecostal movement without exception as diabolical.'[66] His view of the self-unmasking is that the girl worked herself up into the role of one possessed and believed that she was doing a service to the leaders of the Evangelical movement by her revelations.[67] Ideas which she had picked up from Seitz during his Bible study hours reappeared in the exorcisms as statements by the Pentecostal demon. This had already become clear to Essler.[68] It is also notable that the prophecy of the 'Pentecostal demon', that the driving out of the demon would bring the end of the Pentecostal movement, was not fulfilled.

> From what we have said, no doubt remains that this case, to which Seitz and the opponents of the Pentecostals have so often referred, had nothing to do with true possession or with diabolically inspired spiritualism. Seitz and, following him, the leaders of the Evangelical movement, allowed themselves to be completely influenced by statements of a hysterical girl. This is all the more striking, when we remember that the 'Berlin Declaration' explicitly criticized the Pentecostal movement on the grounds that men, and their whole work, were placed in slavish dependence upon the 'messages' of women and young girls.[69]
>
> M. Michaelis fell victim to a similar error to that of Seitz. Accepting a hysterical girl as inspired by the Spirit, he accused a City Missionary of being a fanatic. Krawielitzki wrote to one of the brethren: 'I do not believe that the brethren of the Pentecostal movement have been possessed by demons, and equally do not believe that the poor mentally ill girl [he refers to the case

> described by Seitz] was really possessed. I am profoundly convinced from my own experiences and tests that both the prophecies of the Pentecostal brethren, and the alleged demonic utterances exploited by the opponents of the Pentecostals, have one and the same origin – their own psyche, by which they allowed themselves to be deceived, so coming to regard the tangle of thoughts in the sub-conscious mind as divine prophecies or demonic possession.[70]
>
> In my view it is incomprehensible that the leaders of the Evangelical movement at the present day should maintain their former view, when an unprejudiced judgment of the events fifty years ago by a psychiatrist, and an objective study of the present-day position, would lead to a completely different position from that laid down in 1909. Consequently, the Berlin Declaration now urgently requires serious revision and correction of its contents. It can no longer be maintained in force, because it is based on numerous false assumptions about demonic possession.[71]

More cautious observers, particularly doctors, had already expressed similar views more than fifty years ago. Jansen regarded the emotional outbursts in the Pentecostal movement as 'epidemic' and asked, with reference to the theologians who accused the Pentecostal movement of 'demonism', 'Has civilization with all the achievements of laborious scientific investigation completely passed them by?'[72]

Another doctor, F. Mohr, who is clearly a Freudian, claims to find in Dallmeyer an 'erotic impulse' which forms a sub-conscious part of the force underlying his religion.[73] According to Mohr, 'the same spirit is at work in those who speak in tongues and in the opponents within the Evangelical movement'.[74] For Mohr, however, there is no question

> that with the whole movement of speaking in tongues we have an explicitly pathological phenomenon. The whole enormous emotion which is to be found there, the abdication of the critical faculty to the point of imbecility, the over-emphasis placed on certain ideas derived from religious tradition and not even rightly understood, and above all the phenomenon of over-excitation or alternatively of paralysis of the motor nervous system, are all pathological.[75]

Mohr comments on Jonathan Paul: 'He is as it were a visible example of the way in which sexual energy can be forcibly diverted into other directions.'[76]

For the moment I record this interpretation without comment. However, important aspects of non-pathological speaking with tongues seem to me to be ignored by it.[77] One thing is certain, and that is that the categories of psychiatry and psychology are wholly sufficient to explain the weaknesses of the Pentecostal movement. The theologians of the Evangelical movement have no need to drag in the devil!

In a study which is still of value today Mosimann affirms:

> The speaking in tongues mentioned in the New Testament and that in the Pentecostal movement are identical from the phenomenological point of view. The speaking 'with other tongues' at Pentecost was essentially the same

phenomenon as the speaking with tongues at Corinth and that at the present day, an incomprehensible ecstatic utterance.[78] But tradition magnified it into a miraculous speaking in unknown foreign tongues, and the author of the Acts of the Apostles then perpetuated this tradition.[79]

All this, however, has not prevented widely published church journals from hawking around up to the present day the untenable assertion that the Pentecostal movement is of satanic origin.[80]

The reason for this indiscriminate condemnation on the part of many German theologians of the Evangelical movement is the fact that their links with the Pentecostal movement are too close, with the result that the only remaining difference is the labelling of the same phenomena as 'spiritual' in their own camp and 'satanic' amongst the Pentecostals. In particular, they share with the Pentecostals an unrelieved fundamentalism, while as early as 1910 critical biblical scholars could have shown them the way to a judgment which was more just and more in accord with the facts.

NOTES

1. Sources, documents, literature: 05.07.001. The German Evangelical movement, the *Gemeinschaftsbewegung*, takes the form of fellowships of members of the established churches who meet regularly outside normal service times, under the leadership of pastors or laymen, for prayer and Bible study. Their beliefs and position in the established Protestant churches make them comparable to Conservative Evangelicals in the Church of England.
2. E. Lohmann, *Auf der Warte* 2/43, 22.10.1905, pp. 3f.
3. E. Lohmann, *Auf der Warte* 2/2, 8.1.1905, p. 3.
4. *Reichgottesarbeiter* 2, 1905, pp. 157ff. A similar opinion is expressed by the American AoG, *PE* 2697, 16.1.1966, p. 7.
5. W. Goebel, *Auf der Warte* 2/12, 19.3.1905, pp. 3f.
6. E. Kunze, *Auf der Warte* 2/10, 26.2.1905, p. 10.
7. *Auf der Warte* 2/7, 12.2.1905, p. 11.
8. M. Schian, *Zeitschrift für Theologie und Kirche* 17, 1907, pp. 254f.
9. S. Keller, *Am Lebensstrom*, quoted by M. Schian, *op. cit.*, p. 253.
10. Fleisch I, p. 297.
11. *Auf der Warte* 1903, no. 16, quoted in Fleisch I, p. 297.
12. Fleisch I, p. 99.
13. Fleisch I, p. 443.
14. J. Lepsius, *Das Reich Christi*, 1904, pp. 21f.; quoted by E. von Eicken, *Heiliger Geist*, pp. 86f.
15. Quoted in Fleisch I, p. 443.
16. M. Schian, *op. cit.*, p. 256.
17. *Ibid.*, p. 245.
18. *Ibid.*, p. 269.
19. *Ibid.*, pp. 267f.
20. Dietrich, *Auf der Warte* 1/38, 17.12.1904, p. 1.
21. *Auf der Warte* 2/24, 10.6.1905, p. 3.

22. Dietrich, in J. Paul (ed.), *Verhandlungen der vierten Gnadauer Konferenz*, 1894.
23. *Auf der Warte* 2/25, 18.6.1905, pp. 3f.
24. *Auf der Warte* 2/3, 15.1.1905, p. 3.
25. Fleisch I, p. 447.
26. Fleisch I, p. 447; *Allianzblatt*, 1903, no. 18.
27. *Licht und Leben*, 1903, no. 7.
28. Quoted in Fleisch I, p. 464.
29. Fleisch I, p. 464.
30. H. Dallmeyer, *Zungenbewegung* (1924), 2nd ed., no date, p. 15.
31. Modersohn, *Das Buch mit den sieben Siegeln*, pp. 13f.; quoted in H. Dallmeyer, *op. cit.*, pp. 16f.
32. E. Lohmann, *Auf der Warte* 2/49, 3.12.1905, p. 4.
33. M. Abrahams, *Auf der Warte* 3/39, 23.9.1906, pp. 6f.; translated from *Missionary Review of the World* 19/8, Aug. 1906, pp. 619f.; originally in *Indian Witness*, 26.4.1906.
34. K. Reuber, *Mystik*.
35. Full documentation: 05.07.002.
36. J. Lohmann, *Sabbathklänge*, 4.8.1906; quoted in A. Goetz, *Mehr Licht*, 28/19–20, 1954, p. 7.
37. *Reichgottesarbeiter* 2, 1905, p. 189.
38. *Reichgottesarbeiter* 3, 1906, pp. 17ff., 36ff.
39. *Ibid.*, p. 138.
40. *Auf der Warte* 2/45, 22.10.1905, pp. 6f.
41. Busch, quoted in Jansen, *Zeitschrift für Religionspsychologie* 1, 1907, p. 329.
42. E. Lohmann, *Auf der Warte* 3/1, 1.1.1906, pp. 7f.
43. The words of the 'Berlin Declaration' of the German Evangelical Movement.
44. The Blue Cross (Das Blaue Kreuz) is a temperance organization.
45. Documents: 05.07.002c, aa.
46. H. Dallmeyer, *Zungenbewegung*, 2nd ed., p. 5.
47. *Ibid.*, p. 6.
48. *Ibid.*, p. 7.
49. *Ibid.*
50. *Ibid.* (Schrenk, Kühn, Modersohn).
51. J. Rubanowitsch, *Das heutige Zungenreden*, pp. 14, 19, 97.
52. E. Lohmann, *Pfingstbewegung und Spiritismus*.
53. J. Seitz und E. F. Ströter, *Selbstentlarvung*.
54. B. Kühn, 'Zur Unterscheidung der Geister', in H. Dallmeyer, *Die sogenannte Pfingstbewegung*, p. 40; B. Kühn, *Pfingstbewegung*, p. 82.
55. Cf. p. 227.
56. F. Simon, *Christliche Welt* 22, 1908, pp. 211f.
57. A. Bruckner, *Erweckungsbewegungen*, pp. 177ff. (W.H.'s italics).
58. W. Nitsch, *Christliche Welt* 21, 1907, pp. 918ff.
59. T. Sippel, *Christliche Welt* 28, 1914, pp. 234f.
60. T. Sippel, *Christliche Welt* 28, 1914, pp. 100ff., 125ff., 146ff., 176ff.
61. Ch. 21, pp. 291ff.; ch. 24.2, pp. 322ff.
62. J. Seitz and E. F. Ströter, *Selbstentlarvung*. According to Haarbeck, the Chairman of the Gnadau Union, this work provoked 'more shaking of heads than agreement'. 'I took energetic steps to see that the work, which he [Seitz] had had printed as it stood in manuscript, was not published. If this had happened, I should have had to come out against it.' (Letter of T. Haarbeck to E. Edel, 21.11.1911; quoted in E. Edel, *Kampf*, p. 37.) Haarbeck was not to know that the work would be reprinted fifty years later.
63. J. Paul, *Zur Dämonenfrage*.

64. A. Lechler, *Die Pfingstbewegung in ärtzlich-seelsorgerlicher Sicht* (dupl.). Summary in A. Lechler, *Zum Kampf.* I quote from the fuller duplicated version, which gives more medical detail.

65. A. Lechler, *op. cit.*, p. 45. Fleisch II/2, p. 231.

66. Lechler, *op. cit.*, p. 46.

67. *Ibid.*, p. 50.

68. *Ibid.*, p. 51.

69. *Ibid.*, p. 52.

70. *Ibid.*, p. 53.

71. *Ibid.*, p. 63.

72. Jansen, *Zeitschrift für Religionspsychologie* 1, 1907, p. 337.

73. F. Mohr, *Psychiatrisch-neurologische Wochenschrift* 10, 1908, p. 61.

74. *Ibid.*, p. 64.

75. *Ibid.*, p. 69.

76. *Ibid.*; in reality, a compliment!

77. Cf. below ch. 24.5, pp. 342ff.

78. Mosimann uses here the term 'ecstatic', a technical term of the academic study of religion, as do almost all psychologists who study the Pentecostal movement. But the expression is misapplied, because the element of inner compulsion in ecstasy is not typical of speaking in tongues as it occurs in the New Testament and in Pentecostalism, and because there is not only 'enthusiastic' but also 'recollected' speaking in tongues.

79. E. Mosimann, *Das Zungenreden*, p. 130.

80. E.g. A. Müller, *Das missionarische Wort* 13/5, May 1960, pp. 135ff.

17

The Attempt to set up a Pentecostal Movement within the Reformation Tradition: The Mülheim Association of Christian Fellowships[1]

1. *Historical Background*

(*a*) *The failure of the theologians of the Evangelical movement and the movement's 'bill of divorcement'*

On 15 September 1909 the leaders of the Evangelical movement met in Berlin, and in the absence of the Pentecostals passed sentence on the Pentecostal movement. Many passages of the 'Berlin Declaration', which was drawn up there and which represents the 'bill of divorcement' of the German Evangelicals, are aimed not merely against the teachings of the Pentecostal movement, but also against cherished ideas which had been defended for years within the Evangelical movement itself.[2] The reply of the Pentecostals[3] and the attempts at mediation by the 'neutrals'[4] were without effect.

> The Berlin Declaration soon proved to be a firm defence against further enthusiastic excesses. And it also healed the rift in the Evangelical movement. The period of revival and Holiness movements was over.[5]

Since an outstanding scholarly history of the Pentecostal movement up to 1945 exists in German,[6] this period can be dealt with very briefly.

(*b*) *Early organization*

The Christlicher Gemeinschaftsverband GmbH Mülheim/Ruhr (Mülheim Association of Christian Fellowships) regards itself not as a 'new church organization' but as 'a "movement", the working of the Spirit in the life of members of all churches'.[7] Nevertheless a minimum of organization came into existence. In particular the new Pentecostal movement had to make it clear what constituted the leadership of the church, with power to install pastors:

> This takes place according to the example of holy Scripture through men of God who are divinely authenticated and also possess the full trust of the fellowship.[8]

These 'men of God' included Edel, Paul, Humburg and Friemel. There were, however, objections to the exercise of authority in the church by 'divinely authenticated brethren', on the part of those who regarded any organization which went beyond local congregations as a betrayal of the gospel. From amongst them arose what became known as 'free Pentecostal Congregations'. These later joined together to form the Arbeitsgemeinschaft der Christengemeinden (Working Fellowship of Christian Churches),[9] which itself was centrally organized on a national level.

(*c*) *The encounter with National Socialism*

In its attitude to the perversion of Nazism the Pentecostal movement was not basically more resolute, but was certainly not more co-operative than the Evangelicals and other Christians in Germany. As early as the first world war, there was enthusiastic support for the war in the ranks of the Pentecostal movement, which in this respect displayed the same naive jingoism as the rest of the Evangelical movement. For example in the journal *Pfingstgrüssen* ('Pentecostal Greetings') we read that the hearts of the French and Russians were filled with hate, because they had turned against the gospel of God. 'It is perfectly clear why this hatred and envy is now directed against our fatherland, so richly blessed by God's grace for forty years.'[10]

> Two calls ring out like the peal of a mighty bell through our whole German nation. The Kaiser calls to arms, and God calls to repentance. The whole of Germany has followed the Kaiser's call. The single-minded response upon the part of our beloved German people is magnificent, splendid and without example in history of Germany, or indeed in the history of the world. A nation of 66 millions has decided to pledge everything that it is, possesses and is capable of to the defence of its existence. The magnificent and unparalleled mobilization is like the earlier Germanic migrations, but has taken place with exemplary order, like a gigantic machine in which all the skilfully assembled parts work without stoppage or friction. In all this the singlemindedness of our whole people is an ineffably great miracle, an unsuspected gift of divine grace. No human skill or effort would have been capable of achieving this – only God could have done it. Everyone, high and low, has understood that the existence or non-existence of our fatherland, our state, our people and our families are at stake.[11]

> What a marvellous spectacle is the mobilization of our army! Everyone says it is a 'lofty artistic experience' to see how all the great and tiny cogs of this mighty war machine have fitted together. There was no creaking and groaning. There was only a marvellous harmony.
>
> The Kaiser called – and everyone, everyone came, the North Germans and the south Germans, the Poles and the Alsatians, the Conservatives and the Socialists, the reserves and the territorials, the conscripts and the volunteers.
>
> It is in the blood of Germans to follow the ancient tradition of rendering military service when the Prince calls for troops. There can be no hesitation

and no delay. Wives and children, hearth and home, are bidden farewell, to follow the Prince to war.

And what is it like now in the field! When the order is given: 'The brigade will maintain its position under all circumstances', then the position is held – to the last man. And when the order is: 'See if that village is held by the enemy' the answer is 'Yes, sir!' and the rider gallops away. Dangers are ignored. Nothing is impossible. What is ordered is carried out. This is true of all, whether 'old hands' or young volunteers. Cheering they go into the attack.[12]

Mrs Ella Penn-Lewis, of Wales, who was already in disgrace for her writings against the Pentecostal movement, had now been impudent enough to describe 'the person of our universally honoured Kaiser as acting under the influence of demonic spirits' and to write: 'The demons have seized hold of the German nation, to carry out their will.'[13]

During the rise of Nazism that part of the Pentecostal movement known as the Mülheim Association tried to stand aloof from political conflict, in accordance with its basic attitude of quietism. But politics could not be completely ignored. Voget wrote of the catastrophe which threatened Germany:

In the East the hammer and sickle, in the South the *fasces*, in the West the French Air Force. And here, the sign to which millions of our compatriots look with enthusiasm for salvation turns out to be the swastika, 'the sign of hope of our heathen ancestors', not the cross of Christ. 'It is not our task to adopt an attitude to political questions.' 'The disunity of Christians is the greatest misfortune of our nation, and no one cares about it.' 'If we could kneel together around the altar of repentance, Evangelicals and Pentecostals, members of the established churches and the free churches, then fire would fall from heaven.'[14]

It is characteristic of the feeling amongst his readers in the 'Mülheim movement' that Voget was accused of having attacked Hitler's Nazi party. Voget defended himself:

My concern is to look at everything, including political parties, with the eyes of Jesus ... This excludes every prejudice ... If this is my approach, ... I cannot be other than a true friend, a faithful, reliable and genuine friend of Hitler ...

He willingly affirmed

that in the National movement, probably in the main through the influence of Hitler and other persons of understanding, there has been a clarifying of philosophical ideas which has consciously rejected the foolish project to bring back the old Germanic Gods.'[15]

In 1940 Mütschele attacked the British for their 'hypocritical, pious language and the false reasons which they have given' for their declaration of war. He praised in contrast the very modest demands of the Führer and his numerous efforts to bring about peace, and concluded his review of 1940 by expressing the following wish: 'May it bring to the nation we love so much, and to our beloved Führer Adolf Hitler at its head, and to all nations, an era of peace'.[16]

Krust describes this period in somewhat different terms:

> But some of our brethren were issued with 'warnings', and others with 'prohibitions', and others again were arrested and put in prison. Others, by miraclous divine interventions, barely escaped with their lives . . . Hardly any of our brethren had any training in political thought, and therefore our resistance to the regime had no political motive on our part. But we were aware of the 'subterranean spiritual current', of the demonic nature of what had come to power in Germany, and this awareness resulted in resistance on our part. This resistance did not primarily take the form of attacks and struggles, as in the case of those who looked at the situation from a political point of view, but consisted of suffering and bearing the cross, which as Jesus' witnesses we were bound to do. If God had asked us to sacrifice our lives, we would have been ready.

As evidence Krust points to an article by Humburg and a vision seen by Schober, but in their carefully chosen words they avoid the real problems at issue.[17]

By contrast, the Swiss Pentecostal movement did not withhold its criticism, although this was not aimed at its sister organization in Germany, for the political blindness of the latter was scarcely known in Pentecostal circles. The Swiss described Nazism as 'the uttermost blasphemy':

> This is the beginning of the reign of the beast in the idolized state, in the picture of the world monarchy in the book of Daniel, and we refuse to co-operate in building it up, for one day it will be destroyed stone by stone without the aid of human hands.[18]

The Mülheim movement kept at a safe distance throughout the church struggle of the Nazi period. On the other hand, it took part in discussions with the 'German Protestant Church', but this did not lead to any binding decisions.

> The answer to the objection that the new German Protestant Church is not really the form which Christ foresaw for his church . . . is that at the present day this form does not exist anywhere; it has been lost through unfaithfulness and cannot be restored by human artifice, but can only be given back to the church by the mercy of God. Of course in every discussion one must keep away 'from all the arts of diplomacy'.

A report dated Easter 1934 affirms that 'the Pastors' Council can be quite happy with what its representatives have done so far'.[19] The Swiss Pentecostals also criticized the Confessing Church, when the latter expressed its certain conviction 'that God will not abandon his cause':

> No promises of the kind which are widely imagined have ever been made about 'the cause of God', that in this age it will not be abandoned . . . It looks

very much as if those who fight on behalf of the Confessing groups in the established churches are expressing by their formulation of the cause of God, which he will not abandon, the hope that the church as such will be saved. It is at this point that they may well be disappointed in their hopes . . . For as they hope the final age draws rapidly closer.[20]

(*d*) *The tensions between the Mülheim movement and the rest of the Pentecostal movement*

The strength of the Mülheim movement lies in its criticism of the rest of the Pentecostal movement. These criticisms, however, almost invariably fell upon deaf ears. The observation was sometimes made that in spite of its relative closeness to the churches of the Reformation, it was much more firmly rejected by the latter than were, for example, the North and South American Pentecostal groups with their much more radical theology.

The Mülheim movement rightly acknowledges that the fragmentation of the Pentecostal movement does immense damage to its testimony. The total rejection of all established churches by the American Pentecostal churches, when compared with the more qualified view of them held in the Mülheim movement (although until recently it received very little genuine theological help from them) makes it hard for American Pentecostals to understand what they see as the 'lukewarm' Mülheim movement. For this reason, those who report to the American Assemblies of God omit from their report about Germany the largest Pentecostal group in Germany, the Mülheim movement.[21] Instead they emphasize the 'ineffectiveness of state-supported churches'[22] and make the false assertion that in East Berlin 'only one meeting place is allowed for all Protestant Christians'.[23] At the Fifth World Pentecostal Conference in Toronto in 1958, the Mülheim movement made an appeal to the Reformation principle of 'Scripture alone', in a declaration which drew attention to the traditionalism of Pentecostalism, which it was claimed, threatened to overshadow the testimony of Scripture.[24]

2. *On Doctrine*

Krust's book, *Was wir glauben, lehren und bekennen* ('What we Believe, Teach and Confess'), written with the co-operation of the Pastors' Council, is a considerable theological achievement. By contrast to many Pentecostal publications, it is very brief and concise, so that it is difficult to summarize. It also differs from the usual run of Pentecostal works on dogmatic theology, in that on most points there had to be a mention of the particular view of the Mülheim group. This book is indispensable for a knowledge of the *present-day* theology of the Mülheim group. It begins with the classical Christian creeds (the Apostolic, the Nicene, and the Athanasian Creeds), and then deals with various points of dogmatic theology. It gives a sentence summarizing the view put forward, which is then interpreted by commentaries from Reformation writings, from the work of modern academic theologians, and by the opinions of the author. We shall summarize a few of the main points.

(*a*) *Speaking in tongues and the baptism of the Spirit*

In the very first number of *Pfingstgrüsse* Jonathan Paul wrote: 'It is not our view that only those who have spoken in tongues have received the Holy Spirit.'[25] Speaking in tongues is to be desired as a gift of the Spirit, but – by contrast with the teaching of many other Pentecostals – it is not the sign that the baptism of the Spirit has been received.[26] The fact is also recognized that speaking in tongues is a natural human gift which the Holy Spirit can use if he wishes.[27]

In his book Krust makes a sharp attack on the doctrine that speaking in tongues is an obligatory accompaniment of the baptism of the Spirit.[28] In fact he goes further and rejects the doctrine of two stages of salvation taught by the Holiness movement and all the rest of the Pentecostal movement.

> The attempt to present the baptism of the Spirit as a second spiritual experience, to be fundamentally distinguished from rebirth, has no basis in Scripture. There is no basis for a way in which this teaching was presented in the Holiness movement by Murray and Torrey, nor as it is put forward at the present day by such as Markus Hauser – however many the inspirations which have come to us from these servants of God. Moreover, the Pentecostal circles which are favourable to this dogmatic pattern also teach the doctrine, equally untenable on a biblical basis, that the baptism of the Spirit must in all circumstances be associated with speaking in tongues as the initial sign. No movement of the Spirit at the present day or in the future, however blessed and however great it is, has the right to call itself a repetition of Pentecost, or the latter rain before the second coming of Jesus, by comparison with the early rain at the feast of Pentecost. This would be to impair the uniqueness of Pentecost in the history of salvation. Genuine movements of the Spirit can claim only the distinction of being at best revival movements, in which the forces of the Spirit present in primitive Christianity again appear. Whether a world-wide revival of this kind will have come about before the church is finally taken up is questionable, however glad we should be to see it.[29]

> [We proclaim] on the basis of the vital and unique event in which is represented by Pentecost . . . the necessity and possibility of receiving power from on high not only for a godly life, but also as an authoritative testimony to Christ, and of being endowed with the gifts of the Spirit (according to I Cor. 12, Rom. 12 and Eph. 4) for effective service . . .
>
> If anyone should say, 'This is the same as other denominations teach,' we should reply: Thank God! We do not wish to preach any unique message of our own; we desire to be unique only in proclaiming the central issue effectively and with authority and in demonstrating it in our personal lives and in our church life.[30]

Hermann Schöpwinkel, one of the leaders of the Gnadauer Gemeinschafts-verband (the Gnadau Evangelical Union – the association which unites the evangelical fellowships within the established churches) has made the following criticism of this summary:

> Dear Brother Krust,
>
> I found your second book no less disappointing than the first. In the first you put abroad false historical accounts, and in the second you conceal the fact that Mülheim has for many years taught quite differently, and as a result has brought about much evil and confusion . . . So long as you remain associated with the world-wide Pentecostal movement, and so long as you do not retract your first book and withdraw it from sale, and do not admit in your second book that for many long years Mülheim has spread a false doctrine, it is impossible for me, and certainly impossible for Gnadau to offer you the hand of fellowship. With deep sadness,
>
> Your old friend,
>
> Hermann Schöpwinkel[31]

There is no doubt that Krust's hope represents an advance upon the earlier teaching of the Mülheim movement. But Krust can appeal to a powerful tradition within the history of his movement. In the teaching of Jonathan Paul in particular, different views seem to exist in parallel with each other.

(*b*) *Sanctification and baptism*

Jonathan Paul's doctrine of sanctification must be interpreted against the biographical background of this unassuming and learned theologian, for whom even his opponents have a high regard. On 17 June 1890 Paul underwent an experience of sanctification which was associated with a vision, and which led him amongst other things to abstain from smoking; he did not regard smoking as a sin in itself, but he wanted to devote the money saved to the church's mission. In Giese's view Paul's description of this experience of sanctification[32]

> is by no means of a mystical or ecstatic nature. If the account is read closely, it can clearly be seen that it is dictated not by any extraordinary mental impulse, or any exalted emotion, but by a perfectly sober self-criticism, which was the basis of this critical and decisive experience. Therefore Paul never regarded himself as a mystic or ecstatic.[33]

According to Scripture this experience of sanctification, also known as the baptism of the Spirit, ought to occur suddenly. But Paul is unwilling to deny that those who have not experienced this sudden baptism of the Spirit possess the gift of the Holy Spirit.[34] On various occasions Paul testified about his experience, and he lays particular stress on one point:

> I would like to express the wish that . . . what I have said should not be understood as a doctrine but as what it is, a testimony of what the death and resurrection of Jesus has brought me.[35]

I here cite a few characteristic aspects of Paul's doctrine of sanctification, from his own testimony:

> One who is reborn, therefore, not only desires to do the will of God, but is also able to do it.[36]

> It was at the beginning of the century that there was intense interest in the question of sanctification, brought to the fore by Pastor Paul, to such an extent that scarcely a single conference at that time could ignore it. I was once present when a speaker in a public address expressed wonder that amongst those taking part in the conference, who included Pastor Paul himself, there were some who imagined that already, in their ordinary life, they had reached perfection. When this challenge failed to produce its effect, since Pastor Paul did not allow himself to be provoked into replying, the speaker went on to make a personal attack and cried out to the meeting, 'I must now ask Paul, who is amongst us, whether he regards himself as perfect.'
> Very quietly Pastor Paul rose from his seat, went to the rostrum and replied as follows: 'If anyone wants to know what I think about myself, I now declare that I am a perfect rotter!'[37]

Paul's teaching has not been properly understood, either by his opponents[38] or by his friends. Admittedly, Paul has been to some extent responsible for this by reason of his obscure and contradictory accounts, which are the result of the different pastoral situations in which they were made. If one attempts to reduce to a clear formula the doctrine of sanctification, expressed, in a laborious, inflated style, in his voluminous writings, it turns out to be a doctrine of perfection such as had already been taught by Wesley.[39] This can be clearly seen from his concept of sin:

> Only culpable failings are sin, not blameless ones . . . Where there is disobedience there is sin; and where there is obedience, there is no sin, but human shortsightedness and limitation . . . Consequently, a pure heart is a heart purified of disobedience (Heb. 8.10). We see from this that what matters is not the extent of the knowledge one possesses, but obedience . . . Thus what matters is that according to one's knowledge one is obedient to the Spirit of God and allows oneself to be led by him.[40]

The judgment just quoted is confirmed by his comments on his translation of the New Testament (the 'Mülheim' Testament; e.g. the commentary on John 1). I hope that I have done something here towards reconciling the completely opposed positions adopted by Erich von Eicken[41] and Ernst Giese.[42] Paul believed in perfect redemption from known, wilful sin.

In its doctrine of baptism the Mülheim movement adopts a middle position. Jonathan Paul and his colleagues in the established churches were champions of infant baptism, although they did not reject believer's baptism. In several theological treatises Jonathan Paul, the founder of the German Pentecostal movement, defended infant baptism[43] – an abomination in the eyes of most present day Pentecostals outside the Mülheim movement. In Paul's view it was clear that the Bible does not make rebirth a condition for baptism.[44]

(*c*) *The inspiration of the Bible*

Both Jonathan Paul[45] and other representatives of the Mülheim movement reacted against the fundamentalist understanding of the Bible which dominates the world-wide Pentecostal movement at the present day. For Krust the Holy Spirit speaks to us 'in the Scripture'. 'This neither prevents nor makes superfluous the objective scholarly study of the Scripture.'[46]

An important contribution on the subject of verbal inspiration had already been made by P. Gericke, a doctor and a prominent member of the Mülheim movement. His position, which differs from that of Pentecostal fundamentalism, is too little known.

> I still regard it as my duty to make clear from the first my attitude to what is known as 'verbal inspiration', that is the literal inspiration of holy Scripture by the Spirit of God. When I declare that I accept the full and total inspiration of Scripture, but not verbal inspiration, I realize that many readers will regard this with hostility or at least with astonishment. For many groups of believers cling to verbal inspiration as an unassailable fact. I would like them to consider whether it is right either out of pure piety or even from tradition to persist in a view with which, if one is honest, one cannot oneself be satisfied, and which must also bring one into conflict with those who think differently, since one is not able to refute their opposing view. Is it not now the time to be clear about this very important matter? As is well known, supporting evidence of the doctrine of verbal inspiration is chiefly sought from II Tim. 3.16: 'All scripture is inspired by God and profitable for teaching, for reproof, for correction, and for training in righteousness.' It is accepted of course that the Scripture, or the 'Scriptures', the books, gospels, epistles etc., are inspired by God. That is, God clearly showed the writers through his Spirit what they should write. But the instrument through whom God desires to speak to men and does speak is a man himself. Besides, every man has his own personal nature, and also his own particular way of expressing himself. God, of course, knows this; and so he lets men exercise their individuality. For example, when two people wish or need to express the same idea, it is possible for them to do so in the same way as far as the meaning is concerned, but not in exactly the same words. And human imperfections, such as an inability to concentrate, lapses of memory, and so forth also play their part. Even the writers of the word of God are not necessarily free from these. One may perhaps consider an event to be less important than the other does, so that he does not record it, or mentions it only in passing ...
>
> Or else, for example, both may have been present at the same conversation. But some words will have remained in one's mind, other words in the other's, and they will write them down accordingly. This explains many of the variations in the way the four evangelists record events or conversations.[47]

After referring to the different traditions of the question put by the sons of Zebedee, and of Jesus' words on the cross, he continues:

> But these two examples are sufficient to show that the idea of verbal inspiration is untenable. Is it possible, in spite of this, to call the Bible the word of God? Absolutely! We are concerned with the content, not the form. The former is of divine origin. Through it God sought to make his divine will known to man, and since he chose the written word for this purpose, he had to take into account the imperfection of human writers. How can we get round this if we cling obstinately to the strict doctrine of verbal inspiration? Take the New Testament alone. Many variations can be found even in the different Greek copies of the original text. Again, one must remember that there are many different translations into modern languages. How can we speak here of literal agreement? . . .
>
> It follows from what we have said that it is not only perverse but also dangerous to cling to the letter of the Scripture. It is not the letter that matters, but the meaning. But the meaning cannot be understood until it is made clear to us by the Holy Spirit, for the natural man apprehends nothing from the Spirit of God, but his Spirit explores all things, even the depths of the Godhead. Paul's statement that 'the written code kills but the Spirit gives life' should be our guide in this matter.[48]

3. *Still Brethren*

On 4 July 1959 a discussion took place in Hagen between the Mülheim movement and the German Evangelical Alliance, which led to a union.[49] But the Gnadau Union remained as distrustful as before, although at a meeting on 30 October 1963 in Darmstadt H. Haarbeck affirmed that 'all the principal objections which Gnadau has felt obliged to make against the Mülheim movement on the basis of the holy Scripture have been settled in a clear doctrinal fashion'.[50] This attitude can only be explained by the fact that the Gnadau movement regards its battle against the Pentecostal movement as its life work.[51]

Hutten's assessment of the situation is more positive. On 27 May 1964 he wrote to Krust:

> I have done my best to study as profoundly as possible the history of the Mülheim Association, and can clearly see that its leaders, after the early period of confusion, devoted themselves with great energy to ensuring that the Association was guided by holy Scripture and rejected dangerous temptations and developments with increasing clarity and decisiveness. As a result it has come to have a unique position in the whole Pentecostal movement. In this way it could and really must form a point of reference for the other Pentecostal bodies in Germany and in the world. This would avert numerous dangers. Unfortunately the others are too convinced that they are right and follow their own way . . .[52]

In the meantime the Arbeitsgemeinschaft christlicher Kirchen (Working

Association of Christian Churches, a kind of German Council of Churches) in Frankfurt intervened. More discussions and contacts with the Mülheim movement took place, but Gnadau continued to stand aside. The consultation in June 1967 between the Mülheim movement and the Working Association was particularly important.[53]

The second working party (November 1969), on the understanding of the Holy Spirit in the Old and New Testaments,[54] included not only representatives of the established churches (Lutheran, Reformed and Roman Catholic), the Free Churches and the Mülheim movement, but also pastors from the Pentecostal Arbeitsgemeinschaft der Christengemeinden (Working Fellowship of Christian Churches).[55] The teaching and religious practice of the last group is somewhat similar to that of the Assemblies of God. The discussions turned out to be very valuable, although Ferdinand Hahn, the New Testament professor in Heidelberg, stated quite frankly in his introductory paper that he regarded critical and historical exegesis, if not as the only possible method of Bible study, at least as one which was essential and valuable in the present discussion. The future is likely to bring the Pentecostal movement and the other churches in Germany closer together. This can also be seen from the fact that the Mülheim movement sent its secretary, Christian Krust, as an observer delegate to the Fourth Full Assembly of the World Council of Churches in Uppsala (1968). It could well be that his paper in Uppsala on the subject of the Pentecostal movement and ecumenism[56] may be the beginning of a new ecumenical phase in the history of the Mülheim movement.

It is even more important for the Mülheim Association to enter into dialogue not only with the churches, but also with biblical scholars. This is the only way in which it can maintain the Reformation position which it has come to adopt and represent so emphatically within the rest of the Pentecostal movement. With its congregations in mind, it may be hard for Mülheim to admit that it has on occasion advanced teachings contrary to the spirit of the Reformation – though the German Evangelical movement has done just the same. Because of its numerous publications aimed against the Pentecostal movement, it will be some time before Gnadau can finally renounce the 'Berlin Declaration'. To do as Gnadau does, and demand that Mülheim should break with the world-wide Pentecostal movement, is short-sighted parish pump politics. In Africa and Latin America the Pentecostal congregations will one day form an essential part of the Protestant churches there. It would be a real ecumenical aim for an open-minded German Pentecostal movement, recognized by its fellow Protestant churches, to show them the way towards a Reformation theology.

NOTES

1. In German: Christlicher Gemeinschaftsverband GmbH [= Ltd or Inc.] Mülheim/Ruhr. Sources, documents, literature: 05.07.008. Statistics: at least 25,000 members; journal: *Heilszeugnisse*.

2. Sources, documents, literature: 05.07.003.

3. Reply of the 'Mülheim Conference': Fleisch II/2, pp. 143ff.; L. Steiner, *Mit folgenden Zeichen*, pp. 198ff.

4. *Vertrauliche Erklärung*, reprinted from *Pfingstgrüsse* 3, 1910, pp. 89–91 (but without agreement on practical details); Krust I, pp. 83f.; Fleisch II/2, pp. 176ff.

5. E. von Eicken, *Heiliger Geist*, p. 32.

6. Fleisch II/2.

7. *Der Kampf der Pfingstbewegung*, reprinted from *Pfingstgrüsse* 2–3, published by the Verlag der Gesellschaft für Mission, Diakonie und Kolportage, Mülheim/Ruhr.

8. Fleisch II/2, p. 194.

9. Cf. above, ch. 16, pp. 231ff.

10. Emil Humburg ('E.H.'), *Pfingstgrüsse* 6/47, 23.9.1914, p. 363.

11. G. von Viehbahn, *Allianzblatt*; *Pfingstgrüsse* 7/8, 22.11.1914, p. 57.

12. *Pfingstgrüsse* 7/28, 11.4.1915, p. 217, 'Heeresfolge' (from *Heilig dem Herrn*).

13. *Pfingstgrüsse* 7/10, 6.12.1914, pp. 77f.

14. *Heilszeugnisse* 17, 1932; Fleisch II/2, p. 345.

15. Fleisch II/2, p. 345.

16. Fleisch II/2, p. 346. On the history of the *Gemeinschaftsbewegung* during the Third Reich, cf. E. G. Rüppel, *Gemeinschaftsbewegung*.

17. There are the usual extreme appeals for sanctification, which avoid any concrete examples. The only reference to the actual situation is perhaps the sentence: 'People ignore the fact that there is a leader (*Führer*) who is above all leaders, who alone can help us, and who is near to everyone in his mercy.' (Krust I, pp. 175ff.)

18. *VdV* 25/4, April 1932, p. 15.

19. Fleisch II/2, p. 347.

20. Richard Ruff (?), *VdV* 27/7, July 1934, p. 14.

21. C. Carmichael, *PE* 2467, 20.8.1961, pp. 25f.; N. Nikoloff, *PE* 2398, 24.4.1960, pp. 4ff.

22. C. Carmichael, *loc. cit.*

23. W. Argue, *PE* 2711, 24.4.1966, p. 9.

24. *P* 46, 1958, p. 11.

25. J. Paul (?), *Pfingstgrüsse* 1/1, Feb. 1909, p. 2. Cf. also C. Krust, *Heilszeugnisse* 52/2, Feb. 1967, pp. 24ff.; 52/3, March 1967, pp. 38ff.

26. J. Paul ('P'), *Pfingstgrüsse* 2/1, Oct. 1909, p. 8; J. Paul (?), *Pfingstgrüsse* 2/19, 24.7.1910, p. 151. *Der Kampf der Pfingstbewegung* (see n. 7 above), pp. 6f.

27. Fleisch II/2, pp. 79f. Fleisch comments: 'This is different from what was reported in the first accounts in 1906/07 [i.e. before the rise of Pentecostalism in the German Evangelical movement, W.H.].'; R.S., *Pfingstgrüsse* 2/6, 23.1.1910, p. 7; similarly, J. Paul, *Pfingstgrüsse* 8/26, 26.3.1916, pp. 201ff.; 8/27, 2.4.1916, pp. 209ff.

28. Krust II, p. 74.

29. *Ibid.*, p. 107.

30. *Ibid.*, pp. 109f.

31. H. Schöpwinkel, letter to C. Krust, 29.10.1963.

32. J. Paul, *Ihr werdet die Kraft des Heiligen Geistes empfangen*, 1896, pp. 399ff.; quoted in E. Giese, *Jonathan Paul*, pp. 24ff. The passage is omitted in the third edition of Paul's book (1956).

33. E. Giese, *op. cit.*, p. 27.

34. J. Paul, *Kraft des Geistes*, 3rd ed., p. 17.

35. Fleisch, I/1, p. 127.

36. J. Paul, *Kraft des Geistes*, 1896, p. 41. Quoted by E. Giese, *Jonathan Paul*, p. 51. I could not find this passage in the third edition of Paul's book.

37. *Heilszeugnisse* 1931, pp. 328f.; quoted E. Giese, *Jonathan Paul*, p. 105.

38. Thimme, *Auf der Warte* 1920/21; Fleisch II/2; J. Paul, *Pfingstgrüsse* 6/22, 1.3.1914, pp. 168ff.

39. 'In the view I hold I am in the fullest sense a follower of John Wesley; I have also been conscious of being in full agreement with the substance of Stockmayer's doctrine in his tract *Gnade und Sünde* ['Grace and Sin'], even though I have used other expressions, in accordance with my own understanding of Scripture.' J. Paul, *Lied des Lammes*, Oct. 1919, quoted in E. Giese, *Jonathan Paul*, p. 223.

40. J. Paul, 'Das reine Herz', *Die Heilung* 139, April 1910, pp. 19f.

41. E. von Eicken, *Heilger Geist*, p. 28: 'This amounts to perfectionism. He has gone beyond the limits to untramelled enthusiasm.' Cf. also H. Haarbeck, *Meiner Gnade*, p. 63.

42. 'Thus there can be no question of perfectionism.' E. Giese, *op. cit.*, p. 329.

43. J. Paul, 'Taufe im Vollsinn', *Pfingstgrüsse* 3/3, 16.10.1910, p. 23; Krust II, p. 136; Fleisch II/2, pp. 351f.; K. Hutten, *Seher*, 8th ed., 1962, p. 495; *MD* 26, 1963, p. 68; cf. also L. Eisenlöffel, 'Taufe und Kirchenverständnis', in W. J. Hollenweger (ed.), *Die Pfingstkirchen*.

44. J. Paul, *Taufe und Geistestaufe*.

45. Cf. above, ch. 16.1(*a*), p. 219.

46. Krust II, p. 117. Cf. also C. O. Voget, *Pfingstbotschaft* 1921, pp. 201ff.; quoted in Krust I, pp. 237ff.; Krust II, p. 120.

47. P. Gericke, *Christliche Volkommenheit*, p. 16.

48. *Ibid.*, p. 18.

49. Sources, documents, literature: 05.07.008d.

50. Minutes of the session of 30 October 1963.

51. H. Haarbeck, *Meiner Gnade*, 1965; reply by C. Krust, *Heilszeugnisse* 51/8, Aug. 1966.

52. K. Hutten, letter to C. Krust, 27.5.1964.

53. W. J. Hollenweger, *Oekumenische Rundschau* 17/1, Jan. 1958, pp. 57ff.; O. Schulz, *Evangelische Welt* 21/14, 16.7.1967, p. 416; C. Krust, *Heilszeugnisse* 52/9, Sept. 1967, pp. 131ff.

54. Minutes, Oekumenische Centrale, Frankfurt; C. Lemke, *Der Leuchter* 21/2, Feb. 1970, pp. 5f.

55. For reasons of space the chapter on the Arbeitsgemeinschaft der Christengemeinden in Deutschland ('Working Fellowship of Christian Churches in Germany') has been omitted from the English edition (German edition, pp. 231ff.).

56. Ecumenical relations have frequently been discussed in the Mülheim movement: Chr. Krust, *Heilszeugnisse* 52/7, 1.7.1967, pp. 98–102; L. Steiner, *Heilszeugnisse* 52/1, 1.1.1967, pp. 3–4; Chr. Krust, *Heilszeugnisse* 53/8, 1.8.1968, pp. 114f.; 53/10, 1.10.1968, pp. 146–59; 53/11, 1.11.1968, pp. 163–6, 171–4 (ample reports from Uppsala); 53/12, 1.12.1968, pp. 180–5 (report of Section I from Uppsala); H. Rottmann, *Heilszeugnisse* 53/12, 1.12.1968, pp. 179–80; cf. below, ch. 30.4(*d*), p. 451.

18

Charismatic Revival within the Established Churches: A New Chance?

1. *First Steps*

IN THE last few years the way has been prepared within the established Protestant churches and the free churches in Germany for a new 'charismatic revival'. According to Wilhard Becker[1] three elements go to make up this process:

(*a*) *The rediscovery of the laity in the church*

This movement, which can be observed in every church in the world, received a great impetus in Germany as a result of the war, when congregations grew accustomed to existing without their ministers, who were at the front.

(*b*) *The ecumenical element*

> In trenches, concentration camps and prisoner-of-war camps, or during air raids, people of different denominations and groups were forced together by external pressure and shared a common fate and life.

Confessional boundaries were of secondary importance. A common eucharist was celebrated against all church regulations.

> These experiences proved strong enough to lead to the formation of lasting contacts after the disappearance of the external circumstances, and to lead to the formation of new groups.[2]

(*c*) *Eschatological character*

The war was interpreted as a period of trial, preparation and sanctification. Evangelistic movements, team missions, and associations resembling religious orders[3] sprang into life, and prophecy, speaking in tongues and the healing of the sick through prayer occurred spontaneously in them.

> Through the ecumenical church conferences of the Swiss Christian Service Association, which has been held for many years in Rüschlikon (Switzerland),

the first contacts were made with Russian Orthodox and Roman Catholic Christians, who have also undergone charismatic experiences. But these fellowships and groups rarely discussed the gifts of the Spirit at work amongst them, and published no 'news letters', so that the charismatic life present amongst them exercised an effect only on those who came into direct contact with such groups.[4]

2. *A German Pastor Discovers Pentecost outside 'Pentecost'*[5]

Pastor Arnold Bittlinger, who at the time was head of the Home Mission Department of the Church of the Palatinate, was undertaking a study tour as the guest of the Lutheran World Federation. His host, the Lutheran delegate to the American Government and head of the Washington branch of the National Council of the Lutheran Church, introduced him to the charismatic movement which had broken out in numerous Lutheran congregations in America. In the course of his official tour he visited several Lutheran and Anglican congregations which had been seized by this revival, and 'became convinced of the non-enthusiastic and non-ecstatic character of this movement'. But Bittlinger rejects the interpretation which most of its adherents give to the movement in America, and attempts to assess the phenomenon without adopting the dogmas of Pentecostalism: 'I am disturbed at the development in the USA, where the Pentecostal vocabulary is simply transferred to the new charismatic revival.'[6] He gives a warning against a fundamentalist attempt to reconcile the statements concerning the gifts of the Spirit in the New Testament, and follows Eduard Schweizer in distinguishing *different* forms of the church in the New Testament. He is clear – and here again he differs from the Pentecostals – that the lists of gifts of the Spirit given in the New Testament are not complete. He decisively rejects a distinction between natural and supernatural gifts:

> If we clearly realize that marriage is as much a charisma as prophecy, and administration as much as speaking in tongues, then it is clear that we must follow Paul in making no distinction between natural and supernatural gifts, between ordinary and extraordinary gifts; rather, all gifts are supernaturally natural and extraordinarily ordinary . . . The tragedy of the Pentecostals is that they place the so-called 'extraordinary' gifts such as the healing of the sick, prophecy, speaking in tongues, etc. in the foreground, and in the process forget the so-called 'ordinary' gifts. On the other hand, I have the impression that in our church work a higher value is placed on the 'ordinary' ministries than on the 'extraordinary', and indeed, that the latter are something to which we have hardly paid any attention . . . Thus we too make the fateful distinction between 'ordinary' and 'extraordinary' gifts. But there are no charismata which always remain pure charismata without the danger of abuse. I am convinced that in our present-day congregations the charisma of marriage is much more seriously abused and deformed than speaking in tongues amongst the Pentecostals.[7]

With regard to the hierarchy between 'natural' and 'supernatural', and between fruit and gift, he refuses to resolve the problem by recalling in a facile way that love is greater than speaking in tongues. (Logically he would also have to add faith and knowledge, for they are likewise both subordinate to love – which shows that for Paul the theological concept of love is not one opposed to the gifts of the Spirit, but is the principle of their application.) Instead, he tries to present a functional understanding of the gifts of the Spirit: 'The greatest and most important gift is always that which is necessary at the time.'[8]

In numerous publications and practical experiments he tried to arrive at a clear picture of the significance of charismatic congregations in the framework of an established church and on the basis of Reformation theology. He had to give special consideration to the disputed gift of speaking in tongues, not only because it is mentioned in writings both in favour of and opposed to the Pentecostal movement, but also because 'to some extent it is wrongly described in scholarly studies, as a result of the misconception of it in Pentecostalism and of the alleged parallels to it in paganism'. But he pointed out that:

> Abuse is avoided not where there is opposition to charisma, but where charisma is properly exercised . . . The church can certainly learn from the errors of the Pentecostal movement, but should not adopt the theology and practice of this movement; rather, it should rethink the question of the gifts of the Spirit with the aid of holy Scripture.[9]

3. *The Movement Takes Root in Germany*

On his return Bittlinger was invited by many congregations and movements to describe his experiences in the USA. The pastor who was his host, Larry Christenson, visited Germany several times. One of the first meetings took place in August 1963 in Enkenbach in the Palatinate. Following this, there came into being both in West Germany and East Germany groups which regularly met in private houses for prayer meetings at which prophecy, speaking in tongues and the healing of the sick through prayer were practised. Those who belonged to these prayer circles remained members of their own churches, whether established or free. 'There were no tendencies to break away into separate sects, or when they occurred they were immediately corrected.'

The way New Testament scholarships forms part of the training of those who take part in these meetings is of particular importance. The meetings include theologians who do not conceal the exegetical discoveries made by New Testament scholarship. Another feature is the considerable participation by Roman Catholic and Orthodox Christians in the 'Ecumenical Church Conferences' at Königstein/Taunus and in the Ecumenical Academy at Schloss Crahein.

4. *Differences between this Movement and the Pentecostal Movement*

In this section I compare the religious practice and teaching of the Pentecostal movement with that of the charismatic groups within the established churches in Germany. The source from which I draw my account of the teachings of the 'charismatic revival' are the writings of A. Bittlinger, R. F. Edel,[10] and above all the definitive account given by Wolf-Eckart Failing, which is based on an extensive study of the literature.[11]

Failing lists the following main theological principles:

1. It is God himself who is the basis of his mission and who carries it out (*missio Dei*).
2. The sending of his Son, that is the cross and resurrection of Christ, cannot be improved upon, and cannot be supplemented, as the expression of God's 'once for all' and of his final and ultimate promise.
3. The church is in its essence the body of Christ, and as such the presence in this world and the 'instrument' of the divine mission. Mission is its fundamental structural principle.[12] It is the will of Jesus Christ to work today in and upon this world through the church. Thus the form the church should take is missionary, charismatic and ecumenical.
4. In order for the church to take this form in reality, God promised and bestowed upon his church the power of the Holy Spirit, which is expressed in the fruit and gifts of the Spirit 'as the individuation of grace' (Käsemann), and so takes concrete shape.
5. Every reborn Christian is a 'charismatic': 'We Christians do not look for a special act of the reception of the Spirit in "sealing" or "the baptism of the Spirit", but we know that the Holy Spirit dwells in every Christian and desires to be visible in every Christian.'[13]
6. A charismatic is a person who is liberated by God's activity through his Holy Spirit for the use of his own proper gifts (proper in the sense of being willed by God), and who makes them available primarily for the building up of the church and its service in the world.[14]
7. Anyone who exercises a charisma acts as a member of the body of Christ. All members are of equal value and have equal rights.[15] There are three ways in which charismatic activity can be distinguished and more closely defined. It takes place:
   (*a*) in dependence upon Jesus Christ (I Cor. 12.3).
   (*b*) according to the measure of faith (Rom. 12.3).
   (*c*) as a realization of love (I Cor. 13).
8. In relation to the forms in which charismata are manifested, a hierarchy of value is unthinkable.[16]
9. Every gift of God, however 'natural' it is, is a charisma if it serves to glorify the Lord of the world and the church and to spread the kingdom of Christ . . .[17]

10. Where all are charismatics, there cannot be any ministerial authority bestowed institutionally. 'This means concretely that authority and charisma is only manifested as genuine in the act of ministry, so only he who ministers can have authority, and that only in the actual exercise of his ministry.'[18] Thus ministerial authority depends on charisma and spiritual authority.
11. 'If the Church order is understood as a manifestation of the Spirit, and a witness to the Lord who lives in the church, it must be apparent particularly in the worship of the Church.'[19] Thus charismatic worship at prayer meetings in the new movement is important as providing an example. It has a particular function as an exercise and training in dependence on God and in experiencing the fact that he disposes of man and not man of him. It is a constant and concrete renewal of the experience 'that the church can only exist as the community of Christ in so far as grace repeatedly lays hold on us and re-creates us as instruments of his service, and that we must leave him to care for the continuity of the church, who alone is able to ensure the continuance of grace.'[20] These services are also an opportunity to learn to listen to one another in the fulness of the gifts of the Spirit. The climax of this is the eucharist. Services are not seen here as a changed form of 'cult', but as an occasion for recollection in 'reasonable worship', and the first steps towards it, in the midst of the everyday life of the world.
12. The most urgent theological question with regard to the church is the following: How can institutional churches, groups firmly settled in their ways, and traditional movements take on a charismatic structure?[21] How can they become dynamic and mobile, and charismatically 'permeable', that is, permeable to the will and the action of *God*, so that the Kingdom of Christ is visibly manifest in space and time?[22]

If these guiding theological principles are compared to the teaching of the Mülheim Association of Christian Fellowships (ch. 17), differences can be seen in the theological climate in which they are propounded and in the style in which they are expressed. W. Failing goes to some trouble to adopt the language in use among German theologians, while that adopted by the Mülheim Association derives from pietism.

When a comparison is made with the Working Fellowship of Christian Churches a number of fundamental theological differences appear:

1. The Working Fellowship sees the baptism of the Spirit as a particular experience, usually characterized by speaking in tongues. This view is rejected by the 'charismatic revival' (see para. 5 of the summary above).
2. The distinction between natural and supernatural which is of fundamental importance to the Working Fellowship is rejected by the 'charismatic revival' (para. 8 and 9 of the summary above).

3. Although there are differences in the atmosphere of their worship and religious outlook,[23] these have no theological relevance, because the sociological composition of the 'charismatic revival' is different from that of the Working Fellowship. On the other hand it must be clearly stated that the American 'charismatic revival' is theologically closer to the Pentecostal free churches than the charismatic revival in Germany, although it must be admitted that it has much in common from the sociological point of view with the German charismatic movement.

In conclusion, we can affirm that the groups involved in the German charismatic revival have succeeded in breaking down the Pentecostal system of stages of salvation. It could well be that the theological assessment called for by the scholar who is best acquainted with the German Pentecostal movement, Paul Fleisch,[24] is being undertaken – a truly ecumenical contribution on the part of German theology. It is an important and welcome fact that none of the publications of this group are examples of the works of edification, hostile to scholarship, which are produced for purposes of evangelization. On the contrary, it represents a noteworthy contribution to the overcoming of the fundamentalism which is found in the Pentecostal movement, without abandoning the ideas and practices which charismatic churches wish to defend.

The Pentecostal movement itself has shown great joy at the acceptance and development of Pentecostal ideas and practices in the established churches.[25] Think of the possible significance for Pentecostals, opposed and mocked by the fundamentalists who form the rest of their brethren, of the occurrence of charismatic phenomena which are not interpreted according to the fundamentalist system that exists in Pentecostalism and which are experienced by people who are not afraid of academic theology, and do not have a negative and hostile attitude to existing established and free churches.

Unfortunately, there has not yet been in the Pentecostal movement any very serious attempt to come to terms with the *theological* work of the 'charismatic revival'.

NOTES

1. W. Becker, in R. F. Edel (ed.), *Kirche und Charisma*, pp. 160f.
2. W.-E. Failing, in W. J. Hollenweger (ed.), *Die Pfingstkirchen*, p. 132.
3. E.g. 'Evangelische Marienschwestern' (Protestant Sisters of Mary), 'Vereinigung vom gemeinsamen Leben' (Society of the Common Life).
4. W.-E. Failing, *op. cit.*
5. In the USA, see above, ch. 1, pp. 3ff.
6. A. Bittlinger, letter to W.H., 18.12.1963.
7. A. Bittlinger, 'Bedeutung der Charismen', pp. 9f. For a discussion of the gifts of the Spirit see below, ch. 25.4, p. 370; also Bittlinger, *Gifts and Graces*, pp. 70ff.
8. A Bittlinger, 'Bedeutung der Charismen', p. 11.

9. A. Bittlinger, *Das Sprachenreden*, Preface.

10. See bibliography.

11. W.-E. Failing, in W. J. Hollenweger (ed.), *Die Pfingstkirchen*, pp. 131–45.

12. Cf. T. Wieser (ed.), *Planning for Mission.*

13. A. Bittlinger, *Der früchristliche Gottesdienst*, p. 9.

14. E. Käsemann, *Exegetische Versuche* I, p. 119; ET: *Essays on NT Themes*, pp. 75f.: 'Paul's doctrine of the charismata is to be understood as the projection into ecclesiology of the doctrine of justification by faith and as such makes it unmistakably clear that a purely individualistic interpretation of justification cannot legitimately be constructed from the Apostle's own teaching.'

15. 'A situation in which all Christians are regarded as endowed with charisma is a situation which does not admit the possibility of sacred space, sacred time, the right of representative action in the cult, of sacred persons, . . . persons thought of as specially privileged . . . The fenced-off boundaries of "religion" are broken through when grace invades the world and its everyday life.' (E. Käsemann, *op. cit.* I, pp. 121f.; *Essays*, p. 78.)

16. Cf. A. Bittlinger, above p. 245 and *Charisma und Amt*, pp. 14ff.

17. W. Becker in R. F. Edel (ed.), *Kirche und Charisma*, p. 167. Käsemann writes: 'The charismata are validated not by the *fascinosum* of the preternatural but by the edification of the community . . . No spiritual endowment has value, rights or privileges on its own account' (*op. cit.*, p. 112; *Essays*, pp. 66f.).

18. E. Käsemann, *op. cit.*, p. 121; *Essays*, p. 78.

19. E. Schweizer, *Gemeinde und Gemeindeordnung*, 2nd ed., 1960, §27a; ET: *Church Order in the NT*, §27a (p. 220).

20. E. Käsemann, *op. cit.*, p. 134; *Essays*, p. 94.

21. Cf. the writings of H. Küng and N. A. Nissiotis on the 'charismatic structure of the church'.

22. Quoted and abbreviated from W.-E. Failing, in W. J. Hollenweger (ed.), *Die Pfingstkirchen*, pp. 139–42. References taken from the original.

23. Emotional or sober, loud or quiet, etc.

24. 'I have not tried to pass any judgment. I have only sought to present and preserve the material necessary for a thorough theological and psychological assessment.' Fleisch II/2, p. 6.

25. A. Bittlinger emphasizes that he came across the phenomenon of charismatic reality outside the Pentecostal movement. He discovered this revival in the American Lutheran churches. But the connection between the charismatic revival in the American Lutheran churches and the Pentecostal movement has been demonstrated. Cf. L. Christenson, *Trinity* 1/2, 1962, pp. 32ff.; *PE* 2493, 18.2.1962, p. 25.

19

'The Religion of the Proud Poor': The Pentecostal Movement in Italy

1. *From a Tiny 'Sect' to the Leading Protestant Church*

THE father of the Italian Pentecostal movement is Luigi Francescon, the founder of the Congregação Cristã do Brasil.[1] Francescon, who came from a Waldensian congregation in Cavaso Nuovo (Udine), joined the Pentecostal movement in North America and was baptized by William Durham.[2] He in his turn converted Giacomo Lombardi to the 'full gospel'. In 1908 Lombardi returned to Italy and at first tried without success to bring the Pentecostal message to Italian Protestants. When he was walking in Rome he heard a voice which said to him, 'Follow the man who is walking in front of you and speak to him of my name.'[3] Lombardi spoke to this man. He was converted and became the first Italian Pentecostal.

The movement rapidly spread over the whole country. In 1929 there were Pentecostal congregations in 149 places in Italy, 25 of which owned their own place of assembly. There was an attempt to set up a link with what is today known as the 'Christian Church of North America'[4] in the United States, but this failed.

The first national conference took place in 1928 with Francescon as its chairman.[5] The 27 representatives who were present discussed the 'Council of Jerusalem' (Acts 15); they followed the apostolic decree in so far as they also forbade the eating of blood. At the second national conference in 1929 there were already 58 representatives. This time, the theme was the baptism of the Spirit. From 1935 to 1958 the Italian Pentecostals had to endure severe persecutions. All meetings, 'in whatsoever form they were held',[6] were forbidden. This led to arrests on ridiculous grounds; for example, when Pentecostals met each other on the street, or called to visit each other, this was regarded as a forbidden meeting 'in whatsoever form it was held'.[7] 'It was a period of frequent court cases, arrests, exiles, threatenings, beatings and martyrdom.'[8] The legal provisions were made even more severe by the decrees of 28 August 1939 and

13 March 1940. The Italian Pentecostal pastor Roberto Bracco points out that the intensification of the persecution coincides first with the outbreak of the Abyssinian war, and secondly with the Italian declaration of war upon England and the USA. Many pastors were arrested. Others fled, but the work went on in secret. 'The word of God was carried to inaccessible places, was preached in the prisons, was proclaimed before Fascist judges and authorities.'[9] After the war the *Assemblee di Dio* (Assemblies of God) tried to organize themselves in order to achieve final religious freedom. This attempt was first made with the aid of the *Chiese Christiana del Nord America* (Christian Churches of North America),[10] but the attempt failed. In 1947 an agreement was concluded with the American Assemblies of God, which guaranteed a degree of financial help to the Italian congregations, but on the other hand made them doctrinally dependent on America. The *Consiglio Federale delle Chiese Evangeliche* (Federal Council of Protestant Churches), with the aid of the advocates Leopoldo Piccardi, Carlo Arturo Jemolo and Giacomo Rosapepe succeeded in 1954, in an appeal to the Council of State, in obtaining a legal decision declaring the persecution of Pentecostals illegal.[11] Since then the Assemblies of God have always carried local cases on to the highest court in Rome and won them with the aid of the advocates named above – who do not belong to the Pentecostal movement. In this process they have received the support of both Catholic and Communist lawyers.

The total number of Pentecostals in Italy is over 200,000, which is twice as many as all other Protestants together.[12]

(*a*) *Assemblee di Dio* (Assemblies of God)[13]

The *Assemblee di Dio* is now the second largest Pentecostal denomination in Italy. It publishes several newspapers, runs an orphanage in Ventosa, and has a Bible school in Rome with 100 students. Unfortunately it withdrew at the last minute from the newly constituted Federal Council of Protestant Churches, although the latter had assisted the Pentecostals during the time of their persecution.

Their doctrine can best be described as an uncritical fundamentalism, and includes the usual characteristic Pentecostal teachings: baptism by immersion, the baptism of the Spirit, the plenary inspiration of the Scripture, the necessity of conversion in order to escape eternal damnation, and the imminent second coming of Christ.[14] It has gone a long way in its evolution into an organized church. This can be seen particularly from the heavy emphasis placed on the office of the pastor:

> In the Christian church there are those who teach and those who are taught, that is, the pastor and the layman . . . The pastor has the duty of exercising the ministry, and therefore has the duty of applying himself constantly 'to the word and to prayer' (Acts 6.4), and the layman has the duty of listening to the word and of submitting to the authority of the minister . . . Just as he who has

received the ministry has the obligation to teach the layman, so the layman who enjoys the fruits of the ministry has the obligation to support him who teaches him from his own possessions.[15]

This is an astonishing development and may be related to the educational tasks that have to be undertaken within the Italian Pentecostal movement.

Ethical doctrine is rigorist. Thus the assembly in Rome expels those who are 'unbelievers'.[16] Pentecostals

> must demonstrate their liberation from the vices and passions of the old nature, and therefore must abstain from smoking, from alcohol and from any other vice which might subject them to dangerous habits. Similarly they must abstain from attending the cinema or the theatre, gymnasiums and playing fields, casinos and dance halls.[17]

This rigorism does not prevent the solo clarinettist of the Venice Opera from accompanying the hymns in the services of the Assembly of God. But he would never allow his wife or his sister to go to an opera in which he himself was playing. This gifted musician, who made his first public appearance at the age of nine, won his first competition when he was eleven, was teaching music at the Venice Conservatory by the time he was twenty-five, and has won first prize in every competition in which he has taken part, plays for the children of God in the services of the Assemblies of God, and plays for the children of the world in the theatre.

The ethical regulations pay particular attention to women's dress. Every means is used to prevent woman from becoming the 'accomplice of hell' by means of elegant low-cut dresses and seductive clothing.[18] This she would certainly become if she adopted the attitude of the modern movement for woman's emancipation.

> It is not the woman's part to decide when the husband can become a father. The father must decide when the woman shall become a mother . . . The woman is the gentle, tender, brave but submissive 'helpmate' of him who has a more direct responsibility before God than she for the life of the family.[19]

Here fundamentalism is associated with the patriachal image which the Italian man has of himself.

(*b*) *Chiesa Apostolica* (Apostolic Church)[20]

This group is much smaller than the *Assemblee di Dio*. It was founded by missionaries of the British Apostolic Church.[21] It has been growing constantly since 1950. In its teaching it follows its mother church in Britain, and like the Apostolic Church it lay emphasis on the prophetic and apostolic offices.[22]

(*c*) *Chiesa di Dio* (Church of God)[23]

An orphanage in Melito in Calabria and a number of congregations in southern Italy were founded by Umberto Lasco, formerly a partisan leader and a member of the Communist party. At first he was supported by the 'Free Swiss Mission for Calabria', based on Biel in Switzerland, which has since ceased to exist, and by the congregations led by Pastor Fritz de Rougemont.[24] By 1963 at the latest the work had been taken over by the *Chiesa di Dio*.[25] It is difficult to say whether its teaching is similar to that of its mother church in North America.[26]

(*d*) *Chiesa Evangelica Internazionale*

This is the youngest (and largest) Pentecostal church on the Italian scene (200 congregations, 200,000 members). It has drawn together many independent Pentecostal assemblies in Italy. It was founded by John McTernan, a pastor of the International Evangelical Church in the USA.[27] Its paper is called *Dialogo Cristiano*, and in fact all members of this church are asked to refrain from polemics against other Christians, in particular against Roman Catholics. It is not surprising in these circumstances that McTernan was introduced to the World Council of Churches by a Roman Catholic priest, and this introduction led to an official candidature of the Chiesa Evangelica Internazionale for membership in the World Council.

2. *The Mistrust of the 'Proud Poor': The Italian Pentecostal Movement and Ecumenism*

When the Buffarini-Guidi circular was brought into force on 9 April 1935,[28] the Italian Pentecostal movement was bitterly persecuted. Giorgio Spini has argued that the criminal Buffarini-Guidi (Mussolini's Minister of the Interior) signed and sent out the circular because Italy needed the support of the Pope in her policy of aggression against Abyssinia, and in fact from then on received it.[29] The Waldensian G. Peyrot has described it as the 'most serious act of religious intolerance'[30] since modern Italy came into being.

Peyrot, Pestalozza, Spini and others have published a depressing collection of material from the records of the Italian courts. Even worse is the fact that the Italian Pentecostals were still subjected to persecution after the second world war. A. C. Jemolo, Professor at the University of Rome, pleaded in 1944, from the point of view of a liberal, both for the continuance of the Roman Catholic Church as the established church and also for political and religious freedom. He exhorted the Catholic Church not to stick to the letter of the Lateran Treaties. The Fascist state had persecuted Protestants because its conscience was uneasy, and for reasons of mere opportunism. It hoped thereby to gain support of the Catholic Church. The Catholic Church should reject these tendencies of its own accord.[31] Unfortunately neither the Italian bishops nor the priests were at that time prepared to listen to this wise advice. For example, on 30 July 1952 Curci Michele, an elder in the Pentecostal church, was trying to get a workmate out of a well and was asphyxiated by the poisonous gases. The burial was to take place on 1 August. A large crowd wished to show their respect to their courageous fellow-citizen and attended the Protestant funeral service. But the Roman Catholic priest took objection to this. For days the civil parish refused burial in the cemetery, which was not church property. Finally, an energetic protest by the Communists enabled the Curci family to obtain its rights.[32] Spini's comment is:

> All this happened in 1952, the fourth year of the republican constitution, and eighty-two years after the fall of the temporal power of the Popes.[33]

It is easy to understand Spini's bitter words: the Minister of the Interior thinks that he must respect the republican constitution when it is a question of dealing with those who were convicted by the Fascist puppet government in Salò, but treat it as a joke when he is dealing with citizens who want to hold their religious services in peace.[34] On the basis of the circular the Pentecostals were punished for their resistance to Fascism right up to 1955!

> There is a risk that the defence of the freedom provided by the constitution will become a monopoly of the Communists. The way this confuses the issues in the political life of Italy is obvious to everyone. . . . What do the wretched clergy of Italy hope to achieve by stirring up the government to persecute Protestants? Do they believe that refusing residence permits, and arrests, are reasonable methods of converting a Protestant to Catholicism? Do they believe that the police are capable of stopping the drift away from the Catholic Church? When they close a chapel, the Protestants divide into groups which reassemble secretly in various houses . . . One of the *Carabinieri* would have to be placed on guard in front of the house of every Protestant believer to check that no one was going in to take part in a gospel meeting. But even this would not be enough. Besides the police there would have to be a priest to check that the policeman himself was resisting the temptation to listen to the gospel in secret. During the Fascist period there was a Pentecostal elder who took the opportunity during every spell of imprisonment to convert his guards.[35]

Against the principles of the constitution, the Protestants, and Pentecostals in particular, were deprived of their rights. In the census they were automatically counted as Catholics,[36] since from 1951 the form did not ask a person's religious denomination, but only to which Catholic parish he belonged. 'This went beyond even the wickedness of Fascism. Whether he wished or not, every Italian was from that moment made a parishioner of the church.'[37]

For years the old catch-phrase was applied, that Pentecostal worship was dangerous to health and should be forbidden for 'reasons of morality and public order'.[38]

> Article 8 of the Italian Constitution might well read: 'All denominations are equal before the law', but the Catholic-Conservative government and its judges made shabby excuses for not applying the provisions concerning

> religious freedom. They said that not every article of the Constitution was obligatory, but merely set out a programme. But even the obligatory articles, they would continue, cannot be put into operation at once, because they have to be more closely defined by a law drafted for the purpose. The provisions concerning religious freedom were naturally included in these articles.[39]

Il Mondo said of the Minister of the Interior, Scelba, who had still been appealing to the Buffarini circular, that he might add to the many titles he already possessed that of the 'Supreme Guardian and Healer of our Nerves and Health'.[40] Although the Federal Council of Evangelical Churches succeeded in bringing about in 1955 the withdrawal of the Buffarini circular, years passed before the provincial authorities noticed that the persecution of Protestants was against the Constitution. Persecutions still take place from time to time at the present day, but they are regularly quashed by the Supreme Court.

Peyrot leaves open the question

> whether the withdrawal of the Buffarini-Guidi circular is the first step in the direction of a policy of constitutional legalism with regard to religious freedom, or only the abandonment by the authorities of a policy which has become impossible to carry out.[41]

Since the *Assemblee di Dio* are continually becoming more fundamentalist under American influence, they distrust the moderately critical theology of the Waldensian Church,[42] although they owe a great deal to the Federal Council of Evangelical Churches, in which the Waldensians play the principal part. Conversations between the Waldensians and the Pentecostals are continuing. No one can tell what their outcome will be.

There is extreme distrust of the World Council of Churches. Italian Pentecostals are afraid that the World Council of Churches is making too many concessions to the Catholic Church.

> These apostles of unity would like to strengthen themselves by swallowing up movements which are still in full vigour, just like the wine-growers who improve a quantity of poor wine by mixing it with a quantity of wine of better quality. But this adulteration always does harm to the better wine.[43]

Pentecostals have not forgiven the Catholic Church for its alliance with Fascism against the Pentecostals. Many Italians, both Catholic and Protestant, regard this as a severe hindrance to relations between Catholics and Protestants.[44] The Catholic canon lawyer Jemolo writes:

> It is a bitter pill for us to swallow, but we have to admit that things can happen in Italy which would be unthinkable in the United States, in France, in Finland, in Denmark, in Switzerland or in England. These 'pogroms', forcible entries into houses where people are singing psalms or praying, the insults, threats,beatings, arrests . . . can only cause us disgust and shame. For Italy to be ranked with Spain and Greece among the countries which still maintain religious intolerance is shameful to us . . .[45]

Various attempts by high dignitaries of the Catholic Church to justify this[46] do not improve matters, and the wearisome reiteration of the claim that Pentecostal worship is dangerous to health would be absurd, until one remembers that it is a camouflaged remnant of Fascist ideology. Cavalli has written in an article that has become notorious, that because of its divine privileges, and because it is the only true church, the Catholic Church must claim the right to religious freedom for itself alone. This freedom extends only to the truth, and not to error.[47] The Archbishop of Milan expressed regret for the abolition of the Inquisition, and desired 'for overriding religious and political reasons' that in particular the freedom of lapsed priests should be restricted.[48] S. Lener, S.J., has described in many articles the dangers of Protestantism, its links with the Communists, the flooding of Italy with preachers and evangelists, and the passion of the Pentecostals to obtain conversions.[49] According to Lener, the latter misrepresent the Catholic interpretation of the Italian Constitution as a Fascist one, and do not hesitate to draw on Communist help to guarantee what they understand as religious freedom, although the missionary societies in their homelands (e.g. the Assemblies of God in the USA) are firmly opposed to Communism. The Federal Council of Evangelical Churches is said to have formed

> a real united front . . ., on one hand in order to oppose the Catholic Church and the religion of the Italian people, and on the other hand to exercise pressure on the legislative, judicial and administrative authorities, to obtain, as we shall show, equal rights for every sect, without any limitations from the point of view of public order . . .[50]

The same churches which bewail the progress of liberalism in their countries of origin are making a deliberate attempt in Italy to call on the aid of the principles which in their own countries have led to liberalism.[51]

> The Catholic Church cannot possibly consent to this turning upside down of all values and privileges. It cannot tolerate numerous people without dignity or scruples, outsiders, sometimes motivated solely by the hope of financial gain, and the search for popularity, inspired by passion or vindictiveness, camouflaged in their newly acquired clerical garb and a recently acquired American citizenship, who attack the Catholic laity, insult the church and the religion of the Italian people, and force those who are in error not into a different religion but to the final abandonment of all religion and every supernatural belief.[52]

In their literature, it is claimed, that they spread lies about the Pope and sow the seeds of doubt of the Catholic religion.

> They lead astray simple souls, who still believe in God and his only-begotten Son, into a vague, alien, Communist-inclined religiosity. When the Supreme Pontiff gives audience to a group of athletes, they accuse him of mixing religion and culture. If he gives audience to scientists and philosophers, there

is again an outcry that he is making political propaganda. If he shows his fatherly care for the poor, the workers and the wretched, they trot out their morbid jokes about the riches of the Vatican. When the clergy of the Catholic church, in their loyalty to the sacrosanct law of God, which is accepted without discussion by Protestants themselves, . . . insist that marriage should remain holy and chaste, they accuse them of using the confessional to satisfy an unhealthy and morbid curiosity . . .[53]

'Do these sectarians really deserve toleration?' Lener asks at the end of this long list of misdeeds.

What these accusations show is not the wickedness of the Pentecostals, but Lener's inability to encounter those whose faith is different with anything but insults and aspersions upon their morality. It is easy to understand why Pentecostals at the present day, even after the Vatican Council, find it difficult to believe in any real change of heart in Catholicism.

I leave it to Carlo Falconi[54] to reply to these accusations. In a brilliant chapter, not without a polemic tone, entitled 'The Anti-Protestant Persecution', he rages against the Catholic press, which he says is devoted to a *fortissimo* rendering of laments for the persecutions suffered by the Catholic Church. The other side of the record consists of hosannas in praise of its constantly increasing power. But the persecution of Protestants in Italy and elsewhere is subjected to an efficient conspiracy of silence in the so-called independent press in Italy, although an adequate and reliable documentation is available.[55] It is impossible, says Falconi, to regard Protestantism, and the Pentecostal movement in particular, as the first stage to unbelief. One has only to read the letters of the Pentecostals in *Nuovi Argumenti* and in *Il Mondo*.

[These] form, without exaggeration, a chapter of popular religious literature which with its direct spontaneity and burning faith is comparable to the literature of early Christianity.

With regard to the ecstatic convulsions seizing members of the Pentecostal movement, in Italy at least these can be dismissed as legends.[56]

Falconi also refutes the charge that Protestantism is anti-Italian, and he quotes the history of the Waldensians in support of his argument. Besides, at the present day, when the role of nation-states must decline, the artificial fostering of Italian nationalism is a crime against all humanity.

It is an unpardonable sin against Christianity to try to resist the ecumenical efforts of Christian churches throughout the world by trying to increase the isolation of national and racist enclaves from the outside world.[57]

The influence of finance from abroad is exaggerated. In any case, these gifts of money are infinitely smaller than the donations which Cardinal Spellman is able to send to Italy every day. As far as methods of proselytism are concerned, the Catholic Church is in no position to accuse Protestants. And why should there be such an outcry on account of 150,000 to 200,000 Protestants in a

Catholic population of 50,000,000? This is because the Catholic Church refuses at any time to abandon its hegemony. And this is the reason why Falconi sympathizes with the Protestants. Their faith is more or less a matter of indifference to him, but he supports them in their efforts to resist the absolutist claims of Catholicism.

In Peyrot's view:

> Considering the presence in Rome of the Holy See and its influence in Italian public life, the religious policy of the Government and the juridical position reserved to the non-Roman Catholic minorities are an index of the attitude, at least unofficial, which the Vatican assumes towards the problems of religious liberty.[58]

But this church does not consist only of the majority of priests and bishops, with their outdated views. It also contains Christians like Jemolo and Rosapepe, who are doing a service to their church by recalling it to reason and tolerance.

The fact that the Communists have come out strongly in defence of the Pentecostals[59] has led many Catholic writers to suppose that the Pentecostals are paving the way for Communism. What is in fact the case? In his work 'The Right Not to Tremble', the writer Luigi Pestalozza, whose sympathies are with the Left, cites a statement by Gaetano Salvemini: 'If the Tremblers are denied the right to tremble, what then becomes of my right not to tremble?' This extremely well documented pamphlet takes Scelba, the Minister of the Interior, sternly to task:

> In the conflict with the Pentecostals, there took place in 1953 a most regrettable official intervention by the executive, in the person of the then Minister of the Interior, Scelba. It showed the treatment which is handed out to Italian citizens who do not profess the Catholic, Apostolic and Roman religion, and the way in which our government regards the provisions of the constitution which establish full liberty of religion, whatever form or manifestation it may take. It must be remembered that Pentecostal worship had been forbidden in Italy by the Buffarini-Guidi circular of 9 April 1935 (no. 600/158), on the grounds that 'its services have been shown to be harmful to the physical and mental health of the race'. At that period, when Nicola Pende was elaborating his fantastic biological theories to establish the existence of an Italian 'type', exemplified in Mussolini, alongside Hitler's Germanic 'type', the motivation of the action taken against the Pentecostals by Buffarini-Guidi, as Minister of the Interior, had at least the merit of being in accordance with the tragic stupidity of the times. But Sr Scelba cannot have held this view when, on 10 February 1953, he replied to a question by Deputy Preti about the persistent intolerance to which the Pentecostal church was subjected, and felt it necessary to state, in these words: 'The practice of Baptist or Pentecostal worship is not permitted in Italy because of the particular nature of the services, which have been shown to be harmful to the physical and mental health of their adherents.'

It is obvious that the Christian Democrat Minister of the Interior was not aware of repeating the very words of his Fascist colleague and predecessor, since he thought it wiser to replace the widely discredited term 'race' by the word 'adherents'. The fact remains that for our government the notorious circular, and the ideas that motivated it, are still valid, and it is still regularly enforced by the organs of the state, notwithstanding the clear contradiction between it and Articles 8 and 19 of the Constitution.[60]

Pestolozza knows that the Pentecostals have no political interest.

The Pentecostals certainly do not offer any constructive alternative to the present order of society; they find consolation for earthly sorrow in the certainty of joy outside this world, and compensation for the wretchedness of daily life in a mystical participation in the life of the religious community, which compensates for human conflicts in the reading of the gospels, and in resignation to suffering. In fact from the point of view of the class struggle these are negative attitudes. But against the background of the social structure of the South, oppressed by age-old constraints, they appear different. In so far as – and only in so far as – they represent a reduction of the spiritual tyranny of traditional authority, these attitudes, with their premises and consequences, can represent a social factor tending towards the liberation of the individual.[61]

The point here is that Pentecostals in general are not Communists, although many vote for the Communist Party. But how can the Catholic Church regard this as a serious reproach against Protestants, for in *Catholic* Italy a third of the population votes for the Communist party. It would make more sense to say that the Catholics had voted the Communists into Parliament. Moreover, who are the Pentecostals to vote for? The 'Christian Democrats', with their long-standing policy of persecution? Pestalozza, on the other hand, is right to defend his standpoint against Ottaviani, who supposes that most Protestant converts are actual Communists.[62] Mario Miegge describes this policy as 'the childish fantasy of someone who tries to tar all his opponents with the same brush'.[63]

3. *The 'Proud Poor' Will Not Remain Poor: The Italian Pentecostal Movement from a Sociological Point of View*[64]

Elena Cassin has called the Pentecostal movement 'the religion of the proud poor'.

The success of sects of Pentecostal type is largely explained by the real and egalitarian solidarity which they create amongst their members. In a country where society is deeply divided into hierarchical orders, where the great families create and dismiss mayors and elected representatives, where ideologists of every kind have always to come to terms with those who have prestige, and therefore who alone have any influence, and where even the Catholic Church cannot break away from this rule, social equality is in the eyes of the poor a trap, and even equality before God seems illusory to them.

> For the members and sympathizers of the dissident group things are different. They meet in a simple room with whitewashed walls, and thanks to the communion on a basis of equality which is established amongst them, they have the impression that they are receiving directly the message of God. Sometimes they think, as in the case of the members of the Assemblies of God, that the Holy Spirit, the supreme gift given to a Christian, will descend upon any one of them, with no necessity for a consecrated person, such as a priest, to act as an intermediary between the deity and the believer. The fact that Pentecostalism lays a greater emphasis than the other sects on its egalitarian character is probably the reason why it has spread more widely than the rest in Calabria and throughout Southern Italy . . .
>
> Its adherents are drawn without exception from the most deprived classes: fishermen, labourers, hired farm labourers, low grade municipal employees (grave diggers, road sweepers). They are the poor, but poor people proud of their poverty, proud of their ignorance, which permits them to be closer to the truth of the Gospel.[65]

The history of these poor people, the peasants of Calabria who are still condemned to silence, has not yet been written,[66] by contrast to studies of the philosophers and soldiers of Calabria. In her study Elena Cassin seeks to give a sketch of this part of the history of Calabria. But her observations are true not only of Calabria. The same story can be told of the rest of Southern Italy. The Pentecostals in Southern Italy do not wait for permission from a church official. Spontaneously and on their own intiative they evangelize the next village:

> Now in Italy everything is permitted and tolerated. But this phenomenon, which is taking place today in the midst of the rural South, is something which is intolerable to the ruling classes of Italy. For a working man in the South to join the Reds is bad enough. But that can be overlooked. He will still be voting for a lawyer or a teacher; he will still be under the control of elements from the bourgeoisie. But for him to do something on his own account, really on his own account, and thumb his nose at the lawyers and the school-teachers, that is really something that goes beyond what can be tolerated in Italy.[67]

This explains both the protest and the attempt to maintain a shamed silence about the rise of Pentecostalism in Southern Italy. The Pentecostal movement made it possible for Pastor Gelsomino of Benevento in Campagna, who had returned from Brazil, to improve his standards of literacy. He himself had learned to read after a fashion in the two years he spent at school. But he then forgot how to read. However, obligatory Bible reading succeeded in doing what the Italian elementary school could not. Similarly, his position as leader of the congregation obliged him to undertake a public debate about the faith with the priest, an immense achievement and an enormous step forward in establishing the rights of the individual as such, even though he was no match for the priest in public debate. He describes how the priest brought his stick crashing down on to the table with such force that everyone fell through into the cellar; no one was hurt except the priest. The policeman ordered one of the Benevento elders: 'Trembler, hold our your hand.' The policeman disappointed, had to admit: 'Ma tu non tremi! (But you do not tremble).' Once again the policeman and the priest, the representatives of hierarchial order, had shown themselves helpless and ignorant. *Il Mondo* adds that an engineer and a student belong to the Assembly, and that the Pentecostals of Benevento vote mainly for the Liberals, but also for the Social Democrats and the Monarchists. 'They possess a critical discernment.'[68]

Nello Finnochiaro visited the Pentecostal congregation of Raffadali, on the southern coast of Sicily. The houses of the village are wretched and poorly built, with the exception of the church, which has recently been renovated. The average income is 60,000 lire (about £35) a year, and bean soup the sole nourishment. The village has 12,000 inhabitants, of whom 4,000 are Communist, 2,000 members of other parties, and 800 Pentecostals. There are 555 inhabitants per sq. km. on average. There is one room to every four persons. Of the 4,761 houses, 1,048 are without water or wash-basin, 545 without water, 2,126 share a toilet, only 11 have a bath, and only 2,161 have electric light.

Before any political protest took place, criticism of these miserable living conditions expressed itself in a religious revolt.

> In certain places the Pentecostals have obtained about a thousand adherents and continue to increase their numbers. The propagandists, returned Sicilian emigrants from distant America, have been joined in the missionary work by young peasants ... In deserted churches, the representatives of the secular clergy rail at them in vain from their pulpits. In the simplicity of the new religion there is something which profoundly touches and at the same time educates the soul of the peasant. Usually the Protestant pastors do not carry out any political activity, but many of their followers have joined the Communist trade union and vote for the Communist Party.

But there is no organizational link between Pentecostals and Communists. The same factors are responsible for the rise of both.

> The peasant sees ... in the priest an individual elector in whose hands is placed the carrying out of the tasks required by those who govern him, and therefore he considers him the person really responsible for his wretchedness. If he has any political perception, the peasant reacts by becoming a Communist; if on the other hand his inclinations tend more to religion, he becomes a Pentecostal. But at the elections he still votes Communist.[69]

4. *Summary*

In the Pentecostal movement the despised and exploited Italian finds his human dignity. As a child of God, alongside other children of God, he is taken seriously. He receives a task (the evangelization of his village) which he can only carry out if he has the courage to see the centuries-old hierarchical structure of his village in its proper perspective. Thus a process takes place in his social psychology which is of vast importance. With a hymn he has learned by heart and a guitar he goes into the next village and sings: 'Tell me the story of Jesus!'[70] and the rejection of Jesus, his insults, 'the years of His labour, the sorrows He bore', His fear and loneliness are described in such a way that the listener can recognize his own fear in the suffering of Jesus. In the glorification, resurrection and kingdom of Christ he can see the way to the restoration of his own humanity and his resurrection to a new life. Only one thing is necessary: the doors of the human heart must be opened from within. There is no bolt on the outside. 'If you want Jesus to come to you, open the door from within!'[71]

For the Pentecostal, this decision is of great importance in his life and for his social psychology. He has taken the first step in overcoming a hierarchical social and ecclesiastical structure which has lasted for centuries. Whether this will lead to the freedom of the gospel or to the uncertainty of the Western European is an open question, and a risk which the Catholic Church in this part of the world has not yet been willing to take.

Unlike Falconi, I regard Lener's criticism of the excesses of Pentecostal propaganda as to some extent justified. The Pentecostals are unaware that their criticism of Catholicism only applies to the forms of Catholic piety with which they come into daily contact, that is, to fanatical and often superstitious misinterpretations of Catholicism. They are ignorant of the growing number of Catholic works which take the Pentecostal movement seriously and try to learn from it.[72] If the Italian Pentecostal movement recognized that even in Italy there exists a more evangelical Catholicism, it would show that from the campaign of vilification conducted by the Catholic Church against Pentecostals it had learnt to judge its own opponents with greater discrimination. But the hostile attitude of the Catholic Church,[73] often in defiance of the constitution, does not help the Pentecostal movement to take this view of Catholicism. In contrast to Lener I hold that 'these sectarians' should be treated as brothers in Christ, because I believe that our Master has shown us to think, believe and love the truth, but never to try to impose it by force. This ultimately shows the difference between faith and unbelief. *Because* 'the gates of hell shall not prevail against the church', the church can renounce the use of force. But if it uses the secular arm, it shows that it has not taken seriously this promise to Peter.

The question remains open. How far is the Catholic Church in Italy ready, in a concrete encounter in Italy itself, to make a reality of the documents of the Second Vatican Council, and of the spirit of ecumenism? And how far is the Pentecostal movement ready to forgive the Catholic Church its past, and to see that the real aims of Pentecostal religion are taken seriously by the Catholic Church throughout the world and are carefully studied? And how far can the Waldensian Church act here as an interpreter, and how can all the churches of

Italy help each other to be truly 'churches for others', that is, for the others for whom the gospel means nothing?

The Waldensian G. Peyrot, who was kind enough to make a thorough critique of this chapter, regards the account given as 'one of the best studies of Pentecostalism in Italy carried out up to the present day', but does not agree with my conclusions. The Catholic Church, he says, still makes a distinction at the moment between different kinds of Protestant. They are ready for dialogue with the traditional churches, but the conditions for dialogue with the 'sectarians' are not yet present on either side. A direct confrontation between Pentecostals and Catholics could only lead to confusion. In his view it is necessary first for Protestants to achieve more unity amongst themselves, and only then to make a common approach to Catholicism.[74]

NOTES

1. Ch. 7, pp. 85ff.
2. Ch. 2.4, pp. 24ff.
3. R. Bracco, *Risveglio*, p. 11.
4. The 'Christian Church of North America' is a fusion of the 'Italian Christian Church of North America' and the 'General Council of the Italian Pentecostal Assemblies of God'. (The original name of the latter was: The Unorganized Italian Christian Churches of North America = Assemblee delle chiese innorganizzate italiane; cf. 02a.02.120.)
5. R. Bracco, *op. cit.*, pp. 17f.
6. Decree of the Minister of the Interior, 9.4.1935.
7. R. Bracco, *op. cit.*, p. 22.
8. R. Bracco, *PE* 2412, 31.7.1960, pp. 2f.
9. R. Bracco, *Risveglio*, p. 26.
10. 02a.02.120.
11. U. N. Gorietti, *Risveglio Pentecostale* 9/6, June 1954, p. 2; *Risveglio P* 13/11–12, Nov.-Dec. 1958, p. 19. G. Rosapepe, *Risveglio P* 9/5, May 1954, pp. 2ff.; *PE* 2399, 1.5.1960, p. 10.
12. AdD, 120,000; Chiesa Apostolica, 2,500; Chiesa Evangelica Internazionale, 200,000. No statistics available for International Pentecostal Assemblies, Chiese Cristiane del Nord America, United Pentecostal Church and individual independent assemblies. Total of Protestants in Italy according to *WChH* 1968, 67,545 (now out of date).
13. Sources, documents, literature: 05.15.006. 120,000 members, 25,000 children attending Sunday school, 550 congregations, 300 pastors. Journal: *Risveglio Pentecostale*. Declaration of Faith: cf. Appendix: 9, pp. 520f.
14. Assemblee di Dio, *Statuto*, 1957; *Risveglio P* 8/11, Nov. 1953, 2: 'Gli Articoli'.
15. R. Bracco, *Verità*, pp. 5f.
16. R. Bracco, *Risveglio P* 8/9, Sept. 1953, pp. 1ff.
17. R. Bracco, *Battesimo*, pp. 25f.
18. R. Bracco, *Verità*, pp. 20f.; detailed discussion below, ch. 28.5, p. 403.
19. R. Bracco, *Verità*, pp. 45f.

20. Sources, documents, literature: 05.15.007. 60 churches, 2,500 members, Journal: *Richiezza di Grazia.*

21. Cf. ch. 13.4, pp. 191ff.

22. See above, p. 192.

23. Sources, documents, literature: 05.15.003. 24 churches, 4,449 members.

24. Cf. *PGG*, pp. 298ff.

25. *European Pentecostal Perspective* 1/1, July–Sept. 1963, p. 6.

26. Above, ch. 4.2, pp. 50ff.

27. See 02a.02.118.

28. Detailed documentation and court records from the period of persecution 05.15. On the Buffarini-Guidi circular cf. G. Peyrot, *La circolare.*

29. G. Spini, *Il Ponte* 9/1, Jan. 1953, p. 5.

30. G. Peyrot, *La circolare*, p. 5.

31. A. C. Jemolo, *Per la pace*, p. 35.

32. G. Peyrot, *Protestantismo* 8/1, Jan.–March 1953, p. 25. C. Falconi, *La Chiesa*, p. 304. Cam. Dep. Res. Somm. Interr. no. 9710 (on Preti); letter of the *Alto Commissariato per l'Igiene e Sanità Pubblica*, 12.12.1952, n. 970/2. 160.

33. G. Spini, *Il Ponte* 9/1, Jan. 1953, p. 8.

34. *Ibid.*, p. 2.

35. *Ibid.*, pp. 12–14.

36. G. Peyrot, *Protestantismo* 8/1, Jan.–March 1953; ET: *Intolerance*, p. 11; *La Luce*, 14.12.1951.

37. C. Falconi, *La Chiesa*, p. 51.

38. Government decrees in G. Peyrot, *Intolerance*, p. 28, and *La circolare.*

39. A. Guggenbühl, *Geschäftsmann und Christ* 2/9, June 1962, p. 15.

40. *Il Mondo* 5, 1953, no. 211, p. 2. Pestalozza also heads the first chapter of his *Diritto di non tremolare*: 'Scelba worries about the health of non-Catholics.'

41. G. Peyrot, *La circolare*, p. 6.

42. Cf. the controversy between G. Miegge and R. Bracco about the new *Dizionario Biblico* in *Risveglio P* 12/5, May 1957, pp. 6–9; 12/7–8, July–Aug. 1957, pp. 18ff.

42. G. Scalzi, *Risveglio P* 11/12, Dec. 1956, pp. 3f.

45. Numerous sources in C. Falconi, *La Chiesa.*

45. A. C. Jemolo, quoted on the cover of L. Pestalozza, *Il diritto.*

46. F. Stephano, Bishop of Teggiano, *Fides*, May–June 1958, pp. 151–7; Cardinal Schuster, Archbishop of Milan, *Osservatore Romano*, 15.10.1953; Bishop of Padua in *Gazzetino del Lunedì*, Venice, 2.6.1952; *L'Avvenire d'Italia*, Bologna, 17.6.1952; Cavalli, *Civiltà Cattolica*, 3.4.1948.

47. *Civiltà Cattolica*, 3.4.1948.

48. I. Schuster, *Osservatore Romano*, 15.10.1952.

49. S. Lener, S.J., *Civiltà Cattolica* 104, 1953/IV, p. 254.

50. *Ibid.*, p. 255.

51. Cf. below ch. 21.1, pp. 291ff.

52. S. Lener, *op. cit.*, p. 266.

53. *Ibid.*, p. 267.

54. C. Falconi, *La Chiesa*, pp. 219ff. In this chapter Falconi answers another Catholic polemicist (I. Giordano, *Crisi*, who makes essentially the same charges against Protestantism as Lener).

55. 05.15.006c.

56. C. Falconi, *op. cit.*, p. 308.

57. *Ibid.*, p. 309.

58. G. Peyrot, *Protestantismo* 8/1, Jan.–March 1953, p. 1, ET: *Intolerance.*

59. Cf. R. Willenegger: 'There the Communists, however paradoxical it may sound, are paving the way for the gospel!' (*Ich komme bald!* 11, 1953, p. 177).

60. L. Pestalozza, *Il diritto*, pp. 3f.

61. *Ibid.*, p. 25.

62. *Ibid.*, pp. 25f.

63. M. Miegge, *Archives de Sociologie des religions* 4/8, July–Dec. 1959, p. 87.

64. This sociological summary has had to be kept very short. For statistical surveys and the religious and economic background cf. 05.15.015, J. Meyriat (ed.), *La Calabria*, and M. Miegge, *op. cit.*

65. E. Cassin, in J. Meyriat (ed.), *La Calabria*, pp. 366f.

66. E. Cassin, *op. cit.*, p. 368.

67. G. Salvemini, *Il Mondo* 4/32, 9.8.1952, pp. 3f.

68. G. Russo, *Il Mondo* 10/465, 14.1.1958, p. 5. G. Peyrot (in a critical comment on this chapter, 16.6.1967) takes a less positive view of the Pentecostals' political involvement and draws attention to their widespread abstention from politics.

69. N. Finnochiaro, *Il Mondo* 9/412, 8.1.1957, pp. 5f.

70. F. J. Crosby, *Redemption Hymnal*, 1958, n. 150; Italian, 'Dimmi la storia di Gesù', sung on the record *Uomini Nuovi*, BIEM UN 4501, sung by Remigio and Delia Nussia.

71. H. A. Parli, sermon on the record quoted in n. 70 above.

72. Cf. ch. 1.1(*c*), pp. 7ff.; ch. 8.3(*c*), pp. 105ff.; ch. 30.3, pp. 436ff.

73. Italian Catholic publications about the Pentecostal movement compare very badly from the theological and historical point of view with the Catholic works mentioned in n. 72. E.g. L. Cristiani, *Enc. Catt.* IX, cols. 1153–4.

74. G. Peyrot, comment on this chapter, 16.6.1967. For direct dialogue between Catholics and Pentecostals cf. ch. 8.3(*b*), pp. 101ff., and ch. 30.3, pp. 436ff.

20

Christsomol versus Komsomol:[1] The Pentecostal Movement in Russia

1. *The Origins of the Russian Pentecostal Movement*

(*a*) *Ivan Efimovich Voronaev, founder of the 'Christians of Evangelical Faith'* (*Pentecostals*)

VORONAEV was born in Russia in 1886, and served in a Cossack regiment under the Tsar. After his conversion in 1908 he became a Baptist pastor in Irkutsk and Krasnoyarsk. In 1911, under the pressure of the persecution of Protestants by the Orthodox Church,[2] he left Russia by way of Manchuria. He became pastor of the Russian Baptist church in San Francisco. Later he moved to Seattle, where he shared a church building with Ernest Williams, a prominent leader of the Assemblies of God. Three years later he went to New York as pastor of the Russian Baptist Church. His daughter experienced the baptism of the Spirit in Glad Tidings Tabernacle, a church of the Assemblies of God. Together with twenty Russian Baptists, who had received the baptism of the Spirit with speaking in tongues, he founded the first Russian Pentecostal church in New York on 1 July 1919.

On 15 July 1920 he travelled to Bulgaria, where in a short time he founded eighteen congregations, which formed the basis of the important Bulgarian Pentecostal movement.[3] From Bulgaria he travelled on to Odessa and Leningrad. Everywhere he set up Pentecostal churches. A number of leading Baptists and 'Evangelical Christians',[4] including D. L. Ponomarchuk and D. S. Ponurko,[5] joined him. The work grew apace. For example, the church in Odessa already had 1,000 members. In 1927 the first Pentecostal Congress for the whole Soviet Union took place, where I. E. Voronaev was appointed president of the 'Union of Christians of Evangelical Faith',[6] and D. S. Ponurko was appointed secretary.[7] In his journal *Evangelist* Voronaev already listed 350 congregations, and Donald Gee estimates that at this period there were 80,000 members.[8]

Since the Pentecostals filled their ranks partly at the expense of the 'Evangelical Christians', the Chlysti and other sects of the Orthodox Church,[9] and also of the Baptists, the Baptists issued a warning against Voronaev and his followers. They were called deceivers, who taught that all Christians had to be able to work miracles and speak in tongues. The Communist author F. I. Garkavenko[10] described Voronaev as a Pentecostal missionary who, disguised as a Baptist, was sent to Russia by American Imperialism. (Voronaev was given financial support by several Pentecostal missionary societies.) But Voronaev conscious of his success, wrote:

> The Baptists are right to fear the 'Tremblers',[11] for in fact when these 'Tremblers' come in the power of the Holy Spirit into the churches of the Baptists or 'Evangelical Christians', then these congregations tremble and shake in their inmost being, and we leave only fragments and splinters behind us.[12]

In 1930, according to Communist sources, Voronaev renounced his faith.[13] The journal *Nauka i Religiya* published a photocopy of his renunciation in his own handwriting.[14] But his wife, Katherina Voronaev, denied that this account was genuine. According to her version, Voronaev was arrested on 6 July 1930, with 800 other pastors, cooped up in a cattle wagon and carried off to Siberia in inhuman conditions. Three years later Katherina Voronaev was also arrested. After several appeals she succeeded at least in being placed in the same concentration camp as her husband. In 1935 the couple were freed for a short time. From 1936 to 1940, they were once again exiled in Siberia. On their release Voronaev tried to emigrate a second time to the USA. Instead of receiving a passport, he was once again arrested. His wife went to Siberia to look for him and wandered from one concentration camp to another. But she was recognized and also imprisoned for six years. On her release she made contact by letter with her children in the USA, which led in 1949 to a third, even more severe and cruel imprisonment. Finally, in 1953, after personal intervention by President Eisenhower, she was allowed to leave for the USA.[15]

As far as Voronaev's renunciation is concerned, it is conceivable that it was made under the brutal torture carried out by his tormentors. But during his brief release (1935–36) Voronaev preached in the Baptist church of Kaluga (south-east of Moscow), and he was not used by the Soviet Atheist Associations, as is usually the case with lapsed Christians, in their propaganda for atheism. So it must be assumed either that the documents mentioned above are forgeries, or else that they are the product of a momentary weakness under torture.

(*b*) *Finnish evangelists*

Voronaev was not the only pioneer of the Pentecostal movement in Russia. Finnish evangelists worked in the Baltic regions, since until 1918 Finland belonged to Russia. According to Baron von Uexküll, Reval[16] and many accounts in Finnish Pentecostal journals, flourishing Pentecostal congregations must have existed in Estonia before 1910[17] and eye-witnesses report that they still exist today. In Riga in 1932 the Swiss Pentecostal pastor Heinrich Steiner found a Pentecostal church with seats for 2,000.[18] Thomas Ball Barrett, the Norwegian Pentecostal leader, evangelized in 1911 in St Petersburg.[19] Russian Pentecostal literature was printed in Finland and Norway.

In 1911 the missionary Urshan returned from the USA to Finland. He converted N. P. Smorodin and N. I. Ivanov, formerly leaders of the 'Evangelical Christians' ' church in Helsinki, to Pentecostalism. These two then moved to St Petersburg, and set up a new church there.[20] This church belongs to the 'Jesus Only'[21] or 'Oneness'[22] type of church. They spread elsewhere in Russia. In Moscow even the Baptist Church and the 'Evangelical Christians' both, as a body, joined the 'Jesus Only' Pentecostals. Whether these Pentecostals still exist within other churches, or continue as 'unregistered' churches, is not known.

(*c*) *Influence on the 'Evangelical Christians'*

The origins of the 'Evangelical Christians' in Russia go back to the last century. The translation of the Bible into Russian, the revival in Southern Russia under the German Stundists (Juliane von Krüdener, Johann Gossner, the Russian Bible Society), the Baptist revival, the revival movement in Leningrad (Lord Radstock, Dr F. W. Baedeker, Georg Müller, Count Korff), occasional contacts with the 'Spiritual Christians of Biblical Faith' in Bessarabia, the *Molokane* and *Sakharovtsy*, combined to provide a foundation on which Voronaev could begin his Pentecostal missionary work. The pioneers of Pentecostalism did not work only by founding independent Pentecostal churches, but also through the powerful influence they had upon the Evangelical Christians. According to Zhidkov, the leader of the Evangelical Christians, the majority of the adherents of the Evangelical Christians are Pentecostals.[23]

Up to the time of the Russian revolution the Pentecostals and Evangelical Christians were cruelly persecuted by the Orthodox Church. In August 1891 the Holy Synod under Pobedonostsev resolved that anyone who left the Holy Orthodox Church to join another religious denomination should be punished 'with the loss of all civil and personal rights, and in less serious cases with 18 months of correction in a "reformatory" '.[24] Heretical propaganda was punished by exile to Siberia. This severe policy of persecution did not prevent the spread of the Evangelical Christians. V. A. Pashkov attempted on 1 April 1884 in St Petersburg to unite the above mentioned groups, together with the Dukhobors, as one Protestant church. The common ground between them was summed up in the statement: 'No union in dogma, but in the Spirit and in truth.'[25]

Although the Evangelical Christians in many places could be described as a kind of internal revival movement within the Orthodox Church,[26] they were and are opposed to the Orthodox Church. The reasons for this are partly sociological – many Pentecostals shared a prison cell with the Communist leaders.

But there are also ecclesiological reasons, for they protested against the general and uncommitted form of Christianity represented by Orthodoxy. 'People greet each other with the glorious Easter greeting: "He is risen!" But they know nothing of the life of the risen Christ.'[27] But the protest against the neglect of social and economic tasks in the history of the Orthodox Church is just as sharp. The 'Evangelical Christians' tried to carry out these tasks of social criticism – which the Lutheran Reformation also ignored.[28]

At first the Pentecostals and 'Evangelical Christians' were loyal to the Communist state. They regarded the Communists as those who had set them free from the yoke of Orthodoxy. They co-operated with enthusiasm and received much praise. The following resolution was adopted with respect to them:

> A specially attentive attitude must be shown to the sectarians, of whom many were cruelly persecuted by the Czarist regime and among whom there is now much activity. Through a skilful approach we must bring it about that the considerable economic and cultural potentialities of the sectarians are directed into the channels of Soviet work . . .[29]

The Pentecostals and Evangelical Christians had founded collective farms and other production co-operatives which functioned better than the state ones – which is why they were later forbidden. On the other hand, they prophesied that the state agricultural production co-operatives would not last:

> As they owe their origin to expediency alone and not to any deep conviction, as they are supported by state assistance and not by the energy of the individuals concerned, they will disintegrate with the same rapidity, and even if they continue to exist they will remain a great handicap for the State.[30]

Then a period of severe persecution followed for the 'Evangelical Christians'. However, the movement continued, in part officially and in part unofficially. Many engine drivers and guards of the Trans-Siberian Railway were part-time Pentecostal preachers and evangelists, and used their long journeys to Siberia to strengthen the faithful and take services. The continuous series of complaints in the Russian papers about the propaganda of the 'sectarians' shows how effective the evangelizing activity of the Pentecostals is at the present day – if they are in fact the sectarians referred to. They are prominent even in secondary schools and the officer corps of the Red Army. Bonch-Bruyevich describes the sectarians as 'exemplary workers' whom 'to fail to use as an economic and cultural vanguard for the Russian economy would be odd, and indeed criminal'.[31] At the moment they are fighting for a new translation of the Bible. The existing translation is written in the old orthography and in archaic language, so that the Russian government can refuse to allow it to be distributed with the claim that 'we do not wish young people to learn a false orthography and the language of the past'. According to *Kracht von Omhoog*[32] modern Russians find the present translation of the Bible totally incomprehensible.

We meet the power of this evangelical movement even in the mocking descriptions of its opponents. Putintsev describes an evangelist:

> In the regular creaking of the cart I heard the cry of the whole world, not only of my own people. From every land, from the lips of millions, their cries rise up, sometimes complaining, sometimes threatening. 'You know you possess the secret of life, the secret of happiness! How can you keep silence? Millions of souls are struggling towards the light, and do not know where to find it . . . You cannot keep silent!' I knew the secret. Yes, I cannot deny it, I knew it! I knew that happiness, joy, the secret of reconciliation with life, the secret of enduring joy, the brotherhood of all men for all nations, all generations, all classes is to be found – in Christ![33]

The religious practice and feeling of Russian Pentecostals and Evangelical Christians is much more Russian than that of Russian Lutheran and Reformed Christians.[34] They believe that Russia may yet one day become Protestant, and will then have a missionary task in the world. Thus many of them take part in the cultural and economic development of the country. Because of its past history the evangelical movement is protected against the usual charge made by the Atheist Associations – that Christianity can be equated with capitalism. The usual slogans against Christians do not on the whole strike people as having any application to Pentecostal and Evangelical Christians. Stupperich's view is:

> There can be no doubt that the gospel movement still represents a genuinely popular movement. The Evangelical Christians had already gained a moral authority amongst the people in the course of the persecutions under the Czarist regime. Even more today, everyone knows that one who proclaims the gospel in word and deed is someone who has committed his whole existence to the truth he acknowledges. Inasmuch as this has made their preaching more worthy of acceptance, it has made a greater impression and has a much more powerful effect. It is not too much to say that the gospel in Russia has never been listened to by the mass of the people as it has been in the last few years.[35]

The Orthodox Church also admits this.[36]

It is difficult to give exact figures for the members of this movement. Those available vary between 400,000 and 15,000,000.[37] The reasons for these wide variations are related to the following facts:

1. The number of effective members varies as persecution is enforced or relaxed.
2. Sometimes all members of the family are counted, but sometimes only adult baptized members.

3. Sometimes the figures cover only the actual Evangelical Christians, and sometimes the whole complex of Evangelical Christians – Baptists – Pentecostals.
4. Sometimes the Christians themselves deliberately give too low a figure, in order to avoid provoking persecution by an increase which gives the lie to atheistic theories.

There is all the more justification for this tactic in that the leaders of congregations quite rightly do not keep membership lists.

(*d*) *Amalgamation with the 'All-Union Council of Evangelical Christians – Baptists' (AUCECB).*[38]

In 1944 the Evangelical Christians (section *c* above) united with the Baptists to form the AUCECB. On 24 August 1945 the 'Christians of Evangelical Faith (Pentecostals)' (section *a* above) joined the AUCECB. At the present day this Union forms the largest Protestant movement in Russia.[39] By contrast to the Reformed churches and Lutherans, who look to other countries for their inspiration, the AUCECB has not only held its own, but has constantly extended its influence.

Within the Union the Pentecostals have always exercised a considerable influence. Many articles in the Union's journal, the *Bratskiy Vestnik*, show the influence of the Pentecostals, and of their doctrine of the baptism of the Spirit and speaking in tongues.[40] Similarly, prayer for the sick has spread throughout the Union, in spite of numerous warnings from the central administration in Moscow.

The Soviet anti-religious press has paid close attention to the controversies within the AUCECB. P. Kaushansky affirms:

> The AUCECB devotes much attention to miracles in their sermons . . . As to where these signs are today Mitskevich[41] modestly points out: 'The Holy Spirit . . . discontinued the phenomenon.' Why? Only Mitskevich knows. However, to spread religious superstitions without believing in miracles is very difficult even for the experts such as the Baptist theologians.[42]

But the Pentecostals point out that Christ today does the same miracles as in the time of the apostles. The gifts of the Holy Spirit, including prayer with the sick and speaking in tongues, have been given to the church even today.

2. *Main Outlines of the Theology of the Russian Pentecostal Movement*

I have not yet been able to lay hands on the original Russian text of the confession of faith of the 'Christians of Evangelical Faith (Pentecostals)'. But I have had access to a Polish translation of this Russian confession of faith.[43] It differs in important features from those of West European and American

Pentecostal churches. Particularly striking is the remarkable insight into the historical process by which the Apostles' Creed came into being, and above all the realization that all confessions of faith show the limitations of their own period and must always be understood in relation to the errors which they are meant to refute. And by contrast with other Pentecostals, the great service performed by Wesley is seen not in his emphasis on holiness, but in the fact that he affirmed man's personal illumination and free will.[44] These elements, and particularly the detailed treatment of christological and trinitarian questions, are no doubt due to the Russian background of the author. The somewhat primitive rejection of materialism and Darwinism in relation to the belief in creation[45] is an obvious polemic against Communism. The speculations about the angels and the archangel Michael ('Many Christians suppose that it is he who will be the archangel who will sound the trumpet to announce the second coming of the Lord') no doubt takes up Russian apocalyptic traditions.[46] The confession of faith follows Zwingli in seeing original sin as 'an inherent disposition to sin (*przyrodżona*) and therefore the cause of all other different sins'.[47] The healing of the sick through prayer is practised. 'Nevertheless not every illness and not every death is a punishment to sin.'[48] The doctrine of the baptism of the Spirit and the gifts of the Spirit are similar to those of the rest of the Pentecostal movement.[49] There is a detailed polemic against the doctrine of 'eternal security' (that anyone who is converted is always assured of not being damned) which is evidently also widespread in Russia and Poland.[50] A surprising feature, but understandable against the background of Orthodoxy, is the description of the church as the communion of all believing and reborn Christians, 'not only those who still live, but also those who have died in the true faith and in holiness'. In a witty play on words, the house church is described as the *dom* (house) led by a patriarch or priest (*kaptan*) and is related to the civil parish. The Lord's Supper is understood in a Zwinglian sense (memorial – *pamiątka*). 'Someone who cannot lead his family aright cannot become a presbyter, but may be an evangelist who bears witness to the all-forgiving love of God.'[51] With regard to the second coming of Jesus the confession of faith tries to avoid choosing any particular one of the various apocalyptic patterns.

> As far as details are concerned the members of our church have freedom to study the holy Scripture under the guidance of the Holy Spirit. We do not wish to discuss details and so ruin the cause of God.[52]

3. *A New Revival*

(*a*) *The rise of the* Initiativniki

As early as 1945 some Pentecostals rejected the union with the AUCECB.[53] According to the Russian author F. F. Fedorenko they set up a headquarters of their own in Dneprozerzhinsk.[54] In 1957 the 'Christians of the Evangelical

Faith (Pentecostals)' asked Khrushchev 'to grant them full religious freedom', that is, to allow them to organize independent Pentecostal congregations. Since the leadership of the AUCECB, he reports, does not allow the Pentecostal services, a hundred thousand Pentecostals have already broken the law, that is, they have organized themselves as so-called 'unregistered', illegal, Pentecostal churches, which do not acknowledge the authority of the AUCECB.[55] The Soviet writer V. M. Kalugin confirms the existence of this underground Pentecostal group.[56] In 1963 a group of these illegal Pentecostals sought asylum in the American Embassy in Moscow.[57] The history of the Russian Pentecostal movement contains repeated examples of large exodus movements. For example, Harriet P. Wilson tells of the migration of a Pentecostal group two hundred strong from the Ukraine to Mongolia, and on to China, in the 1920s. Later, on the basis of promises by prophets, they continued their journey overseas.[58] Many of these emigrants are working today in the Slav branches of the South American, North American and Philippine Pentecostal movements.[59]

The growth of these Pentecostal groups has accelerated since about 1966. Both those who remain within the Baptist Union (AUCECB) and also the underground Pentecostals have organized themselves into 'initiative groups' (*Initiativniki*). Many of the decisions of the Moscow leadership of the AUCECB show that the AUCECB is prepared to some extent to accommodate them, but considerable differences still exist. These are:

1. The Pentecostals demand that speaking in tongues should not be forbidden in public worship (cf. I Cor. 14.39: 'Do not forbid speaking in tongues').
2. The Pentecostals wish to set up Sunday schools.
3. They have held informal meetings in public places – once even in front of the Kremlin – and in public transport vehicles.

In spite of St Paul, the AUCECB rejected the first demand on theological grounds, and the second and third requests under pressure from the Communist Government. They rightly point out that the second and third demands are not permitted by the constitution in Russia, to which the Pentecostals replied that in this case the constitution is contrary to the Charter of Human Rights and Christ's missionary command to the church.

Since in 1961 the AUCECB, together with the Russian Orthodox Church, joined the World Council of Churches, the protest of the Pentecostals in Russia is also directed against the World Council of Churches. They suspect that the World Council is supporting the AUCECB in its cautious policy of maintaining the *status quo*. In fact the AUCECB is afraid that to give way to the Pentecostals would deprive them even of the small degree of freedom that their Union enjoys in Russia at the present day.

There has been much discussion of the question whether agents of the state Council for the Affairs of Religious Cults (CARC), or even of the Russian secret police, are active in the headquarters of the Baptist Union. An interview with Mikhail Zhidkov[60] suggests that the first at least is true. He asserts that CARC workers were 'planted' amongst the *Initiativniki* 'in order to stir up hostility against the registered churches in an attempt to divide and disrupt the work of unity'. It can at least be concluded from Zhidkov's statements – and he is the son of the second most important person in the AUCECB – that in Baptist circles the possibility of the intervention of CARC workers in the life of the church is accepted. The latter question is answered by Steve Durasoff, a minister of the Assemblies of God in the USA, who is now a Professor of Oral Roberts University, and is the grandson of a Russian priest of the Old Believers. He says that the investigation 'neither revealed any of the AUCECB leaders to be KGB agents, nor did it exclude the possibility that one or more could be included'.[61]

There are great difficulties in categorizing exactly the denominational position of the *Initiativniki.* Steve Durasoff rightly points out that J. C. Pollock overlooked the hidden Pentecostal element in the *Initiativniki.*[62] The same is true of Michael Bourdeaux. Certainly, not all the *Initiativniki* are Pentecostals. It probably even includes strictly anti-Pentecostal fundamentalist groups. The undercurrent of Pentecostalism, an atmosphere of Pentecostal piety, and distinctive doctrines which are explicitly Pentecostal[63] are all clearly to be seen in their published documents.

It is equally difficult to ascertain their numbers. Estimates vary between 26,500 in 1966 and 3,000,000 in 1968.[64] Although the latter figure seems to be exaggerated, one must bear in mind Bourdeaux's argument that the decline of the AUCECB, for which there are reliable statistics, has benefited the *Initiativniki* and their successor organizations.

One thing that is certain is that neither the Baptist headquarters in Moscow nor the state has succeeded in suppressing the Pentecostal movement, neither that part of it which is illegal nor that part which has organizational links with the AUCECB. This can be seen from information received by letter from Russia, from various interviews, and the increasing abuse poured on the Pentecostals in the Soviet press. Thus *Komsomolskaya Pravda* of 25 September 1962 contains an account by I. Voevodin, the chairman of the Atheist Association of Krasnoyarsk, a town of 500,000 inhabitants in Siberia:

> Recently, I attended a trial session in the criminal case against the leader of the fanatical Pentecostal sects, Leonid Shevchenko. Every time I entered the courtroom one particular contrast would strike me. The people of Krasnoyarsk are usually exceptionally healthy – physically and mentally. In the room, all the faces are fresh, rosy – what we call 'blood and milk'. On the other hand, on the benches and in the corners of the room, I saw black clothing, sallow complexions, sunken eyes, cheerless young men with their heads shaven, girls with their heads covered with scarves in the fashion of old women. Sectarians. Like dead grass withered in the spring. This is not an accidental contrast and

not only an outward one. The tiredness of the sectarians is the result of their nightly 'zealotry', unnatural rites and exhausting prayers.

It was not the first time that I met sectarians, when attempting to snatch fellow citizens out of their claws. But, at this trial, the stink and dirt of this little world opened to me with its full strength. When you look for a word best suited to express the 'program' of the Pentecostals, you will find in it – hostility. Hostility, reaction, hatred of humanity. The leaders of the sect forbid their members everything 'secular', i.e. everything that is ours: Soviet books, radio, the Pioneer scarf, participation in social activities. Even the joining of a Labour Union is declared to be a godless thing. The sects are hostile to everything that is bright and good in man. All talks about sympathy, sharing and plenty of love which allegedly exist in their midst – are nothing else but fairly tales. . . . Yet they have sufficient 'sympathy' to fawn on a person in distress and to catch him in their spider web. Then the man-hating zealotries follow.

Even if you know, very well, all the wild, immoral and inhuman character of the sect, you have a hard time answering questions like this: 'Why is it that the sectarians still find new partisans? Where do they get their strength from?' An assembly of fanatical, half-illiterate old women . . . And, among them, Lelia Bordysheva, a sickly, secretive girl, Nadezhda Davidova, a young woman not yet deprived of her charm, who not long ago graduated from the Pedagogical Institute of Krasnoyarsk . . . What was it that attracted them to Leonid Shevchenko, to Elena Puchinskaya? I do not hesitate to reply for myself: it was the determination and activity of the soul catchers . . .

The witnesses told about broken families, about women who wound up in mental institutions, about children with their souls crippled. People 'doped' by Shevchenko and his assistants, refused to fulfil their citizen's duties, tore off their Pioneer scarves, trampled the red flag with their shoes. How much time and energy was used to create so much evil! And what was it that we, the activists, the Komsomol members, did in opposition to this strategy of the sectarians?

Well, practically nothing. Judge for yourselves: in all Krasnoyarsk, a city of half a million inhabitants, there is only one more or less active group of Komsomol members – atheists, consisting of fifteen students. But even they have little training in the art of convincing, the difficult job of dealing with those gone astray. Now, what about those gone astray? . . . We don't even know how to help a man who entered on the pathway of co-operation with religion. Her pious aunt told Valya N.: 'You are not going to enrol in the Institute. The teacher is against God!' Valya did not follow the order. But this is as far as she was able to go. In her aunt's home the sectarians would meet as before. Now how did Valya's school-mates help her, the Komsomol member? How did they support the weakening will to fight? In no way at all.

Gena Kulikov's mother forced him to pray, beat him, locked him up in the store-room. The boy starved, suffered humiliation, but would not give in. He escaped from home and started the life of a homeless wanderer. And we, the atheists, to our shame, did not even know about this struggle . . .

Why this indifference, this inactivity among the Komosol leaders? They

> ask persistently for waste paper, for scrap metal, for membership dues. They even impose punishments. But it does not cause them any headache that people get lost, that through sectarian channels, hostile ideology penetrates into our midst, through the failure of other Komsomol members. We cannot rely only on the essential influence of our basically very healthy Soviet environment. Even the greenest meadow is not secure from rotten grass. We should act in such a way that the forces of the healthy environment strengthen the failing growth and kill the roots of malicious thistle.[65]

Voevodin does not mention any verdict by the court against Leonid Shevchenko, who is described as a skilled engineer, educated, strong-willed, diabolically clever and politically reactionary.

If one looks carefully at this attack by Voevodin, two features can be noted. First of all, the Pentecostal movement is a religious, economic and political factor in the Soviet Union. Voevodin and his atheists are helpless when faced with the phenomenon of the Pentecostal movement. As a result, they must use the familiar method of Christian and non-Christian sects, and make moral accusations against their opponents, whose beliefs they cannot refute.

(*b*) *Have the* Initiativniki *made theological innovations?*

The trial of Feoktist Ivanovich Subbotin, Lyubov Milhailovna Khmara, and the brothers Nikolai Kuzmich Khmara and Vasili Kuzmich Khmara took place on 24–7 December 1963.

> They were convicted of bringing up minors in isolation from social life by drawing them into their group, of calling unbelievers to reject their responsibilities as citizens; they were convicted of inciting citizens to disobey the auxiliary police, to refuse to join trade unions and in general to avoid all forms of social activity. They held illegal prayer-meetings at night in insanitary conditions and with minors present.

On the intervention of the AUCECB from Moscow, the older members of the congregation had yielded, but the younger members continued to hold their secret meetings. Consequently they were condemned to terms of imprisonment of from three to five years.[66]

One of those convicted, N. K. Khmara, died two weeks later from the results of torture.

> The palms of his hands were burnt, as were the toes and the soles of his feet. The lower part of his abdomen showed marks of deep wounds made by the insertion of a sharp jagged object; his right leg was swollen; the ankles of both legs seemed to have been beaten; on his body were black and blue bruises.[67]

The 120 members of the congregation who signed the above description of the dead body of Khmara were expressing their grief at the cruel death of their brother, who had only been converted in the summer of 1963 from a life 'of uninterrupted drunkenness'. But they were brave enough to sing at Khmara's grave and to testify: 'Fear not those who can kill the body but cannot kill the soul.' But the document signed by the 120 members of the congregation contains in addition an important detail from the indictment. The accusation was made against the *Initiativniki* that they 'analysed various biblical texts, permitted arbitrary and incorrect interpretations, criticized and did not accept the new constitution of the AUCECB'. They rightly wonder:

> One might think that the witnesses were members of the Holy Synod, people with higher theological education, were versed in biblical truths and called to defend their purity. But not at all! ... Since in the Penal Code there is no article against incorrect interpretation of the Bible, the prosecutor called it reactionary activity, harmful to society. Thus he put the 'incorrect' interpretation of the Bible and the criticism of the constitution of the AUCECB under article 227 of the Penal Code.[68]

Although the above text does not make any direct statement about the nature of the interpretation of the Bible which the *Initiativniki* put forward, it is nevertheless clear that they were prepared to risk their lives for the freedom to work out their own interpretation of the Bible. To understand the theological characteristics of this protest group it is probably necessary, as in the case of the independent Zionists of South Africa and the Brazilian Pentecostals, to rely on oral tradition. But there is literary evidence for this oral tradition, in their hymns. We possess some of these hymns. I quote one as an example. It takes as its starting point modern man, exposed to technological development.:

1. Man, whose life is a perpetual struggle,
For whom life means a conquest,
You have subdued all in this world,
But you have failed to subdue yourself.

2. You have gained fame as a ruler on land,
You have penetrated the depths of the sea,
You have reached the heights, but you are still a slave
Of your own base passions.

3. You have split the invisible atom,
You even know how to conquer space,
You have reached the age of great discoveries,
But you have failed to conquer yourself.

4. Yes! You are strong and at the same time weak,
You are great, as well as insignificant,
By the power of your mind you are a god,
But by your lust you are a slave.
You were high, but how low you have fallen.

5. In your selfishness you scorned the Creator,
You did not find him in the stratosphere,
You returned to earth victoriously like God,
Robbing him of his glory.

6. You are firmly resolved, as in past ages,
To make your name immortal,
And have forgotten the Tower of Babel
In your senseless struggle with God,

7. What of it that you can soar above the earth,
With transient glory on your mortal brow?
You will take off into space again,
But you will still die here on earth.

8. The hosts of planets, in lofty majesty,
Follow their courses above you.
But it was decreed to mankind: No!
You will not reach a single one of them.

9. Oh, unfortunate, haughty, and earthly man!
Give glory to the Supreme God.
Only with him can you be truly happy,
With him you will reach the region beyond the clouds.

10. Without your space-ships and all your efforts,
The Lord will transform your body,
In the first Resurrection, he will give
An immortal body to the faithful saints.

11. God is spirit, and the eternal ruler of the stars,
And if you want to reach the starry sky
You must fall down before him, earthbound man,
And you must conquer yourself in this life.

Amen[69]

It is easy to understand the young members of the Komsomol who go over to the *Initiativniki* because they are bored in the Komsomol.[70] The reason for this lies not merely in the new hymns, which are accompanied on the guitar,[71] but just as much in the fact that these hymns attempt to pose the question of the meaning of life, technology and civilization;

> What is the use of all this modern technical and scientific knowledge . . . We are merely left wandering and erring at random by ourselves, only to end by coming to the horror of emptiness and purposelessness.[72]

It must of course be admitted that the hymn quoted above presents a remarkable mixture of existentialist and pietist interpretation, modern anthropological questions and mythological images. But it is perhaps this very fact which makes it so attractive.

(*c*) *Steps towards a political theology*

It is easy to understand why Christians in Russia become apolitical, and make up their minds 'to become radishes' – that is, outwardly and officially they are red, but underneath they are white.[73] But there must be a significant number of Christians who reject this attitude. The documents we possess, however, do not suggest that they adopt an attitude of undiscriminating anti-Communism. On the contrary, at a very early stage there was an unambiguous expression of support for the Soviet Union from the ranks of Russian Pentecostals, in the form of a resolution which explicitly called for service in the Red Army,[74] much to the displeasure of the American Assemblies of God. It stated that Communism was no 'hindrance to the work of evangelism'. They fully maintained that the socio-economic principles of Communism 'are not contradictory to the teaching of our Lord Jesus'.[75] These statements cannot simply be dismissed as Russian propaganda manoeuvres, even though some political declarations – for example, in connection with the Korean war – cannot but give the impression that they are simply a repetition in religious terms of the official line.[76]

On the other hand, the *Initiativniki* have come into conflict with the tenets of the Marxist criticism of religion. The first indication of such a conflict was the letter of which they succeeded in smuggling several copies out of Russia to the Secretary-General of UNO, U Thant. One of those who passed it on – the letter must have reached the West through several different channels – told me of the dramatic circumstances in which the letter was handed to him in a forest. He had been invited to go for a walk by one of the members of the *Initiativniki*. 'Please bring your Bible with you,' he had told him. The Russian asked my acquaintance to read Hebrews 11: 'Some were tortured, refusing to accept release, that they might rise again to a better life. Others suffered mocking and scourging, and even chains and imprisonment . . .' 'That is our story; will you take this letter for U Thant?' asked the Russian. My acquaintance declined, because the task was too risky for him. Then the member of the *Initiativniki* fell on his knees and uttered a heart-rending prayer. My acquaintance did not understand the words of the prayer. But he allowed himself to be persuaded and accepted the mission. 'Good,' the Russian told him, 'You will now carry on in the direction I tell you for a certain distance. There you will find a man who will walk past you and hand over to you the letter to U Thant.'

The letter was published in the press numerous times.[77] It is a very carefully compiled document, which describes the oppression of the Pentecostals in full detail. The tortures, the illegal trials, the deportations, the sudden arrests by the Russian police were exactly described with the place, date and name of the persons concerned. A description is given amongst others of the testimony of an invalid who was refused urgently necessary treatment in prison. There is an account of the interrogation of children about the religious practices of their parents. The letter ends with a list of the names of those arrested (giving the sentences in each case) and a request to U Thant for help.

The first interesting feature of this document is the fact that the Pentecostals of Russia turn for help to the Buddhist U Thant, and not to their fellow Christians in the West, far less to the Baptists and Pentecostals of America. The second striking thing is the courage of these Christians. They know that to some extent their demands go beyond what the Russian constitution allows them. (However, they stress very strongly that in innumerable cases the Russian state, in its persecution of the Pentecostals, was itself unwilling to grant even the limited religious freedom accorded by the Russian constitution). The Pentecostals are appealing *against* the Russian constitution to a higher human right, and explicitly refer to the 'Declaration of Human Rights', which in 1960 was ratified by the United Nations and published on 2 November 1962 in the Soviet Union.

The document shows that the *Initiativniki* (or Council of Evangelical Christians and Baptists, as they later call themselves) does not consist of uneducated and ill-advised fanatics, although the AUCECB tries to present them as such.[78] In another context they emphasize:

> All this is not happening in some underdeveloped colonial country, and not under a fascist regime, but in a country where it has already been proclaimed to all the world for fifty years that the most just, democratic and humanitarian society has been built, and that there is equality of all people, irrespective of race and creed.[79]

Their knowledge of the history of the Russian constitution had already been shown in a petition made on 14 April 1965 to Comrade L. I. Brezhnev.[80] Referring to Lenin[81] and Bonch-Bruyevich, the Pentecostals of Soviet Russia demand full religious freedom:

> 'The Russian Tsars showed no mercy on schismatics and sectarians', wrote the Social Democrats, 'they persecuted, tortured, drowned, executed them, they pilloried them, threw them mercilessly into prisons and dungeons and drank their blood. As so it has gone until now, when the mentality, laws and customs of people have become less severe. No longer are sectarians and schismatics executed before the very eyes of the people. Now they are merely put on trial, arrested, exiled, imprisoned . . . Soon the day will come, and is indeed already near, when all people will have the right to believe in what they want, observe whatever religion they prefer. The day will come . . . when the church will be entirely separated from the state. Everyone will have the right to meet freely, to speak freely and everywhere to propagate whatever views he likes. Everyone will have the right freely to print and disseminate whatever he wishes anywhere in the world . . . Sectarians! the hour of freedom is at hand and it is drawing nearer.'[82]

The Pentecostals are trying to hasten the arrival of the age of freedom promised as long ago as 1904. For in this age – so they believe – the Russian Pentecostal movement will evangelize not only Russia, but the whole world.

4. *A New Phase in the Conflict between Communist Atheism and Christianity*

Since the protest movement has already encroached upon the Orthodox Church,[83] primitive authoritarian measures, such as the closing of churches,[84] and even punishment by imprisonment and torture, are no longer sufficient. In an article in *Kommunist* in 1965 Mchedlov was already calling for an end to the primitive witch-hunts and slanders against Christians.

> Certain authors seem incapable of being satisfied by an objective analysis of new phenomena and through laziness restrict their criticism to features which their ideological opponents have rejected.[85]

This is also true of polemics against Pentecostals, for 'Not all Pentecostals are fanatics', in the lapidary words of *Nauka i Religiya*.[86]

The call here is for the conflict to be conducted with more discrimination. It has not yet penetrated, however, to the works of Soviet atheist propaganda – mostly of a popular or even pseudo-scientific character, as for example in the journal *Nauka i Religiya*. Hans Bräker, in his essay on the debate on religious philosophy in the Soviet Union, discusses the articles that have appeared in Soviet specialist journals,[87] and I give his conclusions here.

One of his main conclusions seems to me to be of fundamental importance. Neither Soviet legislation on the subject of religion since the beginning of 1918, nor the Soviet criticism of religion, has ever been concerned to any extent with the wide current of Russian Christianity which lies outside the institutional framework of the official churches. This manifestation of Christianity (which Bräker rather rashly compares to the latent non-practising Christianity of the West), which took shape before the revolution in the Russian sects, and since then has in part continued to exist in the Pentecostal movement and the *Initiativniki*, is one which it is difficult to assess in the categories of the Soviet criticism of religion. Thus Bräker reports M. V. Vagabov as stating bluntly and emphatically

> that on the Soviet side there exists hitherto no research from the point of view of sociology and social psychology on the extent of religious belief in the Soviet Union, and that there is as a result, 'it must be admitted to our shame' – Vagabov's actual words – a very inadequate knowledge of the number of believers . . ., of their intellectual world and of their psychology.[88]

But the Soviet criticism of religion is ill-informed in another and more important sphere. This is in the field of modern Protestant theology, which a Soviet work calls 'one of the most impressive ideological phenomena in contemporary Western history'.[89] Bräker refers explicitly to the growing encounter with Bultmann, Tillich, and particularly Bonhoeffer; but he goes on to ask why there is no detailed analysis of these theologians, who have an open-minded approach not only to atheistic humanism, but also, and not least, to Marxism, or at least to the early Marx, and are prepared to be known as 'Marxists' in this sense. Bräker suspects that discussion on this manifestation of Protestant theology has already begun, even though there is no literary evidence of it. But at the present moment, he thinks, its publication is regarded as inopportune, because such a theology would make available to the Soviet reader an interpretation of Christianity

> in which there is no longer any need for an absolute and profound gulf between Marxism and Christianity, Marxism and religion, a pattern of thought which could have some attraction for intellectuals who are beginning to have doubts and are not so sure about their 'historical and dialectic materialism'.[90]

What role do the *Initiativniki* play in this coming conflict? Until recently there was a tendency to class them as evangelical fundamentalists who could only fight a rearguard action in this conflict. Against the *orthodox Communism* of the Komsomol, the *orthodox fundamentalism* of the Christsomols (as one might call the young *Initiativniki*) has an unquestionable advantage. The *Initiativniki* (like the Baptists) offer their members in the secularized Russian state a warm-hearted community and the mutual help of a brotherhood, which can be attractive not only to peasants and workers, but also to engineers, officers of the Red Army, students and secondary school teachers. But what attitude will the *Initiativniki* adopt to a criticism of religion which has progressed in the direction described above? Will they be able to cling to their present untenable affirmations, such as the defence of the biblical creation story against the theory of evolution, and the affirmation of the infallibility of the Bible understood in an historical and scientific sense, and persist their narrow cultural and ethical attitudes? Or will they develop a theology which takes man as its starting point in the sense of the hymn quoted above?[91]

It seems at first sight that both the atheists, and also the Christians (both Russian Orthodox, Baptists and *Initiativniki*) are afraid of modern theology. For the atheists, this theology destroys the caricature which they have painted of Christians. It shows that a Christian need not in every case be anti-Marxist and ill-informed, and that the gospel has an essential contribution to make even in a secularized and technical society; and that Christians are not automatically defenders of the *status quo* (Bonhoeffer). The Christians are afraid, because the 'adulthood' of the churches demands humility and a readiness for dialogue from ministers, and the venture of faith from believers, whereas the old-fashioned creed of fundamentalism gives something firm to hold on to in the vicissitudes of persecution.

The strength of the *Initiativniki* is their return to these sources. Their weakness is that they are trying to give a present-day significance to the statements of Lenin, like those of the Bible, by ignoring the intervening historical development. But if in the midst of all the physical and mental pressure upon them they can develop a method of interpretation that can abandon 'Christian principles' which have long been untenable, they will not merely have made an essential contribution to the interpretation of the gospel in Russia, but will also have helped in overcoming the Communist form of fundamentalism, which can be seen in the way in which Marx and Lenin are quoted.

NOTES

1. *Komsomol* is the name of the Soviet Communist youth organization. The sources for this chapter were the dissertation by Steve Durasoff, both in its original form (*AUCECB, 1944–1964*, New York 1967, manuscript) and in its published form (*Russian Protestants*, 1969), a selection made by Christian D. Schmidt from two recent Russian books about sects in Russia (F. I. Fedorenko, *Sekty, ikh vera i dela*, Moscow 1965; A. I. Klibanov, *Istoriya religioznogo sektantstva v Rossii*, Moscow 1965), a number of interviews (names not given) and the report of a commission sent to Russia in 1969 by the WCC, together with the sources and reports quoted in the footnotes.

2. See below, p. 269.

3. Sources, documents, literature: 05.04.001.

4. Russian: *Evangel'skie Khristiane*, see below, pp. 269ff.

5. D. I. Ponomarchuk, *Bratskiy Vestnik* 5–6, 1960, p. 74.

6. Russian: *Soyuz Khristian Evangel'skoy Very.*

7. F. F. Fedorenko, *Sekty*, p. 180.

8. D. Gee, *Upon All Flesh*, p. 31.

9. F. M. Putintsev, *Politicheskaya rol' sektantstva*, p. 445.

10. F. I. Garkavenko, *Chto takoe religioznoe sektantstvo*, p. 83

11. Russian: *tryasuny*, another name for the Pentecostals.

12. I. E. Voronaev, *Evangelist* 1928/12, p. 23.

13. G. M. Livshits, *Religiya i tserkov'*, pp. 135f.

14. *Nauka i religiya* 5, 1960, p. 28.

15. The above is an attempt to reconcile the somewhat conflicting accounts of S. Durasoff and *Pentecost* 1961, p. 3: 'Release of Mrs Voronaev'. Both accounts are largely based on statements by Mrs Voronaev. Since his last arrest nothing more has been heard of Voronaev.

16. Baron von Uexküll, *The New Acts* 3/4, July–Aug. 1907.

17. Particularly reliable Finnish sources are the early numbers of *Toivon Tähti* and *Ristin Voitto.*

18. H. Steiner, *VdV* 24/12, Dec. 1931; 25/1, Jan. 1932, pp. 3ff.; 25/2, Feb. 1932, pp. 9ff.; 25/3, March 1932, pp. 10–12.

19. W. Schmidt, *Pfingstbewegung*, p. 86.

20. Evangelical Christians in the Apostolic Spirit (Russian: *Obshchina evangel'skikh kristian v dukhe apostol'skom*): F. I. Federenko, *Sekty*, p. 178.

21. *Ibid.*, n. 20. Russian: *Isusovtsy* (from Russian *Iisus*, Jesus). Cf. above, ch. 3.1, pp. 31f.

22. Russian: *Edinstvenniki* (from Russian *edinstvenny*, only, sole).

23. *P* 58, 1962, p. 10.

24. J. H. Rushbrook, *Baptist Movement*, p. 80.

25. M. M. Korff, *Am Zarenhof*, pp. 65ff.; quoted by R. Stupperich, *Die Furche* 20,

1934, p. 141; S. Durasoff, *Russian Protestants*, pp. 44ff.; I. Motorin, *Bratskiy Vestnik* 2, 1946, pp. 24f.

26. N. S. Leskov, *Velikosvetskiy raskol'*, p. 59; S. Durasoff, *op. cit.*, p. 43.

27. *Dein Reich komme* 9, 1930, p. 215.

28. I. S. Prokhanoff, *In the Cauldron of Russia*, pp. 231f.; *Erfolge* (German version), p. 7.

29. *KPSS v Rezolyutsiakh i Resheniakh S'ezdov* I, 1953, p. 858; ET: W. Kolarz, *Religion*, p. 293.

30. Letter of Tregubov, the follower of Tolstoy, to Stalin in: Putintsev, *Kabalnoe*, p. 92; ET in: W. Kolarz, *Religion*, p. 293.

31. *Pravda*, 1924, n. 128; ET: W. Kolarz, *Religion*, p. 288.

32. *Kracht van Omhoog* 26/14, 15.1.1963.

33. Based on R. Stupperich, *Die Furche* 20, 1934, p. 145.

34. F. F. Fedorenko, *Sekty*, pp. 82, 83, 86; A. I. Klibanov, *Istoriya*, pp. 194f.

35. R. Stupperich, *Die Furche* 20, 1934, p. 149.

36. M. Artenjev, *Orient und Occident*, vol. 6, p. 36.

37. R. Stupperich, *Die Furche* 20, 1934, p. 143 n. 29.

38. *Soyuz evangel'skikh kristian – baptistov.*

39. A. Karev, in J. Meister (ed.), *Bericht*, 1959, p. 242.

40. I. Z. Zhidkov and A. V. Karev, *Bratskiy Vestnik* 1955, 1, p. 5; V.S., *Bratskiy Vestnik* 1952, 3, p. 11; A. V. Karev, *Bratskiy Vestnik* 1960, 3, p. 18.

41. A. I. Mitskevich, *Bratskiy Vestnik* 1959, 2, p. 49; 3, 1960, pp. 96ff.

42. P. Kaushansky, *Nauka i religiya* 1961, 12, pp. 18ff.; ET: S. Durasoff, *AUCECB*, p. 186.

43. N. I. Pejsti (ed.), *Zasady*, printed in Polish and German: 05.23 004.

44. N. I. Pejsti (ed.), *op. cit.*, preface and ch. 6.

45. *Ibid.*, ch. 4.

46. *Ibid.*

47. *Ibid.*, ch. 7. The phrase *eph ho pantes hemarton* (Rom. 5.12) is translated not following the Latin Vulgate (*in quo omnes peccaverunt*) but correctly as '*because* they have all sinned' (*ponieważ wszyscy zgrzeszyli*).

48. *Ibid.*, chs. 9 and 20.

49. *Ibid.*, ch. 13.

50. *Ibid.*, ch. 12.

51. *Ibid.*, chs. 14, 16 and 18.

52. *Ibid.*, ch. 9.

53. R. C. Torbet, *History of the Baptists*, p. 203, speaks of 700,000 Baptists, who later split.

54. F. F. Fedorenko, *Sekty*, p. 183.

55. *P* 42, 1957, p. 16.

56. V. M. Kalugin, *Sovremennoe*, p. 19.

57. *Times*, 4 Jan. 1963, p. 8; M. Bourdeaux, *Religious Ferment*, pp. 16ff.

58. Their leaders were Sergei Shevchuk, Alexander Shevchenko, Joseph Lotkeff, Dancheko.

59. H. P. Wilson, *European Evangel* 12/5, May 1963, pp. 6ff. Cf. also D. Shakarian, ch. 1.1(*b*), p. 8.

60. Interview by M. Zhidkov with S. Durasoff, 5.7.1965; S. Durasoff, *Russian Protestants*, p. 202.

61. S. Durasoff, *AUCECB*, p. 324.

62. J. C. Pollock, *Faith of the Russian Evangelicals.* S. Durasoff, *AUCECB*, p. 16.

63. S. Durasoff, *Russian Protestants*, pp. 140ff.; *Nauka i Religiya*, 1966, 9, pp. 22f.

(M. Bourdeaux, *Religious Ferment*, pp. 8ff.); F. Garkavenko, *Nauka i Religiya*, 1966, 9 pp. 24f. (M. Bourdeaux, *Religious Ferment*, p. 25). *Bratskiy Listok* (journal of the *Initiativniki*), quoted by M. Bourdeaux, *op. cit.*, p. 26. Even the General Secretary of the AUCECB, A. V. Karev, puts forward in a remarkable article a Pentecostal doctrine of the baptism of the Spirit, although without the 'initial sign' of glossolalia postulated by the American Pentecostals for the baptism of the Spirit: 'One must make a separation between being born of the Holy Spirit and being filled with his power . . .' (A. V. Karev, *Bratskiy Vestnik* 1960, 3, p. 16; ET: S. Durasoff, *AUCECB*, pp. 172ff.

64. Novosti Press Agency, Oct. 1966; English in *Religion in Communist Dominated Areas* 5/21, 15.11.1966; M. Bourdeaux, *Religious Ferment*, p. 3.

65. I. Voevodin, *Komsomolskaya Pravda*, 25.9.1962. English version based on that in R. Wurmbrand (ed.), *Soviet Saints*, with corrections from the version by S. Durasoff, *AUCECB*, pp. 214f. and the German version of Joachim Müller, Stuttgart: 'Wie Sie ihres Glaubens Leben. Bericht von den evangelischen Christen in der Sowjet-Union' (Ms., 1963). Wurmbrand gives the Russian name for 'Pentecostals', *pyatidesyatniki*, which, for a reader unfamiliar with Russian, obscures the fact that Shevchenko is a Pentecostal.

66. *Sovetskaya Yustitsiya* 9, 1964, p. 27; ET: M. Bourdeaux, *op. cit.*, pp. 77f.

67. Duplicated letter by 120 brethren and sisters from Barnaul and Kulunda (Siberia), 16.2.1964; ET: *Religion in Communist Dominated Areas* 3/16, 30.9.1964, pp. 122ff.

68. *Ibid.*

69. Quoted in M. Bourdeaux, *op. cit.*, pp. 64f.

70. S. Khudiakov, *Molodoi Kommunist* 3, 1957, pp. 118ff.

71. *Sovetskaya Moldaviya* 15.9.1966, p. 4.

72. Y. Kruzhilin and N. Shalamova, *Pravda Vostoka* (Tashkent), 22.10.1966, p. 4; ET: M. Bourdeaux, *op. cit.*, p. 137.

73. A. T. Ohrn (ed.), *Eighth Baptist World Congress*, 1950, p. 49.

74. Resolution by G. Ponurko and I. E. Voronaev at the second Ukrainian Pentecostal Congress, 1927; F. F. Fedorenko, *Sekty*, pp. 180f.

75. *Bratskiy Vestnik* 1947, 4, p. 7; ET: S. Durasoff, *Russian Protestants*, p. 243.

76. *Bratskiy Vestnik* 1953, 1, pp. 4f.

77. In full and with great care in *Religion in Communist Dominated Areas* 7/4–5, 15–29 Feb. 1968, pp. 1160ff.

78. *Bratskiy Vestnik* 1967, 5.

79. Quoted in M. Bourdeaux, *op. cit.*, p. 122.

80. *Posev* (Frankfurt am Main), 5.8.1966, pp. 4f.; ET: M. Bourdeaux, *op. cit.*, pp. 105ff.

81. 'The Social Democrats go on to demand that each individual should have the full right to confess any creed whatever quite openly . . . In Russia . . . there still remain disgraceful laws against people who do not hold the Orthodox creed, against schismatics, sectarians, Jews. These laws either forbid the existence of such a faith or forbid its propagation . . . All these laws are most unjust and oppressive, they are imposed by force alone. Everyone should have the right not only to believe what he likes but also to propagate whatever faith he likes . . . No civil servant should even have the right to ask anyone a single question about his beliefs: this is a matter of conscience and no one has the right to interfere.' Quotation from V. I. Lenin (1903), Vol. 6, pp. 325ff.; ET: M. Bourdeaux, *op. cit.*, p. 108).

82. Bonch-Bruyevich, in *Rassvet*, Geneva, 1904, no. 1; quoted in V. D. Bonch-Bruyevich, *Izbrannie Sochineniya* 1959, vol. I, pp. 197f.; ET: M. Bourdeaux, *op. cit.*, p. 107. The passage is quoted in the petition.

83. *Kampf des Glaubens. Dokumente aus der Sowjetunion*, Berne, 1967. G. Simon,

Die Kirchen in Russland. Cf. particularly the letter of A. E. Levitin-Krasnow to Pope Paul VI, in: *Religion in Communist-Dominated Areas* 9/19–20, Oct. 1970, pp. 151–8.

84. *Nauka i religiya* 10, 1961, p. 92.

85. Mchedlov, in *Kommunist*, quoted in *Information* 14, 2nd ed. June 1965, pub. by the Evangelische Zentralstelle für Weltanschaungsfragen, Stuttgart.

86. *Nauka i religiya* 1964, 8, pp. 3ff.; ET: S. Durasoff, *op. cit.*, p. 211.

87. H. Bräker, 'Die religionsphilosophische Diskussion in der Sowjetunion' in U. Duchrow, *Marxismusstudien* 6, series 1969 (Weltreligionen und Marxismus vor der wissenschaftlich-technischen Welt), pp. 115ff.

88. M. V. Vagabov, 'Bol'she vnimaniya sovetskomu islamovedeniya', in *Voprosy Filosofii* 12, 1966, p. 174; quoted by H. Bräker, *op. cit.*, p. 126.

89. V. M. Boriskin, 'Krisis khristiantva i ego otrazhnie v evangelicheskoy teologii', *Vestnik Moskovskogo Universiteta* 3 (VIII), 1965, p. 69; quoted by H. Bräker, *op. cit.*, p. 132.

90. H. Bräker, *op. cit.*, p. 148.

91. Cf. above pp. 278f.

PART TWO

Belief and Practice

21

'Back to the Bible!': The Pentecostal Understanding of Scripture

1. *'The Bible, the Inspired Word of God': The Fundamentalist Understanding of the Bible*

ALMOST all Pentecostal denominations and holiness groups teach:

> The Bible is the inspired word of God and its content is infallible divine revelation.[1]
> [It] is the infallible rule of faith and conduct, and is superior to conscience and reason, but not contrary to reason.[2]

Often the remarks are even more specific. We believe in 'the whole Bible',[3] 'Old and New Testament',[4] 'in verbal inspiration'[5] or even 'in the supernatural plenary inspiration of Scripture'.[6] Others describe the operation of inspiration as a Pentecostal 'experience of infusion':[7]

> God the Holy Spirit gave the men who wrote the original autograph copies of the Scripture His own thoughts, so that the words as well as the thoughts are God's revelation to us.[8]

Sometimes even the translation is indicated. The Authorized Version or Luther's Bible are preferred, though Jonathan Paul of the Mülheim Association of Christian Fellowships has produced a good translation of the New Testament with a Pentecostal commentary.[9] The 'serving brethren' of the 'Gemeinde der Christen "Ecclesia"' have to swear an oath that they will never criticize the Bible or call it in question.[10]

No wonder, then, that European and especially German biblical scholarship is vehemently rejected, because this ' "higher criticism" undermines faith in the supernatural, especially in the inspiration and authority of the Word of God'.[11] Elementary findings in 'Introductions to the Old Testament', e.g. the distinction between the three Isaiahs, are contested:

In 1890 the 'liberal' was debating whether there were two Isaiahs; in 1930 the extreme 'modernist' was debating whether there was a personal God.[12]

This free thought, which has never produced a Luther or a Niemöller,[13] is said to repeat the old mistake of Erasmus in taking this world, the state, man, more seriously than God and the world beyond.[14] Such a remark overlooks the fact that Niemöller is not a fundamentalist. At a consultation between twenty-three European Pentecostal preachers and representatives of the World Council of Churches, Martin Niemöller was asked by the Pentecostalists: 'How can you work with people who do not believe in the inspiration of Scripture?' Niemöller replied:

> When I founded the Pastors' Emergency League in 1933, I expected that every pastor who believed in the Bible would know who his leader was. To my disappointment, I discovered that belief in inspiration could very easily be combined with National Socialist compromises.[15]

Among American and European Pentecostals, knowledge of the German Church struggle and of European theology is very superficial. The Americans dismiss it out of hand as modernism. G. F. Atter mentions Karl Barth among the sectarians, alongside the British Israelites, Moral Rearmament and the 'Jesus Only' groups. According to Atter, neo-orthodoxy, of which Barth was a spokesman, was a reaction against liberalism. Barth understands revelation as event, in other words, as a meeting of the divine and the human. Dogma is not a revelation, but at best a pointer to revelation. Theological expressions are paradoxical. The Bible contains three kinds of writing, true, imaginary and mythical. All have their value, once their different functions have been recognized. Atter concludes his enumeration with the remark: 'Thus will be seen how very far the heirs of the Reformers are from the truly Scriptural position of the Bible doctrine.'[16]

For the healing evangelist T. L. Osborn, it is particularly important to make and indelible mark for aggressive evangelism:

> In Switzerland, where Barthian theology holds that all men are already saved in Christ, and need only to hear the news, [Osborn's] straightforward questions were laying the axe at the very roots of the religious traditions of the land.[17]

It does not disturb the authors of the quotations above (Osborn and Atter) that the leader of the Apostolic Church (in Switzerland the 'Gemeinde für Urchristentum'), Pastor Robert Willenegger, should describe Brunner and Barth as 'theologians who stand near to the Bible'.[18]

With this ignorance of theological work it is possible to obtain a doctorate in theology at a Pentecostal Bible school without knowledge of ancient or modern languages, without knowledge of the origin or composition of the Bible, without secondary education, and simply on the basis of six years' instruction on the Bible, a few essays, tests in shorthand, business management, church history and practical theology, and regular visits to meetings (the number of services attended is taken into account in the examination for the doctorate).[19]

The first task of Pentecostal Bible schools is to build up a spiritual bulwark against evolutionary theories and biblical criticism. Pentecostal Bible schools, unlike 'secular' universities, are not 'naturalistic and man-centred but supernaturalistic and God-centred'.[20] Nor are they, as e.g. the Baptist Bible schools, 'honeycombed with bastard modernism'.[21] The Pentecostal Holiness Church is proud of the fact that not a single modernist preacher can be found in its ranks.

> Every minister and every layman, without exception, holds to the same traditional orthodox, evangelical dogma which characterized the teachings of the Church before the infiltration of German rationalism and modernism.[22]

C. W. Conn of the Church of God (Cleveland) accuses the traditional churches of allowing the ideas of Kant, Emerson, Newman, Voltaire, Schleiermacher, Carlyle and 'a mixture of theologians, philosophers and poets' to exercise more influence in many pulpits than the word of God.

> The most famous of these critics was Renan, who stated in his biographies of Christ that He was but a mere man and that both the New Testament and the Old Testament contained numerous myths and legends. Both modernism and socialism resulted in much scepticism among the masses of the people.[23]

George Jeffreys, a well-known British Pentecostal evangelist, can write:

> We do not hesitate to say that modernism is the most pernicious and poisonous influence at work in the Christian Church today. It paves the way for Unitarianism, Spiritism, Russellism, Buddhism, Theosophy and many other similar delusive doctrines. Modernism invariably means mutilation of the Book. The pulpits should be purged of this pestilence.[24]

The Assemblies of God in distant Australia have stated the goal of their union to be a battle against all sects and 'higher criticism'.[25] The Belgian, French and Swiss Pentecostal movements affirm in their confession:

> We accept the Bible as the inspired word of God and we continue in the evangelical faith, far removed from all modernism, higher criticism, new theology and whatever ends up by undermining belief founded on Jesus Christ, the Son of God.[26]

The tragedy of modern biblical criticism works itself out in producing empty churches, and alienation from the church is in turn a cause of international conflict. That is the result of our 'theologizing to death'.[27] The theological intellectuals had their chance in past centuries and now have lost it. They have shown what *man* accomplishes. 'Now there is a theology emerging that is proving what *God* can do.'[28] The best thing is 'to have nothing to do with biblical criticism, but to rely simply, like a child, on the eternal ground of truth. . . .'[29]

> Much as we rejoice in the fact that God also makes use of learned men to demonstrate the authenticity of his word, we must assert with great regret that despite everything, biblical criticism is taking on more disastrous dimensions and that many of those who study theology are losing their faith. From this we can see clearly that this way is not the most reliable one. My professor of religion used to try to persuade me that the study of theology was the only means of understanding the Bible. But he himself was a bad example of that. When I began to read my Bible with prayer and to put into practice what it contained, I found my way towards understanding the Bible . . .'[30]

The unhappy alternative, that the Bible is not the word of God but merely contains it, is rejected:

> The liberal religionist compromises to assert that the Bible only *contains* the Word of God. Evangelical Christians, however, believe the entire Bible to be equally inspired. We believe that all Scriptures, as originally written, are the living oracles of God and should be accepted as such.[31]
>
> The most dangerous opponents are the 'faithless believers', truly Christian people, who, through innocent fearfulness, have been misled by deceitful misrepresentation of the facts about the Biblical inspiration. They have accepted a half truth; they believe the written Word of God to be reliable in matters of faith and practice, but open to error in matters of fact and history.[32]

Writers join Bengel in asserting that not only the ideas of Scripture but also the words are inspired, though a mechanical doctrine of inspiration is rejected.[33] Granted,

> the Bible contains many words of man and even words spoken by the Devil. But in its totality it is the inspired word of God, the truth . . . Jesus believed in what the prophet Daniel wrote; he also believed what happened to Jonah.

We cannot go wrong if we keep to the teaching of Jesus and his apostles,[34] for

> from the first verse in Genesis to the last in Revelation there is not one single contradiction. You may search in vain to find inaccuracies because they are only supposed. The one divine Author, moving each of its writers, has given us a complete Bible that will stand the tests of all time.[35]

Often this biblical exegesis gets caught up in grotesque questioning. The Church of the Living God may not be so far from the truth when, as a negro church, it asserts that Jesus, David, Job, Moses' wife and other holy people of the Bible had dark skins,[36] but it seems strange for Jesus to be regarded as a freemason.[37] W. V. Grant is able to provide information about men in 'flying saucers';[38] Williams and Sauer have to answer questions raised by evidently not uncritical readers, e.g.: will the Third World War take place before the great tribulation? Yes. Is the new Jerusalem (in heaven) inhabited now? No, it is uninhabited and will come down from heaven uninhabited.[39] Will the final rapture take place at the beginning, the middle or the end of Matt. 24?[40] It is recognized that the Babylonian flood stories are earlier than those in the Bible.

> [They] may perfectly well be the product of conversation with Noah. This narrative, circumstantial agreement with the Scriptures to a degree simply astounding, puts the fact of the flood beyond all cavil or doubt.[41]

Schneider, a Swiss missionary in South Africa, hits the nail on the head when he writes:

> Certainly, the Bible is in the hands of all the Ethiopian bishops[42] and all the Zionist prophets . . . But it is not enough to have the Bible. It is also necessary to know how to read it . . . It is necessary to know how to interpret it.[43]

One of these negro churches 'explains the Bible from the following chapters, Amen: Jer. 1.4–5; Prov. 8.22–26. Amen.'[44] Another not unjustly offers as the key to exegesis: 'We believe in the Old and New Testament "by the interpretation of the river" ',[45] and a third believes in the Old and New Testaments and the teaching of John Dawi.[46]

The creation narrative in Gen. 1–3 is understood literally.[47] Therefore Edith C. Stevenson objects to the new *Oxford Bible Atlas*, which 'would seem to discredit his belief in the Genesis account of man's beginning upon this earth'.[48] Mink explicitly asserts:

> I find it much easier to believe that God made man from earth than that he developed from a cell to an ape and then to a human being. . . Why should we pay homage to the theory of evolution when we believe in the almighty God for whom nothing is impossible?[49]

The *Elim Evangel* attacked the BBC for giving information in one series on the prehistory of the earth. This information was condemned as 'both unscientific and anti-Christian'.[50] That the universities teach these 'beastly doctrines' only makes matters worse.[51] 'Hitler believed the axiom that the bigger the lie the more inclined people will be to believe it. Modern scientists appear to work on a similar principle.'[52]

Modern theology is a 'monstrosity inspired by the devil'. 'It is a clear, proven fact that evolution leads to atheism or agnosticism. . . .'[53] The origin of giants from the association of angels with women (Gen. 6.2) 'is a fact. This still happens today' (Matt. 24.37).[54]

For Bruce Williams, 'the Biblical account of the creation of man is more plausible and satisfying than the theories of natural evolution'.[55] We can refute the scepticism and mockery of unbelievers and avoid the traps of the modernists with the words 'In the beginning God'.[56]

Obviously, Moses is regarded as the author of the Pentateuch (the so-called five books of Moses).[57] Jost Müller-Bohn admonishes his readers:

> Friend, do not believe these bewildering assertions. It has long since been proved that they are not true and established sciences. Believe rather in the unchanging word of God.[58]

It should not be assumed that this superficial castigation of the natural sciences is an invention of the Pentecostal movement. The traditional churches have for long enough defended positions which have been quite untenable.

> If the Bible does not give us a true account of the six-day work of creation in its first chapter, then none of its statements is trustworthy.[59]

In the same way, in 1962 the Lutherans of the Missouri Synod were still designating the theory of evolution as a 'foolish theory without any proof', which is 'degrading mankind'.[60] The Holiness movement[61] and the German[62] and Swiss[63] Conservative Evangelicals have been waging a polemical campaign against reasonable biblical scholarship for years. Even a conservative theologian like Schlatter was not safe from their attacks,[64] because he detected legendary traits in the book of Jonah.

> The Lord Jesus bears unmistakable testimony to the historical truth of Jonah's sojourn in the great fish (Matt. 12.40). If it is assumed that the story of Jonah is a saga, then either the Lord did not speak the truth or he was wrong. In this case the whole Bible and therefore all the words of Jesus are put in question.[65]
>
> The Bible knows only full inspiration. It designates the Holy Scriptures as being God's Word completely, and knows no half or quarter inspiration. It bears witness with powerful authority to the fact that the word spoken by God is identically the same as that written down by man.[66]

This understanding of the Bible leads to a confusion between the Bible and a book of oracles. Thus Gordon Lindsay can spend 52 pages answering the question *Why do the righteous suffer?* He knows *Forty signs* which foretell the imminent return of Jesus and he knows *All about the Gifts of the Spirit.*[67] Naturally, he contests the theory of evolution:

> If you have a child in school, this is a must book for your home. Authoritative information is given proving that the theory of evolution is fake.[68]

Even worse, this theological conservatism often runs parallel to an unimaginable social and political blindness. The German Conservative Evangelicals demand that a Bible-based radicalism of the right be set over against the teachers' radicalism of the left.[69] In a pamphlet of the Anchor Bay Bible Institute on Communism and its prehistory, 'a number of French infidels and immoral philosophers' (Weishaupt, Marx, Prudhon [*sic*]) are mentioned, 'the most infamous of whom was one Jean Jacques Rousseau'. Communists and socialists are condemned root and branch. The only difference between them is the tactical question of the method to be applied. Darwinism (evolution) is a denial of ancestral authority, Nietzscheism (modernism) a denial of divine authority, and Marxism (atheism, Communism, socialism, Bolshevism) a denial of all authority.[70] As in America there is doubt about the literal understanding of hell even in the teaching of English, it is now time to protest against the surrender of children to communism in American schools.[71]

Martin Schian rightly remarks: 'The recognition of the authority (of the Bible) is more a principle than a matter of practice'.[72] Thus in that period, shaken by social struggles, it could be said in an incomprehensible misunderstanding of the real situation:

> No one saves a man by fulfilling his needs. Bring him into contact with Jesus and he will soon be able to buy his own bread and butter.[73]

Social and political blindness, fruitless political conservatism and fundamentalist ignorance were present in many of the so-called 'believing' circles of the Protestant churches at the time of the first rise of the Pentecostal movement. No wonder that the movement took much of it over. What is much more surprising is that despite continuing polemic against biblical criticism and against a true social and ethical engagement on the part of the churches, there are Pentecostals who do not succumb to this polemic. They must be mentioned next.

2. '*Are we Fundamental Enough?*' *Self-criticism of Fundamentalism*

Within the Pentecostal movement there is a minority, small indeed but not to be underestimated, which has become weary of these fundamentalist cries. Among them is Donald Gee, though he was once theologically a fundamentalist. After the fundamentalist fighting-cocks in the Pentecostal movement made it impossible for him to take part in the Third Full Assembly of the World Council of Churches in New Delhi (1961), he wrote the fiery article, already mentioned, entitled 'Are we fundamental enough?'[74]

At the conference of the German Pentecostal Movement held from 6–9 August, 1928, there was an account of a vision directed against polemic:

> You yourself stood there in the smithy and watched your sword being made ready. With flashing eyes, filled with lust for battle, you stood there and watched closely. You followed the work of the heavy hammer, and when the sword was made ready, you took it to yourself. Then there was a great clash of arms in your midst and you drew your sword against your brother. Thereupon the heavens opened and the great hand of God descended and stilled your work-place. You are surprised that you can no longer hear the buzzing and whirring and roaring of the wheels in your factory. You are seized with great anxiety because of your lack of work. But you must also know that you have been given notice and dismissed by your employer . . .'[75]

Alongside these general appeals for peace, there were also attempts to think out the problem of verbal inspiration once again. Russell Evans, teaching at Swansea University, wrote an article for the youth of the Elim Foursquare Gospel Alliance in which he attempted to establish, with the help of the theory of relativity, 'realms of non-physical reality' in which the laws of causality do not apply, and then through a new understanding of the creative activity of

God in the present (*creatio continua*) to arrive at a new understanding of the relationship between natural science and faith. How far this article can be understood by the average Pentecostal teacher is, however, another matter.[76] Wilbur O. Fogg, one of the leaders of the Pentecostal movement within the American church, wants

> to avoid as much the Scylla of a superficial fundamentalism as ... the Charybdis of a washed-out liberalism ... The appeal to the spirit of the scripture must not be used to explain away the truth and power contained and embodied in the letter itself. The point is that the Spirit interprets the letter, and that spiritual understanding is always consistent with miracle-working power.[77]

Some Pentecostal groups go even further. The Associated Brotherhood of Christians asserts that in our time 'none of the statutes of the Mosaic Law are binding'.[78] The Pentecostal Church of Christ requires the whole Bible to be read and studied, but only the New Testament is accepted 'as our infallible guide in matters pertaining to conduct and doctrine'.[79] Pentecostal Quakers regard the Bible as secondary. For example, the Full Salvation Union regards the people who wrote the Bible as having been inspired, but not the book. The Union is clear that some passages of the Bible have no direct significance for the individual reader of it. Although the Union recognizes that the Bible is necessary for a clear recognition of the will of God in certain situations in life and that it is a pointer and a stimulus for worship and practice, on the other hand it asserts that the Bible should never have to compete with God's direct guidance of an individual.

> God has not confined himself to the written word. He still speaks direct to his children as the Bible plainly teaches he has done in the past. He does not direct anyone contrary to the standard of righteousness as taught in the Bible, but in his direct leadings, he often makes known his will to a person entirely apart from any written statement of scripture known to that person.[80]

In the Associate Brotherhood of Christians a preacher is expressly allowed to hold and preach other dogmatic views than those laid down in the confession of the group. He is merely expected to be converted, to believe in God and to lead a normal Christian life. No difficulties are to be made for him if light has not yet fallen on all the articles of faith; it is the view of the Brotherhood that 'many unnecessary divisions have arisen within the Pentecostal movement because of disputed points of doctrine'.[81] Occasionally one still meets the primitive Pentecostal view that 'the Word of God is not taught in his church to be discussed but to be obeyed',[82] but it is increasingly giving place to a fundamentalist rationalism, as Horton Davies[83] and F. Lovsky[84] have also established.

However, this rationalism leads individual groups to put their pre-Enlightenment theology in question. Thus, for example, the negro preacher Arthur M. Brazier gives a good survey of the questions of the canon and authorship of the

New Testament in an article on the beginnings of the New Testament, but does not draw any conclusions.[85] Roberto Bracco, who finds the new *Dizionario Biblico* of the Waldensian church not fundamentalist enough, prints the reply of the Waldensian theologian Giovanni Miegge to his [Bracco's] criticism of the dictionary in his Pentecostal newspaper.[86] It is to be hoped that the Italian Pentecostals will resist the temptation to allow themselves to be prodded into a theological feud against the Waldensians by their American sister organization; during the period of persecution they relied for years on the help and support of the Waldensians.

V. Pfaler, formerly a Lutheran pastor and later a Pentecostal preacher, rejected the rigid biblicism of the Finnish Pentecostal movement:

> God preserve us from treating each other in this way in word and writing. God preserve us from saying of a brother or sister in the faith that they do not stand on the ground of the Word because they do not recognize all 'our views' as being biblical.[87]

An account has been given above of the way in which the founder of the German Pentecostal movement, Pastor Jonathan Paul, explicitly distinguished his position from that of fundamentalism in the context of the dispute with Lepsius.[88] Today, however, there are many circles in the German-speaking Pentecostal movement which deny the theological fundamentals of their founder. But with what right?

Even so, the Mülheim Association of Christian Fellowships which has been most strongly influenced by Paul, never seems to have been strictly fundamentalist. One of its leaders, a doctor, P. Gericke, has carried on an outspoken controversy with fundamentalism and has rejected it without qualification.[89]

3. *Fundamentalism as a Ritual:* *The Function of the Fundamentalist Understanding of the Bible*

Any perceptive observer of fundamentalism will agree with Schian's judgment[90] that fundamentalist belief in the Bible is more a matter of principle than of practice. But in that case, what role does fundamentalism play in the Pentecostal understanding of faith? The answer to this question seems to me to lie in the direction of a comment made by James Barr. James Barr feels 'the criticism of fundamentalism which has become very customary to be faulty'.

> The fundamentalist use of the scripture can thus be better described as a ritualistic than as a propositional procedure. It is a form of poetry, an almost aesthetic expression of harmony with the true faith, i.e. the tradition. This is why particular verbal forms, such as the King James Version, are highly prized. . . . The Bible . . . comes to have attached to it attributes of perfection and of sublime superiority to human feelings and to human judgment; and the

> nearest analogy to the way in which these attributes work is the idea of the Immaculate Conception of the Virgin in popular Roman Catholicism of some kinds. Like the Virgin, the Bible is the human visible symbol involved in salvation; and like her freedom from all contagion of human imperfection, it has a kind of perfection and sublimity which makes it sacrilegious for us to analyse and criticize its seamless fabric. . . . The degree to which the unthinking and uncritical attitudes towards the Bible, which we regard as fundamentalistic, are damaging and dangerous, is related to the social situation. There can be situations in which a certain naivety of this kind can seem so natural as to be inevitable.[91]

Barr thus explains fundamentalism as ritualism. If this is the case, then in some social conditions Pentecostal fundamentalism would have to be understood as the natural and inevitable expression of the understanding of the Bible. In a world of the transvaluation of all values, in which what yesterday was good is today bad, most people need an assured point of reference; for the Pentecostal this is, of course, the Bible. This point of reference becomes all the more certain, the more naive and unreflecting the faith that the Bible is infallible. This would explain the unwillingness of many Pentecostal preachers to enter a discussion of particular, clearly defined, exegetical questions; for the discussion of the infallibility of the Bible itself takes away the nature of the rite.

A rite is not discussed; it is celebrated. And as in ancient religions, the celebration of the rite guarantees the salvation of the world. It is a protection against the attack of demons which would destroy fellowship and order. All rational objections to this rite of preserving the world leave Pentecostal fundamentalists untouched. When anyone agrees to discuss the rite of preserving the world, then the world, his world, collapses.

So far so good. But what if 'social conditions' change, and regular contacts are made with other 'rites for preserving the world'? In that case, one's own rite is made relative. It can be altered, adapted, combined with other methods of mastering the world. This happened, for instance, in one of the most rapidly growing Pentecostal churches of Indonesia, the Geredja Isa Almasih, which – like most other Pentecostal groups – practises the baptism of the Spirit with speaking in tongues.[92] Its Pentecostal devotion did not, however, prevent it from transcending fundamentalism as a rite of preserving the world. It sent one of its younger preachers, Liem Khiem Yang, to the Theological High School at Djakarta and then to Germany, where his passed his doctorate examination. Nevertheless, the Geredja Isa Almasih has remained a Pentecostal church. Prayer is offered in rotation in each community from four in the morning to ten at night. But the church has profited from the theological work. It is far removed from the rigorist ethics and narrow-minded segregationist tendency of other Pentecostal groups, and invites theologians like Dzao Sze Kwang, J. Verkuyl (the Dutch secretary of missions), Andrew Gih and Hans Hoekendijk (now teaching as a professor of theology in New York and regarded by Pentecostals and many local churchmen as a radical modern theologian) to preach in its congregations.

A similar development may be noted among Catholic Pentecostals. Pentecostal fundamentalism, the religious climate of American revivalism, the 'simplistic and individualistic Christian ethics', the ban on smoking, drinking, dancing, make-up, theatre-going or other amusements, are regarded as culturally conditioned adiaphora which do not belong to the centre of the Pentecostal message. They may be natural and inevitable for certain sociological situations, but not for all.[93]

On the other hand, the traditional churches cannot overlook the fact that many of the present Pentecostal preachers have been instructed by the traditional churches. The parents in the traditional churches see in the Pentecostal movement a child in which they can recognize again, in a sorry distortion, their own sins and weaknesses. It is necessary and salutary for the traditional churches to look upon this child. We are reminded how long we in the Protestant churches have 'been afraid to share our knowledge about the Bible with church folk'.[94] It demonstrates unmistakably that instruction in the Bible which is limited to those *under* fifteen years of age will be regarded by some – the majority of those who are the future academics – as inadequate to their intellectual demands. By others – the stratum of the population which could potentially be won over by the Pentecostals – it is seen as unbelieving, 'liberal' instruction, because the church tries to communicate to children in confirmation classes minimal knowledge of biblical criticism at a stage when most of the children do not even understand the questions that are being asked. If we have to acknowledge that we have not succeeded in fulfilling Luther's demand in expressing the *literal* meaning of Scripture better than the fundamentalists, with the help of our exegetical training, the first conclusion to be drawn is not that we need better instruction of young people, but that we need to look carefully at *the concentration of all instruction on children and young people*.[95] It should not be objected that adult instruction is impossible to carry out. Only carefully prepared experiments could clarify the question. Such experiments are now being carried out. One need only think of the work in the Evangelical Academies, the Lay Training Institutes for Adult Education, the contribution made by religious programmes on radio and television, etc. Several ecumenical working parties are attempting to assess the significance of this adult education, where each person is at the same time both teacher and pupil, in other words, where adults educate each other rather than the minister introducing the so-called laity into theology. It is 'a matter for *all* members to be trained or equipped'.[96] The first results of these working parties and study groups are now available[97] and were the object of detailed consideration at the Fourth Assembly of the World Council of Churches at Uppsala.[98]

4. *Biblical Criticism at the Service of Scripture: An Example*

In his most friendly criticism of my *Handbuch*,[99] Leonard Steiner courteously but clearly rejected my attempts at loosening up Pentecostal fundamentalism. Nevertheless I shall make one more attempt to enter into conversation with those Pentecostals for whom social conditions have, in my opinion, so changed that fundamentalism seems neither natural nor inevitable to them.

First of all, it must be pointed out that the aim of modern biblical criticism – with exceptions that will not be discussed here – is to illuminate the literal meaning of a particular passage of the Bible. At any rate, that is the way in which critics understand their own work. More general works like Klaus Koch, *The Book of Books*, or commentaries like J. H. Eaton's *Psalms* in the Torch series are examples, easily accessible to Pentecostals, of the way in which commentators attempt to let individual passages from the Bible say what they particularly have to say, even if this contradicts the so-called fundamental statements of the Christian faith or other passages of the Bible. When fundamentalist interpretation of the Bible assimilates the statements of different biblical authors to each other on the grounds that the Bible is a harmony without contradiction, it is using a criterion (namely the 'harmony of the Bible') which it has *not* taken from the Bible itself. The fundamentalists ought first to prove *from the Bible* that the Bible is only significant when and because its statements are in harmony with each other.

The kind of consequences to which a fundamentalist understanding of the Bible can lead is shown by the example, mentioned above, of the author of the enquiry section of the *Pentecostal Evangel*, Ernest S. Williams.[100] Williams was asked:

> Will you please explain why the Lord punished David for numbering Israel when he moved David to do so? II Samuel 24.1f. *Answer:* If you have an Oxford Bible you will find a marginal reading to show the reference is to Satan. Thus it would read, '*Satan* moved David . . . to say, Go, number Israel and Judah.' This is in harmony with the same account recorded in I Chronicles 21.1: 'And Satan stood up against Israel, and provoked David to number Israel.' If God lifts His protecting hand from any of us because we have provoked Him to anger, the way is open for Satan to tempt us to err.[101]

What kind of reverence for the Bible do we find there? No critical exegete would proceed in the same way as E. S. Williams. The whole Hebrew tradition clearly says, God tempted David (II Sam. 14.1). The fact that the book of Chronicles (thought to have been written later) takes offence at this difficult passage and replaces God by Satan does not allow Williams to interpret II Sam. 24.1 clean contrary to the wording of the biblical text. Furthermore, the marginal note in the Oxford Bible merely points to the differently worded parallel passage in I Chron. 21.1; it does not mean that we have the right to twist the biblical text so that it means the opposite, as Williams does. The firm fact is that the book of Samuel gives God as the one who incited David, while Chronicles gives Satan. If people are intent on harmonizing even at the cost of truth, they will end up turning the text of the Bible into its opposite.

What do so-called unbelieving, modernist exegetes do with this text? At any rate, they begin by leaving it as it is. Let me take an example. In Gerhard von Rad's *Old Testament Theology*, which a Pentecostal can understand quite easily, we read:

> The fact that Jahweh's anger once again broke out against Israel, and that he incited David against his people, is noted at the beginning with a matter-of-factness almost of the kind found in annals – in just the same way as it is later regarded as self-evident that the destroying angel was visible to everyone when it appeared over Jerusalem. It is certain that the census which David organised served a military purpose; it meant some sort of reform in the army. The measure marked an important turning-point, namely the transition from the old holy war to the war of tactics. David wanted to have figures available in order to be able to make his arrangements. In so doing, the King brought serious guilt upon himself: he 'acted foolishly', that is, he deliberately broke a sacral regulation. But afterwards David was not punished like the commonalty of his people – his favoured position as the anointed of Jahweh is expressed in the fact that he is himself allowed to choose his punishment, that is, he is confronted with quite individual decisions. The story obviously starts from the presupposition that by this choice of his the King can still make things turn out very much for the better or very much for the worse. David chooses – for so the passage is to be understood – the most severe punishment, pestilence, which was regarded as a visitation coming directly from Jahweh. For the ancient readers this was utterly unexpected, for who in those old days would have chosen a visitation that came directly from the deity rather than a calamity brought about by men? The story-teller shows us a decision of a highly dramatic character. David did what was quite unexpected, but precisely in so doing he flung himself through the thick curtain of the divine anger directly on God's heart.
>
> The story was a *hieros logos* belonging to Jerusalem, that is, it gave the answer to the question how there came to be an altar of Jahweh in the previously Canaanite city of the Jebusites. The answer shows that this saving appointment was preceded by the anointed's deep humiliation, but also that by his confidence in Jahweh's mercy he brought about the turn for the better. In our opinion, the story's strange beginning can only be understood in the light of its end: if the final upshot of the matter was a wide-reaching and important saving appointment on the part of Jahweh, then a human offence could not have been the releasing factor. If a complex of events resulted in a revelation of divine salvation such as this, the moving initiative must have come from Jahweh. The Chronicler could no longer endure this great theological tension: he says 'Satan led David astray' (I Chron. 21.1).[102]

As far as the author of II Samuel was concerned, the founding of the temple was a divine ordinance of salvation. It could not therefore be derived from an initiative on the part of Satan. Therefore – von Rad concludes – the driving force behind history must come from Yahweh, even when it includes leading David astray to transgress the divine will. Ernest S. Williams may want to reject this picture of God, but that is his affair. He may not read into the biblical text (of II Sam. 24) a meaning which he has drawn from a later text, the book of Chronicles. It would now be the task of a further analysis to investigate why the author of the book of Chronicles seeks to ascribe the initiative in the story of the foundation of the temple to Satan. Was it, as von Rad supposes, that he could 'no longer sustain the theological tension', or is the temple no longer a divine ordinance for him, so that its foundation can be ascribed to Satan? At this point I shall break off the analysis. The reader himself may decide which of the two exegetes, the Pentecostal Ernest S. Williams or the Old Testament professor, Gerhard von Rad, takes the text more seriously.

'Critical interpretation of the Bible' does not mean an interpretation that criticizes the Bible. In academic terminology the adjective 'critical' denotes an appropriate method of relevant interpretation. Part of this method is the critical investigation of one's own conceptions, one's own *understanding* of the Bible, that e.g. in the case of Williams stood in the way of understanding the Bible. 'Critical interpretation of the Bible' means 'to learn to discriminate' (Greek *krinein* = 'discriminate') between what is helpful for life and faith today and what is less helpful. Therefore confessions of faith must continually be formulated anew, and preaching must keep on changing.

Within Pentecostal circles this fact has been recognized by, for example, the Russian and Polish Pentecostal movement.[103] Other representatives of the Pentecostal movement too, however, cannot get by without critical interpretation of the Bible. They distinguish between essentials and inessentials: for some foot-washing is important, whereas others reject it as historically conditioned; for some speaking with tongues at the baptism of the Spirit is obligatory, others regard it as unnecessary; some baptize 'in the name of Jesus' and reject all other forms of baptism, others baptize 'in the name of the Father, the Son and the Holy Spirit', a third group baptizes in the name of the Trinity but immerses three times and reject other forms of baptism as invalid. Donald Gee accuses certain Pentecostal evangelists of taking Matt. 10.9–15 literally because they take 'no bag on the way', 'nor two tunics, nor sandals, nor a staff'. Here Gee takes over the liberal tradition of interpretation and says, 'Obviously in such passages a distinction needs to be made between abiding principles and local circumstances.'[104]

All these Pentecostals distinguish between what seems essential to them and what seems inessential. All claim to believe in the Bible as the inspired word of God. How then does it come about that there is no point of Pentecostal doctrine on which they are agreed? These differences are so significant that no expense or trouble is too much to introduce the forty-three varieties of Pentecostal faith to the Japanese, the Polynesians or the Yorubas. If they are so unco-ordinated in their mission round the world, the differences must be important.

Why is this? It comes about because people cannot be bothered to acquaint themselves with the beliefs of their fellow-Pentecostals or with the interpretations given by biblical criticism. They have no time for that. What others have thought and believed, matters to which they have devoted a lifetime of thought, are unimportant to them, for what good can come from an unenlightened human understanding?

If the Pentecostal movement were to get to know the thought of theologians other than through the caricatures of non-Pentecostal fundamentalists, they would discover that Protestant theology is not concerned to choose between the alternatives of a belief in the meaning of the Bible and a belief in the words of the Bible. Protestant theology sets out to take the words of the Bible quite seriously in their contemporary significance. It therefore pays careful attention to the original language of the Bible and to history. That is why it devotes so much trouble and labour to translating and interpreting the Bible.

It is impossible to present an introduction to the Protestant understanding of the doctrine of Scripture within this introduction to the Pentecostal movement. Nor is it necessary, for the work has already been done. I would suggest that my friends in the Pentecostal movement look, for example, at the small booklet by the Methodist preacher Rolf Knierim, *Bibelautorität und Bibelkritik*. It contains an expert and well-arranged discussion with fundamentalism and an excellent account of biblical criticism. The Baptists in Germany train their preachers in accordance with the principles of historical-critical scholarship without giving up their evangelical elan, their free-church understanding of the Christian community and their allegiance to scripture. They regularly publish contributions on this theme in their *Zeitschrift für Mitarbeiter in der Verkündigung und der Gemeinde* (Journal for fellow-workers in preaching and the community).[105] Anyone who would like to know how one can believe and preach the gospel while accepting that the first chapters of the First Book of Moses were not written by Moses but by various authors at various times on the basis of old mythological material ought to consult the writing of, for example, Gerhard von Rad or Alan Richardson, who – unlike many fundamentalist elaborators – prove exciting and refreshing reading, like the Bible itself.[106]

Finally, it might be appropriate to make another reference to Martin Niemöller whom the Pentecostals rightly regard as a friend who is well-disposed towards them. The publishing house of the American Assemblies of God commended Niemöller's biography with the words: 'We praise God for the grace and the courage given Martin Niemöller for the stand he has taken for the Lord Jesus Christ. His trust is in God.'[107] It is all the more astonishing in that Niemöller is not a fundamentalist. In a lecture which was unjustly described by the Pentecostals as 'Niemöller's Confession of Unbelief',[108], he said:

For me, a personal knowledge of Jesus has become decisive, and I am certain that if that had not happened, I would be an atheist pure and simple.[109]

Niemöller than went on to tell how he came to believe. For Niemöller this belief is 'a personal, loving relationship of trust':

I know that I am loved by God, the Father in heaven, and I love him in turn as my Father; I know that I am loved by Jesus Christ, my Saviour and brother – he became a man like me, and I love him in gratitude – and both of them, the Father and the Saviour, live. I speak with them and bring my worries and needs and questions to them in prayer.

After this lengthy introduction, Niemöller went on to the subject of 'modern theology'. He did not fail to speak up on behalf of Rudolf Bultmann, the professor of theology, who was under attack. He remarked: 'I have known this professor for thirty years, and if even half the members of our church synod were as real Christians as he, I would thank God.' Of the young theologians, 'who are atheists, because God, too, is a myth for them', Niemöller said:

Things will not be otherwise until Jesus meets up with them. Then the myth will suddenly become reality. I am not at all surprised; anyone who does not join company with Jesus must in all honesty become an atheist.

Niemöller then went into more details about the question of history and freely acknowledged:

It is well known, and should no longer be disputed, that there are many historical mistakes in the Bible. [But] we are paying a heavy price in church preaching today for the fact that in our sermons for one hundred and fifty years we have kept quiet in front of our congregations about theological developments. The result is that people still believe in verbal inspiration.

We cannot hold out against the truth and against reality. The view of the world accepted by those who wrote the Bible of the Old and New Testaments no longer holds today . . . And all the statements in the Bible that are bound up with this false picture of the world – such as the ascension of Christ – cannot be allowed to stand. They certainly did not happen in this way. To affirm the contrary today is simply ridiculous, whereas in the time of Luke the evangelist no one took any offence. What is lost from the message that Jesus has been exalted to God as the living Lord and shares in God's rule over the world if we can no longer accept and present the external happening of the so-called ascension as true reality? Nothing at all! It does not affect my belief in Jesus in the slightest.

These quotations from Niemöller make at least one thing clear. For the normative pioneer of the 'Confessing Church', who put his faith in Jesus Christ to the test in a concentration camp, confession of Jesus Christ and confession of the Bible as the word of God are not coupled, for better or worse, with the confession of the historical infallibility of the Bible.[110]

If Pentecostals asked me the straight question 'Is the Bible the Word of God or does it only contain it?', I would reply without hesitation, 'It is the Word of God.' But this is not the end of the conversation. It is only the beginning. For what does 'the Bible is the Word of God' mean? First of all, which Bible is the Word of God? Obviously, the original text, is the reply. But I must go on to ask, Which original text? Even today there is still dispute among the Christian churches over which books belong in the Bible. The oldest of these churches, the Abyssinian church, for example, accepts the Apocalypse of Enoch as canonical. The Roman Catholic church includes the Apocrypha (as did the first Spanish Protestant Bible of 1569). Furthermore, the various manuscripts of the Bible differ from each other. For example, does the story of Jesus and the woman taken in adultery, which is missing from most ancient manuscripts, belong in the Bible? What about the conclusion of the Lord's Prayer? And what if we have two competing texts, e.g. a very early text on the birth of Jesus, which states: 'Jacob begot Joseph. Joseph, to whom was betrothed the Virgin Mary, begot Jesus, who is called the Christ',[111] or: 'Joseph, to whom Mary, a virgin, was betrothed, was the father of Jesus'?[112] Every decision, even the fundamentalist one, is an estimate in most passages; the Pentecostals would say that it is a hypothesis, the result of human consideration. What is the use of talking about the historical accuracy of the original text of the Bible if this original text is lost for ever and we can only reconstruct it approximately? The reconstruction is quite enough for us to be able to believe in Jesus as the redeemer and lord of the world. But it is not enough for the historical accuracy postulated by the fundamentalists and considered by Martin Niemöller to be inessential.

NOTES

1. Schweiz. Pfingstmission, *VdV* cover.
2. K(ristova) P(entekostna) C(rkva), *Temeljne*, point 1; AoG, *Early History*, pp. 17–19, cf. Appendix: 2, p. 514; AdD, *Vérités*; cover *Viens et Vois*.
3. H. T. Spence, *Pentecost*, n.d., p. 4.
4. PChOG of America, *This We Believe*.
5. ChoG (Cleveland), Declaration, cover *ChoGE*, Appendix: 4; Int. P. Assemblies, *General Principles*, pp. 1–5; A. A. Allen, Prospectus of the Bible School, pp. 3f.; M. A. Daoud, *M. A. Daoud's Miracles and Missions Digest*.
6. N. Bhengu, *Back to God*, 1958/1, pp. 2, 6, 9; W. Diener, *Medio Seglo*; cited by I. Vergara, *El Protestantismo*, pp. 75–7.
7. L. J. Willis, *ChoGE* 52/8, 23.4.1962, pp. 4f.
8. Apostolic Church, *Fundamentals*, p. 23.
9. *Das Neue Testament in der Sprache der Gegenwart*. Neue Mülheimer Ausgabe (with notes and concordance), Altdorf bei Nürnberg, 1914, 7th ed., 1967.
10. *MD* 21, 1958, pp. 155f.
11. J. A. Synan, 'God's purpose in the Pentecostal Movement for this Hour', in: D. Gee (ed.), *Fifth Conference*, 1958, p. 33.

12. G. G. Atkins, *Religion*, p. 86; cited by J. E. Campbell, *PHCh*, 1951, p. 8.
13. On this see pp. 305f.; ch. 30.4(*c*), p. 443.
14. J. E. Campbell, *PHCh*, p. 16.
15. W. J. Hollenweger, *Ökumenische Rundschau* 17/1, Jan. 1968, p. 58.
16. G. F. Atter, *Cults*, pp. 18f ; cf. also ch. 3.3. p. 40.
17. T. L. Osborn, *Faith Digest* 5/12, Dec. 1960, p. 3.
18. R. Willenegger, *Ich komme bald!* 19, 1961, p. 146.
19. The Anchor Bay Bible Institute, *Full Gospel Center*.
20. C. W. R. Scott, *PE* 2472, 24.9.1961, pp. 12f.; cf. ch. 3.2(*d*), p. 39.
21. GPH, *A Defence*.
22. J. E. Campbell, *PHCh*, p. 104.
23. A. Hyma, *World History*, p. 355, cited by C. W. Conn, *Army*, p. XX.
24. G. Jeffreys (?), *Elim Evangel* 17/6, 7.2.1936, pp. 81f.
25. AoG Australia, *United Constitution*.
26. Union des Églises Évangéliques de Pentecôte, 1962 yearbook, pp.4–6; *Viens et Vois*, cover; *Promesse du Père*, cover. Cf. *PGG*, p. 592.
27. J. v. Gijs, *Het feest*, p. 26.
28. J. J. Chinn, *Christianity Today* 5, 1961, p. 880, cf. ch. 4.2(*b*), p. 51.
29. P. Mink, *Maranatha* 15/4, 1960, pp. 423–7.
30. *Ibid.*
31. L. J. Willis, *ChoGE* 52/8, 23.4.62, pp. 4f.
32. H. G. Greenway, *Labourers*, p. 6.
33. *Ibid.*, p. 14.
34. P. v. d. Woude, *Pinksterboodschap* 1/1, May 1960, p. 3.
35. G. Jeffreys, in D. Gee (ed.), *Phenomena*, pp. 48f.; L. Steiner, *VdV* 29/5, May 1936, p. 19.
36. From the catechism of the Church of the Living God (Christian Workers for Fellowship), cited by Clark, *Small Sects*, p. 121.
37. F. S. Mead, *Handbook*, 3rd ed., 1961, p. 84.
38. W. V. Grant, *Men in the Flying Saucers Identified*.
39. Cf. ch. 3.3, pp. 40f.
40. J. G. Sauer, *Midnight Cry* 24/1, Jan. 1963; 24/6, June 1963.
41. *Redemption Tidings* 43/29, 21.7.1967, pp. 12–15 (The Dawn).
42. Cf. ch. 12, pp. 149ff.
43. T. Schneider, *Verbum Caro* 6, 1952, p. 125.
44. Sundkler, p. 276.
45. Sundkler, p. 208.
46. I.e. John Dowie (cf. ch. 9.2, pp. 116ff.; so Sundkler, p. 55).
47. P. Newberry, *Redemption Tidings* 45/50, 11.12.1969, pp. 8f.; A. J. R. Sharp, *Redemption Tidings* 43/5, 3.2.1967, pp. 12f.
48. E. C. Stevenson, review, *P Testimony*, July 1963, p. 32.
49. P. Mink, *Maranatha* 15/4, 1960, pp. 428f.
50. *Elim Evangel*, 30, 1949, p. 513; cited by B. R. Wilson, *Sects*, p. 86.
51. *Elim Evangel* 11, 1930, pp. 129–31; cited by B. R. Wilson, *loc. cit.*
52. *Elim Evangel* 34, 1953, p. 28; cited by B. R. Wilson, *loc. cit.*
53. *VdV* 58/1, Jan. 1965, pp. 8, 19. Cf. *PGG*, p. 273; *VdV* 29/6, June 1936, pp. 17–19.
54. D. M. Panton, *VdV* 23/6, June 1930, pp. 13–16; cf. *PGG*, p. 273, n. 108.
55. B. Williams, *PE* 2471, 17.9.1961, pp. 4f.; cf. ch. 3.2(*d*), p. 39.
56. T. Rees, *Unity* (Tenets of the Apostolic Church 1), pp. 10f.
57. H. H. Barber, *Pentecostal Testimony*, special ed. Cf. also J. Paul, *Das Geheimnis*.
58. J. Müller-Bohn, *Dennoch* 3/4, April 1962, 7; cf. *PGG*, p. 236.
59. *Evangelischer Brüderbote* 21, 1909, p. 162.

60. C. A. Mueller, 'Science', *Senior Bible Lessons* 11/4, July–Sept. 1962, pp. 9–11.
61. E.g. R. A. Torrey, *Talks to Men about the Bible*.
62. Cf. ch. 16.1(*a*), pp. 218ff.
63. The Swiss Methodist Church is an exception. As early as 1906 it issued a warning against the underestimation among conservative Evangelicals of theological work (in detail 05.28.004b, bb, n. 174).
64. E. Lohmann, *Auf der Warte* 2/34, 22.00.1905, pp. 3f.
65. E.g. W. Malgo, *Mitternachtsruf* 3/10–11, Jan.–Feb. 1959.
66. G. Wasserzug-Traeder, *Gottes Wort*, 3rd ed., 1962, p. 9; similarly some of the American Anglicans who have experienced baptism of the Spirit with speaking with tongues, cf. ch. 1.1(*a*), p. 5.
67. See bibliography.
68. G. Lindsay, *Evolution*.
69. W. Goebel, *Auf der Warte* 2/12, 19.3.1905, pp. 3f.
70. M. L. Dye, *The Murderous Communist Conspiracy*.
71. T. Wyatt, *March of Faith* 15/11, Dec. 1960, p. 10.
72. M. Schian, *Zeitschrift für Theologie und Kirche* 17, 1907, pp. 254f.; cf. ch. 16.1(*a*), p. 220.
73. *Auf der Warte* 2/24, 10.6.1905, p. 3 (Torrey). Cf. also ch. 16.1(*a*), p. 221.
74. D. Gee, *P* 57, 1961, p. 17; cf. ch. 15.2(*b*), p. 210.
75. Fleisch II/2, pp. 295–7.
76. Evans, *Youth Challenge* 2, 1963, pp. 6f.
77. W. O. Fogg, *Trinity* 1/3, 1962, p. 17.
78. Associated Brotherhood of Christians, *Articles of Faith*, pp. 6–8; cited by Moore, pp. 283–6
79. P. Church of Christ (Los Angeles), *By-laws*, pp. 7–13; cited by Moore, pp. 230–4.
80. Full Salvation Union, *Manual*, p. 20, cited by Moore, p. 294.
81. Associated Brotherhood of Christians, *Articles of Faith*, p. 16; cited by Moore, p. 188.
82. Congregação Cristã do Brasil, *Estatutos*.
83. Horton Davies, *Christian Deviations*, 1961, pp. 83f.
84. F. Lovsky, *Réveil*, *Digeste Chretien* 4, 15.4.1952, pp. 14–16.
85. A. M. Brazier, *Christian Outlook* 39/4, April 1962, p. 3; but cf. Brazier, *Black Self-Determination*.
86. R. B(racco), *Risveglio P* 12/5, May 1957, pp. 6–9; G. Miegge, *Risveglio P* 12/7–8, July–Aug. 1957, pp. 18–20.
87. V. Pfaler, *Ristin Voima*, 1931: 10–11, p. 79; cited by W. Schmidt, *Pfingstbewegung*, p. 197.
88. Cf. ch. 16.1(*a*), p. 219.
89. Cf. ch. 17.2(*c*), pp. 239f.
90. Cf. above, ch. 16.1(*a*), p. 220.
91. J. Barr, *Old and New*, pp. 203–5.
92. J. Verkuyl quotes the relevant passages from the confession of faith of the church in his history of the church in Indonesia (J. Verkuyl, *Geredja*, p. 39; in detail, 03.08.015a).
93. K. and D. Ranaghan, *Catholic P*, pp. 154, 257; *Spirit*, pp. 1, 131; D. J. Grepi, *Pentecostalism*, p. 123.
94. A. Robertson, *That Old-time Religion*, p. 176; cf. also A. Comba, *Nuovi Tempi* 4/23, 7.6.1970, p. 8.
95. The theme is developed further in W. J. Hollenweger, *Ev. Missionsmagazin* 112/1, 1968, pp. 7–16.
96. WCC, *The Church for Others*, 1967, p. 25.

97. WCC, *The Church for Others*; W. J. Hollenweger, 'The Church for Others: A Discussion in Latin Europe', *Study Encounter* 3/2, 1967, pp. 84–96 (in the same volume as a report on 'Adaptation to Minority Situations' and 'The Congregation for Others: a DDR Report'); 'The Church for Others in the DDR', *Study Encounter* 5/1, 1969, pp. 26–36; W. J. Hollenweger, 'The Church for Others in Belgium: Can the Church be pluralistic?', *Study Encounter* 4/3, 1968, pp. 162–4; see also the *Monthly Letter on Evangelism* (WCC Geneva) for the period in question.

98. N. Goodall (ed.), *Uppsala Report* 1968, Section II, pp. 21–38; cf. also WCC, *Drafts for Sections*, Section II, pp. 28–51.

99. Cf. *PGG*, pp. 577–83, and ch. 32.2, p. 500.

100. Cf. ch. 3.3, pp. 40f.

101. E. S. Williams, *PE* 2488, 14.1.1962, p. 7.

102. G. von Rad, *Old Testament Theology* I, pp. 317f.

103. N. I. Pejsti (ed.), *Zasady*, Preface; cf. ch. 20.2, pp. 272f.

104. D. Gee, *Ministry*, p. 16.

105. E.g. M. Metzger, 'Historisch-kritische Forschung und Verkündigung', *Wort und Tat* 21/9, Sept. 1967, pp. 309–15.

106. E.g. G. von Rad, *Genesis*; Alan Richardson, *Genesis* 1–11, SCM Press, 1953.

107. Review of Basil Miller, *M. Niemöller*, *PE* 1500, 6.2.1943, p. 8; *PE* 1639, 6.10.1945, p. 14.

108. *VdV* 57/10, Oct. 1964, p. 5; cf. E. Giese, *VdV* 58/2, Feb. 1965, p. 4; R. Joop, *Friede sei mit euch* 11/12; W. Malgo, *Mitternachtsruf* 9/6, Sept. 1964, pp. 17f. cf. ch. 21.2, p. 292; ch. 30.4(*c*), p. 443.

109. M. Niemöller, *Zeichen der Zeit*, 14/4, 1964, pp. 149–52.

110. Only after I had finished the manuscript of this book did I discover the excellent little book by the Neo-Pentecostal professor of theology, J. Rodman Williams, *The Era of the Spirit*, in which he gives a positive evaluation of the theological work not only of Barth and Brunner, but also of Tillich and Bultmann.

111. *Jerusalem Bible*: notes on Matt. 1.16.

112. *NEB* note.

22

A Crimson Stream of Blood: The Doctrine of the Trinity and Christology

MOST Pentecostals adhere to a doctrine of the Trinity which is formulated in orthodox terms, but seem no longer to understand it. This can be seen, for example, in the translations of the incomprehensible confession of faith of the Assemblies of God[1] into Portuguese[2] and Serbo-Croat.[3] Both attempt to make the undigested fragments of traditional Protestant orthodoxy accessible to the faithful. By simplifying the Apostles' Creed and taking over scholastic terminology, they ascribe to God all the attributes which he has in orthodox theology.

> We believe that there is one God, infinitely perfect, who exists eternally in three persons, the Father, the Son, and the Holy Spirit.[4]

> We deem believe . . . in one God, Father, Son and Holy Spirit.[5]

Statements concerning the Holy Spirit which are made in the context of the doctrine of the Trinity are also taken over directly, but without comprehension, from the orthodox doctrine of the Spirit:

> We believe that the Holy Ghost, the third person in the Godhead, is a Spirit, a personality, which eminated (*sic*) out from God the Father, and God the Son, and is one in essence, co-equal in power and glory with the Father and Son.[6]

The first controversy in the Pentecostal movement about the doctrine of the Trinity arose when a considerable proportion of Pentecostal pastors declared that trinitarian baptism in accordance with Matt. 28.19 was invalid, and prescribed re-baptism 'in the name of Jesus', referring to the Acts of the Apostles.[7] This doctrine of baptism is associated with a condemnation of the orthodox doctrine of the Trinity. The Father of the Old Testament and the Holy Spirit of the present time are stated to be no more than alternative forms in which the Christ who appeared in Jesus is manifested. To speak of three persons is nonsense. There is only one God, who has revealed himself under three different forms. This modalist doctrine of the Trinity,[8] which is more in accordance with religious feeling and practice of Pentecostalism than a doctrine of the Trinity taken over without understanding from the traditional churches, was bitterly resisted by the trinitarian Pentecostals. The Pentecostal Assemblies of Canada, the founders of which had almost all been baptized a second or third time 'in the name of Jesus', but had then renounced their error, make a detailed attack on the 'Jesus only' doctrine in their confession of faith, and strongly emphasize that the three persons are different and not to be confused with each other.

The 'doctrine of the two natures' (Christ is true man and true God) is simply repeated without comment in Pentecostal confessions of faith. Its function is unknown to Pentecostal writers.

On the other hand, the fall and the atoning death of Jesus are of the utmost importance to them. When they confess 'We believe in the fall of the two first human beings and the hereditary corruption of the whole of mankind',[9] this is the expression of an existential reality, the experience 'that all men . . . have become morally helpless (*bezbronnymi*) creatures'. The Polish and Russian Pentecostal movement follows Zwingli's doctrine of original sin in rejecting hereditary *guilt*,[10] but teaches the hereditary 'corruption of human nature by sin'.

Only two articles of orthodox christology are of real importance in Pentecostal religion, the virgin birth of Jesus and the atonement through his blood. The virgin birth is fiercely defended; according to Pentecostal theology, everything depends on the truth of this doctrine. A Pentecostal lady explained to me during an extramural course on fundamentalism at Zürich University: 'If Jesus is not the son of a virgin, he cannot redeem us.' For the fundamentalists and many of their hidden supporters in the traditional churches see the act of conception as having a contaminating effect. The Church of Jesus Christ (Gemeinde Jesu Christi – a Pentecostal denomination) is considered to have been called into being by God in order to restore the ruined inheritance.

> But the question is: 'What is the ruined inheritance?' It is certainly not the churches destroyed by the war, but the destroyed truth of the gospel in Christ. In our churches it is taught in the creed that Jesus Christ was conceived by the Holy Ghost and born of the Virgin Mary, while in our theological seminaries the divinity of Christ is denied. The gospel of Christ has been abandoned, and we find ourselves drawing from the leaking cisterns of a church religion of our own making.[11]

In spite of the traditional way in which the doctrine of the virgin birth is formulated in the Pentecostal movement, the underlying motive is not faithfulness to an ancient dogma. While there is a commitment to the infancy narratives of Luke and Matthew, the main motive is an unconscious one, in which sexual taboos are an important determining factor. It is Jesus 'conceived by the Holy Spirit in the womb of the Virgin Mary',[12] 'Mary's son and Mary's God'[13] who has shed his pure sinless blood for us. And faith in the 'death and shed blood of our Lord Jesus Christ for the remission of every sin of every sinner'[14] is the central article of Pentecostal christology. This is obvious from the numerous hymns in Pentecostal hymn books which praise the blood of Jesus:

> I see a crimson stream of blood,
> It flows from Calvary,
> Its waves which reach the throne of God,
> Are sweeping over me.[15]

The author of the words and music of the hymn above – G. T. Haywood, one of the Negro pioneers of the American Pentecostal movement – describes in the verses of this hymn the power of the blood of Jesus:

> When gloom and sadness whisper
> You've sinn'd, no use to pray,
> I look away to Jesus,
> And He tells me to say:
> I see a crimson stream of blood . . .[16]

In hundreds and thousands of prayers the blood of Jesus is called down to sprinkle the meeting room and purify the hearts and minds of those present. The South African Latter Rain Assemblies have developed this theology of the blood even further. There members must 'continually imbibe through faith this blood, this life'.[17] In a public round table discussion an elder of the Zürich Pentecostal Mission referred to the many unbelieving pastors in the established churches. I asked him, 'How can one recognize an unbelieving pastor?' The answer was, 'An unbelieving pastor does not believe in the blood of Jesus.' He was usually receptive to someone else's point of view, and I tried to explain to him:

> When I speak nowadays of 'blood', my unsuspecting hearer may be reminded of a wound, a slaughterhouse, or perhaps a blood orange, and possibly of the war, but certainly not of the atoning death of Jesus.

'But that's what it refers to,' interjected the Pentecostal. I replied:

> Certainly, but in New Testament times streams of blood flowed from sacrifices in Jerusalem, Rome, Corinth, and Alexandria, and indeed in Switzerland too amongst the Celts and Alemanni. Anyone who said to people then, 'The blood of Jesus has been shed for you, you no longer need to offer sacrifices,' was talking in a language which they could understand. By the expression 'the blood of Jesus' they were saying that the redemption in Christ was unique and final. At the present day we have to express the same thing in other words.

But the Pentecostal was not content with this: 'If the Bible speaks of the blood of Jesus, we must not be too proud to speak of the blood of Jesus as well.'

I cannot at this point give a general summary of Protestant christology and the

Protestant doctrine of God. Emil Brunner, described by the leader of the Apostolic Church in Switzerland as 'a theologian close to the Bible'[18] has written an outstanding chapter on the question 'Is there a God?';[19] in his *Dogmatics* he sets out his disagreement with the doctrine of the virgin birth in terms anyone can understand.[20] Günther Bornkamm gives a discussion in easily accessible language of the event in world history represented by God's imperishable act in Jesus of Nazareth.[21]

NOTES

1. AoG, *Early History*, cf. Appendix: 2.
2. E. Conde, *Testemunho*, 3rd ed., 1960, pp. 183ff.; cf. Appendix: 2.
3. Kristova Pentecostna Crkva, *Temeljne*, p. 6; cf. Appendix: 2.
4. W. Diener, *Medio Siglo*, quoted in I. Vergara, *Protestantismo*, pp. 75ff.
5. Quoted from J. L. Neve, *Churches*, pp. 364f.
6. P. Church of Christ, *By-laws*, pp. 7ff.; quoted in Moore, pp. 230ff.
7. Cf. ch. 3.1(*b*), pp. 31ff.
8. For details: United Pentecostal Church: 02a.02.140.
9. *Pinksterboodschap* 3/3, 1960, p. 3.
10. N. I. Pejsti (ed.), *Zasady*, ch. 7.
11. Gemeinde Jesu Christi, *Gemeinde*.
12. From the *Manual del Ministro* of the Iglesia Pentecostal de Chile.
13. PAoW, *Minute Book*, pp. 44ff.
14. W. F. P. Burton, *God Working With Them*, p. v.
15. G. T. Haywood, *Hymns of Glorious Praise*, 1969, no. 99.
16. *Ibid*.
17. Latter Rain Assemblies of South Africa, *The Blood of Jesus*, no pag.
18. R. Willenegger, *Ich komme bald!* 19, 1961, p. 146.
19. E. Brunner, *Our Faith*, ch. 1.
20. E. Brunner, *Dogmatics* II, pp. 350ff.; *The Mediator*, pp. 322ff.
21. G. Bornkamm, *Jesus of Nazareth*.

23

'Rolled away': The Doctrine of Justification

THE fundamental experience, necessary to salvation, for the Pentecostal believer is conversion or regeneration. In numerous hymns and choruses he sings of

> the miraculous transformation which takes place in the soul and life of the sinner in the moment in which he repents and declares his sincere faith in Christ Jesus as his Saviour.[1]

When at the end of the gospel meeting the Pentecostal preacher makes the call to sinners to turn to Jesus, the angels look down with rapt attention from heaven. Their harps are silent and they fold their wings, for 'they have never felt what moves a poor sinner whom Jesus leads home.'[2]

A faint reflection of the urgency of the call to conversion – which in a good evangelist does not sound sentimental – can be found in a record by Gerhard Klemm.[3] In clear concise terms he describes the hill of Golgotha and the hopeless situation of his hearers 'in a world of sin . . ., unrighteousness and lovelessness, in a world in which a man is virtually nothing more than a number and a file.' How happy are those who can fly to Golgotha, who have the privilege 'of pouring out their hearts at last, of shedding their tears, of telling their distress and finding comfort and peace like a child in its mother's arms'. Preaching of this kind is only effective with people who are actually suffering from loneliness, sickness and lack of understanding. But it is these whom the preacher attracts.

> How I long to take you by the hand and lead you to this quiet hill. It is not high. However heavy your burden, you can climb it, even if your body is weakened with illness. But it is not an outward path; no, you sink to your knees, close your eyes and say: Lord Jesus Christ, be merciful to me a sinner: Saviour, let me rest in your heart, forgive me, wash me clean through your blood.[4]

Jimmie Davis turns to the woman over forty who is standing by herself, describes her life – without showing her up, and without even naming her – and asks her: Have you lived a life worth living,[6] or 'have you wandered alone on life's pathway, have you lived without love a life of tears? Have you searched for the great highest meaning? Is your life filled with love or wasted years?' And his voice drops; he hurries after her as she returns home in the night ('as you walk on in darkness and fear') and speaking over her shoulder in friendly tones, says:[7] 'Turn around, turn around, God is calling. He is calling you from a life of wasted years.'

The Finnish Pentecostal preacher Hokkanen finds it difficult

> to describe the process of regeneration, and yet something happens. The godless life comes to an end. Someone no longer dances, no longer drinks, loves God's word and God's people. 'If you are not reborn, open your heart to Jesus the King of sorrows, and the miracle of grace will take place in you too – you will be reborn to a living hope.'[8]

The conditions for regeneration have been fulfilled on God's side in Jesus.

> It is received quite freely through grace alone; yet for a man to accept it rests on a conscious and free decision of his will . . . Regeneration does not take place gradually, but in a moment.[9]

The International Church of the Foursquare Gospel declares:

> We believe that the change which takes place in the heart and life at conversion is a very real one; that the sinner is born again in such a glorious and transforming manner that old things are passed away and all things are become new.[10]

The same is the experience of the Chilean peasant, torn from his traditional extended family and harnessed to the processes of industrial work, and still, after years, ill at ease in the life of a large modern city. Without the help of the Pentecostals, he often falls victim to drunkenness, hopes to win large sums of money by gambling, or tries to forget his misery in the arms of prostitutes. Often the only people to have any concern for him are the street singers of the Iglesia Pentecostal. They visit the shanty towns and sing to the accompaniment of guitar and mandolin:

> Rolled away, rolled away, rolled away,
> All the burdens of my sins rolled away,
> I remember when my burdens rolled away,
> That I feared would never leave night or day;
> Jesus showed to me the loss,
> So I left them at the cross.[11]

At first he may laugh with the rest of the bystanders, but then he is convinced by the faces of these Pentecostals: in the midst of the filth of the city they are already in heaven. Through curiosity and boredom he walks along with them. He hears a preacher who like himself has to struggle for daily bread for himself and his children. He says to himself, 'This is one of us', and after attending a number of services is converted to the Pentecostals. He is now no longer at the mercy of uncertainty, hunger, unemployment, drunkenness, boredom and homelessness, because he has once again become part of a 'family', because he has 'brothers' and 'sisters' who help him and give his life moral direction. They may not teach him to write, but they teach him to read and underline the important passages in the Bible for him. He learns to read not only the Bible, but the newspapers as well, and sends his children to school. And because he no longer throws his money away, he may be able to send one of his sons to study at the university. All this he owes to the Saviour who has rolled away the burden of his sin, who has led him out of the prison of sin, indifference and hopelessness, and to the Holy Spirit, who has not just to be believed in, but whom one can experience in all sorts of marvellous healings, visions and utterances in tongues which one has not learned.

One can understand the Hungarian immigrant who found a new hope in an American Pentecostal assembly, and wrote:

> God saved my husband and my children too and brought us to Portland, so that we could live amongst His children. I am grateful to God for fellowship with them. This is my people. Their God is my God! I adore my heavenly Father with all my heart.[12]

Conversions of ministers, doctors and other educated persons take place more often than is commonly supposed, but form the exception. The older Pentecostal churches know that the experience of conversion was more dramatic in the early days:

> We have the courage to be quiet when the Lord does not move the water. We stand praying earnestly before God for a new and powerful descent of the Spirit.[13]

Today even Pentecostals, and especially their children, become

> Christians in a milder manner, without being able to point to a definite emotional crisis taking place at a definite time. Some of the very best saints of the church bear testimony to this quiet type of conversion experience, which results from a lengthy period of Christian training . . . On the other hand there are thousands in modern society who are unreachable except by means of a crisis experience.[14]

J. E. Campbell, therefore, accuses the Reformation churches of neglecting the preaching of conversion and of not believing in a supernatural new birth.[15]

> We believe that the church lost something vital when she began to neglect that old landmark, the altar, where people may come together and 'pray through' until empowered and unified.[16]

There are numerous lamentations at the 'largely unbelieving clergy'.[17]

Is it not a well known fact that the vast majority of the theologians who preach in the pulpits of the established church have experienced neither conversion nor regeneration, far less biblical sanctification or endowment by the Holy Spirit? Someone who will not let himself be renewed by the Spirit of God has not been called by God to preach his word. No honour can be given to God by unbelievers and people who are addicted to vicious habits. How many theologians sit in their studies in a cloud of cigar smoke? Can people like this free other slaves to the vice of tobacco, or preach liberation? Anyone who associates with such people and makes an alliance with them is an abomination to the Lord. We need men of God in our pulpits and not idolators. The friend of the world is the enemy of God. If the higher church authorities do not see and admit this, they are blind. And when the blind lead the blind, they both fall into the ditch ... Woe to those who baptize children in the cradle, and convince them later of the lie that this has made them Christians! Woe to those who confirm young people of fourteen years of age, and tell them that now the baptismal covenant has been renewed ... How can anyone take such pious play acting seriously! In the morning they utter devout words and make vows, and after that there is a party. O, this formalism, this playacting, this mass murder ...

But the Pentecostal movement consists of people who have mostly been brought by pastors without theological training, in the course of missions, to have a living faith in Jesus Christ, and have experienced a decisive conversion (repentance) and the ensuing regeneration (John 3). In these meetings the word of God is ... a power such that every person who receives it is made new and set free from all the constraints that weighed upon him, all vices and sins, all fetters and lusts ... The present-day church cannot deny these signs, but says nothing about them ...[18]

In practice things are not so easy. Even in the Pentecostal movement there is – fortunately – no exact way of knowing who is really saved. Of course bitter attacks have been made on Bishop James A. Pike because he will not limit salvation to people 'who happen to have heard the news and heard it well'.[19] On the other hand, it is asserted that 'innocent children' who have been neither converted nor born again will take part in the rapture.[20] There are also Pentecostal groups who declare the conversions which normally take place in the Pentecostal movement to be invalid, because in their view confession is necessary for a valid conversion. Some say that it must take place before the pastor, others before the person who has been offended, and others again before both.[21]

All endeavours in prayer and singing, in weeping and fasting, and all other devotional practices are worthless in the eyes of God if sins are not confessed with godly repentance and contrition, and the past restored to purity.[22]

Other Pentecostal groups require only contrition and readiness to repent before God. The most recently formed organizations are not content with the confession of *remembered sins*, but require a 'complete confession', that is, the confession even of forgotten sins, made possible by the aid of prophetic messages.[23] With regard to the condition of man before confession, Pentecostal doctrine is the strictly orthodox one of 'the utter depravity of human nature' bringing as its consequence 'the necessity for repentance and regeneration'. Most Pentecostals believe that it is possible to fall back from the state of grace after conversion,[24] while others believe in the 'eternal security' of the converted. All agree that

> However great a sin may be committed by a person before he receives the Lord Christ, if he believes in him and accepts him, the sin is forgiven.[25]

> Salvation is not only reforming ourselves and turning over a new leaf, nor is it becoming a church member – although all saved people should do so – but salvation is being washed in the precious blood of Jesus Christ and becoming a new creature in Christ.[26]

Sins committed after conversion fall into the wide field of Pentecostal pastoral care. There is disagreement about what to think of children of God who sin. In the view of the Congregação Cristã do Brasil:

> Sins committed after the Lord has been received should be judged by the church, always in accordance with the word of God, with the exception of mortal sin, which in accordance with the word of God is unforgivable. One of the mortal sins is committed when there is resistance to the work of the Holy Spirit (Matt. 12.32.)[27]

The view of the Russian and Polish Pentecostal movement is the same:

> Not every sin committed after conversion is a mortal sin or a blasphemy against the Spirit, as many falsely teach. But any sin not confessed to God can bring man to the point where he falls outside the forgiveness of God. Consequently every Christian must 'work out his own salvation with fear and trembling'.[28]

Sins committed by the converted led the Holiness and Pentecostal movements to add a second stage to regeneration or conversion. This is the experience of sanctification, through which sins are finally rooted out. Ultimately salvation depends on the final overcoming of sin. Only those who overcome it will inherit the kingdom of God. The result of this, as Hutten has frequently affirmed, is that in spite of the formal affirmation of the doctrine of justification by faith, the doctrine of justification is emptied of meaning and reduced to a preliminary stage for beginners in Christianity. Röckle expresses the view of the majority of Pentecostals when he makes this charge against Hutten:

> Hutten's basic error is that he speaks of grace without conditions, and the Bible knows of no such thing. The doctrine of grace without conditions is a master stroke of Satan, with which he has already deceived millions of people and led them to damnation.[29]

Kurt Hutten has given a clear, brief and comprehensible account of the evangelical doctrine of justification in his book *Die Glaubenswelt des Sektierers* ('The

World of the Sectarian's Faith') especially in the chapter about the *theologia crucis* as taught by the Reformation.[30]

NOTES

1. AdD, Dominican Republic, *Reglamento*, 1944.
2. *Pfingstjubel*, 1956, no. 205, v. 2.
3. G. Klemm, Record *Evangeliumsklänge* A 35 L.
4. G. Klemm, *ibid.*
5. J. Davis, *Songs of Faith*: 'Wasted Years', Decca DL 4220.
6. A. A. Allen also takes up this theme on a more primitive level. Cf. below, ch. 25.2(*c*), p. 366.
7. Associations which are not made explicit in the hymn and are therefore supplied unconsciously, but all the more effectively, by the hearer.
8. L. Hokkanen, *Oletko*; quoted in W. Schmidt, *Pfingstbewegung*, p. 211.
9. N. I. Pejsti (ed.), *Zasady*, ch. 11.
10. Declaration of Faith compiled by A. S. McPherson for the ICh4G. The crucial text for Pentecostals is II Cor. 5.17, but the AV here follows the false reading of Marcion, which introduced the word 'all' into the Pauline text: 'The old has passed away, behold, *all things* have become new.'
11. A 'chorus', which has been carried by oral tradition throughout the world. Minnie A. Steele, *Hymns of Glorious Praise*, 1969, no. 452, has a slightly different version.
12. *Apostoli Hit*, May 1961, p. 2.
13. K. Schneider, *Kirchenbote Zürich* 51/8, 1.8.1965, p. 8.
14. J. E. Campbell, *PHCh*, pp. 122, 132.
15. *Ibid.*, p. 60.
16. T. Wyatt, *Birth*, pp. 10ff.
17. K. Hutten, *Seher*, 11th ed., 1968, p. 529.
18. H. Lauster, *Die Wahrheit* 15/4, April 1962; *MD* 23, 1962, p. 108.
19. J. A. Pike, *Christian Century* 77/51, 21.12.1961, pp. 1496ff.; *PE* 2444, 12.3.1961, p. 3; cf. ch. 3.3, pp. 41, 45 n. 88.
20. E. S. Williams *PE* 2443, 5.3.1961, p. 11; *PE* 2696, 9.1.1966, p. 17.
21. ChoG in Christ, *Year Book*, 1951, pp. 88f.; quoted in Moore, pp. 178ff.
22. J. Widmer, *Im Kampf* II, 2nd ed., 1949, p. 108. Cf. also Drollinger, *Offener Brief*, 28.10.1937, p. 17.
23. Cf. above ch. 11.2(*a*), p. 142.
24. Apostolic Church, *Fundamentals*, p. 3; C. W. Conn, *ChoGE* 50/50, 15.2.1960, p. 13.
25. Congregação Cristã do Brasil, *Estatutos*, Art. 27.
26. O. Vouga, *Our Gospel*, p. 8.
27. Congregação Cristã do Brasil, *op. cit.*, Art. 27.
28. N. I. Pejsti (ed)., *Zasady*, ch. 9.
29. C. Röckle, *Philadelphiabrief* 15/165–166, March–April 1963, p. 3.
30. K. Hutten, *Glaubenswelt*, pp. 58ff.

24

'Showers of Blessing': The Doctrine of the Spirit

1. *'Firm are the Promises Standing': The Dependence of the Doctrine of the Spirit upon the Doctrine of Inspiration*

FOR Pentecostals the Acts of the Apostles are regarded as a normative record of the normative primitive church. 'The apostolic church is its obligatory model.'[1] The Pentecostal understanding of the Bible leads to the question: Why is the present-day church so very different from the church of the apostles? The reason cannot lie in God, because

Firm are the promises standing, nor can they ever fail.
Sealed with the blood of our Jesus, they must, they shall remain.
Heaven and earth may perish, mountain and hill may vanish;
Yet stands the word we cherish, ever to faith made sure.[2]

Since God has not changed, the disobedience of Christians (Acts 5.32) must be the cause of this degeneration of the church. Accordingly, Pentecostals ask: In what way have we departed from the commandments of God, so that the gifts of the Holy Spirit, the healing of the sick, prophecy, and speaking in tongues have disappeared, and the church has become lifeless and powerless? How can we overcome its 'deepfreeze theology'?[3] What must we do for the wind of revival to begin to blow again, and the 'showers of blessing' to descend once more?

Showers of blessing, showers of blessing we need;
Mercy drops round us are falling, but for the showers we plead.[4]

This is the Pentecostals' prayer. It is a biblical starting point, or rather a biblicist one. The critics of the Pentecostal movement who accuse it of neglecting the written word in favour of individual illuminations by the Spirit are ignorant of the role which the Bible plays in the Pentecostal movement. Pentecostals live with the Bible. They read it every day and know many passages by heart. The words of the Bible are woven into their prayers and writings. Many of them hardly read any books apart from the Bible, since they often come from levels of society in which the practice of reading is uncommon,[5] and the intellectual effort of reading two chapters a day is enough for them. But these two chapters are absorbed by a memory which is not over-burdened. They fall upon virgin ground and put down firm, immoveable roots. I can recall a labourer in Zürich municipal gas works. In his rough Zürich German he gave a testimony which culminated in a description of his attempt to avoid taking part in a mission by Smith Wigglesworth. His relations had gone to hear the famous evangelist. He stayed behind at home, distracted and discontent, and to take his mind off the matter, drank a beer glass full of *Schnaps*. But he did not become drunk as he had hoped. Then he tried to play with the children in the park. But they avoided him. Returning home, he picked up the Bible by chance and read in Gal. 5.19–21: 'Now the works of the flesh are plain: immorality, impurity, licentiousness, idolatry, sorcery, enmity, strife, jealousy, anger, selfishness, dissension, party spirit, envy, drunkenness, carousing, and the like. I warn you, as I warned you before, that those who do such things shall not inherit the kingdom of God.' The labourer continued, 'This was God's photograph of me. I cried out to the God whom I did not know, and from whom up to now I had fled, for grace.' When the family returned home from the gospel meeting and told him that they had been converted that evening, he told them that he had undergone the same experience. Since then, the daily practice of prayer, Bible reading and regular attendance at meetings (four times a week) had brought about such a psychological and cultural change in this man that although one can tell where he comes from, one is astonished to notice the improvement in his character.

The former Baptist preacher James Brooke tells how, after he read the Bible, 'the truth concerning the Body of Christ as set out in the Acts of the Apostles and in the Epistles, streamed like sunlight into my being'.[6] Someone who lives by the Bible in this way has only one desire: to experience the Holy Spirit in *exactly* the same way as the first disciples. Thus I agree with Professor Horton Davies[7] and Professor F. Lovsky,[8] who regard the Pentecostal movement as a revival movement based on the premises of fundamentalism.

2. '*Above the World . . .*': *The Pattern of Salvation*

John Wesley, the founder of the Methodist Church, under the influence of Catholic works of edification, distinguished between the ordinary believer and those who were 'sanctified' or 'baptized with the Spirit'. Emotional outbursts were no novelty to Wesley. In his diary he describes the 'howling of those upon whom the power of God came'.[9] The way in which Wesley's doctrine of sanctification was taken over and coarsened by the American Holiness movement has been described above.[10] This Holiness movement taught a doctrine of a two-stage way of salvation. It distinguished between the 'converted' ('the born again' or 'saved') and those who had in addition been 'sanctified'. This 'sanctification', also known as the 'second blessing' or 'baptism of the Spirit',[11] is regarded as a precisely definable experience 'subsequent to and different from regeneration'.[12] Thus the Christian and Missionary Alliance, a denomination of the Holiness movement, teaches as follows:

> This experience of Christ our Sanctifier marks a definite and distinct crisis in the history of a soul. We do not grow into it, but we cross a definite line of demarcation, as clear as when the hosts of Joshua crossed the Jordan and were over in the Promised Land and set up a great heap of stones, so that they never could forget the crisis hour.[13]

Many circles in the American, South African,[14] English, Scandinavian, Swiss[15] and German[16] churches, however, maintained this doctrine long *before* the coming into being of the Pentecostal movement. The elaboration of this two-stage pattern, as taught by the Holiness movement, by the addition of a third stage is described in the history of the Church of God.[17] But the greater part of the Pentecostal movement rejects this three-stage pattern, and has once again reduced it to a two-stage pattern of (1) conversion and (2) the baptism of the Spirit, understanding sanctification as a process which continues throughout life. The Assemblies of God, as a classic example of a Pentecostal movement teaching a two-stage pattern of salvation, have also been described above.[18]

But this does not exhaust all the possibilities. Ultimately, a further stage can be added at any time. For example, the Pentecostal churches of the Apostolic type[19] add to the Pentecostal theory of stages of salvation the acceptance of the authority of the apostles of the Apostolic Church. The American 'Latter Rain movement' seems to add to the Pentecostal experience which every believer must undergo a further experience of 'ascension'.[20] Röckle adds to the three-stage pattern a fourth stage, at the moment a final one, that of 'total shattering'. This is complete redemption from one's religious or even 'sanctified' ego. Unfortunately this shattering is possible only rarely, and only when God intervenes 'in a supernatural way'.

> Hitherto the Lord has only been able to reveal himself in very few of the brethren with the power and clarity which is necessary to prepare us for the day of the first resurrection.[21]

One cannot object that these differences concern only matters of detail. For the Pentecostal groups concerned they formed sufficient reason to found separate organizations. For example, in the Finnish Pentecostal movement there was disagreement between the Pentecostals who taught the three-stage way of salvation and those who taught the two-stage way. Smidt, one of the founders of the Pentecostal movement, had been won over to the 'two-stage' Pentecostal movement by William H. Durham, while he was in America, whereas the Norwegian Barratt, who exercised a considerable influence in Finland, was a former Methodist and taught the 'three-stage' way of salvation. Barratt wrote explicitly:

> We do not accept the opinion of Durham, that all, in the moment in which they are born again, are wholly sanctified. We do not deny that many who have received sufficient light with respect to the crucifixion of the old Adam may possibly receive the complete purification of the heart in regeneration. But the word of God and experience [this is a typically Pentecostal way of arguing] show us that most people do not find this higher life in regeneration. They must therefore undergo an act of purification, through which this happens. Many have this before the baptism of the Spirit, others after. But it must come after the baptism of the Spirit, if a person has not received it before, for otherwise he lapses into pride, party spirit, worldliness and sensuality, so that the power of the Spirit, which he has received, is not vindicated in him. This purification has been called the second blessing. But the name is an unsuitable one . . .[22]

The dispute between the two-stage and three-stage Pentecostals has not yet been resolved, and, together with the unsolved questions of the doctrine of the Trinity, it is the most difficult problem faced by Pentecostal theology. Whether the Pentecostal has reached the first, second or third stage, he must continually pray: 'Lord, lift me above the world!' Except on a few specially blessed days of his life, he will never be able to say sincerely, in the words of Phoebe P. Knapp:

> I rise to walk in Heav'n's own light
> Above the world and sin,
> With hearts made pure, and garments white,
> And Christ enthroned within.[23]

At the beginning of the 1930s, under the influence of the Reformed pastor Voget, the German Pentecostal movement completely abandoned the theory of stages of salvation. In the Mülheim Association of Christian Fellowships

> one theory after the other disappeared: the three-stage pattern of salvation, the baptism of the Spirit with gifts, and then even the baptism of the Spirit with, at least, the sign of speaking in tongues. Now even the expectation of the days and gifts of Pentecost was given up. It was replaced by the mystical Nothingness . . . This was in fact the complete reversal of what had taken place at the beginning.[24]

> [One sister] saw people who had been imbued with indescribable riches of gifts and treasures. Instead of delighting in them and taking of them, they desired Nothingness. As the Nothingness was so great and mighty to them they regarded the whole glory as worthless. It was as if they were lifted above everything, and they worshipped! Where there is everything, Nothingness is gloriously revealed![25]

Leonhard Steiner has tried to replace the weary climb up the ladder of salvation by an evangelical outlook.[26] But these are exceptions. Bruckner's warning is still true: The false, mechanical view of Scripture maintained by the Evangelical movement leads to 'a completely unbiblical fragmentation of the doctrine of the process of salvation'.[27] In spite of profession of belief in justification by faith, the Pentecostal movement does not understand the meaning of *sola gratia*, redemption by faith alone, for without holiness 'no one will see the Lord' (Heb. 12.14). But in Pentecostal belief and practice the stress is not on contempt for beginners in Christianity, for Pentecostals have all been amongst the beginners for long enough themselves, and it is never certain when they may be sent back to the first stage. Their whole urge is forward and above:

> I stood so long in the courtyard, by holy awe dismayed,
> How often and how fearfully for blessed peace I prayed!
> The holy place with splendour
> Of heavenly glory shone,
> And yet the door was closed to me,
> I still could not go on.[28]

3. '*Storms Obscure the Light of Day*': *The Understanding of Sanctification*

No outsider can imagine the anguish undergone by earnest Pentecostals who struggle to live a holy life. In their worship they sing the hymns of total victory:

> Troubles almost 'whelm the soul;
> Griefs like billows o'er me roll;
> Tempters seek to lure astray,
> Storms obscure the light of day;
> But in Christ I can be bold,
> I've an anchor that shall hold.[29]

Their pastors promise them, on the basis of the Bible, the 'total and complete sanctification of the sons and daughters of God'.[30] But their everyday lives bring numerous sins. What can be done? The answers given by Pentecostals vary, and the same group or the same pastor can hardly ever be tied down to any one of the possible answers. Sometimes they follow John:

> The biblical norm is: Do not sin! (I John 2.1). For this we were redeemed and born again. But supposing that you are a young child and make a slip and sin, what then? Come to Jesus and tell Him that you have sinned, confess your sin to Him, and then He will forgive you them, for He intercedes for you.[31]

But at the same time they affirm:

> When many people say that we are not delivered from our sins, the devil has the last word, for then the trick the devil tried to play in paradise has succeeded. This makes the devil more powerful than God. But these are thoughts

that border on blasphemy. Redemption consists of the total removal of the consequences of the fall.[32]

There are many descriptions of experiences of sanctification from the Holines movement:

> Lord, I cried, let this moment be the beginning of my full redemption! Baptize me now with the Holy Spirit and with the fire of pure love! Now create in me, oh God, a pure heart![33]

All the phenomena which were later to form the basis of the charge of excessive enthusiasm made by the Holiness movement against the Pentecostal movement can already be found in the experience of sanctification in the Holiness movement. Moody tells how at the height of his success two elderly women in his growing congregation told him that they were praying for him, that he might be 'filled with the Spirit'. Moody suggested they pray for the people, but they were insistent. 'It is you that need the power of the Spirit.'

> I, Moody thought, with the largest congregation in Chicago, with conversions by the hundred in and out of the city, a program feature for conventions all over the country, moving thousands of others to work, raising buildings where others were content to dream – I need such power?[34]
>
> But the more he thought about it the more it wore on him. At last he asked the two Free Methodists to come and talk with him. They came, prayed, and Moody began to hunger as never before for a further instalment on his Christian experience. Each Friday afternoon he met with the two for prayer. One, Mrs Sarah Cooke, had become 'burdened for Moody that the Lord would baptize him with the Holy Ghost and fire'. Finally, she recounted, after a number of prayer meetings together, 'Mr Moody's agony was so great that he rolled on the floor and in the midst of many tears and groans cried to God to be baptized with the Holy Ghost and fire.'[35]
>
> Now, in a dramatic rounding of doctrinal insemination, which made him sympathetic with as well as suspicious of all denominations, he was seasoned with Pentecostalism.[36]

Markus Hauser, the founder of the Chrischona congregation in Zürich, describes his experience of sanctification as follows:

> Heaven opened up round about me, a sea of light surrounded me. A wave of fire swept slowly through spirit, soul and body. Wave upon wave flowed through me. The Holy Spirit took possession of me.[37]

Apart from certain exceptions, the experience of sanctification does not open the way to perfection.

> We do not believe it is impossible for the sanctified to commit sin; but we do believe that it is possible for a sanctified person not to commit sin.[38]

The doctrine and experience of sanctification is sufficient reason for the

Pentecostal movement to step in where there are established mission churches of the Reformation churches:

> It is a difficult work because before the missionaries [in this case, missionaries of the Apostolic Church] it was taken for granted that if a native [in the New Hebrides] was baptized as a confession of faith, that was all that was necessary, and our missionaries are faced with the task of leading the natives into a life of sanctification after conversion and baptism . . .[39]

Although Serena M. Hodges, the historian of the missions of the Assemblies of God, admits that the church history of the *traditional* churches in Samoa reads like the Acts of the Apostles, and that whole tribes had been converted, that the Bible had been translated into the indigenous languages and that from the very first the Samoan church had sent missionaries to neighbouring islands, she considers that the intervention of the Assemblies of God in that church was necessary, for 'of late years, most of these early churches had become very formal.'[40]

Occasional objections are made to this doctrine of sanctification. For example, it is pointed out that it is incorrect to apply the expression 'sanctified' to Christians who have received a 'second experience' after conversion. Paul uses the term 'sanctified' for all Christians.[41]

The early Pentecostal movement believed that 'whoever is purified and loves him cannot sin'.[42] This view, since given up by the older Pentecostal churches, is today being advocated again by the Latter Rain Movement:

> The mystery of the new covenant is that these laws are now written in our hearts . . . We now no longer steal or curse or kill, not because the law forbids it, but because grace has given us a life that *cannot* steal or curse or kill.[43]

> If the Lord has purified us and set us free from sin, then the source from which all the hateful sins appeared in the past is now empty . . . and now – glorious truth! – the heart cannot sin, because there is no longer any sin in it, so that sin can no longer come forth from it (I John 3.6, 9 and 5.18).[44]

It is easy to understand the attraction the 'Children of the Latter Rain' have for the Pentecostals. In the beginning the Pentecostal movement taught and bore witness to these doctrines and they are still sung in hymns, yet nowadays they are rejected as errors.[45] But they can still be experienced – 'glorious truth!' – in the Latter Rain movement by a continual 'slow cauterization' of the flesh.[46]

A further possible way of solving the problem is by making a distinction between temptation and sin:

> We cannot prevent the birds flying above our heads, but we can prevent them from building nests on them.[47]

But even this advice must be difficult to work out in practice, because the Pentecostal constantly discovers nests of evil in his life. Thus other groups attempt to take the sting out of sin with statements that repeat the teaching of the Holiness movement:

> Only culpable transgressions are sins, not blameless ones.[48]
>
> Sin is a wilful transgression of the law. This means that one's motive is to do wrong.[49]

Wesley had already said that only 'the voluntary transgression of a known law'[50] was sin. Unintentional or forced acts, or those which spring from good intention or ignorance, he did not call sin.

The *Kirchenfreund* criticized Pentecostals because they

> dismiss the whole matter with the aid of a brand new principle. Since the facts of life naturally are not in accord with their lofty assertions, the way out is simply to call things by a different name from what they are in reality. The term sin is no longer attributed to what the untroubled evangelical conscience would otherwise feel to be a sin. Thus they simply make a distinction of moral judgment, which makes no difference to the real nature of things . . .[51]

The reduction of sin to what can be experienced psychologically has two consequences: 1. Sin that is experienced is taken more seriously than in the Reformation churches. 2. *Unconscious* sin (the neglect of social and ethical responsibility, the condemnation of other Christians through ignorance and mental inertia) is done with a good conscience. 'No one ever does wrong so fully and so happily as when he does it with a clear conscience.'[52]

The Pentecostals who believe in a 'three-stage way of salvation' teach that sanctification

> is received as a definite experience subsequent to regeneration . . . And it surely is instantaneous [i.e. not a process of growth].[53]

The account we have given shows that the doctrine of sanctification found in the Pentecostal movement forms part of an influential tradition within the history of the church. It can be found in the Roman Catholic Church, in the Methodist Church, and in the Holiness movements within the Lutheran and Reformed Churches.

The difficulty inherent in all these doctrines of sanctification – both where sanctification is thought to be an instantaneous experience, and also where it is understood as a lifelong process – lies in the fact that it takes away from man his certainty of salvation. If a person's salvation depends upon his sanctification, this does away with the grace of God, given unconditionally. It reminds one of the story of the man who was condemned to death for embezzlement. Those present took pity on the young man, who had fallen into evil ways. The King gave £1,000 from the treasury to make good the debt, the Queen gave £500, the young Crown Prince gave £490, and the people in the public gallery passed the hat round and collected another £9 19*s* 6*d*. But since the condemned man owed £2,000 in all the judge said: 'It is no use, the man must be executed.' In despair the man went through his pockets and to the applause of those in the court produced the last vital sixpence from his trouser pocket.

This example illustrates the way sanctification is understood in Pentecostalism, and in the Holiness movement within the traditional churches. Admittedly, the last sixpence is a very small contribution compared to the large donations made by the King and the Crown Prince,[54] but this last sixpence is the one that matters. Without this sixpence, without the minimum of sanctification for which God looks, there is no redemption.

It cannot be disputed that this view is also present in the New Testament, especially in the Epistle to the Hebrews, which is often quoted by Pentecostals in this context. It is also found in other New Testament epistles of the second and third generations. But this view cannot be found in the teaching of Jesus. He guaranteed his unity with us and his love unconditionally. Once again we come up against the fact that the same thing is not always right at different times and in different places. The varying statements of the New Testament on the subject just discussed are evidence of this. Consequently, the doctrine of sanctification found in the Pentecostal movement cannot be dismissed out of hand. There may be times and places where its effect is a wholesome one. But I can give striking examples of the way it can make Christians uncertain in their faith, and inculcate fear or even indifference.

A former Pentecostal, about thirty-five years old, who to this day gratefully recalls her time in the Pentecostal movement, but has now left it, told me of the following dream she had had:

> Opposite my house stood a large, ugly house. From the very top floor three black women (perhaps they were only shapes, I did not know if they were women) looked out, one of them masked like a devil. I was rather afraid and shut the window at once. Shortly afterwards there was a knock at the door, and the three women stood there. As I opened the door, they reached,[55] came in and closed the door behind them. They said, 'You must not be afraid, we shall do nothing to you if you do what we tell you.' Then they carried me off with them. (I was obliged to go.) Then we were suddenly in a large house. There was a large room there with many corridors, doors and staircases. There was some talking going on, I did not know whether it was a real service, but they were talking about God and everything was terribly holy. The preacher was very conspicuous. He was a cross between God – the way you think of him – the apostle of peace Dätwyler[56] and Pastor X.[57] He had a beard and wore long dark clothes (difficult to describe). I had only one idea all the time, to get out of there as fast as I could. I was quite free to walk about anywhere and to go out of all the doors. But when I went to the big main door, 'God'[58] was standing there again and said, 'You can't go out this way any more.' And he took my arm and stopped me. My husband was waiting for me outside.[59]

The interpretation of this dream could only be worked out together with the woman who dreamt the dream, for the associations which the figures in it have for her are clearly the most important factors in interpreting it. But certain things seem clear. The woman felt herself under pressure from the three figures (the three Maries?). She was certainly free to go out of any door. But when she came to do so, she found herself back in the hands of 'God' (personified here by the pastor), who cut off her way to freedom – and to her husband!

4. *'The Power that Fell at Pentecost' : The Doctrine of the Baptism of the Spirit*

According to Pentecostalism, the traditional churches are still stuck between Easter and Pentecost. Although they know that Jesus died and rose again, they lack the Pentecostal power which fell on the disciples when they were behind closed doors, drove them out,[60] and made them into courageous witnesses to the gospel. All Pentecostals agree:

> The pow'r that fell at Pentecost, when in the upper room,
> Upon the watching, waiting ones, the Holy Ghost had come,
> Remaineth evermore the same;
> Unchanging still, O praise His name.[61]

> The Saviour himself did not preach until he had received this baptism, and he did not let his disciples preach without this baptism with the Holy Spirit. We see how important this baptism is. The true aim of the Church of Jesus Christ is to restore this ruined inheritence amongst our people.[62]

But there are differing views within the Pentecostal movement about the signs by which the baptism of the Spirit is known. The view of a large majority is:

> The Baptism of believers in the Holy Ghost is witnessed by the initial physical sign of speaking with other tongues as the Spirit gives utterance.[63]

'I have received the baptism of the Spirit' is not merely an expression of faith. The person baptized in the Spirit requires an external, verifiable criterion.[64]

> We are against hair-splitting distinctions, but the distinction between speaking in other tongues, as the initial sign of the baptism with the Spirit, and the operation of the gift of tongues, is as palpable as a vital distinction can be.[65]

> Speaking in unknown tongues is the normal and biblical 'manifestation' of the Holy Spirit, the external proof of an inner fulfilment.[66]

> We believe in the baptism of the Holy Spirit, as in a mighty divine power which penetrates into man after salvation and is visibly manifested by the scriptural sign of speaking in new tongues.[67]

Even the Pentecostals who have been involved in ecumenical dialogue,

Donald Gee and, until recently, David J. Du Plessis, shared the teaching of the majority of the Pentecostal movement, that speaking in tongues was an obligatory sign of the baptism of the Spirit. Donald Gee defended this view in innumerable publications.[68] Harold Horton and many others held the same view:

> The evidence of water baptism at Jerusalem, Caesarea, Ephesus, was not faith nor love, but wetness! It is the same today. The evidence of baptism in the Spirit at Jerusalem, Caesarea, Ephesus was not faith nor love, but tongues. So it is today. To be baptized merely 'by faith' or tradition without evidence, is not to be baptized at all – either in water or the Holy Ghost . . .[69]
>
> The leader of a modern fundamental denomination that is not Pentecostal wanted to persuade me some time ago, that a sufficient evidence of the baptism is love. But I want to know, what degree of love will warrant a poor sinner saved by grace the claim, that he has received the baptism? What degree of flowing, we might as reasonably ask, would be sufficient indication that water is boiling. Flowing is certainly a proof that water is not stagnant, but only steam is an evidence of its boiling. Flowing is a characteristic natural to river water. Steam is not. It is the result of a further and non-natural process. However strongly a river flows, it never boils that way. It might froth with flowing. That looks a bit like boiling, but it is not. Love may look like the baptism, for both those who are baptized and those who are not have love. But love is not the baptism . . . Love is a fruit of the new life we have in Jesus. It is natural to that life. It is an expected result of the life in the Tree. If the tree bore diamonds and pearls instead of fruit, that would be the result of some mighty supernatural enduement that the tree had enjoyed. That is exactly the comparison between love and tongues. Love is a fruit of the Spirit . . . But speaking with tongues is not a natural exercise but a supernatural exercise. Some mighty supernatural enduement is necessary to cause a natural man to speak perfectly a language he has never learned. That language is the evidence of the baptism.[70]

Karel Hoekendijk speaks for the great majority of Pentecostals when he says that many Christians reject speaking in tongues as evidence of the baptism of the Spirit only because they do not possess this gift:

> They have something against it, they find it 'uncanny' and 'weird'; consequently they try to push speaking in tongues back to an earlier period, to the time of the apostles, or if they cannot get away with this, they call it a speciality of very 'emotionalized' Pentecostal groups, which make 'unrestrained' use of it . . . and this is why the overcoming of demon-possession and sicknesses caused by demons is so little in evidence among them.[71]

This Pentecostal dogma has been adopted by those Pentecostals within the traditional churches in America whose mouthpiece is the journal *Trinity* – but not by the charismatic movement within the established Protestant churches in Germany:

The Holy Bible makes it very clear that when the Holy Spirit came upon the disciples they spoke with other tongues.[72]

The Apostolic Faith Mission in South Africa cannot treat speaking in tongues as the sole sign of the baptism of the Spirit, because in South Africa many independent African churches practise speaking in tongues. Speaking in tongues is recognized as an initial sign of the baptism of the Spirit, but not as the sole valid sign of it. All who are baptized in the Spirit must speak in tongues, but not all who speak in tongues have been filled with the Holy Spirit. This compromise is a dangerous one for Pentecostal pastoral care and teaching, because it leads to the introduction of further criteria, while explanations have to be sought for the speaking in tongues which is not brought about by the Spirit of God.

A sharp distinction is made between regeneration and the baptism of the Spirit:

Yes, a person can be born again without being filled with the Holy Spirit, because the latter experience is not the same as regeneration.[73]

As early as 1915 the Assemblies of God rejected the identification of rebirth and the baptism of the Spirit as a false doctrine.[74]

Most Pentecostals do not regard the baptism of the Spirit as necessary to salvation.[75] It is the arming of a person with power for missionary service. It is meant for the church on earth, but it is of immeasurable worth, because without it, as the history of the church shows, the church cannot be a missionary church. Only a minority – mostly 'Jesus only' groups – maintain that the baptism of the Spirit is necessary to salvation.[76]

The experience of the baptism of the Spirit has often been described.[77] It must be understood as a liberating, disinhibiting experience, integrating emotional and sometimes even erotic urges. For anyone who has experienced it spontaneously and genuinely – in the setting of the psychological group pressure of a Pentecostal meeting there are also baptisms of the Spirit which are forced and strained – it is of fundamental importance for the course of their life.

For the Pentecostal pastor, the baptism of the Spirit is an indispensable equipment for the exercise of his calling. In terms of the phenomenology of religion, a Pentecostal pastor might be described as a modern *shaman*. Through the baptism of the Spirit he learns to use levels of his soul and his body hitherto unknown to him, as sense organs with which to apprehend a psychological climate, a group dynamic situation. The descriptions of baptisms of the Spirit which follow are examples of this extension of awareness:

On 28 January, at about half past eleven at night, Jesus fulfilled his promise and baptized me with the Holy Spirit. This was the greatest experience of my life . . ., when I suddenly felt my shoulder shaking, and there was immediately a feeling like an electric shock from outside which went through my whole body and my whole being. I understood that the holy God had drawn near to me. I felt every limb of the lower half of my body shaking, and I felt involuntary movements and extraordinary power streaming through me. Through this power the shaking of my body grew continually, and at the same time the devotion of my prayer increased, to an extent that I had never experienced . . . My words dissolved in my mouth, and the quiet utterances of my prayer grew louder and changed into a foreign language. I grew dizzy. My hands, which I had folded in prayer, struck against the edge of the bed. I was no longer myself, although I was conscious the whole time of what was happening. My tongue jerked so violently that I believed it would be torn out of my mouth, yet I could not open my mouth of my own power. But suddenly I felt it opening, and words streamed out of it in strange languages. At first they came and went, with times of silence, but soon my voice grew louder and the words came quite clearly; they came like a stream from my lips. The voice grew louder and louder, at first sounding clear and bold, but suddenly changing into a terrible cry of distress, and I noticed that I was weeping. I was like a horn that someone was blowing. A great chasm was open before me, into which I was shouting, and I understood immediately the meaning of what I was uttering, even though the words were strange to me. According to the account of people who were in a neighbouring room, this speaking and singing lasted about ten minutes. When it ceased it became quite silent, and there followed an almost silent prayer, which was also uttered in a strange language . . . When it was over my soul was filled with an inexpressible feeling of happiness and blessedness. I could do nothing but give thanks, give thanks aloud. The feeling of the presence of God was so wonderful, as if heaven had come down to earth. And indeed heaven was in my soul . . .[78]

The baptism of the Spirit of the Presbyterian minister Dr Charles Price can be understood in the same category. He was a minister in Santa Rosa, California, and some of the members of his congregation attended a gospel meeting to hear Aimee Semple McPherson. He intended to preach about 'this humbug' and give a sermon on the theme 'Divine Healing Bubble Explodes', so that he had to go to the meetings himself. When he arrived he found there was still room in the places reserved for cripples. 'That is where I belonged, but I did not know it at that time.'[79] He was profoundly impressed by the people who came foward during the call for conversion. The next evening he went again. His modernistic theology was punctured by the evangelist until it looked like a sieve. The following evening Price went forward and knelt at the penitents' bench:

> Something burst within my breast. An ocean of love divine rolled across my heart. This was out of the range of psychology and actions and reactions. This was real! Throwing up both hands I shouted, 'Hallelujah!' I ran joyfully through the whole tent, for through the corridors of my mind there marched the heralds of Divine truth carrying their banners on which I could see emblazoned: 'Jesus saves', 'Heaven is Real', 'Christ Lives To-day'. [80]

He soon received the baptism of the Spirit, which he describes as an electrifying feeling which flowed from the ends of his fingers through his arms and his body.

G. T. Lindsay also describes his baptism of the Spirit as 'like pulsating electricity.'[81] The South African geologist and tutor at the University of Stellenbosch, A. V. Krige, had to wrestle for a long time for the 'baptism of the Spirit and power' because 'my brain, a part of the body over which the Holy Spirit must also take control, was too active to yield unconditionally'.[82] J. B. van Kesteren, a Flemish Pentecostal pastor whose father was a Reformed pastor, 'received the fullness of the Holy Spirit, when the Lord wrote the strange language for me in clear letters [as a text on a wall]'.[83]

In the case of the Norwegian Methodist minister and later pioneer of the European Pentecostal movement, T. B. Barratt, flames of fire were actually visible.[84] The Danish opera singer Anna Larsen Bjørner describes her baptism of the Spirit as follows:

> My whole body shook; it was like waves of fire going through me, over and over again, and my whole being was as bathed in light.

She took courage to invite her fellow actors and actresses to her villa and had Barratt speak to them. Another singer, Anna Lewini, was also converted and became a missionary in Ceylon. On Barratt's advice, Anna Larsen Bjørner gave up her work at the Opera. She was taken into a mental hospital for observation, because she was regarded as mentally ill. But the Director of the hospital said of her:

> If I was to give a certificate of your condition, it would be to say that you are the only sane person in this hospital, and all the rest of us are mad.[85]

Innumerable writings give instructions how to prepare for the baptism of the Spirit, and what conditions have to be fulfilled for it to be received. In the older Pentecostal denominations, in which the majority of members have not received the baptism of the Spirit, these writings are of increasing importance.[86] The preparation usually advised is prayer, faith (that is, the expectation of the baptism of the Spirit), and full repentance, with confession and reparation for sins. The Jesus Church teaches that fasting, prayer and tithing are preconditions for the baptism of the Spirit.[87] In the Swiss Pentecostal Mission the baptism of the Spirit tends to be received during Bible Weeks. On one such occasion I observed a mighty outburst of emotion. Strong men roared like hungry lions and beat with powerful blows of their fists on the seats – for in Pentecostal fashion the whole assembly was kneeling facing the seats. A confusion of weeping and laughter came from the women. The noise was so great that one of the Pentecostal pastors who had not yet received the baptism of the Spirit with speaking in tongues decided to withdraw into the kitchen and peel potatoes there, until the noisy prayer-meeting was over. Sometimes what are called 'waiting meetings' are held, where the baptism of the Spirit is awaited. But this practice is condemned by Harold Horton:

There is absolutely nothing in the scripture one degree like what we call a 'waiting meeting' today; where, say, a dozen come to seek the Spirit and all go away disappointed, to come again by invitation next week to wait and seek, and go away again empty, and so on week after week, month after month, year after year.[88]

At the first European Pentecostal Conference in Stockholm in 1939, the first and most important subject of debate was a thesis formulated by Leonhard Steiner, who was a young pastor at the time:

Is it right to base our conception of the baptism of the Spirit on the Acts of the Apostles, and the experience of the twelve apostles? Can this experience be deduced from the epistles written by them?[89]

Undeterred by the criticism implied in the above question, the leaders of the European Pentecostal movement advanced the usual view. The one exception was George Jeffreys, who demanded that any one of the 'supernatural gifts of the Spirit' should be recognized as a sufficient sign of the baptism of the Spirit.[90] This opinion by Jeffreys did not appear in the official Swedish report of the conference,[91] but it can be found in the monthly journal of the Swiss Pentecostal Mission.[92] Jeffreys's view is held today by the Elim Pentecostal Churches,[93] the Swiss Pentecostal Mission, the Chilean Pentecostal movement,[94] and a number of other denominations. Similarly, the German Pentecostal movement has from the first resisted the theory that only one who speaks in tongues has received the baptism of the Spirit.[95] To regard speaking in tongues as in general the sign of the baptism of the Spirit is regarded by Leonhard Steiner as 'a great mistake':

In our day the testimony of the whole gospel is constantly disturbed and deformed by movements of exaltation and of sectarianism within the Pentecostal Movement. The false doctrine of the baptism of the Spirit has played a large part in this . . . The number of those which it has not helped[96] is greater than is supposed . . . One of the most urgent necessities at the moment is the correction of the doctrine of the baptism.[97]

In a memorandum address to the leaders of the Pentecostal movement, Steiner completely rejects the Pentecostal theory of stages of salvation.[98] In 1960, Leonhard Steiner wrote me a letter in which he sums up his studies of the baptism of the Spirit:

My conclusion, then, is that one can no longer maintain the doctrine of stages of salvation. This inevitably leads to the rejection of the distinctive doctrines of Pentecostalism. This does not entail the rejection of the Pentecostal movement, that is, the *experience* of the Spirit which is to be found in it. There are numerous genuine examples of the *experience* of the Spirit, without there being present a correct *understanding* of the Spirit.[99]

I agree with this view.

In my view Carl F. Henry summarizes the situation correctly:

> While tongues remain for most Pentecostalists the decisive experience of a Spirit-centred life . . . here and there a spokesman may be found who insists that the tongues-phenomenon of the first Pentecost . . . ought not to be regarded as repetitive at all [i.e. present in every Baptism of the Spirit][100].

The Holiness movement had propagated the Pentecostal doctrine of the baptism of the Spirit for years.[101] In many of his works, E. Schrenk has distinguished between the élite who have received the baptism of the Spirit, and form the 'general staff' or 'bodyguard' of God,[102] and those Christians 'who have come nowhere near so far as the apostles had at the time of Jesus's ascension', but who nevertheless assert with enthusiasm: We have received the Holy Spirit.[103] Johannes Seitz and the greater part of the European church press were at one time extremely enthusiastic about the emotional outbursts in Wales.[104] The German,[105] Swiss, French, Belgian, Scandinavian and other church journals put forward Pentecostal doctrines. Nowadays they would prefer to forget this, and issue warnings against the diabolical imitations of the Spirit to be found in the Pentecostal movement.[106]

In the traditional churches there is still too little realization of the fact that the experience and doctrine of the baptism of the Spirit occur in the history of doctrine and religious practice in many places outside the Pentecostal movement. In the early church there was already a distinction between baptism (which a priest could carry out) and confirmation (the imparting of the Spirit, which only the bishop or his representative could carry out). In Catholic piety there are famous works of edification which identify the progress from the stage of the ordinary Christian to that of the more spiritual Christian with particular experiences. This devotional pattern, together with similar currents in the Anglican Church, influenced Wesley. They have found their way into European Protestantism through the Anglo-Saxon Holiness movement.[107]

When we look for the biblical roots of the baptism of the Spirit, we discover that the Pentecostals and their predecessors based their views almost exclusively on the Gospel of Luke and the Acts of the Apostles. Luke has a particular interest in the Holy Spirit. This can be seen at once from the fact that the word *pneuma* as a title of the Spirit of God occurs in his gospel three times as often as in Mark. With thirty-seven occurrences, the first twelve chapters of the Acts of the Apostles show the greatest relative frequency in the New Testament.[108] Luke, who was not an apostle, states himself (Luke 1.1–4) that he depended upon written and oral sources .In one particularly interesting passage we possess his original, as it is quoted literally by Matthew (Matt. 7.11). Luke shows his special interest in the Holy Spirit by replacing the word 'good things' in this sentence by 'Holy Spirit'.[109] For him the Holy Spirit is the good thing which the Father in Heaven will give to those who ask him for it. With this saying, which he quotes in a different context from Matthew, Luke concludes the parable of the friend at midnight. The lesson he intends to teach is that one must ask for the Holy Spirit.

Luke also makes a distinction between the reception of the Spirit and the reception of salvation. According to Luke, one can be a Christian without having received the Holy Spirit. For him the Spirit is something additional to salvation. Thus for example the Christians of Samaria believed and were baptized. Who – apart from Luke and the Pentecostals – would say of such Christians, 'The Holy Spirit had not yet fallen on any of them, but they had only been baptized in the name of the Lord Jesus' (Acts 8.16)? According to Luke the reception of the Spirit is manifested in outward and visible signs, frequently but not exclusively that of speaking in tongues: 'Now when Simon *saw* that the Spirit was given through the laying on of the apostles' hands . . .' (Acts 8.18). According to Luke, Paul had to receive the laying on of hands, *after* he had already had his vision of Christ (Acts 9). How does Peter know that Cornelius has received the Spirit? By his faith? By his love? By the fruits of the Spirit? Not at all. According to Luke Cornelius had already been devout and god-fearing before.[110] Peter knew that Cornelius had received the Spirit by his speaking in tongues (Acts 10.14). The same situation occurs in Acts 15. As a sign that the heathen have believed Peter points out: 'God who knows the heart bore witness to them, giving them the Holy Spirit just as he did to us' (Acts 15.8). The Christians of Ephesus were not asked: Have you believed in Christ, have you grown in faith, in patience, in doctrine? Rather, the decisive question was: 'Did you receive the Holy Spirit when you believed?' (Acts 19.2). The reception of the Spirit here means nothing other than what follows: 'The Holy Spirit came on them; and they spoke with tongues and prophesied.' 'The peculiarity of Luke's testimony lies in its demonstration that a church which has no special power to fulfil its missionary task in a concrete way is a church without the Spirit.'[111] According to Luke believers who pray receive the Holy Spirit; but according to Paul – as we shall shortly see – prayer and faith are a consequence of the action of the Spirit.

By contrast to Luke, Paul recognizes expressions of the Spirit which are not extraordinary in nature. For example, by contrast to the Corinthians he includes service (Rom. 12.7; I Cor. 12.5), exhortation (Rom. 12.8), acts of mercy (Rom. 12.8), liberality, (Rom. 12.8), and even being single or being married (I Cor. 7.7) amongst the gifts of the Spirit (*charismata*). Yet Paul speaks in tongues more than the Corinthians (I Cor. 14.18). Visionary experiences are likewise nothing new to him (II Cor. 12.2). Paul neither considers the extraordinary to be of greater worth than the ordinary, nor the reverse. 'The greatest and most important gift is always that which is necessary at the time,'[112] that is, that which most serves 'the common good' (I Cor. 12.7). He strongly refutes the widespread religious conception that the unusual, the supernatural, is more divine. There are no phenomena which for him are closer to God because they are unusual. But neither are they closer to the devil because they are unusual, because of their abnormal and irrational character. The standard by which he judges is that the Spirit is present where faith comes into being and reliance on oneself is overcome, where Christ can be Lord and the body of Christ is built up. The contrast with Luke is clear. For Paul the Spirit is not something additional to faith.

Not only has Paul a different understanding of the Spirit from Luke, but there are also considerable differences between Luke's account of Paul's theology, and Paul's testimony to his own views. For example, according to Luke (Acts 22.30 – 23.11):

> Paul must give an account of himself . . . because he is an arch-Pharisee, and is advocating the Pharisaic doctrine of the resurrection of the dead and the messianic hope.[113]

Acts 23.6 is to be compared with Phil. 3.5–9.[114] Paul retained his Pharisaism 'for one purpose, that he might win Christ'.

> What he [Luke] cares about is the truth that the bridges between Jews and Christians have not been broken. It is Luke's genuine conviction that in the last resort fellowship between Judaism and Christianity is still possible: the Pharisees also hope for the Messiah and expect the resurrection of the dead. In that they are one with Christians. Their only mistake is in not connecting their hope and faith with Jesus. The resurrection of Jesus and the messiahship which this demonstrates are not contrary to the Jewish faith.[115]

For a critical exegete the contrast between the statements of Paul and Luke about the Spirit does not mean that one should be regarded as of less value than the other.[116] Nevertheless the above exegesis is unacceptable to the Pentecostal Leonhard Steiner.[117] His principle argument is that Luke was the disciple and companion of Paul. How can he then describe Paul's theology in a non-Pauline way? One might answer that both German and Swiss Pentecostals regard themselves as disciples and successors of Jonathan Paul. Some of them were his companions for a long period. Nevertheless, some of the most important doctrinal teachings of Jonathan Paul (resistance to fundamentalism, rejection of the Pentecostal doctrine of the baptism of the Spirit, the defence of infant baptism)[118] were rejected by the very same disciples. Charles Parham and W. J. Seymour were leading pioneer figures in the American Pentecostal movement. It was they who converted most of the early Pentecostal preachers to the Pentecostal movement. In spite of this, their doctrinal views[119] did not become the characteristic doctrines of the Pentecostal movement. The same is true of the pioneers of the British Pentecostal movement, Alexander Boddy and Cecil Polhill.[120] Moreover, it cannot be deduced from the text of the Acts of the Apostles that the author of Acts was a companion of the apostle Paul. Individual 'we' passages (e.g. Acts 16.10ff.) can be shown to be quotations or a trick of style in common use at the time. The titles of books in the Bible have not been retained in their original form. Neither the third gospel itself nor the

Acts of the Apostles give the name of an author, nor do the two works themselves lead to any conclusion about their authorship.[121] That Luke was the author of the gospel and the Acts of the Apostles was first asserted *towards the end of the second century*, that is, more than hundred years after they were written, in the so called Muratorian Canon and in Irenaeus.[122]

If these internal indications (the difference in theology) and external indications (the original text does not assume that Luke was the author) are considered together they do not, of course, prove that the author of Acts was not Paul's companion, but this is the most probable conclusion.

One may object that if it is a matter of judgment whether or not the Acts of the Apostles was written by Luke, the companion of Paul, then anyone may choose to hold the traditional view. This view is also taken within the churches. But for the fundamentalists it ought to be unacceptable, for it is they above all who must insist on an exact study of the biblical text. Moreover, the Acts of the Apostles has been preserved in two texts which disagree in essentials. On every page of the Greek text there are differences of *content* between the two (and not merely of orthography). Once again, the establishment of the original text is a matter of judgment, a question of probability which must be resolved as carefully as possible. Here too the Pentecostals cannot escape making a judgment, unless they abandon the establishment of the biblical text to the critical exegetes whom they otherwise reject.

The churches' defence against the Pentecostal movement has mostly consisted of an unconsidered advocacy of the view found in the Pauline writings within the New Testament canon, the testimony of the Lucan writings being represented as an exception in a transitional situation, as though we were not in a transitional situation at the present day. For example Hutten (to name one of the most searching, careful and friendly critics of the Pentecostal movement) feels obliged to base his argument on this arbitrary choice between two strands in the New Testament canon:

> What was extraordinary in the New Testament now becomes normal in the Pentecostal movement; what was experienced as an overwhelming force from outside becomes the fruit of an achievement; the personality and sovereignty of the Holy Spirit becomes a supernatural power which one can use and call upon, to raise the quality of one's state of salvation. Associated with this is a lowering of the value of the church's sacrament of baptism.[123]

Not everyone will accept without question this basic principle of interpretation, that Paul is to be preferred to Luke. Some will ask instead of those who claim that the age of the Apostles is past: 'Yes – the difference is quite considerable! But how do we know what we usually take for granted, that this is the will of God? What gives us the right to say that his promises no longer hold?'[124] This argument – quoted here from one who is himself a theologian of one of the established churches – is that which will be put forward by someone who regards the Acts of the Apostles as the normative document of the normative church.

I shall now attempt to understand the *relative* justification of the views contained in the Lucan writings. I understand 'relative' here not in a pejorative, but in a literal sense. The statements of the evangelist Luke must be seen against the connection or relation they have to the church of Theophilus to whom he writes. In this sense the statements are not 'absolutely' true, that is, true in isolation from the situation to which they belong. Just as the testimonies of Pentecostal faith must be interpreted having regard to the place and time in which they arose, so the biblical writings must be understood as primarily a testimony for their own times. This is the reason why in Pentecostal and Reformation churches the Bible is not simply read, but interpreted in its meaning for our present situation. And this is also the reason why in different churches and different places, the preaching must be different, as every Pentecostal pastor knows from his own experience.

The Lucan writings must be understood as a pastoral document written by a theologian concerned for his church, and composed in a time when to be a Christian and be a missionary were not, as in the time of Paul, automatically the same thing. But Luke knows that the Church will perish if it dispenses Christians from their missionary task. Luke's approach to this defusing of Christian existence is a pastoral and theological one. He attempts to reunite the two elements, being a Christian and being a missionary, which have become separated from each other, by means of his theory of two definite stages. He says it is sufficient to believe in Christ. But one only believes in Christ if the result of this faith is to become a witness to it. The church is not the church unless it lives as a missionary church. If the church replies: We are not able to be a missionary church, Luke says: That is true. That is why God sent his Holy Spirit at Pentecost. And for the same reason he sends him again and again. God will help you. All you have to do is pray earnestly for the gift of the Spirit. If you then, who are evil, know how to give good gifts to your children, how much more will the heavenly Father give you the Holy Spirit if you ask him for it. He will give you the Holy Spirit, who made those terrified disciples missionaries at Pentecost, who made the apostle Paul a missionary, and who turned that wretched, timid, inward-looking group in Ephesus into a church which in two years turned the city of Ephesus upside down (Acts 19).

In presenting this theological sketch Luke uses older testimonies. But he is not a church historian in the modern sense. For example, Peter's sermon at Pentecost is a composition by Luke. It is difficult to imagine a disciple who spoke Aramaic not only preaching in the words that are used, but expressing the main ideas of the sermon, for the scriptural proofs are based on mistranslations of the Greek Old Testament (Septuagint). This can be verified by a comparison of the texts in an English version. Acts 2.20 quotes the prophet Joel from the Greek New Testament: 'Before the day of the Lord comes, the great and *manifest* day.' But in the Hebrew original of the prophet Joel (2.31) we read: 'Before the great and *terrible* day of the Lord comes.' Acts 2.27 quotes Psalm 16.10. The psalm speaks only of protection from death. The Greek translation which Luke quotes turns this into a liberation from corruption. It is only the mistranslation into Greek which makes it possible to interpret this text as referring to the resurrection of Jesus.[125] We are not arguing that the Old and the New Testaments are contradictory, but that it can be shown that the author of the sermon in Acts 2 used a *Greek* Old Testament. Anyone who believes that Peter gave this sermon must accept the unlikely thesis that a Galilean fisherman who spoke Aramaic preached in Jerusalem on the basis of a Greek mistranslation. This is not wholly impossible, but it is unlikely.[126]

Thus we cannot, on the basis of the text of the New Testament, refute Paul with Luke, nor Luke with Paul. Nor must we attempt to harmonize them. We have simply to ask which categories of presentation and thought are best appropriate to our own situation and our own congregations. Luke and Paul share a concern that the church should be sound in belief and full of missionary zeal. Paul's language is more theological, more precise, but less concrete. Luke separates into a temporal succession things that belong together. It is not accident that the picture presented by Luke has been accepted as the true biblical view by people who are not capable of dialectic thought.

Readers who are Pentecostals will have noticed that this attempt at an interpretation of the Acts of the Apostles is based on the results of theological scholarship. It is close to some of the interpretations which Pentecostals have put forward themselves. Thus for example in the Mülheim Association of Christian Fellowships the difference between natural and supernatural gifts is rejected.[127] The confession of faith of this Association, edited and commented by C. Krust, is wholly based on the Pauline witness in the New Testament.

> The attempt to present the baptism of the Spirit as a second spiritual experience, to be fundamentally distinguished from regeneration, has no basis in Scripture . . .[128]

Here Krust has begun the process of leading his Association back to a Reformation and Pauline theology. On the other hand the Pentecostals who have remained within the Reformation churches[129] do not hold this Pauline doctrine of the Spirit, as do Catholic Pentecostals, together with Christian Krust. 'Since the incarnation of Christ there is no radical dichotomy between the supposedly natural and the supposedly supernatural.'[130]

But there are many people for whom the Lucan testimony is more comprehensible and therefore more appropriate than that of Paul.

5. '*Set Hearts and Tongues Afire*':[131] *Speaking in Tongues*

For most Pentecostals 'Speaking in tongues . . . is a sign that the recipient is possessed by the Holy Spirit.'[132]

> [It is] *the* sign of the baptism of the Spirit . . . All gifts which the Spirit brings and gives had already been given individually before Pentecost, except for speaking in other tongues with interpretation! Thus this was the new sign by which the baptism of the Spirit was known . . .[133]

By this Pentecostals mean speaking in a tongue of men or angels which the speaker has never learnt. In their literature they quote many testimonies of speaking in languages which have been identified. They tell of pastors to whom the gospel was preached in Latin in Pentecostal Assemblies, of Rabbis who found themselves hearing the 'mighty acts of God' in Hebrew, etc.[134] The question whether real languages are used in speaking in tongues can only be clarified when there are sufficient tape recordings of speaking in tongues available. Pentecostals hesitate to make themselves available for such experiments.

Pentecostal teaching and practice distinguishes between two functions of speaking in tongues: (*a*) speaking in tongues as the initial sign of the baptism of the Spirit; (*b*) speaking in tongues as one of the gifts of the Spirit. In the case of the second kind of speaking in tongues, a distinction is made between public speaking in tongues in Pentecostal services, which according to I Cor. 14.27 must always be interpreted, and personal speaking in tongues, which can be described as a non-intellectual prayer and praise too deep for words (Rom. 8.26). However, it has sometimes happened in Pentecostal services that

> [the worshippers] were caught up in an ecstatic volume of united worship. Speaking in tongues which occurs at such a time is not for the edification of others, but is devoted to the worship of the Most High God. These special movings of the Spirit we always welcome and encourage.[135]

Behm asserts: 'Any subsequent phenomena of glossolalia in Church history can only be hollow imitations of this first springtime of the Spirit.'[136] But in the bibliography which Behm himself gives he includes the work of E. Mosimann, whose view in my opinion is the correct one: 'The speaking "with other tongues" at Pentecost was essentially the same phenomenon as the speaking in tongues in Corinth and at the present day. . . .'[137]

As a result of the spread of speaking in tongues in the traditional churches, a great deal has been written about speaking in tongues, but most of these works simply repeat the well-known Pentecostal view. Exceptions which may be mentioned are the works of Cutten,[138] who gives a valuable historical account, Lombard,[139] who tries to classify the various forms of speaking in tongues, the Lutheran pastors Christenson[140] and Bittlinger,[141] who take the phenomenon of tongues seriously and try to understand it against the background of Lutheran theology, and the Pentecostal Vivier-van Eetveldt, who made speaking in tongues the subject of his thesis in psychiatry.[142] The Anglican priest Morton T. Kelsey,[143] who does not speak in tongues himself, but has a group of members of his congregation who speak in tongues, makes an attempt to understand the phenomenon of speaking in tongues against the background of Jungian psychology. He sees speaking in tongues as an expression of the collective psyche. In Kelsey's view, it has for certain people – not only primitive or uneducated people – a similar therapeutic function to that of dreams, and should certainly not be despised as a pathological phenomenon, 'hollow imitations of the first springtime of the Spirit', or as the work of demons. On the other hand he believes that speaking in tongues which occurs under external pressure damages the character and mental health both of the person who imposes the pressure and the recipient. Kelsey regards speaking in tongues as an extremely effective therapeutic instrument, which, however, when applied to the wrong patients, can be dangerous. K. McDonnell, a Benedictine, goes further and states: 'Even the speaking in tongues to be found among pagans cannot *a priori* be excluded from the workings of the Holy Spirit.'[144] This of course is to follow D. J. Du Plessis in not restricting the gifts of the Spirit to Christians.[145]

There are nowadays no scientific grounds for explaining away speaking in tongues as a pathological form of expression.[146] The sociologist Bryan Wilson[147] and the anthropologist Malcolm Calley[148] describe speaking in tongues as a necessary form of expression for people for whom this form of speaking is the only possible way of speaking in public.

Psychologists interpret speaking in tongues as a form of expression which is valuable under certain circumstances. Pentecostals and theologians are astonished that 'liberal' ministers are not excluded from it.[149] When someone is praying, and through psychological inhibition, weariness or despair 'does not know how to pray as he ought' (Rom. 8.26) he is helped by the 'liturgy of speaking in tongues':

> Breathe on us now the Holy Ghost,
> The young and old inspire;
> Let each receive his Pentecost,
> Set hearts and tongues afire!
> Thou wonderful transforming power,
> Come now in this accepted hour.[150]

When in spite of St Paul's teaching in I Cor. 14.39, the Reformation churches attempt to reject or ridicule speaking in tongues, they can hardly be surprised that those for whose mental health speaking in tongues is necessary turn to the psychiatrist or set up in separatist groups. Paul himself believed that a person speaking in tongues edified himself (I Cor. 14.4), and that it consequently formed an important element of the personal life of prayer, but should be limited to a subsidiary function in public worship. Thus we would have to have very strong reasons to deny the wholesome effect of speaking in tongues.

It is possible that the origin and function of speaking in tongues may at some time in the future be 'explained'. For example, the Professor of Psychiatry at the University of Berne, T. Spörri, is working on such an explanation. His view is:

> The solemn assertion of people who are of themselves trustworthy, that they have heard someone who speaks in tongues speaking in Italian, Hebrew or Latin, cannot simply be rejected as an invention.[151]

Spörri suspects that this is a phenomenon similar to that of people who are able to imitate a language, its melodic accent, and its rhythm in a convincing way, without ever having learnt the language. A striking factor in the testimonies of speaking in comprehensible languages is that the person who received the message was usually addressed in his own native language, and the message finally resolved a long-standing conflict.[152] Here speaking in tongues would represent a *non-verbal* archetypal form of communication, an interpretation which has been borne upon me by many examples of speaking in tongues and their interpretation in Pentecostal services.

If this interpretation is true, then two important conclusions follow:

1. The explanation of speaking in tongues deprives it of none of its significance. Ultimately, one can give a medical explanation of why man needs food and sleep. In the same way, man needs the possibility of meditation and the relaxation of tension, and these are not limited to intellectual forms. For some people art fulfils this function, for others, speaking in tongues; and those who can unload their mental burdens in both ways are not so rare as commonly supposed.

2. It is becoming clear that communication is one of the most important present-day problems, and therefore the possibility of non-verbal communication should not be taken lightly. Because this form of communication is incomprehensible and uncontrollable by those who are not initiates, they are suspicious of it. Their first reaction is a defensive one. A more rational reaction would be an attempt to understand this phenomenon better. To this end the function of speaking in tongues as a form of group therapy – although it must not simply be called mass suggestion – is dealt with below.[153]

Since the uninformed view that speaking in tongues is of its nature ecstatic appears ineradicable, it must be explicitly stated here that this is not so. There exists not only 'hot' speaking in tongues (which can be described as ecstatic, although the person speaking in tongues is never 'outside himself'), but also 'cool' speaking in tongues, sometimes mystical, and sometimes sounding like an incomprehensible foreign language – something like listening to a foreign station on the radio speaking in a language you do not understand. I have come across an example of the second kind in a Negro spiritual.[154] This is not surprising, since spirituals and the Pentecostal movement originate in the same milieu, the religion of American Negroes.[155]

6. '*Your Sons and Daughters Shall Prophesy*': *Prophecy*

It is clear that we could not recognize the false coin if we did not have good coin.[156]

> Prophecy is the ability to reveal future events, and can be recognized by the following signs: First, that it is fulfilled in due time. Secondly, that it is fulfilled without doubt in exact accordance with the prophecy. And it must be such that it could not have been spoken on the basis of human foresight, the prophet being solely dependent on the inspiration of the Spirit.[157]

In Pentecostal churches of the Apostolic type, and in various African churches,[158] prophecy plays an important part. A Basak pandit in Indonesia 'for many years foresaw the death of members of his congregation, often weeks in advance, which gave him the opportunity to prepare the person for death.'[159] Pastor W. W. Verhoef is certain about the possibilities of subjective influence in prophecy. The same, he believes, must have been true of the prophets of the Old Testament. In spite of this the risk involved in prophecy must be taken.[160] The older Pentecostal denominations reject prophecy as the foretelling of the future, and permit it only as edification.

> We have known marriages arranged, church business conducted, personal friendship dissolved, family matters dealt with, money matters handled, by such methods, with obvious disastrous results. Missionaries directed by such unattested predictions ... have ... gone over the ocean only to come back later disillusioned ... One could easily fill a magazine with the stories of such happenings.[161]

Wherever the Pentecostal movement has taken on organizational forms, spontaneous prophecy which goes beyond exhortation for edification has necessarily been rejected as 'Satan deceiving and misdirecting simple souls'.[162]

Where conditions of life are difficult prophecy recurs as concrete prediction of the future. Thus for example in 1963 in Czechoslovakia, in the border district adjoining Poland (Česky Těšín, Tčinec) there was a Pentecostal revival within an existing church. Visions, dreams and prophecies of catastrophe occurred. The group amongst which this happened had originally been a Pentecostal church (in Polish it was called Związek stznowczych chrześcian) and belonged to Christian Endeavour. It had united with the Jednota Českobratrská (Unitas Fratrum). But under the influence of the revival it divided again. Associated with the revival was the wish of the Ukrainians in that area to emigrate to Poland, as well as an outbreak of suicides amongst Christians who believed they had committed the sin against the Holy Ghost.

Apart from a few exceptions, which are, however, important,[163] biblical prophecy seems to me to be absent in the Pentecostal movement, for biblical prophecy contains more than the edificatory exhortation known as prophecy in the Pentecostal movement at the present day. One of the most impressive prophecies in the Pentecostal movement comes from the British evangelist Smith Wigglesworth. Unfortunately most Pentecostals of the present day are unaware of it, although it has been fulfilled in a most remarkable way. Wigglesworth visited David J. Du Plessis in 1936, and laying his hands on Du Plessis' shoulders he pushed him against the wall and began to prophecy:

> You have been in 'Jerusalem' long enough . . . I will send you to the uttermost parts of the earth . . . You will bring the message of Pentecost to all churches . . . You will travel more than most evangelists do . . . God is going to revive the churches in the last days and through them turn the world upside down . . .[164]

Then he began to tell him details of visions he had been seeing that morning and which God had told him to share. It was all too fantastic. Even the Pentecostal movement would become a mere joke compared with the revival which God was bringing to the churches. Wigglesworth went on to specify that all this would not happen until after Wigglesworth's death. Wigglesworth died in the 1950s, shortly before his prophecies began to be fulfilled.[165]

The Pentecostal movement and the traditional churches, in consciousness of their poverty, may co-operate in their search for present-day forms of prophecy, both spontaneous and the fruit of thoughtful reflection. It is not so important to establish that there are examples of foreknowledge which are difficult or impossible to explain.[166] Much more important would be the experience of the guidance of the church brought about by thanksgiving and thought, question and answer, a guidance which would not evade the problems for which both the world and the church cannot find answers.[167]

A starting point can be found in the work of the Evangelical academies, the Lay Training Centres, the Pope's various social encyclicals, and the conference of the World Council of Churches, 'Church and Society', at Geneva in the summer of 1966.[168]

I shall conclude this chapter by pointing to one or two examples of theologians who have given attention to the prophetic task of the church, by way of introducing Pentecostal pastors to the important but somewhat complex literature on the subject. An outstanding example in the German-speaking world is Arthur Rich, the successor of Emil Brunner at the University of Zürich. He was an apprentice mechanic before studying theology. His main work has been concerned with the question of what it means to be a Christian in an industrialized and technological world, a question which no Pentecostal pastor can avoid, for he has to speak every day to people who are trying to be Christians in this industrialized world.

In the English-speaking world, William Temple took up the Christian socialist tradition from F. D. Maurice. Two years before his death he published *Christianity and Social Order* in which he discussed the question whether 'Middle axioms' could be found halfway between general theological principles and particular policies.'[169] He was the chairman of the first national Christian Conference on Politics, Economics and Citizenship (COPEC) in 1924. He was greatly influenced by – and influenced in his turn – Reinhold Niebuhr, whose works are also concerned with the Christian task in the modern world.

NOTES

1. *Bases Bibliques de l'Église Évangélique de Réveil de La Chaux-de-Fonds* (Switzerland), Prospectus.
2. L. Pethrus, *Redemption Hymnal* 1958, no. 494.
3. D. J. Du Plessis, *Volle Evangelie Koerier* 21/2, Aug. 1959, pp. 4ff.
4. J. McGranaghan, *Redemption Hymnal*, 1958, no. 245; *Hymns of Glorious Praise*, 1969, no. 217.
5. J. E. Campbell, *PHCh*, p. 275; B. R. Wilson, *Sects*, p. 87.
6. J. Brooke, *A Testimony*, p. 4.
7. H. Davies, *Christian Deviations*, pp. 83f.
8. F. Lovsky, *Réveil*, *Digeste Chrétien* 4, 15.4.1952, pp. 14ff.
9. J. Wesley's *Diary*, quoted in *Schweizer Evangelist* 29.7.1905, p. 238. F. Dale Bruner (*Theology*, pp. 35–47), deals in detail with Wesley and the forerunners of the Pentecostal Movement. J. D. G. Dunn (*Baptism*, p. 1) deals with similar teachings and phenomena in Britain.
10. Cf. above ch. 2.1, pp. 21f.
11. P. Breese; quoted in T. L. Smith, *Called*, p. 51.
12. All confessions of faith of the Holiness movement.
13. A. B. Simpson, *Fourfold Gospel*, no pag.
14. Cf. above, ch. 9.1, pp. 111ff.
15. Cf. *PGG*, pp. 252ff.
16. Cf. above, ch. 16.1(*b*), pp. 221ff.
17. Cf. above, ch. 4, pp. 47ff.
18. Cf. above, ch. 3, pp. 29ff.; ch. 15, pp. 206ff.
19. The Apostolic Church is a representative of this type; cf. above, ch. 13.4, pp. 191ff.
20. Details, 02a.02.D.VI.
21. C. Röckle, *Philadelphiabrief* 101/102, 1957; K. Hutten, *Seher*, 11th ed., 1968, p. 228.
22. P. Brofeldt, *Helluntaiheräty*, p. 108; quoted in W. Schmidt, *Pfingstbewegung*, p. 97.
23. P. P. Knapp, *Hymns of Glorious Praise*, 1969, no. 386. I have noticed that the Pentecostal hymnbook used in Switzerland and Germany (*Pfingstjubel*) contains significantly more hymns of sanctification from the classical Holiness tradition than the *Redemption Hymnal* of the British Assemblies of God and the *Hymns of Glorious Praise* of the American Assemblies of God.
24. Fleisch II/2, pp. 343ff.; details, with many references, 05.07.008a, dd.
25. Fleisch, II/2, pp. 343f.
26. Cf. p. 335 and 05.28.025d, hh.
27. A. Bruckner, *Erweckungsbewegungen*, pp. 177ff.; cf. ch. 14.2, pp. 209f.
28. J. Paul, *Pfingstjubel*, 1956, no. 393, v. 2.
29. W. C. Martin, *Hymns of Glorious Praise*, no. 297.
30. Confession of Faith of the 'Bruderschaft: Der König kommt!'

31. G. Krüger, *Glaube, Liebe, Hoffnung* 15/11, Nov. 1962, pp. 1f.
32. Regehly, *Auf der Warte* 3/31, 29.7.1906, pp. 4f.
33. E. A. Rogers's memoirs, quoted in Fleisch, *Geschichte*, p. 70.
34. R. E. Day, *Bush Aglow*, p. 123; W. R. Moody, *D. L. Moody*, pp. 146f., quoted in R. K. Curtis, *They Called Him Mister Moody*, p. 149. Details, 02a.02.004.
35. W. M. Smith, *Annotated Bibliography*, quoted in R. K. Curtis, *op. cit.*, p. 149.
36. R. K. Curtis, *op. cit.*, p. 150.
37. M. Hauser, *Gnadenthrone*, pp. 143f.
38. J. A. Synan, 'Doctrinal Amplifications', in PHCh, *Discipline*, 1961, pp. 32ff.
39. T. N. Turnbull, *What God Hath Wrought*, p. 129.
40. S. M. Hodges, *Look on the Fields*, pp. 67f.
41. Full Salvation Union, *Manual*, 1944; Moore, pp. 298f.
42. From a sermon by T. B. Barratt in Zürich, quoted in *Kirchenfreund* 5, 1910, p. 328; cf. above n. 33.
43. A. V. Krige, *Rundbriefe der Deutschen Spätregenmission* 3/6, Aug. 1961, p. 3 (italics in the original).
44. A. V. Krige, ''n Paar Grondwaarhede', p. 19.
45. E.g. *Kracht van Omhoog* 26/12, 12.12.1963, pp. 18f.
46. A. V. Krige, ''n Paar Grondwaarhede', p. 33.
47. Congregação Cristã do Brasil, *Estatutos*, 1946, Art. 8.
48. J. Paul, 'Das reine Herz', *Die Heiligung* 139, April 1910, p. 19.
49. E. P. Paulk, *Neighbour*, p. 89.
50. Wesley, *Works* XI, p. 396. For Wesley's doctrine of santification see: J. Wesley, *Plain Account*, *Works* XI, pp. 366–446. Cf. also 05.28.004a, and the literature noted there.
51. *Kirchenfreund* 5, 1910, p. 327.
52. 'Jamais on ne fait le mal si pleinement et si gaiement que quand on le fait par conscience.' Pascal, *Pensées*, Frag. 895.
53. P. F. Beacham, *Scriptural Sanctification*, 9th ed., n.d., p. 12.
54. Since the story originates in Catholic circles, the Queen (i.e. Mary) plays a certain part in it. Pentecostals would probably have the Crown Prince paying the whole sum of £1,999 19*s*. 6*d*.
55. Not quite clear. The expression (German *zogen sie*) means that the woman felt herself from the first in the power of the three figures, who wanted to draw her along with them.
56. The 'Apostle of Peace' Dätwyler, a well-known Swiss pacifist, rather Utopian, with a long beard.
57. Pastor X, the pastor of the Pentecostal church which the woman had previously regularly attended.
58. 'God', i.e. the above mixture of 'God', Dätwyler and Pastor X.
59. Noted down by W.H.
60. John 20.
61. C. H. Morris (1862–1929), *Redemption Hymnal* 1958, no. 219.
62. W. A. Waltke, 'Gemeinde', *Lebendiges Wasser*, no date, number, pagination. (The 'Church of Jesus Christ' is the German Pentecostal *Gemeinde Jesu Christi.*)
63. AdD, Dominican Republic, *Reglamento*, 1944; cf. AoG, USA, Appendix: 2.
64. P. v. d. Woude, *Volle Evangelie Koerier* 21/4, Oct. 1959, p. 2.
65. UPCh, Tract, no. 126, n.d.
66. C. Le Cossec, *Le Saint-Esprit* (Vérité à connaître 3), p. 16.
67. AdD, Italy, *Risveglio P* 8/11, Nov. 1953, p. 2.
68. For a fuller account see ch. 13.2(*b*), pp. 208ff.
69. H. Horton, *Baptism*, 1956, pp. 13f.

70. H. Horton, *PE* 1661, 9.3.1946, pp. 3, 7; cf. also R. E. Orchard, *PE* 2892, 12.10. 1969, pp. 8f., 27.

71. K. Hoekendijk, *Waffenrüstung*, pp. 48f.

72. *Trinity* 1/1, 1961, pp. 51f.

73. *Trooster* 32/5, May 1962, p. 25.

74. Cf. above, ch. 3.1(*b*), p. 32.

75. E.g. J. A. Cross, *ChoGE* 53/3, 18.3.1963, p. 9.

76. Cf. ch. 3.1(*b*), pp. 31f. Documents, etc., 02a.02.137; 02a.02.137A; 02a.02.139.

77. E.g. T. B. Barratt (05.21.007; 07.093.001), A. Larsen Bjørner (07.141.001), J. R. Flower (07.449.001), D. Gee (07.093.001), J. V. van Kesteren (07.752.001), A. V. Krige (07.781.001), G. T. Lindsay (07.855.001), A. S. McPherson (07.932.001), T. C. Newby (08.025.001), A. N. Ozman-La Berge (08.080.001), J. Paul (08.097.001), C. Price (08.156.001), V. Pylkkännen (08.160.001), E. Roberts (10.731.001, 05.13.001), L. Steiner (08.399.001), L. Wreschner (80.645.001).

78. V. Pylkkännen, *Toivon Tähti* 1914/18, pp. 68ff., quoted in W. Schmidt, *Pfingstbewegung*, pp. 115ff.

79. C. Price, *Story*, p. 33.

80. C. Price, *op. cit.*, pp. 36, 37.

81. G. T. Lindsay, *Story*, p. 40.

82. A. V. Krige, ''n Paar Grondwaarhede', p. 48.

83. P. van Kesteren, letter to W.H., 17.8.1963.

84. T. B. Barratt, *Free Gospel Mission Journal* 10/3, quoted by F. G. Henke, *American Journal of Theology* 1909, pp. 193ff.; Barratt, *Da jeg fik; When the Fire Fell; Latter Rain*, pp. 127ff.; C. Björkquist, *Svenska Pingstväckelsen*, p. 25.

85. A. Larsen Bjørner, *Teater og Tempel*, pp. 95f., 117; ET, *P* 10, 1949, cover.

86. J. E. Stiles, *Gift*; cf. ch. 1.2(*a*), pp. 12ff.

87. 02a.02.138.

88. H. Horton, *Study Hour* 9, 1950, p. 69.

89. Basis and formulation of Question 1 in Förlaget Filadelfia, *Europeiska Pingstkonferensen*, pp. 50ff.; German: *VdV* 33/2, Feb. 1940, pp. 15ff.; 33/3, March 1940, pp. 12ff.; cf. above, ch. 5.5, p. 67.

90. Cf. n. 89; details in G. Jeffreys, *Pentecostal Rays*, 2nd ed., 1954, p. 35; cf. B. Wilson, *Sects*, p. 57.

91. Cf. n. 89.

92. G. Jeffreys, *VdV* 33/5, May 1940, pp. 11f.

93. Cf. ch. 14.2, p. 200.

94. E.g. 02b.08.049b, 11.

95. Cf. above, ch. 17.2(*a*), pp. 236f.

96. I.e. the number of Pentecostals who have not received the baptism of the Spirit.

97. L. Steiner, *Baptême*, p. 6.

98. L. Steiner, *Sind wir nun keine Pfingstler mehr?*

99. L. Steiner, letter to W.H., 20.2.1960.

100. C. F. Henry, *Christianity Today* 5/17, 22.5.1961, p. 737.

101. Cf. above, ch. 9.1(*b*), pp. 114f.; 02a.02A; 05.07A; 05.28A.

102. E. Schrenk, *Wir sahen*, 1888, pp. 66f.; quoted in H. Klemm, *Theologie*.

103. E. Schrenk, *Suchet*, n.d.; quoted in H. Dallmeyer, *Zungenbewegung*, 1924, 2nd ed. n.d., pp. 12f.

104. Cf. ch. 13.1, pp. 176ff.

105. Cf. above, ch. 16.1(*b*), pp. 221ff.

106. E.g. W. Malgo, *Mitternachtsruf* 7/9, Dec. 1962, p. 20.

107. 05.07.A; 05.08.A; 05.13.001; 05.20.001; 05.21.A; 05.28.A.

108. In the following pages I have drawn on E. Schweizer, art. *pneuma*, *TDNT*

VI, pp. 332–451, and the literature given there, without losing sight of my main purpose, which is to be comprehensible to Pentecostal pastors without higher theological training. For those who have no Greek, the article is summarized in: E. Schweizer, *Spirit of God* (Bible Key Words).

This interpretation is in opposition to F. D. Bruner (*Theology*), who does not see any justification of the Pentecostals' teaching in the Lucan writings. 'To confuse what Luke records with what he teaches is as erroneous as it is frequent.' (*Theology*, p. 194)

To a lesser extent this interpretation is also in opposition to the recent analysis of J. D. G. Dunn (*Baptism*). Dunn maintains that for the writer of Acts 'it is only by receiving the Spirit that one becomes a Christian' (p. 5). Dunn says in his preface that the Pentecostal doctrine of the Baptism of the Spirit 'cannot escape heavy criticism from a New Testament standpoint'. In spite of his eirenic and thorough research Dunn's 'Pauline' interpretation of Acts did not convince me. It remains my conviction that the Catholic *and* the Pentecostal teaching have some justification in Acts, but not in Paul.

109.

Matt. 7.11:	Luke 11.13:
'If you then, who are evil, know how to give good gifts to your children, how much more will your Father who is in Heaven give *good things* to those who ask him!'	'If you then, who are evil, know how to give good gifts to your children, how much more will the heavenly Father give *the Holy Spirit* to those who ask him!'

110. It is characteristic of Luke – in common with certain Pentecostal groups (cf. below ch. 28, pp. 399ff.) to look favourably on those who 'fear God' – even on Pharisaism properly understood. He goes far beyond what P. Volz finds good in the Pharisees ('sacrifices were replaced as the dominant practice by the ethical practice of piety', *RGG*, 2nd ed., vol. IV, col. 1179). This leads him to give a very individual picture of Pauline theology.

111. E. Schweizer, *Spirit of God*, p. 50.

112. A. Bittlinger, 'Bedeutung der Charismen', p. 11; cf. ch. 18.2, p. 246, and A. Bittlinger, *Gifts and Graces*, pp. 70–2.

113. E. Haenchen, *Apostelgeschichte*, 12th ed., 1959, p. 569.

114.

'. . . cirumcised on the eighth day, of the people of Israel, of the tribe of Benjamin, a Hebrew born of the Hebrews; as to the law a Pharisee, as to zeal a persecutor of the church, as to righteousness under the law blameless. But whatever gain I had, I counted as loss for the sake of Christ . . . For his sake I have suffered the loss of all things, and count them as refuse,' Phil. 3.5–8.	'Brethren, I am a Pharisee, a son of Pharisees; with respect to the hope and the resurrection of the dead I am on trial.' Acts 23.6.

Literature discussed in Haenchen, *op. cit.*, p. 45.

115. E. Haenchen, *op. cit.*, p. 571.

116. Cf. p. 340.

117. Cf. *PGG*, pp. 580f., and below, ch. 32.2, p. 500.

118. Cf. ch. 17.2, pp. 235ff.

119. British Israel theory (Parham, cf. below ch. 2.2, p. 22); three-stage theory of salvation (Seymour, ch. 2.3, pp. 22ff., and Appendix: 1).

120. Cf. ch. 13.2, pp. 184ff.

121. S. Schulz, *Stunde*, p. 235,

122. References in S. Schulz, *loc. cit.*, and E. Haenchen, *op. cit.*, p. 7.

123. K. Hutten, art. 'Geistestaufe', *RGG*, 3rd ed., vol. II, col. 1304. Cf. 05.07.046; 06.004.003b.

124. Pastor Eppler, Thanksgiving sermon for the former parish minister and later Pentecostal pastor P. Hug (dupl.) (05.28.025b).

125. Cf. E. Haenchen, *Apostelgeschichte*, 13th ed., 1961, p. 145.

126. Cf. also E. Schweizer, *Neotestamentica*, pp. 418ff.

127. *Heilszeugnisse* 45/8, 1.8.1960, p. 61.

128. Krust II, p. 107; cf. above, ch. 17.2(*a*), pp. 236f.

129. Germany is an exception (cf. above ch. 18, p. 244).

130. Ranaghan, *Catholic P*, pp. 204, 123.

131. C. H. Morris, *Redemption Hymnal*, 1958, no. 219.

132. J. H. Schat, *Spreken.*

133. F. Kramaric, *VdV* 52/12, Dec. 1959, p. 12.

134. Details in C. Brumback, '*What Meaneth This?*'; cf. above ch. 1, pp. 3ff.

135. F. S. Williams, *PE* 2714, 15.5.1966, pp. 6f.

136. J. Behm, art. 'Glossalalia', *TDNT* I, p. 726.

137. E. Mosimann, *Zungenreden*, p. 130.

138. G. B. Cutten, *Speaking with Tongues.*

139. E. Lombard, *Arch. de Psych.* 7, 1907, pp. 1ff., 300ff.

140. L. Christenson, cf. Bibliography.

141. A. Bittlinger, cf. Bibliography.

142. L. M. van Eetveldt Vivier, *Glossolalia*, 1963. Eng. summary: Vivier, 'The Glossolalic and his Personality', in T. Spörri (ed.), *Beiträge sur Ekstase*, pp. 153ff.

143. M. T. Kelsey, *Tongue Speaking.*

144. K. McDonnell, *Worship* 40/10, Dec. 1966, p. 611.

145. Information supplied by D. J. Du Plessis.

146. Cf. the outstanding article by V. H. Hine, *Journal for the Scientific Study of Religion* 7/2, 1969, pp. 211ff.; cf. also G. J. Jennings, *Journal of the American Scientific Association*, March 1968, pp. 5–16 (including bibliographies).

147. B. R. Wilson, *Sects and Society* and *Social Aspects of Religious Sects.*

148. M. J. Calley, *Aboriginal Pentecostalism.*

149. Squintus, *Elim Evangel* 43/51–52, 25.12.1962, p. 824.

150. C. H. Morris, *Redemption Hymnal*, 1958, no. 219.

151. T. Spörri, 'Ekstatische Rede', in Spörri, *Ekstase*, 1968, p. 151.

152. Cf. the example given above, ch. 1, pp. 3ff.

153. Cf. below, ch. 31.1(*c*), p. 366.

154. Brother Cleophus Robinson, with Spirit of Memphis (Dickens): 'Jesus, I can't live without you.' Europäischer Plattenclub, *Negro Spirituals* no. 2 (Gospel Songs II) 51 BIEM (passage with speaking in tongues after 2 minutes 10 seconds).

155. Cf. above ch. 2.3, pp. 22ff., and details in 02a.02c.

156. Congregação Cristã do Brasil, *Estatutos*, 1946, art. 5.

157. *La Voz Pentecostal*, June 1962, pp. 7f.

158. Cf. ch. 12.4(*d*), pp. 157ff.

159. T. Müller-Krüger, *Ev. Missionszeitschrift* 7, 1950, p. 163.

160. W. W. Verhoef, *Vuur* 6/3, May 1962, pp. 2ff.

161. *Elim Evangel* 21, 1940, p. 568; W. G. Hathaway, *Spiritual Gifts*, pp. 67ff.; B. R. Wilson, *Sects*, p. 25.

162. E. S. Williams, *PE* 2486, 31.12.1961, p. 21.

163. Cf. e.g., ch. 6.1, p. 75

164. Quoted by M. Harper, *As at the Beginning*, p. 51.

165. Details in M. Harper, *op. cit.*, pp. 51ff.; cf. also *Vie et Lumière* 30, Jan.–Feb. 1967, pp. 19ff.

166. E. Kuchynka, 'Neue Wissenschaft', *Zeitschrift für Parapsych.* 5/1, 1930, pp. 1ff.

167. Cf. J. B. Souček, in volume in honour of J. L. Hromádka, *O Svrchovanost viry.* pp. 24ff.; French transl. *Communio viatorum* 4, 1961, pp. 221ff.

168. M. M. Thomas and P. Abrecht, *Christians.*

169. R. Preston, 'William Temple after Twenty-four Years', *Church Quarterly* 2/2, Oct. 1969, p. 116.

25

'The Day of Miracles is Still Here':[1] Healing by Prayer and the Doctrine of Miracles

1. *'They will Lay their Hands on the Sick . . .': The Practice of Healing through Prayer*

(*a*) *The longing for the supernatural*

THE longing for the supernatural and for the healing of sickness by prayer is a constant feature of nineteenth-century works of edification, as anyone who reads them can tell. In 1885 a Divine Healing Conference was held in London, and a number of well-known Swiss pastors took part. The Reformed pastor Otto Stockmayer believed that sickness and death could be conquered in the life of a sanctified Christian. Elias Schrenk, who took part in the conference, used to pray with the sick, and had started to keep a book in which he collected the testimonies of those who had been healed. The South African Reformed pastor Andrew Murray stated:

> Wherever the Spirit acts with power, there He works divine healings. . . . If divine healing is seen but rarely in our day, we can attribute it to no other cause than that the Spirit does not act with power.[2]

> Your submission is nothing else than spiritual sloth in view of that which God commands you to do.[3]

The Swiss Evangelical movement made pilgrimages to Vialas, where the French peasant Vignes practised healing, and Hermann Ruetschi's healing meetings were publicized by a minister of the established church in Switzerland.[4] Ruetschi was put on trial for practising quack medicine and was acquitted. 'One can only be pleased that the shares of the Berne-Worb Railway have gone up [because so many patients were travelling out to Worb to see Ruetschi].'[5] One of the forerunners of the Pentecostal movement, the 'Restorer', 'Elias III', John Alexander Dowie, who took the title of 'Doctor', believed he had been sent 'to destroy sin, to prepare the people of God and to restore the Kingdom of the Lord'.[6] His Zion City in Illiniois, USA, its subsidiaries in Zürich, Amsterdam and South Africa, and his sermons and healings, exercised a considerable influence on the early Pentecostal movement. The American healing evangelists appealed directly to him, and many leaders of the Assemblies of God, as well as the funds for the Swiss,[7] Dutch and South African Pentecostal movements, came from Dowie's Zion Church.[8]

Later the Jeffreys brothers,[9] Smith Wigglesworth, Douglas Scott and other healing evangelists drew audiences of thousands. After the death of this first generation of evangelists many Pentecostal pastors were seized with fear: Will the same thing happen to us as to other denominations? Will the miracles disappear? This must not and cannot be.

(*b*) *William Branham and his followers*

On 7 May 1946, at approximately 11 o'clock at night, an angel clad in white visited William Branham, an American Baptist preacher. The angel was clean-shaven, his hair hung down to his shoulders, and he had a friendly, sun-tanned face. He said to Branham:

> Fear not. I am sent from the presence of Almighty God to tell you that your peculiar life and your misunderstood ways have been to indicate that God has sent you to take a gift of divine healing to the peoples of the world. *If you will be sincere, and can get the people to believe you, nothing shall stand before your prayer, not even cancer.*[10]

From then on Branham was never without the guidance of the angel. The angel gave him signs to help in him his task. The most important was Branham's ability to name with astonishing accuracy the sickness, and often also the hidden sins, of people whom he had never seen. The author, who knew Branham personally and interpreted for him in Zürich, is not aware of any case in which he was mistaken in the often detailed statements he made. It was characteristic of Branham's kind-heartedness that he gave certain personal revelations to those who were seeking healing in a whisper, so that they were not picked up by the microphone and revealed to the spectators.

In the years that followed Branham filled the largest stadiums and meeting halls in the world. He was reported in the newspapers, sometimes favourably, often critically, and in fact in most cases unfavourably. Much that was written about him in Pentecostal journals seems to be exaggerated, but there are a number of well-attested cases of miraculous healings. It has even been asserted that he raised the dead.[11]

Branham died on Christmas Day in 1965 as a result of a head wound – as he had prophesied[12] – which he received when he was putting petrol into his car, and another car full of drunken youths ran into him. But he had announced that a great miracle evangelization campaign would begin on 25 January of the following year. His followers had his body embalmed and refrigerated, because they expected him to rise from the dead on 25 January. When this did not happen, the date was put off until Easter 1966. This postponement of his burial is probably the reason why European Pentecostals heard nothing about Branham's death.[13] When he did not rise at Easter 1966 either, he was buried.[14] Nevertheless, a profusion of legends had already grown up about his life and death, in which even someone familiar with his life is soon at a loss, and which led the traditional Pentecostal churches to look with disfavour on Branham's friends. The friendly reception Branham received at first from the Pentecostal movement turned into an almost unanimous rejection when Branham announced that the Millennium would begin in 1977,[15] and preached baptism 'in the name of Jesus',[16] but a vigorous protest had already been provoked by his healing campaigns. Some regarded Branham's talent as a natural gift,[17] whereas others declared that it was the result of some occult tendency.[18]

It is clear that what Branham achieved was not of equal value on every occasion and in every place. To be fair, one must take into account his extremely limited education and his inadequate English. He seems to have been aware of his limitations in this direction, and in his writings asks for indulgence because of his poor education. However generously he is judged, it must be admitted that his sermons were not merely simple, but often naive as well, and that by contrast to what he claimed, only a small percentage of those who sought healing were in fact healed. The Pentecostal pastor Leonhard Steiner had a poor opinion of Branham's campaign in Zürich. He wrote that the call to make a decision for Christ was 'disturbingly vague. No real call to repentance could be distinguished . . . The convincing miracles of God, the true evidence of his Spirit and of power, were absent.'[19]

The following much abbreviated extract from a letter which was sent to me describes both the diagnostic gifts which Branham exercised, and also his therapeutic failure in the meetings at Zürich.

> Two years ago I came, suffering from a long-standing and severe bile and liver complaint, to one of Brother Branham's evening meetings in Zürich. Although I had not drawn the slightest attention to myself, his son gave me a little card, but those who received them were not called up that evening – but regardless of the cards, some of the sick people were called up, either directly by Brother Branham, or by you yourself. To my unspeakable joy I was one of those who was spoken to (although I was right at the back and out of sight of Brother Branham). You had to call me three times (with an accurate diagnosis by Brother Branham), until I understood that it was actually I who was meant. This word was given to me: 'Be comforted, my daughter, your faith has helped you, you will be healed.'

The sick woman gave a detailed account of her further misfortunes, the worsening of the pain, and the onset of new diseases and her increasing loneliness. In her despair she wrote the above letter and begged me to tell Branham of her sickness:

> Please, my dear brother in the Lord, could you make my great desire your own and say a single word to Brother Branham from these hands, stretched out to you in distress? Surely you will be seeing him? This will be the greatest act of love which you could ever show me.

Unfortunately, to avoid yet more disappointment, I had to decline. But I considered it would be right, since the journals of the Swiss and foreign Pentecostal movement had for years publicized the testimonies of those who had been healed, to publish at least once a testimony from one of the majority who had not been healed (such as the above letter). This suggestion was turned down by the leaders of the Swiss Pentecostal Mission.

Branham became the inspiration and example of the healing evangelists who imitated him, and whose mouthpiece was the journal *Voice of Healing*. For many Pentecostal pastors, spurred on by his example, had taken new courage. A great number of them underwent an experience of a call similar to that of Branham.[20] They travelled the world to heal the sick. Some of them, such as T. L. Osborn and Hermann Zaiss,[21] were welcomed into the traditional churches in spite of, or perhaps even because of their extreme healing practices. They made tentative contacts with the Anglican Order of Saint Luke, an association of American doctors and theologians.

Gordon Lindsay was the literary and organizational manager of the healing evangelists, and published their reports in the journal *Voice of Healing*, which he edited. Later the Full Gospel Business Men's Fellowship International[22] took over the financial and publicity organization of the healing evangelists. More recently, evidently for financial reasons and because of dogmatic differences, some of the healing evangelists have set up their own supporting organization, while others have returned to ordinary pastoral work. One section has united with groups from the New Order of the Latter Rain to form the Full Gospel Fellowship of Churches and Ministers International.[23] W. A. Raiford has been chosen as the executive secretary of the new denomination. He was formerly a detective, but is now an honorary doctor of theology. Velmer Gardner was very disturbed at the feeble testimonies of healing in the Pentecostal congregations with which he was acquainted, and the vast difference between the religion of the Acts of the Apostles and that of the Pentecostal movement. He therefore founded the Velmer Gardner Evangelistic Association. Jack Coe was revolted by the cold, unemotional services in most Pentecostal churches, and at the tendency to found colleges, make constitutions and draw up confessions of faith, and to neglect the old-fashioned revival meetings. He wished to fight against the 'tragedy of a powerless Pentecostal movement', and therefore set up the Coe Foundation.

In a flood of literature the healing evanglists proclaim that it is the will of God – with or without the help of doctors – to heal the sick. 'Expect a miracle and you can have one.'[24] Gordon Lindsay knows God's 'master key' to success and prosperity.[25] The healing evangelists live in a constant dialogue with angels and demons, the Holy Spirit and the spirits of diseases from the abyss; some experience electric currents through their hands when they pray with the sick, others have a halo around their heads when they are photographed, and others again have oil appearing on their hands when they pray. If the healing of a sick person does not take place, this can be the result of one of ten, fifteen or twenty reasons why prayers are not heard (unbelief, sin, etc., on the part of the persons seeking healing).[26]

(*c*) *Self-criticism*

The attitude of individual Pentecostal groups to the healing of the sick by prayer in general, and to the healing evangelists in particular, varies a great deal. On the whole one can say that the more recent and more enthusiastic groups look with favour on the healing evangelists.[27] On the other hand, the older Pentecostal groups have gone to some trouble to keep the healing evangelists at a distance, for until recently they held and taught the view of the healing evangelists which they now condemn as false: 'Anyone who believes is healed; anyone who is not healed has not believed aright.'

Brumback accused the healing preachers of attacks upon local Pentecostal pastors, moral lapses, egotism, arrogant behaviour and over-estimation of the value of bodily healing, and the false teaching that prosperity is an irrefutable sign of piety. This led the *Pentecostal Evangel* to refuse to publish any further reports of the healing evangelists. But when Brumback expressed the view that they had lost their following[28] he was probably too optimistic. For if this is so, how can they pay for their broadcasts, their massive missionary work in Europe, and the tons of printed material they publish? The older Pentecostal denominations are now paying the penalty for often lacking the courage to make an open admission of their mistakes, for they spread and encouraged for many years the practices of the healing evangelists, which they now condemn.[29] It is possible that it is not only this false teaching which makes the older Pentecostals look unfavourably upon the healing evangelists, but also the fact that with the aid of their organizations they divert money from local congregations to pay for evangelistic radio broadcasts. This alarms the traditional Pentecostal churches. The following observation gives support to this suspicion. At the World Pentecostal Conference in Toronto in 1968, Leonhard Steiner gave a lecture on 'Divine Healing in God's Plan of Redemption'.[30] In this lecture Steiner pointed out that the healing evangelists wanted so to speak to make God their servant, and in their prayers for healing had ignored the limitation that man must always make: 'Thy will be done.' Consequently God has not confirmed their preaching in the last ten years. It had to be stated with sadness that in the healing campaigns, after the first rush of enthusiasm, those who remained healed were only a very small percentage. 'The apostles practised divine healing without making a special point of preaching it, whereas we preach it, but fail to practise it.'[31]

Like the critical remarks made by Jeffreys at the conference in Stockholm in 1939,[32] the passage of the lecture referred to was suppressed in the conference report, for besides a lively expression of agreement, it also provoked violent objections.

(*d*) *The doctine of healing through prayer*

It must be stated that many traditional Pentecostal denominations taught until recently the doctrine of the healing evangelists which they now reject; and some still teach it. One example is the French Pentecostal pastor Le Cossec:

> Whatever your sickness and its cause may be, you know that it is an oppression by Satan, a work of the devil. Put your trust in Jesus Christ, who has come to destroy the works of the devil and to set free the oppressed, and you will be healed.[33]

The Assemblies of God, USA, taught the same doctrine. One of their members, Dr Lilian B. Yeomans, was cured of severe addiction to morphia by Dowie after she had been treated without success by several specialists.[34] She wrote several books for the Assemblies of God and expressed her belief in the doctrine which Brumback opposes:

> Many of us have been taught to pray, 'If it be Thy will, heal me.' That wasn't the way David prayed . . . Ps. 6.2–9 . . . there were no ifs or buts in that prayer . . .'[35]

F. F. Bosworth regrets the passing of the period of revival with which the Assemblies of God began:

> The modern idea that God wishes to let some people suffer was never mentioned in those days, and it cripples the prayer of faith of the sick, and prevents all from being healed.[36]

As recently as the Fifth Pentecostal Conference (1958) the evangelist Richard Vinyard, of the Assemblies of God, repeated the same theory:

> If you will turn your faith loose tonight you can take heaven home with you. If there is going to be any healing for that body in that heaven, there is healing down here now.[37]
>
> Healing does not fail because of the will of God, but because of the unbelief of his children.[38]

In a 'discussion in the power and demonstration of the Spirit' the Church of God (Cleveland) resolved in 1907: 'We should take Jesus as our Physician.'[39] As the Church of God (Cleveland) increasingly took on the form of an organized church, this view was abandoned. One of its splinter groups, the Church of God of Prophecy, brought it back into force, but only imposed sanctions when the taboo against medicine was transgressed by *pastors*.

The majority of Pentecostal groups believe in healing through prayer, but at the present day no longer reject medical assistance. The healing evangelists, who are extremists in other ways, constantly emphasize their gratefulness for the help of doctors. They admit that many are not healed through their prayers, but point out that many also seek help in vain from doctors. Enrique Chávez wrote to me:

> All the Pentecostal churches accept divine healing, without making it a doctrinal principle, except as a manifestation of the power of God and of his love.[40]

The Italian Assemblee di Dio teach:

> We believe in divine healing according to Holy Scripture: by prayer, by anointing with oil, and by the laying on of hands.[41]

The Jugoslav Kristova Pentekostna Crkva proclaims:

> Deliverance from sickness is provided for in the atonement at Golgotha, and is the privilege of all believers.[42]

The confession of the Brazilian Assembléias de Deus states:

> Since divine healing is a privilege for those who believe it is clear that it cannot be a law, nor a reason for resisting or despising science and medicine.[43]

Its sister organization, the Congregação Cristã, affirms:

> We are sometimes asked to pray for someone who is a stranger to our faith. Let us always do this without hesitation, unless the Lord determines otherwise. On the other hand, we should say that we are neither doctors nor healers, and that in faith we place his case before God, and if his faith is sufficient to believe that Jesus Christ can cure him, he will be made well by Him . . . We should never speak against doctors and medicine, and no commandment should be laid down about this matter.[44]

Sometimes we hear of spectacular healings,[45] and even of people raised from the dead:

> But we learn of the apostles and the Lord that they did not surrender even when death had taken place. They were not grave-diggers or cemetery chaplains, but people to whom the Lord had given power even over death![46]
>
> Jesus raised from the dead. His disciples did the same (Matt. 10.8; Acts 9.4; 20.12). The gates of death are in our possession. Even today, through faith, the dead are called back to life. The author of this article has once experienced this himself.[47]

Jonathan Paul said the same thing:

> We do not say that a Christian can no longer sin, be ill or die. But we assert with the word of truth in Christ Jesus that the living members of the body of Christ no longer have to sin. And since he has borne their sickness, they no

longer have to be sick. And the hour is near when they will no longer have to die either.[48]

Accounts of raisings from the dead – both unsuccessful and successful – are not rare in the Pentecostal movement.[49] For example Lura Johnson Grubb, an evangelist of the Assemblies of God, who has risen from the dead, has described her experiences during death. She even produces her doctor's death certificate.[50] On the other hand Paul Hug, formerly a Reformed pastor, and later a Pentecostal pastor, tried in vain to bring a dead person back to life.[51] Pentecostal writers do not seem themselves to place much reliance on most stories of persons raised from the dead. Thus Kristian Heggelund says that in thirty-seven years in the ministry he has travelled in many places and has come to know many servants of the Lord with great gifts, 'but I never met one who had raised someone who was really dead'.[52]

(*e*) *Significance for Africa and Latin America*

Prayer for the sick is of particular importance in the African churches. The scientific treatment of illness as practised by Europeans is unacceptable to many Africans, even if they are not intellectually capable of explaining what prevents them from accepting it. European medicine seems to them to be a new and worse magic, which claims to be able to overcome the tragedy of sickness and the link between body and soul with the tools of modern science. In these circumstances, a responsible integration of academic medicine (including psychiatry) and the African practice of hypnotherapy (healing by hypnosis) with healing through prayer is an urgent necessity. This view has been impressed upon me in conversation with young Africans. The same idea is expressed in a report by an African psychiatrist to the conference 'West African Workshop: The Church in Action in Urban and Industrial West Africa'.[53]

A further example of such an integration is the Etodome Nyanyuie-Presbiteria Hame Gbedoda Kple Doyo-Habobo (The Prayer and Healing Group of the Evangelical Presbyterian Church at Etodome in Ghana). This prayer group was founded by the bricklayer Frank Kwadzo Do, a faithful member of the Presbyterian Church in Etodome. With the permission of the authorities of his church in Ziofe, where he works during the week, he began to hold Presbyterian services, because the nearest Presbyterian Church was too far away. Since those who came to these services did not know any Protestant hymns, he put on a special singing practice for them. A dying child was brought to one of these practices, and was healed by the prayers of the assembled congregation. At the same time Do received visions and the gift of speaking in tongues. This prayer and healing group in Etodome, which had formed around Do, worked with the permission of the church authorities within the Presbyterian Church, although the speaking in tongues and other peculiarities caused a great deal of tension with neighbouring congregations. Its healing services are quite different from

American ones. They consist of friendly pastoral care for individual patients, with confession of sins, and advice for combating diseases, the difficulties of pregnancy, the fear that the children will fall ill, and miscarriages and still-birth, together with help to prepare expectant mothers for the task of bringing up their children. In addition, all the greater and lesser difficulties of marriage and the up-bringing of children which occur in daily life are dealt with in a sympathetic, good humoured, but never frivolous way, in what amounts to an unselfconscious form of group therapy.[54] In Africa the church is faced with the alternative either of taking seriously the problem of healing as a unified process concerning both body and soul, or of losing a large proportion of its adherents to Pentecostal groups and sects.[55]

Binder, who is a disciple of Albert Schweitzer, provides an example of the integration of South American Indian medical practice with European scientific medicine. He does not fight against the Indian medicine men, but accepts them as colleagues on a basis of equality. While he learns from them, he also passes on to them important elements of the knowledge of medicine and hygiene. Binder's dealings with the medicine men seem to me to be a classic example of what theology understands by 'dialogue'. The distinction between pupil and teacher is no longer present. Both, the European doctor and the Indian medicine man, are pupil and teacher simultaneously. This would seem to be the proper method for an evangelical mission, for 'where one of the partners [thought himself] confirmed in his views, there no dialogue took place, but a monologue with stopped ears. There Christ did not speak, rather he was silenced'[56] or talked down. Since Binder has recognized the fact that not only what might be called practical help is important, but also the discovery of new ideas and hitherto unknown possibilities amongst the Indians and mestizos of Peru, the same problems of communication occur with him as in missions. He wishes neither to confirm the Indians in their former practices, nor force them abruptly out of the context of their civilization. And yet the way in which the Indians approach and experience life, their religion and their economy must be fundamentally altered if they are to survive. But Binder does not simply impose these new values on them as an outward veneer. He does not offer them a new religion, a new feeling for life, but helps the Indians to discover for themselves the new ideas and attitudes which they need.[57]

The Christian Medical Comission, a sponsored agency of the Division of World Mission and Evangelism of the World Council of Churches, is conscious that the church's work of healing does not consist in the maintenance or even the erection of traditional hospitals. Hospitals, especially in the third world, but also, for example, in the USA, are becoming increasingly expensive and increasingly ineffective in raising the general level of health of the population, because they are 'bed-centred' and 'care-centred', instead of being 'person-centred' and 'health-centred'. What is the use of treating infectious diseases when the water supply and the air are increasingly polluted? What is the use of treating heart ailments when modern patterns of living and work (even in the churches) impose an excessive burden on the heart? The most important question a sick man asks – to choose an example from Africa[58] – must not be constantly avoided. This question is not: 'What is my disease (appendicitis or a broken arm)?' but: 'Why am I ill? (evil spirits, crime against society)?' The African wants to see treatment for what he regards as the root of the disease, not its symptoms. Thus a decisive factor for the work of healing in Africa is the co-operation in health work of Africans who have not necessarily had medical training, but are aware of this background and take it seriously.

Before we discuss the function of miracles within Pentecostal religious thought, and contrast it with the Protestant understanding of miracles, I shall try to give a more detailed picture of this pattern of belief and practice by looking at three of the healing evangelists, Hermann Zaiss, Oral Roberts and A. A. Allen.

2. *'God is a Good God': The Fight against Illness*

(*a*) *Hermann Zaiss*

Hermann Zaiss who 'wants to make a row for Jesus', knows God's telephone number. It is Heaven 1.[59] 'Every illness can be ended in the moment in which you believe; for the Lord is the Lord.' For a woman ill with cancer he asks point blank: 'Father in heaven, please send this sister a packet of anticancerin, because she is ill with cancer.'[60]

In spite of the weakness of Zaiss's doctrine of healing, indisputable healings have taken place. Thus for example the *Schwarzwälder Bote* (13.12.1955) describes a case in Heilbronn. A man of fifty years of age who had been unable to walk or stand for months because of a painful curvature of the spine, resulting from a nervous complaint, was healed by Zaiss. Dr Kötteritz observed that this person was not the only patient from his practice who had obtained relief after meeting Zaiss.[61]

Of course Zaiss has overestimated his success in healing. Someone who had received a temporary improvement wrote to Zaiss only the second day after her 'healing': 'Everything is as before, I am deaf again, please help me, dear brother Zaiss.' But in Zaiss's office records this person had already been registered as 'healed', and so, in spite of her disavowal, she could have read in Zaiss's journal *Mehr Licht!* the thanksgiving she uttered in the first hours.[62]

Zaiss had already been converted as a boy through the testimony of a Christian blacksmith, known as the 'Hallelujah Blacksmith', but then, as the result of all kinds of disappointments, 'consciously went away from God for twenty years'.[63] On 22 July 1944, the day on which these twenty years were up, he went with his wife into the bombed church of Ohlig to pray: 'If you will have us again, here we are!' His style of preaching is described by the *Heilbronner Stimme* as follows: 'An elderly, cheerful-looking gentleman in a well-fitting suit. With close-cropped, greying, thinning hair, he looked exactly like what he is, a contractor and manufacturer ... Like an explosion the torrent of words streams out over the packed room, and the quieter it is round the lonely man on the stage, the wilder are the gesticulations which emphasize each particularly telling phrase.'[64]

(*b*) *Oral Roberts*[65]

Oral Roberts, the tall, dark-haired talented television and radio evangelist, combines the boldness and toughness of his Indian ancestors with the simple and indeed over-simplifying outlook of the Pentecostal Holiness Church, in which he grew up. His mother composed comic ballads about the grocers who charged too high a price to them – they were small cotton farmers – for their goods. It is from her that he must have inherited his exceptional talent as a speaker, which enables him to speak every Sunday for half an hour, on 500 radio and television stations, to a potential audience of eighty per cent of the population of the USA. With his gigantic tent, which holds 12,000 persons and cost £100,000, he travels throughout America, stirring consciences and praying for the sick. Every year, according to his own figures, a million people are converted, and these, like Billy Graham, he directs to the existing churches. He asks for cases of healing by prayer to be medically tested, and publishes only accounts of cases where recovery has been maintained for a long period under medical supervision. But his religious activities do not prevent him from being a member of the Rotary Club, like any 'successful American', and of being received by President Kennedy, Chiang Kai Shek, Ben Gurion, the Polish Minister for Religious Affairs, and other important personalities.

He has at his disposal the most modern printing works, film and recording studios. By contrast to the books of other healing evangelists, his works are well written and tastefully produced. His sermons are carefully prepared, but their effect is both spontaneous and direct. His followers can share in his work by means of the 'Blessing Pact': 'Test God to see if he will bless you if you invest your money in his work' (this does not refer solely to the Oral Roberts Evangelistic Association). At first he said he was willing to repay investments if the promised prosperity was not achieved.

His teaching is as follows. God is a good God, and the devil is a bad devil. God's will for you is good (health, riches, well-being); The devil's will for you is bad (sickness, poverty, depressions). Therefore make your choice for the good, for God!

Behind this dualistic world-view lies the experience undergone by Oral Roberts, at the age of seventeen, when he was suffering from tuberculosis. The devout visitors who stood round his sick bed tried to convince him that this illness came from God. He rejects this interpretation to this day. If he had accepted these religious insinuations, he would never have been healed from his sickness. The sudden cure of his tuberculosis is the basis of his ministry of healing. He holds firmly to his teaching, although he is realistic enough to admit that only twenty-five per cent of the people with whom he prays are healed or improved. He says in as many words: 'No one in the whole world has prayed with more sick people who have *not* been healed than I have.'

In Tulsa, Oklahoma, Oral Roberts built for £2,000,000 a shining white marble administrative building. The glittering marble cube, adorned with large coloured stones, and built in imitation of the 'heavenly Jerusalem' in the book of Revelation, has no windows and is artificially lit and ventilated. Typewriters linked to 'electronic brains' answer 30,000 letters a day. The most striking thing is that because God is a good God, the 'employees of God', from the director and his wife down to the office junior, not only wear well cut, striking modern clothes, and the women faultless make-up, but they have always to radiate happiness: with friendly smiles they lead every visitor through this miracle of technology and optimism.

In spite of what sometimes appears in German and Swiss papers, Oral Roberts is in no way rejected by the fundamentalists[66] or the traditional churches. On the contrary, he has good relations with the Anglican Order of St Luke,[67] and with Billy Graham, with whom he sometimes shares a platform at conferences of the Full Gospel Business Men's Fellowship International.[68] When the magazine *Life*[69] accused Oral Roberts of using methods of psychological suggestion and of seeking to enrich himself, the *Tulsa Tribune* (Roberts' headquarters is in Tulsa) replied at the beginning of 1962: He is still not as rich as the Archbishop of Canterbury or the Pope, and cares for more people than they do. To the charge of hysteria, the paper replied: Perhaps the emotional tension of a tent meeting is necessary for some people in order to overcome their complexes; the psychiatrist's couch and the silence of the cloister are not the only places where a person can find relief. Whether his healings come about through suggestion or something else, we do not know but at any rate he gets results. 'We are proud to have him in Tulsa.'

In 1962 Oral Roberts University was founded. It contains all faculties, including a faculty of medicine. It is equipped with the most modern apparatus. Any student can use the electronic communication system to dial a request from his place to the research centre for the tapes he needs. Similarly he can use the dial to put the films he needs for his studies automatically on to his individual television screen. A lecturer has the most modern teaching aids at his disposal. His desk in the lecture hall is like the cabin of an airliner. He can project simultaneously or successively, on to several screens, films or slides which are delivered to him immediately by electronic means from the fully automated research centre of the University. The aims of study are described as follows:

> If a young person wants to become say an architect, a journalist or a linguist, and he goes to a highly accredited University, he faces a battle. There are forces within some of these schools which are atheistic and materialistic. God

> has an answer for this problem. It is our objective to build the greatest academic University founded on the Word of God that has ever been built . . . We want every professor in the University to have a doctor's degree or its equivalent and to be baptized with the Holy Spirit.[70]

This last requirement has since been modified to state that lecturers must be sympathetic to Pentecostal speaking in tongues.

The sponsors and directors are the managers of the Full Gospel Business Men's Fellowship International. The founding of the University represented for Oral Roberts the fulfilment of a long cherished dream. As the highly talented but penniless son of a pastor of the Pentecostal Holiness Church, Oral Roberts had to suffer many humiliations during his youth. For example, he tells how on graduation day he was chosen as 'king of the school'. He provided himself for the festival with a new shirt, a new pair of trousers and white tennis shoes, which cost $2.16. The 'queen', a girl from a rich family, appeared in a dress of white satin. It was not surprising that the teacher asked him: 'Oral, shouldn't you go straight back home and get changed?'

Nevertheless Roberts succeeded in becoming a famous television evangelist and the founder of a University. In this way he was able to heal the wounds caused by the way his classmates despised him because of his lowly origin. Something of the satisfaction of having made it, in spite of the poor conditions of his early life, was visible at the inaugural ceremony of his University, when Oral Roberts, honoured by the governor of Oklahoma, and applauded by the notables of Tulsa, called up onto the platform his father, who was of partly Indian ancestry and was pastor of a small Pentecostal congregation, and presented him to the cheering crowd.[71]

On 18 March 1968 he surprised his colleagues by stating that he was joining the Methodist Church. The pastor of the largest Methodist church in Tulsa said on receiving Oral Roberts into the Methodist Church: 'Oral Roberts has not changed his faith at all. He will remain the same, but there will be greater possibilities for his work.' This means that the healing campaigns and the television programmes will continue in the same style. He will naturally continue to be president of the University. Some of his colleagues, including his friend of many years, Corvin, the Chancellor of the university, were evidently not in agreement with this change. They left his university.

Roberts has not been immediately accepted as a pastor in the Methodist Church, since he has not obtained the academic qualifications required by American Methodists. He has been provisionally accorded the status of a lay preacher. It is stated that he is going to carry out the required course of study so as to be ordained as a Methodist pastor in the near future.

(*c*) *A. A. Allen*

A. A. Allen has published a record[72] which includes a healing service. He opens the service with the words of the song he takes up later: 'I'm going to a city, friends – are you? – where the roses never fade, where there'll be no more crutches, no more wheel chairs, no more stretchers.' Tonight, he continues, there is in the invalid section 'a little woman laying on a stretcher. Helpless, she can't walk. She has to take 25 pills every night, so she'll not be in agony. She jumped out of an upper storey to window end it all. God's going to heal her tonight.' There are interjections now and then from the audience. He breaks off. The spotlights shine across his vast tent; loudspeakers carry his voice to every one of his audience of thousands, and he sings:

I am going to a city, where the streets all with gold are laid,
Where the tree of life is blooming, I am going where the roses never fade.
Here they bloom but for a season, soon their beauty is decayed.
I am going to a city, I am going where the roses never fade.

He makes contact with his audience:

Loved ones gone to be with Jesus,
– 'How many have some gone?' he interjects –
In their robes of white arrayed,
Now they're waiting for my coming,
They're waiting where the roses never fade.
– 'How many going with me?' –

The last question makes Allen, a rather weak singer, the unquestioned master of the audience. He calls for prayer, for the 'little woman'. 'Jumped out of a window, upper storey window, 'cause life wasn't worth living. How many'll pray that God'll make life worth living tonight?' The audience join in the next song, 'Leave it there'.

When your youthful days are gone, and old age is creeping on,
And your body bends beneath the load of care,
Jesus will never leave you then, he'll be with you to the end,
If you take your burden to the Lord and leave it there.

He speaks to the woman of her suicide attempt: 'Are you sorry you did that, lady?' She is near to tears as she replies: 'Yes, yes . . .' (It may well be the first time in her life that she has been addressed as 'lady' – and with maximum publicity by someone who, in that situation, occupies a position of the highest status.) Allen's voice breaks with emotion as well:

'You do want Jesus to hear you tonight?'

'I want Jesus to hear me . . . I'm tired of suffering.'

'And you want him to heal you tonight?'

'I want him to heal me tonight'.

'In the name of Jesus,' Allen cries, 'In the name of Jesus, my God, heal this woman from the effects of this fall . . . Heal this spine, and heal, O Lord, this nervous system, heal this spinal cord and this spinal column. Lord, from her head down to the toes, put this spinal cord back in place.' His voice rises constantly and the words come faster. 'Take away this nervousness, and, let this woman walk normally again as she used to walk. O God, in Jesus's name' – his voice grows hoarse – 'give her something to live for.' He rebukes the demon. 'I rebuke this melancholy devil. In the name of Jesus I curse this melancholy, suicide devil! Can then these tears be dried, this broken heart be bound up?' The rest comes suddenly, like lightning:

> Remember Peter stopped at a gate one time and said to the man who couldn't walk, 'In Jesus's name rise up and walk'? Well, I'm going to do more than that, because God's doing a new thing today. I'm going to say, 'Jump up and run.'

There is a pause, then, word by word, formally, solemnly, he pronounces:

> 'In the name of Jesus Christ of Nazareth – Jump!'

The audience bursts into shouting and enthusiasm, and a commentator described to the radio audience how the woman has jumped up and is running round the tent. At this point the recording seems to have been cut, and we hear Allen saying 'Let's praise the Lord!' There is apparently another cut, and what follows is a jam session with significantly fewer people, probably in a studio. The conclusion is interesting for the way in which, against a background of a dance-like rhythm ('There'll be a great day when we all gather round') another blues-like melody is superimposed quite independently.

It is impossible to say on the basis of this record whether this healing in fact took place. It can be thought of either as a transitory cure in the tense atmosphere of the tent meeting, or even as a permanent cure, if the woman 'found something that made her life worth living' in the framework of a Pentecostal assembly.

3. *'The Proof of Divinity': The Function of Miracles*

In spite of the considerable weaknesses of the healing evangelists, who are being subjected to an increasingly acute criticism from the more thoughtful leaders of the Pentecostal movement,[73] the connection between salvation and healing cannot simply be denied. Why are we told of so many healing miracles by Jesus? Why has the gospel always been accompanied by healing activity throughout the course of history?

As an increasing number of Pentecostals are being trained as doctors,[74] the rejection of medical assistance is being abandoned. Röckle writes:

> The saviour actually healed a blind man with clay and a dumb man with spit. But they (certain Pentecostals) do not even use the plants which God has made to grow, and heal everyone through the prayer of faith. They even forbid the use of such means, without considering that according to I Tim. 4.1 this prohibition is the doctrine of the devil.[75]

In the Polish and Russian Pentecostal movement it is clearly understood that not every sickness is a punishment for sin.[76]

The Pentecostal doctrine of the healing of the sick cannot be understood until it is seen in its relationship to the Pentecostal understanding of Scripture. The fundamentalists who say 'Back to the Bible!' are told: 'It would be better not to speak of a complete return to the Bible if you then draw up a list of "exceptions".'[77] The explanation of the expectation of miracles in Pentecostalism is to be found in the rock-like belief that Jesus Christ is the same, yesterday, today and for ever (Heb. 13.8), that those who believe are accompanied by the signs of faith (Mark 16.17–18), that Jesus Christ has come to preach good news to the poor, to proclaim release to the captives and recovering of sight to the blind (Luke 4.18), and that he has borne our sicknesses and carried our pains (Isa. 53.4). Other fundamentalists *preach* the miracles of the Bible, but Pentecostals experience them. 'Take away the supernatural from Christianity, and Christianity ceases to exist.'[78]

> Miracles are to Christianity what movement is to the body. That is, if the body no longer moves, if it is incapable of moving, it is nothing but a dead shell, a corpse ... To take miracles away from Christianity is to make it simply a moral code, that is, to reduce it to a philosophy of existence and life.[79]

> It is not enough to preach the word of God. The word of God must constantly be confirmed anew (Mark 16).[80]

Although Gee is of the opinion that what is normal is the will of God,[81] he still maintains:

> We believe the Pentecostal Movement will absolutely fail in obedience to the heavenly vision that God placed before it, if it goes back to dependence upon purely natural gifts for the work of the ministry, never mind how deeply people may be consecrated, or how efficiently they may be educated in Bible schools or elsewhere ... The early church 'turned the world upside down' in a generation. But they did it through spiritual gifts and not through natural gifts.[82]

The view that the gifts of the Spirit are 'supernatural' gifts can also be heard in the traditional churches.[83] Similarly the 'Evangelical Association' in Berne defended the healer Vignes in Vialas with the argument: 'He has great faith, his faith is successful.'[84] These groups within the existing churches agree with the Pentecostal movement in seeing in the healing of sick through prayer 'a proof of divinity':

> The heathen have a more religious view of nature than many Christians at the present day ... But the whole of Christianity stands and falls with miracles ... Divine healing is on the one hand a proof of the divinity and the rule of Jesus Christ for the world, and at the same time is the manifest revelation of divine love.[85]

Sometimes these proofs miscarry. For example, in 1955 August Waltke was condemned to six months' imprisonment for manslaughter by criminal negligence, following the failure of an attempt to heal a sick person by prayer. He showed himself unconcerned at the sentence:

> When the Bible speaks, it speaks only to the children of God, the natural man cannot understand it. [I take it that I] have to spend six months in the prison hospital of Hohenasperg for the sake of the gospel. I am not the first and will not be the last who has had to suffer for the gospel.[86]

The person who died, a sixteen-year-old boy called Rolf Kober, had stated explicitly that he did not wish to be taken into hospital for the treatment of his diabetes. He said, 'If I am not cured in this way [i.e., by the driving out of the 'sugar demon' and Waltke's laying on of hands], I would rather die.' But in spite of Waltke's irresponsible use of prayer, it must be asked: What right have the public authorities and doctors to enforce the use of a particular kind of cure against the will of a patient and his mother? Such an assault on the rights of the individual seems possible to me only on the basis of the kind of Catholic theology which is 'based on an objectively recognized order of things'.[87]

The main question posed by Waltke is: Are there spheres of reality which are accessible only to the spiritual eye? A large number of ministers and theologians within the traditional churches are inclined to say that there are. In connection with the dispute about Sadhu Sundar Singh many ministers and laymen in European churches believed Sundar Singh's fantastic accounts, basing their view on I Cor. 2.13.

> For a Christian who possesses the gift of the discernment of spirits, because he has a living converse of prayer with God, there can simply be no doubt that Sundar Singh is genuine – 'we judge spiritual things spiritually.'[88]

Heiler, a professor of theology, and his followers take the view:

> Our method of historical criticism is a wholly inadequate instrument and our scepticism about all miracle stories, even those in the Bible, is based on the narrowness of our intellectual and religious horizons.[89]

But what does it mean to judge 'spiritually'? If 'spiritually' consists of giving preference to what is 'inward' over what is 'outward', to the 'spiritual' over the 'bodily', to the 'eternal' over the 'historical', to the 'spontaneous' over the considered', this 'spirituality' can certainly not claim to be based on the Bible. The attitude that can be called 'spiritual' is that which does not fear the critical investigation of 'miracles', which exposes its interpretation of the Bible, whether it be 'spiritual' or that of 'historical criticism', to the understanding and sight of one's fellow men and, when they offer a different interpretation, does not disqualify and rule them out as 'unspiritual' or 'uncritical', in order to ensure for one's own interpretation of the Bible a monopoly of 'spirituality' or 'integrity'.[90]

4. *Assessment*

Healing through prayer is sought by those who, through lack of time, money or confidence, cannot or will not be treated medically.[91] They are not to be blamed if in the final instance – this at least is how they see it – they turn to God. Purely as a phenomenon, healing through prayer can be seen to be an effective form of support, and in some cases a substitute, for medical healing. The healing powers of group-psychological and sociological factors – to which a Pentecostal has access in the form of prayer – are more important than people were prepared to concede a few years ago. But precisely because we are dealing with forces which cannot be ignored, their application should not be left solely to the intuition, still less to the craving for recognition and success of individual star evangelists. I am not clear how a useful dialogue between medical science and the Pentecostal practice of healing by prayer can be carried out. That it is necessary and of great importance to certain classes of people and countries seems to have been clear for some time.[92]

In a provocative sermon on Mark 5.1–43, Walter Vogt, a doctor himself, said:

> Medicine has developed an unsuspected skill in restoring health without healing . . . The encounter with mental illness can no longer take place in freedom. Society avoids confrontation with what cannot be healed, because it has itself become unhealthy.[93]

In a very valuable book Hans Schaefer[94] investigates the underlying principles and effects of present-day medicine. Because of its strict scientific method, together with an openness towards what is 'not yet explicable',[95] it provides a good basis for dialogue. Because the author argues strictly from observed phenomena, he avoids hasty definitions,[96] takes into account the economic and sociological factors of our 'health industry', and also poses the questions of ethical principle. Similar questions are being raised in the English-speaking world. The English doctor Michael Wilson, in a short but very instructive article, describes present-day medical practice as 'violence'. The patient, without being informed, is subject to a series of unpleasant, painful and often dehumanizing procedures.

> My hunger continues for one who will relate to me personally in terms of myself, and not technologically in terms of defects. The church has a non-violent task of friendship . . . not a power which erupts from outside, but an invitation for us to dance with one another the dance of life, crippled though we both may be.[97]

When we look for the *religious theme* in Pentecostal miracle stories, we find an attempt to provide a proof of God appropriate to an age of empirical investigation. It is easy to give a theological refutation of this proof of God, and to denounce it as heretical, heathen, or at least as Catholic. But in my view this is to blur the problem concealed within this admittedly inadequate proof of the existence of God. The problem should be formulated somewhat as follows. In the age when all authorities are declining, the authority of preaching grows weaker every day. When the Reformation churches reply that this is the scandal of the cross, which is a stumbling block to some and foolishness to others, they are forgetting that Paul, who said this, also spoke of the cross as a power of God, and that he came to Corinth 'in demonstration of the Spirit and power' (I Cor. 2.4).

The modern world asks such questions as: Is God alive? Is this God the Father of Jesus Christ? Is there any sense in praying to and trusting this God? Is the whole business of the church simply a vast and useless enterprise run at public cost, like an elaborate religious version of one of Tinguely's mobiles, or at best a 'necessary illusion'? The answer the Pentecostal gives to all these questions is that of the man who was born blind: 'Whether he is a sinner, I do not know; one thing I know, that though I was blind, now I see' (John 9.25). I conclude this chapter with a list of theses on the subject:

1. Miracles are ambiguous and not specifically Christian. There are many modern and ancient miracle stories. The Bible itself tells of miracles performed by enemies of God (Matt. 12.27; Ex. 7.11f.; Acts 8.9–11). From the period before, during and after the composition of the New Testament,[98] and from our own time, there is an extensive literature of miracle stories. These cannot be described as nothing but fiction or deception. From the phenomenological point of view they must be described as inexplicable events, though the question must remain open whether they can ever receive an explanation.

2. This does not mean that miracles and signs are excluded as forms of Christian witness. The biblical authors were not afraid to use even heathen words and conceptions such as Logos, Saviour, Lord and son of God in their works. In the New Testament period the emperor was known as 'Lord' and 'Saviour'. In direct competition with this 'Saviour' the Christians professed belief in their 'Saviour'. Philosophers and miracle workers were venerated as 'sons of God', stories were told that a god had visited their mothers in the absence of their husbands and seduced them. The 'Logos' was the slogan of numerous sects. They understood by it a kind of world reason, which pervaded the universe. If it was possible for the New Testament writers under certain conditions to use these heathen conceptions, so human abilities which up to now remain inexplicable, such as the healing of the sick by the laying on of hands, or foreknowledge through intuition, can be used to serve the Christian witness.

3. These signs are not qualified for this use simply by the fact that they are remarkable. But neither does this fact disqualify them, any more than does the possibility that in a short time it may be possible to 'explain' them. There are times and places in which the 'remarkable sign' is properly shown more attention than what is ordinary and unremarkable.

4. Paul does not distinguish between natural and supernatural gifts. He assesses them on the basis of the following criteria:

- they serve the common good [of the church] (I. Cor 12.7);
- they point to the fact that Jesus is Lord (I Cor. 12.1–3);
- they are not contrary to what has come about in the incarnate Word of God, in Jesus (I Cor. 12.3).

5. The list of gifts of the Spirit in the New Testament is arbitrary in so far as it is determined by the situation of those who received the epistles. Consequently, it is neither complete, nor obligatory in the legal sense. That is, there can be new gifts of the Spirit (which are not listed in the Bible). Other gifts can die out or become less prominent. What is decisive is not what kind of gift it is, but whether it fulfils the criteria given in para. 4 above.

6. This does not mean that speaking in tongues, healing through prayer, visions, etc., which rarely occur in our traditional and established churches, are without significance. Perhaps we underestimate their importance. Speaking in tongues has an important psycho-hygienic function. Anyone who rejects it must offer a substitute which has the same function and effect. The healing of the sick through prayer must not be seen as an alternative to the practice of medicine. Many people may learn that prayer is concerned with concrete matters from prayers in accordance with James 5, more than from numerous sermons. For people who have difficulty with abstract thought and live in the age of illustrated papers and television, visions are an important means of communication.

7. The New Testament signs must be qualified by being integrated into the process of preaching. This is true both of the 'remarkable' and the 'ordinary' signs, sacramental (*verbum visibile*) and profane. When Christians buried both Christian and heathen dead during the plague in Rome, at a time when the Roman doctors had fled, they had to give a reason for this remarkable behaviour. They said: We believe in the risen Christ who has taken away the power of death. This gave a purpose to the sign (the burial of the dead) and power to their profession of faith ('I believe in the risen Christ'). When they bought slaves in the market and set them free, they had to give a reason for what in Roman eyes was pathological behaviour: 'Christ has set us and all men free from slavery and made us his fellow workers.'

8. It follows that signs (both 'remarkable' and 'ordinary') need the word which accompanies them. But this does not mean that it must be possible to draw a logical deduction from the sign to the existence of God. When at the present day something is observed to happen which conflicts with the sociological, psychological or physical norms of behaviour which are familiar to us, a practised observer will not proceed straight to the 'hypothesis of God'. Rather, he will formulate the description of the norms of behaviour in such a way as to take in the exception that has been observed (e.g. the sacrificial courage of a missionary, the raising of a person from the dead).

With regard to the Pentecostal movement it must be affirmed:

(*a*) To define a miracle as a breaking of the laws of nature is inadmissible both theologically and scientifically. It is theologically inadmissible, because the Bible does not speak in terms of a sphere of nature, governed by natural laws, and a sphere of the Spirit, governed by supernatural laws which take preference over natural laws. It is scientifically inadmissible because the so-called laws of nature are statistics based on experience. Consequently if new experience is discovered, they must be changed. Thus they cannot be used to mark a boundary between God and the world.[99]

(*b*) We must look beyond the gifts of the Spirit which are manifested in the Pentecostal movement to find modern gifts of the Spirit: the gifts of service to society and science. That is, we need gifts that will help us to understand better our sick world of politics, economics and science and to contribute to the task of healing it.

NOTES

1. *PE* 1466, 13.6.1942, pp. 1, 10f.
2. A. Murray, *Divine Healing*, p. 16; cf. also above, ch. 9.1(*c*), pp. 115f.
3. *Divine Healing*, p. 71.
4. Pastor Wyss, *Feierabend* (a free supplement containing matter of religious interest and edification, given with the *Emmenthaler Nachrichten*) 22/31, 5.8.1911, p. 248.
5. *Pfingstgrüsse* 4/19, 4.2.1912, p. 151.
6. *Blätter der Heilung*, 15.12.1899, p. 15.
7. Cf. *PGG*, pp. 257ff.
8. Cf. above, ch. 9.2, pp. 116ff.
9. Details: 05.13.024.
10. G. Lindsay, *W. Branham*, p. 77.
11. *Ibid.*, p. 93.
12. *MD*, 29, 1966, pp. 141ff.; 30, 1967, pp. 81ff., 105ff., 118ff., 140f., 185.
13. *MD* 29, 1966, p. 46.
14. Verbal communication from David J. Du Plessis.
15. W. Branham, *Seven Church Ages*, quoted by Hutten, *Seher*, 11th edition 1968, p. 758.
16. E. Frank, *Das Wort Gottes bleibt in Ewigkeit*, Nr. 7.
17. P. Frehner, *Tagesanzeiger*, Zürich, 2.7.1955.
18. K. Koch, *Deutsches Pfarrerblatt* 56/13, p. 293.
19. L. Steiner, *VdV* 48/7, July 1955, pp. 8f. Cf. also D. Gee, *P* 36, 1956, p. 17.
20. Details, 02a.02.D.VII.
21. Cf. pp. 362ff.
22. Cf. above ch. 1.1(*b*), pp.
23. Documents: 02a.02.D.VI; 02a.02.159.
24. O. Roberts, *God is a Good God*, p. 180.
25. G. Lindsay, *God's Master-Key to Success and Prosperity*.
26. Cf. the study by R. P. Shuler, *McPhersonism*; quoted by A. J. Pollock, *Modern Pentecostalism*, p. 49.

27. Examples: AdD in France (05.09.003a, ee), Stromen van Kracht, Holland (05.20.010), Kracht van Omhoog, Holland (05.20.009) and others.

28. C. Brumback, *Suddenly*, p. 334.

29. 'We have erred by refusing any place in our doctrine [on divine healing], or at least a very insufficient place, for the sovereign will of God. To ask for Divine healing without the accompanying "nevertheless not my will but Thine be done" seems to pose an attitude out of keeping with every other right attitude we take in prayer.' D. Gee, *Trophimus*, p. 27.

30. L. Steiner, in D. Gee (ed.), *Fifth Conference*, pp. 139ff.

31. L. Steiner, Letter to W.H., 14.4.1960.

32. Cf. above, ch. 5.5, p. 67 and p. 73 n. 39.

33. C. Le Cossec, *La guérison*, (Vérité à connaître 4), p. 24.

34. Her testimony is given in *Leaves of Healing* 4, 1897.

35. L. B. Yeomans, *Healing*, pp. 22f.

36. F. F. Bosworth, '*Deshalb*', p. 13.

37. R. Vinyard, in D. Gee (ed.), *Fifth Conference*, pp. 67ff.

38. P. Mink, *Ich bin der Herr*, pp. 17f.

39. ChoG (Cleveland), *Second Book of Minutes*, 1907, p. 25; quoted by C. Conn, *Army*, p. 76.

40. E. Chávez, letter to W.H., 23.1.1963.

41. AdD Italy, *Risveglio P.* 8/11, Nov. 1953, p. 2 (cf. Appendix: 9).

42. Kristova Pentekostna Crkva, *Temeljne* (cf. Appendix: 2).

43. E. Conde, *Testemunho*, 3rd ed., pp. 183ff. (cf. Appendix: 2).

44. Congregação Cristã do Brasil, *Estatutos* 1946, Art. 7.

45. *PE* 1466, 13.6.1942, pp. 1, 10f.

46. P. Mink, *Ich bin der Herr*, p. 17.

47. E. Buchmann, *Die ganze Fülle* 2/10, Oct. 1962, p. 5.

48. J. Paul, *Pfingstgrüsse* 3, 1911, p. 299.

49. Details: 05.07.008a, aa2; 01.36.013b.

50. L. Johnson Grubb, *Living to Tell of Death.*

51. Documents: 05.28.025c.

52. K. Heggelund, *Våre Sykdommer*, p. 13.

53. 'West African Workshop: The Church in Action in Urban and Industrial West Africa', All Africa Conference of Churches, Lagos, 25 Aug.–2 Sept. 1965. T. R. A. Otolorin, *The Ministry of Healing in the Community and the Work of Aro in the Field of Mental Health* (dupl. speech).

54. C. G. Baëta, *Prophetism*, pp. 94ff.; 01.12007.

55. Detailed discussion on the problem can be found under Ghana 01.12 (esp. 01.12.005; 01.12.007; 01.12.008; 01.12.009; 01.12.014; 01.12.018; 01.12.020); Nigeria 01.28 (esp. 01.28.001; 01.28.008; 01.28.017; 01.28.018; 01.28.022; 01.28.024; 01.28.068); Republic of South Africa (esp. 01.36.019b; 01.36.B). Cf. above, ch. 12.4(*e*), pp. 159ff.

56. M. Heryan, *Red Concept* XII, Sept. 1966 (WCC, Geneva), pp. 25ff.

57. J. Mendelsohn, *The Forest Calls Back.*

58. F. Donaldson, *The Sister Buck Memorial Hospital Project.*

59. *MD* 19, 1956, p. 217.

60. *Mehr Licht* 12/3; *Fröhliche Nachrichten*, 1.3.1956; documents, 05.07.030.

61. *MD* 19, 1956, p. 227.

62. *Für Arbeit und Besinnung*, Württembergische Beilage 1.7.1954; *MD* 19, 1956, p. 231.

63. For his divorce, the bankruptcy of his business, etc., cf. 08.663.001.

64. *MD* 19, 1956, p. 217. For the legends that grew up at his death, 08.663.001.

65. Documents: 02a.02.177.

66. J. E. Campbell, *PHCh*, pp. 557f.
67. E.g. with W. S. Reed, a doctor.
68. W. P. Sterne, *Abundant Life* 16/10, Oct. 1962, pp. 8f.; *FGBM's Voice*, 10/9, Sept. 1962, pp. 2ff.
69. H. B. Jacobs, *Harper's Magazine*, Feb. 1962; *Life*, Aug. 1962.
70. O. Roberts, *Daily Blessing* 5/1, Jan./Feb. 1963, p. 10.
71. Documents: 08.192.001.
72. A. A. Allen, *Miracle Revival Service*, M-110.
73. D. Gee, *P* 36, 1956, p. 17; L. Steiner, *VdV* 48/7, July 1955, pp. 8f.
74. *A Seara* 2/6, Nov.-Dec. 1957, p. 50; L. Eisenlöffel, *Ein Feuer*, p. 85.
75. C. Röckle, *Weckruf* 2/10.
76. N. I. Pejsti (ed.), *Zasady*, ch. 9; cf. above ch. 202, p. 273.
77. A. van Polen, *Pinksterboodschap* 4/1, Jan. 1963, p. 3.
78. G. Jeffreys in D. Gee, *Phenomena*, p. 50.
79. C. Parizet, *Vie et Lumière*, May–June 1961, pp. 3, 26f.
80. J. de Wilde, sermon in Zürich, 27.11.1961 (noted by W.H.).
81. D. Gee, *VdV* 56/6, June 1963, pp. 14f.
82. D. Gee, *Ministry*, pp. 14ff.
83. D. O. Schmitz, *Bedeutung*, p. 2.
84. *Brosamen* 44, 3.11.1895.
85. P. Pirscher, *Brosamen* 46, 17.11.1895.
86. K. Hutten, *MD* 19, 1956, pp. 196f.
87. 'When certain sects reject medicine, and forbid injections and blood transfusions, it is the duty of the civil authorities to intervene to save human life. No one will regard this as an attack on religious freedom. But in order that these interventions should never be arbitrary, they must be regulated by just laws which apply equally to everyone and are based on an objectively recognized order of things.' Fr. Jérome Hamer, adviser to the Secretariat for Christian Unity at the Vatican Council, in *Oek. Pressedienst* 33/2, 20.1.1966, p. 5 (omitted from the English version).
88. F. Heiler, *Wahrheit*, p. vi.
89. F. Heiler, *ibid.*, p. xi; similarly H. Lilje, *Die Furche* 20, 1934, p. 465.
90. Full details in 03.07.014a.
91. Roche Report, *Frontiers of Clinical Psychiatry* 7/4, 15.2.1970, pp. 5f.
92. Cf. above, pp. 360f.
93. W. Vogt, *Reformatio* 19/2, Feb. 1970, pp. 76ff.; cf. also the critical reply to Vogt in the same number by Christian Müller, Christian Maurer, Walter Nussbaum and Dorothee Hoch.
94. H. Schaefer, *Die Medizin*, 2nd ed., 1963.
95. Cf. for example his chapter on 'quacks' (*op. cit.*, pp. 267ff., etc.).
96. Schaefer begins his book with the words: 'Medicine is concerned with ill people. But it will be shown that one cannot define what "illness" is, and when a person is "really" ill. Of course in numerous extreme cases illness is a phenomenon that science can define and influence, but this is not so in the majority of cases. A reality, which we can call illness, does not exist.'
97. M. Wilson, *Christian Century* 87/24, 17.6.1970, pp. 756ff.
98. A characteristic of these miracle stories is that, the further away they get from the event they describe, the more marvellous and detailed they become. For example, in the Gospel of Nicodemus (ch. 7), the woman with the issue of blood is given the name Veronica, while in Macarius Magnes I.6 she becomes a princess of Edessa. Luke gives the ruler of the synagogue the name Jairus (Luke 8.41), which does not occur in Matt. 9.18–26. In the Gospel of the Nazaraeans the man with the crippled hand becomes a mason, who begs for Jesus's help in the following words: 'I was a mason

and earned my living by my hands; I pray you, Jesus, restore my health, so that I do not have to beg shamefully for food.' Luke specifies that it was the right hand. Similarly as Sadhu Sundar Singh and the Pentecostal healing evangelists retell their stories, they elaborate them.

99. The Reformed pastor D. G. Molenaar, who is very close to the Pentecostals, tried to break down the distinction between 'natural' and 'supernatural'. (D. G. Molenaar, *De doop*; cf. below, ch. 30.2, pp. 433f.).

26

Against Principalities and Powers: Demonology

THAT our battle is not against 'flesh and blood' but against 'principalities and powers',[1] Pentecostals can testify from their own experience. Here they are in agreement with the Conservative Evangelicals. There are demons of sickness, of lies, of fornication, Hitler demons and divorce demons.[2] Pentecostals say:

> We believe in the personality of the Devil, who by his influence and power brought about the downfall of man and now seeks to destroy the faith of every believer in the Lord Jesus Christ.[3]
>
> We believe in the personal existence of the Devil and his angels, the evil spirits.[4]
>
> Satan is the chief of the fallen world of angels, the father of lies, the deceiver of men and the prince of this world.[5]
>
> We believe in the existence of the demons, who provoke evil amongst men.[6]
>
> What is offered nowadays as theology is often nothing but Satanology.[7]
>
> Critical exegetes are 'servants of the Devil' and 'disciples of Satan'.[8]
>
> There are people possessed! Many are possessed. Here in the midst of what is called Christianity.[9]

The Indian Pentecostal Lam Jeevaratnam has published a demonology in which he describes the signs of demon possession; peculiar appearance, irritation, bad temper, pains all over the body, bad dreams, irregular periods in women, miscarriages.[10] The healing evangelists are specialists at driving out demons, particularly A. A. Allen, who has published a small illustrated book with pictures of demons.[11] He has put on sale a record which includes the expulsion of the chief devil Lucifer from a woman.[12] In the *Glaubenhaus* in Warngau

> we experienced more than once the demons crying out so loud and uninterruptedly that the police came. In one case the devil grinned and said: 'Now

I have set the police on you.' When we replied, 'That's right, now the public will learn that devils are driven out here,' he cried: 'What an idiot I am!' and the possessed woman beat her brow with her long pointed fingers.[13]

Full grown men were thrown by the devil through the air into the middle of the room where prayers were being held. A man was pulled through an oven door up to the shoulder. A boy possessed by a 'pig devil' can still only grunt. Beer by the litre came out of a peasant woman whose father and grandfather had been drunkards. For days from a woman in prayer there came down serpents of saliva, sometimes with blood. When hands were laid on one man there was the sound of the violent barking of dogs, and from another the sounds of the hooves of a whole troop of horses. The devils 'cry out, they roar, they bellow, they spit, they snarl, hiss and give cries of terror, and finally they stink so strongly of sulphur when they come out that the meeting room has to be aired.'[14]

Johannes Widmer, one of the founders of the Apostolic Church in Switzerland (Gemeinde für Urchristentum) entitled his principal work, in three volumes, 'In the Battle Against the Kingdom of Satan'.[15] Widmer fights without intermission against the devil and his accomplices, who try to do harm to the children of God, their domestic animals, and even their cheeses – a serious matter for a Berne cheesemaker.[16] In the Apostolic Church they tell how

> in our bedroom the spirits were piled up so high that there wasn't a cubic centimetre of empty space left anywhere . . . The only way I could get through was to take hold of the New Testament and beat back the hellish disturbers of the peace in front of me step by step.[17]

'The devil does not even disdain to go into dogs and cocks!'[18] Of course the gospels record the same kind of thing (Mark 5.13).

According to Johannes Widmer there is often a connection between sickness and possession:

> And how the devil is pleased when he stays undiscovered for a long time in his hiding place and can go with the sick person to visit a beautiful health resort and take the waters! He laughs at all the chemicals that are swallowed and all the solutions that are injected.[19]

The Latter Rain Assemblies report the existence of 'calling voices'. This term refers to demonic powers who continually call up other powers, because the first powers are already bound. They pray:

> Father, I pray, send a mighty angel with a two-edged sword to hack away all the undermining threads of thought[20] and nets, so that my prayer can rise up to Thy throne of grace.[21]

Lester Sumrall, an evangelist of the Assemblies of God, tells of a girl who was bitten by a devil.[22] E. Kopf expresses surprise that

> those amongst our present official theologians who are supposed to believe

most in the Bible admit that Jesus believed in a pure world of spirits, but say that this does not stop us from abandoning this belief altogether.[23]

This question is of decisive importance for the African[24] and Latin American[25] churches. Anyone who approaches 'this superstition' with the superiority of the European will get nowhere. For many Africans and Latin Americans the demons are realities. In discussion with them the biblical writers provide a useful starting point, for they do not teach us to 'believe in the personal existence of the devil', but in the *overpowering* of Satan and his accomplices. Paul does not believe in the demons, he believes that Christ has conquered them.

Neither Pentecostals nor Protestant Christians, then, are able to believe strongly enough that demons have been so far overcome that they have to leave the battlefield. In spite of the battles against demons described above, and in spite of the detailed and reasonable account of spiritualist phenomena given by Raphael Gasson, a former spiritualist,[26] the phenomenon of possession is an unsolved problem in Pentecostal belief and practice. The Working Association of Christian Congregations in Germany (Arbeitsgemeinschaft der Christengemeinden in Deutschland) makes two paradoxical statements:

> Even the regenerate can remain under a curse or come under one through sin . . .
>
> The regenerate are made wholly free by redemption and need no further redemption.[27]

The conference of Pentecostal pastors which discussed these theses made no attempt to reconcile the contradiction, but dismissed the pastoral difficulties with the statement that 'many of our members are not yet regenerate'.[28]

But this picture is rejected by Charles W. Conn of the Church of God (Cleveland). He maintains 'on the authority of God's holy Word that a demon cannot possess a Christian spirit, soul or body', because this suggests that Christ 'will share a Christian with the devil'.[29]

A demonology similar to that of the Working Fellowship of Christian Churches in Germany has been developed by the 'Russian Orthodox Church Outside Russia'. Both the Orthodox and the German Pentecostals are in agreement that the immortal soul is made sick by sin.

If at the moment it takes its leave of the body

> the soul is not saved or on the way to salvation . . . it remains for ever in the condition of 'the death of the soul', an expression which must be understood metaphorically and which signifies eternal torment.[30]

Sin sets up a 'diabolical circle' around the soul, which in certain cases is manifested in hopeless depression. The thoughts of dejection

> are insinuated by the demons into the soul which is being converted; in this way they try to work against the conversion. The only proper attitude here is that of the Prodigal Son (Luke 15). The absolution of the priest, who acts here

> as Christ's representative (Matt. 16.9 and 18.18), if repentance and resolution to amend are honestly present, brings about something that can be compared to the erasing of a magnetic tape.[31]

Further means which are suggested for the healing of a soul made sick by sin and demons are the 'breathing' of the soul, that is, prayer; participation in the eucharist; attendance at services; and active love.

> If everything is brought into order, then all the fearful cares and states of anxiety, all complexes, inhibitions, neuroses, depressions and such like suddenly disappear. They vanish like smoke in the wind. A person is once again *free*, but this time *truly* free; once again he finds joy in his work, in life, in nature, and in every little thing. In a word, he once again has courage and takes pleasure in life. He does not give in.[32]

Although Pentecostal pastors are clever enough to recognize the limits of their ministry and to tolerate with resignation, when there is no other alternative, the work of the psychiatrist,[33] to have recourse to a psychiatrist implies the admission of a spiritual failure on the part of the pastor and the believer, and this is done only with great reluctance. For example Wim Malgo advised a mother who asked him whether in a difficult matter of upbringing she should call in a psychiatrist:

> Pray a great deal with the children and for the children. If you do this consistently, looking earnestly to the Lord, you will have splendid children.[34]

Wim Malgo would have learned better from King David by taking to heart the history of David's family in the Old Testament. Nevertheless, Malgo sticks to his advice:

> Your boy does not need a psychologist. He needs a mother who will pray more for him, and more seriously . . . The psychologist can undoubtedly give transitory relief to the soul by certain psychological methods, but he does not go to the root of the trouble, that is, unforgiven sin, a hard, disobedient heart.[35]

It is not surprising that Donald Gee has gone his own way here. In *Study Hour*, a journal for Pentecostal pastors, he published an article which tried to obtain understanding for the treatment of the mentally ill. He argued for an appropriate psychiatric treatment for the depressed within the Pentecostal movement, and commented sympathetically on the work of Werner Gruehn, Freud and Jung.[36]

It is not possible for me to give a conclusive judgment on this subject, even though I am certain that most phenomena of possession can be explained within the framework of modern psychiatric knowledge, even if they cannot be healed. But I agree with Albert Moll in believing that there is possibly an 'inexplicable remnant'.[37] This 'inexplicable remnant' points to the fact that our methods of apprehending and describing reality are relatively accurate only in certain spheres, for which the method used is particularly appropriate. Thus the 'inexplicable remnant' does not point to the existence of demons, but to the inaccuracy (perhaps only temporary) of our explanation of reality. But it prevents us from making statements in this field which go beyond our competence, that is, statements which it is impossible for us to test. Anyone who uses the devil as a stop-gap to explain the 'inexplicable' makes him a meaningless figure.

For a reader familiar with the literature of the driving out of demons, the most impressive account is that by Blumhardt concerning his struggle to set free the possessed girl Gottliebin Dittus.[38] This girl, into whom, according to Blumhardt, the devil had magically introduced nails, frogs and other substances, was finally set free before witnesses by months of prayer on the part of Blumhardt. I am not able to conclude whether there were parapsychological phenomena at work, or whether it was a phenomenon of psychiatric practice which can be interpreted in terms of modern knowledge. But I quote Benedetti's useful interpretation of this driving out of a demon 'in the light of modern psychotherapeutic knowledge':

> A modern psychiatrist who, in treating a psychosis, allowed so much of its content to infect him as well, as Blumhardt did, would be bound to cause us serious concern for his mental health. For the 'reality' in which we live today has much less room for the possibility of such experiences than did the world view that existed a hundred years ago. Nowadays, the occurrence of such experiences implies a far greater departure from the outlook and mode of experience of the healthy social environment in which they are situated. At that time, the world was much more open to many of the experiences of psychotic people than is our modern world, formed by science. And I wonder whether this may not be the reason why patterns of symptoms like that of Gottliebin Dittus hardly ever occur at the present day. In our age sufferings of this kind have become a rarity.[39] Extreme mental distress is expressed in different forms today from those that expressed it in the past. We observe it more in the autistic loneliness of schizophrenia or depression than in the colourful images of a spreading and contagious hysteria, occasional occurrences of which were still being studied at the beginning of this century by the early psychoanalysts. Consequently I think that to diagnose hysteria in the modern sense in the case of Gottliebin Dittus would be to fail to give a full account of the nature of her affliction. Hysteria at the present day is something different from what Blumhardt describes.[40]

In bringing the demons 'face to face' with him, Blumhardt became in part subject to them. This is the meaning which we can perceive in the 'mythological' narrative that exists. Hallucinatory experience which he shared with his patient show us how far he himself was affected by the stimulus of the psychotic situation. But the effect was not like that upon people who completely shut themselves off from the affliction of the mentally ill person, and yet fall victim to it themselves as a defence against it. The cruelty of the persecution of witches was an expression of the fact that the persecutors had succumbed in this way. By entering into the situation of the psychosis, Blumhardt finally overcame it.[41]

A theologian, Joachim Scharfenberg,[42] has also studied the case of Gottliebin Dittus in detail. He follows Benedetti in regarding Blumhardt's relationship with the sick girl as a realization of, and pointer towards, 'the classical pattern of psychotherapeutic dialogue'.[43] According to Scharfenberg, the healing took place because Blumhardt abandoned the attitude of pastoral care as instruction and consolation, and entered into an open dialogue with the girl, 'setting the faculties of experience free to receive a new experience. But it is the area of consciousness which is enlarged in this way which is able to exercise a healing effect, both on the mental situations and on the social conflict situations in which the younger Blumhardt was trying to carry forward the line of development begun by his father.'[44] It is therefore not surprising that in the revival movement sparked off by Blumhardt the sermon was replaced by an activity in which 'as far as possible all members were involved in the dialogue'.[45] In these meetings – nowadays they would be called charismatic gatherings –

> the fateful division between the profane and the sacred is really broken down, here . . ., a style of life is realized in which dialogue can develop, in which all who take part both give and receive. Here Blumhardt also learned to abandon and leave behind his earlier 'sharp' style of preaching,[46] and there was even a visible replacement of pastoral concern for the individual by this group dialogue as a form of life. The effect of these impulses and promptings will spread far and wide, without setting up a situation of sectarian dependency upon them. Here people find liberation and – as Blumhardt set out as his aim – consciousness and 'knowledge of themselves'.[47]

W. Schulte, a doctor, had already given a similar reply, in a fine article written twenty years ago, to the question: 'What can a doctor say to Johann Christoph Blumhardt about illness and possession?'[48] Schulte states 'It is not possible to give a diagnosis which distinguishes between sickness and possession . . . They represent two possible aspects of the same event.'[49] From this Schulte concludes:

> No discerning doctor will deny that the healing of a disease can only come about with the help of God. But this should not mean abandoning all medical activity in the sphere of psychological and mental illness and looking for help from a miracle of prayer.[50]

As so often in our discussion we have come to a point where the historic churches and the Pentecostal movement are faced with the same questions. How can we get away from a form of pastoral care which provides only instruction, and find our way to open dialogue, even if demons appear in it? Perhaps there are even people at the present day who can best be helped by entering into the 'situation of the psychosis', in Benedetti's words. And perhaps a Pentecostal pastor, who because of his understanding of the Bible is more open to this 'situation of psychosis', may be able to give more help than a psychiatrist.

And is it not possible on the basis of Schulte's interpretation – that possession and illness are two possible aspects of the same event – that a dialogue with Pentecostalism might be both necessary and meaningful?

NOTES

1. Eph. 6.12.
2. A. A. Allen, *Divorce*.
3. AoG, Australia, *Doctrinal Basis*.
4. Congregação Cristã do Brasil, *Estatutos*, 1946, art. 37, para. 6.
5. R. Willenegger, *Ich komme bald!* 9, 1951, pp. 118ff.
6. Iglesia Pentecostal de Chile, *Manual*, n.d., p. 6.
7. W. Malgo, *Mitternachtsruf* 7/1, April 1962, pp. 9ff.
8. J. Vetter, *Die Bibel, das Schwert des Geistes*, quoted in Fleisch I, p. 443.
9. Christiansen, *Auf der Warte* 3/33, 12.8.1906, p. 3.
10. L. Jeevaratnam, *Concerning Demons*, 3rd ed., 1948, pp. 4f.
11. A. A. Allen, *The Curse of Madness*.
12. A. A. Allen, Miracle Revival Recordings, no. 111: 'I am Lucifer.' 'Actual recording of demon possessed women, the demon declaring "I am Lucifer". Greatest lesson in demonology ever heard! Convincing. Spiritual. Biblical.' Psychological commentary on it in T. Spörri (ed.), *Ekstase*, pp. 139ff.
13. *MD* 22, 1959, p. 69.
14. K. Hutten, *Seher*, 11th ed., 1968, p. 538.
15. Joh. Widmer, *Im Kampf gegen Satans Reich*.
16. Joh. Widmer, *Im Kampf* III, 2nd ed., 1952, pp. 142f.
17. O. Ellenberger, in Widmer, *Im Kampf* II, 2nd ed., 1949, pp. 99f.
18. Widmer, *ibid.* I, 3rd ed., 1948, p. 57.
19. *Ibid.*, pp. 54f. Cf. *PGG*, ch, 19.21(*b*), pp. 282ff.
20. A network of undermining threads of thoughts is woven above the saints by evilly inclined persons, so that ultimately a complete network is made above them and their prayers can hardly reach the throne of grace.
21. L. Eisenlöffel, *Die Spätregenbewegung*, pp. 25f.
22. L. Sumrall, *The True Story of Clarita Villanueva*.
23. E. Köpf, *Nicht Worte*, p. 5.
24. Cf. above ch. 12.4(*c*), p. 157.
25. Cf. above ch. 8.2, p. 97.
26. R. Gasson, *The Challenging Counterfeit*, cf. ch. 15.3, pp. 215f.
27. *Der Leuchter* 14/4, April 1963, pp. 5ff.
28. *Ibid.*
29. C. W. Conn, *ChoGE* 51/27, 11.9.1961, pp. 3f.
30. O.S., *Orthodoxe Stimmen*, 12/47, 2nd and 3rd quarters, 1965, p. 8.
31. *Ibid.*, p. 10.
32. *Ibid.*, p. 11.
33. But exceptions are common: e.g. J. La Valley, *PE* 2450, 23.4.1961, p. 15.
34. W. Malgo, *Mitternachtsruf* 6/7, Oct. 1961, p. 15.
35. W. Malgo, *Mitternachtsruf* 8/2, May 1963, p. 20
36. *Study Hour* 9, 1950, pp. 7ff., 33ff.
37. A. Moll, *Zeitschrift für Religionspsychologie* 1, 1907, pp. 353f.
38. Blumhardt, *Kampf*, 8th ed., n.d.; cf. also E. Gordon, *PE* 1539, 6.11.1943, pp. 6f.

39. Here Benedetti seems to be wrong. For psychological and sociological reasons such afflictions are hardly ever observed by psychiatrists. The 'possessed' do not go to psychiatrists, but to Pentecostal pastors.

40. G. Benedetti, *Reformatio* 9, 1940, pp. 474ff., 531ff.; quotation, p. 533, n. 1.

41. G. Benedetti, *op. cit.*, p. 487.

42. J. Scharfenberg, *Theologia Practica* 4/2, April 1969, pp. 140ff. (with bibliography).

43. J. Scharfenberg, *op. cit.*, p. 150.

44. *Op. cit.*, pp. 154ff.

45. *Seelsorgerliche Mitteilungen*, Bad Boll, 1884, op. 47.

46. J. C. Blumhardt, *Ausgewählte Schriften*, vol. III, p. 260.

47. J. Scharfenberg, *op. cit.*, pp. 153f.

48. W. Schulte, *Ev. Theologie* 9, 1949–50, pp. 151ff.

49. *Op. cit.*, p. 163.

50. *Ibid.*, pp. 166f.

27

'To them that Obey Him': The Sacraments

1. *'The Old Rugged Cross': The Lord's Supper – Belief and Practice*

THERE is no fully developed eucharistic doctrine in the Pentecostal movement. When statements are made about the Lord's Supper, it is interpreted on Zwinglian lines as a memorial of Jesus's death.[1] But there is a clear and well-developed pattern of eucharistic *devotion and practice*. One would not expect it of a free church which lays emphasis on the Spirit, but the service of the Lord's Supper is the central point of Pentecostal worship. It is as it were the holy of holies, where those who have been 'bought by the blood', and who have 'washed their garments clean in the blood of the Lamb', come together and celebrate the Lord's Supper 'as a sign of the cruel death of our Lord Jesus Christ, our Saviour and Master',[2] so in the commemoration of his suffering and death, 'sharing the divine nature of our Lord Jesus Christ',[3] by 'eating and drinking, to speak symbolically' his body and blood.[4] In these services they sing with their eyes closed, from memory, many of the mystical prayers with which the Pentecostal liturgy is so rich:

> On a hill far away stood an old rugged cross,
> The emblem of suffering and shame;
> And I love that old cross where the dearest and best
> For a world of lost sinners was slain.
>
> So I'll cherish the old rugged cross
> Till my trophies at last I lay down;
> I will cling to the old rugged cross
> And exchange it some day for a crown.[5]

The Lord's Supper is

> a solemn service . . . we consider the suffering and the great love which he showed for us on the cross, and by faith, in that moment, feeling ourselves in

intimate communion with Him, it means for us that we have seen Him in agony and dying, the Just One, pouring out his precious blood on the cross, suffering for the unjust and sinners.[6]

When we receive the bread and the wine, we can have sweet communion with the living Christ.[7]

The Italian Assemblee di Dio express their belief in Catholic terminology, although their eucharistic worship is no different from that of other Pentecostal groups: 'We believe that the Lord's Supper symbolizes the sacrifice of the Son of God. . . .'[8] Pentecostals expect from this communion with the Son of God the strengthening of their inner being, strength in everyday temptations, and the healing of sickness:

For ev'ry contrite, wounded soul,
Calv'ry's stream is flowing,
Step in just now, and be made whole,
Calv'ry's stream is flowing.[9]

By taking part in the Lord's Supper

the believer expresses his love for Christ, his faith and hope in Him, and pledges to Him perpetual fidelity.[10]

How matchless the grace, when I look'd in the face
Of this Jesus, my crucified Lord;
My redemption complete I then found at His feet,
And Calvary covers it all.[11]

Although the basic pattern is the same everywhere, there are great differences within it. Children under twelve years of age are generally not allowed to take part in the Lord's Supper (even when they have been baptized with water and in the Spirit, which is an inconsistency in Pentecostal teaching), 'because they have not the necessary understanding to discern the body of the Lord.'[12] Some churches use wafers but most use ordinary bread. The Congregação Cristã requires that the Lord's Supper

should be celebrated with a single loaf . . ., which is broken by hand at the moment when it is to be distributed, and with a single cup; in this way the word of God is honoured.[13]

In Anglo-Saxon countries it is celebrated once a week, in many European churches once a month, and in a few churches once a year.[14] Pentecostal churches of the Anglo-Saxon tradition (though not the European churches) use non-alcoholic grape juice, fruit juice or water, and this in its turn has provoked the protest of the Pentecostal Assemblies of the World, who regard these as 'modern substitutes that have been invented by the formal church today'.[15] The few Quaker Pentecostals reject the literal eucharist altogether:

We hold then, that partaking of natural or literal elements is not essential to

> our salvation, and therefore refrain from partaking thereof; but with due Christian courtesy we respect those who may hold an opposite view.[16]

A service of the Lord's Supper, in the course of which there is room for the gifts of the Spirit in a Pentecostal assembly, faces the older Pentecostal denominations with liturgical problems which are not easy to solve. Donald Gee points out that liturgical forms controlled by the pastor do not satisfy those Pentecostals who long for the 'pure working of the Spirit':

> Sometimes we hear it suggested that the Breaking of Bread service must be left quite 'open': that in it there ought to be no set preaching by the pastor; that there must be no intercession, but only what is called 'worship', etc. The result of all this mere traditionalism is to produce meetings so stereotyped that, for all their boasted freedom, they become more barren than the very liturgical services they deprecate – and with less aesthetic appeal . . . In Assemblies where this part of the service is regularly deadened by the same one or two unanointed persons praying every time, it should be urged that the remedy is not in their forcible suppression, but in quicker response by all the others.[17]

Pentecostal eucharistic devotion is a combination of the 'love of Jesus', that is love for the faithful friend who is called Jesus, 'blood and wounds mysticism', an absorption in the suffering and death of Jesus, and a looking forward to the coming marriage feast with Jesus, in the experience of the sacrament. The latter aspect is clearly expressed in the record 'The Lord's Supper'.[18] The close and intense concentration of words and associations such as 'mother', 'Come home!', the mother's death-bed, 'evening shadows', sunset, and 'the gates of glory' bring powerful subconscious emotions into play. Some people feel that there is a significant human experience, while others reject it as sentimental and false. Some weep, others are physically sick. It would be useful if a psychologist could study and interpret reactions to this record. The bodily reactions (tears, vomiting) on the part of supporters and critics respectively may well have a common cause.

Most ministers of traditional churches find the record unbearably sentimental rubbish; but many of their church members, after the record has been played to a church audience, write down the number and the publisher of the record, in spite of their minister's criticism, so that they can order the 'beautiful record'. This shows once again that the criticism made by the Reformation churches carries weight only when they are able to present as an alternative to the devotion and practice of the Pentecostal movement a eucharistic service which, while it possesses evangelical sobriety, provides a real experience (and not merely a spectacle which can be observed). In recent years there have been movements in this direction in Catholicism. The Catholic liturgist Theodor Klauser, in his significant *Short History of the Western Liturgy* has given a description of the worship of the early church, on the basis of the oldest extant liturgical book of the city of Rome (the *Apostolic Tradition* of Hippolytus). At the beginning of the service the faithful bring their gifts to the altar; oil, olives, cheese, bread, wine, fruit, flowers. Over these gifts the bishop prays the prayer of thanksgiving (*eucharistia*). He recalls the death and the resurrection of the Lord (*anamnesis*) and calls the Holy Spirit down upon the gifts (*epiclesis*). Then he distributes the bread and wine amongst the people. The greater part which remains is used for the maintenance of the bishop and for the charitable works of the early church. 'The clergy, like the poor, lived so to speak from the altar. The eucharistic sacrifice was at the same time the very source of the charitable activity of Christians.'[19]

This simple form later became mutilated. Under the influences of Roman emperor worship the oriental ceremonial of the Roman court was adopted. 'Since the Bishop of Rome had acquired almost the same degree of dignity as the Emperor, like the Emperor he could claim the right to have his portrait hung in public buildings (i.e. in churches) and to be greeted on his arrival at church by a choir of singers.'[20] Here begins the history of the 'introit', the chant sung while the priest enters the place of worship.[21] A further borrowing from Roman court ceremonial was the representation of Jesus as emperor and Mary as the queen mother. 'The apostles were turned into a senate, the angels now constituted the household of a heavenly court, and the saints were represented as guests seeking audience and bringing their gifts.' People began to speak of a heavenly court (*curia*) and palace (*palatium*).[22] At the same time the congregation became increasingly immature, dependent and passive. It was excluded from the liturgical action. A priest could even celebrate mass on his own. In congregational services, the priest celebrated in a strange language with his back to the people. The altar was so arranged that the people could not see what was happening. The most important words were whispered. It would have been irreverent to say them aloud. As wafers of unleavened bread began to be used, the offertory procession also disappeared. It is not surprising that the laity, who were still present, but no longer took part, came to ignore the eucharistic action and occupied themselves during services with 'non-liturgical subjective, pious exercises'.[23]

The final comment of this Catholic scholar about the mass is:

> No longer do we see before us today that majestic and orderly inner sanctuary which at one time crowned the structure of the eucharistic liturgy, but a chapel whose architecture has run wild and is cluttered with turrets and brass in such a way that the untrained eye can scarcely detect its basic outline.[24]

What we need today, Klauser writes, is a liturgy 'of common action'. Thus Klauser, following the second Vatican Council, calls for a prayer of intercession which 'arouses the attention of the faithful at the service, because it stresses concretely what they are concerned about at the moment'.[25]

If, like the Pentecostals, we take the worship of the early church as the norm for the church today, eucharistic services should be based on the following criteria:

1. The eucharist should be a liturgy 'of common action'. This requirement is fulfilled by many Pentecostal eucharistic services. They do not consist of a priest or pastor celebrating for the congregation, but the whole congregation is responsible for the form and content of the service. For traditional churches in present-day society this brings difficult but not insoluble problems in the preparation and conduct of services.

2. The eucharistic service in which someone states at length and in detail that something is now happening, but nothing visible does happen, is in obvious contradiction to the tradition of the early church. The offertory procession of the congregation was visible, as was the distribution of the 'one body and one Bread' of Christ in the world, when the hungry mouths of Corinth were fed with 'the loaf broken for many'. This was a revolutionary act on the part of the early Christians, for what other religious group would use its holy of holies to appease ordinary bodily hunger? A eucharist that has lost this visible dimension of social criticism may well remain an impressive religious spectacle (and is not without significance as such), but cannot stand up to the test of comparison with the practice of the early church.

3. Naturally there is no question at the present day of simply reinstituting simple forms developed by a world dependent on an agricultural economy; as it were, to turn the eucharist into a permanent harvest festival, enshrining the folk lore of the past. More important is to translate the dimension of social criticism in the eucharist into the terms of our own society.

Examples of such a translation exist already. One example is the Catholic 'Shalom Group' in Holland. When the members of this fellowship, at their eucharistic worship, drew up an aid programme for the black Christians in the South of the United States, and carried it through in a co-ordinated way ('Delta Ministry'),[26] and resolved in the course of the eucharistic service to hand back the tax reductions made by the Dutch Minister of Finance with the request that these contributions should be used for increased aid to developing countries, these were modern forms of bringing the one bread, broken for the world, to the hungry of our own time.[27] The social dimension of the eucharist was likewise made visible when at the official Swiss National Thanksgiving Day it was not the pastor, as usual, but a group of Italian and Spanish immigrant workers who distributed communion,[28] or when the Bishop of Guernavaca (Mexico) sent the labourers and mestizos after mass to the factory director with the question: How is it that we are brothers at the table of the Lord, but not at the conference table?;[29] or when in the *paroisse oecuménique des jeunes* in Lausanne the eucharistic celebration, the dialogue (which replaced the sermon) and the help given to backward school children were felt and celebrated as a unity;[30] or when during the disturbances of May 1968 in Paris, Catholics and Protestants bore witness to their revolutionary solidarity around the table of the Lord.[31]

2. *'Buried with Christ'*:[32] *The Doctrine of Baptism*

Most Pentecostals hold a view of baptism close to that of the Baptists. In general, those who are converted are baptized on the basis of the testimony of their conversion, and baptism in water is understood as

> an outward sign, seal or expression of an inward death, burial and resurrection, signifying the believer's identification with Christ.[33]

> The ordinance of Baptism by a burial with Christ should be observed as commanded in the Scriptures, by all who have really repented and in their hearts have truly believed on Christ as Saviour and Lord. In so doing, they have the body washed in pure water as an outward symbol of cleansing, while their heart has already been sprinkled with the blood of Christ as an inner cleansing.[34]

Let us compare a Reformed Church baptismal service with a Pentecostal service. In the Reformed Church eight children are being baptized. The pastor goes to considerable trouble to explain to the parents and godparents the significance of baptism. He comes up against a brick wall of embarrassment, because the parents and godparents are not expecting an explanation, but a celebration. They can make nothing of what the pastor has to say, because it is months or perhaps years since they have attended a service. The pastor's congregation listens in boredom to his sermon. The most human thing about the whole service is the crying of two of the babies. They form the centre of interest. Their godmothers try to quiet them with 'Hush!', 'Ssh'!, and the congregation smile sympathetically. They can now let the pastor's words pass over their heads and accept them as a religious celebration, as 'background music'.

A Pentecostal baptismal service is quite different. At five o'clock on Sunday morning the Pentecostals gather at a bathing place on the shore of Lake Zürich. While the candidates for baptism change, the congregation sings. The pastor appears dressed in white tennis clothes, wearing a white tie, while those to be baptized wear long flowing white robes. Before the assembled congregation they are asked:

> Do you believe in the Lord Jesus Christ, as the Son of the living God? Have you broken every ungodly link with the world, and with every known sin . . . so that now, freed from a bad conscience through the sprinkling of your heart with the precious blood of Christ, you now wish to come to the bodily cleansing with pure water?
>
> Will you also give yourself through baptism to be crucified to the world in the death of Jesus, and to die to sin? Will you . . . place the interests of the kingdom of God in all circumstances and in every place above your own earthly interests?[35]

They answer 'yes' to each question. One at a time they climb down into the water, an elder calls out a verse of the Bible to each, and two pastors baptize them, one of them saying: 'N., I baptize you in the name of the Father and of the Son and of the Holy Spirit, into the name of Jesus.'[36] The congregation sings, and sometimes there is speaking in tongues. The baptized are allowed to to go into the changing hut. A few early morning boatmen row by on the lake, pause and look from a respectful distance at the unusual service.[37]

Read describes a baptismal service in the Brazilian Congregação Cristã do Brasil. Only one condition must be fulfilled for baptism – the personal acceptance of Jesus Christ as Saviour. No application has to be made, and no baptismal instruction is required. All one has to do is to come forward during the baptismal service, put on the baptismal garments and be immersed, in the baptistry of the church. At a service observed by W. R. Read 130 were baptized. In ten months this congregation had baptized 3,801 people, which means that every second Sunday was a baptismal Sunday. For the baptized the simple baptismal service represents their acceptance into the church and the turning point of their lives. It is as though the baptisms described in the Acts of the Apostles had returned.[38]

In the Musama Christo Disco Church the baptized are given 'heavenly names' at their baptism;[39] in the Church of the Twelve Apostles (Nackabah) they are soaped and bathed before baptism.[40] In the 'The King Comes' Brotherhood prophetic sayings are called out over the candidates for baptism, instead of Bible verses; e.g. 'The sound of your harp will be sweet!', 'The mouths that have mocked you are dumb and will no longer be able to do so!'[41]

In most cases 'water baptism takes place by immersion',[42] for 'Jesus Christ himself commanded that water baptism should be carried out by immersion, because the Greek word *baptisma* itself means immersion.'[43] But a not inconsiderable minority of the Pentecostal movement practises baptism by sprinkling. The Chilean Pentecostals

> believe in water baptism by sprinkling as an outward sign and act of obedience of an inner faith.[44]

Most other Pentecostals reject this baptism as invalid. Thus for example Lilly Wreschner, who on her conversion from Judaism to Christianity received baptism by sprinkling in a Reformed church, had to undergo another baptism by immersion. A large minority in the Pentecostal movement practices not only the baptism of believers but also infant baptism.[45] This minority includes almost the whole of the Chilean Pentecostal movement, the largest German Pentecostal group,[46] and a Yugoslav Pentecostal group.[47] It also included the Finnish and Norwegian Pentecostal movements in their early days, as well as others. The bulk of the Pentecostal movement disagrees with infant baptism. Armin Reichenbach suspects that behind the reasons given for infant baptism lies the work of the 'old prince of lies, who from the very first has tempted men with the question, "Did God say. . .?" '[48]

> Nor is it God who acts in baptism, as is often stated so finely, but wrongly.[49]
>
> It is illogical and not in conformity with the word of God to baptize infants.[50]

The Australian Assemblies of God state:

> Baptism is for believers only. While some churches practise infant baptism, the Word of God shows clearly the error of this.[51]

Thus a large part of the Pentecostal movement rejects both infant baptism and baptism by sprinkling.[52] This has led, for example in Chile, to great tension between the large indigenous Pentecostal churches and the American Pentecostal missionary churches. Chávez, a Chilean Pentecostal leader, and a member of the Central Committee of the World Council of Churches, rightly comments:

> The Pentecostals who in Chile originate from the Methodist church maintain the baptism of infants and adults by sprinkling. Only when Pentecostal missions came to Chile . . . did they introduce baptism by immersion.[53]

Jonathan Paul, the founder of the German Pentecostal movement, firmly defended infant baptism,[54] and the Quaker Pentecostals consider the dispute about baptism altogether irrelevant. Their view is that the main question is not whether the early Christians practised water baptism or not, but whether it was intended to be a permanent institution in the church:

> We believe that water baptism was not provided as a permanent requirement and that any and all ceremony as insisted on by fixed rules and practices is inconsistent with the leadership and control of the Holy Spirit.[55]

Besides the attitudes described – baptism by immersion for adults, baptism by sprinkling for infants and adults, and the rejection of baptism altogether – there is also a not inconsiderable group of Pentecostals for whom the only valid baptism is that carried out 'in the name of Jesus'. The dispute about the correct *formula* of baptism between Pentecostals who baptize in the name of the Trinity, following Matt. 28.19, and those who follow Acts 2.38 and similar passages and baptize 'in the name of Jesus', has not yet been resolved. It has such consequences as the practice of the Apostolic Faith Mission in South Africa of emphasizing trinitarian baptism by threefold immersion,[56] while others have proposed a compromise formula between the two baptismal formulae.[57]

As far as possible the 'Jesus only' groups are ignored by Pentecostals who baptize in the name of the Trinity, although, for example, the largest Pentecostal denomination in Colombia[58] and the majority of Indonesian Pentecostals belong to them. Baptism 'in the name of Jesus' is often regarded as necessary to salvation.

> It is important for us to know why we do whatever we do . . . Many of us have been baptized once before [as adults].[59]

> The Acts of the Apostles and the Epistles are the only inspired books that we have which give an accurate account of how the apostles obeyed Matt. 28.19, under the direction of the Holy Spirit.[60]

These books clearly show, it is claimed, that the apostles always baptized 'in the name of Jesus' (Acts 2.38; 8.16; 10.48; 19.5) and so fulfilled the baptismal commandment of Matt. 28.19. Which of us dares say that we know better than they do?[61]

S. C. Johnson of the Church of the Lord Jesus Christ of the Apostolic Faith, Inc. has discovered that a baptism 'in the name of Jesus' is not sufficient. Since in the New Testament there are three people whose name is Jesus, it is necessary to state precisely that 'Jesus Christ' is meant. Thus the correct baptismal formula is 'in the name of Jesus Christ'.[62] Other Pentecostals will only baptize 'in the name of the Father'.[63]

The disputes about baptism in the Pentecostal movement have led in certain places to the loss of the original significance of baptism as a single unique act. Apart from the fact that the Pentecostal view of baptism as a sign of a forgiveness of sin which has *already taken place* is irreconcilable with the Acts of the Apostles ('Be baptized everyone of you . . . *for* the forgiveness of your sins.' Acts 2.38), the repetition of baptisms practised by other churches – even Pentecostal churches! – has led in South Africa, for example, to the transformation of baptism into a rite of purification which is constantly repeated. Sundkler describes such an act of purification in detail:

Ehhe-ehhe-ehhe-ehhe ee ee	Ehhe
Ngiyamazi uBaбa	I know my father
owangenzayo	who made me
Ngiyalazi idlozi	I know the spirit
elangenzayo	who made me
Ehhe-ehhe-ehhe-ee ee	Ehhe

> It is dawn – there is still half an hour to go before the sun rises out of the Indian Ocean. Near Ekukhanyeni the diviner Dlakude approaches with her novices (*amathwasa*). The pupils dance around the leader as they come half-running down the slope to the Ihlekazi stream, chanting songs to the ancestral spirits.
>
> They are not alone. On the opposite side of the stream another group approaches, some of them clad in white robes with green or yellow sashes. It is the prophet Elliot Butelezi of the Sabbath Zionist Church and his followers. Half-running, dancing in circles around the prophet as they move along, they sing with shrill voices:
>
> | | |
> |---|---|
> | *Thixo, Baбa, ngidukile,* | God Father, I have erred, |
> | *nasekhaya ngisukile.* | and have gone astray from home. |
>
> The diviner group arrives at the stream first. All the members of the group have brought their calabashes and, when these have been filled with water,

u6ulawu-medicine is added and the concoction is stirred until froth is formed. The diviner gives each to drink from the frothy water, and they begin to vomit.

The Zionists look on silently for a while, but presently Elliot asks the *isangoma* leader: 'When are you going to finish, preacher?' This joke produces laughter from the Zionists, whereas the diviner and her pupils remain silent, intent on their vomiting rites. To conclude the ceremony, Dlakude finds some white clay, which she smears upon herself and her followers. One of them starts the spirit-song:

Ehhe ehhe
Ngiyamazi uBa6a . . .

The whole group leaves the stream, returning to Dlakude's kraal. The leader dances round her group in joy, beating them with twigs as they run homewards.

Now comes the Zionists' turn. 'The water has been defiled, because the diviners have entered it,' complains one in the group. But Elliot replies: 'Pay no heed to that, for this is running water, and the impurity has been removed by its flow.' He intones a hymn. The older Zionists follow suit, but newcomers to the congregation follow with 'Amen, Amen' to the same tune. There follows blessing of the water. Elliot stirs in the stream with his index finger and looking up to heaven says a short prayer to the Lord of the Living Waters (*inkosi yamanzi aphilayo*) that the stream may be cleansed of vile things. One of the group is brought to Elliot by a prayer-woman. With both hands he scoops water into the mouth of the patient, at the same time shouting: 'In the name of the Father and of the Son and of the Holy Ghost. This blessed water will take away illness from this sick person. Drink!'

Elliot then takes the patient with him in the middle of the stream and makes the woman stoop until the water goes over her head. He places his hands upon her head and in the same moment becomes filled with the Holy Spirit. His whole body shakes, and he shouts, first slowly, but soon faster and faster: '*Hhayi, hhayi, hhayi, hhe, hhe, hhe!*' The patient drinks repeatedly from the water, praying in the intervals: 'Descend, Spirit, descend like a dove!' Soon she also gets the Spirit, begins to shake and to speak with tongues: 'Di-di-di di-didi.' While this is happening, the faithful on the banks sing a hymn. The sick woman comes up from the stream and begins to vomit on the rocks.

Other patients follow her into the water and go through the same process ending with vomiting. One of Elliot's brothers, Philemon, an elder in the Church, is suddenly possessed by the Spirit. He dashes round the group in his long white gown, beating the air with a long white cross. He sings, shouts, and speaks with tongues. After the 'water and vomiting' ceremony, Elliot takes white ashes and mixes them with water. He smears the patients' faces and shoulders with this mixture. To complete the cure, green sashes are tied around their shoulders.[64]

That the baptismal practice of our existing established and Free Churches is an ailing one is clear to everyone who shares in the agony of the existing churches.

But the problem is not to be resolved simply by adopting adult baptism without further consideration. This can be seen from the immense difficulties which result from Pentecostal baptismal practice. The Chilean Pentecostals, who practise both kinds of baptism, and so express the two most important themes of baptism, God's unconditional promise to man and man's profession of faith in this promise of God, seem to me to point to a solution which is not merely possible but indeed necessary for the existing churches, if we are not to go on being a 'church without decision'. The retaining of the sprinkling of infants together with believer's baptism would assure that the promise of God to man was not made dependent upon man's response. Moreover, most of the church orders of the traditional churches offer the possibility of such practice. The baptism of adults takes place fairly frequently, but because of a false understanding of baptism on the part of congregations–and the opportunity to correct this on the occasion of the baptism of an adult is regularly missed – it takes place privately in the sacristy.

3. *'The Whole Bible': The Washing of Feet*

Bobby Lauster of the Church of God (Cleveland) writes:

> In their constitutions present day Pentecostals write that they believe in the whole Bible. But when they come to the passage in the Scripture which states that believers should wash each others' feet they have great difficulties in accepting it. But in spite of all eloquent arguments God's word remains.[65]

The Pentecostals who reject the washing of feet advance the following arguments against the numerous 'foot-washers' amongst the Pentecostals.[66] In New Testament times the washing of feet was a practice which was adopted by the early Christians, but need no longer be carried out at the present day. One might ask of course, why the practice of immersion in water is necessary to salvation, while that of the washing of feet is not, since according to the letter of the New Testament both rites were explicitly commanded by Jesus, and Pentecostals never weary of stressing that God gives his Holy Spirit 'to those who obey him' (Acts 5.32). For Pentecostals, but also for many Christians from the traditional churches, this question is unanswerable. Those who practise the washing of feet have at least this to be said for them, that on this point they are obedient to the whole Scripture – in the framework of the fundamentalist misunderstanding of Scripture. They are only outbid by the Pentecostal seventh day adventists who take the ten commandments more seriously than ordinary Pentecostals.[67]

Within the framework of a fundamentalist understanding of the Bible, there are no grounds for the disobedience of other Pentecostals to the command to wash one another's feet. The only alternative is to be concerned, in patient and detailed exegetical work, and in dialogue with the 'beginners' in other churches, about the *one thing* which is necessary. But the question of what belongs to this *one thing*, and whether it includes all the burdens which Pentecostals impose upon their faithful, is a matter of dispute among Christian denominations. The Bible points to the foundation of our faith, Jesus Christ. But what does it mean for Jesus Christ to be the foundation of our faith? All Christians, and all sectarians, appeal to Jesus Christ as the foundation of their faith, not least amongst them the Pentecostal foot-washers and seventh day adventists, the former by pointing to Jesus's own example (John 13.14).

It would be useful to consider further here this sole foundation of faith. But such a consideration must take into account not merely the washing of feet and the commandment to keep the sabbath. These two issues are merely the magnifying glass which shows us in greatly enlarged form the weaknesses of a literalist understanding of Scripture. If these weaknesses are recognized, then the whole fundamentalist understanding of Scripture must come under scrutiny. We must be able to give an account of why 'Jesus as the witness of faith',[11] but not a single provision in the New Testament, can be the foundation of our faith. The theology of the Reformation will help us in this examination and scrutiny. For its most important theme is: How can we let Jesus 'as the witness of faith, be the basis of faith'?[69] What does it mean to have to do with him and to enter on his way, and thus to participate in that which is promised to faith, namely, the omnipotence of God?[70] This question is common both to the religious thought and practice of Pentecostalism and to Reformation theology.

NOTES

1. N. I. Pejsti (ed.), *Zasady*, ch. 16; *Risveglio P* 8/11, Nov. 1953, p. 2; Appendix: 9.
2. Iglesia Pentecostal de Chile, *Manuel del Ministro*, p. 13.
3. Kristova Pentekostna Crkva, *Temeljne*, art. 6; AoG, *Early History*, art. 6. Cf. Appendix: 2.
4. F. P. Möller, *Die Apostoliese Leer*, p. 38.
5. G. Bennard, *Hymns of Glorious Praise*, 1969, no. 87.
6. Congregação Cristã do Brasil, *Estatutos*, 1946, art. 14.
7. Source no longer ascertainable.
8. *Risveglio P* 8/11, Nov. 1953, p. 2; cf. Appendix: 9.
9. L. H. Edmunds, *Hymns of Glorious Praise*, 1969, no. 98.
10. P. Free Will Baptists, *Faith*, 1961, pp. 1ff., art. 24.
11. W. G. Taylor, *Hymns of Glorious Praise*, 1969, no. 93.
12. Congregação Cristã do Brasil, *Estatutos*, 1946, art. 14.
13. *Ibid.*
14. The Jesus Church, *Assembly Report*, 1952–3, pp. 11f.; quoted in Moore, p. 308.
15. PAoW, *1963 Minute Book of PAoW*, pp. 9f., art. 7.
16. Associated Brotherhood of Christians, *Articles*, n.d., pp. 6ff., art. 6; quoted by Moore, pp. 283ff.
17. D. Gee, *Study Hour* 5/2, 15.2.1946, pp. 27ff.

18. Evangelisations-Team Königs-Quartett, BIEM 101: 'Komm heim zum Abendmahl!'

19. T. Klauser, *A Short History of the Western Liturgy*, p. 109.

20. T. Klauser, *ibid.*, p. 34.

21. A musical prelude with the entry of the pastor is not customary in many Pentecostal churches.

22. T. Klauser, *op. cit.*, p. 37.

23. *Ibid.*, p. 97.

24. *Ibid.*, p. 24.

25. *Ibid.*, p. 59.

26. B. Hilton, *Delta Ministry*; WCC, *Church for Others*, pp. 116ff.

27. H. J. Herbort, *Monthly Letter on Evangelism*, May–June 1967 (WCC, Geneva).

28. W. J. Hollenweger and A. v. d. Heuvel, 'Sylvester: Psalm 121', in: E. Lange (ed.), *Predigtstudien* V/1, 1970/71, pp. 79–90.

29. W. J. Hollenweger, *Neues Forum* 126/192, December 1969, pp. 711ff.

30. Jacques Nicole, Georges Kolb, *Monthly Letter on Evangelism*, Nov.–Dec. 1969.

31. Claudette Marquet, *Monthly Letter on Evangelism*, May–June 1970. On the whole matter cf. W. Simpfendörfer, *Offene Kirche*, pp. 158ff. The texts mentioned in notes 27 to 31 have been published with many others in: W. J. Hollenweger (ed.), *Kirche, Benzin und Bohnensuppe*, and in Hollenweger, *Theologie* (English translation for both volumes in preparation).

32. T. Ryder, *Redemption Hymnal* 1958, no. 692 (baptismal hymn).

33. G. G. Kulbeck, *What God hath Wrought*, pp. 351ff.

34. Kristova Pentekostna Crkva, *Temeljne*, art. 5; cf. also AoG, *Early History*, pp. 17ff.; Appendix: 2.

35. Baptismal vows of the Swiss Pentecostal Mission.

36. A compromise formula between the Pentecostals who baptize in the name of the Trinity and the 'Jesus only' groups, who baptize in the 'name of Jesus'.

37. I have taken part in many baptismal services myself.

38. W. R. Read, *New Patterns*, pp. 27f.

39. 01.12.020.

40. 01.12.014.

41. K. Hutten, *Seher*, 8th ed., 1962, p. 499.

42. *Die Wahrheit* 15/11, Nov. 1962, pp. 6, 10.

43. N. I. Pejsti (ed.), *Zasady*, ch. 16.

44. Iglesia Pentecostal de Chile, *Manuel*, n.d., p. 16.

45. Baptism by sprinkling is practised by: Apostolowo Fe Dedefia Habobo (01.12.018); Musama Christo Disco Church (10.12.020), other African churches, and the groups mentioned in notes 46 and 47.

46. Mülheim Association of Christian Fellowships (ch. 17.2(*b*), pp. 237ff.) (both forms of baptism). This led to severe tensions, not yet resolved, in the German Pentecostal movement; the statement that 'baptism is much too holy for us to agree now in our assembly on one formula' (Fleisch II/2, pp. 382f.) was not enough to settle the difficulties.

47. Kristova Duhovna Crkva 'Malkrštenih' (05.16.005).

48. A. Reichenbach, *VdV* 55/10, Oct. 1962, p. 4.

49. *Ibid.*

50. C. Le Cossec, *Le vrai baptême* (Vérité à connaître 2), p. 8.

51. AoG Australia, *You Have Accepted Christ*, pp. 2f.

52. *Ibid.*

53. E. Chávez, letter to W.H., 23.1.1963.

54. J. Paul, *Taufe*.

55. Full Salvation Union, *Manual* 1944, p. 27; quoted in Moore, p. 295.

56. Cf. ch. 9.3(*a*), pp. 120ff.

57. Cf. SPM, above p. 391; O. Vouga, *Our Gospel*, pp. 15ff., rejects these mediating formulae.

58. Iglesia Pentecostal Unida (02b.20.010).

59. F. L. Smith, *What Every Saint Should Know*, 3rd ed., n.d., p. 9.

60. O. Vouga, *Our Gospel*, pp. 15ff.

61. *Ibid.*

62. S. C. Johnson, *Who is This*, p. 6.

63. School of the Prophets (02a.02.141).

64. Sundkler, pp. 238ff. Other examples: St Paul Apostolic Faith Morning Star (01.36.412); Zion Apostolic Church of South Africa (01.36.449). Cf. above ch. 12. 4(*b*), pp. 156ff.

65. B. Lauster, *Die Wahrheit* 15/12, Feb. 1962, p. 6; also P. H. Walker, *ChoGE* 52/19, 9.7.1962, pp. 4f.

66. Most Pentecostals who believe in a three-stage way of salvation, and 'Jesus Only' groups.

67. '. . . for however much I look, I have never found in the New Testament the words which lay down the first day of the week instead of the seventh.' P. Mikkonen, *He huusivat*, quoted by W. Schmidt, *Pfingstbewegung*, p. 125. Pentecostal seventh day adventists: 02b.08.066; 05.08.003e, cc; 05.28.042; a few African groups.

68. The whole sentence reads: 'Jesus as the witness of faith in the pregnant sense of the author and finisher of faith' (G. Ebeling, *Nature of Faith*, p. 71). This book gives, in concise modern language, 'an introduction to the understanding of Christian faith'.

69. *Ibid.*

70. The whole sentence reads: 'What does "faith in Jesus" mean? It means to let him, as the witness of faith, be the basis of faith, and thus to have to do with him and to enter upon his way, and thus to participate in that which is promised to faith, namely, the omnipotence of God.' (*Ibid.*)

28

'Religion is what you must not do': Ethics

1. *'Bring Ye All the Tithes into the Storehouse' : Tithing*

MANY Pentecostal groups require from their members an offering of ten per cent of their gross income.

> We believe that the method ordained of God to sustain His Ministry . . . is 'Tithing'.[1]

Tithing is praised as the surest way, the 'master key'[2] to financial prosperity.

> Give until it hurts and then give until it stops hurting . . . Many put zero into the collection and then complain the church is cold . . . Salvation is free, but not cheap . . . Is it fair to expect to get gold out of the sermon when you put coppers into the service?[3]

Tithing is often obligatory for pastors. In the Church of God of the Mountain Assembly pastors who do not pay the tithe are dismissed.[4] The Jesus Church believes that anyone who does not pay tithes receives no gifts of the Spirit,[5] and in Lebanon an Arabic pamphlet was published to explain to Arab Christians that the tithe is meant for church expenses, to maintain the pastors, and not, for example, for the poor.

2. *'Remember the Sabbath Day . . .': the Observance of Sunday*

Most Pentecostals believe in a quiet Sunday rest.

> In these days when the Lord's day is being desecrated by so many, we as a church feel it our duty to take a stand against the practice of buying and selling on Sunday, attending meetings for worldly amusement, visiting resorts, promiscuous and questionable joy-riding, etc., on the Lord's day.[6]

When the choir of the Evangelical Association (Berne) were involved in an accident on the occasion of a trip on a Whit Monday, the Apostolic Church (Switzerland) received 'the following instructive prophecy':

> Avoid the filth of this earth, take food from My word . . . I had showers of blessing ready . . . But they [those who went on the coach trip] were not ready . . . Therefore I could not help, My hand could not be at the wheel and drive. My foot did not press the brake, and so they received their lot . . .[7]

In 1950 the Elim Pentecostal Church was campaigning against television, which kept the faithful away from services on Sunday, although I observed television sets in the houses of Elim pastors as early as 1948. To desecrate the Sabbath is a sin. 'If you begin by making it Funday, it will end by making it Sinday.'[8] Albert W. Edsor fought against Britain's joining the Common Market, because England would then fall more and more under the power of Catholicism, which would endanger the traditional Sunday, 'the Lord's Day, the day which Almighty God has commanded to be kept holy'.[9]

Other Pentecostals find this attitude legalist.

> We do not hold that our Salvation is contingent upon the keeping of certain days, or times.[10]

> If someone should lose his calendar and all record of time yet if he rested and worshipped one day out of seven regardless of when he started he would be approved of God as keeping the commandment.[11]

In the opinion of these Pentecostals the Sabbath was made for man and not man for the Sabbath.

In a fine and eloquent chapter of his *Church Dogmatics* Karl Barth has discussed at length the sanctification of the day of rest.[12] If Pentecostals were to read this chapter, which is easily comprehensible by non-theologians, they would not find that everything in it pleased them. At the same time it would be worthwhile for them not to ignore the thinking of this 'biblical' theologian. The questions which are posed at the present day by the commandment to keep the day of rest holy are discussed in two short volumes entitled *Verlorener Sonntag*[13] and *Industrielle Sonntagsarbeit*.[14]

3. *'Thou Shalt Not Kill': Military Service*

At first there were a number of Pentecostals – including Russian sailors – who refused military service.[15] A refusal of military service still seems to be widespread amongst the Working Fellowship of Christian Churches (Germany):

> Many young men refuse armed military service for reasons of conscience, although there is no doctrinal requirement that they should.[16]

From 1917 to 1921 the Church of God (Cleveland) placed several of its members under discipline because they wished to fulfil their duty of military service. From 1928 to 1945 these sanctions were limited to members of the Church of

God (Cleveland) who carried out their service in fighting units. At the present day the Church of God (Cleveland) has ceased entirely to condemn military service.

The American Assemblies of God declared that they could not participate 'conscientiously in war'.[17] The General Council passed a resolution 'which expressed the unwillingness of the members of the Assemblies of God, as followers of Christ, to participate in armed conflict.'[18] But only twenty young Pentecostals belonging to the Assemblies of God were registered as conscientious objectors. In an article 'The Plight of the Conscientious Objector in the Present World Conflict', J. Roswell Flower[19] reported that to refuse military service imposed too great a financial burden, be it on the individual or the church which supported him, since a person who refused military service had to maintain himself during the whole course of the civilian service which replaced it. Moreover, in the course of civilian service he was exposed to dangerous, non-Christian influences. It is not surprising that in 1961 Ernest S. Williams, another leader of the Assemblies of God, decided to leave the question of military service to the conscience of the individual, although he was able to give precise answers to the question of whether women should wear make-up, whether one might play volley-ball on Sunday, and other similar questions.[20] Similarly, he expressed support for capital punishment.[21]

In the Swiss Pentecostal Mission every war, even war in defence of one's freedom, has been condemned 'as an expression of violence, which is emotional and not godly'.[22] But there are no conscientious objectors in the Swiss Pentecostal movement.

In Great Britain many Pentecostals refused military service during the first world war.[23] In the 1930s the leaders of the Elim Pentecostal Churches strongly stressed the incompatibility of the gospel call with a Christian's participation in war. But in 1940 James McWhirter, of the same church, declared that pacifism was unbiblical,[24] while Donald Gee did not deny conscientious objectors the right to refuse military service, but told them they should show the same 'tenderness of conscience' in business.[25]

Surveying the whole picture, one can say that whereas during the first world war,[26] and to some extent also during the second world war, German Pentecostals joined with other German Christians in manifesting an astonishing enthusiasm for war, they are resolutely putting this attitude behind them at the present day. On the other hand, American Pentecostals are trying to prove their loyalty and conformity to the American government by forgetting their critical past.

4. '*Faithful in Little*': *Taboos on Pleasure and Food*

Most Pentecostals – but not all – reject smoking as unchristian. A Christian does not smoke, he burns: 'If God wanted men to smoke, then He would have made men with chimneys on their heads!'[27]

All Pentecostals except those on the continent of Europe practise total abstinence from alcohol, and also, with reference to Acts 15.28–29, from eating blood, e.g. black-puddings.

> When you eat the blood the character of the animal enters you. Consequently you lose control of your intelligence. You will have to suffer the consequences. This is why so many people can no longer control their sexual urges, but are controlled by them. That is why the marriage of the divorced is so alarmingly widespread. Through the continuous eating of blood for generations people's characters have become animal in nature.[28]

> We believe that it is necessary to abstain from things sacrificed to idols, from blood, from what is strangled and from fornication.[29]

Sometimes pork is also condemned. 'Anyone who eats pig's flesh is a pig.'[30] Some independent African Pentecostal churches practise other food taboos: Stink-fish (because its smell is unclean), the flesh of sharks (because sharks eat men), snakes (because they crawl through the dirt), etc.

The Associated Brotherhood of Christians prohibits alcohol, but leaves other matters to the individual.[31] In many Pentecostal groups the transgression of a food taboo brings the imposition of church discipline.

5. '*A Life of Overcoming*': *Sex Taboos*

The way which leads to the Kingdom of Heaven is so narrow that all unnecessary ballast in the form of worldly pleasures must be unloaded. For some Pentecostals this ballast consists of all musical instruments (except the violin, the mandolin, the guitar and the concertina),[32] but for others it consists of the 'worship of the Silver Screen'.[33] A Christian in a cinema is like a 'sheep in a pigsty'.[34]

> One who has Christ does not need the theatre or any worldly pleasures . . . One who has Christ is peaceful and satisfied and no longer hurries to the theatre. I have a horror of modern Christianity which permits everything: attending services and trips to the theatre, fearing God and serving idols.[35]

For others again, this ballast consists in the use of slang, foolish talking, jesting, visits to open-air swimming baths, fairs and theatres, the wearing of make-up, loud ties, skirts with slits up the side, short sleeves and any clothes 'which tend to inflame lust in the opposite sex'.[36] Consequently, the Pentecostal Assemblies of the World forbid all their members to wear 'all unnecessary jewelry, such as rings (not including wedding rings), bracelets, ear-rings, stick-pins and flashy breast pins . . . showy colors in dress, attractive hosiery, short dresses, low necks, short sleeves (that is, above the elbow), and bright ties.'[37]

Unfortunately the wives of ministers of the established churches give a bad example in this respect, for they wear their hair short and their skirts above the knees, or tight trousers and make-up, and worship images in the form of the television.[38]

The International Church of the Foursquare Gospel, whose founder, Aimee Semple McPherson, made up with great care and made a great – but ill-fated – impression by her striking beauty, deals in its Declaration of Faith, under the heading 'Moderation', not with the usual taboos on clothing, but with fanaticism and idle gossip about third persons.[39] But most Pentecostals consider that fashionable clothes are not for Christians. Women's hair should not be waved; powder and make-up should be left to the world.[40]

> It is God's will that our vile bodies should be covered. This should be done by wearing generously cut, flowing clothes . . . Satan does not wish to cover but to expose. Because the fashion of semi-nakedness cannot be practised in winter, then they are made at least to display the shape of the body . . . Are we not responsible when a teacher says that the way girls wear their sweaters nowadays is a trap for a teacher . . . And unfortunately the same flimsy stockings . . . the same scanty underwear . . . can be found on believers as well.[41]

Roberto Bracco regrets that in the Italian Pentecostal movement

> one can no longer tell where the world finishes and the church begins. Skirts and sleeves grow shorter, necklines lower, and accessories more startling . . . A Christian woman should never be a motive of temptation, if she is not to become an accomplice of hell. But everyone knows that the thousand arts of fashion serve above all to make woman pleasing and attractive: that is, they serve to excite the insane desires of men. A skirt which stops at a certain point or which clings to the body in a certain way, a neckline which displays the bare body indiscreetly, the bodice which exaggerates the outline of the body, are all things which encourage lust.[42]

The Pilgrim Holiness Church regards the prohibition of worldly pleasures (the cinema, the theatre and sports grounds) as an important article of faith.[43] 'Stages for plays set up within a church are nothing other than a symbol of unbelief and degeneracy.'[44]

And the ministers of the established churches – as Conrad Lemke tells in describing his crossing of the Atlantic – never thought 'to demonstrate that they were accompanied by Jesus on their way'. They were 'usually to be found in the bar. Mostly they were everywhere where they were not expected.'[45]

On the basis of the wooing carried out by Eliezer for Isaac, Hermann Müller concludes:

> The Bible knows nothing of the concepts of friendship and courtship [between young men and women] . . . nor do they exist for Christians . . . but only a short period of preparation for the marriage that is to follow.[46]

As far as divorce is concerned, the letter of the New Testament is strictly observed. Originally divorce and remarriage were rejected. But at the present day this practice has been somewhat relaxed. Divorce in the case of adultery[47] and remarriage of the innocent party[48] is possible in the older denominations. In the Pentecostal Assemblies of Canada these provisions are only applied to officials.[49] In the groups in which a high dignitary of the group concerned obtained a divorce and remarried, these regulations have been lifted altogether.[50]

Marriage between believers and unbelievers (that is, those who are not converted) is forbidden, but in certain circumstances can be carried out in the Pentecostal church.[51]

In Latin America[52] and amongst gypsies[53] Pentecostal pastors endeavour to introduce European marriage customs. A problem which has not yet been solved is that constituted by Pentecostal West Indians in Great Britain who live together according to West Indian custom, but are not legally married. In general they do not marry until they have at least one child. The Pentecostal pastors are completely incapable (and in this they are no different from most other English ministers) of helping them in this matter with the necessary freedom but with clarity as well. The Pentecostal movement is faced with an equally difficult problem by the Independent Australian Pentecostals, because according to Australian aboriginal custom their women live with several men.[54]

The mighty apparatus which is mobilized against the wicked flesh in the Pentecostal churches no longer seems to be very successful. More often than their pastors like to acknowledge, Pentecostals struggle unsuccessfully for a 'pure life', although in their services they sing:

> A life of overcoming,
> A life of ceaseless praise,
> Be this thy blessed portion
> Throughout the coming days.[55]

This ethical attitude cannot be explained solely from the underlying hostility to creation which has always been present in the Pentecostal movement. It is also the expression of (*a*) an uncertainty with regard to the emancipation of women and (*b*) a protest against the ethical perplexity of our times.

With respect to the emancipation of women, the Pentecostal movement would prefer to leave women in the position that they have in the East. The feeling is that the woman's place is in the home. 'Be a wife, be a housekeeper, be a mother and be glad and rejoice because God has seen fit to bless you with a good husband and loving children.'[56] There is an unconscious protest against the growing independence of women, although women are compensated indirectly in Pentecostal churches by the exercise of a very considerable influence. An expression of this protest is the copying of oriental practices:

> Whenever a woman prays or prophesies she must have her head covered with a veil.[57]

> Hair cut short still means today that power has been lost (Judg. 16.17).[58]

> It is also important that according to apostolic teaching our sisters should not have their hair cut, for Paul describes this as shameful.[59]

In his exposition of I Tim. 2.15 (woman will be saved through bearing children), Roberto Bracco writes:

> The woman is the gentle, tender, brave but submissive 'helpmate' of him who has a more direct responsibility before God than she for the life of the family. Paul intended to teach . . . that every married woman should seek her approval before God by complete submission to her husband, by heroic fulfilment of the task of motherhood, and by accepting the pains of childbirth.[60]

For Pentecostals, rigorist ethics seem to be the only way of protesting against the moral perplexity of our times. A Pentecostal shop assistant hears her workmates saying: 'I am surrounded all day by beautiful things which I will never possess. And I sometimes ask whether it is really worth being respectable. There isn't much difference: the same man every night or a different one every night.'[61] At least a Pentecostal has an answer to the question 'Is it worth it?' If she has to renounce on earth what is apparently or really beautiful, she does not lose heart, 'for this slight momentary affliction is preparing for us an eternal weight of glory beyond all comparison, because we look not to the things that are seen but to the things that are unseen' (II Cor. 4.17–18).

In older Pentecostal churches one can observe a relaxation of this ethical rigorism, which is due to sociological reasons. Nowadays a Pentecostal assistant in a beauty parlour can be described as 'a preacher in a beauty shop'[62] – a practical idea which is worth imitating. Ernest S. Williams had to admit that many young Pentecostal girls, and wives of pastors, use make-up,[63] and that the young people of the Assemblies of God were rock and roll fans[64] – even though Davies and Greenway of the Elim Pentecostal Churches described the blues as the expression 'of the covetous moans of a lost generation, unable to fill its vacuous soul with the toys that bring no true salvation',[65] and David Wilkerson called rock and roll 'the devil's heart-beat'.[66] In spite of protests against the cinema, many Pentecostals who are still at school go to the cinema either after or before Pentecostal young people's classes, a fact that for reasons beyond my comprehension seems to be unknown to Pentecostal pastors.

However, some have approved of the relaxation of rigorism. Philip J. Brewer writes to a girl who has been called 'Jezebel' because she uses make-up:

> You may think that your face needs the help of cosmetics. It would be rude of me to agree with you! . . . The Crusader motto 'Our best for God', must apply to personal appearance and attraction as well as other things. Please always look your best – but make sure it is for God.[67]

A number of independent Pentecostal churches in Africa maintain, in spite of the teaching of European missionaries, 'African marriage', that is, polygamy. The North American Negro church, the Pentecostal Assemblies of the World,[68] declares: 'Whatever adventures a person may have had before marriage' they are nothing to do with how he is judged by the church. The Pentecostal Assemblies of the World refuse to force the separation of divorced and remarried couples who have been converted because of their irregular union.[69]

Here again we must pay special attention to Donald Gee. The value of his ethical writings can hardly be overestimated, although unfortunately they are almost unknown in Pentecostal circles. His healthy outlook upon sexual ethics and family planning is too often ignored in the Pentecostal movement. He mocks Pentecostal couples who pray for liberation from 'God-given desires':[70] 'Rather pray for commonsense.' We cannot simply transfer the sociological circumstances of the ancient East into our own society:[71]

> It is much more Christian to bring planned, wanted, loved children into a happy home lovingly prepared for them, than produce a string of children, so-called God-sent, that spend most of their time at clinics and hospitals trying to find the health that their poor wretched mother has been unable to give them.[72]

On the other hand, these concessions in their turn provoke protests from the newer Pentecostal churches:

> The women of the United Pentecostal Church practically stand alone today, as church after church falls into the peril of the painted face.[73]

The relaxation of rigorism,[74] which can be observed in most of the larger Pentecostal denominations, is the reason why every twenty years, at the most, a new Pentecostal denomination has to be formed. The older churches become more reasonable, abandon taboos and enthusiastic practices. Soon a handful of disappointed members forms into a church which can once again return to the primitive gospel, this time, and they suppose, for good, only to be subjected in their turn, after a generation, to the same process of transformation into an organized church under the same sociological pressures. Thus at the present day the Latter Rain movement reproaches other Pentecostals:

> Why is it that so many sisters paint themselves and curl their hair? Who are they awaiting? With hair all made up, there are far too many Jezebels looking through windows today (II Kings 9.30) . . . Far too many vain peacocks who cannot possibly kneel down when they pray, for the god of Fashion has seen to it that their dresses are far too short to allow them to kneel.[75]

One may well ask whether the excessive pressure imposed by numerous restrictions is not partly responsible for the failure of Pentecostals in their struggle, and whether a less restrictive morality (for example, the official lifting of the ban on the cinema and dancing) might not resolve some of the difficulties that prevent a moral effort in other directions.

The Protestant Church is aware that it has no right to confuse gospel ethics with the respecting of taboos, but that on the other hand it is expected to provide *practical* help in ethical matters. Within the sphere of marriage ethics I would like to draw the attention of Pentecostals to an attempt to give counsel based not on legalism, but on human sympathy, which because of its roots in the Bible and its open attitude towards present day problems offers real assistance.[76] The World Council of Churches, in its Fourth Full Assembly at Uppsala in 1968, dealt in Section VI with questions of personal ethics, under the title: 'The Search for a New Style of Life'. This deals with questions of sexual morality, but also with new questions such as 'What does "sanctification" mean in a world in which two-thirds of the population are hungry?'[77]

6. *'The Crowning Day': the Origin and Function of Ethical Rigorism*

The tragedy of Pentecostal ethics is that it is only ever relaxed with a bad conscience, as a concession to the flesh, to worldly lust. This means that valuable suggestions are not developed, as for example, the very reasonable advice given by Robert Willenegger[78] and George Johnstone[79] to those about to be married. For example, Johnstone states that it is necessary for a married couple to take out life insurance – a certain sign that the Pentecostal Assemblies of Canada no longer await the imminent second coming of Jesus. It is very rarely that legalism is really overcome. This has happened in the Congregação Cristã do Brasil, which explicitly rejects Pentecostal rigorism, and in the Original Gospel Movement in Japan, which under Buddhist influence rejects American and European pharisaism.

If we look for the origins of Pentecostal ethics, we find on the one hand a constant basic pattern of ethical prescriptions, and on the other hand powerful influences from the national background of each particular group. But the belief is always held that these distinctive national features have been derived from the Bible. Thus a biblical basis is found for the passionate defence of Sunday by British Pentecostals, and also for the demand for archaic patriarchal rights for the father of the family in the Assemblee di Dio in Italy.

Amongst the regulations based on the social and national background of a particular church, one can find reasonable rules of good manners and practical advice for conduct. Thus the Congregação Cristã do Brasil lays down detailed regulations for gifts to the church, and specifies that the church may accept land as a gift only if it is going to build a church on it. Think of the landed property owned by the Catholic Church in Latin America![80] Regulations for conducting a well ordered members' meeting, such as are found in the statutes of the Church of God of the Mountain Assembly,[81] would not come amiss in many European Pentecostal assemblies, which regard such outward things as beneath them.

The International Pentecostal Assemblies lay down that letters (especially letters from headquarters) should be answered.[82] The rules which Prophet Wovenu makes about taking oaths are impressive, and their point can be seen against the African background.[83] It is impressed upon pastors of the Pilgrim Holiness Church that they have nothing to do except save souls. To this end they should read (not only in the Bible), write and pray. During prayer they should close their eyes. If they are travelling as evangelists, then as soon as they arrive at their host's house, they should withdraw for prayer. In the morning they should get up punctually, be punctual at meals and services, should not be fussy about their food, should eat only rarely in a restaurant, and keep their rooms tidy.[84]

The main concern in ethical questions is not seen to be that of living with one's fellow men in a bearable and human fashion. From the Pentecostal point of view more is at issue. What matters is not to lose eternal glory; to keep and guard the white garment, the sign of purity, and the ring, the sign of the love of God, for the coming marriage feast, 'the crowning day'.[85]

The function of ethics is to keep the believer on the narrow way which leads to heaven. For this reason there is even opposition to cremation. A whole life of sanctification should not be destroyed by a heathen cremation. As long as ethics has the function of preserving the white garment for the kingdom of heaven, the concern of Pentecostal ethics can never be for one's fellow man, but only for oneself: I must endeavour not to get my hands dirty, not to have any stain on the marriage garment, so that I may be ready when Jesus comes. To this extent it is also necessary to behave respectably towards my fellow men, otherwise my account in heaven is blotted. And so a Pentecostal is friendly and patient with his neighbours and business colleagues. Even more, he regards them as potential objects of evangelization. In his eyes they are candidates for hell. A Pentecostal's love for these candidates is genuine in so far as he seeks to save them from hell. Consequently, he does all he can to deliver them from the future anger of God. Everything is subordinated to this single aim, even the love of one's neighbour. The idea that a person might lie as a matter of moral responsibility (for example, during the persecution of Jews in Germany) is beyond him.[86] He is concerned not with saving earthly life – what do a few years more or less matter? – but with the 'interests of the kingdom of God', that is, that as many people as possible get to heaven.

One may compare to this ethical attitude that of Moses, who, in order to save his people, was willing to be blotted out of the book of life (Ex. 32.32; so too Paul: Rom. 9.3).

In recent years the German theologian and martyr, Dietrich Bonhoeffer, faced these questions in his own suffering. No theologian of the present day or of the past has more to offer to Pentecostals, particularly with regard to their special forms of religious practice and the problems that arise from them, than this devout thinker, who prayed and meditated on the Bible every day. He very soon recognized the falsehood of Nazism. He intervened on behalf of the Jews when Pentecostal journals were still full of enthusiasm about the Führer sent by God,[87] and many members of the German Evangelical movement had sided with Hitler.[88] By contrast to Wernher von Braun, whose belief in 'Jesus Christ as Saviour and Lord'[89] and in the 'last judgment'[90] did not prevent him from developing Hitler's murderous V1 and V2 rockets, Bonhoeffer was forced by his belief to pray for the defeat of the German armies. He called the attempt of the Oxford Group Movement to convert Hitler 'a ridiculous failure to understand what has been going on – it is *we* who are to be converted, not Hitler.'[91]

When the Lutheran Pastor Hitzer, now a Pentecostal pastor, criticized the practice of infant baptism, Bonhoeffer agreed with him 'in considering the existing custom as such to be hardly acceptable, and to be very largely a mockery of the sacrament'.[92] But he did not share Hitzer's hope that the church would be renewed by believer's baptism for adults. In Bonhoeffer's view, something more fundamental was needed. Above all, the church must stop blowing its own trumpet. It must learn to be silent until the gospel is sought once again and the precious content of its words once again becomes urgent.

> Bonhoeffer's desire for an 'arcane tact' and a possible silence is, of course, more than can reasonably be asked of a 'Church of the Word' that is continually speaking. But what he means is clearly that when the Gospel is preached the relationship between God's Word and his world is not an obvious thing and cannot be established artificially or by a trick. The invention of new words achieves nothing. This relationship is something Pentecostal. Banging on the recruiting drum destroys any Pentecostal beginnings. To force something on people is to abandon any hope of its really making a mark on them.[93]

When Bonhoeffer was arrested in April 1943, a manuscript was found on his desk which stated:

> The cross of atonement is the setting free for life before God in the midst of the godless world; it is the setting free for life in genuine worldliness.[94]

What does he mean by 'genuine worldliness'? It means to exist for the world, for others. In Bonhoeffer's actual situation it meant amongst other things to take the part of the Jews – including those amongst them who were not baptized. It meant to pray for the defeat of Germany. And it meant to take part in a plot to remove Hitler. In prison Bonhoeffer said

> that, as a pastor, it was his duty, not only to comfort the victims of the man who drove in a busy street like a maniac, but also to try to stop him.[95]

> To stop this madman 'the use of camouflage became a moral duty'.[96]

For the sake of his Christian responsibility Bonhoeffer decided to lie intelligently and consistently. The Dutch theologian Hans Hoekendijk had to make similar decisions.[97] It should be noted that Bonhoeffer made no compromises with the world (to use the language of Pentecostals). On the contrary, the ideology of lies by which Germany was bewitched had to be unmasked. But when it was a question of 'how to exist for others', the usual ethical principles turned out to be inadequate in extreme cases. Every Pentecostal pastor should be urgently pressed to read the biography of this man. In it he will find a devout witness to Jesus Christ, who in all seriousness exposed himself on our behalf to the problems that oppress us at the present day. Granted, Bonhoeffer's religious practice does not fit the Pentecostal stereotype. When he was imprisoned he could take a childish delight at the gift of a cigar from Karl Barth, and at the same time write his astounding *Letters and Papers from Prison*, which later became so famous.

As he lived, so he died. Ten years later the camp doctor recalled Bonhoeffer's execution. He described how Bonhoeffer prayed before his death.

> I was most deeply moved by the way this lovable man prayed, so devout and so certain that God heard his prayer. . . . In the almost fifty years that I worked as a doctor, I have hardly ever seen a man die so entirely submissive to the will of God.[98]

NOTES

1. *Declaration of Faith* compiled by A. S. McPherson for the International Church of the Four Square Gospel, n.d., art. 22.
2. G. Lindsay, *God's Master Key*.
3. All in *The Bridegroom's Messenger* 50/11, Aug 1962, pp. 3f.; 51/2, Nov. 1962, pp. 3f.
4. ChoG of the Mountain Assembly, *Minutes*, 1962, p. 14.
5. The Jesus Church, *Assembly Report*, 1952–53, p. 16; quoted by Moore, pp. 308f.
6. P Free Will Baptists, *Faith*, 1961, pp. 1ff., art. 17.
7. Johann Widmer, *Im Kampf* II, 2nd ed., 1949, pp. 177f.
8. *Elim Evangel* 14, 1933, p. 11.
9. A. W. Edsor, *Pattern* 24/1, Jan. 1963, p. 15.
10. Associated Brotherhood of Christians, *Articles*, n.d., pp. 6ff., art. 12.
11. Full Salvation Union, *Manual*, 1944; quoted by Moore, p. 302.
12. Karl Barth, *Church Dogmatics* III/4, §53/1, pp. 47–72.
13. *Verlorener Sonntag*, no. 22 of the series 'Kirche im Volk', ed. by Friedrich Karrenberg (whose father was a leading figure in the German Pentecostal movement) and Klaus von Bismarck.
14. Werner Reiser, Dieter Hanhart, Christian Gasser, Hans Wenger, *Industrielle Sonntagsarbeit*.
15. For the numerous examples of the refusal of military service in the Swedisch Pentecostal movement cf. B. Wirmark in W. J. Hollenweger (ed.), *Pfingstkirchen*, pp. 256–61.
16. L. Eisenlöffel, *Ein Feuer*, p. 116; cf. also, W. Sardaczuk, *Ich hatt' einen Kameraden*; a similar development can be observed in France, cf. *Viens et Vois* 35/2, Feb. 1967, p. 24; *ibid.* 36/1, Jan. 1968, p. 21; R. Copin, *Viens et Vois* 36/2, Feb. 1968, p. 11.
17. E. S. Williams, *PE* 1362, 15.6.1940, p. 4.
18. J. R. Flower, *PE* 1518, 12.6.1943, pp. 6f.
19. J. R. Flower, *PE* 1521, 3.7.1943, pp. 2f.
20. E. S. Williams, *PE* 2440, 12.2.1961, p. 11. In 1966 the 'current spirit of disobedience' was 'deplored', *PE* 2708, 3.4.1966, p. 11.

21. *PE* 2385, 24.1.1960, p. 4.
22. R. Ruff, *VdV* 28/11, Nov. 1935, p. 19.
23. M. Harper, *As at the Beginning*, p. 46.
24. J. McWhirter, *Bible and War*.
25. D. Gee, *Redemption Tidings*; *PE* 1356, 4.5.1940, p. 4.
26. *Pfingstgrüsse* 7/28, 11.4.1915, p. 217; cf. ch. 17.1(*c*), pp. 232ff.
27. M. Jarvis, *Redemption Tidings* 43/5, 3.2.1967, p. 3.
28. *MD* 22, 1959, p. 68.
29. *Risveglio P* 8/11, Nov. 1953, pp. 2, 8 (cf. Appendix: 9); R. Bracco, *Il battesimo*, p. 15; Congregação Cristã do Brasil, *Estatutos*, 1946, art. 37, para. 11.
30. *MD* 24, 1961, pp. 182ff.
31. Associated Brotherhood of Christians, *Articles*, n.d., pp. 6ff., art. 15.
32. Iglesia Misionera de Cristo (02b.08.050a).
33. L. Sumrall, *Worshippers of the Silver Screen*.
34. R. Riggs, *VdV* 55/11, Nov. 1962, pp. 1ff. On the other hand, the Church of God (Cleveland) regretted that a 'sex-laden' film by Ingmar Bergman received a prize, while 'King of Kings' took no award (L. Ward, *ChoGE* 51/42, 1.1.1962, pp. 4f.). On pornography, *PE* 2893, 19.10.1969, p. 11; on homosexuality etc. cf. the Working Fellowship of Christian Churches in: W. J. Hollenweger (ed.), *Pfingstkirchen*, pp. 357f.
35. J. Vetter, *VdV*, May 1936, p. 16.
36. Pentecostal Fire Baptized Holiness Church (02a.02.107b) (from Moore, pp. 238, 219); cf. also *Zeitschrift für Religionspsychologie* 1, 1907, pp. 230ff.
37. PAoW, *1963 Minute Book*, p. 25.
38. *MD* 26, 1963, p. 214.
39. *Declaration of Faith* compiled by A. S. McPherson for the International Church of the Four Square Gospel, n.d., art. 13.
40. PAoW, *1963 Minute Book*, p. 25.
41. *Die Wahrheit* 15/7, July 1962, pp. 1f.
42. R. Bracco, *Verità*, pp. 21, 23f.
43. Pilgrim Holiness Church, *Manual*, 1962, Section 30 (10).
44. E. Lüscher, *Weckruf* 25, 1961, p. 19.
45. C. Lemke, *Der Leuchter* 13/12, Dec. 1962, p. 5.
46. H. Müller, *Christus unser König*, May 1959, pp. 56ff.
47. P Free Will Baptists, *Faith*, 1961, art. 21; *ChoGE* 50/50, 15.2.1960, p. 13.
48. *ChoGE* 53/5, 1.4.1963, p. 14.
49. W. E. McAlister, *P Testimony*, Nov. 1960, p. 9.
50. E.g. Church of God, Inc. (Pulaski, Va.) (02a.02.071a). The biography of A. S. McPherson is particularly impressive in this respect (07.932.001).
51. Apostolic Church, *Principles*, 1937, 2nd ed. 1961, pp. 145f.
52. AdD, Dominican Republic, *Reglamento*, 1932, 1944 (02b.10.008b).
53. AdD, France, (05.09.003a, cc, n. 10).
54. 05.13.021a; 04.01.015b, ff.
55. F. H. Allen, *Redemption Hymnal* 1958, no. 439.
56. J. Franklin, *ChoGE* 53/12, 20.5.1963, pp. 11, 19.
57. Congregação Cristã do Brasil, *Estatutos*, 1946, art. 28.
59. P. Mink, *Maranatha* 15/4, 1960, pp. 476ff.
60. R. Bracco, *Verità*, pp. 47, 49.
61. *Tagesanzeiger*, Zürich, 13.3.1965, p. 14.
62. N. Brownell, *PE* 2741, 20.11.1966, p. 24.
63. E. S. Williams, *PE* 2449, 16.4.1961, p. 13.
64. E. S. Williams, *PE* 2448, 9.4.1961, p. 15.
65. J. H. Davies and H. W. Greenway, *Youth Challenge* 1, 1962, p. 25.

66. D. Wilkerson, *PE* 2357, 12.7.1959, pp. 4f.
67. P. J. Brewer, *Elim Evangel* 43/37, 15.9.1962, p. 586.
68. Cf. 02a.02.139.
69. PAoW, *Ministerial Records*, 1952, pp. 27f.; quoted in Moore, p. 249; PAoW, *1963 Minute Book*, p. 24.
70. Very occasionally sexual relations within marriage are condemned: E. Köpf, *Geistliches Leben.*
71. D. Gee, *Study Hour* 9, 1950, pp. 154ff. E. P. Paulk, *Neighbour*, pp. 210f., holds the same view.
72. D. Gee, *op. cit.*
73. T. F. Tenney, *P Herald* 38/3, March 1963, pp. 10, 12.
74. 02a.01.013a, dd, ff; 02a.02.115a, ff; 05.13.024b, gg; cf. above ch. 3.2(*c*), pp. 35ff.
75. M. Fraser, *Deplorable State of Pentecostal Movements.*
76. T. Bovet, *Love, Skill and Mystery*. Cf. also British Council of Churches, *Sex and Morality.*
77. WCC, *Drafts For Sections*, pp. 112–36; N. Goodall (ed.), *Uppsala Report*, pp. 86ff.
78. R. Willenegger, *Ich komme bald!* 15, 1957, pp. 129ff.
79. G. Johnstone, *P Testimony*, 44/1, Jan. 1963, pp. 28f.
80. Congregação Cristã do Brasil, *Estatutos*, 1946, art. 35.
81. ChoG of the Mountain Assembly, *Minutes*, 1962, pp. 3f.
82. International Pentecostal Assemblies, *Statement*, 1960, p. 3.
83. C. K. N. Wovenu, *Adzogbedede na Mawu*, p. 5.
84. Pilgrim Holiness Church, *Manual*, 1962, section 169 (4 and 5).
85. E. Nathan, *Redemption Hymnal*, 1958, no. 753.
86. C. M. Ward, *PE* 2840, 13.10.1968, p. 7.
87. See quotation above, ch. 17.1(*c*), p.
88. Cf. A. Boyens, *Kirchenkampf und Oekumene*; E. G. Rüppel, *Die Gemeinschaftsbewegung im Dritten Reich* (a very important documentation which shows the political blindness of many German Conservative Evangelicals during the Nazi regime); W. J. Hollenweger, *IDOC* [Transconfessional Documentation Center for Religious and Human Renewal, Rome and Geneva], North American Edition, 18.7.1970, pp. 61–8; *id.*, *Study Encounter* (WCC, Geneva) 6/1, 1970, pp. 16–25.
89. The shallowness of such faith was never discovered by the Assemblies of God (L. Shultz, *PE* 2720, 26.6.1966, p. 26).
90. W. von Braun: 'Where does the desire for ethical action come from? What makes us want to be ethical? I believe there are two forces which move us. One is belief in a last judgment, when every one of us has to account for what we did with God's great gift of life on the earth. The other is belief in an immortal soul. . . .' (*PE* 2712, 1.5.1966, p. 11). Cf. also *PE* 2882, 3.8.1969, p. 14 and W. M. Ward's booklet *Wernher von Braun: 'The Farther We Probe Into Space the Greater My Faith. . . .'*
91. E. Bethge, *Bonhoeffer*, p. 415; ET, p. 285.
92. E. Bethge, *ibid.*, p. 795; ET, p. 612.
93. *Ibid.*, p. 990; ET, p. 786.
94. *Ibid.*, p. 809; ET, p. 625.
95. *Ibid.*, p. 955; ET, p. 755.
96. *Ibid.*, p. 707; ET, p. 532.
97. Cf. W. J. Hollenweger, *Reformatio* 16/10, Oct. 1967, pp. 663ff.
98. E. Bethge, *op. cit.*, p. 1038; ET, p. 830.

29

'In these Last Days . . .': Eschatology

1. *'Mercy Drops': The Pattern of History*

A PENTECOSTAL pastor knows that he is the servant of the final age of revival, which has returned to the earth in the days before the end. The final phase of the history of the church will restore its earliest days, or even surpass them, for Jesus himself said: 'Truly, truly, I say to you, he who believes in me will also do the works that I do; and greater works than these will he do' (John 14.12). The early rain at Pentecost was followed by the long period of drought, of the wilderness, in which only a very few 'mercy drops'[1] fell upon mankind in its thirst. But now 'streams of grace are falling down', the 'showers of blessing', the latter rain has come. Consequently, the history of the church, apart from a few 'mercy drops', such as the Reformation, is of no importance. There is no time to bother with the past. What matters is the present. Even the history of the Pentecostal movement is little known.

> It seems to me to be an interesting thing to gather together all kinds of facts about the Pentecostal movement. But all the same it is more worthwhile to undergo the experience of Pentecost for oneself.

So wrote several of the Pentecostal pastors whom I asked for information.[2]

Of the Reformers, Luther is sometimes quoted, and it is believed by some that he too spoke in tongues and saw visions. As a German Pentecostal denomination sees it, the first breakthrough of grace came with Luther, the second with the German Evangelical movement, and the third in Röckle's 'Philadelphia movement'. The Apostolske Kerk i Danmark sees Luther as the Bible teacher who rediscovered the gospel of the atonement, understood as the experience of conversion, Wesley as the one who taught the church the truth about full sanctification, the Baptists as the source of the restored doctrine of baptism, and the Pentecostals as the discoverers of the baptism of the Spirit; while it was the Pentecostal movement of the 'apostolic type'[3] which restored to the church the 'ministries' (apostles, prophets, pastors, teachers, evangelists).[4] Doctorian's description of the 'conversion of Luther' as a Pentecostal experience of illumination is typical of the understanding of the Reformation amongst Pentecostals. Doctorian describes a conversation with a priest on the steps of St Peter's in Rome:

> The same moment I remembered about the great reformer, when he was going up the stairs kneeling; suddenly enlightened by the light of God's Word, he jumped down and shouted: 'The just shall live by faith.'[5]

This tiny trickle of grace, which began to flow from the time of the Reformation, has been blocked by the present-day Reformation Churches.

> Martin Luther said: 'As surely as Jesus Christ is the Son of God, even so the Pope of Rome is the devil incarnate.' But what has the Reformed,[6] Protestant Church turned into since Martin Luther's time? It has become the brother Church of Rome, and soon they will be ashamed of anyone like Martin Luther.[7]

Sometimes the Pentecostal movement is understood as the 'logical continuation of the Reformation', which is struggling 'to realize what the Bible represents as the ideal church'.[8] And therefore the Zulu leader of an independent Pentecostal church in South Africa can indulge in the gross exaggeration of justifying the founding of the two hundredth or three hundredth Pentecostal group with the words: 'We do as Luther did on October 31, 1517.'[9] Among certain groups of the African Pentecostals, the central theme of the Reformation is not merely overshadowed, but completely lost, as for example when 'the forgiveness of sins' is interpreted as 'to live respectably'; because for these Africans the concept of forgiveness is incomprehensible. 'Legalism is directly comprehensible to man.'[10] I agree with Dale Bruner who describes the theology of the Holiness and Pentecostal movements, and particularly their doctrine of two or, in some cases, three stages of salvation, as the precise opposite of what Luther intended. On the contrary, it was this Catholic view of salvation which was the very object of his theological attack.[11] But there are a number of notable exceptions, of theologians from the Pentecostal movement who come seriously to terms with the Reformation. These include Christian Krust,[12] Karl Ecke[13] and H. R. Gause.[14]

Against the background of this picture of history, the period before the rise of the Pentecostal movement is described as a dark, hopeless period.

> The Darwinian hypothesis of evolution had unsettled the convictions of some. Higher Criticism was undermining the faith of others. The Gospel of socialism appealed to still others more than the Gospel of the crucified Christ. The clouds of world war were hanging low, ready to burst in a thunderclap at Sarajevo. God's answer was the revival of the Pentecostal movement.[15]

In a theological dissertation a leader of the Pentecostal Holiness Church, Joseph E. Campbell, describes the contribution of his church as a struggle against free thought. In his account of German liberal theology he draws entirely on the second-hand accounts of inferior American fundamentalist literature. He makes German biblical scholarship, of which he is completely ignorant, and which he sees as closely linked with Darwin's theory of evolution, responsible for all the evil in the world, and especially for socialism[16] and the ecumenical movement.[17] And since this German biblical scholarship, partly in the form of the social gospel, is threatening to swamp America, in spite of Karl Barth's 'emphasis upon personal religion',[18] the Pentecostal Holiness Church has been called to be the guardian of biblical doctrine.

The increase in crime in Anglo-Saxon countries is imputed to 'Jesuit-inspired modernism that started in the German theological seminaries', a modernism which has 'the intention of destroying Protestant Biblical foundations'.[19]

2. '*When the Roll is Called up Yonder*': *The Imminent Expectation of the Second Coming*

The Pentecostal movement arose in an atmosphere of fervent expectation of the second coming of Jesus. 'The cry, "The bridegroom comes!" is extraordinarily powerful at the present day,' wrote Markus Hauser in 1903.[20] This imminent expectation is revealed in the titles of Pentecostal journals: 'The Bridal Call', 'The Last Trump', 'I come quickly', 'The Evening Light and Church of God Evangel', 'Maranatha', 'The Midnight Cry', 'The End-Time Messenger', 'The Bridegroom's Messenger'. As each denomination grows older, these titles for their journals tend to be abandoned. But in most churches – officially at least – the expectation of the second coming of Jesus still predominates:

> The consummation of God's plan of salvation will take place in the following stages:
> The rapture of the church.
> Great tribulation under the Antichrist.
> The return of Christ to redeem Israel and to set up the millennial kingdom of peace.
> The resurrection of the dead for the last judgment.
> The destruction and re-creation of heaven and earth, the new Jerusalem, God as all in all.[21]

Sometimes the details of the timetable for the final age are disputed. Will Jesus come before or after the tribulation? Will he come twice, once for the elect[22] and the second time to judge the unbelievers? Are there chosen persons who are carried up individually like Enoch, before the second coming of Jesus (this was believed, for example, of Aimee Semple McPherson). In the journal *Bantu-Klänge* there was an account by O. T. Swart of how he picked up a hitch-hiker. The hitch-hiker said to him, 'Friend, the coming of the Lord is nigh.'

Suddenly the stranger disappeared from the car as it drove along. 'Only two prints in the car showed clearly where his feet had rested.'[23] Hermann Zaiss gives a colourful description of the ascension to heaven of the faithful in a Mercedes 3000.[24] Zaiss's followers believed that he had been taken up to heaven during a car accident. There was in fact a human failure on the part of his secretary, who drove too fast across a building site.

Gerhard Klemm, in a sermon on Acts 1.8, describes how he himself – following I Cor. 15 and I Thess. 4 – sees the rapture of the church:

> I have heard of an impressive drama of nature in Norway. Thousands of migrating birds gather along the banks of the fjord. On a certain day they all fly up and with a cry of triumph they begin their journey to the south. But the sick and weak birds do not dare to fly with them. These who have remained behind begin a heart-breaking crying and complaining . . . Only winter and death is in store for them. For us Christians too, the day will come, of which the Bible says that the trumpets of God will sound and we shall be lifted up the Lord Jesus Christ in the clouds in the air. Will you be there?[25]

Nothing shows how the life of Pentecostals is set upon the world to come as clearly as their hymns. Unceasingly they sing of the day of death, when it will be seen that they have not believed and fought in vain, the day in which the derision of those who mock them will be changed into an embarrassed silence. To a boogie-woogie tune Jimmie Davis sings of the 'Sunset of Life', when all earthly hopes will fade and Jesus will take the child of God by the hand and lead him through the cold river of death.[26] I have heard Einar Ekberg, formerly a baritone at the Stockholm theatre, singing in London's most modern theatre, before an audience listening with bated breath: 'I am a pilgrim, I am a stranger', but I am on the way to my home above.[27] Before praying with the sick woman whose healing is described above, A. A. Allen sings of the heavenly city of Jerusalem[28] and asks the obstinate sinners, constantly varying the questions: What will happen to you once the last prayer has been spoken, the last sermon given, the last hymn sung?[29] Mahalia Jackson takes up the same theme.[30] Presumably the author and performer of the above songs are expressing a genuine experience of their own. It seems that they look forward to death and greet it as redemption. These hymns are not quite so convincing when they are sung by young girls or boys[31] of the second or third generation. It is hard to believe that their life is directed towards death the same way.

Many 'signs of the time' are related to the expectation of the end of the world. Examples are the Common Market, the Labour Party victory in 1945,[32] the non-aggression pact between Russia and Germany,[33] the journal *New Christian*,[34] the growing power of Russia,[35] the growth of technology, the World Council of Churches as a sign of Antichrist, and in some cases the British Commonwealth (interpreted in terms of the British Israel theory, which asserts that the Anglo-Saxon people are descended from the ten lost tribes of Israel), the 'spirit of the air',[36] that is, the increase in air traffic, and the footnotes to the Zürich translation of the Bible.[37] In 1939 the *Pentecostal Evangel* actually asserted that Hitler would conquer Palestine together with the Arabs.[38] Bulgarian Pentecostals know from the Revelation of John[39] that they are living in the final age. They are therefore not afraid of going into public baths, stations and hospitals – where ministers of the official churches are not allowed access – to 'catch souls'.[40]

A closer link with the dead members of the church is expressed in the confessions of faith of the Russian, Polish[41] and Greek[42] Pentecostals – presumably taken over from Orthodox belief.

The fact that the attention and concern of Pentecostal believers is directed towards the event of Christ's second coming makes them indifferent to the political and social problems of the world. It works as a palliative which prevents them from despairing in the wretched circumstances in which they live. One can hardly deny them this consolation as long as their conditions of life are not improved. And so they sing:

When the trumpet of the Lord shall sound, and time shall be no more,
  And the morning breaks, eternal, bright and fair;
When the saved of earth shall gather over on the other shore,
  And the roll is called up yonder I'll be there.[43]

As social conditions improve the fervent expectation of the imminent second coming disappears. It is still taught in theory, but is no longer a matter of experience. Pension funds are set up for pastors, and building and training programmes which take years to complete are carried out. The *Elim Evangel* laughs at the hymns which express a longing for the world to come and writes: Nobody believes in them. We have all become worldly, even those amongst us who do not go to the cinema, for we have built up our own entertainment (i.e. film) industry.[44]

As the expectation of the second coming of Jesus declines in the older Pentecostal denominations, new Pentecostal churches, which once again stress the second coming, became necessary. The 'The King Comes' Brotherhood

> confesses the truth of Jesus, in the light of the onset of his coming kingdom, that 'the last' shall be 'the first'. It believes and prays fervently for the making up of the full numbers of the members of Christ from the nations. It believes that God is giving the promised latter rain, which is to fall upon all flesh, and which can bring about the regeneration and incorporation into the body of Christ even of the 'latecomers' amongst the members of Christ.[45]

Although Jeffreys believed that he could identify the crisis year 1932 as the very end of time,[46] in the older Pentecostal denominations at the present day insurance policies are taken out as a matter of course. The younger Pentecostal churches protest against this: a Christian 'does not go in for life insurance'.[47]

Heaven and hell are believed in in a literal sense. Hell is

a real place, not an imaginary place, and not simply a state or condition . . . the fire is literal and sinners will never have another chance to repent and accept the salvation which God has so wonderfully offered.[48]

After the re-awakening of their body the unbelievers will come into the pit of eternal, despairing pain.[49]

All those whose names are not found written in the Book of Life shall be cast into the Lake of Fire, burning with brimstone, which God hath prepared for the devil and his angels.[50]

Only the Quaker Pentecostals are not in agreement with this picture. According to the Full Salvation Union there are three different doctrines concerning the second coming of Christ:

belief in his bodily return to this earth
belief in his spiritual coming to each individual
belief in his second coming without specifying exactly what this means.

To insist that Christians believe exactly this or that concerning future events is a waste of time. Our spiritual welfare depends on historical facts and present realities, but not on future contingencies.[51]

In my view we are now paying for the high-handed suppression of the book of Revelation by the Reformers. What they suppressed is now producing subconscious repercussions in the traditional churches and amongst the Pentecostals. The Protestant Church is paying for its failure to provide fundamentalists and sectarians within and outside the established churches with any insight into exegetical work on the apocalytic passages in the New Testament. It is not enough to assert that the New Testament does not give a timetable for the final age. The book of Revelation should be applied, with the aid of the most modern exegetical methods, to the interpretation of that dimension of faith which is concerned with world history and cosmology.

The book of Revelation was written in a situation of persecution. Outwardly the church was a tiny sect with nothing to say to the world. That this church did not turn into a religion of the inner life, quietism, individual ethics, moralism, speculation about the origin of evil, and a longing for the spiritual world (as many religions of that time did) is due in part to the author of Revelation. This church could believe in heaven; it could adopt from the ideas of the time the conception of the city paved with gold and the gates of pearl, and draw comfort from the hope of the day when all tears will be wiped away, and death, disease and the devil will be conquered; it took over the conception of the millennium from the Apocalypse of Enoch, *without abandoning this world.*

The book of Revelation helped the church not to give up this world as an unsatisfactory first attempt on the part of God, as a first version full of mistakes, shortly to be followed by a second corrected edition. It did not regard the redemption through Christ as a fiasco. It was convinced that Christ would bring the history of mankind to the consummation he had established, with or without the consent of the authorities of Rome, and in the same way would guide the history of the church to its conclusion, with or without the co-operation of its members. This faith gave the church the power neither to despise nor to sacralize the world. With the eyes of faith it saw in this world the theatre where God's drama was being acted out, and did not exclude from this the arena where Christians were persecuted. In its confident prayer for the victory of the righteousness of God, it recognized the world as a creation which was not autonomous, and which had not fallen prey to demons.

At the present day we can take courage from the book of Revelation in two ways.

1. It can give us the courage to interpret the apocalyptic images which oppress the men of the present day as they did those of New Testament times. The author of Revelation took these images from his own time and his own environment. He made them comprehensible against the background of the act of God in Jesus Christ. Films, television and the modern theatre overwhelm us at the present day with apocalyptic images. Men who are called to bear witness by him whose 'eyes were like a flame of fire' (Rev. 1.14) can and must interpret these images.

2. It gives us the courage to testify that this world is proceeding towards the goal laid down by God. Nothing can change this. The question is whether at the consummation of the creation we will be present, looking on in wonderment, or whether it will take place against our will.

In recent years theologians have rediscovered the significance of eschatology. This rediscovery began with Albert Schweitzer's work on the New Testament. But it took effective form above all in the preaching and pastoral care of the two Blumhardts,[52] and the preaching of the Kingdom of God by Hermann Kutter and Leonhard Ragaz,[53] and was continued by Emil Brunner and Karl Barth. More recently Jürgen Moltmann has written his work *The Theology of Hope*, which takes as its starting point Karl Barth's famous statement: 'If Christianity be not altogether and unreservedly eschatology, there remains in it no relationship whatever to Christ.'[54] But Moltmann goes on to ask: 'Yet what is the meaning of eschatology here?'[55] This is the basic question for Moltmann, for as he sees it:

> The eschatological is not one element *of* Christianity, but it is the medium of Christian faith as such, the key in which everything in it is set, the glow that suffuses everything here in the dawn of an expected new day.[56]

Consequently the concept of the 'doctrine of the last things' (eschato-logy) is in Moltmann's view a false one.

> There can be no 'doctrine' of the last things, if by 'doctrine' we mean a collection of theses.[57]

In his search for this 'key in which everything is set' Moltmann studied the

Old Testament. The heathen of that period, the Babylonians and Canaanites, believed in gods who at the beginning had fixed the world as it is for all time. For these people there were 'no new horizons towards which a people could be led, no God who is on the way letting men see what they have never yet seen.'[58] By contrast with this, the God of Israel was a God of nomads, who were continually travelling, and who – as exemplified in the story of Abraham – were always setting out towards new horizons on the basis of God's promise.

But the promise was always greater than its fulfilment. This 'overplus of promise'[59] by contrast to history was the driving force behind the history of Israel.

> The overspill of promise means that [events] have always a provisional character. They contain the note of *provisio*, that is, they intimate and point forward to something which does not yet exist in its fullness in themselves.[60]

The horizon moves on ahead of the traveller, it is a 'boundary of expectation which moves along with us and invites us to press further ahead.'[61]

Moltmann now applies this Old Testament insight to the understanding of the church. Just as the Old Testament people of God was travelling towards the land where milk and honey flow, so the New Testament people of God is travelling towards the new earth and the new heaven.

> This hope makes the Christian Church a constant disturbance in human society, seeking as the latter does to stabilize itself into a 'continuing city'. It makes the Church the continual source of new impulses towards the realization of righteousness, freedom, and humanity here in the light of the promised future that is to come.[62]

Significantly, Moltmann does not limit the hope to the salvation of individual souls. It includes the world and society. According to Moltmann it is not possible to hope for a new heaven and a new earth and at the same time to abandon this world. 'Hope then fades away to the hope of the solitary soul in the prison of a petrified world.'[63] Someone who knows that God will wipe away all tears will not accept with resignation the tears of those who are tormented and tortured. Anyone who knows that there will be no more disease can already look forward to a provisional and symbolic conquest of the sickness of individuals and of society. And someone who knows that the enemy of man and God, the devil, will be conquered, will already perceive him in his machinations in the family and also in society. Either hope for this world which God created and loves, or no hope at all! Thus the Christian mission is not concerned with maintaining what exists in the world, but in transforming it to be like what is to come. This transformation of the world to be like what is to come brings in the social and political aspect of hope. It is in these areas in particular that there is a need for people who are not embittered by resignation and hardened by cynicism, for according to Moltmann resignation is only a particular sort of pride, which camouflages its despair by saying with a smile: *Bonjour tristesse!* Moltmann is not ready to follow the French writer Camus in 'thinking clearly and hoping no more', 'as if thinking could gain clarity without hope'.[64] On the contrary, 'positivistic realism proves to be illusory, so long as the world is not a fixed body of facts.'[65]

In his chapter on the relationship between the exposition of the Bible and mission, Moltmann takes up a primary concern of Pentecostals:

> The question as to the correct exposition of the Old and New Testament scriptures cannot be addressed to the 'heart of scripture'. The biblical scriptures are not a closed organism with a heart, or a closed circle with a centre. ... Thus if we are to understand the biblical scriptures ... we must look in the same direction as they themselves do.[66]

But the scripture looks forward to the second coming of Jesus and to the mission which precedes it and is related to it. Moses (Ex. 3.11), Jeremiah (Jer. 1.6), Isaiah (Isa. 6.5), and Paul (Acts 9) did not understand God's word, God's forgiveness, and God's future until they were taken by God into his service. Thus the so-called conversion of these men was identical with their calling, with their being taken into the service of God's mission. And 'missions perform their service today only when they infect men with hope.'[67] Thus to be converted and called means to live by a hope which goes beyond what is now present and at hand, and for that reason changes what is present.

A theologian who reads the simplification of Moltmann's thesis which I have been forced to make here may raise his eyebrows at it. To a Pentecostal pastor it will seem very complicated and difficult. But I would ask him for indulgence. It is worth his while to come to grips with this vision of the last things, because here he is being shown a vision of the last things which believes in heaven without betraying the earth, which hopes for the second coming of the Lord without giving up any part in the work of society, and which indeed draws inspiration and power from the hope of what is to come to change the present world in the light of the future.[68]

NOTES

1. Quoted from a hymn by J. McGranahan, *Redemption Hymnal* 1958, no. 245.
2. Quoted from B. Elling, Stadskanaal, Holland; letter to W.H. 17.7.1963.
3. E.g. the Apostolic Church; cf. ch. 13.4, pp. 191ff.
4. S. Beck, *Daaben*, p. 63.
5. S. Doctorian, *The Evangelist* 4/1, June 1964, p. 4.
6. The difference between 'Reformed' and 'Lutheran' is virtually unknown.
7. H. Lauster, *Die Wahrheit* 15/8, Aug. 1962, p. 4.
8. L. Eisenlöffel, *Der Leuchter* 10/1, Jan. 1959, pp. 4f.
9. Sundkler, p. 170.

10. K. Schlosser, letter to W.H., 3.3.1964, p. 7.
11. F. D. Bruner, *Doctrine* I, pp. 26ff.; II, p. 27, n. 61.
12. Krust II.
13. K. Ecke, *Der reformierende Protestantismus*; *Schwenkfeld*; *Pfingstbewegung*; *Sektierer*; K. Ecke and O. S. v. Bibra, *Reformation.*
14. H. R. Gause, *ChoGE* 51/33, 23.10.1961, pp. 8ff.
15. G. G. Kulbeck, *What God Hath Wrought*, p. 24.
16. J. E. Campbell, *PHCh*, p. 34.
17. *Ibid.*, p. 60.
18. Here Campbell is summarizing W. W. Sweet, *Story*, pp. 584–90; J. E. Campbell, *PHCh*, p. 29.
19. D. H. Macmillan, *Churchman's Magazine*; *Pattern* 20/11, Nov. 1959.
20. M. Hauser, *Komme*, p. 81.
21. Gemeinde für Urchristentum, *Wer wir sind*, p. 10.
22. J. Paul, *Pfinstgrüsse* 3/14, 1911, p. 111; cf. also Elim Missionary Assemblies (02a.02.121, esp. b,9).
23. O. T. Swart, *Bantu-Klänge*, June 1961, no. 93, p. 2.
24. *Fröhliche Nachrichten* 14, 15.2.1956.
25. G. Klemm, *Bald kommt der Herr*, Evangeliumsklänge A 51 L.
26. J. Davis, *Songs of Faith*, Decca DL 4220: 'My Lord Will Lead Me Home'.
27. Einar Ekberg, *Jag är en främling*, Hemmets Härold P 5055.
28. A. A. Allen, *Miracle Revival Service* (E), M-110; cf. above ch. 25.2(*c*), p. 366.
29. A. A. Allen, *What Then?* M-109.
30. Mahalia Jackson, *What Then?* Metronome, MEP 1099.
31. Cf. the longing for eternity expressed in the song 'Komm heim zum Abendmahl' (Come home to the Lord's Supper), Evangelisations-Team Königs-Quartett, BIEM 101; commentary, above, ch. 27.1, p. 387.
32. *PE* 1632, 18.8.1945, p. 8.
33. *PE* 1395, 1.2.1941, p. 10 (NB: a year and a half after it was signed!).
34. *PE* 2704, 6.3.1966, p. 10.
35. *PE* 1563, 22.4.1944, p. 16. But the fact that Finland became allied to Germany in its fight against Russia can best be attributed to spiritist influences (*PE* 1570, 10.6.1944, p. 16).
36. S. MacCennan, *VdV* 25/1, Jan. 1932, p. 9.
37. R. Ruff, *VdV* 6/1, 1.1.1914, pp. 8ff.
38. *PE* 1323, 16.9.1939, p. 9.
39. H. Popoff, *T'lkuvanie.*
40. *Tschernomorski Front*, quoted in *MD* 23, 1960, pp. 285f.
41. N. I. Pejsti (ed.), *Zasady*, ch. 4.
42. G. Krissilas, *Rundschreiben*, in modern Greek and German: 05.11.004a.
43. J. M. Black, *Redemption Hymnal* 1958, no. 763.
44. Squintus, *Elim Evangel* 43/37, 15.9.1962, p. 581.
45. Declaration of Faith of the Bruderschaft: Der König kommt! (The 'The King Comes!' Brotherhood).
46. *Elim Evangel* 12, 1931, p. 266; quoted by B. R. Wilson, *Social Aspects* I, p. 91.
47. P. Mink, *Ich bin der Herr*, pp. 32f.
48. C. L. Brasfield, Jr., *ChoGE* 51/48, 12.2.1962, p. 7.
49. N. I. Pejsti (ed.), *Zasady*, ch. 20.
50. PAoW, *1963 Minute Book*, pp. 9ff.
51. Full Salvation Union, *Manual*, 1944, p. 82; quoted in Moore, p. 302.
52. On Blumhardt cf. above, ch. 26, pp. 381ff.
53. On Ragaz, see *W. J. Hollenweger*, *Theologie* (ET in preparation).

54. K. Barth, *Römerbrief*, 2nd ed., 1922, p. 298; ET, *The Epistle to the Romans*, 1933, p. 314.
55. J. Moltmann, *Theology of Hope*, p. 39.
56. *Ibid.*, p. 16.
57. *Ibid.*, p. 17.
58. V. Maag, *Malkût Jhwh*, *Vetus Testamentum* Suppl. VII (Congress Volume, Oxford, 1959), 1960, p. 150, quoted by Moltmann, *op. cit.*, p. 101.
59. J. Moltmann, *op. cit.*, p. 106.
60. *Ibid.*, p. 108.
61. *Ibid.*, p. 125.
62. *Ibid.*, p. 22.
63. *Ibid.*, p. 69.
64. *Ibid.*, p. 24.
65. *Ibid.*, p. 25.
66. *Ibid.*, p. 283.
67. J. C. Hoekendijk, *Mission – heute*, p. 12.
68. Cf. also what Catholic Pentecostals have to say about eschatology (K. and D. Ranaghan, *Catholic Pentecostals*, p. 247).

30

Not an Organization but an Organism: Ecclesiology

1. *The 'Host Redeemed by the Blood': The Pentecostal Understanding of the Church*

THE Pentecostals are trying to return to the church of the New Testament, which they understand as the 'host redeemed by the blood', the 'church of the regenerate' and 'those guided by the Holy Spirit':

> So long as persons who are more or less consciously not born again are accepted into a church, it becomes a mere organization. Human religious organization is of its nature in conflict with the church of the living God. Outwardly it is always more powerful than the church; and therefore, time and again in the course of the years, it has persecuted the church.[1]

In the early publications of the Pentecostal movement there was a vigorous polemic against all 'human organizations which fight against holiness and resist the working of the Spirit'.[2] But after a very few years all the churches were forced to accept some form of organization. This process is in full swing at the present day. Thus for example the Free Will Baptists of the Pentecostal Faith disagree with the view of Armin Reichenbach quoted above, They state: 'The Church is an organized body of believers in Christ.'[3] The Jesus Church lists the three following marks of the true church of Jesus: (i) it bears his name; (ii) it has a biblical church constitution; (iii) it does not choose its pastors by majority vote.[4] But here the members of the Full Salvation Union disagree with most other Pentecostals: they regard every association which is led by the Spirit of God as belonging to the church, regardless of the name it bears. Yet the Full Salvation Union likewise regards majority votes in the church as wrong, because through them the church comes to rely on the groupings of church politics, instead of waiting for the guidance of the Spirit. On the other hand most American Pentecostals regard democratic votes as a primitive Christian feature. Most Pentecostals believe that 'the church is the totality of all members of the body'. But Pentecostals of the 'Apostolic' type go on to add that the church 'is guided by its heavenly Head through apostles, prophets, evangelists, pastors and teachers who are filled with the Spirit'.[5]

The view predominates that

> the church of Christ is a people set apart from the world which professes and maintains faithfulness to the Lord . . . It is composed of those who are born again through the Holy Spirit, whose names are written in heaven.
>
> Entry into it is by faith in Jesus Christ . . . by true repentance . . . by verbal confession of faith in Him.[6]

The accusation is made against the established churches:

> Murderers are venerated as saints (because they have served the church's purpose), church constitutions are held in high regard, confirmations and blessings are administered. They juggle with huge statistics of 'faithful', and everything is done to demonstrate the 'life' of the church.[7]
>
> . . . that there should 'also' be true children of God in the traditional churches is an unintentional irony. One might ask whether the church of Jesus does not consist only of the regenerate.[8]

There is no agreement about the control of doctrine by the church. Originally the Pentecostal movement hoped that its churches could be kept free from doctrinal disputes.

> We do not preach rigid dogmas, but the written word of God, and believe that God himself confirms it. We do not speak of a 'new faith' which one must accept to be saved, but of the divine person of Jesus Christ . . . We do not assert that 'salvation' is achieved by belonging solely to our church, but we do believe that it is the will of God in this last age of grace to gather together once again a living, hoping and serving church of Christians who have made a free commitment.[9]

But only a few years after the founding of the Pentecostal movement violent disputes broke out about baptism, the significance of speaking in tongues, visions, and present day apostles. In the older Pentecostal churches dogmatic conflicts and declarations of faith play an increasingly important role. The distinctive focal point of a denomination is no longer the Pentecostal *experience*, but Pentecostal doctrine; this has come about since the majority of members and quite a few pastors have no longer undergone the experience of baptism of the Spirit.

There is great diversity in church constitutions. Pentecostals who teach the three-stage way of salvation mostly have an episcopal church constitution, while many others have something between a congregationalist and a presbyterian constitution. In all Pentecostal denominations the rights of those who are not pastors are severely restricted. In most Pentecostal churches lay people are not represented in the highest governing body of the church. The Congregação Cristã do Brasil forms a exception here: apart from the treasurer it has no full-time officials. There was a controversy about church order which lasted for years between the Scandinavian and American Pentecostals. Reacting against the Lutheran state church, the Scandinavians advocated an extreme form of congregationalism. The Americans wanted to set up a denomination which was more centrally organized.

In general the view of Pentecostals is that 'the church of Jesus rejects . . . every state church.'[10] These contentious opponents of the establishment of the church must have been unaware that quite a few Pentecostal churches have a status similar to that of a state church.[11] The Norwegian Pentecostal movement receives a state subsidy worth £46,000[12] and the Australian Apostolic church finances its mission amongst the Australian aborigines with state subsidies.[13] This is true of most of the Pentecostal mission stations in former colonial areas. Homer A. Tomlinson, the son of one of the greatest pioneers of Pentecostalism, has called for the union of state and church in America.[14]

The relationship between various Pentecostal groups varies from country to country and from group to group. In general this difficult problem is avoided: 'In this conference no single problem was discussed, let alone resolved,' said A. van Polen at a conference of the Full Gospel Business Men's Fellowship International.[15] In many countries national committees are beginning to be formed, which are representative to a varying degree. It seems that the older denominations are growing weary of the permanent fragmentation of their movement and are trying to begin the task of organizing national Pentecostal denominations, an undertaking which meets with embittered resistance from the smaller, more recent and more enthusiastic groups.

This development has not yet progressed so far on the international level. C. Lemke regrets this fact, in the context of a false announcement that the Pope's nephew had joined a Pentecostal assembly. When the Vatican denied this, *Der Leuchter*, which together with many other Pentecostal and non-Pentecostal journals had printed the report,[16] published a correction, but added to the denial a general exhortation

> to the responsible persons in our world-wide Pentecostal movement . . . to co-operate rather more. Is there not a Pentecostal church in Rome where one could have checked up? . . . The committee of the World Pentecostal Conference should have been more effectively in evidence here . . . There is no need immediately to raise the bogey of uniformity and a super-church when this is pointed out.[17]

Here Lemke is touching on a fundamental problem, An international Pentecostal information office, as an organ of the World Pentecostal Conference, could only work satisfactorily with a full-time secretariat. But this secretariat would either have to be financed by one group within the Pentecostal movement (which would then presumably dominate the other groups, as is already happening at the present day with the headquarters of the Assemblies of God in Springfield, Missouri), or else it would have to be financed by all the Pentecostal groups, a measure which would lead to all the structural and organizational problems which face the world federations of individual denominations and the World Council of Churches.

So far the World Pentecostal Conferences have no body which functions satisfactorily between the conferences. It could not even pay the travelling expenses for the committee of the World Pentecostal Conference. In spite of this some of the World Pentecostal Conferences have drawn the world Pentecostal movement closer together.[18] In North America there exists the Pentecostal Fellowship of North America, which functions satisfactorily. In Europe there are two competing Pentecostal regional alliances, while in other countries there are national federations of Pentecostal denominations (Great Britain, Switzerland).

In concluding this summary I think it is important to do as I have in the previous chapters, and give a brief outline of the understanding of the church as it is seen by New Testament scholarship. Anyone familiar with ecumenical discussion knows that this is the most difficult theological question between the churches. Since the ecumenical movement was founded, there have been those within it who have advocated the Pentecostal understanding of the church![19] But New Testament study shows that that New Testament presents different understandings of the church. We have on the one hand the Johannine type of church, in which the sacraments play a subordinate part – or are they even eliminated in the Johannine Epistles? – where the account of the institution of the Eucharist is replaced by the narrative of the washing of feet, and which shows an aversion to hierarchical structures and a preference for informal groups. But there is also the idea of the church found in the pastoral epistles, with the beginnings of a structured church ministry. And one must also remember that Paul interprets both ministry and charisma strictly in terms of their functions. These different understandings of the church, each of which is due to the situation in which it arose, are well described by Eduard Schweizer in his book *Church Order in the New Testament*. It is really incomprehensible that a work which takes as its theme one of the main concerns of Pentecostalism, the question 'What is the New Testament church?' should not be made obligatory reading for every Pentecostal pastor and every student in Pentecostal Bible schools.

Other scholars, like Adolf Martin Ritter[20] and Colin Williams[21] have made further investigations into the ecclesiological pluralism of the New Testament. Ritter agrees with Ernst Käsemann and in the New Testament we find

> our own situation in microcosm . . . at best an ancient ecumenical confederation without an Ecumenical Council. The tensions between [the different writers and traditions of the New Testament] are as great as those of our own day. One-sided emphases, fossilized attitudes, fabrications and contradictions,

> opposites in doctrine, organization and devotional practice are to be found in the ecclesiology of the New Testament no less than among ourselves. To recognize this is even a great comfort and, so far as ecumenical work today is concerned, a theological gain. For, in so doing, we come to see that our own history is one with that of primitive Christianity.[22]

If Jesus has founded something like a church, this church was certainly very different from anything we consider today to be a church.

> There is no sign to distinguish those who gather round Jesus from the other Israelites – neither a rite such as the baptism of John, nor a set creed such as that daily recited by faithful Israel, 'Hear, O Israel . . .' (Deut. 6.4), nor a given place of assembly like the monastery at Qumran by the Dead Sea, nor a common rule such as the *Manual of Discipline*. Jesus gives his disciples no special name and no special rite (Mark 2.18). There is nothing to distinguish his group of disciples from other people except the fact that they have been reached by his word, and that . . . they are . . . prepared to go under for other people (Mark 8.34f.; John 12.25f.).[23]

The church can therefore be considered as being the outcome of the work of Jesus, but *not his foundation*, the circle of his disciples being open, with everybody being a minister and where there is no distinction 'between ordinary believers and those called to service',[24] a concept which was accepted in the early Pentecostal denominations.

These are well-known results of New Testament scholarship, although they are consistently disregarded by many systematic theologians, by most ecumenical conferences and by almost all church bureaucrats. Ritter asks rightly whether Jesus was not asking too much from his disciples, in failing to integrate them in a fixed order. After all they were no longer at home in the Jewish tradition, they had lost the Jewish place of worship, the Jewish law, priesthood and sacrifice. Jesus did not replace these things. He abolished them! Anyone experienced in ecumenical dialogue knows the arguments which can be advanced here for a safe 'both and'. But the extreme position in this instance is not taken by a youth delegate or some way-out theologian, but by Jesus himself. Never mind, one can still ask: Did not Jesus expect from his disciples a measure of idealism which was unrealistic? On Good Friday the whole world, not excluding Jesus's disciples, answered 'Yes' to this question, and thus – openly or secretly – declared him to be guilty.

> But Jesus deliberately and publicly took that very way. He did everything to attain no success, no growth and no fortifying of the Church, but to allow himself and his followers to be broken in pieces – for the world.[25]

Yet God did not allow the cause of Jesus to end with his death. It was this act of God, the resurrection, which made the church possible. Ritter examines the different ecclesiological positions in the New Testament. He compares particularly the Pauline with the post-Pauline and Lucan ecclesiology. The central term for Paul's understanding of the church is *charisma*, which for Paul is not something supernatural. All Christians are – according to Paul – charismatic, or they are not Christians at all. To everyone the Holy Spirit has been visibly given, the goal of this doctrine of charisma, or – as Käsemann says – the transformation of the *sola gratia* into the level of ecclesiology – being the coming of age of the congregation. The sole purpose of any church order is 'to make room for the Spirit to carry out his work of edifying the Church with as little hindrance as possible'.[26]

It seems clear from this that Käsemann, Ritter and Schweizer are theologians of the first importance for Pentecostalism. One could safely say that they have contributed more to a Pentecostal ecclesiology than the fundamentalists.

2. *Greater and Lesser Babylon: Relationships with Established and Free Churches*

For Harold Horton the church of Christ is neither 'a Lecture Course, a Social Rendezvous' nor 'a Conservatory of Aesthetics. The Church of Christ is a deliverer from human woe and sin and disease and despair, from Satan and Hell.' And nothing of it is to be found 'inside the organized churches'.

> Revival is *outside* the churches today – and will be till Jesus comes. Revival is in Pentecost – not in the gorgeous temples where the ritual of Pentecost is travestied still, but in the back street upper rooms where the power of the Spirit of God is mightily distributed in soul-satisfying Spiritual Gifts and outpourings.

It has been outside ever since the day of Pentecost. 'Pentecost means the triumph of the inexpert, the unprofessional, the non-ecclesiastical.' Naturally the churches try to imitate Pentecost.

> You must have something. If you have not got the authentic Glory in Light and Cloud and Unction, it must be simulated with tallow candles and stinking incense smoke. [But] Pentecost is not parade but Power. Not show-off but Revelation. Not incense but Unction. Not side-shows but Salvation.[27]

This excludes any possibility of co-operation between the Pentecostal movement and the historic churches:

> First, Pentecost does not consort with Bible criticism and ritualism and worldliness. Second, the churches do not wish for the introduction of power that would sweep them clean of every vanity they cherish. It has been tried again and again. There is not a single church or denomination as such that has received Pentecost. Pentecost remains despised and rejected but all-glorious and vital 'without the camp'. Every individual Christian who receives his miracle-Pentecost goes ablaze with love and zeal and heavenly astonishment carrying his glowing brazier with him into his cold and dead church. Everyone without exception, if he presses his flaming good tidings, is evicted. The Upper

Room[28] is despised, and even persecuted, by the Temple still as in the Acts of the Apostles. But it is the Upper Room and not the Temple that has the power of Pentecost.[29]

The early years of a new Pentecostal denomination are characterized by a rejection of the 'greater and lesser Babylon',[30] that is, the established churches and the free churches. When the law of religious freedom was passed in Finland in 1923, the Finnish Pentecostal Movement breathed a sigh of relief, 'because the faithful will now leave Babylon and can freely join the new Jerusalem.'[31]

> Out of Babylon! . . . Are you afraid of outward things? Do you love the church with all its inadequacies and human doctrines so much that you will not leave it, to gain the freedom of the gospel of Jesus?[32]

The Assemblies of God rejoice because

> God has brought us out of old, dead ecclesiasticism and denominationalism. He has made us a free people and we are not going back into 'Babylon' any more.[33]

In 1910 the Swiss Pentecostal Mission also made an appeal

> to leave the whore church of Babylon. The knell of the previous system of Christianity has been sounded and thousands are following the Lamb out of the camp, bearing his shame.[34]

In 1927 Lewi Pethrus justified the Pentecostals for remaining outside the Alliance.

> Drive rationalism out of yourselves, cleanse your pastors' training colleges of teachers who practise the disparaging criticism of the Bible, drive anti-Christian rationalism away from you and break off your links with whoredom.[35]

In the course of time these aggressive attacks have been replaced by a condescending acknowledgement of the existence of good-will within the churches. But their services offer too little to Pentecostals. Their spiritual hunger is appeased in the assemblies of the Pentecostal movements. There they receive true bread. Co-operation with the traditional churches would only be possible if these churches renounced infant baptism and introduced a New Testament church order on the pattern of I Cor. 12–14 (thus the Swiss Free Christian Church).[36]

In many Pentecostal denominations aggressive attacks, and also the attitude of the Free Christian Church, described above, have been abandoned. An equivocal attitude has been taken up towards the Reformation churches. On the one hand, Pentecostals would be glad to enjoy their recognition and attention, and to be able to hold weddings, burials and larger Pentecostal conferences in their churches.

On the other hand, the existing churches are rejected because of their unbelieving pastors and their contempt for the gifts of the Spirit. But there are frequently sporadic personal contacts. When ministers from the historic churches get to know a Pentecostal pastor personally, they are surprised not to find in him the bigoted sectarian they expected. Pentecostals in their turn are surprised at the interest and understanding which the minister shows for the distinctive forms of religious expression of the Pentecostals, and do not hesitate to regard such ministers as 'believers' because of their friendliness. These ministers can scarcely imagine what it means for a Pentecostal pastor to be taken seriously by one of the clergy of the great church which threatens and condemns him. But these contacts should not, as constantly happens, remain on the level of friendly personal relationships. A minister's love of his neighbour should lead him, after personal trust has been established, to enter into theological dialogue, discussing for example the doctrines of inspiration and baptism, or the division of reality into the sphere of the natural and supernatural. He will find to his surprise that the Pentecostal pastor is capable of stating in simplified and rationalizing terms what the minister himself is aware of in an unspoken form in his church and in his own life. One reason why many ministers avoid this kind of dialogue may be the fear that the Pentecostal pastor may dig up conceptions buried in the minister's own thinking, which he has not overcome but merely suppressed. That Pentecostal 'theology' lumps together these submerged ideas in an inadequate fundamentalist frame of reference is not the question. A genuine dialogue, of value both to the Pentecostal pastor and the established church minister, should be possible as long as questions which are psychologically and philosophically relevant are not excluded.

Even today one still sometimes finds in Pentecostal publications massive attacks on the established churches. Admittedly one hardly ever finds nowadays Pentecostals who will defend the view that as a member of an established church one cannot be saved.[37] E. N. O. Kulbeck of the Pentecostal Assemblies of Canada concedes that a large part of the mistrust of Canadian fundamentalists for the United Church is the product of misunderstandings.[38] J. D. Bright of the Church of God (Cleveland) regards the recognition that 'our denomination is part of the body of Christ, the church, but not to the exclusion of other consistent Christian denominations' as one of the 'most important steps in the Church of God (Cleveland).'[39] But it is hard for Pentecostals to accept the historic church as the church if its members do not seem to take seriously the normative document of the normative primitive church,[40] the Acts of the Apostles.

The fear which Pentecostals have of the superiority shown by ministers with an academic education, and of the state-financed church apparatus,[41] is ventilated in aggressive outbursts:

> Jesus chose simple fishermen, who were to carry his gospel into all the world. He said nothing about great church buildings, or that they were necessary for the proclamation of his word.[42]

The ministers of the established churches are always finding that the Pentecostal pastors are poaching on their preserves. If the Pentecostal pastor is to be faithful to his vision, he must win men for Christ. But he can only do this if he has a stock of faithful fellow workers and financial supporters. But these he has to entice away from the established churches, which in its turn provokes the displeasure of the ministers. The Pentecostal pastors do not understand this displeasure, for the minister has a parish of two thousand to four thousand souls. Why does he grudge the Pentecostal pastor another half dozen to add to his twenty-five or thirty people? Of course the Pentecostal pastor would give other reasons for his work of recruitment:

> It is not always that the 'sheep' are 'stolen'. Very often we fear they have been starved and have sought and found more satisfying pasture on their own initiative [in the Pentecostal Assembly].[43]

Attendance at non-Pentecostal services is usually discouraged:

> The people of God have no need to attend services in other churches, whose faith is different from ours and whose doctrine is not entirely apostolic.[44]

The many ministers of established churches who have either played a leading part in the Pentecostal movement while remaining ministers of the established churches,[45] or who have left the service of an established church to become Pentecostal pastors[46] must be regarded as mediators between the Pentecostal movement and the established churches in Europe. Similarly there are a large number of ministers of traditional churches outside Europe who as ministers of their church have supported Pentecostal doctrines and practices[47] or who have left the ministry of traditional churches to become Pentecostal pastors.[48]

A genuine dialogue between the Pentecostal movement and the established church has taken place in Holland. One example of this is that the best account of the Dutch Pentecostal movement has been written by a Dutch Reformed Church minister, G. A. Wumkes.[49] It is brief and uses reliable sources. Wumkes makes a critical but sympathetic assessment of the Pentecostal movement, and heads his work with a quotation from T. Achelis: 'Ecstasy is really becoming a powerful social ferment.'[50] In various cities in Holland members of the Reformed churches and Pentecostals have held joint services.[51] At the institution of Pastor Verhoef a Pentecostal pastor joined in the laying on of hands. In the series *Oekumenische Leergang*, F. Boervinkel includes a good account of the Dutch Pentecostal movement and its present-day position. He accepts the aims of Pentecostalism and considers that living gifts of the Spirit are necessary in modern church services, by contrast to the usual view that the gifts described in I Cor. 12 and 14 were only given for the age of the apostles. He naturally disagrees with the Pentecostal teaching that only someone who speaks in tongues has received the baptism of the Spirit,

> but unless it is filled with the Spirit in this way the word of the church is only a humanist word of men. Although this is better than nothing, it can be found elsewhere. Only when it is brought to life by the Holy Spirit can this word become a power which renews, a fire that warms and a means to break through the iron and other curtains.[52]

But the decisive publication in the dialogue with the Dutch Pentecostal movement was the Pastoral Letter of the Reformed (*Hervormde*) Church. After a concentrated and accurate description of the Dutch Pentecostal movement, and a critical but sympathetic assessment of it, it continues:

> The first thing that the church has to say about the message of the Pentecostal groups should not consist of blame or criticism, but of the shameful recognition that a movement such as the Pentecostal groups can come into being, because in the church there was so little 'demonstration of the Spirit and power' (I Cor. 2.4), which is why the power of the Kingdom cannot be sufficiently revealed in this world.[53]

In spite of this, the Reformed Church resists the theory of the Pentecostals that the descriptions of baptisms of the Spirit in the Acts of the Apostles should be regarded as binding directions for the reception of the Holy Spirit by present-day Christians. But it does not reject on principle the significance of speaking in tongues for us at the present day.[54]

In their reply the Pentecostal groups thank them for the Pastoral Letter, which they regard not as a 'pointing finger' but as an 'outstretched hand'. 'As a brotherhood we are glad to be able to give a positive answer to a positive letter.'[55]

> The Brotherhood of Pentecostal Churches in the Netherlands takes note with gratefulness and joy of the Pastoral Letter of the General Synod of the Netherlands Reformed Church . . . with gratefulness for the way in which the Synod has described the message of the Pentecostal churches and with joy at the profound study it has made of it. The Brotherhood regards it as very important that both members of the Reformed Church and also the members of the Pentecostal churches should take note of the Pastoral Letter. They would regard it as unsatisfactory if the latter took note only of the answer without studying the questions raised in the Pastoral Letter. In the dialogue between the church and the Pentecostal movement the Brotherhood regards this Pastoral Letter as a great help. The aim of the Pentecostal churches certainly is not to form separate groups alongside the existing churches, but to spread the Pentecostal message in all churches and circles.[56]

Further on, minor corrections are made to the description given in the Pastoral Letter. The Pentecostals point out that the gifts of the Spirit did not cease with Montanus, but that Eusebius still reports their presence. They once again formally affirm that they believe in the Bible as the inspired Word of God, that in the Pentecostal movement the Word is recognized as the highest revealed truth by which the prophetic words of the gifts of the Spirit must be judged and that there can therefore be no disagreement with the church on this matter.

Where Pentecostals disagree with the Pastoral Letter is in believing that the Acts of the Apostles provides a norm for present-day Christians, and that consequently it is necessary for regeneration to be followed by a special baptism of the Spirit.[57] They admit that the New Testament contains no explicit teaching about the baptism of the Spirit, but believe that in this case one should be guided by the experiences of the apostles and the early church, which provide our pattern.[58] The answer of the Pentecostal group describes as fanaticism the view that in the established churches one cannot be saved, and it opposes this view in the isolated cases where it is held.[59] It thankfully acknowledges the work done by the established churches in the sphere of the translation and exposition of the Bible. With regard to the World Council of Churches, the Pentecostal movement feels obliged to adopt an attitude of caution, because the World Council of Churches contains people who deny the fundamental truths of Scripture, that is, the divinity of Christ and the virgin birth.

As far as the question of emotionalism is concerned, the Pentecostals believe that it is far better to show enthusiasm for things of God than for valueless rubbish, but that for the churches to ascribe to the Holy Spirit creations of the human spirit in the cultural sphere is certainly not in accordance with Scripture. For this would mean that people who were not born again possessed the Holy Spirit. 'The natural and the spiritual are distinguished in the Bible.'[60]

The only reaction known to me on the part of the Reformed church to the 'answer' of the Pentecostals appeared in the journal *Vuur*.[61] The review in *Vuur* of the Pentecostals' reply was a friendly one, but it was observed that one must realize that

> The Brotherhood of Pentecostal churches does not represent the whole Dutch Pentecostal movement, but only the older tendency in it, and therefore adopts a more considered and balanced attitude.

The remarks about the cultural sphere are regarded by the journal as a 'theological spanner in the works'. The Pentecostals ought to adopt a more positive attitude to ecumenism. In spite of all the questionable elements in the Ecumenical movement – what more could one expect from two hundred churches, all subject to human frailty! – it is still true that the Holy Spirit is bringing about more unity through this instrument.

On the other hand, Hutten took a more critical view of the whole discussion.[62] In 1963 a book by the Reformed pastor D. G. Molenaar on this subject was published posthumously. The first, exegetical part is marked by an alarming ignorance of the New Testament study of the last thirty years. Thus Molenaar can make a fundamental distinction between the reception of the Spirit and regeneration, and agrees with the basic assertion of the Pentecostals: 'Baptism with the Holy Spirit is a "plus".'[63] More interesting, however, is his philosophical and psychological assessment of speaking in tongues, divine healing and prophecy. His aim, which, however, he does not achieve, is to remove the opposition between natural and supernatural. He discusses and takes further the views of Werner Gruehn (*Die Frömmigkeit der Gegenwart*) and H. C. Rümke's hypothesis ('unbelief is stunted growth'), and attempts to show that for certain persons para-psychological religious experience is a necessity. In particular, he points out that it is not only schizophrenics who experience visions, speaking in tongues and the like, but that at the present day, as in the Bible, it is both possible and necessary, within the framework of a theology and religious practice based on the Bible, to include and accept the possibilities for human life offered by these phenomena. But the examples he gives are somewhat arbitrary. He brings together William Branham and Blaise Pascal, Tommy Hicks and John Calvin, T. L. Osborn and Carl Hilty.

The dialogue produced a number of unexpected side-effects. Thus the ecumenical Pentecostal journal *Vuur* is able to describe pluralism amongst Christians and co-operation with non-Christians as necessities.[64]

And again, very unorthodox views have been put forward about relations with Eastern Europe. It has been suggested that people in Holland have forgotten that not only the Americans but the Russians too had contributed towards the liberation of Holland. A double standard was being applied. When the Russians marched into Czechoslovakia, cries of 'Murder!' went up, though ultimately they were only sticking to the Yalta agreement. But when the Americans did the same in Vietnam and South America, people did nothing.[65]

It would be a good thing if the dialogue which is being begun, and into which in the meanwhile the Catholic Church has also been drawn,[66] was taken further. It would show us the possibilities and limits of co-operation between Reformed Churches and Pentecostals in other countries. A good example has been set by the readiness to discuss issues objectively, although anyone familiar with the subject will realize that in spite of the objective tone of the Pentecostals they have not abandoned the basic fundamentals of the specifically Pentecostal principle of biblical interpretation. But the Dutch have found a way out of the polemics or meaningless politeness which are usual in other countries.[67]

A dialogue between Pentecostals and other churches on a broader basis has also begun in other countries, as for example in the USA between Pentecostals and Anglicans.[68] The General Assembly of the Lutheran World Federation in Evian (1970) was right to affirm that in many countries Pentecostals are 'members of either evangelical or national councils'. 'Regional consultation between Pentecostal and other church leaders have taken place in countries as different as Brazil and Rumania.' It is true that the Lutheran churches have long neglected the questions posed by Pentecostal brothers in the faith.

> The road toward fruitful dialogue seems to be strewn with unsurmountable obstacles. . . . [But] in recent years the ecumenical climate in the Pentecostal movement has changed decisively. Pentecostalism has come to be recognized as one of the most powerful Christian missionary forces in the world. Information about Pentecostal churches has been vastly increased through the

> publications of Catholic, Protestant and non-Christian scholars . . . Some academic circles have been especially receptive to the movement . . .
>
> We recognize that Pentecostalism is a vigorous part of the church universal, nourished on basic elements of Catholic faith; it is not just a marginal movement alongside the church . . .
>
> In preparation for a truly fruitful dialog, Lutherans should give special consideration to the question of dialog procedure. The prospect of a dialog with Pentecostalism offers the challenge of developing a method of theological reflection which is appropriate to both partners in the dialog. This means that we must be willing to think of a dialogic method which includes common experiences in worship and life.[69]

This means that the Lutherans are looking for a theological dialogue in which hymns, testimony and celebrations are regarded as of equal value with theological argument.

3. *The Great Whore Saved? Relationships with the Catholic Church*

Pentecostals agree with many fundamentalists – have they not learnt this from Luther? – in describing the Catholic Church as the great whore:

> She is called 'the great whore', which speaks of her impurity in doctrines and practices. Romanism professes to be the sole spotless Bride of Christ, but in reality she is 'the mother of harlots and abominations of the earth', for the kings of the earth have committed fornication with her, and the inhabitants of the earth have been made drunk with the wine of her fornication (Rev. 17. 1–6).[70]

When John F. Kennedy's election campaign was taking place attacks against the Catholic Church flared up once again both in the American Assemblies of God[71] and also in the Church of God (Cleveland).[72] That Reformation and Catholic Churches were entering into dialogue with one another is a scandal to most Pentecostals (although David J. Du Plessis was invited as an observer to the Vatican Council):

> Protestant pastors and representatives take part in Catholic festivals, attend the laying of the foundation stones of Catholic churches, and soon they will be joining in Corpus Christi processions.[73]

Sometimes there are criticisms of those Anglican priests who are sympathetic towards the Catholic Church: 'Yet these men take Protestant money and do the Pope's work.'[74]

> Rome is well-disposed towards Protestantism today, because she has need for Protestant bayonets and Anglo-Saxon nuclear deterrents to save her from being swallowed by the red tide of communism.[75]
>
> What disturbs us so much at the present day is that the Church of Rome has

begun a great campaign of reconquest. Blind leaders of the blind in the church of the Reformation are selling at give-away prices the basic biblical truths which God in his grace and mercy, through faithful instruments, has given back to mankind.[76]

Pentecostals are not misled by these attempts on the part of the Catholic Church 'to ingratiate itself'.[77] Jorge Buarque Lyra defended the Brazilian Pentecostal Pastor Manoel de Melo against the attacks of a Catholic priest:[78]

> Listen, reporter, . . . these people whom you call fanatics – now listen, church journalists – are people who cause no difficulties to the police, who do not pillage, steal and rob . . ., but who fight against crime and vice . . ., and co-operate with the police to achieve a healthy morality and a spiritual level in society. You should realize this, journalist, smelling of the priest's cassock . . . Dangerous fanaticism is when mobs stirred up by dishonourable Jesuits destroy Protestant churches . . . Fanaticism is when a wild crowd, dangerous to others and to itself, spends millions of cruzeiros in the capital of the Republic to give an image of the so-called Madonna of Capocabano a luxurious diamond-studded crown, while millions are dying of hunger and weakness on the hills round about the city . . . We are certain that the Virgin was saddened by these honours . . . What we call dangerous fanaticism is the ignorance of the word of God amongst our people, who kneel at the feet of priests who, as if it was not enough to steal their souls out of paradise, plunder their finances mercilessly in the mass and the confessional . . . They called our pastor Manoel de Melo 'wily' (*espertalhao*). Properly speaking, he is wily in God's work, and you are wily in the work of the evil one.[79]

This feud in the press led to a lawsuit which was won by Manoel de Melo, though this did not prevent de Melo from calling the Bishop of Recife, the apostle of the poor, Helder Câmara, the pattern of an evangelist.[80] Part of the protest quoted above can be explained from the persecution which the Latin American and Italian Pentecostal movement has had to suffer at the hands of the Catholic Church.[81] Particular warnings against the intolerance of the Catholic Church are given by former Catholic priests, of whom there are many amongst the Pentecostal pastors.[82]

On the other hand, some of the best and most accurate accounts of the Pentecostal movement have been written by Catholic priests. In recent years disciminating judgments on the part of Catholic observers have been on the increase[83] and in Rome David J. Du Plessis, as a Pentecostal observer at the Second Vatican Council, encountered more than polite astonishment. He tells of high Catholic dignitaries who begged him for the laying on of hands, that they might receive the baptism of the Spirit.[84] And already informal consultations are taking place between the Vatican and a number of leading Pentecostal pastors.

With the spread of Pentecostal practices in the Catholic Church[85] a severe blow was dealt to Pentecostal polemics against the Catholic Church. While

Pentecostal journals only occasionally report on the Pentecostal revival in the Catholic Church,[86] Pentecostals are well aware of it. There is occasional co-operation with Catholic priests, especially in the USA,[87] Chile,[88] Holland,[89] France.[90] In the summer of 1970 the leader of the Pentecostal *Chiesa Evangelica Internationale* in Italy (with two hundred churches), McTernan, visited the General Secretary of the World Council of Churches in Geneva and was introduced there by a Catholic priest (K. McDonell). The church has formally asked for membership in the World Council of Churches.[91] Pentecostals and Catholics are beginning to sing the same hymns, they read the same Bible, and they receive the same gifts of the Spirit.

One of the most important questions which preoccupies the Pentecostal movement in Latin America was put to me in almost every discussion: Will the World Council of Churches lead the Protestant Churches back under the rule of Rome?[92] I told the Pentecostals of the existing contacts between Rome and Geneva on the level of the exchange of observers, but stressed emphatically that the Catholic Church had hitherto made no application for membership of the World Council of Churches. But if this application should be made – which is not impossible – it will be all the more important that the Protestants of Latin America (that is, the Latin American Pentecostal movement) should take part in these discussions, regardless of whether these Pentecostal churches were members of the World Council of Churches or not.

4. *Antichrist: Relationships with the World Council of Churches*[93]

(*a*) *Two Chilean Pentecostal churches join the World Council of Churches*

In the 1950s the extreme American fundamentalist McIntire was agitating against the World Council of Churches. He spoke in the *Iglesia Pentecostal de Chile*, seeking to show that it was the intention of the World Council to lead the Protestant churches back into the Catholic Church. Anyone who conducts a campaign in these terms in South America can be certain of stirring up the most violent resistance against the ecumenical movement, for 'in Latin America Romanism is synonymous with paganism', in the words of E. Chávez, the leader of the *Iglesia Pentecostal de Chile* (1962) to G. Theyssen.[94] Chávez gives the following reasons for this violent reaction. One may perhaps understand it better, he says, when one realizes the situation.

> The Roman Catholic Church has bitterly persecuted Protestants wherever they have appeared. In Chile we have been stoned in the public street, we have been dismissed from our jobs solely because we were Protestants, and many times the sick have been refused help and harrassed in the hospitals by demands that they should be converted to the Catholic Church. In Colombia they closed the schools, killed the brethren and persecuted them in many ways on behalf of the Catholic Church . . . There are places such as Argentina, Paraguay, Peru and others where there is no religious freedom. This cam-

paign of persecution . . . provides sufficient reasons why the words of McIntire and his assistants sound out like the voice of a prophet, giving the alarm to the Protestant churches against the World Council of Churches, which they were making out to be a body which would lead them back along the fatal path to the hated Roman Catholic Church . . . McIntire did great damage in Chile, by dividing the Presbyterian Church (*Iglesia Presbiteriana*), which is one of the oldest in Chile, and which has worked in the country for more than a hundred years.[95]

Consequently when Theo Tschuy, a Swiss Methodist and Latin American secretary of the Division for Inter-Church Aid of the World Council of Churches, came to Chile, he was met with considerable mistrust. But it soon became clear that McIntire's prophecies were baseless, and instead Tschuy was welcomed by the Chilean Pentecostal movement as a 'good Samaritan'.[96] As a result Chávez travelled to the United States in order to learn more about the World Council of Churches. He became convinced of its honourable intentions, and proposed to his church that it should join the Ecumenical movement, which it unanimously resolved to do.[97] Thereupon Chávez travelled a second time to the United States, and called personally on Franklin Clark Fry to present to him his church's application. Fry almost fell off his chair when Chávez came into his office with this proposal, as he states in an exact account of this conversation.[98] The care with which the legal documents for this transaction were prepared[99] shows that the proposition had been given thorough consideration and accepted with a full knowledge of the consequences. Chávez felt a link of solidarity with the World Council of Churches and believed that 'it would keep its word', that is, that the Protestants of Latin America would not be handed over to a Catholic Church which persecutes them. 'But we, as members of the World Council of Churches, are doing what we can to combat this false impression.'[100]

Chávez's report on the third Full Assembly of the World Council of Churches, held in 1961 in New Delhi, is particularly interesting. The report reveals Chávez's respect for a body which is able to let even its most bitter opponents make their views heard. He was particularly astonished to find that in New Delhi McIntire had had access to the press rooms and 'spoke at great length'. He observed that for the Russian Orthodox, as for him, New Delhi was a new experience of the ecumenicity of the church, 'in contrast to all previous concepts'.[101]

The reaction of the Pentecostal press to the acceptance of both Chilean Pentecostal churches[102] into the World Council of Churches was one first of embarrassment and then of rejection.[103] An exception is the report of D. J. Du Plessis, who wrote that the two Chilean Pentecostal churches 'were both greeted on their acceptance with such applause that I felt that they were receiving the honour which was ready for the whole Pentecostal movement, if it too had joined'.[104]

But the other Pentecostal journals made light of the matter. The Chilean Pentecostal movement, which hitherto had been praised in Pentecostal literature as a shining example an autonomous national Pentecostal movement, was now suddenly treated as an insignificant group of outsiders, as though it had never taken part in the World Conferences of the Pentecostal movement.

It must be noted that the two Pentecostal churches are amongst the smaller Pentecostal churches in Chile. Nevertheless they are larger and more influential than the financially powerful North American Pentecostal missions in Chile, which have caused a great deal of disturbance in the country. As they have done in some European countries, the American Pentecostal denominations in Chile attempt either to set up their own mission churches or to bring existing Pentecostal denominations under their control. Sometimes there have been attempts to bring massive political pressure to bear.[105]

For some time tension has been evident between the Protestant churches of Chile (including the two Pentecostal churches). Of course sometimes this can happen even in less explosive situations. One of the reasons for this was the intervention of American Pentecostal churches with Enrique Chávez. Thus for example the Pentecostal Holiness Church joined the *Iglesia Pentecostal de Chile* because on the basis of information given by John Nichol, it believed that Chávez and his church 'were at the point of making a final break with the WCC. At a later time we were informed that this was not in your plan, and that your church was still fully participating as a member of the WCC.'[106] But because the Pentecostal Holiness Church believes 'that the WCC makes room for those who are known to be spokesmen for atheistic communism, that in various ways it encourages and promotes Marxism and revolution, the fact that it has so many, many people who are so liberal as to deny the fundamental truths of the Christian faith which are so precious to us, as well as many other reasons', the Pentecostal Holiness Church found it necessary to break off their links with Chávez.[107]

Since then it has appeared that neither the World Council of Churches nor the traditional churches have yet found the means of communication which is necessary in dealing with a church of the proletariat such as the Chilean Pentecostal Church. Our normal statements and books, and the way in which our theological discussion is conducted, are inappropriate to these people – apart from the fact that there is very little Protestant literature in Spanish or Portuguese. What is required is a kind of theology which is closer to the social psychology represented by the means of communication in the New Testament than to the modes of expression of European philosophical thought. Both the ecumenicity of European and Latin American churches, and also the political future of Latin American Protestantism, are dependent upon the solution of this problem. The importance of this task cannot be over estimated, for the Pentecostals of Chile and Brazil represent 20–25% of the electorate. Consequently the decision of the *Iglesia Metodista Pentecostal*[108] to be represented in

Uppsala by two observers is of the utmost importance.[109] But they will find the Ecumenical movement of use to them only if it succeeds better than the American Pentecostal missionaries in setting up contact with them on a profound level of equal partnership and oral and non-literary communication.[110]

(*b*) *Reaction among other Pentecostals*

Before these two Pentecostal churches joined the World Council of Churches, the prevailing attitude to the Ecumenical movement was one of rejection. Officially the World Council of Churches was regarded as being 'allied with the Antichrist',[111] a 'sign of the coming of the end', and as being in contradiction to genuine spiritual unity in the Church of Jesus Christ. The entry of the Russian Orthodox Church was interpreted as 'as shift in the balance towards the East', which 'is bound to have unimaginable consequences'.[112] 'A host of liberals who are committed to a theology and philosophy which are definitely anti-Christian in the Biblical sense' are at work in it. Its links with the Catholic Church 'threaten to weaken if not destroy the distinctive testimony of Protestantism'.[113]

> The pious fraud consists in this: the coming world church will proclaim itself to be a legitimate divine institution, the Church of Jesus, although it is as far from the word and spirit of Jesus as it possibly can be.[114]

The unity in the World Council of Churches is misunderstood as 'compromise', as the 'peaceful co-existence' of different doctrines.[115] This *Una Sancta* is only a 'union of the outwardly holy',[116] an association of 'church organizations set up by men'.[117]

In particular, three charges are made against the World Council of Churches: that it is infected by liberalism, friendly to Catholicism and infiltrated by communism.[118] The Pentecostal movement has adopted these accusations from their most bitter opponents, the non-Pentecostal fundamentalists (e.g. the Bible School of Beatenberg), who oppose them in everything else. They have come to the conclusion that the World Council of Churches

> tolerates in its midst churches which in their teaching deny the divinity of Jesus and contest the essential teaching of the gospel, the holy atoning blood and the reality of the resurrection of Jesus. We refuse to have fellowship with such anti-Christians in an ecumenical movement; and I deny you the right, Pastor, to attribute honest intentions to all these people, as persons 'who to the best of their knowledge and with a clear conscience confess Jesus as their Lord, in the word of truth and in the act of love'.[119]

David J. Du Plessis is accused of having made himself the representative of the Pentecostal movement at the World Council of Churches, and of having no authority to speak in the name of the Pentecostal movement. According to Du Plessis, Catholics see the medium of faith as the church, Protestants as doctrines and Pentecostals as experience. In Du Plessis's view all three aspects are important. He himself does not claim to represent the Pentecostal movement, only Pentecostal experience. But Pentecostals cannot so easily dismiss the ecumenical attitude of Donald Gee, whose authority in the Pentecostal movement is uncontested, if uncomfortable.[120]

(*c*) *Ecumenical consultation in Gunten* (*Switzerland*)

In spite of these negative opinions, there have been important meetings, beginning in 1966, between representatives of the World Council of Churches and the Pentecostal movement. Firstly, we should mention the informal consultation between twenty-three European Pentecostal pastors and representatives of the World Council of Churches in Gunten (Switzerland) in October 1966. The chairman at these discussions was Leonhard Steiner. It showed unmistakably that the criticism of the World Council of Churches made by Pentecostals is already being expressed within the member churches of the World Council. On this subject, the Pentecostals introduced no new views into the debate, but only affirmed more strongly what the World Council had already stated. Thus M. Handspicker of the Secretariat for Faith and Order wrote, on the lines of many documents produced by the World Council of Churches:

> We know what we reject: a centralized 'super-church' which dictates from afar to churches all over the world, and a vague 'spiritual unity' which does not seem to manifest its communion in truth visibly. Each is a mockery of unity rather than its fulfilment.[121]

The German Pastor A. Bittlinger drew attention to charismatic revivals within the established churches:

> I agree with the charismatic understanding of the church, but I have great difficulties with the theological fundamentalism and ecclesiological separatism of the Pentecostals.[122]

Albert van den Heuvel, director of the Department of Communication of the World Council of Churches, who is a Reformed pastor and has close contact with the Dutch Pentecostal movement, emphasized the fact that the World Council of Churches believes that the Pentecostal movement has much to offer it. But co-operation cannot be restricted to reading ecumenical documents. A personal encounter is necessary. Consequently, the Pentecostal movement must set aside its fear of the World Council of Churches and become a partner in the search for revival and unity. The hope that this partnership is possible does not necessarily imply the expectation that Pentecostals will join the World Council of Churches, but it requires a fundamental, critical and systematic dialogue. Albert van den Heuvel said that he was personally sympathetic to many of the criticisms of the World Council of Churches made by Pentecostals. But they seemed to be directed against potential rather than actual dangers. Further, if they were not uttered within the World Council of Churches then they would be fruitless. The effect of Christian criticism is always one of reconciliation. 'The critique we get is often stupid because it is built on ignorance; malicious because it is given without love.'[123] An outstanding feature of the discussion was the dialogue of the Pentecostals with Martin Niemöller, which has already been mentioned.[124]

The results of the consultation were: 1. A description of the 'European Pentecostal Movement'[125] in a form for which Pentecostals shared responsibility was prepared by the Secretariat for Faith and Order; 2. An account of particular aspects of Pentecostal belief and practice written by Pentecostal experts and pastors from all over the world appeared in the series *Die Kirchen der Welt* (The Churches of the World).[126]

There were comments on the discussions at Gunten in the journals of the Evangelical movement and the Pentecostal movement. The Swiss evangelist Wim Malgo wrote:

> Anyone who does not, in the name of Jesus, resolutely decide to have nothing to do with any spirit of enthusiasm, is bound to lay himself open to other spirits. How these 'ecumenical' spirits have already seized hold of these Pentecostal brethren is clear from the text of the 'recommendation' which they laid before the representatives of the World Council of Churches.[127]

Other journals, including Roman Catholic ones,[128] tried to give more accurate information about this movement, which seems to be ultra-Protestant, but which had adopted essential elements of Catholic thought and practice. A few Pentecostal journals made critical comments. At the same time, there were also attempts at a positive judgment.[129] A French Pentecostal journal devoted a special issue to the World Council of Churches. It reproduced an article by D. J. Du Plessis, who saw in the way in which the traditional churches and the Pentecostal movement were drawing closer together the fulfilment of a prophecy by the famous popular Pentecostal evangelist Smith Wigglesworth. The journal quotes ecumenical documents at length, and reproduces a photograph which shows a Pentecostal team of French gypsies in the chapel of the Ecumenical Centre in Geneva.[130]

As this process of drawing together continued, several conferences with Pentecostals took place in Germany,[131] with black Pentecostals in the United States,[132] in Chile,[133] Mexico[134] and Brazil. What at the moment is the latest stage in this dramatic story is the acceptance of the Brazilian Igreja Evangélica Pentecostal 'Brasil para Cristo' into the World Council of Churches,[135] together with the Pentecostal Eglise de Jésus Christ sur la terre par le prophète Simon Kimbangu from the Congo,[136] the beginning of bilateral conversations between the Lutheran World Federation and the Pentecostals[137] and between the Vatican and the Pentecostals and a candidature for membership of the important Italian Pentecostal church Chiesa Evangelica Internazionale. These facts have disturbed and alarmed some Pentecostal churches even more than the acceptance of the two Chilean churches into the World Council.

(*d*) *Analysis of the charges made by the Pentecostal movement against the World Council of Churches*

The charges made by the Pentecostal movement against the ecumenical movement can be summarized as follows:[138]

1. *The World Council of Churches has a false understanding of the Church*
It regards all existing churches as the Church of Jesus. Many circles in Protestant Christianity – and the whole Pentecostal movement – reject this assertion. The Church of Jesus can only consist of those who are born again, and who are characterized by the reception of the Holy Spirit. Does the World Council do anything to bear clear witness to this biblical truth? The World Council wants to maintain existing ecclesiastical institutions, and yet assist in the renewal of the church. What will this renewal look like in practice? The Pentecostal churches believe that a real renewal can only come about by the setting up of so-called 'gathered churches'. The dead burden of the past must be honestly written off.

2. *The World Council of Churches is not based on a firm biblical foundation*
The 'Basis' of the World Council of Churches is formulated in such general terms that it cannot be the basis of a genuine renewal. What is the attitude of the World Council of Churches to the Bible and to the fundamental truths of redemption (christology)? The Church of Jesus can only be renewed and perfected on the basis of the whole word of God.

3. *The World Council of Churches is growing increasingly close to Rome*
Since 1948 the World Council of Churches has followed a path which has brought it increasingly close to Rome, as though the reasons which led to the Reformation and the later spiritual revival no longer existed. Does the World Council of Churches really want a union with the Catholic Church? The inaugural address of the new General Secretary, Eugene Carson Blake, has posed this question in a particularly acute form.

The Pentecostal churches are convinced that the papacy is not of divine institution. What is the attitude of the World Council of Churches to the increasing political activity and the spiritual claims of the Pope?

4. *The World Council of Churches is a political association*
Is the World Council of Churches aware of the dangerous links between 'throne and altar'? Its political commitment glosses over the historical significance of this link, which is wholly unbiblical.

In the calls and recommendations of the World Council of Churches to Christians to involve themselves actively in overcoming the problems of the present day, the Pentecostal churches fail to see a clear witness of the rule of Jesus Christ over the world. Why are those in political authority not told the simple truth that they have only a short time in which to realize their task, because Jesus Christ will come soon? Pentecostal churches see *this* testimony as the greatest responsibility of the Christian towards the state.

Does the World Council of Churches take seriously the prophetic word of the Bible, and does it preach the imminence of the terrible judgment of God, which has been prophesied for a time like our own by Jesus and the apostles?

Are the leaders of the World Council of Churches aware that the coming into being of a world government comprising all nations will bring with it a 'world church' purely earthly in origin, as is stated for example in Rev. 13? The Pentecostal churches are afraid that the World Council of Churches could become an instrument in the formation of this world church.

The well-meaning eirenic purposes of the World Council of Churches seem to us to ignore the fact that the end of civilization *must* come, because the world is trying to establish its peace without Jesus Christ. Why does the World Council of Churches not speak more urgently of the sin, which cries out to heaven, of so-called Christian nations and of the inevitable judgment of God?

When violent measures are taken by the state against non-member churches, will the World Council of Churches defend their freedom of religion and conscience, or consent to these acts of repression?

5. *The World Council of Churches sets too high a value on itself*

What are the biblical facts which permit the World Council of Churches to regard itself as *the* divine movement of the century?

It is difficult to answer these charges, because Eisenlöffel does not give references for a single one of his assertions. He uses the same methods in condemning the World Council of Churches which the churches used for long enough against the Pentecostal movement. That is, he bases his charges on rumours, on hearsay, on newspaper reports, and not on a real knowledge of the documents of the ecumenical movement, whereas it is an elementary Christian duty to obtain exact information about a movement before criticizing it.

I shall now go on to give a brief answer to these charges made by the Pentecostal movement. I base my answers on the official reports of the World Council of Churches and on the collected speeches of the previous General Secretary, Visser 't Hooft.

As far as the first charge is concerned, both free churches and established churches are members of the World Council. But the former are in a large majority; that is, the question of the understanding of the church is still open amongst member churches, and is the object of mutual criticism. The form which the renewal of the churches should take is not only described in theory but tried out in practice.[139] The guiding principle of this renewal is a church dedicated to mission. What is wanted is a church in which

> it is possible to breathe, stop and think, and share a common concern for the direction one's life is taking; a church where taboos are not inviolate, and questions can remain open; where we can wait for the *shalom* of God *and* society.... How can we establish such a place, where more is given than advice which each individual is supposed to carry out on his own (but cannot)?[140]

The preparatory document for Section II ('Renewal in Mission') of the Full Assembly in Uppsala states unambiguously: 'All institutions of church life are provisional.'[141]

> Whenever we sing the *Veni Creator* we have to keep in mind that it was by the guidance of the Spirit that Jesus was driven out into the wilderness (Matt. 4.11; Mark 1.12). It is also by the guidance of the Spirit that the church is to be driven out beyond its own frontiers and definitions into the mission within the world (Matt. 10.16ff.; Heb. 13.12ff.). The Church is not called to be the institute of salvation but to participate in God's action for the salvation of the world. Everything in her structures that suggests sacralization must be tested to see if it hinders or even prevents the Church from being taken up into the divine mission for the salvation of the world.[142]

These two documents of the World Council of Churches (*The Church For Others* and *Section II of the Full Assemly in Uppsala*) make it unambiguously clear to anyone that the World Council of Churches is not concerned with the maintenance of ecclesiastical institutions, but with a search for 'new instruments of mission', which will make the church better able to fulfil its task. In the Toronto Declaration of the Central Committee of the World Council of Churches (1950) the theme 'The Church, the Churches and the World Council of Churches'[143] was dealt with point by point. There was an explicit affirmation:

> The Council is far from desiring to usurp any of the functions which already belong to its constituent Churches, or to control them, or to legislate for them, and indeed is prevented by its constitution from doing so.[144]

> The World Council cannot and should not be based on any one particular conception of the Church. It does not prejudge the ecclesiological problem.[145]

> Membership in the World Council of Churches does not imply that a Church treats its own conception of the Church as merely relative.[146]

Visser 't Hooft has discussed these problems in several articles. At a very early stage he called 'mission an ecumenical action'.[147] The unity of the church does not consist of 'common allegiance to human ordinances or traditions'.[148] In another article he shows that the World Council cannot of its nature attempt to be a 'super-church'.

> It is not enough to affirm that the ecumenical movement does not want to be a super-church. We must show that its presuppositions, spirit, structure are fundamentally different from those of the super-church.[149]

Visser 't Hooft sets out to show this in six theses (which are given here in abbreviated form):

> The ecumenical movement is not motivated by political, social or institutional concepts of unity, but by the biblical affirmation that the Church of Christ is one.
>
> The ecumenical movement does not seek a return to the sociological unity of the *Corpus Christianum*, but promotes the spiritual and manifest unity of churches which seek together to be the Church in the world.
>
> The ecumenical movement stands for religious liberty.
>
> The ecumenical movement does not believe in unity imposed by pressure or constraint but stands for that unity which expresses itself in the free response of the churches to the divine call to unity.
>
> The ecumenical movement does not promote unity as an aim in itself, but as part of the total calling of the Church of Christ.
>
> The ecumenical movement seeks in its own life to avoid the dangers of concentration of power, of centralisation and institutionalism.[150]

I turn now to the second charge. Anyone who ploughs through the mountains of Pentecostal literature will soon observe that there is disagreement within the Pentecostal movement itself about what belongs to the 'whole word of God'. Examples of this are the different views of baptism, the controversy about the baptism of the Spirit, the washing of feet. Not even Pentecostals within the Pentecostal movement itself have so far been able to delineate the 'biblical doctrine' which should provide the basis of true unity. Thus it is far less likely that there should be a biblical doctrine on which all Christians could agree. The counsel 'in essentials unity, in inessentials liberty, and in all things charity' breaks down against the fact that Christians are never in agreement about what exactly is essential. Nevertheless, there is an impressive amount of agreement amongst the churches of the World Council. This is shown, for example, by the long report of the 1963 Faith and Order Conference in Montreal. One section dealt in detail with the theme 'Scripture, Tradition and Traditions'.[151] It is impossible to summarize this work here. Anyone who proposes to criticize the inadequate biblical basis of the World Council of Churches should study this text. With great care it examines the relationship to Scripture, on the one hand of the oral traditions which preceded Scripture, and on the other hand of the interpretation of Scripture which followed.

With regard to the third objection, it is difficult to decide whether the World Council of Churches is growing closer to Rome, or whether Rome is growing closer to the World Council. Closer co-operation is only possible when the Roman Catholic Church abandons its exclusive claims. But this is not out of the question. For there are miracles in the history of the church too, not only in the history of the Pentecostal movement. At a time when an increasing number of Pentecostal churches join with Catholics in ecumenical services[152] this charge is a little surprising. Latin American Pentecostals at least are clear that it is not sufficient for them to come into contact with the fanatical, exclusive kind of Catholicism, but that they must also acquaint themselves with the Catholicism which is ready to enter into an honest partnership with other churches, and is therefore prepared to renounce exclusive claims. No one at the present day can say which party in the Catholic Church will gain the upper hand. Consequently, the question of whether the Catholic Church can be a member of the World Council of Churches must remain in abeyance until this question is clarified. But one must not judge the matter in advance, as Eisenlöffel does, by expecting the Catholic position to harden.

Lukas Vischer, who was an observer for the World Council of Churches at the Vatican Council, expressed a similar view in his report to the Central Committee of the World Council in Enugu (1965):

> The results do not point clearly in one direction. Many movements have taken place which hint at a promising development. There are many signs that the great ideas which were unfolded at the outset can be brought only to partial fruition . . . The movement which was sparked off by the proclamation of the (Vatican) Council has not yet come to an end, and it is still too early to talk about the outcome of the Council. The Roman Catholic Church itself is not yet fully aware of what the Council has really done to it. The broad trends can still only be seen in outline.

But even though the Council has led the Roman Catholic Church to some extent into complicated difficulties, this is no reason for other churches to indulge in

> neutral aloofness or even secret gloating. The defeat of one church is no victory for the others. It is a defeat for the proclamation of the name of Christ in general. The non-Roman churches have therefore a responsibility to exercise. They must attempt through their contribution to bring to development the potential beginnings made in the Council. Dialogue, encounter based on an open confession of loyalty to the truth, is the hope for the way ahead. An inner withdrawal would be a sure way of bringing the movement of the Council to a halt.

Lukas Vischer does not conceal the enormous difficulties attached to such a dialogue.

> We have seen that the big question of how a fellowship of dialogue and co-operation can come about between the churches is still not settled. The decree *de oecumenismo* does not supply an answer to it . . . For this reason the dialogue should begin at this very point.[153]

In 1965 a Joint Working Group of the World Council of Churches and the Roman Catholic Church was set up. Its task was 'to work out the principles which should be observed in further collaboration and the methods which should be used'.[154] The Jesuit Roberto Tucci – who, like the Pentecostal Christian Krust, was invited to speak at the Fourth Full Assembly of the WCC in Uppsala, as a representative of a non-member church – does not regard the obstacles to the Roman Catholic Church joining the WCC as 'insuperable'.[155]

In 1969 the Pope visited the World Council of Churches in Geneva.[156] A particularly important aspect of this visit was that he was received in exactly the same way as a representative of any other Christian denomination – and not as the representative of the whole of Christianity. The representatives of the World Council of Churches (amongst whom were an Indian layman and a British teacher) met the Pope as a partner – and this was given visible expression through the fact that the chairs were all *on the same level.* In the report of the first four years of the Joint Working Group *no decision* was made about the possible entry of the Roman Catholic Church into the WCC. The Joint Working Group

> recognized that the question of membership needed to be examined, and reported that a small group had been asked to study the problem in detail. The Minutes left entirely open the possible outcome of this enquiry. It listed various possibilities which might be considered: the continuation and extension of existing relationships; the establishment of a new fellowship of Churches different from the existing World Council of Churches; the entry of the Roman Catholic Church into the World Council of Churches in its present form or in a slightly modified form. The text does indeed add that it is this third solution which will be investigated first.[157]

Since Pentecostals are carrying out discussions with the Catholic Church at various levels, it is reasonable to ask how they can also contribute to the dialogue between the WCC and the Roman Catholic Church, particularly since the Pentecostal revival in the Catholic Church seems increasingly to be spreading.

The fourth charge, that the World Council of Churches is a political organization, must have been formulated in total ignorance of the work of the World Council. The World Council had a Secretariat for Religious Freedom which – with partial success – intervened on behalf of persecuted minorities throughout the world – including the Jehovah's Witnesses. Pentecostal churches have also benefited from interventions on the part of the World Council of Churches – for example in Italy and Latin America. In numerous publications and official documents[158] the WCC has made clear that religious minorities must also, under all circumstances, have the freedom to profess their religion in public. This religious freedom

> includes freedom to worship according to one's chosen form . . ., freedom to teach . . . freedom to practice religion or belief . . . It is for the churches in

their own life and witness, recognizing their own past failures in this regard, to play their indispensable role in promoting the realization of religious liberty for all men.[159]

In the declaration on 'Christian Witness, Proselytism and Religious Liberty' accepted by the Third Full Assembly of the World Council of Churches in New Delhi (1961), no modifications were made to the above statements. It was affirmed that a Christian's task is to bear witness in every situation. But this witness is corrupted

when cajolery, bribery, undue pressure, or intimidation are used – subtly or openly – to bring about seeming conversion.[160]

Thus this is the definition which the World Council of Churches gives to the term 'proselytism', and it is difficult to see what Pentecostals have against this.

It should also point out in all modesty that at the time when certain sections of the German Pentecostal movement were still welcoming Hitler as a leader sent by God,[161] leading figures in the World Council of Churches were pointing to the anti-Christian element in Nazism. References can be found in Bethge's splendid biography of Bonhoeffer. Moreover, in protesting against racial discrimination in South Africa (which has led a number of South African churches to leave the World Council of Churches), against discrimination against negroes in the USA (which led to a decrease in finances from America), and against certain aspects of the American intervention in Vietnam, the World Council clearly showed that it does not bow down before the mighty of this world. On the other hand, one looks in vain up to the present in the journals of the American Pentecostal movement for similar utterances, and in fact it is this commitment on the part of the World Council of Churches which in the eyes of American Pentecostals casts suspicion on it.

Most ecumenists are clear that all these honest endeavours 'are in vain . . . unless the Lord builds the house'. Thus for example Visser 't Hooft writes:

The world thinks it knows what peace means, and the church, in so far as it is of this world, sometimes also speaks as if it had peace in its pocket. But our Lord tells us that there is a peace which is quite different from the peace of this world. And the city of peace, Jerusalem, must be told that it does not know what makes for its peace. The truth is that peace is like all the other gifts of God. We can only receive them, when we constantly admit that we do not really know them and we do not really possess them. We are only rich when we remain beggars. Thus today we can still do nothing better than to ask time and again what the peace is which our Lord seeks to give us. And since he himself *is* the peace that he gives, we are not trying to define some concept, but asking what he is and what he does.[162]

To the fifth charge, that the World Council of Churches thinks too highly of itself, I would reply as follows. The World Council of Churches does not regard itself as *the* divine movement of this century. There is no text of the World Council of Churches which makes such an assertion.

Finally, one must add how far the Pentecostal movement may have formulated its criticisms in an unfortunate way, and yet is pointing to something profoundly wrong in the ecumenical movement, which the Pentecostal movement could play an essential part in curing. Albert van den Heuvel has already pointed out[163] that the World Council of Churches believes that the Pentecostal movement has a great contribution to make to it. This contribution could be made by helping to answer the following questions: What forms of personal commitment exist for Christians? What is the significance of a 'spontaneous liturgy' for traditional churches and how can the existing traditional liturgies be 'unfrozen'? What means of communication are available with those levels of the population which have lost contact with the traditional churches?

Recognizing a need for co-operation in these areas, the Mülheim Association of Christian Fellowships sent its administrative head, Christian Krust, as an observer delegate to the Fourth Full Assembly of the World Council of Churches at Uppsala in 1968. There he stated: 'I tried constantly to discover more about the relations between the ecumenical movement and the Pentecostalist movement.' He set out his critical contribution under seven heads:

The ecumenical movement as a spiritual unity.
Living faith, not verbal statements of belief.
The testimony of holy Scripture and scholarly study of the Bible.
Variety of members, but unity in spirit.
The renewal of mankind and of the world can come only from God.
The ecumenical movement and the Pentecostalist movement – opportunities for mutual aid.
No salvation apart from Christ.

Krust says: 'However, my own view is that it might benefit both movements tremendously if they were to get to know each other better.'[164]

NOTES

1. A. Reichenbach, *VdV* 55/10, Oct. 1962, p. 5.
2. *VdV* 1909 or 1910; quoted in *Schweizer Evangelist*, 12.2.1910, p. 104.
3. P Free Will Baptists, *Faith*, 1961, art. 22.
4. The Jesus Church, *Assembly Report 1952–1953*, p. 16; quoted in Moore, p. 310.
5. Gemeinde für Urchristentum, *Wer wir sind*, p. 9.
6. AdD, Dominican Republic, *Reglamento*, 1932, 1944.
7. L. Eisenlöffel, *Leuchter* 5/1, Jan. 1957, p. 5.
8. L. Eisenlöffel, *Leuchter* 13/12, Dec. 1962, pp. 7f.
9. Arbeitsgemeinschaft der Christengemeinden in Deutschland, *Wer wir sind*, n.d.
10. P. Mink, *Einheitskirche*, 4th ed., n.d., on the distorted information about the *Volkskirche*-situation in some European countries; cf. V. D. Hargrave (*ChoGE* 51/34,

31.10.1960, pp. 10–13) who states: 'Switzerland constitutionally grants freedom to all religions, but even the Pentecostals must belong to one of the official churches or else suffer the embarassment of being classified as second-rate citizens.'

11. Swaziland: 01.39.007. In socialist countries, in which the Pentecostal church has the same rights as other churches (Poland, Yugoslavia, Rumania, Hungary) pastors are possibly paid by the state. No exact details are available. This suggestion is based on verbal information.

12. *PE* 2526, 7.10.1962, p. 13; *PE* 2887, 7.9.1969, p. 15.

13. T. N. Turnbull, *What God Hath Wrought*, p. 125.

14. *The Church of God*, April 1964; quoted in *MD* 27, 1964, pp. 227f.

15. A. v. Polen, *Pinksterboodschap* 3/12, Dec. 1962, p. 12; cf. ch. 1.1(*b*), pp. 7ff.

16. *Der Leuchter* 18/10, Oct. 1967, p. 2; Nils Taranger, *Mensageiro da Paz* 37/16, 16.8.1967, pp. 1, 7.

17. C. Lemke, *Der Leuchter* 19/2, Feb. 1968, pp. 9f.

18. On the World Conferences cf. ch. 5.5, pp. 67ff.

19. Cf. below, ch. 30.4(*c*), p. 442.

20. A. M. Ritter, G. Leich, *Wer ist die Kirche?*

21. C. Williams, *Where in the World?*; *What in the World?*; *Faith in a Secular Age*; *The Church.*

22. E. Käsemann, 'Unity and Multiplicity in the New Testament Doctrine of the Church', in Käsemann, *Questions*, p. 257.

23. E. Schweizer, *Church Order*, 2a.

24. *Ibid.*, 2l.

25. *Ibid.*, 2m.

26. *Ibid.*, 7m.

27. All these quotations from H. Horton, *Gifts*, 6th ed. 1960, pp. 224–6.

28. For this concept cf. ch. 2.1, p. 26, n. 1.

29. H. Horton, *op. cit.*, pp. 226f. (reprinted in 1960).

30. V. Pylkkännen, *Voitto Sanoma*, 1932, no. 9, pp. 117ff.; quoted in W. Schmidt, *Pfingstbewegung*, p. 190.

31. *Toivon Tähti*, 1923, no. 2, p. 14; quoted in W. Schmidt, *Pfingstbewegung*, p. 145.

32. *Toivon Tähti*, 1913, no. 1, p. 11; quoted by W. Schmidt, *Pfingstbewegung*, p. 144.

33. E. S. Williams, *PE*, 1945, 19.8.1951, pp. 3–4.

34. From *VdV*, 1909 or 1910; quoted in *Schweizer Evangelist*, 12.2.1910, p. 104.

35. L. Pethrus, *Der Heilsbote*; *VdV* 20/7, July 1927, pp. 13ff.

36. Details: 05.28.020b.

32. Broederschap van Pinkstergemeenten in Nederland, *Pinkstergemeente*, pp. 14f.

38. E. N. O. Kulbeck, *P Testimony*, July 1964, pp. 2, 32.

39. J. D. Bright, *ChoGE* 51/25, 28.8.1961, pp. 6f.; cf. also H. R. Gause, *ChoGE* 52/34, 29.10.1962, pp. 3f.

40. Cf. above ch. 24.1, pp. 321f.

41. *Der Leuchter* 14/1, Jan. 1963, p. 2; L. Eisenlöffel, *Ein Feuer*, p. 98; *PGG*, pp. 235ff.

42. W. A. Waltke, *Gemeinde*, p. 5.

43. D. Gee, *P* 22, 1952, p. 17.

44. Congregação Cristã do Brasil, *Estatutos*, 1946, art. 4.

45. E.g. A. A. Boddy (07.134, Anglican, Great Britain), K. Ecke (07.390, Lutheran, Germany), F. de Rougemont (08.212, Reformed, Switzerland), and many others.

46. E.g. A. Béart (07.107, RC, France), C. Glardon (07.511, Reformed, Switzerland), A. Hitzer (Lutheran, Germany), V. Lindblom (07.853, Lutheran, Finland), and many others (cf. 06.002).

47. E.g. in all churches in the USA (cf. above, ch. 1, pp. 3ff; 06.002).

48. Almost all the pioneers of the Pentecostal movement were originally ministers in a traditional church (e.g. C. Price, 08.156, Presbyterian, USA), and the same phenomenon can be observed more recently outside Europe, especially in Latin America.
49. G. A. Wumkes, *Pinksterbeweging*.
50. T. Achelis, *Kulturprobleme der Gegenwart* I, p. 195.
51. E.g. in Haarlem; cf. J. Zeegers, *Pinksterboodschap* 2/7, July 1961, p. 7.
52. F. Boerwinkel, *Pinkstergroepen* (Oekumenische Leergang 5), 1962, p. 13.
53. Nederlands Hervormde Kerk, *De Kerk en de Pinkstergroepen*, 1960, 3rd ed., 1961, p. 34.
54. *Ibid.*
55. A. van Polen, *Pinksterboodschap* 3/11, Nov. 1962, p. 3.
56. Broederschap van Pinkstergemeenten in Nederland, *Pinkstergemeente*, pp. 7ff.
57. *Ibid.*, p. 10.
58. *Ibid.*, p. 12.
59. *Ibid.*, pp. 14f.
60. *Ibid.*, pp. 15–17.
61. W. W. V[erhoef], *Vuur* 7/4, June 1963, p. 9.
62. *MD* 21, 1958, pp. 237f.; 25, 1962, p. 60.
63. D. G. Molenaar, *De doop*, p. 34.
64. Bruno Paul de Roeck (RC), *Vuur* 13/2, Feb. 1969, pp. 4f.
65. G. H. Wallien, *Vuur* 13/6, June 1969, p. 6.
66. J. Zeegers, *Pinksterboodschap* 3/4, April 1962, p. 13; W. W. Verhoef, *Vuur* 6/5, July–Aug. 1962, pp. 11ff.
67. On the Dutch Pentecostal Movement see W. J. Hollenweger, *Nederlands Theol. Tijdschrift* 18/4, April 1964, pp. 289ff.
68. *Ecumenical Press Service* 30/2, 16.1.1963, p. 1.
69. L. K. Grosc, *Sent into the World*, pp. 79–80.
70. M. H. Duncan, *Revelation*, p. 217; so also W. H. Hannah, *Redemption Tidings* 45/23, 5.6.1969, p. 11.
71. M. Gaston, *PE* 2421, 2.10.1960, pp. 6f., 28f.; *PE* 2422, 9.10.1960, p. 10.
72. Cf. ch. 4.2(*b*), p. 53.
73. H. Lauster, *Wahrheit* 15/8, Aug. 1962, pp. 4f.
74. *Elim Evangel* 19, 1938, p. 86; quoted in B. Wilson, *Sects*, p. 94.
75. C. D. Alexander, *Pattern* 24/2, Feb. 1962, p. 11.
76. E. Bischoff, *Wahrheit* 15/9, Sept. 1962, pp. 4f.
77. E. N. O. Kulbeck, *P Testimony*, April 1959, p. 2.
78. *Estado de S Paulo*, 8.7.1959.
79. J. B. Lyra, *A Voz Pentecostal* 7/78, Oct. 1959, pp. 2, 7, reprinted: J. B. Lyra, *Orientação*, pp. 31–4.
80. Cf. ch. 8.3(*b*), p. 104.
81. Cf. ch. 19.2, pp. 254ff.
82. E.g. E. Piccioni, *Risveglio P* 9/7–8, July–Aug. 1954, pp. 7f.; J. Zanin, *Here is the News* (periodical), n.d. On A. Béart: 05.09.027b.
83. H.-C. Chéry, *Offensive*; I. Vergara, *El Protestantismo*; *Mensaje* 3/41, Aug. 1955, pp. 257ff.; A. de Moura, *A importancia*; P. van Dongen, *Oekumene* 5/5, 1966, pp. 26ff.; A. Gaëte, *Un cas d'adaptation*, in Abd-el-Jalil and others (ed.), *L'Eglise*, pp. 142ff.; L. Zenetti, *Heisse (W)Eisen*, pp. 304ff. For the important American publications cf. ch. 1.1(*d*), pp. 8f. For a general summary, see W. J. Hollenweger, *Una Sancta*, June 1970, pp. 150ff.
84. D. J. Du Plessis, *Vuur* 8/11, Jan. 1965, pp. 12f.; E. O'Connor, *Ave Maria* 105, 3.6.1967, pp. 7ff.; M. Sandoval, *Nat. Cath. Reporter*, 12.6.1968.
85. Cf. ch. 1.1(*d*), pp. 8f.

86. F. J. Schulgen, *Testimony*, 4/1, 1st quarter, 1965, pp. 1ff.; L. O'Docharty, *ibid.*, p. 8; *PE* 2860, 2.3.1969, p. 10; *PE* 2785, 24.9.1967, pp. 6f., p. 13.

87. *Acts* 1/5, 1968, pp. 14ff.

88. Interviews with the Catholic priest Jean-Marie Robert and Bishop Mancilla of the Iglesia Metodista Pentecostal.

89. Cf. above, n. 66.

90. Cf. the very remarkable article 'Question oecuménique' in the French Pentecostal journal *Vie et Lumière* 46, pp. 14ff.

91. Verbal communication from Emilio Castro, July 1971.

92. Cf. the interview by *Vie et Lumière* with Lukas Vischer (*Vie et Lumière* 46, pp. 10ff.).

93. On the whole subject see W. J. Hollenweger, *Ecumenical Review* 18/3, 1966, pp. 310ff.

94. E. Chávez, letter to G. Theyssen, 19.6.1962.

95. *Ibid.*

96. E. Chávez, *La Voz Pentecostal* no. 56, June 1962, p. 16.

97. E. Chávez, letter to G. Theyssen, 19.6.1962.

98. Correspondence at the WCC, Geneva.

99. The legally certified documents of authorization in the archives of the WCC in Geneva bear witness to this.

100. E. Chávez, letter to W.H., 23.1.1963.

101. E. Chávez, *La Voz Pentecostal* 56, June 1962, p. 16.

102. Iglesia Pentecostal de Chile (02b.08.054; Misión Iglesia Pentecostal (02b.08.601); W. A. Visser 't Hooft (ed.), *New Delhi Report*, pp. 70. 219.

103. R. C. Cunningham, *PE* 2526, 7.10.1962; F. M. Boyd, *PE* 2526, 7.10.1962, pp. 4f., 19; *MD* 25, 1962, pp. 225, 426.

104. D. J. Du Plessis, *VdV* 55/3, March 1962, p. 9.

105. Cf. the chapter 'Dios y Dolares' in E. Labarca Goddard, *Chile invadido*, pp. 287ff.

106. R. O. Corvin, letter to E. Chávez, 10.9.1968.

107. J. A. Synan, bishop of the PHCh, letter to Chávez, 3.6.1969.

108. The second largest Pentecostal church in Chile, the Iglesia Evangélica Pentecostal (02b.08.045) was not represented at Uppsala.

109. Cf. A. Ramírez-Ramírez, 'I could have danced', *Monthly Letter on Evangelism*, Oct. 1969 (Geneva, WCC). Several meetings have taken place between the leading pastors of the Iglesia Metodista Pentecostal and W. J. Hollenweger and D. J. Du Plessis (*Concepto Latino-Americano* I, Special Issue 26, March 1970, WCC, Geneva).

110. Proposals in *Concepto Latino-Americano* I, II, III (WCC, Geneva). Summarized and interpreted by *W. J. Hollenweger*, *IRM* 60/238, April 1971, pp. 232ff.; cf. also *Theologie* (ET in preparation).

111. *PE* 1748, 8.11.1947, p. 10 (not directly in connection with the WCC, but with a report on E. Stanley Jones's plans for Church unity).

112. K. Schneider, *VdV* 55/8, Aug. 1962, p. 2; *PE* 2849, 21.1.1962, p. 10; cf. also ch. 3.4, pp. 42f. and p. 45 n. 93.

113. *ChoGE* 51/48, 12.2.1962, p. 15.

114. L. Eisenlöffel, *Leuchter*, 13/11, Nov. 1962, pp. 4f.

115. K. Kopelle, *Pinksterboodschap* 4/1, Jan. 1963, pp. 6f.

116. H. Lauster, *Die Wahrheit* 15/4, April 1962; *MD* 25, 1962, p. 108.

117. A. Guggenbühl, *Geschäftsmann und Christ* 3/11, Aug. 1963, pp. 6 ff.

118. Further documents on the attitude of individual Pentecostal denominations to the WCC: 02a.01.13b, ee; 02a.02.115c, bb; 02b.05.012c; 02b.08.054d/e; 05.07.015c, dd; 05.07.028f; 05.09.026; 05.09.027; 05.13.023c, bb; 05.15.B.VI; 05.20.004e/g;

05.23.C; 05.28.025c, ee, etc. Cf. also above ch. 3.4, pp. 42f.; ch. 6.3(*b*), pp. 81ff.; ch. 8.3, pp. 99ff.; ch. 12.5(*c*), pp. 165ff.; ch. 17.3, pp. 240ff.; ch. 19.2, pp. 254ff.

119. W. Malgo, Letters to the Editor, *Mitternachtsruf* 6/6, Sept. 1961.

120. Cf. above ch. 15.2(*b*), pp. 208ff.

121. M. B. Handspicker, *Purpose*, FO/66:63. Oct. 1966.

122. A. Bittlinger, *Fragen*, SE 67:3, Oct. 1966.

123. A. van den Heuvel, *Impulses for Renewal*, Y:66/21. Other preparatory papers: J. H. Davies, *Renewal*, SE 66:32; L. Eisenlöffel, *Renewal*, SE 66:34 (printed in German in *Leuchter* 17/11, Nov. 1966, pp. 5ff.); W. J. Hollenweger, *European Pentecostal Movement*, SE 66:35. A similar consultation took place in 1967 in New Zealand (M. B. Handspicker and W. J. Hollenweger, *The Outlook* 74/1, 18.2.1967, pp. 16f., 21); *MD* 30, 1966, pp. 283ff.

124. Cf. ch. 21.4, pp. 305ff.; ch. 30.4(*c*), p. 443.

125. M. B. Handspicker and L. Vischer, (ed.) *An Ecumenical Exercise* (Faith and Order 49) 1967; also in *Ecumenical Review* 19/1, Jan. 1967, pp. 47ff.

126. W. J. Hollenweger (ed.), *Pfingstkirchen.*

127. W. Malgo, *Mitternachtsruf* 11/10, Jan. 1967, p. 15.

128. Cf. above n. 83.

129. Review of W. A. Visser 't Hooft, *Oekumenische Bilanz*, by L. Eisenlöffel, *Der Leuchter* 18/1, Jan. 1967, pp. 4f.; L. Steiner, *VdV* 59/12, Dec. 1966. pp. 13f.; *Heilszeugnisse* 52/1, Jan. 1967, pp. 3f.

130. *Vie et Lumière* 30, Jan. 1967.

131. Cf. L. Steiner, *Heilszeugnisse* 52/1, 1.1.1967, pp. 3–4; C. Krust, *Heilszeugnisse* 52/7, 1.7.1967, pp. 98–102; H. Rottmann, *Heilszeugnisse* 53/12, 1.12.1968, pp. 179–80; C. Krust, *Heilszeugnisse* 53/8, 1.8.1968, pp. 114f.; *ibid.* 53/8, 1.8.1968, pp. 116–18; 53/11, 1.11.1968, pp. 163–6, 171–4; 53/12, 1.12.1968, pp. 180–5; cf. ch. 17.3, pp. 240ff.

132. W. J. Hollenweger, *Black Pentecostal Concept*, June 1970 (WCC, Geneva).

133. Cf. above n. 109.

134. *Concepto Latino-Americano* III, Sept. 1970 (WCC, Geneva). English summary by W. J. Hollenweger, *IRM* 60/238, April 1971, pp. 232ff., and *Theologie* (ET in preparation).

135. Cf. ch. 8.3, pp. 99ff.

136. M. B. Handspicker and L. Vischer (ed.), *An Ecumenical Exercise* (Geneva, WCC, Faith and Order 49); M. L. Martin, *Kirche ohne Weisse*; *PGG* (French edition); WCC, *Central Committee Minutes*, Canterbury, 1969, p. 11.

137. Cf. above n. 69.

138. The following quotations are taken from an unpublished article by Ludwig Eisenlöffel. Cf. also the attitude of the AoG, USA, Appendix: 3, pp. 516f.

139. Cf. the regular *Monthly Letters on Evangelism* (Geneva, WCC); reprinted in W. J. Hollenweger, *Kirche, Benzin und Bohnensuppe* (ET in preparation).

140. WCC, *The Church for Others* (quotation from the Preface to the German edition, WCC, *Die Kirche für andere*, p. 5).

141. WCC, *Drafts for Sections*, p. 31.

142. WCC, *The Church For Others*, pp. 37f.

143. Most easily available in English in the collection by L. Vischer (ed.), *A Documentary History of the Faith and Order Movement*, pp. 167ff.

144. L. Vischer, *op. cit.*, p. 167.

145. *Ibid.*, p. 170.

146. *Ibid.*

147. W. A. Visser 't Hooft, *Oekumenische Bilanz*, pp. 9ff. (an essay written in 1941).

148. *Ibid.*, p. 10.

149. W. A. Visser 't Hooft, *Ecumenical Review* 10/4, July 1958, p. 375.

150. *Ibid.*, pp. 376f.

151. P. C. Rodger and L. Vischer (ed.), *The Fourth World Conference of Faith and Order, Montreal 1965* 3, 1964, pp. 50ff.

152. Cf. above, ch. 30.3, pp. 438, and Ranaghan, *Spirit*, pp. 114ff.

153. L. Vischer in his report of the third session of the Vatican Council, given to the Central Committee of the WCC in Enugu, 1965, *Minutes of the Central Committee* (Enugu 1965), pp. 100f.

154. L. Vischer, *Ecumenical Review* 22/1, Jan. 1970, p. 37. Cf. also the report of the 'Joint Working Group between the Roman Catholic Church and the World Council of Churches' in N. Goodall (ed.), *Uppsala Report*, pp. 344ff.

155. R. Tucci, 'The Ecumenical Movement, the World Council of Churches and the Roman Catholic Church' in N. Goodall (ed.), *Uppsala Report*, pp. 323ff.

156. The speeches made by E. C. Blake and the Pope are given in *Ecumenical Review* 21/3, July 1969, pp. 265ff.

157. L. Vischer, *Ecumenical Review* 22/1, Jan. 1970, p. 67.

158. 'Statement on Religious Liberty' in W. A. Visser 't Hooft (ed.), *New Delhi Report*, pp. 159ff.; 'Declaration on Religious Liberty', Amsterdam 1958, in WCC, *Evanston to New Delhi*, pp. 253f.; 'Christian Witness, Proselytism and Religious Liberty' (Central Committee, St Andrew's, 1960; Full Assembly, New Delhi 1961) in L. Vischer (ed.), *A Documentary History of the Faith and Order Movement*, pp. 183ff.

159. W. A. Visser 't Hooft (ed.), *New Delhi Report*, pp. 160f.

160. L. Vischer (ed.), *A Documentary History*, p. 271.

161. Cf. above, ch. 17.1(*c*), pp. 252ff.

162. W. A. Visser 't Hooft, *Oekumenische Bilanz*, p. 68 (essay of 1950).

163. Cf. p. 442.

164. C. Krust, 'Pentecostal Churches and the Ecumenical Movement' in N. Goodall (ed.), *Uppsala Report*, pp. 340ff.

31

'Islands of Humanity': A Sociological Assessment

1. *Aspirin or Hope: The Psychological and Therapeutic Function of Pentecostal Belief and Practice*

(*a*) *Help for those on the fringes of society*

THE belief and practice of the Pentecostal movement provides help for people who live on the fringes of society. Black South Africans, without any political rights, pray to the God who saved Daniel from the fiery furnace: 'Thou, God of Meshach, Shadrach and Abednego'.[1] Enok Butelezi sings with his congregation:[2]

Yek' i Jerusalema
Umuzi okhanyayo
(See Jerusalem,
The shining city).

The church members move their bodies to the rhythm. Two or three women are seized by the Spirit. They fall to the ground and speak in tongues, while the others sigh: 'Ooh, hho, hho, hho!' One woman testifies:

> Peace in Zion. Amen. (Amen!) A few days ago there was a terrible row in our kraal. One of my husband's wives hates me because he loves me more than her. She beat me with a stick, just here on the forehead. And I bit her on the ear. May the Lord forgive me for that. Amen. (Amen!)

The prophet Butelezi begins to pray. All kneel. After a few seconds the room is filled with a thunderous noise of praying. Everyone prays together, and everyone tries to pray louder than his neighbour, so that his prayer can rise up to the throne of God. The roaring of the prayers, the brilliantly coloured uniforms, a heavy atmosphere of sweat, urine and cow dung in a small, completely closed room – a real foretaste of Zion! Enok begins to speak in tongues. Some people drum with their fists on the ground. A woman who has not yet received the baptism of the Spirit cries aloud:

> *Woza, Moya, woza* (Come, Spirit, come)! Thou Eagle of Judah, thou who art great in Jerusalem, thou Almighty, thou source of power that flows out from Zion – *woza, woza, woza!*

After a time the meeting grows quieter. Suddenly the drummer girl intones the Our Father. All join in, and at the end sing 'Amen' in different variations for three minutes.[3]

The Harris prophets of Ghana have a prayer garden in which the sick are subjected to a powerful psychological therapy. But they do not reject ordinary medical assistance. The patients stand in the 'prophet's garden' before a white cross, and carry a pitcher of holy water on their heads. The top half of their bodies must be naked. While the congregation gives support to the healing by singing, the prophets and prophetesses walk through the rows of the sick and dip their fingers in the pitcher on the patients' heads. They they touch the sick part of the bodies of those who are seeking healing. As the healings take place there are violent outcries, shouts of joy, signs and convulsions.[4]

In the revival which gave rise to the Chilean Pentecostal movement, which has since become known throughout the world, the Pentecostals were seized by holy dread. In their services, the agricultural labourers of Chile had the experience of being persons of importance in the history of the church and the world.

> The brethren were possessed by dancing and spiritual visions, they spoke in tongues of angels, prophesying about the great spiritual revival. The Holy Spirit seized them in the streets. The authorities took them into the prisons as criminals, but the brethren danced in the prisons, speaking in tongues and prophesying to these officials.[5]

Pentecostal religion enabled the Toba Indians of Argentina to change from a nomadic life to that of cotton planters, without having to give up the mythical and magical conceptions which were important to them. They were able to continue these, under a Christian guise, in the new form of Pentecostal worship.[6]

The Indians of Peru treat tuberculosis by drinking warm cow's blood, with a pulp of shark's eyes or a buzzard soup. For them, the prayers for healing uttered by a missionary – especially where these are associated with elementary medical aid – are the first step towards the abandonment of the treatment of sickness by magic means alone, and yet this does not oblige them to make an abrupt break with their former practice.[7]

But Pentecostal religion also brought relief to the workers of North America. According to Charles S. Snyder Jr., these were lost to the Presbyterian Church not for theological reasons, but because their 'educational and social disadvantages have eliminated them from Presbyterian membership for many generations'.[8]

As early as 1929 Niebuhr identified the reasons for the rise of Pentecostal churches as the rejection of the intellectual and liturgically fixed services of the traditional church, and a preference for a spontaneous form of worship, quite often of a primitive kind.[9]

Whether it exists amongst the agricultural workers of Chile, the Indians of Argentina, the proletariat of North America,[10] the masses of African cities, the gypsies of France,[11] the members of Swedish trade unions,[12] or the poor of Britain,[13] the function of the Pentecostal movement is to restore the power of expression to people without identity and powers of speech, and to heal them from the terror of the loss of speech.

The person who kept the books for a saw sharpener in a suburb of Zürich suddenly died. The craftsman was thereby cut off from his source of ready money. His wife knew that they had a fairly large sum of money in the Post Office She asked the counter clerk: 'Will you please let me have some money, even if it is only 200 fr. (about £20), because we have some money in the Post Office.' A murmur passed along the queue waiting at the counter. The clerk looked at the woman: 'Anyone can say that.' When the woman showed no sign of leaving the counter, he motioned her to go away. What was she to do? Her husband was a quick and accurate tool sharpener, but had no more idea about the world of figures and letters than she, and he told her: 'If you can't get any cash at the Post Office, I shall have to divorce you.' In despair the woman went to the Swiss Pentecostal Mission, heard that Jesus could help her in her distress, asked for someone to pray with her and finally told what her difficulties were. By chance the pastor knew something about accountancy. He helped the couple to find a new person to keep their books and filled in the urgently needed withdrawal form, at the same time instructing the woman how to draw cash from the Post Office. To an outsider, this seems something perfectly straightforward, but for the two people it represented the help of God in great distress. Naturally any social worker would easily have been able to help them. But after the Post Office clerk had not understood them, they would hardly have dared to go to any public agency. Disadvantaged persons cannot bear people laughing at their disadvantages. But when they can express their disadvantages 'liturgically'[14] they need not fear mockery. When they find themselves in the meeting with persons who suffer the same disadvantages, they find the courage to express their *concrete* difficulties.

A French pastor, Daniel Maurer, was disturbed by a Pentecostal service in Paris:[15]

> In a back street in a working-class district we come to the sign of the 'Good News' . . . Let us go in and find a place if we can. The room is almost always full. A hundred, two hundred, three hundred people? . . . Most of those present come from the working-class district where we are: workmen and persons with small independent incomes, all together; equal numbers of men and of women. There is a warm atmosphere of friendliness and fellowship. There is nothing which recalls the unbreakable ice of churches and chapels.

As newcomers, we were picked out and greeted (there is no reception committee). Someone hastened to give us a hymn book . . .

One person speaks, but a hundred people vibrate in unison with his prophetic appeals. A wave of Hallelujahs and Amens, the expression of a spiritual whirlpool rising up from the very depths of faith . . . almost convinces us that we are no longer in the twentieth century, . . . in a harmless mission hall . . . but have been carried back in time to Lystra, Pergamon, Antioch, or Rome, amongst the early Christians . . . The deacon makes an incisive call for immediate conversion. Some hands are raised. The sick are counted and invited to kneel in a semicircle on cushions round the platform. There they receive the laying on of hands . . . There is silence for the message of those who speak in tongues. The interpreters are asked to translate. It is sad to see how far all this is from normal Protestantism and its traditional worship.

We are disturbed. 'Is it these people, and they alone, who have made the Reformation really come about?' Healing by anointing with oil or by laying on of hands; baptism in the Holy Spirit; glossolalia (speaking in tongues); a fervent expectation of the return of Christ. Nothing seems anachronistic to them or out of date to them. With the joy of the newly converted, we step into the uncharted land of a new Acts of the Apostles. A breath of resurrection seems to blow across the pages of the First Epistle to the Corinthians, pages which, for so many Christians, remain a dead letter.

A Catholic observer in France describes the religious practice and sermons in a Pentecostal service and comes to the conclusion.

All these people, their eyes shining with hope, overcome with remorse for their faults, resolved upon a better life, I am sure would mostly have laughed or shrugged their shoulders if a priest had said the same things to them [as Pastor Gallo had said to them in this assembly]. So how can this man do it? I was overcome with pity and with affection for them. I would have liked to cry out 'The [Catholic] Church offers you all this . . .'[16]

He was probably right. Many elements in Pentecostal religion are Catholic, a fact which the Pentecostal historian H. V. Synan also stresses.[17] But why are these practices rejected when a priest offers them? The answer is obvious: to hear a *priest* speak of the love of God, or repentance and of conversion, is not the same as hearing someone who has had to be converted himself, someone of whom the person who hears him can say: He is one of us!

In Southern Italy the Pentecostal movement is the religion of the proud poor, and has assisted the anonymous peasants, robbed of their humanity, to attain a personal and individual identity.[18] Pentecostal religion is not limited to a particular national temperament. Although in various countries it takes on a specific national colouring, its function of overcoming personal and social disadvantages by a religious experience is exercised amongst all nations. Thus in Finland the form taken by this religion is 'subdued, as it were sprinkled with tears'.[19] I give an example from the origins of the Finnish Pentecostal movement:

The schoolmaster Lars Ulstadius of Uleaborg interrupted the minister in Åbo Cathedral in the middle of his sermon. He was seized, but broke loose, leaving the few rags in which he was dressed in the hands of the people who had seized him. 'Ulstadius ran around the church naked, crying in great exultation: "The shame of the pastors will be shown in its nakedness, as I am naked now!" '[20] The newly revived Laestadians (*Udesti Heränneet Laestadiolaiset*), from whom a Finnish Pentecostal movement arose under Barratt's influence, practised a passion mysticism:

> You sinner, seeking the way to heaven! Go into the garden and ask why the clothes of the Strong One are so red, and why his cloak is like his who treads the wine press. Follow him then to Golgotha, and you will understand what your redemption cost. The reason will see no miracles on this path. He who helped others is seen hanging there on the tree, unable to help himself. But where sinners are willing to repent, there the greatest miracles take place.[21]

A striking example of the compensation for a disadvantage (in this case a geographical disadvantage) which religious experiences can provide is seen in the revival in Wales. The Celtic people of Wales were at a disadvantage with regard to the rest of Britain because of the lack of communications, on economic grounds, and because of their Welsh language. In the revival in Wales their disadvantages were transformed into advantages. Their services were characterized by hours of singing in harmony in Welsh, a decline in the role of the sermon, prayer in concert by the congregation, interjections, an emphasis on the experience of the baptism of the Spirit and the guidance of the Spirit, and *hwyl*, the typically Welsh phenomenon of a gradually rising intonation on the part of an emotional orator.[22]

Since in Germany and Switzerland spontaneous forms of religious expression of this kind are socially unacceptable, the need for this sort of service is all the greater. It is also more important for them to be established as a legitimate form of religion, and defended against the services of the traditional churches. Consequently, prayer in concert and singing together in tongues must be shown to be biblical forms of worship.[23] The disadvantages of a form of worship which is too exclusively intellectual in its conception, which leaves no room for spontaneity, and which often presents the faithful with sermons and prayers in written form, cause distress not only to the uneducated, but even to theologians and academics; this is shown by the not inconsiderable drift of ministers and ordinands to the Pentecostal movement.

In this context, one should read the letter which Pastor Fritz de Rougemont of Neuenburg wrote to one of his colleagues after joining the Pentecostal movement:

> They say that the traditional churches provide missionary opportunities. I do not dispute this, but my view is that the missionary opportunities would be greater if the situation were not constantly obscured by the mixture of Christians and half-Christians in our church. It is useless to make a constant appeal

> to the Reformers without following their examples. How many struggles it needed to bring about even the slightest 'little Reformation' with regard to the practice of baptism! Our dear André Frommel says: Patience, God has patience. But this does not seem to me to be the note that sounds in the Bible. 'Redeem the time!' we read there. And if a pastor tries to take this demand seriously, he must first have behind him dozens of devotional hours, funerals, baptisms, weddings, meetings and other ways of passing the time. Why should we not let the dead bury their dead? Must one really fret one's whole life away with a church like this? How many real conversions are there per year in the established church of Neuenburg? In our church a pastor can preach virtually any doctrine he likes. He can reduce the gospel to a point at which it is unrecognizable. But woe on him if he says anything against infant baptism![24]

It would be easy to show that what Fritz de Rougemont was expecting from his conversion to the Pentecostal movement is impossible. But the decisive fact is that here a man from a cultured, devout, aristocratic family, the son of a pastor, psychologically healthy, open to the world, an art lover, a trained theologian and respected by his colleagues, is posing questions that cannot easily be answered, even if one must regard de Rougemont's conclusion as the victory of despair over hope. His statement expresses the sorrow of a man who in his ministry has experienced the disadvantages under which the pastoral office labours in present-day society. The rhetorical claims made upon the pastoral ministry, and the class consciousness which it imposes on the minister himself, and which is accepted by the nuclear congregation which he serves, bear no relation to factual reality. This 'status contradiction'[25] is experienced by the minister as a *misère affective*.

Fritz de Rougemont is not alone in this. It would be a mistake to believe that the experience of being on the fringes of society is shared only by those who suffer from economic and social disadvantages. There are more people than it is usually supposed who suffer from a real or imaginary disadvantage because of the colour of their skin, their education, their sex, their temperament, their outward appearance, a contradiction in their status, and so forth, and wish to compensate for this disadvantage. After the victorious campaign of the Pentecostal movement amongst the poor and the intellectually deprived, we are experiencing at the present day a second wave of Pentecostal revivals amongst high officials, managers in big businesses, scientists and scholars in every subject, artists, diplomats and officers.

What is it which draws these people into the Pentecostal movement? Lotte Denkhaus[26] has expressed what many feel about the inability of the church to communicate its faith:

> More than ever I [that is, every 'serious' Christian] stand in a situation of confusion. I need to have studied philosophy, and learned by heart and understood a whole dictionary of technical expressions, in order to grope my way

in turn round each new movement and theological doctrine. Why? So that I can make an independent decision, which I have a right to do. For – according to what all the theologians assert directly or indirectly – the most important thing in the world is at issue. But it lands me in front of the bars of a cage and they, the theologians, draw the bars closer and closer. Sometimes, perhaps when I have been ill or on holiday and have had time and leisure and have paid good money for thick theological tomes, I have had the fortune or misfortune to dip into them and have a look around this world of scholarship. But it requires endless trouble, patience, courage and determination to make my way back out of the cage and into the park along a path which may finally perhaps have been overgrown ... Who, then, can choose one item from so rich a stock and take it home? And who can ever succeed in entering the warehouse of theology and getting a selection to choose from? Most of us have not got trained minds. Thus we are hopelessly 'naive' and 'primitive', excluded from any possibility of knowing what there is in the church which concerns us, even down to the personal decision about what is false coin and what is good coin.

Even the ministers are disciples of a particular school, either Barthians or disciples of Bultmann, or disciples of his disciples, or followers of Tillich, and so forth. They never make us independent, or at least rarely. Nor can they even seriously propose to do so, because very often they are no longer independent themselves. So we need guidance from somewhere else. In simple terms, we need the Holy Spirit. I wait on him, I pray for him. But I do not pray regularly, and certainly my prayer is often only subconscious ... And so much time is taken up by my daily quota of work, so wearisome and yet so much loved, by care for the family and worry on their account, and by concern for the people whom I meet, who need me or whom *I* need.

People like these, disappointed with a kind of worship which adds the problems of the theologian to their own professional problems, and longing for direct prayer and a simplification of religious faith in the form of spontaneous and personal relationships, find in Pentecostal worship exactly what they need. For it does not teach people to think, but to believe (in the sense of a direct religious experience) and to live (within the framework of tangible personal relationships). Thus the well-known Dr Charles Price, who was himself a colleague of Aimee Semple McPherson, has described one of her services – in which numerous academics felt at home:

Somebody way back in the audience starts to sing in a little soprano voice, 'Oh, it is Jesus.' The multitude take up the refrain and they sing it again and again; the cornets proclaim it in measured tone; the trombones boom out the same sweet story; the grand piano vibrates and pulsates with joy, 'Oh, it is Jesus.' Sister's tambourine is working now, rolling from her finger tips as she leads the great audience in singing the glad story, 'Oh, it is Jesus.' It reminds us of Miriam sounding the timbrel over Egypt's dark sea after the crossing of the waters. ... 'Oh, it is Jesus' shout back the preachers and the choir. The building rings and rings again until it seems as if the great dome must break, and let the whole world hear the music of the pilgrims who have that day seen the King in all His beauty.[27]

(*b*) *Hymns, the outward expression of the personal friendship of Jesus*

There has been no systematic study of the hymns of the Pentecostal movement. Such a study is much to be desired, because hymns are more decisive in their influence on the religious belief and practice of Pentecostals than is the literature of the Pentecostal movement. A Pentecostal lives with his hymns. He knows fifty or a hundred hymns, with several verses, by heart as well as innumerable choruses. Most congregations sing in harmony. Often the congregational singing or a soloist's song is accompanied on instruments. A good pianist in the Pentecostal movement knows how to improvise, providing a rhythmical accompaniment to the melody in the style of the pianist in a bar.

Apart from the classical themes (the church year, revival hymns, hymns of the world to come, etc.) the most striking group consists of the numerous hymns which sing of Jesus as the friend of the soul:

Like a mighty sea, like a mighty sea,
Comes the love of Jesus, sweeping over me.[28]

These hymns (which are not sung in the Pentecostal movement alone) use the imagery and key words of popular songs, and apply them all to the one true friend who never leaves us, to the 'lover of my soul' who 'sought me in tenderness' and who 'leads me in the dark'. For a long time he 'stood at my heart's door', but now the Pentecostal asks 'Draw me nearer!' For he wants 'to go deeper and deeper into the heart of Jesus'.

Another type of hymn typical of the Pentecostal movement is the ballad. In the style of a popular song, a soloist tells a story. It may be the story of his own life,[29] the story of someone in the audience[30] or a Bible story.[31]

The Working Fellowship of Christian Churches in Germany believes that when classical music is played a Pentecostal 'sits like one in the desert':

> The simple songs, performed by inspired singers and players, take hold of every heart – regardless of the level of a person's education – and therefore more use should be made of them.[32]

This statement is only necessary because the first signs are present of a change in the Pentecostal movement with regard to music. The hymns of A. A. Allen[33] have something genuinely primitive about them. Allen carries conviction not by his good singing, but by his total personal identification with the content of the song. But many other records give the impression that the singers are dissociating themselves from the hymns they are singing and trying to understand them as the object of an artistic statement. The result is that the deficiencies of these texts and melodies become embarrassingly prominent.[34]

The Assemblee di Dio go further, and take up the tradition of Italian opera choruses. They try to present the heavenly Jerusalem in the style of a brilliant opera by Verdi.[35] Douglas Gray, and other musicians and composers who have received a full musical education, have expressed the wish that Pentecostal musicians and composers should not be forced to give up all they have learned to take for granted during their musical training.[36]

Ralph Carmichael goes further still. In the style of a modern film score he paraphrases the hymns of the Pentecostals, accompanied by a huge symphony orchestra. In the hymn 'Now I Belong to Jesus',[37] for example, the refrain of the first verse is played by four trombones, while the second verse is accompanied by six bassoons[38] – a vast technical outlay,[39] which is in startling contrast, in my view, to what the composition is capable of bearing. From an artistic point of view the great majority of Pentecostal hymns are probably valueless. But they have the indisputable advantage of being sung by thousands of people. The Pentecostal movement teaches people to sing who would otherwise remain dumb. Sometimes, however, amongst the enormous mass of Pentecostal compositions, there appear works of genuine popular art. For example the Finnish Pentecostal movement has carried on the tradition of Finnish folk song,[40] while in the Brazilian Pentecostal movement we find genuine rumba, cha-cha and samba compositions,[41] accompanied by indigenous accompaniments.

(*c*) *Interpretation and assessment*

It is easy to dismiss this religion of longing for the world to come and inward experience as an opiate, a religious aspirin. As long as we have not found any effective remedy for the sickness of the world and the church, and as long as only 'educated and civilized persons . . . can satisfy their religious (and other) needs',[42] we have no right to deny those who are suffering their means of relief. The group therapeutic function of Pentecostal worship has been described at greater length above.[43] It has been thoroughly studied by the British sociologist Wilson.[44] It is beyond the scope of this study of the Pentecostal movement to review his specialist contributions on the subject. But one view which he advances seems to me worth quoting here. Wilson shows that Niebuhr's thesis that the sects, from a sociological point of view, are the expression of economic deprivation, is a statement which applies only to the circumstances of America.

In reply to this view Wilson argues that it is not economic deprivation alone which is decisive, nor does every deprivation lead to protest. Thus for example as long as a person accepts the class ethics of the Middle Ages, he does not feel deprivation. Only a deprivation which is a matter of conscious experience leads to protest. And this does not necessarily mean that the deprivation is real. It may be the only one which is felt. What is decisive is not the deprivation in itself, but the *feeling* of deprivation. The function of sects, from the sociological point of view, lies in the overcoming of this feeling of deprivation (status contradiction,[45] loneliness, poverty, sickness, racial discrimination, speech and language difficulties, handicaps of character, etc.) and it is not important in the first instance whether the deprivation is really overcome or merely allayed, as it were by a drug.

Christian Lalive d'Epinay, in his ambitious sociological study of the Chilean Pentecostal movement, shows that this movement is a substitute for the *hacienda*, the producer and consumer association of the great land owners. Here the Pentecostal pastor takes over the function of the former land owner. He cares for his congregation, finds work for them – factory managers are glad to turn to Pentecostal pastors as employment agents, because the Pentecostals are known as good and obedient workers – prays for the sick and organizes leisure activities.

The central point of this group therapeutic process is to be found in the Pentecostal service. An astonishing degree of communication, never achieved in other churches, takes place in these services. In Pentecostal worship – which only a casual observer could describe as unstructured and unliturgical – everyone can express himself with the means of speech at his own disposal. The criterion is not conceptual clarity, but communicability. A good Pentecostal pastor does not preach a sermon. The written text of theological or exegetical preparation does not come between him and his congregation.[46] He is not a 'man of fine phrases', who gives 'paper speeches, that is, essays which he reads aloud, and which have lost in the process of being written down the decisive element of speech, the living reality which arises directly from the dialogue between preacher and hearers.' But he is never at a loss for words, for 'the phenomenon of being at a loss for words is one which without question arises from the world of manuscripts, scholarship, and carefully formed and polished language.' Gesture and speech form a unity. He does not speak in an exaggerated or parsonical voice. He allows the social background of his hearers to 'put him off' and in fact these play a great part in determining the content and form of what he says. 'A good Pentecostal preacher is well worth hearing, for he has a genius for communication; his preaching is not a lecture but a dialogue.'[47]

It is here, in a sphere of liturgy and preaching, that the Pentecostal movement seems to me to have made its most important contribution, and not in the sphere of pneumatology, as is constantly and quite wrongly supposed.

But the two advantages of Pentecostal worship (its function as group therapy, and the direct personal contact obtained in preaching) are severely restricted by the unfortunate fact that they are reduced to processes within the mind of the individual. By the second generation, if not sooner, the methods used to overcome deprivation are subjected to a critical examination, and the drug which serves to overcome only the feeling of deprivation, and not the actual deprivation itself, is rejected. This is why, after twenty years, the titles of journals expressing an imminent hope of the second coming disappear, the purely emotional element falls into the background, secondary education becomes more important than the baptism of the Spirit, and ethical rigorism is relaxed. But none of this is possible until the first generation has succeeded, with the aid of the drug, in rising out of the misery which crippled it. The Communists of Chile say to young Pentecostals: 'Your pastors were Moses. They told you of a land in which milk and honey flowed. We are Joshua, we will lead you into it.' But even they have to admit that without the preparatory work of Moses the Pentecostals would not listen to Joshua. The result here is that young Pentecostals are no longer prepared to tolerate social and political injustice. And Donald Gee agrees with them:

> Too many of us have retreated for too long from the application of the principles of the gospel to society . . . If our remedy for the crying problems of social misery and injustice is absorption in evangelism pure and simple – so let it be. But let us take due note that our evangelism in that case must be full and complete. It is not enough to give men an assurance that their souls are securely labelled for heaven because of a decision in some mass meeting . . . Better citizenship should be a direct result of all sound Pentecostal evangelism.[48]

In certain societies the Pentecostal movement is a necessary island of humanity. For the poor it provides a home, relative economic security, care when they are sick and basic educational opportunities. It helps the managers of large factories, engineers, diplomats, artists and university professors, overloaded with responsibility, to discover the other side of their personality, the original, spontaneous, and individually human element, and to experience it in the framework of a liturgy which controls it, but which is spontaneous in form. The Benedictine Kilian McDonnell, in his study of the 'Ideology of Pentecostal Conversion', has rightly pointed out that in the Pentecostal church the problem of the 'unbelieving believer' cannot be approached by referring him to the 'field' of abstract theological assertions, in which he is hopelessly lost. He is capable neither of denying nor accepting the statements that are made about this 'theologians' God'. But – in McDonnell's view – he can experience in the Pentecostal liturgy that he is once again able to pray.[49]

Whether this island of humanity enables those who visit it to make the other spheres of society more human, or whether it betrays them into shutting off the humanity that they possess from the outside world – and so losing it – is a question which in my view still remains unanswered.

2. *Conversion or Politics: The Growing Social Commitment*

The Holiness movement championed conversion as the way to overcome social distress. 'For the converted, are not most so-called social problems in fact resolved?'[50]

> No one can save a man by filling his belly. Bring him into contact with Jesus and he will soon be able to buy his own dinner.[51]

Social problems are seen exclusively as the product of individual sins, amongst which the cinema and alcohol play the greatest part.[52] The Pentecostal movement took over from the Holiness movement this attitude of abstinence from politics:

> Consequently the Assemblee di Dio in Italy stand above and outside all the political competition and every political movement, from which they abstain, in order to concern themselves solely with the service of the Kingdom of God.[53]

'Worldly pleasures' are dangerous:

> If you have confessed Christ as your Saviour . . . tell them of your decision immediately . . . Should they reject him and attempt to draw you back into your old pursuits, remember that 'Friendship with the world is enmity with God'.[54]

Such worldly friendships should be used only as a bridgehead for evangelizing the world.

There are attacks on UNO, although the forbears of the Pentecostal movement, Upham and Mahan, proposed a United Nations Organization as long ago as the last century.[55] In Venezuela, a country where the average age of the population is nineteen, the Pentecostal movement, like the other Protestant churches, is losing the majority of its young members. The slightest deviation from ultra-conservatism is branded as free thinking. But in general, they are completely impotent when faced by economic and political problems.

> [The pastors] preach salvation by the blood of Christ and distribute tracts, but these problems are beyond them. The social movements are going to run us down, and we go on singing 'Onward, Christian Soldiers'.[56]

This abstinence from politics can rapidly, and apparently without motive, be transformed into over-simplified judgments on political matters, whenever Pentecostals come to feel that the kingdom of God is at stake. Thus Ignacio Mosqueda, once an army chaplain with Castro's revolutionary troops, and now working for the Full Gospel Business Men's Fellowship International, believes that Communism can only be fought with the gifts of the Spirit,[57] although the journal of this organization has described Fidel Castro as 'a great man with a deep hunger in his heart for God'.[58]

It is not surprising, then, that in certain American Pentecostal churches one finds the usual attacks on Communism. A speaker at an FGBMFI conference in 1964 could say that, even at the first United Nations conference in San Francisco, we were making every effort

> to accommodate ourselves to the Russian Communists and so to dishonour God. And as we excluded the Bible from our schools, so we did away with the last bulwark against the Communist termites who were gnawing at the very foundations of our God-given Christian Republic.[59]

These American Pentecostals magnanimously overlook the fact that some

Chilean and Brazilian Pentecostals are involved in an intensive dialogue with the Communists, and that many Italian Pentecostals vote for the Italian Communist Party, quite apart from the Russian Pentecostals, many of whom remained loyal to their Government, not only for tactical reasons. The affirmation of the Hungarian, Polish, Yugoslav and Rumanian Pentecostal movements,[60] that the people's democracies were the first to give them full religious freedom, cannot simply be dismissed out of hand as mere propaganda. Although these Pentecostals do not possess all the freedoms which are (theoretically) taken for granted in Western Europe, their situation has vastly improved by comparison with the period before the second world war. For not only are the hands of the majority churches tied, so that they can no longer oppress the Pentecostals, but also, whether they like it or not, they have to seek a *modus vivendi* with them. Donald Gee has contributed to this controversy with a courageous article entitled 'The End of Acts 2'.

> We may find excellent reasons for rejecting the idea of communism, but those professing to be filled with the Spirit of Christ have the responsibility of showing a realistic alternative.[61]

He questions whether resisting Communism 'is to be made a reason for Christians engaging in war and bloodshed'. Nevertheless, many Pentecostals in communist countries show that one can be a Christian even under a Communist government.[62]

The Dutch Pentecostal journal *Vuur* is even clearer in its statements. It recalls that Holland was liberated by the Canadians, the Americans, the British and the French. But Russian troops fought side by side with them. Today, the journal continues, it is only the Americans who can rely on us to be grateful. Whatever they do in Latin America, Greece, Portugal, Spain and Vietnam, they liberated us. Are we so grateful to the Russians that they can now do what they please in Czechoslovakia? It seems to be inherent in man, and even in Christians, to apply a double standard. Why were no obstacles placed in the way of Czech refugees, while it was extremely difficult for refugees from Angola to get into Holland?[63]

Individual Pentecostals have become politically conscious. Attempts to form a political party in Sweden under Pentecostal guidance, however, have not yet succeeded.[64] In Brazil, before the military regime was set up, Pentecostals were federal and provincial deputies,[65] and in Canada[66] and Kenya[67] there were Pentecostal ministers in the government.

The political awakening in the large Black Pentecostal movement in the USA is of great importance. This group, which has between 1,500,000 and 5,000,000 members[68] is posing at the present day a whole series of questions about the political relevance of the gospel. These churches regard political involvement and picketing as a gift of the Holy Spirit.[69] They are organizing job training centres and low income housing,[70] not only for their own members but for all who need it. Nor do those who teach in the job training centres have to be Pentecostals, nor even Christians. The important thing is that they can teach the subjects required. The bishops of the Church of God in Christ – this Negro church is the largest Pentecostal denomination in the United States, not the Assemblies of God, as is often falsely stated – are also clear that those who pass through these schools may very well not join a church, and perhaps not even become Christians at all.[71] Nevertheless, they believe that this work should be taken on as a part of the missionary task of the church.

It is understandable that against this background Black Pentecostals are not satisfied with the feeble attempts of white Pentecostals in America to understand social and political commitment as a task of the individual Christian (and *not* of the churches),[72] and the very tardy and generalized appeals for the Christian love of one's neighbour to be extended to the social field.[73]

> We believe in the content of the Graham message, but we can't go along with its suburban middle-class white orientation, that has nothing to say to the poor nor to the Black people.

In short, mass evanglism practised by the Rev. Billy Graham (and his imitators) – in the words of a Black pastor of the Assemblies of God – never had and never will have any relevancy to the Black community.[74] Their guiding theme is the non-violent resistance of Martin Luther King. During the garbage workers' strike in Memphis – during which King was assassinated – a Black Pentecostal church placed its principal church at the disposal of the strikers for their headquarters. The appeal of the Assemblies of God, 'not coercion, but conversion'[75] will fall on deaf ears as long as it continues to be uttered only to those below, and not equally loudly to those above. One can understand the pastor of the Assemblies of God in Alabama who stated:

> I feel that the greatest indictment against the church of the Lord Jesus in our century is our stand (or lack of one) on racial problems. We must search in our hearts to see if we have any type of racial misunderstanding in attitude or action.[76]

In words of great concern, addressed to the representatives of the Pentecostal revival within the traditional churches, Donald Gee wrote that it is not enough to have received the gift of speaking in tongues. 'Contrary to popular opinion, the highly educated and cultured sometimes make the worst fanatics.' We would not like to see in the new revivals simply a repetition of a pietistic form of religion in a higher level of society.[77]

In the field of charitable works, the achievements of the Pentecostal movement are small. This makes it all the more important to mention the more obvious exceptions. The Assembléias de Deus, Manoel de Melo and the Congregação Cristã do Brasil, have made original and valuable contributions in bringing social help and educational opportunities to large numbers of people in Brazil.

Their hospitals, schools and welfare institutions play an important part in Brazil. The schools and hospitals of the Norwegian Pentecostal movement also form an exception to the normal pattern of Pentecostal missionary activity, since the Norwegians, by contrast to other Pentecostals, have laid the greatest emphasis on this part of their missionary work. One outstanding achievement is the orphanage founded by Lilian Trasher in Assiut, Egypt,[78] where thousands of orphans are supported.

We must not underestimate the contribution of the Pentecostal groups which practise total abstinence, and assist in Africa to reduce the consumption of alcohol. Braide, one of the founders of an independent Pentecostal group in Nigeria, was arrested, officially for incitement to riot, but in fact as much as anything for the considerable reduction which he brought about in the takings from the excise duty on brandy.

The fact that several thousand gypsies have adopted the Pentecostal faith has had important social consequences, and so have the marriage agency of the Musama Disco Christo Church and the work carried out amongst young gangsters and drug addicts.[79]

Christian Lalive d'Epinay has criticized the Chilean Pentecostal movement because of its abstention from politics. The other Protestant churches in Chile are few in numbers, and with regard to their political commitment no better than the Pentecostal movement. Their message too is: Convert the sinner, and then you will convert society. But there is one exception, the Pentecostal Iglesia Wesleyana Nacional; it is a condition of membership in this church to belong to a trade union and to be an active member in a party of the left.[80]

D'Epinay's criticism of the incautious acceptance of Weber's hypothesis is of particular importance.[81] He paraphrases a famous text from Karl Marx:[82]

> The Pentecostal movement in Chile is 'at once the expression of economic wretchedness and a protest against real wretchedness'. It 'is the sign of the oppressed creature, the heart of a heartless world and the soul of soulless conditions. It is the opium of the people.' The abolition of Pentecostal religion as the illusory happiness of a people is a demand for their true happiness. The call to abandon illusions about their condition is the call to abandon a condition which requires illusions. Thus the critique of religion is a critique in embryo of the vale of tears of which religion is the halo.

Whereas in a European or North American society, a person's conversion and the puritan way of life associated with it, can lead to economic improvement, a better education for his children, and ultimately to the decisive degree of capital formation necessary for industrialization, in Latin American society the requirements for economic improvement brought about by conversion are absent. A monthly wage with a purchasing power varying between £5 and £15 does not allow any capital formation, even with a strictly puritan way of life. And even if this were possible, the runaway inflation of the escudo (approximately 20% a year) would swallow it up. Only the very rich can possess capital – that is, those Chileans who can obtain either landed property or foreign shares (or both). The cause of poverty in Chile is not the personal inadequacy of Chilean workers. Its causes lay in the *structural* poverty brought about by the situation of the international market and the capitalist economic system. These cannot be removed by the conversion of the individual, but by a political programme which makes impossible the exploitation of Chile by a handful of rich Chilean families and foreign companies. Only a minority of Pentecostals have yet recognized this. The dogmatic atheism of the Communist party of Chile prevents them from recognizing these structural links.[83]

3. *The Head or the Heart: The Growing Importance of Pentecostal Schools*

As long as attendance at secondary schools and universities was exceptional in the Pentecostal movement, there was agreement that 'God did not want scholars and clever persons. He had no need of science. All he wanted was pure hearts.'[84]

> Education is killing Christianity. I can go back to my young days among the Peculiar People; I had an uncle who couldn't read or write, but he got saved, and after that God taught him to read the Scriptures. But now head knowledge gets into religion. It makes young people query the virgin birth ... The less education the more quickly you can accept salvation.[85]

The Pentecostal experience gave talent to those who lacked it.[86] But Donald Gee criticized the sentimental style of writing and the inadequately prepared sermons to be found in the Pentecostal movement.[87] 'You must either have notes in your memory or on paper. If you have neither you have no message and are wasting the time of the flock.'[88]

In order to satisfy these demands, Bible schools were necessary. The fact that the pioneers of the Pentecostal movement included a number of preachers with no education, but great talents, is an exceptional case which is no excuse for insufficient training.[89] The backbone of Pentecostal schools is formed by the Sunday school. Their work is continued by fundamentalist Bible schools.

> The churches are not ignorant of the material needs of their members and as soon as the desire to improve their income is manifest amongst them, their sons go to the secondary schools and universities, admittedly only a small proportion of them.[90]

The Indian Pentecostal pastors from the United States also see redemption, emancipation and education as inseparable:

> I remember a girl said she couldn't do it, she was just an Indian. That's her defeat. That's the devil talking. Jesus is your help. He wrote my emancipation on Calvary ... God ... will make us free ... Don't give up just because you're

an Indian. You can stand with a white man, any race. You must *be* educated.[91]

H. D. Honsinger of the Pentecostal Assemblies of Canada replies to the charge that they are hostile to education. It is true, he says, that we never want to lose the contribution of self-taught men, who through no fault of their own have not been able to follow the normal course of theological training.

> Our doors will never be closed to men of their calibre. We will not be ashamed of their company . . . [But] we have no pleasure in men who despise education. The fundamental tenets of our statement of faith must always be open to investigation. Knowledge will not tarnish our beliefs but cause them, as their evidences are examined, to become brighter and more convincing.[92]

Polish Pentecostals allow their pastors to be trained at the Theological Academy in Warsaw together with Protestant ministers. They have produced the only scholarly study I know written in Europe about Dwight L. Moody.[93]

The African Pentecostal churches also build schools. Prophet Wovenu of the Apostolic Revelation Society gives an impressive account of how the attack of termites upon his school building was defeated by the concentrated prayer of Wovenu and his colleagues. Today Wovenu runs several schools and a seminary for pastors. Many Pentecostal missionaries have had to undertake linguistic studies because the tribes to whom they were preaching sometimes had no written language and often no translation of the Bible. Thus for example C. Austin Chawner was elected on to the committee for the orthography of the Tsonga language. In 1961 the missionaries of the Assemblies of God in Volta completed a translation of the New Testament from English into the Mossi language. One may have some doubts about the value of translation from English without any knowledge of the process of interpretation from the original biblical languages into English. Nevertheless, this work of translation has obliged the Pentecostals to come to grips with linguistic problems which otherwise they do not regard as worth considering.

The Swedish Pentecostal movement, whose founder, Lewi Pethrus, was awarded an honorary doctorate of Wheaton College, built an education college, the curriculum of which is particularly remarkable for the non-religious subjects it includes (civics, national economy, the working-class movement). The Swedish Pentecostal movement was unable to keep permanently within its ranks the writer Sven Lidman, who for years was the editor of the Swedish Pentecostal journal, and was known as a writer outside his own country.[94]

The development of the educational programme, of secondary schools and seminaries for pastors has been carried on at considerable expense and with remarkable sacrifices.[95] On the other hand the experience of conversion[96] and the gifts of the Spirit are less prominent,[97] and this is sometimes regretted:

> We have in our assemblies many more people, perhaps even members, who only have the forgiveness of sins, but are not born again and have not received the Holy Spirit.[98]

4. *Modern Shamans:*[99] *The Origin and Environment of Pentecostal Pastors as an Aid in Interpreting Pentecostal Belief and Practice*

(*a*) *Social origin*

The following table, 'The Profession of Pentecostal Pastors before their Ministry', is based on short biographies of four hundred leading Pentecostal pastors. The study's limits and deficiencies have been discussed in detail elsewhere. In particular, Latin American pastors are virtually unrepresented.[100]

It is immediately obvious from a study of the table that a large proportion of Pentecostal pastors were ministers of other free churches or of established churches before they joined the Pentecostal movement (I: 26.2%; 42.6%).[101] There is a remarkably large proportion of Anglicans, Lutherans, Reformed and Methodist ministers (60% of I). Small farmers (IV: 1.2%; 2.1%), and semi-skilled and unskilled industrial workers (V: 6.5%; 10.8%) are rather few, and even skilled manual and white collar workers (III: 9.5%; 15.6%) form a smaller proportion than one would expect. What is surprising is the relatively large proportion of upper- and middle-class origin (II: 12.5%; 20.3%) and artists (VI: 5.3%; 8.6%). Out of 400 pastors, 103 (25.7%; 42.0%) have had an academic education. This figure is surprising, even when one takes into account the proportion of pastors (45 out of the 103 with academic education; 11.7%; 18.3%) who up to the end of their lives (or until 1966) remained as ministers of a traditional church in addition to their activity in the Pentecostal movement.

The table can be summarized as follows: 26.2% (42.6%) of the Pentecostal pastors were originally pastors of a traditional church. A large proportion (I+II: 38.7%; 62.9%) were of upper- or middle-class origin. A significant minority were skilled manual or white collar workers, semi-skilled or unskilled industrial workers and small farmers (III+IV+V: 17.2%; 28.5%).

When the professions of the fathers of Pentecostal pastors are studied, the results are similar.[102] The largest group is once again that of ministers and pastors (I: 44.7%),[103] and there is once again a very high proportion of Lutheran, Reformed and Methodist ministers (approx. 40% of I). But we already find a considerable proportion of Pentecostal pastors whose *fathers* have themselves been pastors in the Pentecostal movement (approx. 30% of I). Here too, the upper and middle classes are well represented (II: 20%), but the proportion is smaller than that of semi-skilled workers, unskilled workers and farmers and farm workers (IV, V: 23.6%). The fathers of 21% of the pastors have had an academic education. This latter figure shows that the Pentecostal pastors in general have received a better education than their fathers.

How are these unexpected results to be explained? Almost all specialists assert that the Pentecostal movement recruits its members from the lower levels of society and that the movement becomes bourgeois in the second or third generation, but our statistics show that the Pentecostal movement as a *whole* is a predominantly bourgeois movement. Here one must bear in mind

The Profession of Pentecostal Pastors Before They Became Pastors

					%	%
I *Ministers, pastors*				105	26·2	42·6*
Roman Catholic	1	Baptist	10			
Anglican	9	Chrischona	1			
Lutheran	16	Salvation Army	8			
Reformed	20	Others	7			
Methodist	19	Lay Workers	14			
II *Upper and Middle Class*				50	12·5	20·3*
Kings	2	Doctors	11			
Large landowners	1	Lawyers	5			
Big businessmen	2	Engineers	7			
Managers	4	Teachers	14			
Professors	4					
III *Skilled Manual and White Collar Workers*				38	9·5	15·6*
Office workers, civil servants	19	Painters	4			
Policemen, etc.	3	Carpenters	2			
Nurses	1	Others	3			
Gardeners	6					
IV *Small farmers*				5	1·2	2·1*
V *Semi-skilled and unskilled industrial workers*				26	6·5	10·8*
VI *Artists, etc.*				21	5·3	8·6*
Musicians	6	Photographers	1			
Journalists, writers	3	Partisan leaders and revolutionaries	4			
Artists	1	Others	2			
Sportsmen	1					
Designers	3					
VII *Unknown*				155	38·8	
VIII *Total*				400	100	100
With higher education				103	25·7	42*
Number remaining until death (or till 1966) a pastor in a traditional church				45	11·7	18·3*

* First percentage taken inclusive of the 38·8% unknown, second figure excluding them.

Graph Relating Three Generations

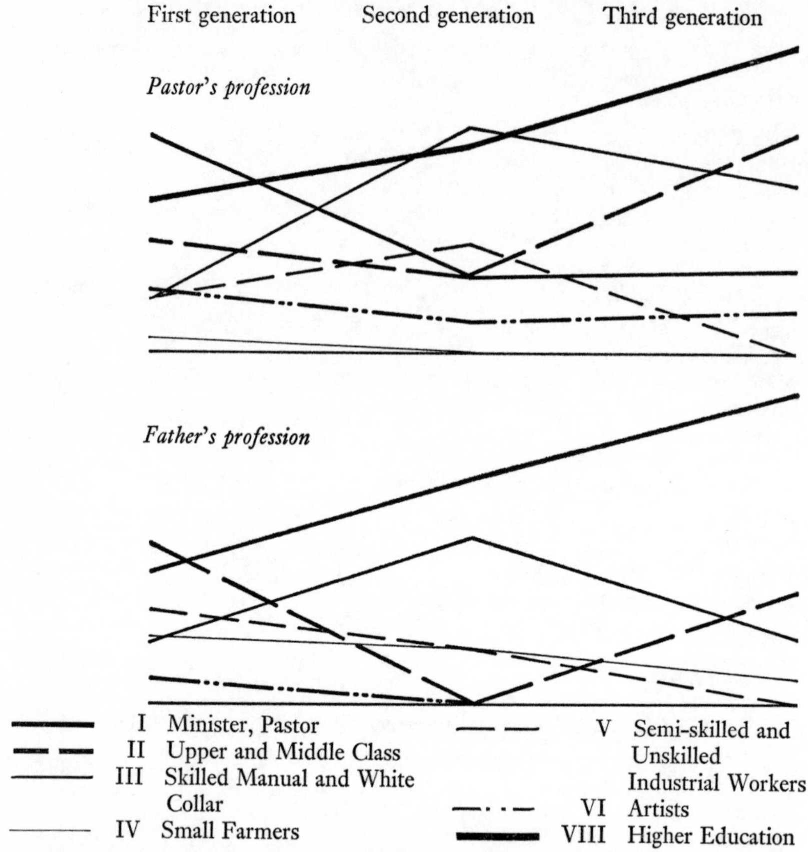

that this study was based on the pastors. Perhaps the social structure of Pentecostal pastors as a group is not the same as that of their congregations.

In order to answer these questions more satisfactorily, it is necessary to break the figures down by generation.[104] The situation is displayed in the simplest possible form in the graph above. The proportion of ministers and pastors (I) falls from the first to the second generation. The proportion of upper- and middle-class origin (II) greatly increases from the second to the third generation. Small farmers (IV) disappear completely after the second generation. The greatest proportion of skilled manual and white collar workers (III) and semi-skilled and unskilled industrial workers (V) is found in the second generation. The proportion with an academic education (VIII) steadily increases.

When one considers the graph of 'Fathers of Pentecostal Pastors' (p. 476), it can be seen that the proportion of pastors whose fathers were already ministers and pastors (I) constantly increases. In the second generation the proportion of pastors whose fathers were upper- or middle-class (II) falls to zero. Small farmers (IV), semi-skilled and unskilled industrial workers (V) and artists (VI) constantly decrease (the latter falling to zero by the second generation). Skilled manual and white collar workers (III) reach the highest point in the second generation. When one compares the graph 'Profession of Pastors before their Ministry' with the graph 'Profession of Fathers of Pentecostal Pastors', it is clear in both cases that curves II (upper and middle class), III (skilled manual and white collar workers), IV (farmers and farmworkers), V (semi-skilled and unskilled industrial workers), and VI (artists) show the same tendency. To sum up, one can say that the number of Pentecostal pastors who, before being called to be pastors in the Pentecostal movement, were already ministers or preachers falls. But the number of those who have had higher education, the number of pastors who come from middle- and upper-class families and from the families of ministers and pastors, increases at a corresponding rate. In both graphs, the lower middle classes (III) reach a maximum figure in the second generation. In both graphs the proportion of farmers and farmworkers (IV), artists (VI) and semi-skilled and skilled industrial workers (V) decreases.

I cannot find an explanation for the remarkable 'kink' which certain curves in the graph show in the second generation.[105] That the sociological structure of the second generation of Pentecostal pastors is different from that of the first can be confirmed by a further observation. It is well known that a large number of the pioneers of the Pentecostal movement were driven out of the denominations they founded after twenty-five years, so that they either had to return to their earlier profession,[106] found new and smaller movements,[107] join another denomination[108] or be deprived of their influence in their own movement and sometimes even be forgotten.[109] In almost every case the official histories of the denomination concerned give explanations to rationalize the reasons for this expulsion: dogmatic deviations, autocratic tendencies, moral failures, etc. Some of these charges may be true. But they are not sufficient to explain the departure of such a large number of prominent Pentecostal leaders. According to B. R. Wilson, who made a thorough sociological analysis of the relationship of G. Jeffreys to the Elim Pentecostal Churches, the reason is that after twenty-five years the Pentecostal denomination has to develop institutional forms and comes to have a new type of pastor, who is at the same time an administrative official. This new kind of pastor inevitably comes into conflict with the type represented by the first generation, the charismatic pioneers.[110]

(*b*) *The motives which lead people to become pastors*

There are two questions which concern us here:

1. What happens when a young man from poor circumstances becomes a Pentecostal pastor?

2. What happens when a minister, an ordinand or someone of middle class origin becomes a Pentecostal pastor?

Examples of (1)

The English Pentecostal evangelist Smith Wigglesworth[111] was born in Menston, Yorkshire, as one of six children in a very poor family. He had to go to work when he was only six years old. When he was seven, he began work in a cotton weaving mill, where he worked with his father from six in the morning to six at night.

> I cannot forget those long winter nights and mornings, having to get out of bed at five o'clock to snatch a quick meal and then walk two miles to be at work at six. We had to work twelve hours each day, and I often said to my father, 'It is a long time from six until six in the mill.' I can remember the tears in his eyes as he said; 'Well, six o'clock will always come.' Sometimes it seemed like a month coming.[112]

With his grandmother he went to Wesleyan services, where he once took part in a dancing service. At that chapel anyone who wished could testify. Wigglesworth tried to do so several times, but after the first words almost burst into tears. One day three old men prayed with him, so that he was freed from this inhibition. Since he had had to work in a factory as a boy, he had no schooling. His wife later taught him to read. He was never very good at writing. The book *Ever Increasing Faith* was written down by those who heard his sermons. He never read it himself. This stocky, uneducated man became one of the greatest evangelists of the Pentecostal movement. In most of the capitals of the world, he preached to large crowds. His preaching was characterized by short staccato sentences. He was adept at summing up his message in a single phrase. Once he had overcome the mute suffering of the exploited proletarian, he became a symbol of the little man, poor and uneducated, despised by the world but loved by God. His sure feeling for the English language was astonishing. Although he had the opportunity to become rich, money meant nothing to him. 'Making a living is the small, time-serving, dwarfed and paralysed man's object. Making a life is the kingly, righteous and holy man's object.' He was very abrupt with God: 'If you ask God seven times for the same thing, six times are in unbelief.' 'If the Spirit does not move me, I move the Spirit.'[113] 'Great faith is a product of great fights. Great testimonies are the outcome of great tests. Great triumphs can only come after great trials.'[114]

When the fourteen-year-old Dane Andreas Enderson (1889–1967) went into the factory, it must have been a cruel shock to him, not only because to the amusement of his instructor, a rough journeyman blacksmith, he could not lift the great sledge-hammer, but also because the latter greeted him with fierce curses and imprecations. 'He said he would have great pleasure in splitting me into pieces, so that at least he could make a walking stick out of me.'[115] Under this man's influence he was soon led into swearing, drinking and stealing materials from the factory. He gives a vivid description of his apprenticeship in his autobiography. There was no one to whom he could utter his distress, for he had no friends. Nevertheless, he prayed the Lord's Prayer every day. A representative of the Blue Cross (the temperance organization), to whom he confided his vice, laid down a probationary period of three months. But how could he go for three months, when he could not even live for three days without alcohol? In 1919, greatly influenced by the words of the pastor at a mission service, he prayed at home: 'Jesus, if it is true that you live, save me and make me as willing to follow you as I have been to follow the devil.'[116] He was certainly freed from his vice. His place in the bar at ten o'clock in the morning and four o'clock in the afternoon remained empty. He told what had happened to the Blue Cross man who had laid down a probationary period of three months for him, but was greeted with disbelief. Four years later he became an evangelist of the Pentecostal Elim Assembly.

Another Danish Pentecostal pastor, Martinus Bjerre, as a small boy, had to drive the cattle fifteen miles to a neighbouring farm at night, so that he lost no time from his work during the day. He used to pray: 'Dear God, it doesn't matter if things go on like this as long as I am young. But please take care of me when I am old, and then I will be able to come up to you when I die.'[117]

Donald Edward Curry has published and commented on a lengthy taped interview with a Brazilian Pentecostal pastor, Antônio José dos Santos. In the north-east of Brazil, in Pôrto do Calvo, dos Santos at the age of thirty-six accepted 'the word of Christ's Gospel'. Then he went ten months into the wilderness to pray. He describes in detail his wanderings in north-east Brazil, his embitterments and miraculous liberations, his healings and prayer meetings. He finally succeeded in founding, with a small congregation of thirty families, a kind of self-governing agricultural co-operative owning its own land. Curry impressively demonstrates the fact that for dos Santos and his followers salvation happens here and now through their liberation from mental subjection, and consequently from economic and political oppression.[118]

Examples of (2) (pp. 477 and 478)

It is clear that the second kind of example will not be so vivid. A well-run upper-class English household,[119] the house of a Lutheran pastor,[120] the court of a rich prince or even a king in Nigeria,[121] or a normal German middle-class family[122] does not provide material for dramatic autobiographies.

Perhaps the best example of a minister who became a Pentecostal pastor can be found in the life story of Fritz de Rougemont, who was a minister in Neuenburg.[123] He is by no means an exception. For example, Otto Witt, a German Lutheran minister, came in contact during the war with the Norwegian Pentecostal movement, and expressed his disappointment at the lack, in his own Lutheran church at home, of a

> deeper and more real experience of the Holy Spirit as the reality proceeding from Christ, giving courage and leading into all truth – not as a 'second blessing', going beyond the fundamental grace of justification, but as the powerful development of a new existence in every direction.[124]

And the talented Dutch organist Peter van Woerden, who became a Christian in prison, describes the first service he attended after his release in the Reformed church as a great disappointment.

> The pastor, standing in the pulpit with his gown, was a wholly sympathetic figure. His sermon was an interesting presentation of a number of biblical truths, his style was polished and every expression he used carefully chosen. But what I found lacking was any practical application of the theological truths which were being so skilfully propounded. One could compare him with someone giving a distinguished lecture about bread to a hungry crowd.

Instead, he found in a Pentecostal assembly the spiritual support and biblical instruction which he sought, although the pastor was not very fluent, and as a trained musician he was irritated by the Pentecostal style of singing.[125]

Out of four hundred Pentecostal pastors, a hundred and five were ministers or pastors in another church before becoming pastors in the Pentecostal movement. Some of them remained ministers in their own church and worked part-time in the Pentecostal movement, while the others left the service of their church. One can sum up by saying that both categories, the ministers and the working men who became Pentecostal pastors, were dissatisfied with the social or ecclesiastical structures in which they lived. The workers saw themselves faced by an anonymous set of circumstances which they had to suffer in silence. The Pentecostal movement made it possible for them to articulate their suffering and so overcome it. The ministers suffered because the church they belonged to had ceased to command a living faith, and they hoped to find in the Pentecostal movement a more lively and missionary-minded group, closer to other people and closer to the Bible, of Christians whose talents were both intellectual and intuitive, both rational and emotional. An examination of their biographies does not confirm the charge that these ministers were looking for a non-institutional and purely enthusiastic fellowship of believers. What they were looking for in the Pentecostal movement was not a church without institutions, but a church which did not carry on its institutions for their own sake, and was ready to give up or replace parts of an institution which had lost their function. This is in fact the most important ecclesiological question in present-day ecumenical discussion. The fact that a large number of ministers and ordinands have joined the Pentecostal movement is the expression of their search for a flexible church structure which is capable of functioning effectively.

The same can probably be said of the artists who have become Pentecostal pastors. The famous Swedish author Sven Lidman[126] found in the Pentecostal movement a meaning for life which he had previously sought in vain in his activity as a writer. The equally famous Danish opera singer Anna Larsen Bjørner[127] found a fuller life as the wife of a pastor than in the opera. Both were to undergo severe disillusionments: Lidman, when he was driven out by the less talented but more vigorous Lewi Pethrus, and Anna Larsen Bjørner when she had to live through a severe schism in the Danish Pentecostal movement, for which her husband, Sigurd Bjørner, the former secretary of the YMCA, was not wholly without blame.

Musicians of average skill from the world of entertainment, such as Joseph Wannenmacher, Douglas Scott and others, found in the assemblies of the Pentecostal movement an attentive and grateful audience, in particular as their music was interpreted in the framework of the scheme of values of Pentecostal evangelization, and sanctified as the handmaid of evangelization. (Summary, pp. 489ff.).

(*c*) *An account of conversion, the baptism of the Spirit and the call as an aid to the interpretation of the doctrine of the Pentecostal pastor*[128]

Conversion: There are many types of description of conversions. Quite a number of Pentecostal pastors were converted when members of a traditional church either by the preaching of a 'minister mighty in the spirit' (see Röckle), by a hymn (M. A. Alt), by the personal exhortation of a 'converted minister' (F. Jéquier), by his own liturgical ministry at the funerals of children (J. Paul), or the pastoral work of the minister who prepared him for confirmation (A. Goetz). Negative judgments on the instruction given by the church can sometimes be found, but are relatively rare (F. Schäufele); for example, the only positive thing which A. Endersen can remember from his confirmation instruction is the fact that because he learned a children's hymn properly he was given a large pear. The confirmation day filled him with dread.

Others were converted by hymns, testimonies, or sermons by Pentecostals, either in open air meetings (L. Jeeveratnam, C. Lemke) or in a Pentecostal service (N. Bhengu, A. Béart). Many were healed from a severe disease and were converted as a result (Adegoke, N. Nxumalo, L. B. Yeomans). Others again were converted by the personal testimony of a Christian (U. Lasco, D. J. Du Plessis, L. Wreschner, H. Zaiss). A few had a vision (M. Fraser, Jakob Widmer). Others were disappointed with life as a result of misfortunes and were then converted (W. A. Raiford). Some were converted when young (A. B. Reuss, R. Ruff and others). Often the conversion represents the close of a period of youthful melancholy.

In general it can be said that the Pentecostal experiences the conversion which is best suited to his blocked expectations and his mental constitution. One must not overestimate the element of 'social deprivation'. It is only one of the possible factors. According to L. P. Gerlach and V. H. Hine the decisive element in joining a Pentecostal assembly is a personal invitation (a statement which is based on a thorough analysis in the USA).[129]

Baptism of the Spirit and call: The baptism of the Spirit has been described in detail above.[130]

In the Pentecostal movement the call to be a pastor must be an experience which in the eyes of the person who is called and of his future followers allows a break with previous loyalties, and indeed demands and gives a positive interpretation to such a break. It can be brought about by visions, dreams, voices, prophecies on the part of another person, the reading of the Bible, or doubts about the established church. The final step is usually brought about by a combination of various factors.

The bishop of the American Negro church, the Church of God in Christ, C. H. Mason, was called by a vision. The healing evangelist T. L. Osborn experienced his call while pasturing cattle 'with many tears', and later had a vision of Christ. The Nigerian steam-roller driver Joseph Babalola did not react to several calls by voices to become a pastor. Thereupon his steam-roller refused to function, which he saw as an unmistakable sign to respond to the call. When the American healing evangelist Philip N. Green was reading a philosophical article, in order to write a book about 'The Believer's Approach to Philosophy', he heard a voice which said to him: 'If you will close your library and read only one Book, I will give you miracles wherever you go.' The German pastor Martin Gensichen was required by his superior in the Berlin City Mission to make written preparation for his sermons. Gensichen tried to carry out this order, but when he tried to write his sermons down, he tells us that his hand was prevented from writing by God. Gensichen thereupon gave up his ministry and became a Pentecostal pastor.

Daniel Berg, a Swedish emigrant to the USA, was shown in a dream that he had to go as a missionary to Pará. He did not know where Pará was, but found in the Chicago public library that it was a state in Brazil. He became the founder of the Assembléias de Deus in Brazil, which now has two million members. Karl Born was called by a prophecy given during a visit of the South African Latter Rain movement to become a full time pastor of the German Latter Rain Mission, after his wife, during the last days of the Benoni Conference in 1960, was set free from an evil force which was made to reveal itself and was driven out with a loud cry. 'Hundreds of people at the conference were present when this happened, to their great joy.'

Sometimes the prophecy or the vision is experienced by someone else. Thus the prophet Job Cartey came to Appiah and prophesied:

> Master Appiah, God has made you a great king. On my way here I saw you in a vision dressed like a king, with a crown on your head, and angels were bringing you down to the earth from heaven. In this way God sends me to tell you that he has made you a great king.

The mother of the prophet C. Wovenu, Mikayanowa, was barren. Wovenu was born as the result of the prophecy of an unknown person who said to his father that 'this son's head will stand higher than my father's'.

G. R. Polman refused a call to become a Salvation Army officer, explaining to another officer that he had to take over his father's farm. The officer replied, 'Anyone can run a farm, but not everyone can save sinners.' The British jazz musician Douglas Scott was called to missionary work by a message spoken in tongues, with an interpretation. He played a decisive part in the setting up of what is the largest free church in France, the Assemblées de Dieu. Many already felt the call to be pastors when they were boys.[131]

Others became certain of their call on being healed from severe illness.[132] The Ghanaian mason Do was told by his pastor that the Bible would become his *dowonu*, that is, his tool. Do took no notice of this statement, because he wanted to become a stonemason. After his apprenticeship as a mason, he worked at digging and lining wells in Togoland, where he was much sought after. Wherever he worked, he was also a keen member of the Presbyterian Church. When he was working in Ziofe, there were no Presbyterian services there. And therefore, with the permission of the church authorities, he began to hold services in Ziofe. Since those who attended did not know the hymns, he organized hymn practices. A dying boy was brought to one of these practices, and the assembled congregation prayed for him, whereupon he was healed. This was the beginning of a prayer and healing group which remained within the Presbyterian church, and of which Do became the leader.

Sometimes, a severe disappointment can lead to a conversion experience, as for example when the American detective W. A. Raiford lost an election. Of greater importance are the doubts which L. Eisenlöffel underwent during his training as a church worker. Eisenlöffel was looking for security and guidance in the training institute, but found instead young people full of questions, 'not because they were thirsting for the truth, but because they wanted to justify their doubts'. His experiences as a teacher in a church children's home strengthened his criticism of the church, and he joined the Pentecostal movement, to which his mother had already belonged. In the case of the founder of the American 'Jesus only' group, F. J. Ewart, the discovery of the baptismal formula 'in the name of Jesus' in the Acts of the Apostles played the decisive part in a new Pentecostal denomination which observed the 'biblical formula of baptism.'

These examples show that a calling to become a pastor is experienced under a wide range of forms, depending on the degree of resistance, the psychological and cultural environment and the individual temperament of the person called. But the decisive element is always that the call is recognized either by the church to which the person belongs, or else by a new congregation which is founded as a result of the call.

(*d*) *Pentecostal dogmatic theology as an expression of the Pentecostal experience of life*

In order to determine the relationship between the experience of Pentecostal pastors and the doctrine they teach, we must ask what the prominent elements will be in a dogmatic system which arises from the experience of life, and the realities in life, which have been described in the above biographies (and in particular in their crucial points, conversion, the baptism of the Spirit and vocation to be a pastor). The material we have given suggests the following conclusions:

1. Anyone who is deprived of nourishment, clothing, education, social recognition and the means of expressing himself has two alternatives.

(*a*) He may develop a system in which these things, or some of them, are seen as of little value or even harmful.

(*b*) Alternatively, he may develop a system which gives him possession of what he lacks.

Both these courses have been followed in the Pentecostal movement.

(*a*) The low value placed on the goods and possessions provided by civilization is expressed in the many rigoristic ethical provisions.[133] A Christian does not smoke and drink. He does not go to the cinema nor to the theatre. A Christian woman dresses modestly and does not wear make-up. Book learning is dangerous to religious life, etc.

(*b*) Alternatively, the reverse argument may be found, especially amongst Pentecostals who as a result of their disciplined way of life have obtained riches and social prestige. There the doctrine is: God is a good God. He cares for his children. And therefore Christians prosper in all circumstances, and particularly in matters of finance and health.[134]

2. But since both groups have experienced the world as a hostile environment, one can expect their theology to be hostile to the world. Their distrust of institutions belonging to this world, such as the structures of the state and the established churches, will crystallize into a pessimistic view of the present. Everything is expected of the future, which is either understood as the second coming of Jesus, or, in a later phase, as a time when the Pentecostal assembly will have a sphere of influence set up and maintained by God, like a tiny island of paradise in the midst of the raging sea of the world. Often both conceptions appear together. The island of paradise is as it were the earthly bridgehead for the coming kingdom of God.

Ministers of traditional churches who become Pentecostal pastors are found in both categories. For them, however, the primary motive is the practical one of being able to work within a team of committed missionaries. But since they have made some study of church history, their effect is to moderate the dualism described above. On the other hand, it is clear to any observer that ministers of traditional churches who become Pentecostal pastors rarely join the older and more moderate Pentecostal groups, but virtually always one of the younger, more dynamic groups, whose outlook is more dualist. They often do so with the explanation, which I find incomprehensible, that they have found a 'sober' Pentecostal church, which avoids the well-known excesses. (They can only say this, of course, because the younger Pentecostal groups are mostly still unknown and often have names which do not include the word 'Pentecostal'.)

One may point as examples to the theologians who in Switzerland have joined not the Swiss Pentecostal Mission, but the more recently formed Apostolic Church; or the ministers in Germany who did not join the Mülheim Association of Christian Fellowships or the Working Fellowship of Christian Churches, but the German Latter Rain Churches. Similarly, one finds in the USA that the many ministers who have experienced the baptism of the Spirit with speaking in tongues very rarely join the Assemblies of God or other more traditional Pentecostal denominations, but instead join the more recent and more dynamic lay organization, the Full Gospel Business Men's Fellowship International, which supports the healing evangelists and includes many rich business men.

When a minister joins the Pentecostal movement, he does so in order to overcome a feeling of deprivation or handicap. In the first instance it is a matter of indifference whether the deprivation is really overcome or merely subdued as by a drug. There is no question that, at first at least, a pastor will feel himself more free in the more informal – but none the less firmly structured – hierarchy of the Pentecostal movement. He will also regard his accession to the Pentecostal movement as a liberation, and develop a theology which regards the group dynamic, subconscious play of forces, controlled by both spontaneous and artificial techniques, which is to be found in the Pentecostal movement, as something more in accordance with the New Testament than the organizational forms of his church of origin.

3. In order to mark the difference between the church and the world, there are likely to be clear landmarks. But the material we have presented shows that conversions are not sufficient to serve this purpose. We have seen that conversion can be experienced in very different ways. Moreover, conversion as a distinguishing mark has been devalued by great evangelization campaigns such as Billy Graham's. Too many people have come forward when the call is made, and there has been no visible change in their lives. Consequently, signs must be found which are clearer and more tangible, in order to make abundantly clear who belongs to one's own 'tribe', the church, and who belongs to the 'hostile tribes', the world. This function of a 'tribal mark' is largely supplied by the baptism of the Spirit, with the objectively ascertainable sign of speaking in tongues. In my view there are sociological reasons why the 'tribal religion' of the Pentecostal church was bound to develop such a doctrine as the baptism of the Spirit, as it is found in Pentecostalism, particularly with the frequent obligatory requirement that it should be accompanied by speaking in tongues.

4. When, however, after twenty years or so, the island of paradise turns out to be a purely human island on which things go on as they always do amongst men – even amongst redeemed men who have been baptized in the Spirit – a crisis occurs in the group's theological thinking. One can naturally expect a

watering-down of the elements of hostility to the world in its theology, and in the 'tribal religion'. But this happens only very slowly. The wounding shock delivered by the 'world' and the 'dead' churches to which they formerly belonged still produces its effects, and is sometimes stirred up again by severe persecutions on the part of majority churches and members' or pastors' accounts, painted in schematic and disparaging terms, of the life of sin lived before joining the Pentecostal movement. The ideology is changed only to the extent to which there are human contacts with other 'tribes' or sub-cultures.[135] In other cases, the suspicion may arise that the tribal tattoo marks are false or imprecise. Additional distinguishing marks have therefore to be introduced, such as baptism 'in the name of Jesus', 'full confession',[136] the setting up of apostolic ministries,[137] a third crisis experience,[138] the keeping of the sabbath and the introduction of the washing of feet.[139] This makes clear the sociological reason why there must always be a variety of doctrinal systems in the Pentecostal movement. The form the varieties take is probably not important. All that matters is that one can wear different tribal marks from the neighbouring tribe, which is related, but for that very reason dangerous.

(*e*) *A contradiction in Pentecostal dogmatic teaching: women preachers*

Not all elements of Pentecostal belief and practice, however, can be explained from the life story of Pentecostal pastors. For example, fundamentalism cannot be explained without more ado from the experience that pastors have undergone in their lives. However, if one follows James Barr[140] in describing fundamentalism as ritualism, it fits well into the scheme of values which one might expect from the life story of Pentecostal pastors.

But the Pentecostal theory about women and the actual roles which women play in the Pentecostal movement are not so easy to reconcile. Three types of women are of particular importance in the Pentecostal movement.

The prophetess: This type is not found in biographical material, because the prophetess never becomes a pastor, and does not write books. She is a 'sister' of the church, who expresses herself during periods of prayer by prophecies. I recall my Sunday school teacher in the Zürich Pentecostal Mission. She was a childless married woman of about 50 years old. Her husband never spoke at the services. But when she began her prophecies, in a voice that went to your very heart, with the words 'Behold, – a long pause! – 'thus saith the Lord . . .,' in immense tension, a silence of almost indescribable concentration, came over the meeting. As far as I can remember, she usually uttered no more than a few short sentences. She was not an exalted personality, but a modest woman, who, when she was asked for advice by the 'sisters', expressed herself very cautiously and hesitantly. Such prophetesses exist in many Pentecostal congregations. Yuasa has given a fine description of their function in the Brazilian Congregação Cristã. They take care of the poor and relieve the pastor of a large part of his personal pastoral care. It is to the advantage of a young pastor to seek the advice of these 'wise women', even if he cannot always follow it. Of course this type of woman also includes domineering scandalmongers, discontented with their marriage or with being spinsters, and this usually leads to tensions or divisions in the church.

The pastor's wife: The pastor's wife is her husband's helpmate. She often has greater intellectual gifts than her husband, with his more spontaneous talents, and takes care of his correspondence, translates letters, reads books for him, goes to most of his services and listens to his sermons. From time to time she may criticize him. For the most part she is the 'gentle, tender, brave but submissive helpmate' of her husband, who, in the words of the Italian Pentecostal pastor Roberto Bracco,[141] 'has a more direct responsibility before God than she for the life of the family'.

> The preacher's wife . . . must stand beside her husband in prayer and travail of tears. He is the champion of God, and she only the helpmate . . . Others may see the anointed giant of God, but she sees the weak mortal who is mere man until the divine spark is struck.[142]

The woman with theatrical talents: This category does not include either the many Pentecostal women missionaries,[143] women pastors[144] nor the women evangelists, who, as in other churches, sometimes work under conditions which are too hard for men (e.g. in Sweden). These are women preachers who by their dominating motherly personality, their beauty, and their outstanding and genuinely theatrical talents play the same role in the Pentecostal movement as great actresses in the rest of society. Women with such talents would, as members of traditional churches, take up a career as actresses or singers. But because these callings are taboo for Pentecostals, the Pentecostal 'actresses' have no other course than to transform the calling of a woman preacher in such a way that it can be carried out by an actress, a 'star of the Kingdom of God'. The most outstanding example is Aimee Semple McPherson. As a girl she already had a sense of the dramatic. Instead of letting herself be laughed at because her mother belonged to the Salvation Army, she invented a Salvation Army game. And even as a child, she succeeded in drawing her friends in the new game. When she was seventeen she was converted by the preacher Robert Semple, whom she later married. Her burning love for Robert Semple united religion, passion and ambition, the three driving forces in her life which enabled her to break down the iron door leading to the wide world. After the death of her first husband, Robert Semple, she married Harold McPherson. But this marriage soon broke up, because Harold McPherson had no understanding of Aimee's ambitions as an evangelist. In 1922 she built the Angelus Temple in Los Angeles (which cost £600,000). It had 5,300 seats and two sets of choir stalls for a hundred singers, and the floors were covered with red fitted carpets. In 1926 she fell in love with her radio operator – in the meantime she had also set up a radio station – and went off on holiday with him, although he was married. This escapade led to a court case, but did not reduce the boundless enthusiasm of her followers for 'Sister Aimee'. From then on one scandal after another took place in her life, including another marriage and a second divorce.

> Thus 'Sister' grappled her followers to her with hoops of steel. Their devotion was not shaken by the many notorious escapades in which she was involved, family quarrels, lawsuits, alleged kidnapping and subsequent criminal prosecution, marriage, separation and so forth. Scandals which would have destroyed any decorous religious leader were used by this prophetess to strengthen her position . . . Her whole career was an interesting study in sexual charm and religious devotion.[145]

She probably died from an overdose of sleeping pills. Her funeral was one of Hollywood's greatest sensations.[146] However, her denomination continued to grow, and at the present day has missions throughout the world.[147] Nor do her critics deny that 'she had actually succeeded in turning criminals into church members and drug addicts into healthy human beings'.[148]

The extravagant Aimee is not the only member of this category. It also includes Lilian Trasher, the orphans' mother.[149] As a young missionary, she went to Egypt and there founded an orphanage, which took the place of home and parents for thousands of Egyptian girls. She sent the more talented of her girls to secondary school, but also introduced them to Pentecostal religion. The girls practised their Christianity by praying every day with their foster mother for the necessary funds. In 1927 and 1936 revivals broke out, with baptisms of the Spirit and speaking in tongues. Lilian Trasher was highly honoured by many Egyptians and even given financial support by the Egyptian State.

We have already mentioned the Danish opera singer Anna Larsen Bjørner. The American Maria Atkinson, known as the 'Woman in White', was originally a Catholic, and became a talented and successful pioneer and founder of churches in Mexico, while Maria Fraser founded the rigorist Latter Rain movement in South Africa. During a dance she heard a voice which said to her: 'What if Jesus came now!' She sold her jewels and gave the money she received to the church and to the poor, but at first remained a member of the Anglican church. Not until later did she and her husband, who was a surveyor by profession, join the Pentecostal movement. In 1927 she founded the Latter Rain movement in Benoni, because the Pentecostals did not agree with her prophecies, which revealed the sins of individuals.[150]

Johanna Nxumalo is a princess from Swaziland. Together with her sister, the queen Nukwase Nxumalo, she helped to spread the Pentecostal movement in Swaziland. Nukwase built the Pentecostals a large cathedral in Lobabma. Following a vision, she wears at services a stole which contains the colours of all the Zionist churches in Swaziland. Three women pastors of different Zionist churches brought her the necessary materials from their churches and sewed it together. This is Nukwase's contribution to ecumenism in the categories of Swazi thought.

One of the most interesting women in the new Pentecostal movement within the existing churches is Jean Stone, the wife of a retired officer of the US Navy, who is now a factory manager at the Lockheed Aviation Works. The 'best society' of California used to meet at her home. Through the laying on of her hands many Anglican, Lutheran, Roman Catholic and Presbyterian ministers experienced the baptism of the Spirit.[151]

To sum up, one could say that while the 'prophetesses' and the pastor's wives fit into the scheme laid down by Pentecostal doctrine concerning the position of women in the church, the women with theatrical talents provide a remarkable contrast to the Pentecostal theory of the subordination of woman. From the methodological point of view this means that the woman with theatrical gifts is a variable. This factor, not previously taken into account this study, illustrates the difference between the hierarchy of persons which one would expect from Pentecostal doctrine, and the informal hierarchy which actually exists. In the Pentecostal movement there are informal systems of value in existence which are in contradiction to the official doctrine that is preached.

One would expect wide degrees of variation (apart from other practical problems) in the degree to which the Pentecostal movement is ready to entertain informal hierarchies, but within the scope of this study I am not able to demonstrate this.

(*f*) *Where sociology and theology coincide*

The results of this sociological study can be summed up as follows:

1. Before taking on the profession of pastor, the majority of Pentecostal pastors in this study belonged to the upper and middle classes (I, II: 38.7%, 62.9%). Many (I: 26.2%, 42.6%) were originally ministers or pastors in other churches. This change of profession cannot be interpreted in the framework of the terminology of American sociology of religion as a professional advancement. The fact that a large number of ministers and ordinands have joined the Pentecostal movement is an expression of their search for a more flexible and serviceable church structure.

The artists (VI: 5.3%, 8.6%) found in the Pentecostal movement a more satisfying motive for the practice of their art, and a more grateful public.

2. There are a considerable number of exceptions to this basic pattern. A considerable minority of Pentecostal pastors were formerly skilled manual or white collar workers, semi-skilled or unskilled industrial workers and farmers or farm labourers (total 17.2%, 28.5%). For them the profession of pastor represented a professional advancement. It is possible that if the sample included more representatives of the Latin American Pentecostal movement, and more representatives of the second generation, the proportion from these levels of society would be greater. The Pentecostal movement made it possible for these underprivileged people to articulate their deprivation and so to overcome it.

3. Not every generation of Pentecostal pastors has the same sociological structure. In a third generation the number of those who have completed a course of higher education, and of pastors of upper- and middle-class origin, greatly increases. The small lower-middle-class group (III), and semi-skilled and unskilled workers, are more strongly represented in the second generation. One must also note that the basic sociological pattern varies from denomination to denomination (and *not* from country to country), according to the history of each individual denomination.

4. A large proportion of Pentecostal pastors come from the family of a minister or pastor. The doctrinal system the pastors present must be interpreted as a function of their life stories. This is also true of fundamentalism, in so far as it can be regarded as a form of ritualism. Both the wide variations and the doctrines which are most strongly emphasized, in Pentecostal belief and practice, can be understood as the rationalized scheme of values of a particular sub-culture, so long as Wilson's important corrections of American sociology are taken into account.

5. The 'prophetesses' have great possibilities open to them in the Pentecostal movement. Pastors' wives are largely overshadowed by their husbands, even though they are more talented than the pastors themselves. In the case of 'women with theatrical talents' the basic feminine urge which is otherwise suppressed in the Pentecostal movement breaks out with great force, so that individual women with special talents can attain an extraordinarily high status, a fact which presents a remarkable contrast to Pentecostal theological teaching about the position of women in the church. This shows that in the Pentecostal movement a manifest talent is of greater importance than rigorous fundamentalism.

The 'woman with theatrical talents' is a variable which we have hitherto not taken in account in our study, and which must be regarded as an exception to the close link which we have postulated between the life story and the doctrines of Pentecostal pastors and evangelists.

At the beginning of this enquiry we asked how far the crucial elements in Pentecostal doctrine (conversion, the baptism of the Spirit, vocation) represent adaptive mechanisms for coping with one's environment. We can now answer that apart from certain exceptions, Pentecostal teaching can be understood as the rationalized scheme of values of a particular sub-culture.

All attempts to understand this sub-culture as an inferior culture, as the expression solely of social, intellectual and economic deprivation, are clearly contradicted by the most recent sociological statistics.[152] N. L. Gerrard describes a study of an enthusiastic Pentecostal group in Minnesota, which is distinguished by the cultic handling of poisonous snakes during services (Mark 16.17–18: 'These signs will accompany those who believe: . . . they will pick up serpents . . .') The results of the psychological study were recorded in individual psychogrammes, and compared to a similar number of psychogrammes of members of a traditional church. The comparison shows that – by contrast to what was expected – the Pentecostal group displayed a lower percentage of abnormal psychogrammes (37%) than the group of traditional Christians (45%). The traditional Christians were more defensive, less ready to admit errors, and displayed more repressions and depressive disturbances, while the Pentecostals presented a more spontaneous, free and independent picture. In particular, in old age the Pentecostals in this group grow more 'normal', while the traditional Christians grow more reserved, unfriendly and fearful. The conclusion of this study is that Pentecostals seem to derive from their worship and their sub-culture more comfort and flexibility to help them master the problems of life than do traditional Christians.[153]

If this sub-culture is not to be described as an inferior culture, what is its characteristic feature? There are still too few studies available on the international level to make possible a conclusive answer to this question. Its central point presumably lies in the experience of being taken into a fellowship which involves a change in one's whole way of life, and which develops a scheme of values which is easier to comprehend and communicate, and the maintenance of which is controlled by group dynamic processes (services).

It is clear that one must not make invidious comparisons between this religious sub-culture and the sub-culture of the established churches, which is equally the product of sociological conditions. Such a comparison would only continue the denominational dispute on the sociological and cultural level. The Draft for Section II (Renewal in Mission) of the Fourth Full Assembly of the World Council of Churches in Uppsala comments:

> Religious sub-cultures of a provisional character spring from disillusionment at the failure of the Church and of society to work for a new humanity. According to anthropologists and sociologists, it is this which accounts for the rise of separatist churches. Their religious sub-culture denies them, indeed, the promise of a renewed mankind, but gives them instead the illusion that within their own membership the new mankind is to be found . . .
>
> If, as in a city, the churches are the places where the people are the most segregated from each other by social and confessional as well as language and national barriers, the theological and social life of the church is almost entirely conditioned by sociological factors. Yet those churches proclaim that within the church these sub-cultures have been covercome. But the opposite is true. Instead of overcoming the sub-cultures, the churches add to the existing secular sub-cultures their own religious sub-cultures.

The question that must be asked here is that of the relative justification for religious sub-cultures, their necessary functions and their relationship to other sub-cultures. In theological terms, this means that the opposite of a sect (for a religious sub-culture which conceives of itself in absolute terms must presumably be described by the theological term 'sect', so long as the concept is understood to include the traditional churches, as well as the Pentecostal churches, when the former also think of themselves in absolute terms) is *not* the church but the *oikumene*, which is not identified here with the World Council of Churches. The function of a sub-culture can be defined in sociological terms. It must be defined sociologically, because a comparison between the dogmatic teaching of the churches and the Pentecostal movement does not give any picture of the functions of dogmatic theology and religious practice (in either the church or the Pentecostal movement).

But it is not enough simply to define these functions. They must be critically evaluated. The question of their necessity, of the needs which they satisfy, and their contributions to the needs of the *oikumene* (to adapt I Cor. 12.7) is something we must now go on to consider.

NOTES

1. Details: 01.36.040f.
2. Details: 01.36.214a: Christian Zion Sabbath Apostolic Church.
3. Sundkler, pp. 183ff.
4. Details: 01.12.014b (bibliography).
5. *Chile Pentecostal*, Sept. 1954; quoted in I. Vergara, *El Protestantismo*, and at length 02b.08.049a.
6. Details: 02b.01.006b (bibliography).
7. Details: 02b.26.001.
8. C. S. Snyder, Jr., in *Presbyterian Survey*; summarized by C. M. O'Guin, *The Pentecostal Messenger* 38/10, Oct. 1964, pp. 4f.
9. H. R. Niebuhr, *Social Sources of Denominationalism*, p. 30.
10. Cf. the analysis of L. Pope (above, ch. 4.2(*c*), pp. 53ff.).
11. Details: 01.09.003.
12. Details: 05.27.006.
13. See ch. 13.3, pp. 187ff.
14. For example in the sacral dance of the Latin American Pentecostal movement, in the 'altar-call' (cf. above, ch. 23, p. 316), in speaking in tongues and its interpretation. The above example is from oral tradition.
15. D. Maurer, *Réforme* 3/115, 31.5.1947, p. 2; 05.09.003a, dd; cf. *PGG* (French translation).
16. H.-Ch. Chéry, *Offensive*, pp. 384ff.
17. H. V. Synan, *P Movement*, pp. 266.
18. Cf. above, ch. 19.3, pp. 260ff.
19. G. Sentzke, *Kirche Finnlands*, p. 57; 05.08.001c.
20. W. Schmidt, *Pfingstbewegung*, p. 27.
21. *Kolkuttaja* 1921, p. 56; quoted in W. Schmidt, *op. cit.*, p. 38.
22. For *hwyl* cf. above ch. 13.1(*b*), pp. 177f.
23. L. Eisenlöffel, *Der Leuchter* 10/1, Jan. 1959, pp. 4ff.
24. F. de Rougemont, letter to a colleague, 9.6.1956. Full text: 05.28.048; cf. also *PGG*, pp. 279f.
25. The concept of 'status contradiction' was applied by B. R. Wilson to Pentecostal pastors. But it is also applicable to ministers of traditional churches, in that within his

church and within a certain section of society a minister has a very high status, whereas outside the church and this particular section of society he has an increasingly diminishing status (05.13.024c/d).

26. L. Denkhaus, quoted from *Deutsches Pfarrerblatt*, in *Wort und Tat* 21/9, Sept. 1967, pp. 316ff.

27. Quoted from D. Gee, *Pentecostal Movement*, 2nd ed., 1949, p. 120.

28. A. I. Zelley, *Hymns of Glorious Praise*, 1969, no. 215.

29. Cf. the hymn *Komm heim zum Abendmahl* quoted above, ch. 27.1, p. 387.

30. Cf. the hymn by Jimmie Davis, *Wasted Years*, quoted above, ch. 23, pp. 315ff.

31. 'One sat alone beside the highway begging . . .', O. J. Smith, in: N. J. Clayton (ed.), *Melodies of Life*, no. 35.

32. R. Franz, *Der Leuchter* 14/7, July 1963, p. 8.

33. A detailed account is given above, ch. 25.2(*c*), pp. 365ff.

34. E.g.: 'Dis-moi pourquoi, o centenier', Edition Croisade, Geneva, 4545B (Eglise Evangélique de Réveil, 05.28.015).

35. Record by Edizioni Uomini Nuovi (25.28.049), BIEM UN 4501: 'Gerusalemme'. The soloist is the Swedish singer Stig Almströn, with Pierre van Woerden at the organ. It is a version of the well-known English song 'The Holy City'.

36. Douglas Gray, *Youth Challenge* 2, 1963, pp. 24–6. Example: London Crusader Choir (05.13.024), 'Blessed Assurance', Herald Sacred Recordings LLR 510.

37. Ralph Carmichael Orchestra, 'Now I Belong to Jesus', Sacred Spectraphonic, Sacred Records, Inc., Whittier, California, LP 8004.

38. To express the idea 'Once I was lost . . .'

39. The sleeve informs us that for the production of this stereo record, which contains paraphrases of several hymns, 200 pages of full score and 1750 orchestral parts had to be written out.

40. E.g. 'Miksi viivyt sä poluill, maailman' (Ruth Jaarla), Celesta CLS-4.

41. Examples on the record PAN-AM (C.P. 4501, S. Paulo) LP 102 (Recordação da 8a Conferência Mundial Pentecostal).

42. E. Buchner, *Christliche Welt* 25, 1911, p. 29; cf. *PGG*, ch. 18.2, p. 262.

43. Cf. above, ch. 31.1(*c*), pp. 465ff.

44. Cf. Wilsons's works in the bibliography.

45. Details: 05.13.024 c/d.

46. The following quotations are taken from E. Altmann, *Predigt als Kontaktgeschehen* (pp. 48–69). Altmann's study, based on comparisons between tape recordings and manuscripts of sermons, shows with merciless clarity why our normal sermons allow no 'contact' to take place, and therefore cannot be 'understood'. Further discussion in: W. J. Hollenweger, 'Preaching Dialogically', *Concordia Theological Monthly* 42/2, April 1971, pp. 243–8.

47. C. Lalive d'Epinay, *Haven of the Masses*, p. 53.

48. D. Gee, *P Testimony* 41/2, Feb. 1960, p. 8.

49. K. M. Donnell, *Journal of Ecumenical Studies*, Winter 1967/68, pp. 105ff.

50. Diettrich, *Auf der Warte* 1/37, 17.12.1902, pp. 1f.; cf. above ch. 16.1(*a*), p. 221.

51. *Auf der Warte* 2/24, 10.6.1905, p. 3 (Torrey on Socialism); cf. *PGG*, ch. 14.1(*a*), p. 205.

52. T. A. Carver in H. W. Greenway (ed.), *Power Age*, pp. 4ff.

53. *Statuto delle AdD in Italia*, pp. 10f.

54. AoG, Australia, *You Have Accepted Christ*, p. 10.

55. Cf. 02a.02.007a, n. 101.

56. W. Scopes, *Christian Ministry*, p. 70.

57. I. Mosqueda, *Voice of Healing*, March 1962, pp. 9, 11, 14.

58. *Full Gospel Men's Voice* 7/2, March 1959, pp. 19ff.

59. M. Arganbright, quoted from *Geschäftsmann und Christ* 5/2, Nov. 1964, pp. 20f.

60. Chile (02b.05.039), Brazil (above, ch. 8.4, pp. 107ff.), Italy (above, ch. 19.3, pp. 260ff.), Russia (above, ch. 20, pp. 262ff.), Hungary (05.33.007), Poland (05.23.006c) and E. Czajko in Hollenweger (ed.), *Pfingstkirchen*, pp. 91–5), Rumania (05.15.002 and T. Sandru in Hollenweger (ed.), *op. cit.*, pp. 82–90), Yugoslavia (05.16.002).

61. D. Gee, *P* 14, 1950, p. 17. Cf. also Joanyr de Oliveira, 'Nem comunismo, nem comodismo', *Mensageiro da Paz* 39/19, 15.10.1969, p. 2; above, ch. 6.2, pp. 79ff.

62. D. Gee, *Study Hour* 9, 1950, p. 167.

63. G. H. Wallien, *Vuur* 13/6, June 1969, p. 6.

64. Bo Wirmark, 'Politik in der schwedischen Pfingstbewegung' in W. J. Hollenweger (ed.), *Die Pfingstkirchen*, pp. 256–61.

65. Cf. above, ch. 8.3(*b*), p. 102.

66. Philip Gaglardi (02a.01.013a, ff).

67. Musa Amalemba (01.17.013a).

68. Depending on whether one counts the ChoG in Christ (02a.02.075 and *Black Pentecostal Concept* Special Issue No. 30, June 1970, Geneva, WCC; the latter gives exact statistics, sources and bibliography) having one or three million members, and whether one is prepared to accept the statistics of the House of Prayer For All People (02a.02.097).

69. E.g. H. D. Daughtry of the House of the Lord (*Black Pentecostal Concept*, pp. 57ff.).

70. E.g., ChoG in Christ (02a.02.075, *Black Pentecostal Concept*, pp. 26ff.), Pentecostal Assemblies of the World (02a.02.139, *Black Pentecostal Concept*, pp. 59ff.).

71. Bishop F. D. Washington of the Church of God in Christ (in J. O. Patterson (ed.), *Holy Convocation ChoG in Christ*, 1969, and *Black Pentecostal Concept*, pp. 29ff.).

72. *ChoGE* 53/24, 19.8.1963, p. 23.

73. AoG, *Our Mission in Today's World*, p. 85.

74. George Dugan, 'Mass Evangelism Called of no Relevancy to Blacks', *New York Times*, 5.4.1970.

75. R. O. Cunningham, *PE* 2840, 13.10.1968, p. 5.

76. AoG, *Our Misson in Today's World*, p. 133.

77. D. Gee, *P* 68, 1964, p. 17.

78. 01.01.006; 05.28.009d.

79. 01.12.020b; cf. above, ch. 3.2(*d*), p. 38.

80. 02b.08.058; C. Lalive d'Epinay, *Haven for the Masses*, p. 143.

81. In a shortened form Weber's hypothesis is: Since North America and Europe owe their riches to the impulses of the Reformation, and the adoption of the Reformation automatically leads to industrialization and capital formation, the first task of Christians in Latin America is to penetrate Latin American society with the ideas of the Reformation.

82. Karl Marx, ed. S. Landshut, *Frühschriften*, p. 208; ET, *A Contribution to the Critique of Hegel's 'Philosophy of Right'*, p. 131. C. Lalive d'Epinay, *op. cit.*, p. 35.

83. This is a summary of Lalive d'Epinay's criticism of Weber's hypothesis (d'Epinay, *op. cit.*, pp. 147ff.).

84. *Frankfurter Zeitung*, 22.10.1907; quoted in *Zeitschrift für Religionspsychologie* 1, 1907, p. 439.

85. Quoted by B. R. Wilson, *Sects*, p. 87.

86. H. Horton, *Gifts*, 6th ed., 1960, p. 226. Cf. also below, ch. 31.4(*b*) on Wigglesworth, p. 478.

87. Cf. above, ch. 15.2(*c*), pp. 211ff.

88. H. Horton, *Preaching and Homiletics*, pp. 114ff.

89. D. Gee, *P Testimony* 38/8, Aug. 1957, p. 8.

90. E. Chávez, letter to W.H., 23.1.1963.
91. D. E. Walker, *A Survey of Nez Perce Religion.*
92. H. D. Honsinger, *P Testimony*, March 1963, p. 32.
93. 05.23.006; 05.23.002; 02a.02.004a, n. 52; Akademia Teologiczna, Warsaw, *D. L. Moody jako ewangelista na tle życia religijno-kościelnego w Stanach Zjednoczonych AP* (1962 acc. to J. Mrózek Jr., etc. (edd.), *Kalendarz* 1963, p. 180).
94. On Lidman, cf. W. J. Hollenweger (ed.), *Die Pfingstkirchen*, pp. 337–9.
95. Examples: P Assemblies of Canada (02a.01.013a,ee). Biographies in 02a.02.110a, cc (PHCh), AoG (above, ch. 3.2(*d*), pp. 37ff.), Oral Roberts University (above, ch. 25.2(*b*), pp. 363ff.).
96. J. E. Campbell, *PHCh*, pp. 122, 132.
97. W. H. Urch, *Spiritual Gifts*, pp. 17f.; *Der Leuchter* 13/2, Feb. 1962, p. 5.
98. R. Willenegger, *VdV* 53/11, Nov. 1960, p. 1.
99. Shaman is *not* a pejorative term. Shamans are not neuropaths, as Eliade (*Myths*, p. 77), Nadel ('A Study of Shamanism', p. 478), Jennings (*Journal of the American Scientific Association*, March 1968, pp. 5–16) have amply demonstrated.
100. 06.002.001. This gap has now been filled by Lalive d'Epinay's study of Chile.
101. The first percentage is based on the total numbers, including the high figure (38%) of those whose profession was not known. The second percentage is more useful for comparison, because it is a percentage only of the number of pastors whose profession before they became Pentecostal pastors is known.
102. Table 3a; 06.002, p. 88.
103. Because of the very high proportion of 'unknown' in the column 'Father's profession', it seemed better not to give a percentage of the whole sample, but only of those whose profession was known.
104. The first generation is formed from pastors who begin their ministry as pastors during the *first ten years* of a denomination. The *second generation* is those who become pastors from the *eleventh to the thirty-fifth year* of a denomination. The third generation consists of those who become pastors in a denomination which is more than *thirty-five years old.*
105. For an attempted interpretation see *PGG*, pp. 271ff.
106. P. R. Ruff (08.218).
107. A. J. Tomlinson (08.482), C. Parham (08.088), Väino Pfaler (08.126), R. Fauvel (07.433), R. Bracco (07.178), A. and S. Larsen Bjørner (07.141, 07.142), S. H. Frodsham (07.476), W. H. Durham (07.382), W. J. Seymour (08.284).
108. S. Jeffreys (07.702).
109. J. Paul (08.097), A. Hitzer (07.463).
110. B. R. Wilson, *Sects*, pp. 15ff.; cf. above ch. 14.3, pp 302ff. Example in the AoG: K. E. M. Clark, *Redemption Tidings* 45/43, 23.10.1969, p. 11; above, ch. 15.3, pp. 213ff. and *passim*. For a summary of the social origin of Pentecostal pastors, cf. p. 475.
111. Sources: 08.606.001.
112. Frodsham, *Smith Wigglesworth*, p. 2.
113. *Ibid.*, pp. 81, 83, 84.
114. *Ibid.*, p. 91. A similar example: Oral Roberts (above, ch. 25.2(*b*), pp. 363ff.
115. A. Endersen, *Frelst i havn*, p. 11.
116. *Ibid.*, p. 68; sources: 07.411.
117. M. Bjerre, *Jeg fik det i tilgift* (07.139).
118. D. E. Curry, *Journal of Inter-American Studies and World Affairs* 12/3, July 1970, pp. 416ff.
119. A. B. Reuss (08.184), C. Polhill (08.146).
120. J. Paul (08.009).

121. P. Mabilitsa (07.883), I. B. Akinyele (07.011).
122. P. Mink (07.955).
123. Cf. *PGG*, pp. 276ff.
124. L. Eisenlöffel, *Ein Feuer*, pp. 34ff. (08.634).
125. P. van Woerden, *Weg mit Jesus*, p. 28 (08.637).
126. Works and biography: 07.851.
127. A. Larsen Bjørner, *Teater og Tempel* (07.141).
128. In order not to overload this section with notes, I would make a general reference to 06.002.003, where the references for all the examples (mostly in autobiographies) are given.
129. L. P. Gerlach and V. J. Hine, *Journal for the Scientific Study of Religion* 7/1, Spring 1968, pp. 23ff. cf. also their important comparison between Black Power and Pentecostalism, *People, Power, Change.*
130. Cf. above ch. 24.4, pp. 330ff.
131. C. Parham, T. L. Osborn.
132. E.g. T. Hicks (07.624.001); Louise Nankivell (08.014.001).
133. Cf. above ch. 28.4, 5, pp. 401ff.
134. Cf. above ch. 25.2(*b*), pp. 363ff.
135. This also explains the violence with which all ecumenical contacts are rejected by Pentecostal churches, but shows how important such contacts are. Nothing shakes tribal religion more than the realization that real Christians also exist in other tribes.
136. Above, ch. 11.2(*a*), p. 142.
137. Above, ch. 13.4(*c*), pp. 191ff.
138. Above, ch. 4.2, p. 50.
139. Cf. above, ch. 27.3, pp. 395ff.
140. Above, ch. 21.3, pp. 299ff.
141. R. Bracco, *Verità*, p. 47 (above, ch. 19.1(*a*), p. 253). Examples: Lexie Allen (07.020); Bertha Augstburger (07.067).
142. *ChoGE* 51/2, 14.3.1960, p. 3; cf. also M. Ray, *ChoGE* 51/44, 16.1.1961, p. 4.
143. E.g. M. A. Alt (07.023); E. A. G. Wilson (08.630).
144. E.g. Paula Gasser (07.492).
145. E. Clark, *Small Sects*, p. 116.
146. *Life* 17, 20.10.1944, pp. 85–9: A. S. MacPherson.
147. International Church of the Foursquare Gospel (02a.02.124).
148. N. B. Mavity, *Sister Aimee*, p. xx; this outstanding analysis is discussed at length in 07.932.001.
149. Literature and biography, 08.191.
150. Cf. above, ch. 11.1, p. 140ff.
151. Cf. above, ch. 1.1(*a*), p. 5. Other examples of leading women, L. Wreschner, Ph.D. (08.645); Louise Nankivell (08.914); M. B. Woodworth-Etter (08.642).
152. L. P. Gerlach and V. H. Hine, *Journal for the Scientific Study of Religion* 7/1, Spring 1968, pp. 23ff.; E. O'Connor, *Pentecost in the Catholic Church*; *The Pentecostal Movement in the Catholic Church.*
153. N. L. Gerrard (see bibliography).
154. WCC, *Drafts for Sections*, pp. 30f., 44f.

32

Practice as a Theological Statement: A Theological Assessment

1. *A Summary of Research*

ATHOUGH in recent years the Pentecostal movement has caused concern to the churches of every continent, and extensive literature has been produced about it and by it, there is still no systematic summary of these publications.[1] This is evident to anyone who consults the scrappy bibliographical details of the Pentecostal movement given in standard scholarly works and lexicons. There seems to be a need, therefore, for a systematic summary of this literature. My *Handbuch der Pfingstbewegung* (Handbook of the Pentecostal Movement) contains some of the preliminary work for this.

In it I list:

approximately 4,700 titles of accounts written by Pentecostals themselves (1,673 authors)

approximately 1,100 titles of accounts of the Pentecostal movement written by others (763 authors)

approximately 1,100 accounts of the Holiness movement by those who belong to it and by outsiders (1,004 authors)

400 short biographies of Pentecostal pastors.

In two research papers[2] I have published a comprehensive summary of this literature.

These papers, and in particular the state of the sources for the early history of the movement which is complicated, but not inaccessible to a systematic study, cannot be summarized here. Nevertheless we shall list here the most important scholarly works on the Pentecostal movement.

(*a*) *Accounts written by Pentecostals*

Pentecostals themselves have published a number of accounts of the movement which satisfy scholarly standards. Naturally, the smaller the area they attempt to cover, the more accurate they are. In my view this is the only method of study which will bring any progress in research in this difficult field. Unfortunately it runs contrary to the requirements of publishers, who mostly call for studies with an international scope, and are not very interested in the publication of special studies.

Amongst the historically reliable studies, based on an exact knowledge of the sources, we would mention the following: Charles Conn's works on the Church of God (Cleveland) and its mission churches,[3] O. T. Hargrave's *History of the Church of God (Cleveland) in Mexico*, Mario G. Hoover's history of the constitution of the Assemblies of God,[4] the splendid but unfortunately unpublished *Handbook of Pentecostal Denominations in the USA* by E. L. Moore, H. V. Synan's extremely well documented history, *The Pentecostal Movement in the United States*,[5] the account of a number of American denominations by Klaude Kendrick,[6] a special study by G. H. Paul of the Pentecostal Holiness Church in Oklahoma,[7] S. Durasoff's history of the Russian Pentecostal movement,[8] the account of the Swedish Pentecostal movement, intended to run to five volumes, by A. Sundstedt[9] and the three-volume study of the Norwegian Pentecostal movement by E. Strand, E. Strøm and M. Ski.[10] The dissertation by J. Campbell on *The Pentecostal Holiness Church* is indispensable, but is not satisfactory in every respect. There are also other American theses, written by Pentecostals for master's and doctor's degrees, on historical aspects of the movement, but I was unable to obtain access to these.[11]

In the wider sense of scholarly accounts of the movement by Pentecostals themselves, one should also include the works on the history of the Reformation and Church history by K. Ecke,[12] R. F. Edel's biography of Thiersch, the leader of the Old Apostolic Churches in Germany,[13] the medical and psychiatric dissertation on speaking in tongues by L. M. Vivier-van Eetveldt,[14] as well as the Polish study of D. L. Moody.[15] With regard to scholarly works on doctrine one must distinguish between works which present normal Pentecostal teaching (most presenting a two-stage doctrine of salvation) in academic form[16] and those writers who, attempting to come to terms with New Testament scholarship, are trying to go beyond this position.[17]

(*b*) *Scholarly accounts by non-Pentecostals*

Until recently, most accounts of the Pentecostal movement by non-Pentecostals were attacks on it, or were works which considered the Pentecostal movement from a particular denominational point of view, either fundamentalist,[18] Lutheran,[19] Reformed,[20] Methodist,[21] Baptist,[22] Anglican,[23] Church of South India,[24] Catholic,[25] Jewish[26] or even Communist.[27]

More recently, a number of works on the Pentecostal movement have appeared which take seriously the fact that the Bible contains a variety of different theologies, patterns of religious practice and ecclesiologies, and that therefore it is not possible to draw a straightforward contrast between the Pentecostal movement and Scripture, Protestant belief or Catholic belief, as was the practice in most accounts until recently – fifty years after K. L. Schmidt's *Rahmen der Geschichte Jesu* (The Framework of the History of Jesus)[28] or Bultmann's *History of the Synoptic Tradition*[29] and ten years after E. Schweizer's *Church Order in the New Testament* and his article *pneuma* in the *Theological Dictionary of the New Testament*, to mention only a handful of exegetic studies which are of particular importance in the dialogue with the Pentecostal movement.

The first attempt at an ecumenical assessment of the Pentecostal movement was by L. Newbigin.[30] In Holland,[31] Germany,[32] Great Britain[33] and Africa, amongst American[34] and French[35] Catholics, and also in publications by the World Council of Churches[36] and in my own works an attempt was made to understand Pentecostalism as an expression of New Testament forms of religious belief and practice which might be following a very independent line, but could not be ruled out on *a priori* theological grounds. In the section that follows we shall see how this interpretation was received by the friends and the opponents of the Pentecostal movement.

2. *The Pentecostal Movement in Dialogue*

The present state of the discussion about the Pentecostal movement can perhaps be best illustrated by the criticisms received of the German edition of the present work, because it is so far the only scholarly document on the subject of the Pentecostal movement which has been discussed at the same time by Pentecostals themselves and also by academic theologians.

The first reaction to this account of the Pentecostal movement was one of astonishment. Kurt Hutten, the leading expert on the German Pentecostal movement, described it as 'an undertaking of mad audacity',[37] which hitherto no World Pentecostal Conference, no church historian and no expert on denominational differences had dared to tackle. Pentecostals were astonished – and partly also a little embarrassed – at the many varieties of Pentecostal belief and practice. They had previously been in the habit of regarding the kind of Pentecostalism prevailing in their own church and their own country as the normal kind, the 'official' pattern. Now they were forced to recognize that it was possible to be a Pentecostal in a quite different way. Protestants and Catholics were astonished at the fact that a marginal section of Christianity, to which little attention had hitherto been paid, could develop so much vitality, and that even though it was able to produce scarcely any theological statements of any value, it could still pose fundamental problems for missionary theology and hermeneutics.

Fundamental criticisms were made from only two quarters. Hermann Schöpwinkel of the Gnadau Association discussed the chapter on Germany[38] and accused me of ignorance of the sources. In his view, the German Evangelical movement would have 'sunk into a quagmire of hell' if the Berlin

Declaration had not set up a timely barrier against Pentecostal enthusiasm. The second fundamental criticism was made by one of my former colleagues in the Swiss Pentecostal Mission.[39] He vehemently attacked the attempt to give a historical interpretation of Pentecostal belief and practice, to draw Pentecostals into an ecumenical dialogue, and to reduce the absolute significance placed on certain passages in the Bible to a relative one against the historical background of the New Testament. In his view co-operation with non-fundamentalist churches, critical exegesis and a Reformation understanding of grace are all irreconcilable with Pentecostal belief and practice, although in the classical Pentecostal movement, as in neo-Pentecostalism, there are well known figures who are at one and the same time critical exegetes, ecumenical theologians and charismatic Christians. But other Pentecostal reviewers are clearly not in agreement with this Swiss critic. Christian Krust[40] is grateful for an 'account which is exact in its scholarship, lively and generally comprehensible'. Ludwig Eisenlöffel[41] regards the 'critical and factually correct' book as 'the first comprehensive account of the great [Pentecostal] revival movement of our century'. It is true that he is also of the opinion that I gave 'excessive preference to current exegetical scholarship', but considers that attention should be paid to my thesis that 'the Pentecostal movement can make a considerable contribution to the life of the church as a whole in the first instance not by its dogmatic theology, but far more by its religious practice'. Leonhard Steiner,[42] an internationally known Pentecostal leader, in his profound postscript to the German edition of this book has also combined a grateful acknowledgement of the account given of the movement with a criticism of the interpretation of the Bible by the methods of historical criticism. He too is afraid that a critical and academic interpretation of the Bible will lead to the loss of fundamental biblical truths. Neither Christian Krust[43] nor the Polish Pentecostal reviewers[44] criticized this point. This is understandable, because the Polish Pentecostal pastors are trained together with other Protestant students of theology at the theological academy in Warsaw. Similarly, the detailed reviews given by Scandinavian Pentecostals do not lay their main emphasis on the different methods of interpreting the Bible, but quite rightly point out that this account of the Pentecostal movement contains an implicit criticism of the representatives of certain structures in the established churches.[45]

Most non-Pentecostal reviewers emphasize the 'element of dialogue' in the book, that is, the attempt to set up a bridge between two different types of religious belief and practice.[46] The book has been called 'a celebration and a monument to the ecumenical coming-of-age of Pentecostalism'.[47] Johannes Althausen[48] of East Germany notes that it has been based on previous dialogue with the groups concerned. 'This is unusual.' In his view the nature of the *encounter* between the partners in the denominational dialogue 'will do a great deal for the future of ecumenism'. Karl Kupisch[49] describes the critical passages of the book as treading 'delicately through this maze' and gives the author credit for having the ecumenical responsibility 'to take care not to regard a single form of religious practice as theologically immaculate'. But it is this imprecision, the unwillingness to use theological criteria and categories to pass judgment on the rigid orthodoxy[50] or the theological weaknesses of the Pentecostal movement,[51] which irritates other reviewers.

Hellmut Gollwitzer[52] asserts:

> It is no longer possible to pass by the Pentecostal movement with one's nose in the air, as academic theology on the continent has done, not only because of its sheer size, which has given it such great significance outside Europe, but also because of its quality . . . A non-Pentecostal reader, and academic theologians in particular, can look forward, if they set aside their prejudices, to exciting reading . . . Anyone who is weary at the dullness of the established churches and the consequences and products of this dullness will find here cause for astonishment at the tumultuous and explosive activities which are going on outside our own narrow circle.

Others emphasize the urges towards a trans-rational mode of communication which this 'first critical introduction to the modern Pentecostal movement'[53] has given them.

> In Pentecostal piety an important beginning has been made of a 'non-verbal communication'. It was this fact which gave me, as a member of an established Lutheran parish 'founded on the Word', most food for thought. Communication has become one of the most urgent problems of our time. We can no longer close our eyes to the fact that we live in a 'post-literary' age as the book and newspaper lose more and more ground to the illustrated magazines and to television. For the majority of people today our 'Word oriented' worship services are no longer comprehensible. The Pentecostal movement with its visions and dreams offers an important non-verbal means of communication to those who have difficulty with abstract thinking. If we do not want to confine ourselves to the shrinking circle of readers capable of intellectual thinking (which would be contrary to our acknowledged task) we cannot but go looking for more relevant expressions for our worship services.[54]

Consequently, Martin Conway rejects 'quick theological condemnations of what the Pentecostals *say*'. They 'only reveal the poverty and narrowness of spirit in much of what the traditional churches *are*'.[55]

S. von Kortzfleisch[56] compares the style of the book to a Pentecostal service:

> In innumerable quotations Hollenweger lets the Pentecostals speak for themselves. He is like a Pentecostal preacher who in his services leaves room for other people's uncensored contributions and yet, without a rigid liturgy, always remains the leader of the worship.

Amongst Catholic reviews[57] that of J. Sudbrack, SJ, is the most interesting. In many places he draws a comparison between the popular mystical piety of Catholicism (the veneration of Mary, pilgrimages, devotion to the Sacred Heart, medals, blessings, novenas) and that of Pentecostalism, and rightly points out that there are many points of agreement. He agrees with J. A. Jungmann:

> The abrupt rejection by the universal church of the second century of the Montanist movement of the Spirit also meant that spontaneity and enthusiastic worship and devotion were excluded from the church, or at least regarded with considerable mistrust. In the course of church history very little has remained of the magnanimity of Paul, who welcomed the fullness of the works of the Spirit in his Corinthian churches: 'Now I want you all to speak in tongues' (I Cor. 14.5). Order and regimentation have swamped almost everything else.[58]

He concluded with a twofold question:

> What should be the form, today and tomorrow, taken by the spontaneity and impulsiveness without which any form of worship only speaks to half of man's being? And again, how can this spontaneity be admitted to the central stream of Christianity?
>
> Is it not right to say that the resistance to jazz and beat masses, to eucharistic liturgies in private and 'unliturgical' settings, to 'political services', which make a call to action, are producing the very opposite effect to what is intended, that is, that they force the tentative steps into extreme positions, which then – and only then! – are maintained and put into practice on the margins of Christianity? With his exhortations to the Corinthians, Paul showed a different way.

In this context, Sudbrack's argument leads him to discuss Harvey Cox's *The Feast of Fools*.

> A German-speaking Catholic is astonished to find that Harvey Cox's sources include Josef Pieper,[59] Hugo Rahner,[60] Josef Andreas Jungmann, Romano Guardini and others.[61]

Here Cox is seen as the interpreter of the 'secular city', deriving his interpretative tools from the piety of Catholicism and Pentecostalism – an unusual and exciting viewpoint.

3. *An Attempt at a Theological Definition of Sectarianism*

Before we look further at the significance of such an interpretation of the 'secular city' with the aid of elements of Catholic and Pentecostal piety (one might almost say that we are making a theological assessment at the point where empirical sociology and historical theology coincide) we must first look briefly at the concept of sectarianism. Academic theology has always tended to regard sects as heretical sects, that is, it has judged them by their doctrinal teachings. The further they have departed from the Lutheran, Reformed, Anglican or Catholic doctrinal position which is regarded as the central message of Scripture, the more they are condemned as an association of heretics. But this definition in denominational terms, that a sect is a body which places the main emphasis on a subordinate doctrinal element, which does not confess Christ as the centre of its faith, which neglects the basis of faith, be it justification or the eucharist, is in my view no longer adequate. For amongst the churches which belong to the World Council, and indeed within the New Testament canon itself, many of these matters are subjects of dispute. That is, even if we have the melancholy courage to make the charge of heretical sectarianism, it is in effect being made not against exotic fringe groups but against other major denominations. But this will not do, for not only the Pentecostal movement, but also the Orthodox Church, the Reformation churches, and the Roman Catholic Church each have their roots in a corresponding tradition in the New Testament. Thus if one were to try to defeat the other with Scripture, Scripture would be used to contradict itself.

But the scholarly study of the New Testament can help us here. It has been shown that the New Testament is not a unified theological textbook. The differences result from the different situations in which the New Testament writers had to work out their message. They were obliged to give a one-sided presentation to the sole matter that was necessary in their situation. If they had not done this, they would be like many modern sermons: correct, but boring and ineffectual. When modern preaching has anything to say, it must also be one-sided. Thus it is a gross over-simplification for the traditional churches to pretend to oppose the Pentecostal movement with the 'message of the Bible'. This kind of apologetics overlooks the fact that on the one hand the Bible is a *collection* of theological outlines, and that secondly, not only in biblical times, but also at the present day, the gospel has to be preached in very different ways to people from different cultures and societies.[62] For the negroes of Georgia, the Lutheran *sola gratia* will never be comprehensible, and the peasant or worker from the Bernese Oberland who has been saved from drunkenness will never understand the meaning of *simul justus*, *simul peccator*. The concept of the 'central message of Scripture' which is so often put forward is not sufficient in our present dialogue. By 'Christ alone' a Salvationist understands the life renewed by regeneration, a Catholic the sacrament, a Lutheran the concept of *sola gratia*, an Anglican a combination of these elements, a Jehovah's Witness his understanding of the Kingdom of God and a Pentecostal the normative document of the normative church, the Acts of the Apostles.

Thus Käsemann is right when he finds present-day denominational differences already foreshadowed in different religious types in the New Testament.[63] Thus to take part in the dialogue with denominations and sects, the present day theologian must be not only 'at home in the Bible' but also 'at home with the conflicts within the Bible'. That is, he cannot simply oppose Pentecostals with the Bible, or in our case with the Pauline doctrine of justification. 'Between Paul and Acts there is a difference in substance, in belief – not merely a difference in the presentation of doctrines, but a difference in belief.'[64]

On this basis we must try to define the nature of sectarianism on some other basis than that of denominational prejudice. A person belongs to a sect if he has excluded himself from the fellowship of the saints, that is, if he asserts that in his *own* ecclesiastical organization, in his *own* theology, and in his *own* experience of faith, God's will is *infallibly* 'incarnate'. Anyone who uses his form of worship or his theology to deny that another Christian is a Christian is making his own worship or theology the standard of what the church is, and therefore denies that the incarnation of God in Jesus Christ is unique.

But this definition is open to the charge of relativism: one can then believe what he wants, so long as one does not bother anybody else. Thus we have to extend the above definition by asking further questions. Is the function of a particular religious practice or doctrine in the social context in which it occurs that of healing and integrating people, giving them a fuller humanity and helping them to reach a critical maturity? Does it set people free from pressures and fears? Does it help them to have an evangelical commitment to help the world and the whole of Christianity? Or does it narrow their horizons, maim them and make them immature? It is clear that the same pattern of practice and doctrine cannot be of equal value in every society, in every age and for all men. And this presumably implies the end of a Christian doctrine which can command assent everywhere, at every time and by everyone.

4. *Are Enthusiasts of Their Nature Sectarians?*

We should now try to apply the principles laid down above to the Pentecostal movement. If in theological terms one regards a group as a sect if it considers belonging to that group to be necessary to salvation, then apart from a number of insignificant examples I know of no Pentecostal groups which would have to be called a heretical sect in this sense.[65] Consequently, I would suggest that the concepts of 'sect', 'heretical sect', or the expression used in America, 'cult', which annoy Pentecostals, should no longer be used in speaking of the Pentecostal movement.

> When we, as a denomination, mistake our own denominational 'arc' for the 'whole circle' we are to be pitied. Each denomination attracts certain types of individuals and social classes which others could never attract . . . The Holiness and Pentecostal sects [sects here is the word used by Campbell himself, who is a pastor of the Pentecostal Holiness Church] need to recognize this truth, and to develop a greater appreciation for those Christians who may differ with them in doctrinal emphasis.[66]

> Every member of a church probably thinks his church is right, but we know that some churches are more spiritual and more scriptural than others. It is extreme narrow-mindedness to think that any one denomination alone constitutes the true Church. The Church of Jesus is made up of born-again believers – persons whose names are written in heaven. Membership in a

visible church does not guarantee membership in the mystical Church. The work of the Holy Ghost is required. The visible church is a means of grace; it is not, in itself, a saviour.[67]

But in my view to dismiss enthusiastic Christians as heretical sectarians is only justified when they try to claim absolute significance for their own enthusiastic Christianity, quite apart from the fact that 'the primitive church in Jerusalem was to a large degree guided by prophetic utterances, which comparative religion would describe as "enthusiasm".'[68] It remains to be shown that an emotional experience has less of the nature of a word than a sacrament does. We do not dispute that the sacraments are preaching in the form of a 'visible word'. Why should not speaking in tongues, visions and healings of the sick on the Pauline pattern be a wholly legitimate form of preaching, if they are integrated into the preaching function? I am not unaware of the criticism that it is just this which fails to happen. Speaking in tongues and visions are often not seen in their function as preaching, but are isolated as actual experiences of God. This may be true; but I can also recall sermons, which, although their outward form was that of preaching, offered not a glimmer of hope, not a breath of the good news of the gospel. Does this mean that the church of the word is a sect, because even the word can be reduced to babbling? And is the church of the Spirit a sect, because genuine emotion can be confused with sentimentality, the Spirit with enthusiastic manifestations, inspiration with sloppy rubbish, and the genuine struggle for words of the uneducated with the slapdash eloquence of the superficial? Now there are people – whose numbers are increasing – to whom sermons are inaccessible. To expect a particular style of religious practice from them is to confuse the obedience of faith with a cultural authoritarianism. As long as the enthusiasts, obedient to their original undertaking, seek to serve the whole church, they are not sectarians. In individual cases this need not prevent their churches taking on fixed organizational forms, but it should stop them from cutting themselves off in a systematic way from dialogue with the religious practice and theology of other churches. If they do this, they betray their own origin.

5. *The Failure of the 'Ecumenical Revival Movement'*

The purpose of the Pentecostal movement was to reconcile the different Christian denominations. Dogmatic barriers were to be overcome not by agreement on a minimum of dogma, but by giving up any attempt to lay down fixed dogma. The bond of union was to be the presence of the living God, the reality of the Holy Spirit, which people looked forward to receiving in conversion, sanctification, the baptism of the Spirit and the gifts of the Spirit. In the expectation of the immediate second coming of Jesus, no attempt was made to achieve theological clarity, and there was also a neglect of political and ethical problems. We are not called to proclaim problems, but the good news of salvation. And therefore there is only a single legitimate aim before the second coming of Jesus on the clouds of heaven: to sanctify and unite the children of God and to evangelize the world within a single generation.

When the Lord delayed, the different ethical and dogmatic views within the Pentecostal movement made a minimum of dogmatic principles a necessity. Only a diminishing minority resisted the temptation to become a large free church, carrying weight in church politics. This group remained faithful to a basic Quaker outlook, refused to lay down obligatory dogma, and refused to make majority decisions. The majority adopted an anti-rationalist dogmatic theology from the arsenal of the previous century and refurbished it by adding the 'initial sign of the baptism of the Spirit', speaking in tongues. The zeal of the churches for sanctification and evangelization grew less. Specialists were used to put through the religious programme of the church, and a beginning was made in the training of pastors. As a result, the questions of church organization, baptism and the instruction of children became urgent. Although the fiction of a universal priesthood was maintained, in all the older denominations one finds a majority of worshippers who listen to the services which the pastor carries out with a small staff of full-time and voluntary helpers. In many churches – not in all – Pentecostal worship offers an opportunity for active participation through prayer, testimony and singing. But it is no longer automatic that those who are not officials are involved in services. From time to time a longing for the Pentecostal ideal makes itself felt. People ask why, with regard to clothing and cosmetics, church government, the relationship of pastors to non-pastors and difficulties with the second generation, they are growing closer and closer to the traditional churches? Such questions result in repentance weeks, penitential prayer, and renewed attempts to achieve complete sanctification. In other words the problem is seen, as in the traditional churches, as a human failure on the part of pastors and church members, and not as the result of adopting unsuitable organizational structures. Often such penitential movements lead to the setting up of new churches, which begin the cycle again a few stages further back.

As far as I know, Pentecostal preaching and literature have so far had little to say about this unfaithfulness to the original vision of an ecumenical revival movement which would take in all churches. The only exceptions are the call to unity, and occasional Pentecostal working fellowships on a national level as an answer to these calls.

The *theological* insights of the Pentecostal movement are neither new nor valuable. They demonstrate to the traditional churches how far their preaching has become incomprehensible, and how much the religious education on which they set so much store is misinterpreted amongst lay people. One should not forget that at least in Germany and Switzerland most Pentecostals have received several years of religious instruction from the historic churches. This is something which the established churches should take to heart. Consequently, the questions posed for traditional churches by the spread of the Pentecostal movement are more important than the answers given by Pentecostalism. It is not enough simply to call the Pentecostal movement a heretical sect because its answers turn out to be wrong. They are no more wrong than other things which are believed by many people within our churches. One may object that while this may be true, the conventional Protestantism found within the traditional churches – or as one might call it, the simple faith of the laity – has no claim to be of theological importance. But this is something that has to be decided. In general we have done ourselves great damage by denying the laity their rights as partners in the theological dialogue.

6. *A Theological Assessment of the Pentecostal Movement Taking Its Social Context Into Account*

To understand the forms of religious practice which occur in Pentecostalism, it is not enough simply to recognize that a variety of forms exist in the New Testament. For example, in order to make a fair judgment on the driving out of demons and other mythological religious practices, it is not enough simply to find out whether or not the particular practice is in accordance with the New Testament. Similarly, to be able – or unable – to identify Pentecostal speaking in tongues with that of the New Testament is not a sufficient standard of judgment. To form a valid judgment, we must consider the *function* of these religious forms in a particular cultural situation. Thus we must also look at the relationship between a particular biblical form of religious practice and the social context in which it occurs. This function must then be compared to that of Pentecostal practice in the social context in which it occurs. Is its function in this context to heal and integrate people, giving them a fuller humanity and helping them to reach a critical maturity? Does it set people free from pressures and fears, and help an evangelical understanding of the world and of the whole of Christianity? Or does it narrow their horizons, maim them and make them immature? In answering these questions, we must always keep in mind the relationship to a particular sub-culture, because *the same element of religious practice* can exercise different functions in a different context.

One example is the different function of Pentecostal religious practice in the first, second and third generations (e.g. in the 'best society' of California and the shanty towns of Santiago, etc.) Since a knowledge of the context is necessary for determining the function of Pentecostal religious practice, a theological judgment upon the Pentecostal movement cannot be made by theologians alone. The attempt to make a fair judgment is seriously hampered by the fact that members of majority cultures proceed from the assumption that in their environment there are no sub-cultures, or alternatively that these are merely stunted versions of the majority culture. It is on the basis of this kind of prejudice that Negroes in South Africa and America are condemned as inferior.

Thus we conclude our study with a question which is not only of fundamental importance for the dialogue between the Pentecostal movement and the traditional churches, but also for the common life of the whole of Christianity. What is the relationship between *contrary* forms of religious belief and practice, which are partly determined by the different social context in which they occur? What form should be taken by an ecumenical Christianity, a church ecumenical in its thinking, forms and purposes, which does not set out to break down sub-cultures by pressure or by education, and which not only tolerates the fact of different forms of religious belief and practice in different sub-cultures, but recognizes that they are theologically necessary? And what form will a church take which tries to include in a single organization the different religious sub-cultures within a region, without smoothing down their particular features until they fit into a normal pattern? What instruments must be developed in order to make a valid assessment within a particular social context of whether a particular form of religious practice functions well or badly? What form will be taken by the religion of those who at one and the same time belong to different sub-cultures?

It is not the task of this 'account of the Pentecostal movement in dialogue' to answer this and other questions which this study has raised. It formed the basis for a study by the World Council of Churches. The results of studies carried out in North America,[69] Western Europe,[70] Switzerland,[71] and East Germany[72] are available. The preliminary theological and sociological studies have been gathered by Thomas Wieser.[73] On the basis of the numerous theologies present in the New Testament and the numerous 'agendas' on which the gospel has to be included at the present day, it will be possible for this 'church for others' to take very numerous concrete forms.[74] Theological and ecclesiological fragments which result from this new reality of the church have formed the content of further studies on the themes outlined here.[75]

A genuine dialogue with the Pentecostal movement will lead the traditional churches not to imitate the Pentecostal movement, but to make a *critical* examination of their own tradition, such as has been begun in fragmentary form in the ecumenical documents referred to. Nor should a dialogue with the traditional churches lead the Pentecostal movement simply to become assimilated to them, it should lead them to look critically at the original task of the Pentecostal movement in the setting of Christianity as a whole.

NOTES

1. A bibliography is being prepared by Ray T. Geiger, 141 Inman Drive, Decatur, Georgia 30030.

2. W. J. Hollenweger, *Una Sancta*, June 1970, pp. 150ff.; 'Ein Forschungsbericht' in *Die Pfingstkirchen*, pp. 307ff.

3. C. Conn, *Like a Mighty Army*; *Where the Saints have Trod.*

4. M. G. Hoover, *Origin and Structural Development of the AoG.*

5. Synan is secretary of the Society for Pentecostal Studies, founded in 1970.

6. K. Kendrick, *The Promise Fulfilled.*

7. G. H. Paul, *The Religious Frontier in Oklahoma.*

8. S. Durasoff, *AUCECB*, printed as *Russian Protestants.*

9. A. Sundstedt, *Pingstväckelsen.*

10. E. Strand, E. Strøm, M. Ski, *Fram til urkristendommen.*

11. I. J. Harrison, *A History of the AoG*; G. F. Bruland, *The Origin and Development of the Open Bible Churches in Iowa.*

12. K. Ecke, *Schwenckfeld*; *Der Durchbruch des Urchristentums*; *Pfingstbewegung*; *Sektierer oder wertvolle Brüder?* K. Ecke and O. von Bibra, *Der reformierende Protestantismus*; *Die Reformation in neuer Sicht.*

13. R. F. Edel, *Heinrich Thiersch.*

14. L. M. Vivier-van Eetveldt, *Glossolalia*; 'The Glossolalic and His Personality' in T. Spörri (ed.), *Beiträge zur Ekstase*, pp. 153ff.

15. Akademie Teologiczna, Warsaw, *D. L. Moody.*

16. C. Glardon, *Les dons spirituels*; Pierre Fuegg, *Le baptême du Saint Esprit*; R. C. Dalton, *Tongues*; O. S. von Bibra, *Die Bevollmächtigten*; L. Dallière, *D'aplomb sur la parole de Dieu*; H. Thulin, *En präst vaknar*; *Kring kyrkan och pingstväckelsen*; *Pingströrelsen.*

17. P. Gericke, *Christliche Vollkommenheit*; A. Bittlinger, *Gifts and Graces* (see also bibliography); J. Paul, *Die Taufe in ihrem Vollsinn*; *Ihr werdet die Kraft des Heiligen Geistes empfangen*; E. Giese, *Jonathan Paul.*

18. J. B. A. Kessler, *Older Protestant Missions and Churches in Peru and Chile.*

19. F. D. Bruner, *A Theology of the Holy Spirit*; E. Briem, *Den moderna pingströrelsen*; 'Den evangeliska kyrkan och de nutida väckelserörelserna' (and also various articles by the same author in *Svensk Uppslagsbok*); E. Linderholm, *Pingströrelsen* (3 vols.); E. Giese, *J. Paul*; W. Metzger, *Fuldaer Hefte* 15 (1964), pp. 46ff.; W. Schmidt, *Die Pfingstbewegung in Finnland*; K. Hutten, *Seher, Grübler, Enthusiasten*; N.Bloch-Hoell, *Pentecostal Movement*; P. Fleisch, *Die Pfingstbewegung in Deutschland.*

20. O. Eggenberger, *Evangelischer Glaube und Pfingstbewegung*; M. Miegge, *Arch. de soc. des religions* 4/8, July–Dec. 1959, pp. 81ff.; G. Peyrot, *Religious Intolerance in Italy*; *La circolare Buffarini-Guidi e i Pentecostali.*

21. E. T. Clark, *Small Sects.*

22. E. Krajewski, *Geistesgaben*; F. Stagg, E. G. Hinson, W. E. Oates, *Glossolalia*; A. Hermansson, *Svenska Missionstidskrift* 53, 1965, pp. 200ff.; 54, 1966, pp. 137ff.

23. M. Harper, *As at the Beginning*; various articles in *The Living Church.*

24. L. Newbigin, *The Household of God.*

25. A. C. Jemolo, *Per la pace religiosa d'Italia*; H.-C. Chéry, *Offensive des Sectes*; I. Vergara, *El protestantismo en Chile*; A. Gaëte, 'Un cas d'adaptation'; P. Damboriena, *Mensaje* (Santiago de Chile) 6/59, June 1957, pp. 145ff.; *Arbor* (Madrid), 50/192, Dec. 1961, pp. 60 ff.; *Tongues as of Fire*; L. Zenetti, *Heisse* (*W*)*Eisen*, pp. 304ff. For American literature cf. above, ch. 1.1(*d*), pp. 8ff.

26. Ben Gurion, *Sixth World Pentecostal Conference* pp. xvii–xviii; Ish-Shalom, *ibid.*, pp. 1f.; A. Gilbert, *Christian Century* 78, p. 1961, pp. 794ff.

27. V. D. Bonch-Bruevich, 'K sektantem', *Rassvet* (Geneva), 1904/1; *Iz mira sektantov*; *Izbrannie Sochineniya*; A. Dolotov, *Tserkov'i sektantsvo v Sibiri*; F. I. Garkavenko, *Chto takoe religioznoe sektantsvo*; A. Iartsev, *Sekta evangel'skikh khristian*; V. M. Kalugin, *Sovremennoe religioznoe sektantstvo*; S. I. Kovalev, *Sputnik ateista*; A. P. Kurantov (ed.), *Znanie i vera v boga*; G. M. Livshits, *Religiya i tserkov*; E. V. Mayat and N. N. Uzkov, *'Brat'ya' i 'sestry' vo Khristi*; V. A. Metsentsev (ed.), *My porvali s religiey*.

28. K. L. Schmidt, *Der Rahmen der Geschichte Jesus*, Berlin, 1919.

29. R. Bultmann, *The History of the Synoptic Tradition*, ET of 3rd ed., Oxford: Blackwell, 1963.

30. L. Newbigin, *The Household of God*.

31. Cf. the literature above, ch. 30.2, pp. 432ff.

32. E. Benz. *Der Heilige Geist in Amerika*; H. Meyer, *Die Pfingstbewegung in Brasilien*.

33. H. W. Turner, *History of an African Independent Church* (2 vols.); *Profile Through Preaching*.

34. Above, ch. 1.1(*d*), pp. 8ff., esp. the works by K. McDonnell.

35. A. M. de Monléon, *Vers l'Unité Chrétienne* 23/9 (227), Oct.–Nov. 1970, pp.81ff.

36. V. E. W. Hayward (ed.), *African Independent Church Movements*; 'The Pentecostal Movement in Europe', *Ecumenical Review* 19/1, Jan. 1967, pp. 37ff.

37. K. Hutten, *MD* 32/17, 1.9.1969, pp. 202ff.

38. Hermann Schöpwinkel, *Enthusiastisches Christentum*.

39. Jakob Zopfi, *Wort und Geist*, 2/2, Feb. 1970, pp. 7ff.; 2/3, March 1970, pp. 15f.; 2/4, April 1970, pp. 13ff.; 2/5, May 1970, pp. 15ff.; 2/8, Aug. 1970, pp. 6ff.; 2/9, Sept. 1970, pp. 11ff.; 3/2, Feb. 1971, p. 23; cf. W. J. Hollenweger, *Heilszeugnisse*.

40. Christian Krust, *Heilszeugnisse* 54/9, 1.9.1969, pp. 132ff., 139.

41. Ludwig Eisenlöffel, *Der Leuchter* 20/9, Sept. 1969, pp. 10f.; and Leuchter Verlag's list of publications.

42. Leonhard Steiner, 'Ein kritisches Nachwort', in *PGG*, pp. 577ff.; *Wort und Geist* 1/8, Aug. 1969, p. 15; *Urchristliche Botschaft* 6/1969, June 1969, p 94.

43. Above, n. 40.

44. E. Czajiko, *Chrześcijanin* (Warsaw) 1970/2, pp. 11ff.; *Jednota* (Warsaw), *Miesięężnik Religijno-Społeczny*; *Powwięcony polkiemu ewangeliczymowi i ekumenii* 14 (28)/3, 1970, pp. 13f.; *Berliner Pressespiegel*, 15.5.1970; Henryk Turnowski (pseudonym), *Więż* 13/2 (142), pp. 120ff.

45. Alvar Lindskog, *Dagen* (Stockholm), 30.12.1969, p. 4; Göran Janzen, *Dagen*, 19.2.1970, pp. 1, 15.

46. *Der Bund* (Berne), 7.11.1969; Otto Brekke, *Vårt Land* (Oslo) 25/215, 17.9.1969, p. 6; Aldo Comba, *Nuovi Tempi* (Rome) 4/23, 7.6.1970, p. 80; Christa Gäbler, *Zürichsee-Zeitung*, 12.6.1970; Helmut Haug, 'Die Brücke zur Welt', Sunday Supplement to the *Stuttgarter Zeitung* 111, 16.5.1970, p. 49; Andreas Lindt, *Reformatio* (Berne) 20/2, Feb. 1971, pp. 127f.; Josef Lundaahl, *Svenska Dagbladet*, 11.9.1969; Rodolfo Obermüller, *Freie Presse* (Buenos Aires), 17.10.1969; Rudolf Renfer, *Le Christianisme au XXe Siècle*, 19.11.1970, p. 11; N. H. Søe, *Kristeligt Dagblad* (Kopenhagen) 74/118, 18.2.1950; Erland Sundström, *Tro och liv. Tidskrift för Kristen och Förkunnelse*, 1969/5, pp. 206ff.; L. Szabo, *Protestantismo* 18/1971, pp. 206ff.; *Tagesanzeiger* (Zürich; weekly issue for circulation abroad), 1.11.1969; *Die Tat* (Zürich), 20.12.1969; Seppo A. Teinonen, *Teloiginen Aikakausi-Kirja* (Helsinki) 15/3, 1970, pp. 207ff.; Hedi Vaccaro, *L'Eco delle valli Valdesi* (Torre Pellice) 107/31–32, 7.8.1970, p. 3.

47. J. H. Yoder, *Ecumenical Review* 23/1, Jan. 1971, pp. 74–6.

48. Johannes Althausen, *Die Zeichen der Zeit* (Berlin, DDR), 1970, pp. 290ff.

49. K. Kupisch, *Christ und Welt*, 10.10.1969, p. 45.

50. Marie-Louise Martin, *Kirchenblatt für die reformierte Schweiz* (Basel), 5.2.1970, p. 43.

51. *Evangelisches Schulblatt*, Dec. 1969.

52. Hellmut Gollwitzer, *Evangelische Theologie* 29/11, Nov. 1969, pp. 619f.

53. Z. K. Zeman, *Canadian Journal of Theology* 16/3–4, 1970, pp. 261ff.

54. Gisela Gorzewski, *Study Encounter* 6/3, 1970, pp. 156ff.

55. Martin Conway, *Theology* 62, Dec. 1969, pp. 563f.

56. S. v. Kortzfleisch, *Christ und Welt*, 10.10.1969, p. 45.

57. *Ephemerides Theologicae Lovanienses* 1969/3, p. 531; B. Holtz, *Neue Zeitschrift für Missionswissenschaft* (Switzerland) 26/1, 1970, pp. 70f.; *Schweiz. Kirchenzeitung*, 1970, p. 39.

58. J. Sudbrack, *Geist und Leben* 43/5, Nov. 1970, pp. 369ff. (both quotations from p. 386). For another Roman Catholic evaluation see K. McDonnell in his valuable review of recent literature on Pentecostalism in *Worship* 45/4, April 1971, pp. 215–19.

59. Josef Pieper, *In Tune With the World: A Theory of Festivity.*

60. Hugo Rahner, *Man at Play.*

61. J. Sudbrack, *op. cit.*, pp. 386f.

62. The ecclesiological and doctrinal consequences which would result from this situation are discussed in W. J. Hollenweger, *Concilium* 6/7, June 1971, pp. 116ff.; and in F. Hasselhoff and H. Krüger, *Ökumene*, pp. 220ff. (ET, W. J. Hollenweger, *Theology: the World's Agenda.*)

63. E. Käsemann, *New Testament Questions*, p. 257; cf. also A. M. Ritter and G. Leich, *Wer ist die Kirche?*, p. 21. (English summary, W. J. Hollenweger, *IRM* 60/237, Jan. 1971, pp. 139–41.)

64. G. Harbsmeier, *Evangelische Theologie* 10, 1950/51, pp. 366f., 352.

65. J. Sudbrack comments: Hollenweger's 'attempt to redefine the concept of a "sect" (above, p. 504), should give Catholic readers food for thought.' But he remarks: 'However welcome the suggestion is that the term "sect" should not be applied to the Pentecostal movement, I am not convinced by the assertion that only "insignificant exceptions" amongst Pentecostal groups adopt sectarian attitudes. The accounts given in the text of the book (cf. the quotation from Doctorian above, ch. 29.1, p. 414) . . . tell another tale.' J. Sudbrack, *Geist und Leben* 43/5, Nov. 1970, p. 382.

66. J. E. Campbell, *PHCh*, p. 121.

67. E. S. Williams, *PE* 2536, 16.12.1962, p. 11.

68. E. Schweizer, *Neotestamentica*, p. 355.

69. WCC, *The Church for Others.*

70. *Ibid.*

71. *Schweizer Concept Suisse* V (Sept. 1966); *Concept*, Special Issue 23 and 24 (July and Nov. 1969) (all WCC, Geneva).

72. *Study Encounter* 3/2, 1967, pp. 84–108.

73. Thomas Wieser (ed.), *Planning for Mission.*

74. W. J. Hollenweger (ed.), *Kirche, Benzin und Bohnensuppe. Auf den Spuren dynamischer Gemeinden* (ET in preparation).

75. W. J. Hollenweger, *Theologie in der Tagesordnung der Welt* (ET in preparation).

APPENDIX

Declarations of Faith

1. *The Apostolic Faith Movement*

Stands for the restoration of the faith once delivered unto the saints – the old time religion, camp meetings, revivals, missions, street and prison work and Christian Unity everywhere.

Teaching on Repentance: Mark 1.14, 15

Godly Sorrow for Sin; Example: Matt. 9.13; II Cor. 7.9, 11; Acts 3.19; 17.30, 31

Of Confession of Sins: Luke 15.21; 18.13

Forsaking Sinful Ways: Isa. 55.7; John 3.8; Prov. 28.13

Restitution: Ezek. 33.15; Luke 19.8

And Faith in Jesus Christ

First Work: Justification is that act of God's free grace by which we receive remission of sins. Acts 10.42, 43; Rom. 3.25

Second Work: Sanctification is the second work of grace and the last work of grace. Sanctification is that act of God's free grace by which He makes us holy. John 17.15, 17: 'Sanctify them through Thy Truth. Thy word is truth.' I Thess. 4.3; 5.23; Heb. 13.12; 2.11; 12.14.

Sanctification is cleansing to make holy. The Disciples were sanctified before the Day of Pentecost. By a careful study of Scripture you will find it so now. 'Ye are clean through the word which I have spoken unto you' (John 15.3; 13.10); and Jesus had breathed on them the Holy Ghost (John 20.21, 22). You know, that they could not receive the Spirit if they were not clean. Jesus cleansed and got all doubt out of His Church before he went back to glory.

The Baptism with the Holy Ghost is a gift of power upon the sanctified life; so when we get it, we have the same evidence as the Disciples received on the Day of Pentecost (Acts 2.3, 4), in speaking in new tongues. See also Acts 10.45, 46; 19.6; I Cor. 14.21. 'For I will work a work in your days which ye will not believe though it be told you' (Hab. 1.5).

Seeking Healing: He must believe that God is able to heal – Ex. 15.26: 'I am the Lord that healeth thee.' James 5.14; Ps. 103.3; II Kings 20.5; Matt. 8.16, 17; Mark 16.16–18.

He must believe God is able to heal. 'Behold I am the Lord, the God of all flesh; is there any thing too hard for Me?' Jer. 12.27.

Text in *Apostolic Faith*, Los Angeles, Sept. 1906, photocopied in R. Crayne, *Early 20th Century Pentecost*, pp. 51–2; cf. ch. 2.3, pp. 22ff.

2. *Assemblies of God*

Here the declaration of faith of the Assemblies of God, USA (ch. 3, pp. 29ff.), is quoted. In the notes examples are given of the variations found in a number of declarations of faith based on the document of the Assemblies of God.

Statement of Fundamental Truths (since 1916)

The Bible is our all-sufficient rule for faith and practice. Hence this statement of Fundamental Truths is intended as a basis of fellowship among us (i.e., that we all speak the same thing, I Cor. 1.10; Acts 2.42). The human phraseology employed in such statement is not inspired nor contended for, but the truth set forth is held to be essential to a full Gospel ministry. No claim is made that it contains all truth in the Bible, only that it covers our present needs as to these fundamental matters.

1. *The Scriptures inspired*

The Bible is the inspired Word of God, a revelation from God to man, the infallible rule of faith and conduct, and is superior to conscience and reason, but not contrary to reason (II Tim. 3.15–16; I Peter 2.2).

2. *The one true God*

The one true God has revealed Himself as the eternally self-existent, self-revealed I AM; and has further revealed Himself as embodying the principles of relationship and association, i.e., as Father, Son and Holy Ghost (Deut 6.4; Mark 12.29; Isa. 43.10–11; Matt. 28.19).[1]

For fuller statement concerning Godhead, see General Council Minutes.

3. *Man, his Fall and Redemption*

Man was created good and upright; for God said, 'Let Us make man in Our image, after Our likeness.' But man, by voluntary transgression, fell, and his only hope of redemption is in Jesus Christ the Son of God (Gen. 1.26–31; 3.1–7; Rom. 5.12–21).

4. *The Salvation of Man*

(*a*) Conditions to Salvation

The grace of God, which bringeth salvation, hath appeared to all men through the preaching of repentance toward God and faith toward the Lord Jesus Christ; man is saved by the washing of regeneration and renewing of the Holy Ghost, and, being justified by grace through faith, he becomes an heir of God according to the hope of eternal life (Titus 2.11; Rom. 10.13–15; Luke 24.47; Titus 3.5–7)

(b) The Evidences of Salvation

The inward evidence, to the believer of his salvation, is the direct witness of the Spirit (Rom. 8.16). The outward evidence to all men is a life of righteousness and true holiness.

5. *Baptism in Water*

The ordinance of Baptism by a burial with Christ should be observed as commanded in the Scriptures, by all who have really repented and in their hearts have truly believed on Christ as Saviour and Lord. In so doing, they have the body washed in pure water as an outward symbol of cleansing, while their heart has already been sprinkled with the blood of Christ as an inner cleansing. Thus they declare to the world that they have died with Jesus and that they have also been raised with Him to walk in newness of life (Matt. 28.19; Acts 10.47–8; Rom. 6.4; Acts 20.21; Heb. 10.22).

6. *The Lord's Supper*

The Lord's Supper, consisting of the elements, bread and the fruit of the vine, is the symbol expressing our sharing the divine nature of our Lord Jesus Christ (II Peter 1.4); a memorial of His suffering and death (I Cor. 11.26) and a prophecy of His second coming (I Cor. 11.26); and is enjoined on all believers, 'until He comes'.

7. *The Promise of the Father*

All believers are entitled to, and should ardently expect, and earnestly seek, the promise of the Father, the Baptism in the Holy Ghost and fire, according to the command of our Lord Jesus Christ. This was the normal experience of all in the early Christian Church. With it comes the enduement of power for life and service, the bestowment of the gifts and their uses in the work of the ministry (Luke 24.49; Acts 1.4, 8; I Cor. 12.1–31). This wonderful experience is distinct from and subsequent to the experience of the new birth (Acts 10.44–6; 11.14–16; 15.7–9).[2]

8. *The Evidence of the Baptism in the Holy Ghost*

The Baptism of believers in the Holy Ghost is witnessed by the initial physical sign of speaking with other tongues as the Spirit of God gives them utterance (Acts 2.4). The speaking in tongues in this instance is the same in essence as the gift of tongues (I Cor. 12.4–10, 28) but different in purpose and use.

9. *Entire Sanctification*

The Scriptures teach a life of holiness without which no man shall see the Lord. By the power of the Holy Ghost we are able to obey the command, 'Be ye holy, for I am holy'. Entire sanctification is the will of God for all believers, and should be earnestly pursued by walking in obedience to God's Word (Heb. 12.14; I Peter 1.15–16; I Thess. 5.23–4; I John 2.6).

10. *The Church*

The Church is the body of Christ, the habitation of God through the Spirit, with divine appointments for the fulfilment of her great commission. Each believer, born of the Spirit, is an integral part of the General Assembly and Church of the First-born which are written in heaven (Eph. 1.22–3; 2.22; Heb. 12.23).

11. *The Ministry and Evangelism*

A divinely called and Scripturally ordained ministry has been provided by our Lord for a twofold purpose: (1) The evangelization of the world, and (2) The edifying of the Body of Christ (Mark 16.15–20; Eph. 4.11–13).

12. *Divine Healing*

Deliverance from sickness is provided for in the atonement, and is the privilege of all believers (Isa. 53.4–5; Matt. 8.16–17).[3]

13. *The blessed Hope*

The resurrection of those who have fallen asleep in Christ and their translation together with those who are alive and remain unto the coming of the Lord is the imminent and blessed hope of the Church (I Thess. 4.16–17; Rom. 8.23; Titus 2.13; I Cor. 15.51–2).

14. *The millennial Reign of Jesus*

The revelation of the Lord Jesus Christ from heaven, the salvation of national Israel, and the millennial reign of Christ on the earth is the Scriptural promise and the world's hope (II Thess. 1.7; Rev. 19.11–14; Rom. 11.26–7; Rev. 20.1–7).

15. *The Lake of Fire*

The devil and his angels, the beast and the false prophet, and whosoever is not found written in the Book of Life, shall be consigned to everlasting punishment in the lake which burneth with fire and brimstone, which is the second death (Rev. 19.20; 20. 10–15).

16. *The new Heavens and new Earth*

We, 'according to His promise, look for new heavens and a new earth wherein dwelleth righteousness' (II Peter 3.13; Rev. 21.22).[4]

Text in AoG, *Early History*, pp. 17–19.

3. *The rejection of the WCC by the Assemblies of God*

1. Setting itself up as an 'ecumenical' ecclesiasticism the council has refused to adopt as a basis of fellowship the absolute minimum of fundamental evangelical Christian doctrine necessary to such a body . . .

2. It has admitted into its membership a host of 'liberals' who are committed to a theology and philosophy which are definitely anti-Christian in the Biblical sense . . .

3. It has created an organization which to all intents and purposes is under the control of an 'oligarchy'. Real control lies in the hands of a few men who are definitely 'liberal' in their viewpoint . . .

4. The ramifications are such that it is already beginning to function as a 'super church', bringing pressures or exerting controls over both member and non-member churches . . .

5. Its concept of the nature of the church, the character of Christ and of essential doctrine is inadequate. It has at no time unequivocally stated its belief in the Bible as the inspired, the only infallible authoritative Word of God; in the deity of our Lord Jesus Christ, in His virgin birth, in His sinless life, in His miracles, in His vicarious and atoning death through His shed blood, in His bodily resurrection, in His ascension to the right hand of the Father, and His personal return in power and glory; in regeneration by the Holy Spirit as essential to the salvation of lost and sinful man; in the present ministry of the Holy Spirit by whose indwelling the Christian is enabled to live a Godly life; in the resurrection of both the saved and the lost – they that are saved unto the resurrection of life and they that are lost unto the resurrection of damnation.

6. It has adopted an approach to the problem of Christian unity which is un-Protestant and un-Biblical and therefore essentially un-Christian.

7. It has seriously threatened the development of a distinctly evangelical foreign missionary programme and formed alliances which will further secularize the whole Missionary Movement.

8. It has encouraged social revolution through liaison relationships with the Commission of Churches for International Affairs and other such bodies.

9. Its relations with the Greek Orthodox Churches and its general attitude toward the Roman Catholic Church threaten to weaken if not eventually destroy the distinctive testimony of Protestantism.

10. It has deliberately omitted or shamefully neglected to include provisions for the preservation and perpetuation of all the values and liberties inherent in historic Protestantism.

Text in: *United Evangelical Action* 13.1.1955 and 15.1.1955, p. 10; also quoted in K. Kendrick, *Promise*, pp. 204–5.

4. *Declaration of Faith of the Church of God (Cleveland)*

We believe

1. In the verbal inspiration of the Bible.
2. In one God eternally existing in three persons: namely the Father, Son and Holy Ghost.
3. That Jesus Christ is the only begotten Son of the Father conceived of the Holy Ghost, and born of the Virgin Mary. That Jesus was crucified, buried and raised from the dead; that He ascended to heaven and is today at the right hand of the Father as the Intercessor.
4. That all have sinned and come short of the glory of God, and that repentance is commanded of God for all and necessary for forgiveness of sins.
5. That justification, regeneration, and the new birth are wrought by faith in the blood of Jesus Christ.
6. In sanctification subsequent to the new birth, through faith in the blood of Christ; through the Word, and by the Holy Ghost.
7. Holiness to be God's standard of living for His people.
8. In the baptism of the Holy Ghost subsequent to a clean heart.
9. In speaking with other tongues as the Spirit gives utterance, and that it is the initial evidence of the baptism of the Holy Ghost.
10. In water baptism by immersion, and all who repent should be baptized in the name of the Father, and of the Son and of the Holy Ghost.
11. Divine healing is provided for all in the atonement.
12. In the Lord's Supper and washing of the saint's feet.
13. In the premillennial second coming of Jesus. First, to resurrect the righteous dead and to catch away the living saints to Him in the air. Second, to reign on the earth a thousand years.
14. In the bodily resurrection; eternal life for the righteous and eternal punishment for the wicked.

Text always printed on the cover of the *Church of God Evangel* (cf. ch. 5, pp. 47ff.)

5. *Declaration of Faith of Nicholas Bhengu*

Our Doctrinal Belief

The members of this mission declare their belief concerning:

1. The Trinity of the Godhead, i.e. Father, Son and Holy Spirit; co-equal and eternally existing in three persons as one God.
2. The deity and humanity of Jesus Christ, that He was begotten of the Holy Spirit, born of the Virgin Mary, possessing a sinless nature; that His death was penal, vicarious and substitutionary; and that he was raised bodily from the dead on the third day.

3. The personality of the Holy Spirit, and that as promised, He came down from Heaven on the Day of Pentecost, to dwell permanently in the Church and in the body of each believer, and that He is the efficient power for godly living, Christian service, and spiritual worship.

4. The supernatural plenary inspiration of the Scripture, that it is inerrant in the original writings and of the supreme, absolute and final authority, in all matters of doctrine, faith and conduct.[5]

5. The ruin of the human race is universal, total, and irremediable by human effort whatsoever.

6. The shed blood of Christ is the only ground of justification by God, forgiveness of sins, and peace with God.

7. The necessity of the new birth as the only ground of entrance into the Kingdom of God.

8. Salvation by grace through faith in the finished work of Christ.

9. The observance of the ordinance of baptism and the Lord's Supper.

10. It is the privilege of all who are born again through faith in Christ Jesus to be assured of their salvation, and that they are in present possession of eternal life, and delivered from judgment and the wrath to come.

11. Satan is a living personality, a veritable being.

12. The true Church which is His body, of which Christ is the absolute Head, is composed of regenerate persons.

13. That the Gospel of Christ issuing from His death and resurrection should be preached without reserve or qualification to every creature under Heaven.

14. That the return of the Lord Jesus will be personal and premillennial, and so far as the Church is concerned it is imminent.

15. The literal resurrection of the body of both the just and the unjust.

16. The eternal blessedness of the just and the eternal punishment of the unjust.

Text in *Back to God*, 1958, pp. 1, 2, 6, 9; cf. ch. 10, pp. 126ff.

6. *Declaration of Faith of the Apostolic Church* (*Great Britain*)

The Apostolic Church states briefly its main doctrines in the form of Eleven Tenets, which are as follows:

1. The Unity of the Godhead, and the Trinity of the Persons therein.

2. The utter depravity of human nature, the necessity for repentance and regeneration, and the eternal doom of the finally impenitent.

3. The virgin birth, sinless life, atoning death, triumphant resurrection, ascension, and abiding intercession of our Lord Jesus Christ; His second coming, and millennial reign upon earth.

4. Justification and Sanctification of the believer through the finished work of Christ.

5. The baptism of the Holy Ghost for believers, with signs following.

6. The nine gifts of the Holy Ghost for the edification, exhortation and comfort of the Church, which is the Body of Christ.

7. The Sacraments of Baptism by immersion, and of the Lord's Supper.

8. The Divine inspiration and authority of the Holy Scriptures.

9. A Church government by apostles, prophets, evangelists, pastors, teachers, elders and deacons.

10. The possibility of falling from grace.

11. The obligatory nature of tithes and offerings.

Text: Apostolic Church, *Fundamentals*, p. 3; cf. ch. 13.4 pp. 191ff.

7. *Declaration of Faith of the Elim Pentecostal Churches*

Elim finds its justification as an independent denomination in the particular doctrinal emphasis which it presents in its evangelical campaigns and church services. The insistent voice of its ministers during the years of its development has been, 'Back to the Bible'. This book, neglected by so many pulpits today, is the basis of Elim's Fundamentalism. Tradition, science, philosophy, all are rejected when they conflict with the living fount of Truth. . . . The tragedy of Modernism and its satellite growths is written all too clearly in the empty churches of our land. Declining church statistics[6] have become a common feature of modern annual reports; who would dare to say that this is not one of the causes contributing to the horrors of international strife?

Elim adheres to the Bible, and we are convinced that the Statement of Beliefs printed below is uncontrovertible, and are prepared to defend this doctrinal position against all critics, whether secular or religious. It is interesting to note that in one town when the agent of a well-known subversive sect called at a certain house, and was well and truly tackled from the Bible, he remarked: 'I suppose you are a member of the Elim Church!'

Well, here is our statement of fundamental truths:

The Bible We believe that the Bible is the inspired Word of God, and that none may add thereto or take away therefrom, except at their peril.

The Trinity We believe that the Godhead eternally exists in three persons: Father, Son and Holy Ghost, and that these three are one God.

The Church We believe that the Church consists of all persons who have been regenerated by the Holy Ghost, and made new creatures in Christ Jesus.

The Saviour We believe that all have sinned and come short of the glory of God, and that through the death and risen power of Christ all who believe can be saved from the penalty and power of sin.

The Healer We believe that our Lord Jesus Christ is the Healer of the body, and that all who will walk in obedience to His will can claim Divine healing for their bodies.

The Baptizer We believe that our Lord Jesus Christ is the Baptizer in the Holy Ghost, and that this Baptism with signs following[7] is promised to every believer.

The Coming King We believe in the personal and pre-millennial return of our Lord Jesus Christ to receive unto Himself the Church, and afterwards to set up His throne as King.

The Fruit We believe that every believer on the Lord Jesus Christ as Saviour should produce the ninefold fruit of His Spirit: Love, joy, peace, longsuffering, gentleness, goodness, faith, meekness, temperance.

The Gifts We believe that the Church should claim and manifest the nine Gifts of the Holy Spirit: Wisdom, knowledge, faith, healing, miracles, prophecy, discernment, tongues, interpretation.

The Ministry We believe that God has given some apostles, and some prophets, and some evangelists, and some pastors and teachers, for the perfecting of the saints, for the work of the ministry, for the edifying of the Body of Christ.[8]

The Future State We believe in the eternal conscious bliss of all true believers in Christ, and also in the eternal conscious punishment of all Christ rejectors.

The Ordinances We believe in the following ordinances: Partaking of bread and wine in memory of our Lord's death; baptism by immersion; the laying on of hands; and the anointing of the sick with oil.

Text in H. W. Greenway, *Labourers with God*, pp. 30f.; cf. ch. 14, pp. 197ff.

8. *Declaration of Faith of the British Assemblies of God*

We believe

in the Bible as the inspired Word of God, the infallible and all-sufficient rule for faith, practice and conduct;

in the unity of the true and living God revealed in three persons: Father, Son and Holy Spirit;

in the fall of man;

in salvation through faith in Christ;

in baptism by immersion in water;

in the baptism in the Holy Spirit with the initial evidence of speaking with other tongues;

in holiness of life and conduct;

in the deliverance from sickness by divine healing;

in the breaking of bread;

in the pre-millennial second coming of the Lord Jesus Christ;

in everlasting punishment, the portion of all who are not written in the book of life;

in the gifts of the Holy Spirit and the offices set by God in the Church as recorded in the New Testament.

Text always printed in *Redemption Tidings*. A longer version of this declaration of faith has been published in AoG (Great Britain and Ireland), *1962–1963 Year Book*, pp. 7f. Cf. ch. 15, pp. 206ff.

9. *Declaration of Faith of the Assemblee di Dio (Italy)*

Gli articoli di Fede della Chiesa Christiana Evangelica Pentecostale (1953).[9]

1. Noi crediamo ed accetiamo l'intera Bibbia, come infallibile parola di Dio ispirata dallo Spirito Santo, sola e perfetta regola della nostra fede e condotta, alla quale nulla si può aggiungere o togliere.
2. Noi crediamo che vi è un solo Dio, Eterno e d'infinita potenza, Creatore di tutte le cose e che nell'unità di esso vi sono le tre distinte persone: Padre, Figliolo, Spirito Santo.
3. Noi crediamo che il Figliol di Dio è la Parola fatta carne. Egli assunse l'umana natura in seno di Maria Vergine. Quale vero Dio e vero Uomo, portò in Sè stesso due nature. Egli è l'unico Salvatore, il Quale realmente soffrì la morte per la colpa primitiva e per i peccati attuali dell'uomo.
4. Noi crediamo che la rigenerazione si riceve soltanto per la fede in Cristo.
5. Noi crediamo che il battesimo dell'acqua deve essere somministrato per immersione nel Nome del Padre, del Figliolo e dello Spirito Santo.
6. Noi crediamo al battesimo dello Spirito Santo, come ad una potente virtù divina che penetra nell'uomo dopo la salvezza e si manifesta visibilmente con il segno scritturale del parlare nuove lingue.[10]
7. Noi crediamo che la Santa Cena simboleggia il sacrificio del Figliol di Dio e che chi la partecipa rammemora in essa la Sua morte e la manifestazione del Suo amore.
8. Noi crediamo che è necessario astenersi dalle cose sacrificate agli idoli, dal sangue, dalle cose soffocate e dalla fornicazione, in ossequio a quanto decretato dallo Spirito Santo nel primo Concilio di Gerusalemme.[11]

9. Noi crediamo alla guarigione divina secondo le 'Sacre Scritture': per la preghiera, per la somministrazione dell'Unzione dell'olio; per l'imposizione delle mani.

10. Noi crediamo che il Signore stesso ritornerà dal cielo e che la risurrezione corporale di tutti i morti avverà e a ciscuno sarà dato in ragione delle proprie opere.[12]

Text in *Risveglio Pentecostale* 8/11, Nov. 1953, p. 2; cf. above ch. 19, p. 251ff.

NOTES

1. The Yugoslav Kristova Pentekostna Crkva (05.16.004) translates this passage as follows: 'The *one* true God has revealed himself as the eternal self-subsistent being (*posebi postojeće bice*), who has revealed himself as the "I Am". He has further revealed himself as a being uniting in himself the principles (*naceka*) of relationship (*srodstva*) and association (*udruženja*), i.e. when Father, Son and Spirit have become one' (many scripture references). (Kristova Pentekostna Crkva, *Temeljne*.)

The Brazilian Assembléias de Deus (above, ch. 6, pp. 75ff.) translate: 'Cremos no único e verdadeiro Deus, criador de tôdas as coisas, que existe de eternidade a eternidade, o qual se revelou a si mesmo como o grande 'Eu Sou', e, posteriormente, nos fêz conhecer que em Sua unidade se incorporam princípios relativos de associação entre as três Pessoas da Trinidade, Pai, Filho e Espírito Santo. Os termos 'Trinidade' e 'Pessoas', quando se relacionam com a Divindade, são palavras que estão em harmonia com as Escrituras; portanto, torna-se fácil transmitir aos outros o nosso conhecimento imediato da doutrina de Cristo, como existindo da parte de Deus, tendo como cooperador eficaz, o Espírito Santo.' (E. Conde, *Testemunho*, pp. 183ff.) God, 'embodying the principles of relationship and association' is translated by 'em Sua unidade se incorporam princípios relativos de associação entre es três Pessoas da Trinidade'. From the doctrine of the Trinity is drawn the pastoral conclusion that it shows that God needs a co-operator, the Holy Spirit.

2. The final sentence is omitted in the Brazilian declaration.

3. In the Brazilian declaration article 11 is omitted. Article 12 is more detailed: 'Nós cremos que no plano da redenção há uma bênção para os crentes em suas enfermidades físicas um privilégio de receber a cura divina pela fé; sendo a cura divina um privilégio para os que crêem, é claro que não pode ser uma lei, nem um motivo para combater ou despresar a ciência e a medicina' (*loc. cit.*).

4. In the declaration of the Brazilian Assembléias de Deus the eschatological passages are much shorter than in the American text. Much of the 'timetable' is omitted. On the other hand the question of an existential interpretation of the justice of God is taken seriously.

5. Cf. S. A. Mamadi, 'Why We Believe the Bible is God's Book', *Back to God*, 1958/1, pp. 5f. Mamadi gives six reasons: 1. It is reasonable to believe that God would reveal himself through the message of a book. 2. The harmony of the Bible speaks in favour of its inspiration. 3. So do the prophecies that have been fulfilled. 4. It claims itself to have been inspired. 5. Its influence cannot be explained in human terms. 6. Its indestructibility argues for its divine origin.

6. Since then the British Pentecostal movement has also had to struggle against 'declining church statistics' (cf. ch. 15.3, p. 215).

7. That is, by contrast to a major section of the Pentecostal movement (e.g. AoG, Appendix: 8, p. 520; ch. 15.2(*b*), pp. 208ff. and *passim*) speaking in tongues is not acknowledged as the sole initial sign (cf. above ch. 14.2, p. 200). The 'Charter of the Elim

Youth Movement', especially drawn up for young people (H. W. Greenway, *op. cit.*, p. 41, and on the cover of every edition of the youth magazine *Youth Challenge*) does not mention the gifts of the Spirit and the baptism of the Spirit at all.

8. By contrast to the Apostolic Church (Appendix: 6, p. 518; above, ch. 14.4(*b*), pp. 191f.) apostles and prophets are not institutionalized in church government.

9. The name Chiesa Cristiana Evangelica Pentecostale is derived from the Christian Church of North America (02a.02.120), which the Italian Pentecostal Movement followed closely for a long time.

10. This doctrine is important in the AdD. Cf. R. Bracco, *Risveglio P* 11/7–8, July–Aug. 1956, pp. 10ff.; D. Gee, *Risveglio P* 13/11–12, Nov.–Dec. 1958, pp. 3ff.

11. The prohibition of the eating of blood is important. R. Bracco, *Il battesimo*, p. 15.

12. Cf. Bracco's comment on the new *Dizionario Biblico*. According to Bracco this is not fundamentalist enough. 'Quasi ad ogni pagina possiamo incontrare dichiarazioni categoriche capaci di turbare la fede semplice, e, forse, ingenua di quanti credono ancora alla totale inspirazione della Bibbia ed accettano con convinzione profonda e, forse, puerile le grande verità affermate . . . del cristianesimo.' Bracco particularly regrets that the doctrine of the immortality of the soul is abandoned. (R. Bracco, *Risveglio P* 12/5, May 1957, pp. 6ff.)

Giovanni Miegge replied by putting forward the well-known Protestant thesis that the Bible does not teach the immortality of the soul, but the resurrection of the dead. In a note Bracco answered the great professor that it seemed to him that in this doctrine there was no longer any place for 'the resurrection of the unrighteous at the last judgment'. (G. Miegge, *Risveglio P* 12/7–8, July–Aug. 1957, pp. 18ff.)

BIBLIOGRAPHY

The following booklist is not a complete bibliography of the Pentecostal movement. It is merely an indication of the books and pamphlets cited (not of all those used) in the present work. Articles in periodicals are not normally included; nor are works which have already been mentioned in the Abbreviations List (pp. xv–xvi). The policy with translations has been to give original editions and English translations only. A full report of research and an exhaustive three-volume bibliography may be found in Part Three of my *Handbuch* (06–11), also a summary account in Hollenweger (ed.), *Die Pfingstkirchen*, pp. 317–466.

Bold type indicates the short titles by which books which are mentioned frequently are cited.

* indicates works or editions mentioned only in the bibliography, not in the text.

AdD (Dominican Republic), **Reglamento** *local de la Iglesia Evangélica de las Asambleas de Dios en la República Dominicana.* Written 1932 by Rafael D. Williams and Francisco Arbizú, Santa Ana, El Salvador; printed 1944 in Trujillo: Prensa Biblica, 27 pp.

AdD (Italy), *Statuto delle Assemblee di Dio in Italia.* Rome: Tipografia Ferraiolo, 1957, 30 pp.

[Adolf, A.] (?), *Nové hnuti, mylne 'letnicni' zvané, ve světle Pisma Sv. a jeho vlastnich dejin, v souhlasu s Crik. vyborem svob. Reform. Cirkve.* Prague: Nakladem Cirk. Vyboru Svob. Ref. Cirkve (1911), 24 pp.

Akademia Teologiczna (Warsaw). *D. L. Moody jako ewangelista na tle życia religijno-kościelnego w Stanach Zjednoczonoych AP*, *1962 (author unknown acc. to J. Mrózek et al., Kalendarz 1963, p. 180; Master-Thesis at the Akademia Teologiczna, Warsaw)

All Africa Council of Churches, **Engagement.** *The Second Assembly. Abidjan 1969.* Nairobi, Kenya: AACC, n.d., 149 pp. (French and English reports)

Allen, A. A., *Miracle Revival Training Centre.* Miracle Valley, Ariz.: Allen, n.d. (prospectus of Allen's 'Miracle-Bible-School')

— **Divorce** *the Lying Demon. A new approach to an old problem.* Miracle Valley, Ariz.: Allen, n.d., 21 pp.

— *The* **Curse** *of Madness.* One of every two seen by doctors complains connected with mental illness. 17,000,000 Americans are mentally ill. 300,000 new patients will enter mental hospitals this year. You can think yourselves into pain. Is insanity a disease or a curse? What are the symptoms of mental illness? What is its cause? How can it be cured? Contains actual pictures and descriptions of demons, by people who saw them, and were visited by them. Miracle Valley, Ariz.: Allen, n.d., 84 pp.

Altmann, Eckhard, *Die Predigt als Kontaktgeschehen* (Arbeiten zur Theol. 1/13). Stuttgart: Calwer Verlag, 1963, 77 pp.

Anchor Bay Evangelistic Association, Inc., *The Anchor Bible Institute, A* **Full Gospel** *Fundamental* **Center** *of Christian Education, Courses and Curriculum.* New Baltimore, Mich.: Anchor Bible Bay Institute, n.d., 12 pp.

Anderson, Sir Robert, *Spirit Manifestations and 'The Gift of Tongues'*. London: Evangelical Alliance and Marshall, 3rd ed. 1909, 36 pp.

AoG (Australia), **United Constitution** *of the Assemblies of God in Australia*, n.p., n.d. (dupl.)

—**You Have Accepted Christ.** *And Now?* Brisbane, Queensland: Executive Presbytery of the AoG in Australia, n.d., 16 pp.

—*Doctrinal Basis*, n.p., n.d. (dupl.)

AoG (Great Britain and Ireland), *1962-1963 Year Book, containing constitutional minutes, lists of assemblies, ministers and missionaries.* London: AoG Publ. House, 1963, 80 pp.

—*Redemption Hymnal With Tunes.* London: AoG Publ. House, 1958

AoG (USA), *Concerning the* **Assemblies of God.** Springfield, Mo.: GPH, Tract 4102, n.d., 6 pp.

—**Early History** *of the Assemblies of God*, prepared by the AoG Public Relations Department, with appreciation of C. C. Burnett for original research. Springfield, Mo.: GPH, 1959, 32 pp.

—*The Minister's* **Service Book.** Springfield, Mo.: GPH, 1942, 147 pp. (a liturgical book!)

—*Hymns of Glorious Praise*, compiled and edited by the music division. Springfield, Mo.: GPH, 1962

—*Our Mission in Today's World. Council on Evangelism. Official Papers and Reports.* Editorial Committee: Richard Champion, Edward S. Caldwell, Gary Leggett. Springfield, Mo.: GPH, 1968, 217 pp.

Apostolic Church, **Its Principles** *and Practices*, Bradford: Puritan Press, *1937, revised 2nd ed. 1961, 163 pp.

—**Fundamentals,** *being 'things most surely believed'. A brief statement of fundamental truths contained in the Scriptures and believed and taught by the Apostolic Church.* Bradford: Puritan Press, n.d., 30 pp.

Arbeitsgemeinschaft der Christengemeinden in Deutschland e. V., **Wer wir sind** *und war wir wollen.* Erzhausen bei Darmstadt: Leuchter-Verlag, n.d., 4 pp.

Associação de Seminários Teológicos Evangélicos (ASTE), *O Espírito Santo e o Movimento Pentecostal, Simpósio.* S. Paulo: ASTE, 1966, 93 pp.

Associated Brotherhood of Christians, *Articles of Faith*, n.p., *n.d.

Atkins, Gaius Glenn, **Religion** *in Our Time.* New York: Round Table Press, *1932

Atter, Gordon F., **Cults** *and Heresies. The Student's Handbook.* Peterborough, Ontario: The Book Nook, 1963, 48 pp. (Karl Barth is included amongst the cults)

—**The Third Force.** *A Pentecostal answer to the questions so often asked by the members of other churches: 'Who are the Pentecostals?'* Peterborough, Ont.: The Book Nook, 1962, 314 pp.

Baëta, C. G., **Prophetism** *in Ghana, A Study of Some 'Spiritual' Churches.* London: SCM Press, 1962, 169 pp.

Baker, John, *Baptized in One Spirit. The meaning of I Cor. 12.13.* London: Fountain Trust, 1967, 24 pp.

Baklanoff, Eric N. (ed.), *New Perspectives of Brazil.* Nashville, Tenn.: Vanderbilt UP, 1966, 328 pp.

Barr, James, **Old and New** *in Interpretation. A Study of the Two Testaments.* London: SCM Press, 1966, 215 pp.

Barratt, Thomas Ball, *Da jeg fik min pintsedaab og tungemaalsgaven.* Oslo, *1907

— *When the Fire Fell, or God's Dealings With One of His Children*, ca. *1907; reprinted under the title: **When the Fire Fell** *and an Outline of My Life.* Larvik, 2nd ed. 1927 (important for Barratt's biography)

— 'The Outpouring of the Spirit in Norway, a Letter From Pastor Barratt, *Free Gospel Mission Journal* (Millvale Station, Alleghany, Pa.), *no. 10, leaf 3; quoted by G. H. Henke, *Am. Journal of Theol.* 13, 1909, pp. 193–206

— *In the Days of the* **Latter Rain.** London: Simpkin, Marshall, Hamilton Kent & Co., 1909, 224 pp.; London: Elim Publ. Co., 2nd rev. ed. 1928, 222 pp.

Barrett, David B., **Schism** *and Renewal in Africa. An Analysis of Six Thousand Contemporary Religious Movements.* Oxford UP, 1968, 363 pp.

Barth, Karl, *Der Römerbrief.* Zürich, EVZ, *1918, 2nd ed. *1921, 3rd ed. *1922, 4th ed. *1924, 5th ed. *1926, 1954, 528 pp.; ET, *The Epistle to the Romans.* London: Oxford UP, 1933, xxi+547 pp.

— *Kirchliche Dogmatik.* Zürich, from 1932; ET, *Church Dogmatics.* Edinburgh: T. & T. Clark, from 1936

Bartleman, Frank, *How 'Pentecost' Came to Los Angeles.* Los Angeles: F. Bartleman, 2nd ed. 1925, 167 pp.

— *What Really Happened at* **Azusa Street.** *The true story of the great revival* compiled by Frank Bartleman himself from his diary. Northridge, Calif.: Voice Christian Publ., Inc. 1962, 97 pp. (edited by John Walker)

Bases bibliques de l'Eglise Evangélique de La Chaux-de-Fonds (folder, Eglise Evangélique de Réveil, La Chaux-de-Fonds, Switzerland, n.d.)

Bastide, Roger, **Les religions** *africaines au Brésil.* Paris: Bibliothèque de sociologie contemporaine, Presses Universitaires de France, 1960, 578 pp.

Bates, E. S., art. 'J. A. Dowie', *Dict. of American Biography*, V (1930), p. 413

Beacham, Paul F., *Scriptural Sanctification.* Franklin Springs, Ga.: Advocate Publ. House, 9th ed., n.d., 14 pp.

Beck, Sigfried, **Daaben** *med den Helligaand.* Kolding, Den Apostolske Kirkes Forlag, 1941, 63 pp.

Becker, Wilhard, 'Die Charismen in der evangelischen Kirche heute', in: R. F. Edel (ed.), *Kirche und Charisma*, pp. 157–67

Behm, Johannes, art. 'glossa', *TWNT* I (1933), pp. 719ff.; ET, *TDNT* I (1964), 719–27

Bennett, Dennis J., *Nine o'Clock in the Morning.* Plainfield, N.J.: Logos and London: Fountain Trust, 1970, 209 pp.

Benz, Ernst, *Der Heilige Geist in Amerika.* Düsseldorf, Diederichs, 1970, 230 pp.

— (ed.), *Messianische Kirchen, Sekten und Bewegungen im heutigen Afrika.* Leiden: E. J. Brill, 1965, 127 pp.

Berg, Daniel, Enviado *por Deus*, *Memórias de Daniel Berg*. S. Paulo: AdD, 1959), 144 pp.

Besson, Henri, *Le* mouvement de sanctification *et le réveil d'Oxford*. Neuchâtel (Switzerland), 1914

Bethge, Eberhard, *Dietrich* Bonhoeffer. *Theologe, Christ, Zeitgenosse*. München: Kaiser-Verlag, 1967, 1128 pp.; ET, *Dietrich* Bonhoeffer. *Theologian, Christian, Contemporary*. London: Collins, 1970, xxiv+867 pp.

Beyerhaus, Peter, 'Die Kirchen und die messianischen Bewegungen' in P. Beyerhaus (ed.), *Weltmission heute* 33/34, pp. 57–72

— (ed.), *Begegnungen mit messianischen Bewegungen* (*Weltmission heute* 33/34). Stuttgart: Ev. Missionsverlag, 1967, 72 pp.

Bhengu, Nicholas B. H., Revival Fire *in South Africa*. Philadelphia: Afro-American Missionary Crusade, Inc., n.d. (1949), 15 pp.

— 'Christ is the Only Answer', in: D. Gee (ed.), *Fifth Conference*, 1958, pp. 89–96

Bibra, O. S. von, *Die Bevollmächtigten des Christus. Das Wesen ihres Dienstes im Lichte des Neuen Testamentes. Eine Untersuchung über die Kennzeichen der echten Diener am Wort nach dem Neuen Testament*. Gladbeck: Schriftenmissions-Verlag, 1947, 103 pp.; Stuttgart: Otto Bauder, 6th ed., 1958, 153 pp. See also Karl Ecke

Bittlinger, Arnold, 'Die Bedeutung der Charismen für den Gemeindeaufbau', in: R. F. Edel (ed.), *Bedeutung*, 1964, pp. 5–18

— 'Die Gnadengaben in der Bibel (1. Kor. 12.7–11)', in: R. F. Edel (ed.), *Bedeutung*, 1964, pp. 24–47

— Der frühchristliche Gottesdienst *und seine Wiederbelebung innerhalb der reformatorischen Kirchen der Gegenwart* (Oekumenische Texte und Studien 30). Marburg/Lahn: Edel, 1964, 32 pp.

— *Das* Sprachenreden *in der Kirche. Seine Bedeutung und Problematik in Vergangenheit und Gegenwart*. Hanover: Bittlinger, 1965, 29 pp. (dupl.)

— 'Disziplinierte Charismen', *Deutsches Pfarrerblatt* 63, 1963, pp. 333f.

— 'Gemeinde und Charisma', *Das missionarische Wort* 17, 1964, pp. 231–5

— *Liebe und Charisma. Eine Besinnung über 1. Kor. 13*. Hanover: Rufer-Zentrale, n.d. (1965), 16 pp.

— *Gnadengaben. Eine Auslegung von 1. Kor. 12–14*. Marburg/Lahn: R. F. Edel, 1966, 104 pp; 2nd enlarged ed. under the title: *Im Kraftfeld des Heiligen Geistes*. Marburg/Lahn: R. F. Edel, 1968, 218 pp.; ET, Gifts and Graces. *A Commentary on I Cor. 12–14*. London: Hodder and Stoughton, 1967, 123 pp.

— *Glossolalia. Wert und Problematik des Sprachenredens. Eine Materialsammlung für Mitarbeiter*. Hanover: Rolf Kühne, 2nd ed. 1966, 100 pp.

— *Gemeinde ist anders* (Calwer Hefte 79). Stuttgart: Calwer Verlag, 1966, 48 pp.

— *Fragen der Kirche an die Pfingstbewegung*. Geneva: WCC, 1967 (dupl. SE 67:3), partially quoted in *MD* 30, 1967, pp. 163–8

— *Charisma und Amt* (Calwer Hefte 85). Stuttgart: Calwer Verlag, 1967, 48 pp.

Bjerre, Martinus, *Jeg fik det i tilgift*. Kolding: Den Apostolske Kirkes Forlag, *n.d.

Björkquist, Curt, *Den svenska pingstväckelsen*. Stockholm; Förlaget Filadelfia, 1959, 121 pp.

Bjørner, Anna Larsen, *Teater og Tempel. Livserindringer.* Kopenhagen: H. Hirschsprungs Forlag, 1935, 183 pp.

Blumhardt, Joh. Christoph, *Ausgewählte Schriften*, ed. by Otto Bruder. 3 vols, Zürich, *1949ff.

— *Blumhardts* Kampf. *Zuverlässiger Abdruck seines eigenen Berichtes über die Krankheits- und Heilungsgeschichte der Gottliebin Dittus in Möttlingen* (mit einer Einführung von Prof. W. Koller). Erlangen, Stuttgart, 1955

Boerwinkel, F., *De Pinkstergroepen* (Oekumenische Leergang No. 5). Den Haag: Plein, 1963, 15 pp.

Bois, Henri, *Le réveil au pays de Galles.* Toulouse: Société des Publications Morales et Religieuses, 1905, 163 pp.

Bonch-Bruyevich, Vladimir, *Iz mira sektantov.* Moscow: Gosudarstvennoe izdatel'stvo, *1922

— *Izbrannie Sochineniya.* Moscow; Izdatel'stvo Akademii Nauk SSSR, 1 1959, vol. I, 407 pp. (vol I: *O religii, religioznom sekantstve i tserkvi*)

Bond, Georgia, *The* Life *Story of the Rev. O. H. Bond.* Oakgrove, Ark., n.d. (1958), 186 pp.

Bonhoeffer, Dietrich, *Widerstand und Ergebung. Briefe und Aufzeichnungen aus der Haft*, ed. by Eberhard Bethge. München: Kaiser-Verlag, *1951; Sibenstern Taschenbuch 1, 3rd ed. 1966; ET, *Letters and Papers from Prison*, London: SCM Press, 3rd ed. 1967, 240 pp.

Born, Karl, *Die waarheid oor die Spade Reën Gemeentes van Suid-Afrika.* Die herstelling von voltooiing van die nuwe-testamentiese Gemeente deur die onbeperkte openbaring van die Heilige Gees. My persoonlike ondervindings in die Europese en Suid-Afrikaanse Geloofshuise van die Spade Reën Gemeente. Benoni, South-Africa: Latter Rain Assemblies of South Africa, 1960, 66 pp.; German: *Die* Wahrheit *über die südafrikanischen Spätregengemeinden.* Die Ausgiessung des neutestamentlichen Spätregens und die Wiederherstellung und Vollendung der neutestamentlichen Gemeinde durch die uneingeschränkte Offenbarung des Heiligen Geistes. Meine persönlichen Erfahrungen in den europaischen und südafrikanischen Glaubenshäusern der Spätregen-Gemeinde. Beilstein, Württ.: Deutsche Spätregenmission, n.d., 79 pp.

Bornkamm, Günther, *Jesus von Nazareth* (Urban-Bücherei 19). Europa-Verlag 1956, 214 pp.; ET, *Jesus of Nazareth.* New York: Harper; London: Hodder and Stoughton, 1960, 239 pp.

Bosworth, Fred Francis, '*Deshalb*'. Leonberg, Württ.: Philadelphia Verlag, n.d., 32 pp.

Bourdeaux, Michael, **Religious Ferment** *in Russia. Protestant Opposition to Soviet Religious Policy.* London: Macmillan; New York: St. Martin's Press, 1968, 255 pp.

Bovet, Theodor, *Das Geheimnis ist gross. Ein Handbuch für Eheleute und ihre Berater.* Bern: Paul Haupt, 1955, 163 pp; ET, **Love, Skill and Mystery.** *A Handbook to Marriage.* New York: Doubleday, 1958, 188 pp.

Boyd, Frank Mathews, *God's Wonderful Book. The Origin, Lineage and Influence of the Bible.* Springfield, Mo.: GPH, 1944, 136 pp.

— *Ages and Dispensations.* Springfield, Mo.: GPH, n.d., 106 pp.

Boyens, Armin, *Kirchenkampf und Oekumene 1933–1939. Darstellung und Dokumentation.* München: Kaiser, 1969, 386 pp.

Bracco, Roberto, *Verità dimenticate e ... punti controversi.* Rome: R. Bracco, n.d., 68 pp.

— *Il risveglio pentecostale in Italia.* Rome: R. Bracco, n.d., 92 pp.

— *Il battesimo. Istruzioni per catecumeni.* Rome: R. Bracco, n.d., 55 pp.

Branham, William, *Seven Church Ages.* Tucson, Ariz.: Branham Campaigns, P.O. 3967, *n.d.

Brazier, Arthur M., *Black Self-Determination. The Story of the Woodlawn Organization*, Grand Rapids, Mich.: Eerdmans, 1969

Brewster, P. S., *The Convert's Handbook.* London: Elim Publ. House, *1939

Briem, Efraim, *Den moderna pingströrelsen.* Stockholm: Svenska Diakonistyrelses Bokförlag, *1924

— 'Den evangeliska kyrkan och de nutida väckelserörelserna'. *Protokoll vid nordiska prästmötet i Helsingfors 1933.* Helsinki, *1933

British Council of Churches, *Sex and Morality. A report presented to the British Council of Churches.* London: SCM Press, 1966, 77 pp.

Broederschap van Pinkster gemeenten in Nederland, *De Pingstergemeente en de Kerk.* De Broederschap van Pinkstergemeenten in Nederland geeft antwoord op het Herderlijk schrijven van de Generale Synode der Nederlands Hervormde Kerk over: De Kerk en de Pinkstergroepen, Rotterdam/Groningen: Stichting Volle Evangelie Lectuur, 1962, 21 pp.

Brofeldt, Pekka, *Helluntaiherätys Suomessa.* Mikkeli, *1933/34

Brooke, James, *A Testimony Concerning Israel in the Last Day.* London: United Apostolic Church, 1939

Brookes, E. H., *A Century of Missions in Natal and Zululand*, *1936

Brooks, N., *Fight for Faith and Freedom.* London, *1948

Bruckner, A., *Erweckungsbewegungen. Frucht und Geschichte.* Hamburg, 1909

Bruderschaft 'Der König kommt!', *Bruderschaft 'Der König kommt!'.* Ferndorf: Kr. Siegen, H. Kocks, 1946 (confession of faith)

Bruland, Gotfred F., *The Origin and Development of the Open Bible Church in Iowa* (unpublished M.A. thesis, Drake University, Des Moines, Iowa, *1945)

Brumback, Carl, *'What Meaneth This?' A Pentecostal Answer to a Pentecostal Question.* Springfield, Mo.: GPH, and London: AoG Publ. House, 1946, 348 pp.

— *Suddenly ... From Heaven. A History of the AoG.* Springfield, Mo.: GPH, 1961, 380 pp.

Bruner, Frederick Dale, *The Doctrine and Experience of the Holy Spirit in the Pentecostal Movement and correspondingly in the New Testament* (theol. Diss. Hamburg, 1963, Manuscript)

— *A Theology of the Holy Spirit. The Pentecostal Experience and the New Testament Witness.* Grand Rapids, Mich.: Eerdmans, 1970, 390 pp.

Brunner, Emil, *Der Mittler. Zur Besinnung über den Christusglauben.* Tübingen: Mohr, 1927, 565 pp.; ET, *The Mediator. A Study of the Central Doctrine of the Christian Faith*, London, 1934, 4th ed. 1946

—*Unser Glaube. Eine christliche Unterweisung.* Zürich: Zwingli-Verlag, *1934, 1951, 1958, 144 pp.; ET, *Our Faith.* London: SCM Press, 1949, 123 pp.

— *Dogmatik*, 3 vols. I: Die christliche Lehre von Gott, 391 pp. II: Die christliche Lehre von Schöpfung and Erlösung, 455 pp. III: Die christliche Lehre von der Kirche, vom Glauben und der Vollendung, 503 pp. Zürich: Zwingli-Verlag, 1953–60; ET, *Dogmatics*, 3 vols. I: The Christian Doctrine of God, 361 pp.; II: The Christian Doctrine of Creation and Redemption, 386 pp.; III: The Christian Doctrine of the Church, Faith and the Consummation, 455 pp. London: Lutterworth, 1949–62.

Burke, Fred, 'Ministry for Ministers', *Monthly Letter on Evangelism* (Geneva: WCC), Dec. 1966/Jan. 1967

Burton, William F. P., *God Working With Them, Being 18 Years Congo Evangelistic Mission History*. London: Victory Press, 1933, 264 pp.

Busch, Moritz, *Wanderungen zwischen Hudson und Mississippi 1851 und 1852* (2 vols). Stuttgart and Tübingen: J. G. Cotta'scher Verlag, 1853/54

Calley, Malcolm J., **Aboriginal Pentecostalism.** *A Study of Changes in Religion*, M.A. Thesis, University of Sydney, 1955, 4 vols (Manuscript)

— **God's People.** *West Indian Pentecostal Sects in England*. Oxford UP, 1965, 182 pp.

Camargo, C. Procópio F. de, 'Igrejas e Religiões em S. Paulo', in: J. V. Freitas Marcondes, Osmar Pimentel, *S. Paulo*, 1968, pp. 365–82

Campbell, Joseph E., *The Pentecostal Holiness Church 1898–1948. Its background and history*. Presenting complete background material which adequately explains the existence of this organization, also the existence of other kindred Pentecostal and Holiness groups, as an essential and integral part of the total church set-up. Franklin Springs, Ga.: PHCh, 1951, 573 pp. (cited as *PHCh*)

Carver, T. A., 'Social Problems of the Power Age', in: H. W. Greenway (ed.), *Power Age*, 1951, pp. 4–6

Cassin, Elena, 'La vita religiosa', in: Jean Meyriat (ed.), *La Calabria*, 1960, pp. 325–72

Cavnar, Jim, *Prayer Meetings*. Pecos, New Mexico: Dove Publications, 1969, 35 pp.

Chéry, H.-Ch., **Offensive** *des Sectes*. Paris (Rencontres 44), 2nd ed. 1954

ChoG, *Minutes of the General Assembly of the ChoG*. Cleveland, Tenn. (from 1906)

ChoG of the Mountain Assembly, *Minutes of the 56th Annual Assembly 1962*, n.p. (Jellico, Tenn.), n.d. (1962), 46 pp.

ChoG in Christ, *Yearbooks*, Memphis, Tenn. (at least from *1951)

Christenson, Larry, **Speaking in Tongues and its Significance** *for the Church*, London: Fountain Trust, 1968, 141 pp.

— **Speaking in Tongues . . . a Gift** *for the Body of Christ*. London: Fountain Trust, 1963, 5th ed. 1969, 32 pp.

— 'Das Charisma des Zungenredens', in: R. F. Edel (ed.), *Die Bedeutung der Gnadengaben*, 1963, pp. 72–86

Clark, Elmer T., *The* **Small Sects** *in America*. New York: Abingdon Press, *1937, 2nd ed. 1949, 256 pp.

Clark, Stephen B., *Spiritual Gifts*. Pecos, New Mexico: Dove Publications, 1969, 35 pp.

Clark, Stephen B., *Baptized in the Spirit*. Pecos, New Mexico: Dove Publications, 1970, 76 pp.
— *Confirmation and the 'Baptism of the Holy Spirit'*. Pecos, New Mexico: Dove Publications, 1969, 20 pp.
Clayton, Norman J. (comp.), *Melodies of Life*. Malverne, N.Y.: Gospel Songs, Inc., n.d.
Conde, Emilio, *Igrejas sem brilho*. Rio de Janeiro: Casa Publicadora das AdD, 1951, 82 pp.
— Etapas *da vida espiritual*. Rio de Janeiro: Casa Publicadora da AdD, 2nd ed. 1951, 110 pp.
— Pentecoste *para todos*. Rio de Janeiro: Casa Publicadora da AdD, 5th ed. 1951, 109 pp.
— O testemunho *dos séculos*. Rio de Janeiro: Livros Evangélicos, O. S. Boyer, 3rd ed. 1960, 194 pp.
— História *das AdD no Brasil*. Rio de Janeiro: Casa Publicadora das AdD, 1960, 355 pp.
Congregação Cristã do Brasil, *Estatutos aprovados em 4 de Março de 1931 e reformados em 23 Abril de 1943, 29 de Novembro de 1944 et de Decembro de 1946, em Assembleia Geral*. São Paulo, n.d.
— *Resumo Comvenção realizada em 20, 21, 22, 24, & 25 de Fevereiro de 1936 e Reuniões de Ensinamentos realizadas em 25, 26, 27 de Março de 1948*. São Paulo, n.d.
Conn, Charles W., *Like A Mighty* Army *Moves the Church of God*. Cleveland, Tenn.; ChoG Publ. House, 1955, 380 pp.
— Where the Saints Have Trod. *A History of the ChoG Missions*. Cleveland: Pathway Press, 1959, 312 pp.
Cossec, C. le, *Le Saint-Esprit et les dons spirituels. Toute la vérité concernant le surnaturel divin* (Vérité à connaître 3). Rennes: Le Cossec, n.d., 55 pp.
— *Le vrai Baptême. L'Eglise. La sanctification* (Vérité à connaître 2). Rennes: Le Cossec, n.d., 51 pp.
— *La guérison miraculeuse de toute maladie et de toute infirmité* (Vérité à connaître 4). Rennes: Le Cossec, n.d., 53 pp.
Cowie, Ian, *The Healing Christ*. Iona (Scotland), n.d., 8 pp.
Cox, Harvey, *The Feast of Fools. A Theological Essay on Festivity and Fantasy*. Cambridge, Mass.: Harvard University Press, 1969
Crayne, Richard, *Early* 20th Century *Pentecost*. Morristown, Tenn.: 1960, 71 pp.
Cristiani, Leone, art. 'Pentecostali', *Enc. Catt* 9, pp. 1153–4 (1952)
Curran, Francis X., Major Traits *in American Church History*. New York: American Press, *1940
Curtis, Richard K., *They Called Him Mister Moody*. New York: Doubleday, 1962, 378 pp.
Cutten, George B., *Speaking With Tongues*. New Haven: Yale University Press, 1927

Dallière, Louis, *D'aplomb sur la parole de Dieu. Courte étude sur le Réveil de Pentecôte*. Valence: Imprimerie Charpin et Reyne, 1932, 54 pp.
Dallmeyer, Heinrich, *Die* Zungenbewegung. *Ein Beitrag zu ihrer Geschichte*

und eine Kennzeichnung ihres Geistes. Lindhorst (Schaumburg-Lippe) and Hanover: Buchhandlung der Landeskirchlichen Gemeinschaft, 1924, 144 pp.; Langenthal, Switzerland; 2nd ed. n.d., 143 pp.

— See also B. Kühn.

Dalton, Robert Chandler, *Glossolalia* (unpubl. B.D. thesis, Eastern Baptist Theol. Seminary, 1940, preparatory work for *Tongues Like as of Fire*)

— **Tongues** *Like as of Fire. A critical study of modern tongue movements in the light of apostolic and patristic times.* Springfield, Mo.: GPH, 1945, 127 pp.

Damboriena, Prudencio, **Tongues As of Fire.** *Pentecostalism in Contemporary Christianity.* Washington and Cleveland: Corpus Books, 1969, 256 pp.

Davies, Horton, **Christian Deviations.** *The Challenge of the Sects.* London: SCM Press, *1954, *1955, *1956, *1957, enlarged 1961 (pp. 83–98 on Pentecostals)

Davies, J. Hywel, *The Renewal of the Church from a Pentecostal Viewpoint* (dupl. Geneva: WCC, SE 66:32, 1966)

Davis, J. Merle, **How the Church Grows in Brazil.** *A study of the economic and social basis of the Evangelical Church in Brazil.* London: IMC, 1943, 167 pp.

Day, Richard Ellsworth, *Bush Aglow.* Philadelphia: Judson Press, *1936

Dewar, Lindsay, *The* **Holy Spirit** *and Modern Thought. An inquiry into the historical, theological, and psychological aspects of the Christian doctrine of the Holy Spirit.* New York: Harper, 1959, 224 pp.

Diener, W., **Medio Siglo** *de Testimonio para Cristo.* Temuco, Chile: Imprenta y Editorial Alianza, *n.d.

Dolotov, A., *Tserkov' i sektantstvo v Sibiri.* Novosibirsk: Sibkraiizdat, *1930

Donaldson, Franklin, *The Sister Buck Memorial Hospital Project in Spiritual Healing, 1966–1967*, 15 pp., n.d. (paper of the Christian Medical Commission, WCC, Geneva)

Douglas, W. M., *Andrew Murray and his Message.* London and Edinburgh: Oliphants, 1926

Drollinger, Christian, **Offener Brief** *auf die Erklärung des Herrn Methodistenpredigers Währer aus Signau, vom 28. Oktober 1937, in betreff der neuen Versammlung in Signau und anderwärts*, n.p. (Signau, Switzerland), n.d. (1937), 23 pp.

Dubb, A. A., *The* **Role** *of the Church in an Urban African Society.* Rhodes University, *1962 (unpublished thesis)

Dumas, André, *Ideologia e fé.* Rio de Janeiro: Tempo e Presença, *1968

Duncan, Mildred H., *A* **Revelation** *of End-Time Babylon. A Verse by Verse Exposition of the Book of Revelation.* Edgemont, South Dakota: M. H. Duncan, 1950, 286 pp.

Dunn, James D. G., **Baptism** *in the Holy Spirit. A Re-examination of the New Testament Teaching on the Gift of the Spirit in relation to Pentecostalism today.* (Studies in Biblical Theology II/15.) London: SCM Press, 1970, 248 pp.

Durasoff, Steve, *The All-Union Council of Evangelical Christians-Baptists in the Soviet Union: 1944–1964.* (Diss., University of New York, 1967, 347 pp., manuscript) (cited as *AUCECB*)

Durasoff, Steve, 'Sowjetunion' in: W. J. Hollenweger (ed.), *Pfingstkirchen*, pp. 50–60
—*The Russian Protestants. Evangelicals in the Soviet Union, 1944–1964.* Cranberry, N.J.: Fairleigh Dickenson UP, *1971
Dye, M. L., *The Murderous Communist Conspiracy. Satan's End-Time Program,* New Baltimore, Mich.: Anchor Bay Evangelistic Association Inc., n.d., 27 pp.

Eaton, J. H., *Psalms.* London: SCM Press, 1967, 317 pp.
Ebeling, Gerhard, *Das Wesen des christlichen Glaubens.* Tübingen: Mohr, 1959, 255 pp.; ET, *The Nature of Faith.* Philadelphia: Fortress Press, and London: Collins, 1961, 181 pp.
Ecke, Karl, **Schwenckfeld**, *Luther und der Gedanke einer apostolischen Reformation.* Berlin: Martin Warneck, 1911, 345 pp.
—**Der Durchbruch des Urchristentums** *seit Luthers Reformation. Lesestücke aus einem vergessenen Kapitel der Kirchengeschichte.* Altdorf bei Nürnberg: Süddeutscher Missionsverlag Fritz Pranz, 2nd ed., n.d. (1950), 131 pp.
—*Die* **Pfingstbewegung.** *Ein Gutachten von kirchlicher Seite.* Mülheim/Ruhr: Christl. Gemeinschaftsverband GmbH, 1950
—**Sektierer** *oder wertvolle Brüder? Randglossen zu einem Sektenbuch.* Mülheim/Ruhr: Christl. Gemeinschaftsverband GmbH, 1950
Ecke, Karl and O. S. von Bibra, *Die* **Reformation** *in neuer Sicht.* Altdorf bei Nürnberg: Süddeutscher Missionsverlag, Fritz Pranz, 1952
—*Der reformierende Protestantismus.* Gütersloh: Bertelsmann, 1952
Edel, Eugen, *Der* **Kampf** *um die Pfingstbewegung.* Mülheim/Ruhr: Emil Humburg, 1949, 63 pp.
Edel, Reiner-Friedemann, **Heinrich Thiersch** *als ökumenische Gestalt. Ein Beitrag züm ökumenischen Anliegen der katholisch-apostolischen Gemeinden* (Oekumenische Texte und Studien 18), Marburg/Lahn, R. F. Edel, 1962, 389 pp.
—(ed.), *Kirche und Charisma. Die Gaben des Heiligen Geistes im Neuen Testament, in der Kirchengeschichte und in der Gegenwart.* Marburg/Lahn: R. F. Edel, 1966, 206 pp.
—(ed.), *Die* **Bedeutung** *der Gnadengaben für die Gemeinde Jesus Christi* (Oekumenische Texte und Studien 33). Marburg/Lahn: R. F. Edel, 1964, 125 pp.
Eggenberger, Oswald, *Evangelischer Glaube und Pfingstbewegung.* Zürich: EVZ, 1946, 61 pp.
—art. 'Pfingstbewegung', *RGG* V (1961), cols. 308–10
Eicken, Erich von, **Heiliger Geist,** *Menschengeist, Schwarmgeist. Ein Beitrag zur Geschichte der Pfingstbewegung in Deutschland.* Wuppertal: R. Brockhaus-Verlag, 1964, 92 pp.
Eisenlöffel, Ludwig, *Die* **Spätregenbewegung** '*Benoni*' *aus Süd-Afrika und die Bibel.* Erzhausen bei Darmstadt, Bibelschule 'Beröa', 1960, 42 pp. (dupl.)
—**Ein Feuer** *auf Erden. Einführung in Lehre und Leben der Pfingstbewegung.* Leuchter-Verlag, 1963, 146 pp.
—'Die Erneuerung der Kirche aus der Sicht der Pfingstbewegung' (dupl. WCC, Geneva, SE 66:34), printed: *Der Leuchter* 17/11, Nov. 1966, pp.

5–7; ET, *The Renewal of the Church from a Pentecostal Viewpoint* (dupl. WCC, Geneva, SE 66:33, 1966)

Eliade, Mircea. *Shamanism: Archaic Techniques of Ecstasy*. New York: Pantheon Books, *1964

— *Mythes, rêves et mystères*. Paris, 1957; ET, *Myths, Dreams and Mysteries*. London: Harvill Press, 1960, 256 pp.

E[llenberger] O[tto], 'Zwei schauerliche Erlebnisse', 1942, in: Johann Widmer, *Im Kampf*, II, 2nd ed. 1949, pp. 99–100

Endersen, Andreas, *Frelst i havn*. Kopenhagen: Forlaget Korsets Evangelium, n.d., 74 pp.

Ewart, Frank J., *The* **Phenomenon** *of Pentecost. A History of the Latter Rain*. St. Louis, Mo.: Pentecostal Publ. House, 1947, 110 pp.

Failing, Wolf-Eckart, 'Neue charismatische Bewegung in den Landeskirchen', in: W. J. Hollenweger (ed.), *Pfingstkirchen*, pp. 131–45

— *Kooperation als Leitmodell. Krise und Strukturerneuerung des Gemeindepfarramtes*. Frankfurt a.M.: Diesterweg, 1970, 226 pp.

Falconi, Carlo, **La Chiesa** *e le organizzazioni cattoliche in Italia, 1945–1955. Saggi per una storia del cattolicesimo italiano ne dopoguerra*. Turin: G. Einaudi, 1956, 670 pp.

Fedorenko, Fedor Illarionovich, **Sekty,** *ikh vera i dela*. Moscow: Gospolitizdat, 1965, 330 pp.

Fleisch, Paul, *Zur* **Geschichte** *der Heiligungsbewegung*, 1. Heft: *Die Heiligungsbewegung von Wesley bis Boardman*. Leipzig, 1910

Ford, J. Massingberd, *The Spirit and the Human Person. A Meditation*. Dayton, Ohio: Pflaum Press, 1969, 177 pp.

— *The Pentecostal Experience. A New Direction for American Catholics*. New York: Paulist Press, 1970, 60 pp.

Förlaget Filadelfia (ed.), **Europeiska Pingstkonferensen** *i Stockholm, den 5–12 Juni 1939. Tal, samtal och predikningar*. Stockholm: Förlaget Filadelfia, 1939, 436 pp.

— *Världpingstkonferensen i Stockholm den 13–20 juni 1955 i ord och bild*. Stockholm: Förlaget Filadelfia, 1955, 150 pp.

Francescon, Luigi, **Resumo** *de uma ramificação da obra de Deus, pelo Espírito Santo, no século atual*. S. Paulo: Congregação Cristã do Brasil, *1942, 2nd ed. *1953, 3rd ed. 1958, 30 pp.

Fraser, Maria M., *The* **Deplorable State** *of Pentecostal Movements in South Africa*. Benoni: The Latter Rain Assemblies of South Africa, 1957 (unpaginated)

— **Getuienis** *van Geestelike Groei, van Geloofslewe en van Werkinge van die Heilige Gees*. Benoni, South Africa, P.O.B. 416, *1952, 2nd ed. 1962, 98 pp.; ET, **Faith Life** *and Diverse Operations of the Holy Spirit as Personally Experienced by Sister M. M. Fraser*. Benoni, South-Africa, P.O. Box 416, 1953, 93 pp.; German: *Persönliche Erfahrungen über das Glaubensleben und die verschiedenen Wirkungen des Heiligen Geistes*. Benoni, South Africa, P.O.B. 416 and Beilstein, Kr. Heilbronn (Germany), Glaubenshaus der deutschen Spätregenmission, n.d., 83 pp.

Frey, Mae Eleanor, *The Minister*. Springfield, Mo.: GPH, 1939, 180 pp. (A novel in which the wish-dreams of a Pentecostal evangelist are fulfilled. He comes to Ferndale in California; the most beautiful girl in the richest and most highly regarded church in Ferndale is converted in his tent mission. She bravely breaks off her engagement to the respected pastor of her own church in order to get to know the full gospel among the Pentecostals. Other very wealthy members of her church also come over to the Pentecostals. A very instructive book, which expresses both the secret and the openly admitted desires of young Pentecostal evangelists in a light, readable style, free of pomposity if somewhat stereotyped.)

Frodsham, Stanley Howard, *With Signs Following. The Story of the Pentecostal Revival in the 20th Century*. Springfield, Mo.: GPH; London: AoG Publ. House, 1926, 254 pp., 2nd ed *1928, 3rd ed. 1946, 279 pp.

— *Smith Wigglesworth, Apostle of Faith*. London: Elim Publ. Co.; London: AoG Publ. House, 1949, 108 pp.

Fuegg, Pierre, *Le Baptême du Saint-Esprit*. Manuscript, 2 vols (Neuchâtel, Switzerland, cf. 05.28.048)

Full Salvation Union, *Manual*, n.p., *1944, 120 pp.

Gaëte, Arturo, 'Un cas d'adaptation: Les "Pentecostales" au Chili', in: R. P. Abd-el-Jali, Daniel Rops, R. P. Houang, Olivier Lacombe, Pierre-Henry Simon, *L'Eglise, l'occident, le monde*. Paris: Libr. Arthème Fayard (Recherches et Débats 15), 1956, pp. 142–9

Garkavenko, Fedor L., *Chto takoe religioznoe sektantstvo*. Moscow: Nauchno-populiarnaia biblioteka, *1961

Gasson, Raphael, *The Challenging Counterfeit. A study of spiritualism*. London: AoG Publ. House, n.d., 92 pp.

Gee, Donald, 'The Initial Evidence of the Baptism of the Holy Spirit', *Redemption Tidings*, *Dec. 1925; reprinted with 'additional considerations'. Kenley, Surrey: AoG Bible College, 1959, 20 pp.

— *Concerning Spiritual Gifts*, *1928; London: AoG Publ. House, enlarged 1937; Springfield, Mo.: GPH, n.d., 119 pp.

— *The Ministry Gifts of Christ*. Springfield, Mo.: GPH, 1930, 110 pp.

— 'The Phenomena of Pentecost', in: D. Gee, P. C. Nelson, Myer Pearlman, George Jeffreys, D. W. Kerr, *The Phenomena of Pentecost*. Springfield, Mo.: GPH, 1931, pp. 5–13

— *Pentecost*, Springfield. Mo.: GPH, and London: AoG Publ. House, 1932, 95 pp.

— *The Fruit of the Spirit*. Springfield, Mo.: GPH, 1934, 94 pp.

— *Upon All Flesh*. Springfield, Mo.: GPH, and London: AoG Publ. House, 1935, 107 pp.; 1947, 118 pp.

— *Proverbs For Pentecost*. Springfield: GPH, 1936, 83 pp.

— *This Is the Will of God*. London: Elim Publ. House, *1940

— *The Pentecostal Movement*. London: Elim Publ. House, 1941, 199 pp.; 2nd enlarged ed. 1949, 236 pp.; 3rd enlarged ed. under the title *Wind and Flame*. London: AoG Publ. House, 1967, 317 pp.

— *Bonnington Toll. The Story of a First Pastorate*. London: Victory Press, 1943, 49 pp.

— *Why 'Pentecost'?* London, *1944
— *Keeping in Touch. Studies on 'Walking in the Spirit'*. London: Elim Publ. Co., 1951, 81 pp.
— **Trophimus** *I Left Sick. Our problems of divine healing*. London: Elim Publ. Co., and Springfield, Mo.: GPH, 1952, 30 pp.
— (ed.), **Fifth** *World Pentecostal* **Conference.** *Pentecostal World Conference Messages, preached at the Fifth Triennial World Conference*, held in the Coliseum Arena, Exhibition Ground, Toronto, Canada, from September 14–21, 1958. Published by the Advisory Committee for the Conference, edited by Donald Gee. Toronto: Testimony Press, 1958, 188 pp.
— 'The Pentecostal Experience', in: D. Gee (ed.), *Fifth ... Conference*, 1958, pp. 43–52; German: *VdV* 50/12, Dec. 1958, pp. 3–6, 15; *Der Leuchter* 10/2, Febr. 1959; 10/3, March 1959, pp. 6–8; Italian: *Risveglio P* 13/11–12, Nov.–Dec. 1958, pp. 3–9; Dutch: *Volle Evangelie Koerier* 21/6, Dec. 1958, pp. 4–5; 21/7, Jan. 1959, p. 5; 21/8, Febr. 1959, pp. 3, 5; 21/9, March 1959, 4–5
— **Fruitful or Barren.** *Studies in the Fruit of the Spirit*. Springfield, Mo.: GPH, 1961, 89 pp.
— *All With One Accord*. Springfield, Mo.; GPH, 1961, 61 pp.
— *To the Uttermost Part. The Missionary Results of the Pentecostal Movement in the British Isles*. Stockport: Redemption Tidings, n.d., 28 pp.
— *Story of a Great Revival*. London: AoG Publ. House, *n.d.
— *The Glory of the Assemblies of God*, published by the Executive Council of the AoG in Great Britain and Ireland. London: AoG Publ. House, n.d., 19 pp.
— and J. N. Gartner and H. Pickering, **Water Baptism** *and the Trinity*. London: AoG Publ. House, n.d.
Gelpi, Donald L., *Pentecostalism. A Theological Viewpoint*. New York: Paulist Press, 1971, 234 pp.
Gemeinde für Urchristentum, *Wer wir sind*. Oberhofen (Switzerland), n.d. (prospectus)
Gemeinde Jesu Christi, *Wer ist die* **Gemeinde** *Jesu Christi in Deutschland?* Stammheim bei Calw (Germany), n.d. (prospectus)
Gericke, P., **Christliche Vollkommenheit** *und Geisteserlebnisse*. Rietenau, Württ.: Gericke, 1950, 224 pp.
Gerlach, Luther P., and Virginia H. Hine, *People, Power, Change. Movements of Social Transformation*. Indianapolis and New York: Bobbs-Merrill Co., 257 pp.
Gerrard, Nathan Lewis, *Scrabble Creek Folk*, Part II, Mental Health (dupl.)
— 'The Serpent-Handling Religions of West Virginia', *Transaction*, May 1968, pp. 22–30
Gesellschaft für Mission, Diakonie und Kolportage m.b.H., *Der Kampf um die Pfingstbewegung*, reprinted from '*Pfingstgrüsse*'. Mülheim/Ruhr: Gesellschaft für Mission, Diakonie und Kolportage, m.b.H., n.d.
Giese, Ernst, *Pastor* **Jonathan Paul,** *ein Knecht Jesu Christi. Leben und Werk*. Altdorf/Nbg.: Missionsbuchhandlung und Verlag, 1964, 354 pp.
Gijs, Jan van, **Het feest** *gaat door!* Gorinchem: Kracht van Omhoog, 1962, 154 pp.

Giordani, Igino, *I Protestanti alla conquista in Italia*. Milan, *1944

Glage, P., *Wittenberg oder Wales?* *1906

Glardon, Christian, **Les dons spirituels** *dans la premiére épître de Paul aux Corinthiens*. Thèse, présentée à la Faculté de Théologie de l'Eglise évangélique libre du Canton de Vaud pour obtenir le grade de licencié en théologie, Lausanne, University, 1966, 123 pp. (dupl.)

Goddard, Eduardo Labarca, *Chile invadido. Reportaje a la intromisión extranjera*. Santiago de Chile: Editora Austral, 1969, 348 pp.

Goldschmidt, Walter R., **Social Structure** *of a Californian Rural Community* (unpubl. thesis in anthropology, University of California, Berkeley, *1942)

Goodall, Norman (ed.), *The Uppsala Report 1968*. Official Report of the Fourth Assembly of the WCC Uppsala, July 4–20, 1968. Geneva: WCC, 1968, 513 pp.

Goss, Ethel E., *The* **Winds** *of God. The Story of the Early Pentecostal Days, 1901–1914, in the Life of Howard A. Goss*. New York: Comet Press, 1958, 178 pp.

GPH, **A Defence** *of the Pentecostal Movement by a Californian Doctor*. Springfield, Mo.: GPH, n.d.

Graham, Billy, 'Billy Graham Speaks to the Churches. A Sermon delivered by the evangelist Billy Graham to the ministers at Sacramento, California, in his 1958 Crusade', *PE* 2348, 10.5.1959, pp. 6f.; *Revivalist* 223, Oct. 1961, p. 6; *Full Gospel Men's Voice* 9/12, Jan. 1962, pp. 20f. (title: The time has come to give the Holy Spirit His rightful place! We need to go back, study and learn against what it means to be baptized with the Holy Spirit!)

— 'Baptized With the Holy Spirit', *P Testimony*, July 1963, p. 5

— 'Something is Happening', in: Jerry Jensen (ed.), *The Baptists and the Baptism in the Holy Spirit*, pp. 16–18, 31

Grant, W. V., *Men in the Flying Saucers Identified*. Dallas, Texas: Voice of Healing, *n.d.

Greenway, H. W., **Labourers** *With God, being a brief account of the activities of the Elim Movement*. London: Elim Publ. Co., 1946, 52 pp.

— (ed.), *Power Age*. London; Elim Publ. Co., 1951, 35 pp.

— (ed.), **World** *Pentecostal* **Conference 1952,** *London*. A brochure setting forth interesting aspects of the great world-wide Pentecostal Revival and the Third World Conference of Pentecostal Churches. London: Elim Publ. Co., 1952, 76 pp.

— *This Emotionalism*. London: Victory Press, 1954, 151 pp.

Grosc, LaVern K., *Sent into the World. The Proceedings of the Fifth Assembly of the Lutheran World Federation, Evian, France, 14–24 July 1970*. Minneapolis, Miss.: Augsburg Publishing House, 1971, 165 pp.

Grubb, Lura Johnson, *Living to Tell of Death*. Memphis, Tenn.: Gruss, 1947, 98 pp.

Gründler, Johannes, **Lexikon** *der christlichen Kirchen und Sekten* unter Berücksichtigung der Missionsgesellschaften und zwischenkirchlichen Organisationen. Freiburg: Herder, 1961, 1 vol. in 2, 1378, 211 col.

Haarbeck, Hermann, *Lass dir an* **meiner Gnade** *genügen. Die Stellungnahme* *des Gnadauer Verbandes zur Pfingstbewegung und zum Christlichen Gemeinschaftsverband Mülheim.* Denkendorf, Kreis Esslingen: Gnadauer Verlag, 1965, 72 pp.

Haenchen, Ernst, *Die Apostelgeschichte, neu übersetzt und erklärt.* (Kritisch-exegetischer Kommentar über das Neue Testament [W. Meyer] 3). Göttingen: Vandenhoeck und Ruprecht, 12th ed. 1959, 661 pp.

Handspicker, Meredith B., *The Purpose of the WCC* (dupl. WCC, Geneva, FO/66:63, 1966)

— and Lukas Vischer (ed.), *An Ecumenical Exercise* (Geneva: WCC, Faith and Order 49), 1967 (also in *Ecumenical Review* 19/1, Jan, 1967, pp. 1–47)

Hargrave, O. T., *A History of the Church of God in Mexico.* (Manuscript, M.A. thesis, Trinity University, 1958, 195 pp.)

Harper, Michael C., **Power** *for the Body of Christ.* London: Fountain Trust, 1964, 2nd ed. 1965, 56 pp.

— *Prophecy. A Gift for the Body of Christ.* London: Fountain Trust, 1964, 32 pp.

— *The* **Third Force** *in the Body of Christ.* London: Fountain Trust, 1965, 32 pp.

— *Life in the Holy Spirit. Some Questions and Answers.* London: Fountain Trust, 1966; Plainfield, N.J.: Logos, 1970, 17 pp.

— **As At the Beginning.** *The Twentieth Century Pentecostal Revival.* London: Hodder and Stoughton, 1965, 128 pp.

Harris, Ralph W., *The* **Cults.** *Teacher's Manual.* Springfield, Mo.: GPH, 1962, 96 pp.

Harrison, Irvine J., *A History of the AoG.* Th.D. thesis, Berkeley Baptist Divinity School, Berkeley, Calif., *1954 (dupl.)

Hartz, E. R., **Social Problems** *in a North Carolina Parish.* M.A. Thesis, Duke University, *1938

Häselbarth, Hans, 'Die Zion Christian Church in evangelischer Sicht', in: Peter Beyerhaus (ed.), *Weltmission heute* 33/34, 1967, pp. 11–25

Hasenhüttl, Gotthold, *Charisma, Ordnungsprinzip der Kirche* (Oekumenische Forschungen I/V). Freiburg: Herder, 364 pp.

Hathaway, W. G. **Spiritual Gifts** *in the Church.* London; Elim Publ. Co., 1933, 123 pp.

Hauser, Markus, *Am* **Gnadenthrone.** *Gedanken über das Gebet nebst köstlichen Gebetserhörungen.* Zürich: M. Hauser, ca. 1897

—*Kraft aus der Höhe. Zeugnisse für den Empfang des Heiligen Geistes* (publ. posthumously by Albert Jung). Zürich 1901; Basel, Brunnen-Verlag, 3rd ed. 1943; Giessen and Basel, Spener-Verlag, 9th ed. 1959

— **Komme** *bald, Herr Jesus!* (compiled from writings of Markus Hauser by Albert Jung). Zürich 1903

Hayward, Victor E. W. (ed.), **African** *Independent Church* **Movements,** Research Pamphlets No. 11, publ. for the WCC, CWME. London: Edinburgh House Press, 1963, 94 pp.

Haywood, G. T., *Apostolic Bible Reading. The Birth of the Spirit and the Mystery of the Godhead.* Indianapolis, Ind.: Voice in the Wilderness Magazine, n.d., 16 pp.

Heggelund, Kristian, **Våre sykdommer** *i lys av Guds ord.* Oslo: Filadelfiaforlaget, 1958, 23 pp.

Heiler, Friedrich, *Die* **Wahrheit** *Sundar Singhs. Neue Dokumente zum Sadhustreit.* München 1927
Herbort, Heinz Josef, 'Catholics in Holland Introduce Bold Changes. Liturgical Reform in Full Swing', *Monthly Letter on Evangelism* (Geneva, WCC), May/June 1967
Heuvel, Albert van den, *What Impulses for Renewal Does the WCC Expect From the Pentecostal Churches?* Geneva: WCC, Y:66/21 (dupl.)
Highet, John, *The Scottish Churches.* London: Skeffington, 1960, 224 pp.
Hill, Clifford S., **West Indian Migrants** *and the London Churches.* Oxford University Press, 1963, 89 pp.
— *Some Aspects of* **Race and Religion** *in Britain* (dupl. address, given at Senate House, 27.1.1969, University of London, Comparative Morals and Religion Panel), 9 pp.
Hilton, Bruce, *The Delta Ministry.* London and New York: Collier-Macmillan, 1969, 240 pp.
Hine, Virginia H., see Luther P. Gerlach
Hitzer, Arnold, *Die sogenannte 'Apostolische Kirche', ihre Lehre und Ordnung,* Kiel: A. Hitzer, 1955, 20 pp.
Hodges, Serena M., **Look on the Fields.** *A Missionary Survey.* Springfield, Mo.: GPH, 1956, 201 pp.
Hoekendijk, J. C., 'Mission – Heute', in: **Mission – Heute!** *Zeugnisse holländischen Missionsdenkens.* Bethel: Studentenbund für Mission in der Evangelischen Studentengemeinde in Deutschland, 1954, pp. 5–12
Hoekendijk, Karel, *De wapenrusting Gods.* Baarn, Holland: Stromen van Kracht, *n.d.; German: **Die Waffenrüstung** *Gottes.* Baarn, Holland: Stromen van Kracht, n.d., 50 pp.
Hokkanen, Lauri, **Oletko** *uudestisyntynyt?* Helsinki, *1932
Hollenweger, Walter J., 'Quer durch die Schweiz. Ein Tatsachenbericht', *VdV* 44/3, March 1951, pp. 11–13; 44/7, July 1951, pp. 10f; 44/10, Oct. 1951, pp. 13–16
— 'An Approach to Pentecostalism. Religion and Emotion', *Methodist Recorder,* 31.1.1963, Supplement III
—'Unusual Methods of Evangelism in the Pentecostal Movement in China', *Monthly Letter on Evangelism,* Nov./Dec. 1965 (WCC, Geneva)
— 'The Pentecostal Movement and the WCC', *Ecumenical Review* 18/3, July 1966, pp. 310–20; reprinted: *The World Christian Digest* (Bala, North Wales) 18/212, Dec. 1966, pp. 26–33
— *The European Pentecostal Movement in Their Own Understanding and the Understanding of Others* (Geneva, WCC, dupl. SE 66:35)
— 'Il risveglio Pentecostale in Italia: religione della fierezza dei poveri', *Concetto italiano* 14, May 1967, pp. 19–32 (Geneva, WCC)
— 'Evangelism and Brazilian Pentecostalism', *Ecumenical Review* 20/2, April 1968, pp. 163–70
— 'The Pentecostal Movement and the Third World', *Ecumenical Press Service* (WCC, Geneva) 36/24, 3.7.1969, pp. 13f.; reprints: *PE* 2892, 12.10.1969, p. 34; *Faith and Unity* (Windsor, Berks.) 13/5, Sept. 1969, pp. 92f.
— 'El movimiento pentecostal y el movimiento ecuménico', *Estudios ecuménicos*

(Mexico), 1969/2, April/May 1969, pp. 11–14; *Concepto Latino-Americano* 26, March 1970, pp. 12f.

— 'Pentecostalism and the Third World', *Lutheran Standard* (Minneapolis, Minn.) 9/19, 16.9.1969, pp. 2–4

— 'Charisma und Oekumene. Der Beitrag der Pfingstbewegung zur weltweiten Kirche.' *Rondom het Woord* (Hilversum) 12/3, July 1970, pp. 300–16; ET in preparation in *One for Christ*

— 'Das Charisma in der Oekumene. Der Beitrag der Pfingstbewegung and die allgemeine Kirche', *Una Sancta*, June 1970, pp. 150–9

— 'Spiel als eine Form von Theologie. Zum geplanten Dialog mit der Pfingstbewegung.' *Lutherische Monatshefte* 9/10, Oct. 1970, pp. 532–4

— *A Black Pentecostal Concept: A Forgotten Chapter of Black History: The Black Pentecostals' Contribution to the Church Universal* (Concept 30), June 1970 (Geneva: WCC)

— 'Pentecostalism and the Third World', *Dialogue* (Minneapolis, Minn.) 9/2, 1970, pp. 122–9

— 'Redécouvrir le Pentecôtisme', *Communion* (Taizé) 1/1, 1970, pp. 74–8

— 'The Unexpected Dialogue Between Pentecostals and Roman Catholics', *Ecumenical Press Service This Month* (WCC, Geneva), Feb. 1970, pp. 4–6

— 'A Little-Known Chapter in Pentecostal History', *Ecumenical Press Service, This Month*, April 1970, pp. 8f.

— art. 'Experimental Forms of Worship', 'Open Air Meeting', 'Ordination, Pentecostal', 'Camp Meeting', 'Worship, Pentecostal', 'Liturgy, Pentecostal', 'Spirituals', in: J. G. Davies (ed.), *A Dictionary of Liturgy and Worship*. London: SCM Press, 1972

— 'O movimento pentecostal no Brasil', *Simpósio. Revista teológica da ASTE* 2/3, June 1963, pp. 5–41

— (ed.), *Kirche, Benzin und Bohnensuppe. Auf den Spuren dynamischer Gemeinden*. Zürich: TVZ, 1971 (ET in preparation)

— (ed.), *Die Pfingstkirchen. Selbstdarstellungen, Dokumente, Kommentare*. Stuttgart: Ev. Verlagswerk, 1971 (Die Kirchen der Welt VII)

— *Theologie in der Tagesordnung der Welt. Sequenzen und Konsequenzen*. Zürich: TVZ, 1972; ET in preparation: *Theology in the World's Agenda*.

Hood, Paxton, *Christmas Evans. The Preacher of Wide Wales. His Country, his Times and his Contemporaries*. London: Hodder and Stoughton, *3rd ed., 1888, 420 pp.

Hoover, Mario G., **Origin** *and Structural Development of the Assemblies of God*. M.A. thesis, Southwest Missouri State College, 1968, 214 pp. (dupl.)

Horton: Harold, *The* **Gifts** *of the Spirit*. London: F. J. Lamb, 1934, 211 pp.; London; AoG Publ. House, 2nd ed. 1946, 3rd ed. 1949; Springfield, Mo.: GPH, 5th ed. 1953; London: AoG Publ. House, 6th ed. *1960, 7th ed. 1962, 228 pp.

Preaching and Homiletics. Presenting the scriptural ideal for all preachers and offering instruction in sermon-making for those who are seeking it. London: AoG Publishing House, 2nd ed., 1949, 119 pp.

— **Baptism** *in the Holy Spirit. A challenge to whole-hearted seekers after God*. London: AoG Publ. House, 1956, 23 pp.

Hutten, Kurth, **Seher,** *Grübler, Enthusiasten. Sekten und religiöse Sondergemeinschaften,* Stuttgart: Quell-Verlag, *1950, 8th ed. 1962 (751 pp.), 11th ed. enlarged 1968 (822 pp.)

— art. 'Geistestaufe', *RGG* II (1958), cols. 1303f.

— *Die* **Glaubenswelt** *des Sektierers. Anspruch und Tragödie.* Hamburg: Furche-Verlag, 1962, 129 pp. (Stundenbuch 6)

Hyma, Albert, **World History.** *A Christian Interpretation.* Grand Rapids, Mich.: Wm. B. Eerdmans, *1942

Hymns of Glorious Praise, compiled and edited by the Music Division. Springfield, Mo.: GPH, 1969

Iartsev, A., *Sekta evangel'skikh khristian.* Moscow: Bezbozhnik, *1928

Iglesia Pentecostal de Chile, *Manual del Ministro* (typescript copy sent by Enrique Chávez to the WCC, archives, WCC)

International Pentecostal Assemblies, **General Principles** *of the Int. Pentecostal Assemblies,* n.d., n.p., 11 pp.

— **Statement** *of Policy,* n.p., 1960, 10 pp.

Iona Community, *Divine Healing.* Iona (Scotland), n.d., 17 pp.

Jager, P. C. de, *Vingerwysings na die Koms van Christus en van die Antichris.* 'n Samevatting van die Tekens van die Tyd sowel as van die rampe wat die gersgestelde mensdom inwag. Benoni, South Africa: Latter Rain Assemblies, 1962, 113 pp.; ET, **Signposts** *Pointing to the Coming of Christ and of the Antichrist.* Benoni, South Africa: Latter Rain Assemblies, P.O.B. 415, 1963, 92 pp.; German: *Die Zeichen der Wiederkunft Jesu.* Beilstein, Kreis Heilbronn: Deutsche Spätregenmission, 1956, 32 pp.

Jeevaratnam, Lam, **Concerning Demons.** *Questions and Answers.* Guidvada P.O., Kistma District, South India, *1936; New York 2nd ed. *1937, Gudivada P.O., 3rd ed. 1937; Madras 4th ed. 1948, 63 pp.

Jeffreys, George. *The Miraculous Foursquare Gospel – Supernatural.* 2 vols., London: Elim Publ. Co., 1929/30

— 'The Gospel of the Miraculous', in: D. Gee. (ed.), *The Phenomena of Pentecost,* 1931, pp. 33–50

— *Healing Rays.* London: Elim Publ. Co. *1932; 2nd ed. *1935; London and Worthing: Henry E. Walter Ltd., 3rd ed. 1952, 121 pp.

— **Why I Resigned** *from the Elim Movement.* London, *n.d.

Jemolo, Carlo Arturo, *Per la pace religiosa d'Italia.* Firenza: La Nuova Italia, 1944, 51 pp.

Jensen, Jerry (ed.), *The Methodists and the Baptism of the Holy Spirit.* Los Angeles: FGBMFI, 1963, 32 pp.

— (ed.), *The Presbyterians and the Baptism of the Holy Spirit.* Los Angeles: FGBMFI, 1963, 32 pp.

— (ed.), *The Baptists and the Baptism of the Holy Spirit.* Los Angeles: FGBMFI, 1963, 32 pp.

— (ed.), *The Lutherans and the Baptism of the Holy Spirit.* Los Angeles: FGBMFI, 1963, 32 pp.

— (ed.), *The Episcopalians and the Baptism in the Holy Spirit.* Los Angeles: FGBMFI, 1964, 32 pp.

— (ed.), *Attorneys' Evidence on the Baptism of the Holy Spirit.* Los Angeles: FGBMFI, 1965, 32 pp.

— (ed.), *Physicians Examine the Baptism in the Spirit.* Los Angeles: FGBMFI, 1968, 32 pp.

— (ed.) *Charisma in the 20th Century Church.* Los Angeles: FGBMFI, 1968, 32 pp.

— (ed.) (?), *The Catholics and the Baptism in the Holy Spirit.* Los Angeles: FGBMFI, n.d., 32 pp. (contributions by Kevin Ranaghan, Bert Ghezzi, Tom Noe, Mary Pat Bradely, Donald E. Knoop, Francis Schulgen, Marc McCarty)

Jerusalem Bible. London: Darton, Longman and Todd, 1966

Jesus Church, *Assembly Report. General Views and Teachings of the Bible and Church.* Cleveland, Tenn.: The Jesus Church Publ. House, 1953, 49 pp.

Johnson, S. C., **Who Is This** *That Defies and Challenges the Whole Religious World On These Subjects?* Philadelphia, *1958

Juillerat, L. Howard, **Brief History** *of the Church of God.* Cleveland, Tenn.: ChoG Publ. House, *1922

Kalb, E., see Lotze, W.

Kalugin, Valerii Maksimovich, **Sovremennoe** *religioznoe sektantstvo, ego raznovidnosti i ideologiia.* Moscow: Gosudarstvennoe iz-vo, *1962

Kampf des Glaubens. Dokumente aus der Sowjetunion. Bern: Verlag des Schweizerischen Ost-Instituts, 1967, 142 pp.

Karrenberg F., and Klaus v. Bismarck (ed.), *Verlorener Sonntag?* (Kirche im Volk 22). Stuttgart: Kreuz-Verlag, 1959, 87 pp.

Käsemann, Ernst, **Exegetische Versuche** *und Besinnungen.* Göttingen: Vandenhoeck & Ruprecht, 2 vols., 1960/64; ET, **Essays** *on New Testament Themes* and *New Testament* **Questions** *of Today.* London: SCM Press, 1964/69

Keller, Samuel, *Am Lebensstrom.* Düsseldorf, *n.d.

Kelsey, Morton T., **Tongue Speaking.** *An experiment in spiritual experience.* New York: Doubleday, 1964, 253 pp.

Kendrick, Klaude, *The* **Promise** *Fulfilled. A History of the Modern Pentecostal Movement.* Springfield, Mo.: GPH, 1961, 237 pp.

Kessler, Jean Baptiste August Jr., *A Study of the Older Protestant Missions and Churches in Peru and Chile.* With special reference to the problems of division, nationalism and native ministry. Goes (Holland): Oosterbaan & Le Cointre N.V., 1967, 369 pp.

Klauser, Theodor, *Kleine abendländische Liturgiegeschichte. Bericht und Besinnung.* Mit zwei Anhängen: Richtlinien für die Gestaltung des Gotteshauses. Ausgewählte bibliographische Hinweise. Bonn: Peter Hanstein, 1965, 245 pp.; ET, *A Short History of the Western Liturgy.* London: Oxford UP, 1969

Klemm, Hermann, *Zur* **Theologie** *Elias Schrenks.* Schramberg (Black Forest): Gatzer & Hand, Graphische Werkstätten, 1934, 87 pp.

Klibanov, Aleksandr Il'ich, **Istoriya** *religioznogo sektantstva v Rossii*. Moscow: Izdatel'stvo 'Nauka', *1965, 345 pp.

Knierim, Rolf, *Bibelautorität und Bibelkritik*. Zürich and Frankfurt: Gotthelf-Verlag, 1962, 64 pp.

Koch, Klaus, *The Book of Books*, London: SCM Press, 1969, 192 pp.

Kolarz, Walter, **Religion** *in the Soviet Union*. London: Macmillan, 1961, 518 pp.

Köpf, Ernst, **Nicht Worte** ... *Kraft* (available from the author, Elsässerstr. 3, Leonberg, Württ.), 1950

— **Geistliches Leben,** *fleischlicher Tod*. Leonberg, Württ. (author), n.d., 34 pp.

Korff, M. M., *Am Zarenhof. Erinnerungen aus der geistlichen Erweckungsbewegung in Russland 1874–1884*, aus dem Russischen übertragen von M. Kroeker, *1927

Kovalev, S. I. (ed.), *Sputnik ateista*. Moscow: Gosudarstvennoe izdatel'stvo politicheskoi literatury, *1959

KPSS v Rezolyutsiakh i Resheniakh S'ezdov, Konferentsi i Plenumov ZK, 1898–1925, Vol. I, Moscow: Gosudarstvennoe izdatel'stvo politicheskoi literatury, 1953, 952 pp.

Krajewski, Ekkehard, 'Schwärmerei oder geistliches Leben', *Die Gemeinde*, *1961, nr. 44–48; reprinted under the title **Geistesgaben,** *eine Bibelarbeit über 1. Kor. 12–14*. Kassel: Oncken, 1963, 64 pp.

Krige, A. V., **'n Paar Grondwaarhede** in die volkaakte Verlossingsplan en 'n Getuienis', *Die Spade Reën Boodskapper* *3, 1930; off-print: Benoni, South Africa, P.O.B. 416, A. V. Krige, 1951, 50 pp.

Kristova Pentekostna Crkva u FNR Jugoslaviji, **Temeljne** *istine Svetog Pisma o vijeri i nauci Kristove Pentekostne Crkve u FNR Jugoslaviji*. Osijek, K[ristova] P[entekostna] C[rkva], 1959, 15 pp. (dupl.)

Kühn, Bernhard, 'Zur Unterscheidung der Geister', in: H. Dallmeyer (ed.), *Die sog. Pfingstbewegung*, 1922, pp. 23–40

— (ed.), *Die* **Pfingstbewegung** *im Lichte der Heiligen Schrift und ihrer eigenen Geschichte*, 2nd enlarged edition of *In kritischer Stunde* (essays by Joh. Seitz, B. Kühn and others). Gotha: Missionsbuchhandlung P. Ott, n.d., 105 pp.

Kulbeck, Gloria G., **What God Hath Wrought.** *A History of the Pentecostal Assemblies of Canada*, edited by Walter E. McAlister and George R. Upton. Toronto: Pent. Assemblies of Canada, 1958, 364 pp.

Kurantov, Aleksandr Pavlovich (ed.), *Znanie i vera v boga*. Moscow: Izdatel'stvo 'Znanie', *1960

Lachat, W. (ed.), *Le Baptême dans l'Eglise réformée*. Textes commentés par un groupe de pasteurs. Neuchâtel: W. Lachat, 1954, 100 pp.

Lake, John G., **Die sichere Grundlage** *für die Heilung der Kranken und Gebrechlichen*. Zürich: E. Weber, 1959, 3rd ed. 1963, 24 pp.

Lalive d'Epinay, Christian, *Le Pentecôtisme dans la société chilienne*. Essai d'approche sociologique, Geneva, 1967, 311 pp. (dupl. theological thesis); ET, *Haven of the Masses*. A Study of the Pentecostal Movement in Chile (World Studies in Mission). London: Lutterworth, 1969, 263 pp.

Lange, Ernst et al. (ed.), *Predigtstudien für das Kirchenjahr 1970/1971*. Perikopenreihe V/1, Stuttgart: Kreuz-Verlag, 1970

Latter Rain Assemblies, *The Blood of Jesus*. Benoni, South Africa: Latter Rain Assemblies, n.d., no pagination; Afrikaans: *Die Bloed van Jesus* (same publisher)

Lawrence, B. F., *The Apostolic Faith Restored*. St Louis: GPH, *1916, 119 pp.

Lechler, Alfred, *Die Pfingstbewegung in Deutschland in ärztlich-seelsorgerlicher Sicht* (ca. 1962, duplicated)

— **Zum Kampf** *gegen die Pfingstbewegung*. Witten (Ruhr): Bundes-Verlag, 2nd ed. n.d., 18 pp. (abridged version of the above)

Lehmann, Jürgen, *Die kleinen Religionsgemeinschaften des öffentlichen Rechtes im heutigen Staatskirchenrecht* (thesis in law, Frankfurt), 1959, 138 pp.

Léonard, Emile G., 'O Protestantismo Brasileiro. Estudo de eclesiologia e de história social.' *Revista de História* (Rio de Janeiro) 2, 1951, No. 5, pp. 105–157, No. 6, pp. 329–79; 3, 1951, No. 7, pp. 173–212, No. 8, pp. 411–32; 4, 1952, No. 9, pp. 165–77, No. 10, pp. 431–75; 5, 1952, No. 11, pp. 129–87, No. 12, pp. 403–43; reprinted: S. Paulo: ASTE, n.d., 354 pp.

— **l'illuminisme** *dans un protestantisme de constitution récente* (*Brésil*) Bibl. de l'Ecole des Hautes Etudes, Section des Sciences Religieuses Vol. LXV, Paris: Presses Universitaires, 1953, 114 pp.

Lepargneur, Francisco, 'Reflexões católicas em face do Movimento Pentecostal no Brasil', in: ASTE, *O Espírito Santo*, 1966, pp. 47–67

Leskov, N. S., *Velikosvetskiy raskol'*. Moscow, *1877

Lewis, William Henry, *And He Gave Some Apostles. A Bible Reading on this Important Subject*. Bradford: Puritan Press, 1954, 25 pp.

Lillie, D. G., *Tongues Under Fire*. Plainfield, N.J.: Logos Books, 1966, 60 pp.

Linderholm, Emanuel, *Pingströrelsen*. I: Dess forutsättningar och uppkomst Ekstas, under och apokalyptik i bibel och nutida folkreligiositet. Stockholm: Bonniers Förlag AB, *1924, 2nd ed. 1929; II: Pingströrelsen i Sverige. Ekstas, under och apokalyptik i nutida svensk folkreligiositet. Stockholm: Bonniers Förlag AB, *1925, 2nd ed. *1933; Suppl. Vol.: Den svenska pingstväckelsens spridning. Stockholm: Bonniers Förlag AB, *1925, 2nd ed. *1933

Lindsay, Gordon (in collaboration with William Branham), *William Branham, a Man Sent from God*. Jeffersonville, Ind.: Branham; Dallas, Texas: Voice of Healing, 1950, 216 pp.

— *The* **Life of** *John Alexander* **Dowie,** whose trials, tragedies and triumphs are the most fascinating object lesson of Christian history. Dallas, Texas: Voice of Healing, 1951, 275 pp.

— *Why do the Righteous Suffer?* Gives twelve reasons why the righteous suffer. Proves that Paul's thorn in the flesh was not sickness. Shows how Job suffered and how he got healed. Dallas, Texas: Voice of Healing, 1956, 52 pp.

— **God's Master Key** *to Success and Prosperity*. Dallas, Texas: Voice of Healing, 1959, 61 pp.

— **Evolution** *the Incredible Hoax. Christ or Gorilla, Which?* Dallas, Texas: Voice of Healing, 1960, 23 pp.

— *All about the Gifts of the Spirit*. Are the gifts of the Spirit for the Church today? The purpose of the gifts. How are the gifts received? Can the gifts

be counterfeited? Their relation to the fruits of the Spirit. Dallas, Texas: Voice of Healing, 1962, 62 pp.
Lindsay, Gordon, *The Gordon Lindsay* Story. Dallas, Texas: Voice of Healing, n.d., 283 pp.
— Forty Signs *of the Soon Coming of Christ*. Dallas, Texas: Voice of Healing, n.d., 63 pp.
Lindsell, H., *Park Street Prophet*. Wheaton, Ill.: Van Kampen Press, *1951
Livshits, G. M., Religia i tserkov' *v proshlom i nastoiashchem*. Minsk, Izdatel-'stvo ministerstva vysshego srednogo spetsial'nogo i professional'nogo obarzovania BSSR, *1961
Lohmann, E., *Pfingstbewegung und Spiritismus*. Frankfurt a.M.: Verlag Orient-Buchhandlung des Deutschen Hülfsbundes für christliches Liebeswerk im Orient e.V., 1910, 81 pp.
Lotze, Wilhelm, 'Dowie und die christlich-katholische Kirche in Zion', in: Ernst Kalb (ed.), *Kirchen und Sekten der Gegenwart*. Unter Mitarbeit verschiedener evangelischer Theologen herausgegeben. Stuttgart: Evang. Gesellschaft, 1905, pp. 485–92
— *Elias III. Ein Wort zur Aufklärung über John Alexander Dowie* (enlarged from Kalb, *Kirchen und Sekten der Gegenwart*). Stuttgart: Verlag der Buchhandlung der Ev. Gesellschaft, 1905, 18 pp.
Lyra, Jorge Buarque, Orientaçâo *Evangélica* (*Interdenominacional*) *para salvar o Brasil*. Niterói: J. B. Lyra, *1960, 2nd ed. n.d., 233 pp.
— *O movimento pentecostal no Brasil. Profilaxia cristã dêsse movimento em defesa de* '*O Brasil Para Cristo*'. Niterói: J. B. Lyra, 1964, 131 pp.

Macleod, George F., *The* Place of Healing *in the Ministry of the Church*. Glasgow: Iona Community Publ. Department, n.d., 13 pp.
Marcondes, J. V. Freitas, and Osmar Pimentel, S. Paulo, *Espírito*, *Povo*, *Instituições*. S. Paulo: Livraria Pioneira Editôra, 1968
Martin, Marie-Louise, Critical Notes on W. J. Hollenweger's Dissertation. Roma, Lesotho, 1964, 4 pp. (manuscript in German)
— 'Afrikanischer Messianismus und der Messias der biblischen Offenbarung', in: Peter Beyerhaus (ed.), *Weltmission heute* 33/34, 1967, pp. 40–56
— *Kirche ohne Weisse*. Basel: Reinhardt-Verlag, 1971
— *The* Biblical Concept *of Messianism and Messianism in Southern Africa*. Doctoral thesis presented to the Department of Theology of the University of South Africa, Morija, Lesotho, 1964, 211 pp.
Marx, Karl, *Die Frühschriften*, ed. Siegfried Landshut. Stuttgart: Kroner Taschenbuch 209, 1953, 588 pp.; ET, *A Contribution to the Critique of Hegel's* '*Philosophy of Right*', ed. J. O'Malley. London: Cambridge UP, 1970.
Mavity, Nancy Barr, *Sister Aimee*. New York: Doubleday, 1931, 360 pp.
Mayat, E. V., and N. N. Uzkov, '*Brat'ya*' *i* '*sestry*' *vo Khriste*. Moscow: Izd. 'Sovetskaia Rossiia', *1960.
Mayer, Philip. Townsmen *or Tribesmen. Conservatism and the Process of Urbanization in a South African City*. Cape Town: Oxford UP, 1963, 306 pp.
McPherson, Aimee Semple, *This is That. Personal experiences, sermons and writings*. Los Angeles, Calif.: Echo Park Evangelistic Assoc., 3rd ed. 1923, 791 pp.

— *Declaration of Faith*, compiled by A. S. McPherson for the Int. Church of the Foursquare Gospel, Los Angeles, n.d.

McWhirter J., *The Bible and War*, *1940

Mead, Frank S., **Handbook** *of Denominations in the United States*. New York: Abingdon Press, *1951, 3rd ed., 1961, 272 pp.

Meister, J. (ed.), **Bericht** *über den Kongress der Europäischen Baptisten*, 26. bis 31. Juli 1958 in Berlin. Kassel: Oncken-Verlag, 1959

Mendelsohn, Jack, *The Forest Calls Back*. Boston: Little, Brown & Co., *1965

Menzies, William W., *Anointed to Serve. The Story of the Assemblies of God*. Springfield, Mo.: GPH, 1971, 436 pp.

Mesquita, A. N. de, **Istória** *dos Batistas no Brasil*. S. Paulo, *1940

Metsentsev, V. A. (ed.), *Mporvali s religiei*. Moscow: Voennoe izdats'stvo ministerstva oborony SSSR, 1963

Meyer, Harding. 'Die **Pfingstbewegung** in Brasilien', *Die evangelische Diaspora. Jahrbuch des Gustav-Adolf-Vereins* 39, 1968, pp. 9–50

Meyriat, Jean (ed.), *La Calabria*. Milan: Lerici, 1960, 463 pp.

Mikkonen, Pekka, **He huusivat** *suurella äänellä*. Porvoo, *1919

Mink, Paul, *Wird die* **Einheitskirche** *kommen?* Hirzenhain, Oberhessen: Maranatha-Mission, n.d. 8 pp.

— **Ich bin der Herr,** *dein Arzt! Betrachtungen über die Heilung durch den Glauben nach dem Wort Gottes*. Hirzenhain, Oberhessen: Maranatha-Mission, n.d., 48 pp.

Molenaar, D. G., **De doop** *met de Heilige Geest*. Kampen: J. H. Kok, 1963, 272 pp.

Möller, F. P., *Die apostoliese leer*. Johannesburg: Evangelie Uitgewers, 1961, 73 pp.

Moltmann, Jürgen, *Theologie der Hoffnung*. Untersuchungen zur Begründung und zu den Konsequenzen einer christlichen Eschatologie. München: Kaiser-Verlag, *1964, 6th ed. 1966, 340 pp; ET, *Theology of Hope*. On the Ground and the Implications of a Christian Eschatology. London: SCM Press, 1967, 342 pp.

Moody, William R., *The Life of Dwight L. Moody*. New York: Revell, *1900

Mosimann, Eddison, *Das* **Zungenreden** *geschichtlich und psychologisch untersucht*. Tübingen: J. C. B. Mohr, 1911, 137 pp.

Moura, Abdalazis de, **Importância** *das Igrejas Pentecostais para a Igreja Católica*. Recife (duplicated typescript, de Moura, Rua Jirquiti 48, Boa Vista), 1969, 44 pp.

Mrózek Jósef jun., Edward Czajko, Mieczysław Kwiecien, Bolesław Winnik (edd.), *Kalendarz jubileuszowi 1963*. Warsaw: Zjednoczony Kościół Ewangeliczny, 1963, 334 pp.

Mummsen, R., *Wittenberg und Wales! Erwiderung auf P. Glages Schrift: Wittenberg oder Wales?* Neumünster: Ihloff & Co., n.d. (ca. 1906), 64 pp.

Murray, Andrew, *With Christ in the* **School of Prayer** (1886). London: Pickering and Inglis, 1957

— *The* **Spirit of Christ.** *Thoughts on the Indwelling of the Holy Spirit in the Believer and the Church* (1888). London and Edinburgh: Oliphants, 1963

— *The* **Ministry of Intercession**: *A Plea for More Prayer* (1898). London and Edinburgh: Oliphants, 1964

Murray, Andrew, *The* Key *to the Missionary Problem.* London: Nisbet, 1901
— *Divine Healing.* London: Victory Press, 1934
— *The* Full Blessing *of Pentecost. The One Thing Needful* (1895). London: Revell, 1908; London: Elim Publ. Co., *n.d. (several reprints until 1970)

Nadel, S. F., 'A Study of Shamanism in the Nuba Mountains', in: William A. Lessa and Evon Z. Vogt (edd.), *Reader in Comparative Religion: An Anthropological Approach.* New York: Harper & Row, 1965, pp. 464–79
Das Neue Testament in der Sprache der Gegenwart. Neue Mülheimer Ausgabe mit Anmerkungen und Wörterverzeichnis, Mülheim/Ruhr, *1914; Altdorf bei Nürnberg, 7th ed. 1967
Neve, J. L., Churches *and Sects of Christendom.* Blais, Nebraska: Luth. Publ. House, 1952, 509 pp.
New English Bible. London: Oxford and Cambridge University Presses, New Testament, 1961, 2nd ed., 1970; Old Testament and Apocrypha, 1970
Newbigin, Lesslie. *The Household of God. Lectures on the Nature of the Church.* London: SCM Press, 1953, 155 pp.
Nichol, John Thomas. *Pentecostalism.* New York: Harper & Row, 1966, 264 pp.
Niebuhr, H. Richard, *The Social Sources of Denominationalism.* New York: Holt, 1929, 304 pp.

O'Connor, Edward D., *The Pentecostal Movement in the Catholic Church.* Notre Dame, Ind.: Ave Maria Press, 1971, 301 pp.
— *Pentecost in the Catholic Church.* Pecos, New Mexico: Dove Publications, 1970, 38 pp. (a revised reprint of articles which originally appeared in 1967 and 1968 in *Ave Maria* and *Ecumenist*)
Ohrn, Arnold T. (ed.), *Eighth Baptist World Congress.* Philadelphia: Judson Press, *1950
Osborn, T. L., *Healing From Christ.* Seven steps to receive healing from Christ. The cream of T. L. Osborn's sermons on faith which have brought healing and deliverance to multitudes around the world. Discloses in seven simple steps your Bible rights to freedom from sickness and sin, *1955, 3rd ed *1956, 4th ed 1961. Tulsa 2, Okla.: T. L. Osborn Ev. Ass., 70 pp.
— *Healing the Sick.* How you can be healed through faith in God. The divine antidote for doubt, fear and defeat. The master-key to world-evangelism. The secrets of Bible ministry today. Tulsa, Okla.: T. L. Osborn, 12th ed. 1959, 239 pp.
— *Impact.* Tulsa, Okla.: T. L. Osborn Ev. Ass., 1961, 104 pp.

PAoW, *Minute Book*, n.p., 1963, 126 pp.
— *Ministerial Records, Codified Rules and Minutes*, n.p., 1952, 82 pp.
Parham, Charles Fox, Kol kare bomidbar. *A Voice Crying in the Wilderness* *1902, 2nd ed *1910, 4th ed. 1944 (Robert L. Parham, Baxter Springs, Kansas, 138 pp.)
— (Mrs), *The Life of Charles F. Parham. Founder of the Apostolic Faith Movement.* Joplin, Miss.: Tri-State Printing Co., 1930, 452 pp.

Pascal, Blaise, *Pensées*. Texte de l'édition Brunschvicg. Introduction par Ch-. Marc Granges. Paris: Garnier Freres, n.d., 342 pp.

Patterson, J. (ed.), *Holy Convocation Church of God in Christ*. Memphis. Tenn.: 1969

Paul, George Harold. *The Religious Frontier in Oklahoma: Dan T. Muse and the PHCh*. Ph.D. thesis, University of Oklahoma, 302 pp. (manuscript)

Paul, Jonathan (ed). *Verhandlungen der Gnadauer Pfingstkonfernz über das Einwohnen des Heiligen Geistes, den Gehorsam des Glaubens und Gemeinschaftspflege in Deutschland*, hgg. im Auftrag des Konferenz-Komittees. Berlin: Deutsche Ev. Buch- und Tractat-Gesellschaft, 1894, 1896, 1898

— **Taufe** *und Geistestaufe. Ein Beitrag zur Lösung einer ungemein wichtigen Frage, besonders auch für solche, welche in Gewissensbedenken sich befinden*. Berlin: Deutsche Ev. Buch- und Tractat-Gesellschaft, 1895, 87 pp.

— *Ihr werdet die* **Kraft des** *Heiligen* **Geistes** *empfangen*. Berlin: Ev. Traktat-Gesellschaft; Elmshorn (Holstein): Bramsted, *1896, 540 pp.; Altdorf bei Nürnberg: Pranz, 3rd ed. 1956, 224 pp. (abridged)

— 'Das reine Herz', *Die Heiligung* 139, April 1910, pp. 1–20

— **Zur Dämonenfrage.** *Ein Wort zur Verständigung*. *1912

— *Die Taufe in ihrem Vollsinn*. Mülheim, 1930

—*Das* **Geheimnis** *der fünf Bücher Mosis durch neueste Forschungen enthüllt. Ein Zeugnis eines von der Tagesmeinung unabhängigen Theologen*. Elmshorn bei Hamburg: Bramsted, n.d., 96 pp.

Paulk, Earl P. (ed.), *Your Pentecostal* **Neighbour.** Cleveland, Tenn., 1958, 237 pp.

Pauw, B. A., **Religion** *in a Tswana Chiefdom*. London: Oxford UP, 1960, 258 pp.

Pearlman, Myer. *Seeing the Story of the Bible*. Springfield, Mo.: GPH, 1930, 123 pp.

— *Successful Sunday School Teaching*. Springfield, Mo.: GPH, 1934, 2nd ed. 1935, 109 pp.

— *Through the Bible Book by Book* (4 vols). Springfield: GPH, 1935, 98, 112, 92, 116 pp.

— *The* **Heavenly Gift.** *Studies in the Work of the Holy Spirit*. Springfield, Mo.: GPH, 1935, 57 pp.

— **Knowing** *the Doctrines of* **the Bible.** Springfield, Mo.: GPH, 1937, 399 pp.

— **Studying the Pupil.** Springfield, Mo.: GPH, 1940, 112 pp.

— *The Life and Teachings of Christ*. Springfield, Mo.: GPH, n.d., 118 pp.

Pejsti, N. I. (ed.), **Zasady** *wiary Kościola Chrześcijan Wiary*. Ewangelicznej w Polsce. Kętrzyn, woj. Olsztyńskie, skrz. poczt. N-4, 1948, 24 pp.

Pentecostal Church of Christ, *By-Laws*. Bell, Calif., 1942, 35 pp.

Pentecostal Church of God of America, *This We Believe* . . . Joplin, Mo.: PChoG of America, n.d.

Pentecostal Free Will Baptist Church, **Faith** *and Government of the Free Will Baptist Church of the Pentecostal Faith*, n.p., 1961, 48 pp.

Pestalozza, Luigi. **Il diritto** *di non tremolare. La condizione delle minoranze religiose in Italia* (L'Attualità 14). Milan-Rome: Edizioni Avanti, 1956, 64 pp.

Peyrot, Giorgio, Commissione per gli Affari Internazionali del Consiglio Federale delle Chiese Evangeliche d'Italia. 'L'Intolleranza religiosa in Italia nell'ultimo quinquennio', *Protestantesimo* 8/1, Jan.–March 1953, pp. 1–39; ET, *Religious* **Intolerance** *in Italy 1947/52*. Geneva: WCC, 1953

Peyrot, **La circolare** *Buffarini-Guidi e i Pentecostali* (Attuare la costituzione 26). Rome: Associazione Italiana per la Libertà della Cultura, 1955, 62 pp.

PHCh, *Discipline*. Frank Springs, Ga., PHCh, *1901 (ed. A. B. Crumpler, Holiness Church); 1925, 106 pp.; 1929, 88 pp.; 1933, 73 pp.; 1937, 100 pp.; 1945, 106 pp. (including King, 'Doctrinal Exegesis'); 1949, 125 pp.; 1957, 125 pp.; 1961, 110 pp. (including Synan, 'Doctrinal Amplifications')

Pieper, Josef, *Bestimmung zur Welt. Eine Theorie des Festes*. München, 1963; ET, *In Tune With the World: A Theory of Festivity*. New York: Harcourt, Brace, *1965

Pfingstjubel. Altdorf bei Nürnberg: Missionsbuchhandlung und Verlag, 1956, 689 pp.

Pike, James A., *Pastoral Letter*. San Francisco. Calif., 1963, 6 pp. (dupl.)

Pilgrim Holiness Church. *Manual*. Indianapolis, Ind.: Pilgrim Publ. House, 1962

Pimentel, Osmar, see J. V. Freitas Marcondes

Plessis, David J. Du, *A Brief History of American Pentecostal Movements* (manuscript, unpublished, not paginated)

— *A Brief* **History** *of Pentecostal Movements* (manuscript, unpublished, not paginated)

— **Pentecost Outside 'Pentecost'**. *The Astounding Move of God in the Denominational Churches*, n.p. (Dallas, Texas?), n.d. (ca. 1961), 30 pp.

— *The Spirit Bade Me Go*. Oakland, Calif.: Du Plessis, 1963, 122 pp.

Plessis, J. Du, *The Life of* **Andrew Murray** *of South Africa*. London: Marshall Bros., 1920

Pollock, A. J., **Modern Pentecostalism**, *Foursquare Gospel*, '*Healing*' *and* '*Tongue*'. London: Central Bible Truth Depot, 1929, 84 pp.

Pollock, J. C., *The Faith of the Russian Evangelicals*. New York: McGraw-Hill Book Co., *1964

Pope, Liston, **Millhands** *and Preachers. A Study of Gastonia*. New Haven: Yale University Press, *1942, 4th ed. 1958, 369 pp. (Yale Studies in Religious Education XV)

Popoff, Haralan, **T'lkyvanie na knigata Otkrovenie**, n.d., 43 pp. (manuscript, Bulgarian, Interpretation of the book of Revelation)

Prokhanoff, I. S., *In the Cauldron of Russia*. New York: John Felsberg, *1933; German: *Erfolge des Evangeliums in Russland*, *1939

Price, Charles S., *The* **Story** *of My Life*. Pasadena: Charles S. Price Publ. Co., 1935, 3rd ed. 1944, 79 pp.

Pryor, Adel, *Tangled Paths*. Springfield, Mo.: GPH, n.d., 192 pp. ('The love story of Dawn Ashley, an exquisite model, and Martin Shann, the young pastor who falls in love with her. A few days after her conversion Dawn marries the suave, debonair London sophisticate, Neil Fairfield. Unhappiness, disillusion and tragedy follow, ending with her husband's death, before she ultimately finds true happiness with the devoted young man who had been the means of her conversion.' (From an advertisement for the book.)

Putintsev, F. M., *Politicheskaia rol' sektantstva*. Moscow: Bezhbozhnik, *1928
— Kabalnoe *bratstvo sektantov*. Moscow, *1931

Rad, Gerhard von, *Theologie des Alten Testaments*, 2 vols. München: Kaiser, 1958/60; ET, *Old Testament Theology*. Edinburgh: Oliver and Boyd, 1962/65
— *Das erste Buch Mose* (Das Alte Testament Deutsch). Göttingen: Vandenhoeck & Ruprecht, 1961; ET, *Genesis*. London: SCM Press, 2nd ed. 1963
Rahner, Hugo, *Der spielende Mensch*. Einsiedeln: Johannes Verlag, 3rd ed., 1954; ET, *Man at Play*. London: Burns and Oates, 1965; New York: Herder, 1967, 105 pp.
Ranaghan, Kevin & Dorothy, *Catholic Pentecostals*. New York: Paulist Press, 1969, 266 pp.
— (edd.), *As the* Spirit *Leads Us*. New York: Paulist Press, 1971, 250 pp.
Raum, O. F., 'Von Stammespropheten zu Sektenführern', in Ernst Benz (ed.), *Messianische Kirchen*, 1965, pp. 49–70
Read, William R., New Patterns *of Church Growth in Brazil*. Grand Rapids, Mich.: W. B. Eerdmans Publ. Co., 1965, 250 pp.
— and Victor M. Monterroso and Harmon A. Johnson, *Latin American Church Growth*. Grand Rapids, Mich.: W. B. Eerdmans Publ. Co., 1969, 421 pp.
Redemption Hymnal With Tunes. London: AoG Publ. House, 1958
Rees, Thomas, *The* Unity *of the Godhead and the Trinity of the Persons therein* (Tenets of the Apostolic Church 1). Bradford: Puritan Press, 1954, 20 pp.
Reiser, Werner, Dieter Hanhart, Christian Gasser, Hans Wenger, *Industrielle Sonntagsarbeit*. Zürich: Flamberg-Verlag, 1960, 96 pp.
Reuber, Kurt, Mystik *in der Gemeinschaftsfrömmigkeit der Heiligungsbewegung*. Gütersloh, 1938
Ribeiro, Boanerges, *O padre protestante*. São Paulo: Casa Editora Presbiteriana, 1950, 215 pp.
Rich, Arthur, *Die Anfänge der Theologie Huldrych Zwinglis*. Zürich: Zwingli-Verlag, 1949, 180 pp.
— *Pascals Bild vom Menschen*. Zürich: Zwingli-Verlag, 1953, 214 pp.
— *Christliche Existenz in der industriellen Welt*. Zürich: Zwingli-Verlag, 1957, enlarged 2nd ed 1964, 284 pp.
— *Glaube in politischer Entscheidung. Beiträge zur Ethik des Politischen*. Zürich: Zwingli-Verlag, 1962, 208 pp.
— *Die Weltlichkeit des Glaubens. Diakonie im Horizont der Säkularisierung*. Zürich: Zwingli-Verlag, 1966, 115 pp.
Riggs, Ralph Meredith, *A Successful Sunday-School*. Springfield, Mo.: GPH, 1934, 128 pp.
Ritter, Adolf Martin, and Gottfried Leich, *Wer ist die Kirche? Amt und Gemeinde im Neuen Testament, in der Kirchengeschichte und heute*. Göttingen: Vandenhoeck & Ruprecht, 1968, 303 pp.
Roberts, Evan, and Mrs Penn-Lewis, *War on the Saints*, *1912
Roberts, Oral, *If You Need Healing, Do These Things*. Tulsa, Okla.: Abundant Life Publ., 1947, 2nd ed. 1948, 3rd ed. 1957, 124 pp.
— God is a Good God. *Believe It and Come Alive*. New York: Bobbs-Merrill Co., 1966, 188 pp.

Robertson, Archie, *That Old-time Religion*. Boston: Houghton Miffling, 1950

Robinson, Ch.E., *The Adventures of Blacky the Wasp*. Springfield: GPH, 1936

Rogers, Esther, *Memoirs*. Cincinnati, *1848

Rossel, Jacques, *Mission dans une société dynamique*. Geneva: Labor et Fides, 1967; ET, *Mission in a Dynamic Society*. London: SCM Press, 1968, 152 pp.

Rubanowitsch, Johannes. *Das heutige Zungenreden*. Neumünster: Vereinsbuchhandlung G. Ihloff, n.d., 120 pp.

Rüppel, E. G., *Die* Gemeinschaftsbewegung *im Dritten Reich. Ein Beitrag zur Geschichte des Kirchenkampfes*. Göttingen: Vandenhoeck und Ruprecht, 1969, 258 pp.

Rushbrook, J. H., *The* Baptist Movement *In the Continent of Europe*. London: Carey Press, Kingsgate Press, 1915, 150 pp.

Santos, Geraldino dos, 'Diversidade e integração dos grupos pentecostais', in: ASTE, *O Espírito Santo*, 1966, pp. 30–2

Sapsezian, Aharon, 'Introducão', in: ASTE, *O Espírito Santo*, 1966, pp. 3–7

Sardaczuk, Waldemar, *Ich hatt' einen Kameraden*. Erzhausen: Leuchter-Verlag, 1968, 55 pp. (clear decision for refusing military service)

Schäfer, Hans, *Die Medizin in unserer Zeit. Theorie, Forschung, Lehre*. München: Piper, 2nd ed. 1963, 415 pp.

Schat, J. H., Spreken *met andere tongen*. Haarlem: Pinkster-Kerkgenootschap, 1963, 6 pp.

Schlosser, Katesa, Eingeborenenkirchen *in Süd- und Südwestafrika, ihre Geschichte und Sozialstruktur. Erlebnisse einer völkerkundlichen Studienreise*. Mühlau: Walter, 1953, 355 pp.

— 'Profane Ursachen des Anschlusses an Separatistenkirchen in Süd- und Südwestafrika', in: E. Benz (ed.), *Messianische Kirchen*, 1967, pp. 25–45

Schmidt, Martin, *John Wesley*, 2 vols. Zürich: Gotthelf-Verlag, 1953/1966, 334 pp., 575 pp.; ET, *John Wesley: a theological biography*, vol. 1, London: Epworth Press, 1962

— art. 'Wales', *RGG* VI (1962), cols. 1535–37

Schmidt, Wolfgang, *Die* Pfingstbewegung *in Finnland*. Helsinki: Kirchengeschichtliche Gesellschaft Finnlands, 1935, 256 pp.

Schmitz, D. O., *Die* Bedeutung *der urchristlichen Geistesgaben für unsere Zeit*. Offprint of the Nachrichtendienst der Pressestelle der Evangelischen Kirche der Rheinprovinz, No. 3/4. Düsseldorf: A. Bagel, 1949, 8 pp.

Schöpwinkel, Hermann. Enthusiastisches Christentum *oder Flugfeuer fremden Geistes?* Bad Liebenzell: Verlag der Liebenzeller Mission, n.d. (1970), 10 pp. (dupl.)

Schrenk, Elias. Wir sahen *Seine Herrlichkeit. Betrachtungen über das hohepriesterliche Gebet*. Kassel: Ernst Röttger, *1888, *1896

— Suchet *in der Schrift*, *n.d.

Schulz, Siegfried. *Die* Stunde *der Botschaft. Einführung in die Theologie der vier Evangelisten*. Hamburg: Furche-Verlag, 1967, 392 pp.

Schütter, Günter. *Die letzten tibetischen Orakelpriester*. Wiesbaden: Franz Steiner, 1971, 162 pp.

Schweizer, Eduard, art. '*pneuma*', *TWNT* VI (1959), pp. 394ff.; ET, art. '*pneuma*', in: *TDNT* VI (1968), pp. 396–451; see also E. Schweizer, *Spirit of God* (Bible Key Words). London: A. & C. Black, vol. 9, 1960; New York: Harper & Row, III/1, 1961

— *Neotestamentica. German and English Essays 1951–1963*. Zürich: Zwingli Verlag, 1963, 447 pp.

— *Gemeinde und Gemeindeordnung im Neuen Testament*. Zürich: Zwingli-Verlag, *1959, 2nd ed. 1962, 220 pp.; ET, *Church Order in the New Testament*. London, SCM Press, 1961, 239 pp.

Scopes, Wilfred (ed.), *The Christian Ministry in Latin America and the Caribbean. Report of a Survey Commission authorized by the International Missionary Council*, issued by the Commission on World Mission and Evangelism of the WCC. Geneva: WCC, 1962, 264 pp.

Secrétan, Louis, *Baptême des croyants ou baptême des enfants?* La Chaux-de-Fonds: Editions du Grenier 20, 1946, 78 pp.

Seitz, Johann and Ernst F. Ströter, *Die* Selbstentlarvung *von 'Pfingst'-Geistern*. Barmen: Montanus u. Ehrenstein, 1911, 29 pp. Reprint: *1962 by Pred. Richard Ising

Sentzke, Gert, *Die Kirche Finnlands*. Göttingen: Vandenhoeck & Ruprecht, 1935, 150 pp.

Sherrill, John L., They Speak *With Other Tongues*. An age-old miracle on the march in a scientific age – and what happened to the reporter in search of its story. McGraw-Hill edition 1964; 1965; Pyramid edition 1965, Spire edition 1965, Westwood, N.J.: Spire Books, 1965, 143 pp.

Shuler, Robert P., *McPhersonism, a Study of Healing Cults and Modern Day Tongues Movements. Containing Summary of Facts as to Disappearance and Re-appearance of Aimee Semple McPherson*. Los Angeles: R. P. Shuler, *n.d.

Sicard, H.v., art. 'Die afrikanischen Religionen und die christliche Botschaft', *RGG* I (1957), cols. 150–2

Simon, Gerhard, *Die Kirchen in Russland. Berichte und Dokumente*. München: Manz-Verlag, 1970, 228 pp.

Simpfendörfer, Werner, *Offene Kirche, kritische Kirche. Kirchenreform am Scheideweg*. Stuttgart: Kreuz-Verlag, 1969, 190 pp.

Simpson, A. B., *The Fourfold Gospel*. New York: Christian and Missionary Alliance, n.d., 8 pp.

Sixth Pentecostal World Conference, published by the Conference Advisory Committee. Toronto: Testimony Press, 1961

Smith, F. L., *What Every Saint Should Know*. East Orange, N.J.: Lutho Press, P.O. Box 31, n.d., 12 pp.

Smith, Timothy L., Called *Unto Holiness. The Story of the Nazarenes. The Formative Years*. Kansas City, Miss.: Nazarene Publ. House, 1962, 413 pp.

Smith, Wilbur M., *An Annotated Bibliography of Dwight L. Moody*. Chicago: Moody Press, *1948

Söderholm, G. E., *Den svenska pingstväckelsens historia 1907–33*, 2 vols. Stockholm: Filadelfia, *1929/33

Souček, J. B., 'O Svrchovanost viry', in volume in honour of J. L. Hromádka,

Prague: Kalich, 1959, 24–35; French translation by D. Urban: 'La prophétie dans le Nouveau Testament', *Communio Viatorum* 4, 1961, pp. 221–31
Souza, Beatriz Müniz de, *A experiência da Salvação. Pentecostais em São Paulo.* S. Paulo: Duas Cidades, 1969, 181 pp.
Spence, Hubert T., *Pentecost Is Not a Tangent.* Franklin Springs, Ga.: PHCh, 3rd ed. n.d., 11 pp.
Spörri, Th. (ed.), *Beiträge zur* Ekstase (Bibliotheca Psychiatrica et Neurologica 135). Basel and New York: S. Karger, 1968, 207 pp.
Stagg, Frank, E. Glenn Hinson, Wayne E. Oates, Glossolalia. *Tongue Speaking in Biblical, Historical and Psychological Perspective.* New York: Abingdon Press, 110 pp.
Stead, W. T., The Revival in the West. *A Narrative of Facts.* London: The Review of Reviews Publ. Office, 4th ed. n.d., 64 pp.; German: *Die Erweckung in Wales. Ein Bericht über Tatsachen* (translated by G. Holtey-Weber), Mülheim-Ruhr: Ev. Vereinshaus, 1905, 75 pp.; French: *Au pays de Galles, le réveil religieux*, Geneva, n.d., 44 pp.
Steiner, Leonhard, Introduction to question no. 1 at the European Pentecostal Conference at Stockholm 1939: 'Ist es richtig, unsere Auffassung von der Geistestaufe auf die Apostelgeschichte und die Erfahrung der zwölf Jünger aufzubauen? Kann dieselbe auch aus den apostolischen Briefen hergeleitet werden?' *VdV* 33/2, Febr. 1940, pp. 15–19; Swedish: Förlaget Filadelfia, *Europeiska Pingstkonferensen i Stockholm*, pp. 50–7
—Mit folgenden Zeichen. *Eine Darstellung der Pfingstbewegung.* Basel: Mission für das volle Evangelium, 1954 (reviewed by A. J. Appasamy, *IRM* 46, 1957, pp. 325f.)
—'Glaube und Heilung', *VdV* 50/4, April 1957, pp. 7f., 10f.; 50/5, May 1957, pp. 2–7; *Der Leuchter* 8/8, Aug. 1957, pp. 5–7; 8/9, Sept. 1957, pp. 5–8; 8/10, Oct. 1957, pp. 7, 9 reprinted, Basel: Mission für das volle Evangelium, n.d.; ET, 'Divine Healing in God's Plan of Redemption', in D. Gee (ed.), *Fifth Conference 1958*, pp. 137–48
—*Sind wir nun keine Pfingstler mehr?* Duplicated memorandum 1960 for all important Pentecostal leaders in the world
—*Le* baptême *de l'Esprit et l'appartenance au Corps de Christ, d'après 1 Cor. 12/13* (une explication de la doctrine du baptême de l'Esprit). Basel, n.d., 7 pp. (dupl.)
Stiles, J. E., *The* Gift *of the Holy Spirit.* Burbank, Calif.: Stiles, n.d. (1963), 156 pp.
Stockmayer, Otto. *La maladie et l'Evangile.* Neuchâtel (Switzerland), 1878, 2nd ed. 1880; German: *Krankheit und Evangelium. Ein Wort an Kinder Gottes.* Basel: C. F. Spittler, 2nd ed. 1880, 3rd ed. 1898, 4th ed. 1924, 5th ed. 1929
Strand, Egil, Erling Strøm, Martin Ski (edd.), *Fram til urkristendommen.* Pinsevekkelsen, gjennom 50 år. Oslo: Filadelfiaforlaget, 1956–59, 3 vols.
Stucki, Alfred, Andrew Murray. *Ein Zeuge Christi in Südafrika.* St Gallen, 1953; Basel: H. Majer, 2nd ed. 1959, 91 pp.
Sumrall, Lester, Worshippers *of the Silver Screen*, with foreword by Edith Mae Pennington, national beauty queen and converted movie actress. Grand Rapids, Mich.: Zondervan Publ. House, 1940, 64 pp.

—*The True Story of Clarita Villanueva.* How a seventeen-year-old girl was bitten by devils, Bilibid Prison, Manila, Philippines. In collaboration with Dr Mariano B. Lara, Chief Medical Examiner, Manila Police Department, Professor and Department Head of Pathology and Legal Medicine, Manila, Central University, and by Rev. Ruben Candelaria, former Superintendent of the Manila District of the Methodist Conference and now pastor in Bethel Temple. South Bend, Ind.: Sumrall, n.d., 177 pp.

Sundkler, Bengt G. M. art. 'Sektenwesen in den jungen Kirchen', *RGG* V (1961), cols. 1664–6

Sundstedt, Arthur. *Pingstväckelsen – dess uppkomst och första utvecklingsskede.* Stockholm: Normans Förlag, 1969, 304 pp. (first volume of a history of Pentecostalism, planned to amount to 5 vols.)

Sweet, William Warren. *The* Story *of Religion in America.* New York: Harper, 1939

Synan, J. A., 'Doctrinal Amplifications', PHCh, *Discipline*, 1961, pp. 27–36

Synan, Harold Vinson. *The* Pentecostal **Movement** *in the United States.* Ph.D. University of Georgia, 1967 (Ann Arbor, Mich., University Microfilms, Inc., 1968), 296 pp.

— *The Holiness-Pentecostal Movement in the United States.* Grand Rapids, Mich.: Wm. B. Eerdmans Publ. Co., 1971 (revised version of the above thesis)

Tavares, Levy. *Minha pátria para Cristo. Discursos e comentários.* S. Paulo: L. Tavares, 1965, 74 pp.

— 'A mensagem pentecostista e a realidade brasileira', in ASTE, *O Espírito Santo*, 1966, pp. 33–6

Temple, William, *Christianity and Social Order.* Harmondsworth: Penguin Books, 1942

Thomas, M. M. and P. Abrecht (edd.), **Christians** *in the technical and social revolution. Report of the World Conference on Church and Society.* Geneva: WCC, 1967

Thulin, Henning, *En präst vaknar.* Stockholm, *1941

— *Kring Kyrkan och pingstväckelsen.* Stockholm, *1944

— *Pingströrelsen – en sociologisk orientering.* Stockholm: Förlaget Filadelfia, *1945

Tognini, Enéas, '**Batismo** no Espírito Santo', in: ASTE, *O Espírito Santo*, 1966, pp. 76–82

Torbet, Robert C., *A History of the Baptists.* Philadelphia: Judson Press, 1950

Torrey, Reuben A., **Talks to Men About the Bible** *and the Christ of the Bible.* London: Nisbet, 1904, 125 pp.

Trinity Society, *Why Tongues, Why Divisions?* Van Nuys, Calif.: The Blessed Trinity Society, n.d., 8 pp.

Turnbull, Thomas Napier, **What God Hath Wrought.** *A Short History of the Apostolic Church.* Bradford: Puritan Press, 1959, 186 pp.

Turner, Harold W., *History of an African Independent Church* (2 vols.) I: The Church of the Lord (Aladura). II: The Life and Faith of the Church of the Lord (Aladura). Oxford: Clarendon Press, 1967, 217 and 391 pp.

— **Profile** *Through Preaching. A Study of the Sermon Texts Used in a West*

African Independent Church, published for the WCC, CWME (Research Pamphlets No. 13). Geneva: WCC, 1965, 86 pp.

Union des Eglises de Pentecôte Belgique, *Annuaire 1962*. Fleurus, 38, rue des Robots, 1962, 26 pp.

United Pentecostal Church, *This is That*. St Louis, Mo.: n.d.

Urch, Walter H., *The Place of* **Spiritual Gifts** *in Pentecostal Churches*. London: Elim Publ. Co., 1955, 31 pp.

Vergara, Ignacio. **El protestantismo** *en Chile*. Santiago de Chile: Editorial del Pacifico, 1962, 156 pp.

Verkuyl, J., **Geredja** *Dan Bidet*[2]. Djakarta: Badan Penerbit Kristen, 1962, 200 pp.

Verlag der Gesellschaft für Mission, Diakonie und Kolportage mbH., *Der Kampf um die Pfingstbewegung* (reprinted from *Pfingstgrüsse* 2–3, 1909–10), Mülheim/Ruhr, n.d.

Vingren, Ivar, **Pionjärens dagbok**. *Brasilienmissionären Gunnar Vingren: hans dagboksanteckingar*. Stockholm: Lewi Pethrus Förlag, 1968, 250 pp.

Vischer, Lukas (ed.), *A Documentary History of the Faith and Order Movement, 1927–1963*. Geneva: WCC, 1963

Visser 't Hooft, William A. (ed.), *The New Delhi Report*. The Third Assembly of the WCC, 1961. London: SCM Press, 1961, 448 pp.

— **Oekumenische Bilanz**. *Reden und Aufsätze aus zwei Jahrzehnten*. Stuttgart: Ev. Missionsverlag, 1966, 268 pp. (reviewed by Ludwig Eisenlöffel, *Der Leuchter* 18/1, Jan. 1967, pp. 4f.)

Vivier-van Eetveldt, L. M., *Glossolalia*, med. thesis, University Witwatersrand, South Africa, 1960

— 'The **Glossolalic** and His Personality', in: Th. Spörri (ed.), *Beiträge zur Ekstase*, 1968, pp. 153–75

Volz, Paul, art. 'Pharisäer', *RGG* 2nd ed., IV (1930), cols. 1178f.

Vouga, Oscar. **Our Gospel** *Message*. St Louis, Mo.: Pent. Publ. House, n.d., 31 pp.

Walker, D. E., *A Survey of Nez Perce Religion for the Research and Survey Staff Institute of Strategic Studies and the Office of Indian Work*. New York: United Presbyterian Church, USA, 1966, 99 pp.

Waltke, W. A., 'Wer ist die **Gemeinde** Jesu Christi in Deutschland? Was ist ihre Lehre? Welches ist ihr Ziel?' *Lebendiges Wasser*, n.d., no number, no pagination.

Ward, C. M., *Dr Wernher von Braun: 'The Farther We Probe Into Space the Greater My Faith . . .'* Springfield, Mo.: AoG, 1966

Wasserzug-Traeder, Gertrud, **Gottes Wort** *ist Gottes Wort. Ein Zeugnis zur Inspiration der Bibel*. Beatenberg (Switzerland): Bibelschule, n.d., 58 pp.

WCC, *Evanston to New Delhi, 1954–1961. Report of the Central Committee to the Third Assembly of the WCC*. Geneva: WCC, 1961

— 'Christian Witness, Proselytism, and Religious Liberty' (Central Committee,

St Andrews 1960, Full Assembly New Delhi 1961), in: Lukas Vischer (ed.), *A Documentary History*, 1963, pp. 183–96

— 'Statement on Religious Liberty', in W. A. Visser 't Hooft (ed.), *New Delhi Report*, 1961, pp. 159–61

— *Central Committee of the WCC, Minutes and Reports of the Eighteenth Meeting*, Enugu, Eastern Nigeria, Africa, 12 to 21 January 1965. Geneva: WCC, 1965

— **The Church For Others** *and The Church For the World.* A Quest For Structures for the Missionary Congregations. Final Report of the Western European Working Group and the North American Working Group of the Department on Studies in Evangelism. Geneva: WCC, 1967, 133 pp. (also in German, Spanish, and Portuguese)

— *Drafts For Sections*, prepared for the Fourth Assembly of the WCC, Uppsala, Sweden 1968. Geneva: WCC, 1968, 136 pp.

Webster, Douglas, **Pentecostalism** *and Speaking With Tongues.* London: Highway Press, 1964, 47 pp.

Weman, Henry, *African Music and the Church in Africa* (Studia Missionalia Upsaliensia 3). Uppsala: Svenska Institutet för Missionsforskning, 1960, 296 pp.

Wesley, John, **Plain Account** *of Christian Perfection, as believed and taught by the Rev. Mr John Wesley, from the year 1725 to 1777*, in: John Wesley, *Works, XI* 1872, pp. 366–446

— 'Thoughts on Christian Perfection', 1759, in: J. Wesley, *Works, XI*, 1872, pp. 394–407

— *The Works of John Wesley*. Grand Rapids, Mich., 14 vols. (photo-mechanical reproduction of the authorized version of 1872)

Whyte, Frederic William, art. 'William Thomas Stead (1849–1912)', in: George Smith (ed.), *Dictionary of National Biography, 1912–1921*. London: Oxford UP (1927), 1966, pp. 507f.

Widmer, Johannes, **Im Kampf** *gegen Satans Reich*, 3 vols. I: 1938, 131 pp. (published first under the title *Mein Kampf gegen Satans Reich*), 3rd ed. 1948, 119 pp.; II: *1942, 2nd ed. 1949, 225 pp.; III: *1947, 2nd ed. 1952, 231 pp. All three volumes: Bern: Gemeinde für Urchristentum

Wieser, Thomas (ed.), *Planning for Mission. Working Papers on the New Quest For Missionary Communities.* London: Epworth Press; New York, WCC, 1966, 230 pp. (This is an adaptation of H. J. Margull (ed.), *Mission als Strukturprinzip. Ein Arbeitsbuch zur Frage missionarischer Gemeinden.* Geneva: WCC, 1965, 3rd ed. 1968)

Wildberger, Hans, *Biblische Welt* (text by Hans Wildberger, pictures by Michael and Luzzi Wolgensinger). Zürich: Silva-Verlag, n.d., 120 pp.

Wilkerson, David R., and John and Elizabeth Sherrill, *The* **Cross** *and the Switchblade*. New York: B. Geis Ass., distributed by Random House, 1963 (GPH edition), 217 pp.; Pyramid Publ. USA 1963, 174 pp.

— *Twelve Angels From Hell.* Westwood, N.J.: Fleming H. Revell, 1963, 152 pp.

Willems, Emilio, 'Religious Mass Movements and Social Change in Brazil', in: E. N. Baklanoff (ed.), *New Perspectives of Brazil*, 1966, pp. 205–32

Willems, Emilio, **Followers** *of the New Faith. Culture Change and Rise of Protestantism in Brazil and Chile.* Nashville, Tenn.: Vanderbilt UP, 1967, 290 pp.

Williams, Colin, *Where in the World? Changing Forms of the Church's Witness.* New York: NCCC USA, 1963; London: Epworth, 1965, 116 pp.

— *What in the World*? New York: NCCC USA, 1964; London: Epworth, 1965, 105 pp.

—*Faith in a Secular Age.* London: Fontana Books, 1966

— *The Church* (New Directions in Theology Today IV). Philadelphia: Westminster, 1968

Williams, J. Rodman, *The Era of the Spirit, including views on the Holy Spirit held by four eminent theologians: Karl Barth, Emil Brunner, Paul Tillich and Rudolf Bultmann.* Plainfield, N.J.: Logos International, 1971, 119 pp.

Wilson, Bryan R., **Social Aspects** *of Religious Sects: A Study of Some Contemporary Groups in Great Britain. With Special Reference to a Midland City.* Ph.D. thesis, University of London, 1955, 2 vols (manuscript)

— **Sects** *and Society: the Sociology of Three Religious Groups in Britain.* London: Heinemann, 1961. (A summary of the foregoing.)

— 'Apparition et persistance des sectes dans un milieu social en évolution', *Archives de Sociologie des Religions* 5, Jan.–June 1958, pp. 140–50

— 'An Analysis of Sect Development', *American Sociological Review* 24/1, Febr. 1959, pp. 3–15

— 'The Pentecostalist Minister: Role Conflicts and Status Contradictions', *American Journal of Sociology* 64/5, March 1959, pp. 494–504

— Typologie des sectes dans une perspective dynamique et comparative', *Archives de Sociologie des Religions* 16, 1964, pp. 49–64

Wilson, Elizabeth A. Galley, *Making Many Rich.* Springfield, Mo.: GPH, 1955, 257 pp.

Winehouse, Irwin, *The Assemblies of God. A Popular Survey.* New York: Vantage Press, 1959, 224 pp.

Woerden, Peter van. *In the Secret Place. A Story of the Dutch Underground.* Wheaton, Ill.: Van Kampen Press, 1954, 64 pp.

— *Mein* **Weg mit Jesus.** Stuttgart: Christl. Verlagshaus GmbH, 1965, 176 pp.

Wovenu, Charles Kwabla Nutornutis, *Adzogbedede na mawu.* Tadzewu, Ghana: Apostolic Revelation Society, 1963, 24 pp. ET, *Vowing to God.* Tadzewu, Ghana: Apostolic Revelation Society, 1963, 24 pp.

Wumkes, G. A., *De* **Pinksterbeweging** *voornamelijk in Nederland.* Amsterdam: G. R. Polman, 1917, 23 pp.

Wurmbrand, Richard, *The Soviet Saints.* London: Hodder and Stoughton, 1968, 189 pp.

Wyatt, Thomas, *The* **Birth** *and Growth of a World-Wide Ministry.* Los Angeles; Wings of Healing, n.d., 15 pp.

Yeomans, Lilian Barbara, **Healing** *from Heaven.* Springfield: GPH, 1926, 139 pp.

Yuasa, Key, notes on a thesis on the Brazilian Pentecostals, ca. 1961

— 'O Pentecostismo e as Igrejas protestantes', in ASTE, *O Espírito Santo*, 1966, pp. 68–70

Zenetti, Lothar, **Heisse (W) Eisen.** *Jazz, Spirituals, Beatsongs, Schlager in der Kirche*. München: J. Pfeiffer, 1966, 328 pp.

INDEX